THE ACADEMIC REVOLUTION

The Academic Revolution

CHRISTOPHER JENCKS & DAVID RIESMAN

With a new Foreword by Martin Trow

The University of Chicago Press
Chicago and London

The University of Chicago Press, Chicago 60637

The University of Chicago Press, Ltd., London

81 80 79 78 77   987654321

ISBN: 0-226-39628-2

Contents

Foreword to the Phoenix Edition

In 1968, when this book was published, American higher education was ending two decades of the most rapid growth in its history. In the twenty years between 1948 and 1968, enrollments in American colleges and universities had grown from 2.6 million to 7 million. That growth was the product of two independent but mutually enforcing factors: a tremendous growth in the college age population, and a rapid and uninterrupted trend among young Americans to continue their formal education beyond high school. These two forces very greatly increased the demand for places in our colleges and universities.

Massive growth had direct or indirect effects on every aspect of American higher education. It altered the social characteristics of the student body as well as the numbers and specialization of college and university administrators; it affected the curriculum and forms of instruction; it enabled many institutions to become academically selective for the first time; and it caused already selective institutions to be even more selective.

This increase in the number of students in those two decades required a parallel increase in the number of college and university teachers, from about 200,000 to over 500,000. And the strong demand for more college and university teachers, together with a very considerable rise in both private and public support for research, promoted the explosive growth of graduate education during these decades.

But the "great leap forward" that took place in American higher education in the two decades after World War II was shaped and conditioned by the history of the American university after the Civil War. Over the hundred years between 1870 and 1970, enrollments doubled every fourteen to fifteen years; in only four years during that century, two of them during wars, was there an absolute decline in the numbers of students. The whole network of interrelated developments over the hundred years since 1870 justifies the authors' use of the term "revolution." Out of all those changes and developments, the authors focus on one—the emergence and growth of an academic profession and the ramified consequences of that development for graduate and undergraduate education. Though they wander from that theme to explore many others, they repeatedly return to it. It is, in a sense, a prism through which they view a variety of other problems and characteristics of American higher education.

There is a certain irony in the title of this book, as the authors themselves acknowledge in the Preface to the second edition, published in 1969. As they noted then, a book bearing this title, coming as it did in the midst of the student upheavals and disturbances of the late 1960s, led many people to expect a study of the student revolts rather than of "the earlier and duller revolution in which the academic profession had freed itself from effective lay control." But the "revolution" that they were writing about was indeed a revolution; whereas the disturbances of the late 1960s, while far more dramatic and "newsworthy," were, as we see now, less a revolution than a revolt, whose effects, though not trivial, are much less sweeping and systematic than the deep and enduring changes of the earlier revolution about which Jencks and Riesman write. Indeed, we can hardly understand the nature and consequences of the student revolts of the late 1960s without understanding the central characteristics of the system in which those disturbances took place.

Although *The Academic Revolution* focuses on a set of transformations in American higher education, the continuing interest and value of the book lie almost as much in its methods of inquiry as in its substance. The analysis is comprehensive in scope, descriptively rich and detailed, eclectic in method, historically rooted, and focused on change. Surely, no other book on this subject has treated so evenhandedly, and without trace of academic snobbery, the enormous range and variety of American colleges and universities: the great research universities, the modest four-year denominational colleges, state teachers colleges, traditionally black colleges, two-year community colleges, as well as the elite, selective liberal arts colleges. Whole reaches of the academic landscape are here illuminated for the first time, placed in broad historical and social context as elements of a national system, and made part of an interacting mix of varied institutions. The book is marked not only by its broad and comprehensive sweep, but also by its empirical detail, its rich particularity. The book is dense with facts, not merely about the hundred or so leading colleges and universities that most students of higher education know at firsthand and write about almost exclusively, but also about the other twenty-four hundred institutions whose names, characteristics, and qualities are likely to be unknown to the ordinary reader, and even to the specialist in the field. And these facts are the product of every kind of research method known to social science; the book shows as little methodological as academic snobbery. Historical accounts, demographic statistics, and survey findings are combined with the insights of direct observation and experience. But the facts, and even the most transient and ephemeral observations, are always placed in broad social and historical perspective. The histories of an institution or a class of institutions an ethnic group a region, a religious denomination, a social class, and a philosophy of education are treated in terms of their ongoing influences on the forms and processes of teaching and learning in America. The search for the nature and sources of change, the tracing and the explanation of academic trajectories, unifies the enormous variety of particular observations that the authors make.

Since this book was written, American higher education has undergone another major shift in direction, perhaps as important in its long-range effects as the century-long revolution described and analyzed in this volume. This current change is associated with a substantial slowing of growth rates, and is felt by almost every institution of higher education in the United States. Just as growth, its correlates and effects, dominated the imaginations of educators for a hundred years, especially during the two decades preceding the publication of this book, so the slowing of growth with the accompanying prospect of no growth or even possible declines in enrollment in the decades ahead dominates academic thinking and planning today. The new austerities and constraints are a shock not only to budgets, but to the hopes and expectations of teachers, students, and administrators as well.

In retrospect, the turning point in college enrollment growth occurred just a year after this book was published, when roughly 47 percent of young white men aged eighteen to twenty-one were enrolled in American colleges and universities. By 1974 that proportion had fallen to a little over 34 percent. (The proportion of women, minorities, and older students has held its ground or continued to rise.) But the growth of the system during the 1960s reflected both the rise in enrollment rates for almost all categories of students as well as a very large growth in the traditional college-age population, a combination of events that will almost certainly never occur again in the United States. Between 1960 and 1973 the number of eighteen- to twenty-one-year-olds in our population grew from 9.7 to 14.7 million. That age group is still growing, though at a much slower rate, and will peak at about 16 million in 1980. By 1985 that age cohort will be smaller than it was in 1973, and by 1990 it will have fallen to around 13 million. These demographic facts are essential to the prediction of a stabilization or decline of enrollments in the 1980s. The major uncertainty, of course, is the future enrollment rates of older men and women. Since that population is so large, even small changes in its enrollment rates will have large consequences for total enrollments.

A series of issues not anticipated in 1968 confronts American colleges and universities today. These have arisen in part as a result of the slowing of growth, and in part as an outcome of the "reforms" of the curriculum and of forms of governance introduced in response to the student disturbances of the late 1960s and early 1970s. They have also resulted from the loss of confidence in academics and academic administrators on the part of politicians and civil servants, and the loss of institutional autonomy that rests ultimately on that trust.

The greater intrusiveness of government—federal agencies, state governors, legislatures, departments of finance, state coordinating councils, and the like—into the affairs of higher education, and especially into the affairs of public institutions, is an important development of the past decade. Some of this reflects the commitment of federal agencies, such as HEW, to the enforcement of government "affirmative action" policies bearing on the admission and employment of minorities and women. The federal government also makes itself felt in the administration of directives designed for the protection of human subjects in scientific research. And it has shown itself ready to enforce its directives through the withdrawal or the threat of withdrawal of federal research grants from recalcitrant institutions. State agencies appear to be more concerned with the issues of academic efficiency and productivity, and through an insistence on greater "accountability" are seeking and finding ways of imposing their own ideas of how to achieve greater efficiency on the colleges and universities within their jurisdiction. The decline in the readiness of both public and lay bodies to trust academics and academic institutions to manage their own affairs is likely to have much larger consequences for American higher education than the more visible campus disturbances of the late 1960s.

The triumph of the specialized undergraduate course, rooted in the research disciplines and in graduate studies, over liberal education does not seem to be the problem it was a decade ago. For instance, the student disturbances of the 1960s accelerated the trend towards the "reform" of the undergraduate curriculum, a reform that has largely taken the form of a reduction in course requirements and a growth in student freedom in the choice and sequence of courses. Moreover, we now see that weakening the influence of the departmental major can impose its own costs on academic standards and values. This is reflected, for example, in trendy and superficial "interdisciplinary" courses that find a lowest common denominator in the academic/political fashions of the day.

Throughout this book there is a concern for the tension between specialized knowledge and liberal education. This tension, and the educational processes which give it different forms in different situations, is never quite resolved, or more accurately, the best undergraduate education can be found where that tension has not been resolved. In 1968, Jencks and Riesman were concerned that the balance was tipping too far toward specialized studies at the expense of liberal education. Today, they may fear, as I do, for the fate of both specialized and liberal studies, in the rise of vocational and pre-professional courses that make claims neither to "breadth" nor "depth," but merely to "relevance." The great numbers of college graduates and their intense anxiety about their careers exert pressures on the undergraduate curriculum at least as strong (though in different directions) as the pressures exerted by the academic profession and its research interests which are described and analyzed in this book.

Other problems of higher education have emerged or become more salient during the past decade. Increasing numbers of college and university teachers are joining unions or professional associations which are engaged in collective bargaining with administrators and state authorities. Collective bargaining is still largely confined to community colleges and state colleges, but it is spreading, encouraged in many states by legislation designed to rationalize industrial relations with public employees. Collective bargaining is likely to have a powerful effect on higher education, changing the ways in which academic decisions are made; in so doing it will also affect what those decisions are. That it will have substantial impact on the governance and administration of colleges and universities is certain. But whether and how it will affect the actual processes of teaching and learning still remains to be seen.

The rise of collective bargaining is perhaps only one form of a more general development in American higher education: the increasing formalization of academic decision processes. Traditional decision-making procedures, based on individual judgment and informal discussions and consultations, are increasingly challenged, both within the colleges and universities, and in the courts. The forms and settings in which those decisions are taken are consequently formalized and subject to more elaborate administrative and legal procedures. Contracts that result from collective bargaining almost always increase the procedural formality and complexity of budgetary and personnel decisions, and even more often, those procedures are elaborated and formalized in anticipation of collective bargaining. Moreover, affirmative action procedures also formalize the processes of hiring, promoting, or firing academic personnel, as well as the processes of student recruitment and admission. Members of academic communities are finding the courts surprisingly ready to hear their grievances and intervene directly into academic decision making, and are taking their grievances to courts more often in consequence. The president of a large urban university recently reported that in his role as president he was currently the defendant in no less than forty lawsuits.

Other processes—for example, the creation or, more rarely, the termination of academic programs—are also subject to more formal procedures when external agencies demand the right to review and pass on those decisions and demand documentation and justification of proposals that affect the costs, the mission, and the character of service of the institution.

The formalization of procedures is enormously expensive: legal and administrative staffs grow to meet the need for more detailed records for use in administrative reviews or court action. The collection of this mass of data becomes a major problem in itself; computerized information systems are developed at great cost, both visible and hidden, but almost invariably they embody such inaccuracies that their use is confined largely to external justification rather than internal administration. And the costs are felt in other ways: in one state system it has become too expensive to refuse an assistant professor tenure, since his inevitable appeal can cost the institution $30,000. The anticipated costs, both in money and in time, of firing faculty become a real deterrent. But the resulting policy of granting tenure to all who are appointed carries with it other very large costs and consequences for an institution.

Even though the problems of the mid-1970s are not those of the mid-1960s, the colleges and universities which are experiencing these problems still are much the same institutions as those about which Jencks and Riesman were writing, and the system continues to show the characteristics that they identified: enormous diversity and vitality; differences of region, social class, religious denomination, and ethnicity; peculiar and variable links to secondary education on one side and to the economy on the other; tension between the inner lift of disciplines and departments and the quite different concerns of academic administration and government. These are still the central characteristics and tensions a decade later. We cannot understand the nature of our current problems without understanding the institutions which house them, the social and historical forces which gave rise to them, and the relations of the colleges and universities to the larger society which supports them. No one has described these aspects of American higher education in all their contradiction and diversity better than Jencks and Riesman in *The Academic Revolution*.

MARTIN TROW
May 1976

Preface to the Second Edition

We finished writing *The Academic Revolution* in August 1967. The events of the ensuing academic year, especially the crisis at Columbia, made some of what we had written seem dated even before it was published in May 1968. Since then there have been more upheavals, notably at San Francisco State. While we do not think these events invalidate our general argument, they do raise questions which we treated rather cursorily in the original edition. Unfortunately, we have been able to make only minor changes in the second edition, clarifying some of the murkier prose and correcting minor errors of fact and interpretation. We have not made any substantial changes in the argument, nor have we tried to bring our examples up to date.

If we were writing today we would probably pick another title. Our choice of *The Academic Revolution* led most people to expect a book about the current student revolts. Many readers felt cheated when they found us writing about the earlier and duller revolution in which the academic profession had freed itself from effective lay control. It is true that we discuss the generational conflict, which underlies today's campus turmoil, in Chapter 2. But we do so from the viewpoint of adults rather than adolescents. Our aim is to explain how the system got to be the way it is, how it maintains itself, and how its internal contradictions may force it to change. We devote relatively little space to explicating the students' feelings about it all: what they want, why they want it, and how they have set about getting it. Under these circumstances we might have called the book *The Academic Professions* instead of *The Academic Revolution*.

A more serious difficulty raised by the upheavals of the past eighteen months is that many people now read the book in a very different spirit from the one in which it was written. When we first began work on higher education in the late 1950s, both educators and laymen seemed appallingly complacent about American higher education. There was much talk after Sputnik about the intellectual deficiencies of elementary and secondary schools, but the only widespread complaints about higher education were that Americans needed more of it and that the professors were underpaid and treated with insufficient respect.

Almost all educators accepted the legitimacy and authority of the academic profession a few years ago, even when they criticized specific aspects of its operation. The adult public accepted academicians as mediators between themselves and their late adolescent children and supported them financially. It seemed necessary and proper to write critically about this situation, stressing the academic world's human and intellectual deficiencies as well as its benefits.

Today all this has changed. The conflict between generations grows more bitter each year. Academicians can no longer mediate this struggle, and they grow annually more vulnerable to attack from each side for being too sympathetic to the other. One consequence is that the public is growing more skeptical about educators' claims for their institutions, money for higher education is harder to raise and autonomy harder to maintain. Another consequence is that educators themselves are far less sure than they were that their traditions and values are worth defending.

The critical spirit with which many students (as well as a growing minority of faculty and administrators) now view the academic enterprise has often been productive, but like all cultural upheavals it has also led to excesses. A small but growing minority seems convinced that the academic system, and indeed the whole fabric of American life, is not just blemished but fundamentally rotten. Destructive members of this minority would like to see the entire system obliterated. In some cases it goes further and seeks to discredit not just the academic system but all forms of rationality and intellectuality. No careful reader of *The Academic Revolution* is likely to suppose that we have much sympathy with these views. But not all readers are careful. Many hear only what they want to hear. Some have read our criticisms of academic professionalism as support for their own broader attack on all aspects of intellectual life. Such readers are still a tiny minority, but their number is likely to grow in the next few years. Anti-intellectualism is on the upswing again in America, and not just among conservatives who rally to George Wallace. If *The Academic Revolution* lends either plausibility or legitimacy to this revival of mindlessness, we will be deeply sorry.

Where, then, do we stand with respect to the current upheavals? There is no simple general answer to this question, for no two insurrections are exactly alike. Some have almost nothing to do with the university except insofar as it is a surrogate for the larger society. Some are concerned with altering the relationship between racial groups, often trying to establish the principle that black students now have a right to push whites around, just as whites have often done to blacks. Some of the disturbances have focused on social restrictions on student behavior. A small but growing number have sought to alter the form and content of the curriculum—an area almost untouched by agitation prior to 1967. We have different reactions to conflicts in each of these areas, depending on the specific demands being made and the tactics used to draw attention to them or implement them. Indeed, if there is a single aspect of the current ferment that we have tried to resist, it is the polarization that leads growing numbers of students and faculty to feel (we wrote "think," but that is too generous) that they can choose sides, either for or against "the revolution," and can then judge issues solely in these terms.

What is required is the closest analysis of what the students want measured against what would be desirable in terms of their own development. Students, like the rest of us, are adroit in arranging matters so that they need not change—sometimes so that they can be entertained or excited by their own or others' dramaturgy instead of discovering whether they have any intellectual interests and how these might be pursued.

Here, everything depends on the institutional context. Reforms that are desperately needed in one place are often inappropriate in another. Student participation in decision-making, for example, often makes good sense on small campuses where there is a strong sense of commitment to the institution. On other campuses, however, the majority of students feel completely alienated from the institution and view themselves as a transient proletariat. They have no sense of identification with the institution, no stake in improving it, and no reason for wanting a voice in its operation except to reduce the extent to which it impinges on their lives while they are acquiring its degree. On such campuses student participation in campus-wide decisions is likely to prove irrelevant, since only a handful of entrepreneurs will take part and the majority will feel no better represented than before. The entrepreneurs, in turn, may want a voice in campus affairs only in order to help bring these affairs to a complete halt. To move on such a campus toward a cure for student discontent should not envisage including students on existing committees but rather discovering or creating units of work and leisure in which student participation and management might become more educative for them.

As these comments suggest, we do not believe there are any universally applicable panaceas for the current ills of higher education. Contrary to what most current critics seem to think, the development of a better system of higher education is an incredibly difficult task, requiring not just good will but patience and attention to detail. This does not mean the task is impossible. It does mean that if we were writing *The Academic Revolution* in 1969 we would expand

Chapter 2 and look far more carefully at innovations that have failed. It also means that we would expand Chapter 12 so as to devote more space to what some better models of higher education might look like. Meanwhile, we can only reiterate that the creation of such incremental improvements, not simply the destruction of present arrangements, should be everyone's aim.

C. JENCKS
D. RIESMAN
January 1969

Introduction

This book attempts a sociological and historical analysis of American higher education. It begins with a general theory about the development of American society and American colleges, then moves on to discuss different species of colleges and their relationships to the various special interest groups that founded them. Not only does it try to describe the past and future of these relationships—it also tries to evaluate them. A book of such ambitious scope plainly cannot hope to be an unqualified success.

As sociology it must inevitably be superficial at many points. There are more than 2,000 institutions of higher education in America, more than 400,000 teachers and administrators, more than 6,000,000 students. We have visited only about 150 of the 2,000 colleges, and in some cases have spent less than a day on a campus. We have talked or corresponded with several thousand professors, but that is only a beginning. Among students the problem is even more acute, for while we have talked with a great many over the years, the turnover is enormous and yesterday's impressions are often out of date. Our sampling has, moreover, been biased, and our ability to learn what we wanted to know about either institutions or individuals has been limited. We have therefore had to rely heavily on "secondary" sources. We have read student newspapers, magazines, catalogues, curricular proposals, and revolutionary manifestos from many colleges we could not visit, as well as from those we could. We have talked with knowledgeable observers in government, the foundations, journalism, business, the professions, and of course academic life itself. We have also read a modest fraction of the books and articles on higher education.

When we began studying higher education more than a decade ago, the number of scholars in the field was small enough so that we could know almost all of them personally and keep up a correspondence with them. Today this is no longer possible. Even keeping up with published reports is a full-time occupation, especially if one defines "the problem" to include not only higher education but its relationship to American society. Given the scope of the questions we have sought to examine and these limitations in our attempts to

answer them, our argument cannot be as fully documented or quanti-
fied as we would like. Much of our discussion is speculative and impressionistic simply because there is no alternative.

As history, too, our work is subject to methodological criticism.
Indeed, it is not history at all as a professional historian usually
defines that term. We have done no original research on the documents that record the evolution of higher education. We have read
only a small fraction of the institutional histories and biographies
that serve as secondary sources in this field. Our interpretations rest
on a small sample of these chronicles and on the general histories done
by traditional historians. The reasons for this are well stated by
Laurence Veysey in his brilliant book on the development of the
American university in the late nineteenth century:

> The development of an institutional framework presents pe-
> culiar problems to the historian who would seek to account for
> it. It is often easy to make general statements about the causes
> for a pattern of institutional arrangements and relationships;
> yet nothing can be more baffling than the effort to relate
> these assumed causes to the abundant documentary evidence
> which is available to illustrate the change. Perhaps this is why
> we have had a number of suggestive general essays about the
> American academic revolution of the late nineteenth cen-
> tury, essays based upon relatively little specific investigation,
> whereas, on the other hand, local histories of individual cam-
> puses, which have more often relied upon archival files, curi-
> ously shy away from the larger issues of interpretation. The
> tendency to chronicle, at least, is understandable enough in
> view of the actual contents of most presidential correspondence.
> For one may read these letters endlessly without coming across
> explicit explanations for the relevant events. Indeed one may
> find the date on which such and such a department was estab-
> lished at such and such a university; one may even uncover a
> spirited debate over the details of certain of the new arrange-
> ments. But exceedingly little direct evidence may be found on
> decisions involving the basic shape of the rapidly emerging aca-
> demic structure. The most fundamental assumptions were not
> being articulated by those who were acting upon them. Many
> of these assumptions would appear in print only tardily—
> perhaps a decade after they had become embedded in the
> institutional pattern—and then would be stated by embittered
> critics.
>
> One would like to know the reasons for such phenomena as
> increasing presidential authority, bureaucratic procedures of
> many sorts, the new functions of the deanship, the appearance

of the academic department with its recognized chairman, and the creation of a calculated scale of faculty rank. These questions were almost always evaded by the participants themselves. Thus President Angell, commenting on the transformation of the University of Michigan during his day, much too casually remarked: "Our rather multifarious usages . . . have grown up without much system under peculiar exigencies." Here was a form of organization which came into being without deliberate debate on the part of its creators and yet displayed such great uniformities that it could not be termed a response to varying local desires or needs. What one sees as one looks at the leading campuses toward the end of the nineteenth century is a complicated but rather standard series of relationships springing to life before one's eyes—yet practically everyone at the time taking the fundamental choices for granted. The lack of self-consciousness that was displayed over the new organization as it came into being points directly toward a predominance of latent elements, rather than manifest intentions, in bringing it about. *One is led, therefore, to reason backward from the evidence of how the academic system functioned toward the causes for its appearance.*[1]

What Veysey found after exhaustive study of late nineteenth-century academic life confirmed our own conclusions, based on more superficial inquiries into many other periods and problems, about the limits of documentary research. Like him we have therefore had to look at what happened and have then tried to reason backward to find out why it happened.

This kind of functional analysis is full of pitfalls. If one focuses on men's unconscious, undebated assumptions about themselves and their institutions rather than on the controversies that they themselves thought important enough to write about, there is very little documentary evidence against which to check one's intuition. Under these circumstances some would argue that it would be wiser to say nothing about motives and intentions, simply concentrating on the events and their consequences. At times we have followed this course. But we have not usually been so cautious. The reader should therefore be forewarned that we are prone to assume—or at least to let the reader assume—that because a given arrangement had a given result, those who instituted the arrangement somehow intended that result or were served by it. This was by no means generally true. American

---

[1] Veysey, pp. 267–68. Italics added. Full citations for all books and documents mentioned in footnotes will be found in the list of references beginning on page 545. Where more than one work by a given author is listed, we have used the initial words of the title to indicate which is being referred to.

educators have seldom been able to give coherent explanations for what they were doing. Even when they did have a consistent theory, it often had little or no relationship to the actual results of their actions. We will try to make this clear in specific cases, but in some instances we may well fail.

Some readers frown on this kind of inquiry, preferring less ambitious but more fully documented analyses. We feel, however, that responsible scholarship must invent methods and data appropriate to the important problems of the day. To reverse this process, choosing one's problems to fit the methods and data that happen to be most satisfactory, strikes us as an invitation to triviality and ultimately as an abdication of social and personal responsibility. The problem to which we have addressed ourselves is the relationship between higher education and American society. Many facets of this relationship can be studied with considerable methodological rigor. The results may even be scientific, in the sense that another investigator can repeat the inquiry with reasonable assurance of getting similar results. But even when the data look "hard," as in the case of the relationship of social mobility to higher education, their meaning is almost always ambiguous, subject to interpretations that vary according to more or less speculative theories about the character of both higher education and society as a whole. When one turns from specific facets of the problem to its over-all shape—trying, for example, to see how students' desire for social mobility fits together with educators' desire to build colleges—nobody can do more than speculate. Ultimately this requires a general theory, and we have tried to move in this direction. We have not, however, been able to develop one that even begins to contain all the complexities of the symbiosis between American colleges and American society. Our description will therefore often transcend and sometimes contradict our generalizations.

Our work is an attempt to generalize and speculate on the basis of many kinds of evidence. The quality of this evidence is limited by the fact that educational institutions, like other small businesses, keep poorer records than large corporations; also, educational statistics are probably even less reliable than economic and demographic statistics. Even so, a good many of our generalizations and speculations could have been more rigorously tested if we had had more time, money, and skilled help. Where we could find data already available we tried to take them into account. But this is an area where academic self-consciousness still often takes the place of institutional research. Where we have found no data, we have had to consult our own experience and that of other informed observers. These observers, like ourselves, were often relying on impressions.

The reader will also be aware of the fact that we have commitments, prejudices, and blind spots. This book is primarily descriptive and is not a polemic on behalf of any given program or policy. The reader who expects a clear-cut evaluation of present or prospective programs is therefore likely to be disappointed. Nonetheless, we have not tried to ignore the major controversies of the day, such as the role of students in university governance, the effects of research on undergraduate teaching, and so forth. We have tried not to let our views on these subjects distort our perspective in that portion of the book—the great bulk of it—that is essentially descriptive. The reader will have to judge for himself whether we have succeeded in this, but he should be cautioned against judging too hastily. Our prejudices are many, but they are often contradictory. The result is that we are ambivalent or uncertain about many issues. This affects our choice of words and tone and leads to a good deal of irony. Many readers may find this puzzling or irritating and want to "know where we stand" and whether to rally round our banner or attack us for our sins. At times, when we argue a position explicitly, this reaction will be both possible and sensible. But those who jump to conclusions about our basic views on the basis of a phrase or sentence are likely to find that a few pages later we are making light of these very views.

The reader may also find a word about our plan of work helpful. This book is the first of two joint efforts on higher education in America. The second will be published under the title *The Academic Enterprise* and discusses what might be called the ecology of higher education in two states: Massachusetts and California. It also includes ethnographic studies of five colleges in these states. Three of these (on Boston College, the University of Massachusetts at Amherst, and San Francisco State College) have already been published.[2] Two others (studies of the evolution of Harvard and of the University of Massachusetts at Boston) have not. Profiles of two "experimental" colleges—New College in Florida and Shimer College in Illinois—will also appear in this volume.

In this first volume, however, we have not gone into much detail about specific colleges. The first chapter outlines a general hypothesis about the evolution of higher education in America and the nature of what we have called "the academic revolution." (The term is not, of course, original. We do not, however, know anyone who has used it in anything like the same sense that we do: to describe the rise to power of the academic profession.) Subsequent chapters examine the relationship of higher education to particular interest groups or subcultures within American society. We have tried to say something about the relationship between most of these interest groups and the over-all system of higher education. At the same time we have also

[2] See Jencks and Riesman, "The Viability."

discussed the evolution of the colleges especially founded to serve each group. In some chapters we emphasize the first approach, in some the second, in some both. Specifically, our first two chapters, which deal with generational conflict and social mobility, say relatively little about special-purpose colleges. Our next chapters, on occupational interests as manifested in professional schools and on class interests as manifested in public and private colleges, focus on particular species of institutions and try to chart the impact of the academic revolution on them. The chapters on geographic interest groups and sex groups strike a middle ground, mingling both perspectives. The chapters on sectarian and ethnic colleges again focus mainly on institutions that serve a specific group rather than on the relationship beween each group and the larger system. Chapter XI takes up two kinds of colleges that have to some extent resisted the academic revolution: the community colleges and what are commonly called experimental colleges. We end with a discussion of the graduate schools, which now shape undergraduate education, and some of the possibilities for improvement there.

This book is the product of a collaboration going back to 1959. Its first fruits were published as "The Viability of the American College" in 1962. The collaboration continued, with frequent interruptions, over the following five years. Over this time our views about higher education have changed, and almost every chapter of this book has been rewritten a number of times to reflect these changes. Even now the reader will detect inconsistencies in both tone and substance.

Since the authors were in the same city for only two months between 1960 and 1967, a division of labor was essential. The organization, quantitative investigation, and writing were done mainly by Jencks. The college visiting and interviewing were done mainly by Riesman. Reading and reflection were divided and at times duplicated. As in any good collaboration, the ultimate product is very much a joint effort. In many cases we ourselves would be hard pressed to say which of us first chose a particular phrase or first elaborated a particular line of thought.

Yet even this puts matters too simply, for in addition to the work of the coauthors, this book is in good part the product of many cooperative colleagues who spent endless hours talking with us, writing to us, reading and criticizing earlier drafts of the manuscript, and turning out manuscripts of their own from which we have learned much. We have tried to acknowledge these unseen collaborators below, but here we wish to apologize to those who have been inadvertently omitted and to thank them all collectively.

We are indebted to Frank Bowles of the Ford Foundation, Richard Storr of the University of Chicago, and Laurence Veysey of the University of California at Santa Cruz for critical comments on an earlier draft of Chapter I. Parts of this chapter will also be published this year in Alvin Eurich's collection of essays, *Campus 1980*.

An earlier draft of Chapter II benefited from critical readings by Frank Bowles, Bruce Eckland of the University of North Carolina, Joseph Gusfield of the University of Illinois, Clark Kerr of the University of California, Michael Maccoby of Cuernavaca, Mexico, and John Finley Scott of the University of Washington. Portions of this chapter appeared in slightly different form in the *Teachers College Record*, Autumn 1967.

Earlier drafts of Chapter III, which is part of a larger investigation of the effects of schooling on social mobility and equality being conducted by the first author, were critically read by Alexander Astin of the American Council on Education, C. Arnold Anderson of the University of Chicago, Samuel Bowles, André Danière, Humphrey Doermann and William Spady of Harvard University, Bruce Eckland, Abbott L. Ferriss of the Russell Sage Foundation, John Folger of the Commission on Human Resources, Seymour Harris of the University of California at San Diego, Robert Hassenger of the University of Notre Dame, Charles Nam of Florida State University, Charles Silberman of *Fortune* magazine, Frederick Rudolph of Williams College, Sydney Spivak of Princeton University, Arthur Waskow of the Institute for Policy Studies, and Finis Welch of Southern Methodist University. Portions of this chapter appeared in somewhat different form in *The Public Interest* (Winter 1968) and *The Harvard Educational Review* (Spring 1968).

An earlier draft of Chapter IV was read by Frank Bowles, Daniel Calhoun of the University of California at Davis, Lawrence Cremin of Teachers College, Columbia University, John Gustad of Ohio State University, Robert Kroepsch of the Western Interstate Commission for Higher Education, Martin Lichterman of the New England Board of Higher Education, George W. Pierson of Yale University, and John and Ruth Useem of Michigan State University, all of whom offered critical comments.

Kenneth Feigenbaum of the Antioch Putney Graduate School, Charles Rosenberg of the University of Pennsylvania, Laurence Veysey, and Dael Wolfle of the American Association for the Advancement of Science made helpful criticisms of Chapter V. Part of this chapter appeared in *Tri-Quarterly* (Winter 1968).

Gary Becker of Columbia University, André Danière, Humphrey Doermann, and Frederick Rudolph offered critical comments on an earlier version of Chapter VI.

An earlier draft of Chapter VIII was critically read by James Luther Adams of the Harvard Divinity School, Larry Bothell of the Episcopal

Theological School, Daniel Calhoun, J. Edward Dirks of the Yale Divinity School, Charles Glock of the University of California at Berkeley, John Gustad, Philip Hammond of the University of Wisconsin, W. J. Kilgore of Baylor University, and Martin Marty of *Christian Century*.

On Chapter IX we are indebted to Sister Marie Augusta Neal, S.N.D., of Emmanuel College, Father Carroll Bourg, S.J., at the Office of Social Research of the Jesuits' Maryland Province, Sister Ritamary Bradley of St. Ambrose College, Frank Buckley of Assumption College, Daniel Callahan of *Commonweal* magazine, Sally Cassidy of Wayne State University's Monteith College, John Donovan of Boston College, Father Joseph Fichter, S.J., of the Harvard Divinity School, Father Andrew Greeley of the National Opinion Research Center, Robert Hassenger, Timothy J. Healey, S.J., of Fordham University, Everett C. Hughes of Brandeis University, Ralph Lane of the University of San Francisco, John Lukacs of Chestnut Hill College, John Noonan, Jr., of the University of Notre Dame, Michael Novak of Stanford University, Michael True of Assumption College, Edward Wakin of Fordham University, and Sister Mary William, I.H.M., of Immaculate Heart College for critical comments on earlier drafts. Portions of this chapter appeared in the Winter 1966 and Spring 1967 issues of *The Public Interest*, and a number of correspondents made comments on these articles which we tried to take account of in revising the chapter for this book.

Richard Balzer of VISTA, Howard Boozer of the North Carolina State Board of Education, Ernst Borinski of Tougaloo College, Lewis Dexter of Belmont, Massachusetts, John Ehle of Winston-Salem, North Carolina, Leonard Fein of Massachusetts Institute of Technology, John Hope Franklin of the University of Chicago, Richard Frost of the U. S. Office of Economic Opportunity, David Fowler of the Carnegie Institute of Technology, Herbert Gans of the Center for Urban Education, Eli Ginsberg of Columbia University, Bernard Harleston of Tufts University, Watts Hill of the North Carolina State Board of Education, Wesley Hotchkiss of the United Church Board of Homeland Missions, Richard Hunt of Harvard University, Bruce Jackson of the University of Buffalo, Esther Jackson of Shaw University, Clifton Johnson and Lewis Jones of Fisk University, James Laue of the U. S. Community Relations Service, Michael Maccoby, Thomas Pettigrew of Harvard University, Richard Plaut of the National Scholarship Service and Fund for Negro Students, Harold Pfautz of Brown University, Richard Robbins of the University of Massachusetts at Boston, Hans Rosenhaupt of the Woodrow Wilson National Fellowship Foundation, Sydney Spivak, Tyson Tildon of Brandeis University, Kenneth Tollett of Texas Southern, Marvin

Wachman of Lincoln University, Arthur Waskow, and Samuel Wig-
gins of George Peabody College provided critical comments on an
earlier draft of Chapter X. It should not need to be said that they
are in no way responsible for what we say in this chapter, but
apparently this does need to be said for other critics have asked
us not to use their names lest they be tainted by any association
with us. An earlier version of this chapter was published in the
Harvard Educational Review (Winter 1967). We have made a few
minor revisions on the basis of published criticisms of that article,
particularly those by Stephen Wright of the United Negro College
Fund, Benjamin Mays of Morehouse College, Hugh Gloster of Hampton Institute, Albert Dent of Dillard University, Paul Garver of Southern University, William Brazziel of Virginia State College, and Julian
Stanley of the University of Wisconsin. These were published in the
Harvard Educational Review (Winter 1967). We have made a few

It must also be said that one of the hazards of extensive correspondence and discussion, especially when spread over many years, is
unconscious plagiarism. A phrase or idea, hardly noticed when first
encountered, often comes back "spontaneously" years later and is
thought to be original. If we have borrowed in this way from anyone
without giving him credit, we apologize, and add in extenuation only
that we have no objection to those who do the same with our
own work. This is particularly likely to have happened with regard to
work published before we began this manuscript. We read and
partially assimilated a great many books on higher education before
deciding to do one of our own, and our citations tend to reflect our
more recent reading better than that done earlier. Nor can citations
readily indicate the extent of our debt to men with whom we have
had personal contact over long periods, or to lecture courses regularly
attended. (The second author is especially indebted in this respect to
Daniel Calhoun, whose course on the history of American education
he audited at Harvard several years ago, and to Everett Hughes,
whose lectures at Chicago he found formative at an earlier point.)

Finally, we must pay tribute to the generous financial assistance
and remarkable patience of the Carnegie Corporation of New York,
which was a model disinterested patron during the years we were
at work on this book, and to the Samuel Rubin Foundation, which
helped support Jencks during 1966 and 1967 at the Institute for
Policy Studies. The substance of our work and our judgments are,
of course, solely our own responsibility.

³ The reader interested in this controversy should also look at the Summer 1967
issue of the *Journal of Negro Education*, devoted to "The Higher Education of
Negro Americans: Prospects and Programs." Many of these articles are critical of
ours, but they were published too late for us to deal specifically with them.

I. *The Academic Revolution in Perspective*

Traditional Colleges and Their Clients

During the seventeenth, eighteenth, and early nineteenth centuries, American colleges were conceived and operated as pillars of the locally established church, political order, and social conventions. These local arrangements were relatively stable, widely accepted as legitimate, and comparatively well integrated with one another. Yet while the pre-Jacksonian college was almost always a pillar of the establishment, it was by no means a very important pillar. An American "college" was in some respects more like today's secondary schools than today's universities. It did not employ a faculty of scholars. Indeed, only a few pre-Jacksonian college teachers, such as James Wyeth, exercised significant influence on the intellectual currents of their time. An upright and usually erudite clergyman served as president. He then hired a few other men (usually young bachelors and often themselves aspiring clergymen) to assist in the teaching. There were only a few professorships in specialized subjects. In most cases everyone taught almost everything, usually at a fairly elementary level.

Nor did these colleges have much impact on the character of the rising generation. Only a minority of those who controlled the established institutions of pre-Jacksonian America sent their children to college, and an even smaller minority had itself been to a college. Even those who attended seldom seem to have regarded the experience as decisive for their later development, at least judging by the relative scarcity of references to colleges in the literature of the time. Unlike leading continental universities, American colleges offered little professional training in fields like medicine, law, or theology. The liberal arts courses were probably in closer touch with the Enlightenment than their nineteenth-century successors would be with the spirit of their time, but they seldom seem to have played a major role in shaping the minds of America's leading thinkers.

With the wisdom of hindsight it is tempting to conclude that these colleges influenced neither the intellectual nor the social history of their era. Indeed, it could be argued that America overinvested in higher education during the pre-Jacksonian years. Perhaps the resources devoted to colleges might have been better allocated to libraries, scientific societies, or primary schooling. But like other more recent victims of colonialism, Americans during these years were eager to have the outward trappings of equality with the mother country, even if these trappings were neither relevant to the American setting nor notably productive in the mother country itself. Many argued that America should go its own way and that social priorities and institutional arrangements had to vary from one country to another. But in America as in Africa today, collegiate promoters could and did charge such critics with selling their country short and perpetuating subordination to Europe. England had a few colleges, so America had more.

By the second quarter of the nineteenth century the character of American society had begun to undergo a radical transformation. The break with England, the formation of a national government, the disestablishment of state churches, and the opening of lands across the Appalachians had all gradually undermined the established institutions and traditions of colonial society. The election of Andrew Jackson has usually been taken as the symbol of this change, even though there had already been a steady progression away from the old order during the fifty years between the Declaration of Independence and Jackson's triumph. The eclipse of established colonial hierarchies after 1828 created a vacuum which almost everyone was eager to fill, but nobody succeeded. The rest of the nineteenth century therefore saw a continuous struggle for power and legitimacy between the many subcultures that flourished in the rapidly growing nation.

Once it became clear that no single group of men had the power to shape society as a whole, many preferred to strike out on their own rather than try to climb the long ladder into existing institutions. Religious dissenters found less and less reason to try to reform the churches within which they had been raised; it was often easier to set up a new church with a new dogma. Rebels against local mores had equally little reason to struggle against them; it was easier to move west where neither law nor entrenched social custom hemmed one in. Entrepreneurs who didn't like the way the family business was run were similarly inclined to go into business for themselves, and they usually had as good a chance of staying afloat as their more venerable competitors. The same pattern was reflected in higher education: the dissidents who disliked Harvard, Yale, or William and Mary did not in most cases try to transform them, as English dissidents did Oxford and Cambridge during this same era. Instead, they set up their own competitive colleges to serve new purposes, many of which had not previously been regarded as appropriate for a college.

Nineteenth-century Americans grouped themselves by occupation, social class, religion, sex, locality, and ethnic background, among other things. As the century wore on almost all these groups felt impelled to set up their own colleges, both to perpetuate their distinctive subculture and to give it legitimacy in the larger society. By 1900 there were special colleges for Baptists and Catholics, for men and women, for whites and blacks, for rich and not-so-rich, for North and South, for small town and big city, for adolescents and adults, for engineers and teachers. We will call these institutions "special-interest" colleges, and will distinguish them from eighteenth-century colleges which served a relatively unified establishment. In many cases a special-interest college served several subcultures simultaneously, blending feminism with the values of the East Coast elite, for example, or mixing Methodism with Texas chauvinism. The number of permutations was almost infinite, and in due course many of them were tried.

In describing this process we do not want to overstress the element of rationality. The entrepreneurs who set up these colleges seldom did anything like market research before opening their doors, and most were ready to redefine or blur their initial aims if this was necessary for survival. Hundreds of colleges owed their existence to the energy and dedication of a single man who felt the call to found a college and was able to rally a few supporters for his cause. (In this they resembled Protestant religious sects, from which they often sprang.) College-founding and college-building were outlets for a variety of talents and dreams that could not be accommodated within either small business or the normal activities of the churches, and they attracted many men with unrealistic ideas about the demand for their services. Yet the influence of such personal factors inevitably diminished over a period of time. Some ill-conceived colleges were stillborn, and others died with their founders.[1] Those that survived and flourished did so less because of their founders' magnetic charm or personal commitment than because they appealed to enduring hopes and passions within American society. Many colleges were founded in improbable places, but all things being equal such colleges were less likely to survive than those that identified with a geographic area at once college-oriented and in some measure self-contained and self-conscious. Similarly, many colleges were founded for religious and pedagogical reasons which are now obscure or forgotten, but most of them quickly dropped these commitments and learned to base their public appeal on the customs, concerns, or practical needs of one or more fairly well-established subcultures. In the evolution of colleges as of species, then, order and apparent rationality emerged

[1] On this process see Tewksbury; his figures indicate that about 800 colleges were probably founded before the Civil War, and that only 180 of these survived into the twentieth century.

through natural selection and adaptation over time rather than from the initial mutations, many of which were freakish and almost random.

The founders of nineteenth-century colleges typically had several contradictory aims. On the one hand, few spokesmen for these sub-cultures really imagined that their followers would soon become a numerical majority in America, or even be able to impose their vision on a majority. This being so, they felt obliged to seek some kind of accommodation with mainstream America, whatever that might be. At the same time they also wanted to redirect this stream into new channels. They were, in short, both diplomats and dreamers, con-cerned with getting on in this generation as well as with laying the foundations for a larger empire in the next.

Thus the pioneers frequently spoke of creating a "Western" culture, which would stand in opposition to the "decadent" East, and the founders of Western colleges sometimes pandered to these prejudices, at least in their propaganda. But the rare pioneer who sent his son to college wanted him to be able to meet Eastern as well as Western standards, or at least to be able to deal with the more Easternized leaders of Western society. Similarly, the Catholic religious orders that founded colleges wanted to create a culture that would be at once literate, respectable, and faithful. In this way they hoped to create a Catholic counter-elite comparable to the Anglo-Saxon upper-middle class. At the same time they frequently wanted to give their alumni the skills and manners they needed to get on in what was still a predominantly Protestant society. The farmers who supported the land-grant colleges were in an analogous dilemma. They wanted to provide their sons with an alternative to the apparently useless classi-cal instruction given at established colleges, but they nevertheless wanted their children to hold their own in conversation with lawyers, bankers, and other big shots educated at traditional institutions. Sim-ilar ambiguities recurred in every special-interest college, for no subculture was ever quite sure whether it wanted its children to stay entirely within the parents' world or make the compromises needed to get on in the larger American society.

On the whole, however, the special-interest colleges were bastions of separatism rather than of social integration. The roots of this separatism are not hard to find. Most nineteenth-century colleges got their money from the particular constituency they served. Church colleges got their money from the church itself, from wealthy phi-lanthropists of the same faith, and from tuition charges which were met by parents and students of that faith. Local colleges got their money from local boosters eager to make a quick profit on land or to develop business opportunities in their town, from taxpayers in the geographic jurisdiction from which they drew their students, and from local students' fees. Women's colleges and Negro colleges, it is true, often depended on philanthropic support from outsiders. Yet even these colleges usually covered most of their costs from tuition and fees, and this made them more inward than outward looking. This pattern was somewhat less marked among vocationally or occupationally oriented colleges. Teachers colleges, for example, were largely supported by taxes on non-teachers, and agricultural colleges relied heavily on taxes paid by city dwellers. In general, however, money was available to special-interest colleges primarily for purposes defined by the subculture to which they catered. The colleges, as we shall see, often redefined these purposes to suit their own internal needs, but they experienced relatively little outside pressure to do so. (The situation was very different at the universities, as we shall also see.)

The choice of college trustees tended to follow the same pattern as financial support. The college whose special mission was defined by geography or religion usually drew all its trustees from within its particular parish, at least initially. The vocational colleges presented a more mixed picture, as did the women's colleges and the Negro colleges. Yet even when whites founded a missionary college for Negroes, or men agreed to serve on the board of a women's college out of noblesse oblige, guilt, or self-importance, or when an engineering school brought lawyers onto the board in order to exploit their special skills and create the appearance of diversity, this usually had only limited direct effect on the character of undergraduate life and learning.

The trustees' most important job was to choose a president, and the most important difference between one board and another was perhaps the criteria they used in making this choice. A sectarian college with a board made up exclusively of Baptists or Catholics was likely to choose a Baptist or Catholic president. A geographically based board composed entirely of Californians or Pennsylvanians, or even one composed entirely of San Franciscans or Philadelphians, was less likely to feel that it could choose only a native of its own area, though of course he would have to make it his own once chosen. An engineering school, on the other hand, even if it had lawyers and businessmen on its board, was unlikely to choose anyone who lacked scientific credentials to run the college. Similarly, boards dominated by whites eventually came to feel they had to find a Negro to administer a college for Negro students, and boards dominated by men sometimes felt that they had to find a woman to preside over a women's college.

Today, as we will argue in more detail later, the pattern of finance, the character of the board, and the choice of a chief

executive probably have less effect on the character of undergraduate
education than the sources of faculty and students. But in the
nineteenth-century colleges we have been discussing, the donors,
trustees, and presidents were probably more decisive. This was an
era when self-confident trustees tended to intervene in college affairs
far more often and more disastrously than is usual today—perhaps
partly because there were fewer financial and architectural decisions
with which the president could divert them, but also because they
were more righteous and sure of themselves. Nineteenth-century
college presidents also tended to be far more domineering than they
are today, carrying the business of the college around in their brief
cases or even in their heads, entrusting very little to committees of
faculty members or lower level bureaucrats, and imposing their personal stamp on the entire college. Most of all, it was a time when
financial solvency was so precarious that colleges responded to even
the smallest external pressures and had only the most limited ability
to reshape the priorities established by their supporters.

In part, of course, this was because the faculty was still quite
unprofessionalized. Relatively few instructors in the colleges we are
describing had had any sort of advanced training beyond the B.A.
Indeed, no such training was available in America except to some
small extent in theology. A few instructors had studied in Europe,
but this too remained exceptional until the last quarter of the
century, and was hardly general even then. The faculty were in many
cases drawn from the same subculture as the rest of the college.
Church colleges tended to hire members of their own faith, professional schools hired members of the profession, upper-class colleges
often hired independently wealthy faculty, and even colleges for
women and for Negroes often came to depend mainly on women
and Negroes to teach. The local colleges were more likely to bring
in outsiders, but these men then tended to take on the protective
coloration of their new environment. The college instructor was,
moreover, very much at the beck and call of the president and
trustees. Tenure seldom existed, and faculty seem to have felt obliged
to move on whenever they got into difficulty with their college or its
public, rather than staying to fight. The vision of a college professor
as an independent expert with a mission transcending the college
where he happened to teach was almost unknown.[2]

The final but perhaps most important element that requires brief
mention is the students themselves. Chapter II will argue in more

[2] On the status of faculty in the pre-Civil War college see Hofstadter and
Metzger, pp. 229–38. These authors make clear that even in that era there was a
gradual improvement in the status and influence of faculty on policy-making at
the better colleges.

detail that students today are less dependent on adults and less influenced by them than they were in the nineteenth or even the early
twentieth century. But there has always been such a thing as student
culture; it has always had a significant effect on the individual
students who came to a given college; and it has always been to some
extent shaped by the mix of student types at that college. This being
so, the recruitment patterns of special-interest colleges meant that
the colleges tended to re-enforce their students' sense of separatism
rather than drawing them into a larger social and cultural milieu.[3] It
is true that some rural and small-town students went away to a
college where they met big-city boys; that some Westerners went
"back East" to college and discovered a more ordered and polished
social style; and that some poor boys worked their way into and
through colleges where most of their classmates came from prosperous and cultured backgrounds. It sometimes even happened that
Negroes broke out of their segregated world into an integrated college, or that evangelical Protestants ended up at a secular college
where their faith was continually under fire. Still, reading college
histories we have the impression that such mixing was less often consciously encouraged then than now, and that it was more difficult both
financially and culturally. Thus, while nineteenth-century America
was an enormously heterogeneous and fluid world, with people moving from region to region, class to class, religion to religion, and farm
to city, this heterogeneity was only partly reflected in the colleges of
the time. Indeed, colleges often seem to have been founded and
maintained primarily as a reaction against the very fluidity of society
and the rapid pace of change, as part of a vain struggle to maintain
the old standards and the old ways.

Still, the special-interest colleges we have been describing were
probably no more important or effective as bulwarks of traditional
values than were their colonial predecessors. Colleges probably
played a far smaller role in nineteenth-century America and did far
less to define people's attitudes toward themselves or one another than
nineteenth-century churches did. Earning a B.A. was of limited value
for getting ahead on the job, and spending four years on a college
campus was of even less value in understanding nineteenth-century
culture. Despite the multiplication of colleges during these years, enrollment remained extremely low, almost all colleges remained finan-

---

[3] We use the term "recruitment" with some hesitation here and throughout
this book to describe a process that might better be called enlistment. Undergraduates at nineteenth-century colleges were almost entirely self-selected, with
almost no systematic recruitment and little screening of applicants. This is still true
in most colleges today. Even in colleges where systematic recruitment and
selection now exist, the character of the student body is still in good part
determined by who wants the college, not by whom the college wants.

cially marginal, and the majority eventually went under. Taken as a group the nineteenth-century colleges portrayed in institutional histories strike us as depressing and sterile places.

The Spread of Meritocratic Institutions

It would take a book considerably longer than this one to describe the changes in American society that led to the establishment of national institutions and of what seems, at least in comparison to earlier times, to be a relatively homogeneous upper-middle class culture. The underlying factors were probably technological, but this should not be interpreted in a narrow sense. Industrial technology (e.g. the assembly line) played some part, forcing many enterprises to reorganize so as to achieve economies of scale. But this was by no means a uniform need or trend. Industrial technology in the narrow sense may have led to the creation of a Ford Motor Company, but it did not account for General Motors and still less for the Bank of America or General Dynamics. These were products of what Kenneth Boulding and others have called the organizational revolution, which enabled a few powerful individuals to exercise effective control over larger and larger numbers of people. This revolution depended on technology (the typewriter, the telephone, later the computer), but in a very different way from the industrial revolution of earlier vintage. There is no clear evidence that the large organizations created in this way were more efficient than the smaller enterprises they usually supplanted, or that they served the public better. All that can be said is that they were not conspicuously less efficient. Probably their spread must be explained in other ways. The agglomeration of power and accommodation of interests within the framework of a single institution inevitably appealed to those in a position to dominate that institution. If such organizations were not egregiously incompetent compared to smaller ones, and if the ideological and legal checks on their growth were weak, they were bound to grow simply because their leaders had more power and resources available than anyone else. The ability of large businesses to retain income and thus free themselves from money-market control has facilitated their ability to grow by their own rather than Wall Street's devising.

There were, of course, many other factors involved in the establishment of overarching national institutions: the closing of the frontier and later the end of migration, the decline of sectarianism and religious fervor, the rise of a national market for both jobs and goods, the emergence of nationwide magazines and more recently radio and television, the growth of the national government as a major force in people's lives, the unifying effect of foreign wars. These changes were accompanied and intensified by changes in the dominant political ideology of American society, in family structure and child rearing, in the character of relationships between individuals, and in individuals' self-perception. The cumulative effect of these changes appears to have been the destruction of the nineteenth-century Jacksonian world in which every dissident could cut loose from his fellows and go into business for himself. Most of the major conflicts and concords of twentieth-century America were shaped within a complex of large, firmly established, loosely interrelated institutions.

Or so it seems. Actually, it might be somewhat more accurate to say that the old Jacksonian world has been overshadowed rather than destroyed. There is, after all, still an enormous amount of small business in America, both in the narrow economic sense and in the larger social sense. On the other hand, there can be no doubt that the over-all economic picture has been radically altered by the fact that the bulk of the nation's business is now done by big corporations, and that most young people considering business careers now choose to work for these corporations rather than take the risk of striking out on their own. A similar line of argument could be developed in other areas. The dissident clergyman who wants to start his own denomination has clearly not disappeared from American life; on the contrary, the number of small fundamentalist sects seems continually to grow. What *has* happened is that big, affluent, highly organized denominations play a much larger role than they did in the Jacksonian era. Analogous changes have taken place in other areas in American life. Whether this has meant an absolute decline in opportunities for independent entrepreneurship is unclear.[4]

The fact that so much of the old Jacksonian world has survived right down to the present time makes it extremely difficult to date the changes we are describing with any accuracy. Historians are always torn between looking for watersheds and looking for continuities. Laurence Veysey has argued that the coming of the railroad was the most important break between the earlier pluralist and loosely federated America and the later, more centralized, unified, and industrialized one. In some respects the Civil War served as a catalyst for changes that began earlier. It both symbolized and

---

[4] The last few decades have seen an absolute decline in the number of self-employed individuals. This includes self-employed businessmen, self-employed professionals, and farmers (see 1960 *Census*, I, 1, table 89, and Blau, p. 478). In many cases, however, this may not reflect an absolute decline in opportunities for self-employment but a relative rise in opportunities for salaried employment. The son of a farmer or small businessman may decline to follow in his father's footsteps even though the farm or business is making a larger profit than it did a generation ago, on the grounds that the increase has been slower than the general increase in salaries.

facilitated a shift of emphasis from the second to the first word in "United States." Yet even today this shift is incomplete, its resolution depending on the nature of the issue, the local as well as the national political climate, and the kinds of deterrents local, state, and federal institutions possess.

Whatever the causes or timing of the change, few would deny that established national institutions play a much larger role today than they did a century ago and that their dominance is likely to increase. The character of American life is in good part determined within such diverse and sporadically conflicting enterprises as the Chase Manhattan Bank and the Treasury Department, the Pentagon and Boeing Aircraft, the Federal Courts and the National Council of Churches, CBS and *The New York Times,* the State Department and the Chamber of Commerce, the Chrysler Corporation and the Ford Foundation, Standard Oil and Sun Oil. It is not determined to anything like the same extent by small businessmen, independent professionals, or eccentric millionaires. This does not, of course, mean that farmers, doctors, or Texas oilmen are without influence. It does mean that they exercise influence through organizations like the Farm Bureau and the American Medical Association, and that they exercise influence mainly on other large institutions rather than directly on other individuals. Big, well-established institutions have in some cases crowded smaller and more marginal competitors entirely off the stage. This is the case, for example, with national news magazines and automobile manufacturers, to take two dissimilar cases. In other enterprises, such as local newspapers and home construction, small entrepreneurs can still break in. In others, such as intellectual quarterlies and fashion design, off-beat individuals can sometimes find a niche. Nevertheless, it seems fair to say that established national institutions set most of the ground rules for both stability and change in contemporary America. (Most, but not all, as Negro rioting and bloody police retaliation have recently been demonstrating.)

The mere existence of well-established institutions does not, however, tell us anything about their management and control. The late C. Wright Mills used to argue that established institutions of this kind were controlled by a small group of men who had been to the same schools, shared the same values, and manipulated the rest of society to suit their own needs. One of the present authors earlier argued the contrary, suggesting that the activities of these institutions are subject to veto by a wide variety of vested interests both within each insitution and within the larger society.[5] Both of us still take this latter

[5] See Riesman, Denney, and Glazer, *The Lonely Crowd,* chap. 11. For further discussion of the difference between Mills and Riesman, see Riesman's preface to the paperback edition (1961). For a full statement of Mills's position see *The Power Elite.*

view. While initiative often comes from the top, this is by no means always the case—especially if the top is taken to mean boards of trustees and directors as against top administrators and professionals.

There are, of course, variations from one institution to another. Control over organized violence is in fewer hands than control over capital, and control over capital is in fewer hands than control over ideas. The Federal Bureau of Investigation is more centralized than the State Department, but both are more centralized than the Office of Economic Opportunity or the Department of Housing and Urban Development. There are similar variations in the private sector. Texas tycoons exercise more personal control over their empires than the Rockefellers over theirs. Almost any profit-making corporation is more managed from the top down than any church, university, or professional association.

Nonetheless, even the managers of the most centralized organizations, public or private, believe they have little room for maneuver. They feel hemmed in by rivals for power within their organization, by competitive organizations, by their prospective clients, by their lawyers and their boards of directors (or fellow directors), and even by their subordinates. The latter, especially, exercise power in many ways that deserve more attention than they have gotten. Boards of directors sometimes go along with their company president because they have no ready replacement and because they fear he may take another job if he is not given his head. President Kennedy ordered resumption of nuclear testing in 1962 because, among other things, scientists threatened to leave the weapons laboratories if their hardware was not tried out. And, of course, as we shall see in more detail later, university trustees and administrators are constantly readjusting both the means and the ends of higher education so as to attract eminent scholars to their institutions.

We hope this view of America will be reflected in our rhetoric. We have chosen to speak of "established institutions," not of "the establishment."[6] We see established institutions as the framework and battleground within which most changes in the American system are now worked out, but we do not see America as ruled by an interlocking directorate or clique. Established institutions are a mixed bag, and their ascendancy does not fully define either the character of modern American life or the expectations and aspirations of the young

[6] It is interesting to note that the English originally used the term "establishment" in the way we use the term "established institutions." It applied to the Church of England and was then extended to include the Civil Service. Only in recent years has it been aimed at individuals rather than institutions, becoming a synonym for something like Mills's "power elite." See the essay by Henry Fairlie, in Hugh Thomas, ed. It was, however, in this latter sense that Americans took over the term in the early 1960s.

people who will live and work within them. Yet the hegemony of these institutions does exclude some possibilities and encourage others.

To begin with, the sources of differentiation in American life are changing. The old nineteenth-century divisions between Irish and Yankee, Baptist and Episcopalian, North and South, country and city seem to be losing their significance. Even the struggles between Negroes and whites and between Catholics and non-Catholics, while certainly far from settled, strike us as legacies of a vanishing past rather than as necessary features of the contemporary American system.[7] This system is increasingly meritocratic, in Michael Young's sense of that term.[8] It tries to divide people according to competence, interest, and achievement rather than according to origin. (Background and competence are very much related, as poor people's failure to meet "objective" middle-class standards indicates. But the correlation is far from perfect.) While there are still plenty of exceptions to the general meritocratic rule, and plenty of reasons for ambivalence about its increasing acceptance, it seems to us an inevitable feature of highly organized societies with a very specialized division of labor.

The partial triumph of meritocracy brings with it what we will call the national upper-middle class style: cosmopolitan, moderate, universalistic, somewhat legalistic, concerned with equity and fair play, aspiring to neutrality between regions, religions, and ethnic groups. Not everyone who has money, power, or visibility in America subscribes to this set of ideals even in theory, much less in practice. There are many who take a narrower and more overtly self-interested view of the world, especially among those who have only recently climbed to within hailing distance of the top. Nor do these attitudes affect all aspects of life equally: men who think America has dealt unfairly with Negroes may, for example, see no comparable source of regret in America's treatment of the Vietnamese. Nonetheless, we would argue that the ethic we are describing, like the institutions which encourage it, is growing stronger rather than weaker.

The Rise of the University

These changes in the character of American society have inevitably been accompanied by changes in higher education. The most basic

[7] The fact that racial conflict can in principle be resolved within the present institutional framework does not, of course, mean that it necessarily *will* be resolved, any more than the fact that Soviet-American conflicts can in principle be resolved necessarily means we will avoid nuclear war. Societies can be destroyed by idiocy as well as by "necessary" conflicts.

[8] See Young, and the discussion in Riesman, "Notes on Meritocracy."

of these changes has been the rise of the university. This has had many consequences. College instructors have become less and less preoccupied with educating young people, more and more preoccupied with educating one another by doing scholarly research which advances their discipline. Undergraduate education has become less and less a terminal enterprise, more and more a preparation for graduate school. The result is that higher education has ceased to be a marginal, backward-looking enterprise shunned by the bulk of the citizenry. Today it is a major growth industry, consuming about 2 per cent of GNP, directly touching the lives of perhaps 4 per cent of the population, and exercising an indirect effect on the whole of society.

The rise of the university has been gradual rather than sudden. The first Ph.D. was awarded in 1861 by Yale. Cornell opened in 1868 with Andrew White as President. Charles Eliot was inaugurated as President of Harvard in 1869. Yet it was not until the 1880s that anything like a modern university really took shape in America. Perhaps the most important breakthroughs were the founding of Johns Hopkins and Clark as primarily graduate universities. Eliot's success in instituting the elective system at Harvard was also important, both in its own right and because it facilitated the assemblage of a more scholarly and specialized faculty. The 1890s saw further progress, with the founding of Chicago, the reform of Columbia, and the tentative acceptance of graduate work as an important activity in the leading state universities. This was also the period when national learned societies and journals were founded and when knowledge was broken up into its present departmental categories ("physics," "biology," "history," "philosophy," and so forth), with the department emerging as the basic unit of academic administration. Medicine and law also became serious subjects of graduate study at this time, with Johns Hopkins leading the way in medicine and Harvard in law.

By World War I two dozen major universities had emerged, and while the number has grown slightly since then, the changes have been slow.[9] These universities have long been remarkably similar in what they encourage and value.[10] They turn out Ph.D.s who, despite

[9] If we arbitrarily define a major university as one which turns out more than 1 per cent of the nation's Ph.D.s each year, we find that twenty-two universities met this test in the period 1926–47. By 1962 the number had risen to thirty. (The absolute number of Ph.D.s needed to meet the criterion had quintupled.) Analyzing the problem another way, the dozen largest producers of Ph.D.s accounted for 55 per cent of all Ph.D.s between 1926 and 1947, compared to 36 per cent in 1962. See Cartter, ed. *American Universities,* pp. 1263–65.

[10] For evidence on this point see Cartter, *An Assessment.* The extraordinarily high degree of consensus about the relative standing of departments in all academic fields suggests that the standards used to evaluate departments must be quite uniform. Rankings over time also show remarkable stability.

conspicuous exceptions, mostly have quite similar ideas about what their discipline covers, how it should be taught, and how its frontiers should be advanced. (This does not mean that there are *no* differences of opinion on these matters within the academic profession. It means only that when contrasted with trustees, administrators, parents, students, or the present authors, the outlook of Ph.D.s in a given discipline seems quite uniform.) These men were not only like-minded at the outset, but they have established machinery for remaining like-minded. National and regional meetings for each academic discipline and subdiscipline are now annual affairs, national journals publish work in every specialized subject, and an informal national system of job placement and replacement has come into existence. The result is that large numbers of Ph.D.s now regard themselves almost as independent professionals like doctors or lawyers, responsible primarily to themselves and their colleagues rather than their employers, and committed to the advancement of knowledge rather than of any particular institution.[11] (For this and other reasons elaborated in Chapter V, we see little distinction between graduate doctoral programs in the arts and sciences and other graduate professional programs. When we use terms like "graduate professional schools," we will mean all sorts of graduate schools.)

These attitudes were greatly strengthened by World War II and its aftermath. Not only in the Manhattan Project but in other less glamorous ones, academic scientists helped contribute to the war effort, and for this and other reasons a dramatic increase in federal support for academic research ensued. This support soon became available not just in the physical sciences but in the biological and social sciences as well. In recent years Washington has even begun to put small sums into the humanities. Unlike previous support for universities, these federal grants and contracts are for all practical purposes given to individual scholars or groups of scholars rather than to the institution where they happen to work. More often than not, if a man moves to a new institution his federal grants are transferred too. Not only that, but these federal grants are made largely on the basis of individual professional reputation and competence. Federal agencies usually give only minimal consideration to an institution's location, sectarian ties, racial composition, and the like. The result has been further to enhance the status of the academician, who is now a prime fund raiser for his institution. Since the amount of research support has grown much faster than the number of competent researchers, talented men have been in very short supply and command rapidly

[11] There is considerable literature on this subject, distinguishing between Robert Merton's terms "locals" and "cosmopolitians," or between Everett Hughes's "home guard" and "itinerant" faculty. The best-known study is Caplow and McGee.

rising salaries. They are also increasingly free to set their own working conditions. The result has been a rapid decline in teaching loads for productive scholars, an increase in the ratio of graduate to undergraduate students at the institutions where scholars are concentrated, the gradual elimination of unscholarly undergraduates from these institutions, and the parallel elimination of unscholarly faculty. The recent effort to enroll black students has to some extent slowed this trend.

From the very start the professionalization of university professors brought conflict on many fronts. Late nineteenth- and early twentieth-century academic histories report many battles in which the basic question was whether the president and trustees or the faculty would determine the shape of the curriculum, the content of particular courses, or the use of particular books. The professors (for instance Veblen) lost most of the publicized battles, but they won the war. Today faculty control over these matters is rarely challenged, and conflict usually centers on other issues. The faculty, for example, have sought the right to choose their colleagues. While they have not usually won this right in the formal sense of actually making appointments themselves, their recommendations are sought at all reputable colleges and universities, and heeded in nine cases out of ten. Faculty committees are, it is true, sometimes overruled. Occasionally this is because the colleague group has rejected a notably popular teacher whose publications may not meet the standards of the guild as locally defined. Sometimes it is because a capable scholar has aroused the Philistines by, in one epoch, backing oleomargerine over butter, or today North Vietnam over South Vietnam. Public universities are in this respect somewhat more vulnerable than private ones, holding quality constant, because of their dependence on the local legislature; but even elected state university trustees are seldom eager to force issues of academic freedom into the open. As long as faculty members stick to problems defined by their disciplines, they almost never run into public controversy except in the most provincial milieus. And while administrators or trustees sometimes reject faculty recommendations, they almost never foist their own candidates on an unwilling faculty. The faculty has also sought to apply to the selection of undergraduates the same meritocratic standards that have long been used to select graduate students. Here again they have largely won the day, although marginal exceptions (geographic distribution, alumni sons, faculty sons) still stir sporadic controversy. The faculty has also sought some voice in choosing top administrators and in this too it has been increasingly successful. Once chosen, these administrators have broad powers to make policy (in the name and with the consent of the trustees). But even here a *unified* faculty has an informal veto at most universities and colleges.

It is important to be clear what these victories mean. College pro-

fessors have not for the most part won significant *formal* power, either
individually or collectively, over the institutions that employ them.
On paper the typical academic senate is still a largely advisory body
whose legal jurisdiction is confined to setting the curriculum and
awarding degrees. Departments, too, have little *formal* power except
sometimes over course offerings and requirements. Budgets and personnel, for example, are in principle subject to "higher" review, and
ultimate control mostly remains where it has always been—with
the administration, the lay trustees, and in some cases the legislature.

The trustees, however, are seldom what they once were. Most are
more permissive than their nineteenth- or early twentieth-century
predecessors. They are also more sensitive to individuals and groups
unlike themselves. They share the general upper-middle class allergy
to "trouble," of whatever sort. If there is strong internal pressure for a
given course of action, they are likely to go along. They are also more
likely than they once were to delegate authority to the college administration, either de jure or de facto. In part this is because the complexity of the university has increased, so that lay trustees feel less
competent to deal with its affairs on a one-day-a-month basis. In part
it is because college presidents are today usually Ph.D.s rather than
clergymen, and can therefore claim apparently relevant but esoteric
expertise which other board members lack. There has been a recent
movement to appoint faculty members and sometimes students to
boards of trustees. This adds expertise but at the risk of involving the
trustees in the details of academic administration. It also reduces the
authority most presidents now possess vis-à-vis lay boards—an authority less common before the professionalization of academic work. The
tremendous competition among leading and aspiring institutions
means that the decisions on recruitment and promotion of faculty
must be made swiftly and would be too much delayed if subjected to
detailed board review. (One reason boards spend so much time on
buildings and grounds is that trustees feel at home in this area, presidents regard it as useful occupational therapy for them, and decisions
can sometimes if not invariably wait. Mistaken judgments about bricks
and mortar are also more obvious to the lay trustees than most mistakes in academic policy or personnel, and the sums of money look
larger in many cases.) To be sure, there are enormous differences in
the degree of self-confidence of trustees. Some still "meddle" regularly
in the affairs of "their" colleges and universities, settling issues the
faculty considers its own prerogative. Those with access to public or
private money also still throw their weight around at times. But the
over-all trend seems to us toward moderation and an increasingly cere-
monial role for trustees. Beyond ceremony, they can be useful as buff-
ers to cope with legislators, potential donors, and other pressure

groups, giving legitimacy to the institution and its activities that would otherwise be hard to achieve.

The transfer of power from boards of directors to professional administrators has not, of course, been confined to higher education. The "managerial revolution," while not so widespread, so complete, or so progressive as some of its prophets have suggested, has taken place in many non-academic enterprises. What is perhaps unusual about the academic world is the extent to which the top management, while nominally acting in the interests of the board, actually represents the interests of "middle management" (i.e. the faculty), both to the board and to the world. Despite some notable exceptions, today's college and university presidents, as already noted, usually start out as members of the academic profession. When they become administrators and have to deal more often with non-academicians, they inevitably become somewhat deprofessionalized. Nonetheless, most university presidents still see their institution primarily as an assemblage of scholars and scientists, each doing his own work in his own way.[12] Most university presidents see their primary responsibility as "making the world safe for academicians," however much the academicians themselves resent the necessary (and unnecessary) compromises made in their behalf. The typical president's greatest ambition for the future is usually to "strengthen" his institution, and operationally this usually turns out to mean assembling scholars of even greater competence and reputation than are now present.

In the course of institution building all administrators find it expedient to pretend that the interests of their institution and of the larger society are identical. Academic administrators are no exception. Many even come to believe their own talk. At that point they may lose sight of some of the distinctive objectives and prejudices of their faculty. More often, however, they compromise in order to fight (or run away) again another day. This usually offends the faculty, which has the luxury of being able to go elsewhere if its insistence on its principles brings reprisal against its institution. In the course of trying to strengthen their faculty, administrators of upwardly mobile institutions also usually offend many of the "weak" faculty currently on the payroll. And in the course of trying to keep the peace among warring departments and contending professors within departments, administrators inevitably offend most professors at one time or another.

Academicians are neither a tolerant nor an easy-going species, and their apparently congenital feelings of irritation and frustration require scapegoats. Administrators serve this purpose and they serve it best

[12] Clark Kerr's much maligned but marvelously perceptive study, *The Uses of the University*, is a good example of this "faculty" view, even though the faculty at Berkeley reacted with horror to the mirror he held up to them.

when their actions can be attributed to non-academic considerations. So they are usually regarded as the enemy. Nonetheless, we would argue that administrators are today more concerned with keeping their faculty happy than with placating any other single group.[13] They are also, in our experience, far more responsive to students and more concerned with the inadequacies and tragedies of student life than the majority of faculty. We have also found that the administrative actions that offend academic liberals and elicit bitter talk about administrative tyranny are usually disapproved by only a minority of the faculty. This minority then finds it convenient to blame the administration instead of blaming its complacent colleagues for what is done with their tacit consent. Sometimes, indeed, the dissidents blame "the administration" for actions the majority of their colleagues insisted on, forgetting that faculties are themselves diverse and assuming if their colleagues do not agree with them it must be because they were "pressured" or "bought," or "manipulated."[14] In our observation, however, where professional opinion is united, trustees and administrators only rarely override and then seldom for long.

The redistribution of power in the universities has been accompanied—and to some extent caused—by a change in the relationship between the university and other established institutions. The universities, especially their graduate professional schools, have become pacesetters in the promotion of meritocratic values. In Talcott Parsons' terms, they are "universalistic," ignoring "particularistic" and personal qualities in their students and professors.[15] This means that

[13] To illustrate: The American Council on Education has for some years sponsored a training program for prospective academic administrators, many of whom are currently professors. In interviewing applicants it proposes various hypothetical problems that might confront the applicant as an administrator and asks how he thinks he would deal with them. One common problem involves a faculty member who is being unreasonable or uncooperative in some way. Most of the prospective administrators respond by saying in effect that they would stand up for their rights and take a tough line. The experienced administrators who are evaluating the applicants are usually said to comment afterward that "that young man obviously doesn't know anything about college faculties"—this despite the fact that he is often a member of such a faculty. The administrators are, we think, usually right. Faculty members have an extraordinarily skewed perception of their own behavior, both individual and collective, and have little sense that their demands are often "impossible."

[14] In a generally liberal academic setting, moreover, faculty members may overlook the significance of a small but vocal group of right wing faculty who are not at all complacent but who tell their right wing political and business cronies that the general run of professors (and students) is even more "subversive" and dangerous than the outsiders realize. Much American anti-intellectualism depends upon the pedantic documentation and conspiratorial interpretations supplied by intellectuals.

[15] For an interesting application of Parsonian categories to the process of education, see Dreeben.

they choose professors almost entirely on the basis of their "output" and professional reputation. Students in the graduate professional schools are selected by similar criteria: by their ability to write good examinations and do good academic work. The claims of localism, sectarianism, ethnic prejudice and preference, class background, age, sex, and even occupational plans are largely ignored.[16]

The graduate professional schools have in turn been leaders in imposing meritocratic values on the professions themselves. The leading law firms hire men who made the law review at the most competitive law schools, and the leading hospitals offer internships and residencies to doctors who did well or were well recommended by the most competitive medical schools. Most conspicuous of all, colleges and universities scramble to hire Ph.D.s who have done well in the most competitive graduate departments. The result is that many traditional prejudices affecting recruitment have broken down: local boys today enjoy little advantage over outsiders; white Anglo-Saxon Protestants monopolize fewer and fewer occupational slots; and family connections count for less than they used to. Even corporation managers with long traditions of self-interested exclusiveness have in recent years frequently yielded to a broader vision of their enterprise and of America. Big employers today recruit university graduates in an increasingly even-handed way, paying ever less attention to "irrelevant" factors like class background, religion, and ethnicity. This is partly because of competition for skilled specialists, partly because of the stirrings of conscience, partly because they fear adverse publicity. Companies have grown larger, have had to rationalize recruitment policy, and can therefore no longer conceal nonmeritocratic discrimination from themselves or (consequently) from the general public. Furthermore, with the growth of democractic ideology and the decline of old-fashioned social snobbery, even college fraternities have become less socially exclusive, as have leading prep schools. This creates cumulative pressures for meritocracy, since even if an employer wanted to discriminate he would have a hard time finding channels that made this easy for him. Legacies of earlier discrimination obviously remain both in recruitment and training—and in judgments about the appropriateness of people for specific posi-

16 There are some exceptions. Law schools admit brilliant students they expect will do well in law school even if they do not plan to practice law, but medical schools take a narrower view. Graduate departments in the sciences will usually admit a good candidate even though they think he will "sell out" and become a scientist in industry, but they will usually reject even the most brilliant candidate if he does not plan to take a Ph.D. In most graduate admissions committees there is also a residual bias against girls, and in the past few years a bias in favor of Negroes. For historical reasons some institutions show other idiosyncrasies, but these are of marginal importance.

tions. A Negro is not likely soon to become president of General Motors, nor a woman president of Harvard University, but both have been Cabinet members and either might become a vice-president of AT&T.

We do not want to exaggerate the extent of the ties between the modern occupational structure and higher education. The big Wall Street and Washington law firms may hire the top graduates of the top law schools, but there is also another legal world where lawyers trained in night schools pick up not-so-good livings chasing ambulances, writing wills, settling insurance claims, and generally acting as brokers between the uninitiated and various bureaucracies. Similar chasms separate the top doctors who practice in teaching hospitals from others who have no hospital privileges anywhere. There are also colleges where, as Everett Hughes has put it, the faculty not only includes no scholars but includes nobody who has even studied under a scholar. There are still many roads into these lower levels of professional practice, and on some of them academic competence counts for less than persistence and animal cunning. There are also many roads to the top in business, from sales and accounting to engineering and law. Academic competence counts for very little on some of them. The Robert McNamaras who come up through graduate schools of business administration are still nothing like a majority.

Nonetheless, the role of graduate education in job distribution seems to be growing. At the same time, and for related reasons, the values and methods promoted in the graduate professional schools seem to be increasingly accepted in the larger society. This does not mean that the outlook of professional school faculty and the professions themselves are ever likely to be the same. On the contrary, there will always be tension between the "theorists" in the graduate schools and the "practitioners" in the field. By the time the AMA accepts compulsory health insurance, group practice, and other reforms long advocated by large numbers of medical professors, for example, professors of medicine will have shifted their attention to new problems and will be attacking the conservatism of practitioners on new grounds. The same is true in other areas. The striking thing, however, is how often the opinions and practices of the professional schools foreshadow those of the profession as a whole a generation later.

The University College

The rise of the university in the late nineteenth century did not at first have much effect on undergraduate education. The overwhelming majority of students continued to attend special-interest colleges, and even those who attended the undergraduate college at a university were for the most part terminal students. While a significant proportion eventually did some kind of work beyond the B.A., competition for admission to most graduate professional schools was relatively slight and had little effect on undergraduate life. Similarly, while administrators at special-interest colleges were often impressed by the scholarly achievements of faculty at leading universities, and some made an active effort to acquire a similar faculty at their own institution, their success was for many years limited by the shortage of Ph.D.s, especially "productive" ones. As in the larger society, the groundwork for a system was being laid, and the giant enterprises that would dominate the system were being organized, but the bulk of the nation's business was still being done by independent enterprises of limited means and limited views.

The pace of change accelerated somewhat after World War I, for the 1920s and 1930s were a period of unprecedented growth in enrollment. (It is always easier to redistribute resources and power in periods of growth, because the progressives can be given more without the standpatters appearing to get less.) By the outbreak of World War II the majority of the nation's college students attended institutions staffed by academic professionals—though there were still many enclaves of provincialism, including all but a handful of teachers colleges, Catholic colleges, devout Protestant colleges, and Negro colleges. The professionalization of the faculty reduced the internal homogeneity of many special-purpose colleges. Upper-class colleges took on literary critics with working-class ancestors, Southern colleges hired more historians who had grown up in the North or even in Europe, women's colleges hired male psychologists, and Methodist colleges took on Unitarian philosophers. Such "mismatching" had, of course, sometimes taken place accidentally even in presumptively homogeneous special-interest colleges, but professionalization made it far more common. It also put trustees and parents who opposed heterogeneity very much on the defensive. A New York millionaire might not like the idea of having his son study under a Jewish radical at Yale, but if the boy's teacher had been publicly defined as "one of the leading economists in the country," the millionaire's objections seemed bigoted and irrelevant (which did not, of course, always prevent him from carrying weight, in Montana if not at Yale).

Until the 1950s, most undergraduates seem to have remained relatively unaffected by these changes. The proportion going on to graduate school in the arts and sciences had risen slowly, but the proportion going into law and medicine had fallen correspondingly.

As a result, the over-all proportion of B.A.s earning graduate degrees probably changed relatively little for some decades.[17] In the late 1950s, however, the effects of the academic revolution on undergraduate life began to multiply. Both the absolute number and the proportion of young people applying to college were rising steadily. This gave many colleges a choice between expansion and greater selectivity. The faculty preferred selectivity. This preference proved influential in colleges of all sorts and decisive in private ones.[18] As a result, the leading undergraduate colleges, both public and private, began demanding higher academic aptitude and more proof of academic motivation from their entrants. These students, in turn, found the academic profession and ancillary activities increasingly appealing, while mostly rejecting careers in business and other fields requiring only a B.A.[19] The proportion of undergraduates who wanted to go on to graduate school therefore began to rise rapidly. The same

[17] Statistical measures of these trends over long periods are hard to come by. Until very recently the U. S. Office of Education's statistics lumped graduate students with undergraduates in law, medicine, theology, and some other professions. Figures on graduate enrollment and degrees included only those taking degrees in fields that offered an undergraduate major—mainly the arts and sciences and education. The proportion of undergraduates going on in professional fields like law and medicine has declined since 1900, but this does not show up in USOE's figures on graduate enrollment. Enrollment in the areas USOE traditionally defined as graduate-level have on the other hand, risen much faster than undergraduate enrollment. The result is that USOE data greatly exaggerated the actual change in the ratio of total graduate to total undergraduate enrollment.

The 1960 Census, I, 1, table 173, shows that among those completing four years of college the proportion going on to complete a fifth year did not change significantly between 1910 and 1950. Among men who were born between 1885 and 1930, about 40 per cent of those completing four years of higher education went on to complete a fifth. For individuals born after 1930, 1960 Census data are not very useful, since such individuals were still returning to graduate school in significant numbers in 1960. The 1960 Census therefore tells us relatively little about trends in graduate enrollment for men earning B.A.s after about 1950. More recent data collected by others is not strictly speaking comparable.

Karel, tables 1 and 2, shows that if one counts all M.D.s as doctor's degrees the proportion of the population earning such degrees rose from 0.68 per cent in 1901 to 1.11 per cent in 1962, while the proportion earning B.A.s rose from 1.32 per cent to 17.76 per cent. But many 1901 M.D.s were not B.A.s, and counting the pre-Flexner medical school as a graduate institution is as misleading as counting it as an undergraduate institution. Since 1950 the lag in medical school growth has been just about offset by the spurt in Ph.D. enrollment. Throughout this century, though, the most rapid expansion in graduate work has been at the Master's level, where the proportion of the population earning degrees rose from 0.12 in 1901 to 3.86 in 1962.

[18] In individual instances there are often other reasons for selectivity, e.g. the failure of a capital bond issue or the lack of building sites for expansion. In some instances, inertia favors growth; in others, stability.

[19] Among the elite students in the elite universities there has been a general rejection of business careers, even those requiring advanced degrees. A certain proportion of men with Ph.D.s and LL.B.s will nonetheless end up in business, holding insurance against their employers by virtue of their professional training.

pattern was repeated to a lesser extent at less selective colleges.[20]

Until World War II many if not most undergraduates came to the old special-interest colleges in order to kill time, get away from home, make new friends, enjoy themselves, acquire salable skills, and so forth. Undergraduates with such aims were not by and large very vulnerable to faculty pressures. Most, of course, wanted a diploma, and that meant they had to meet whatever formal requirements the faculty set. But these requirements served mainly to sift and intimidate the less competent students. The abler students could get C's without doing much work, and most capitalized on this opportunity. The spread of graduate study altered these attitudes appreciably. Today a substantial fraction of the undergraduate population wants not only a degree but an undergraduate transcript sufficiently distinguished to ensure entry into a competitive professional school of some sort. Unlike many employers, these schools are generally reluctant to take undergraduates with undistinguished grades.[21] The faculty can use this fact as a weapon to make undergraduates do far

[20] Since the early 1950s the steady growth of graduate work in fields like education, business, engineering, and the arts and sciences has more than offset the continuing lag in first professional degrees like the LL.B. and M.D. A 1963 National Science Foundation survey of 1958 B.A.s found that 58 per cent had done some graduate work. (See Sharpe, "Five Years.") The NSF figures include some students who had not completed a full year of graduate work, and who in theory would not be entitled to report "five or more" years of higher education to the 1970 Census. It is therefore likely that the increase in the proportion of B.A.s entering graduate school was less than the apparent contrast between NSF and earlier Census figures. But probably not much less.

More recent studies by Alexander Astin and his colleagues at the American Council on Education show that since 1958 the proportion of entering freshmen who *plan* to do graduate work has continued to rise. In Astin's sample of 45 four-year colleges the proportion of all freshmen planning to get some sort of graduate degree rose from 49 to 67 per cent between 1961 and 1965. This sample appears to be representative of other four-year colleges, though the percentages would be somewhat lower if junior college entrants were included. A 1965 follow-up of the students entering 246 four-year colleges in 1961 showed that the proportion planning to do graduate work rose from 42 to 70 per cent over the four college years. These plans were admittedly unrealistic in many cases. (Only 60 per cent of this same sample had even earned a B.A. at the time of the follow-up. Many of the non-B.A.s were not even enrolled in college at the time they outlined their plans for graduate study.) Nonetheless it seems fairly clear that graduate plans and enrollment are today rising much faster than college entrance or graduation rates. Although women are generally less likely to go to graduate school than men, the recent increase has been about equal for the two sexes. This suggests that draft deferment is not the primary cause.

[21] The enormous expansion of institutions seeking to offer graduate instruction has made places available to many who do not have distinguished undergraduate records at distinguished places. Still, the more energetic and competent undergraduate teachers generally want their students to go on to "good" graduate schools and steer them away from the more anemic ones, including the home institution at times. An undergraduate education itself tends to expose its student devotees to the names of luminaries at leading graduate schools, even though many textbooks and readers are produced by men at the less visible places.

more academic work than was common in the traditional terminal colleges. This external threat has been re-enforced in recent years by changes in the mass media's portrait of established national institutions. These institutions are increasingly shown offering prize jobs to men who have intellectual skills. Students are therefore constantly searching themselves for signs of intellectual competence and worrying about signs of stupidity. Many cannot settle for C's, even if the graduate schools would, for they cannot accept the idea that they are only "worth" a C.

The fruition of this change was the birth of what Frank Bowles has called the "university college." In our usage this is a college whose primary purpose is to prepare students for graduate work of some kind—primarily in the arts and sciences but also in professional subjects ranging from law and medicine to business and social work.[22] A university college may be part of a university with big graduate schools, such as Yale or Michigan, or it may be geographically isolated and administratively independent, as Amherst, Oberlin, or Vassar is. But even if it is nominally independent, it is a de facto prep school for a small number of graduate professional schools, in much the same way that Groton, Andover, and Farmington are prep schools for Ivy League and Seven Sister colleges. Such a university college usually draws most of its students from the top tenth of the national ability distribution. It seldom loses more than a fifth of them during the undergraduate years. (More than a fifth may drop out, but many return and most of the others graduate from other colleges.) It usually sends nearly three-quarters of its men and a third to a half of its women to graduate school. If such a university college is administratively part of a larger institution, it is likely to share its faculty with the graduate school of arts and sciences. But even if it is separate, it is almost certain to draw its faculty from the same manpower pool as the graduate schools of arts and sciences, seeking the same virtues and looking askance at the same presumed vices. The university college is the fruition of the academic revolution at the undergraduate level.

Out of more than 2,000 undergraduate colleges, probably no more than 100 today really fit the above description. Yet these are the most prestigious colleges in the country, to which the ablest and most ambitious students usually gravitate. They also attract the ablest faculty and administrators and the most generous philanthropists. And they provide a model which many of the other 1,900 colleges

22 The term "university college" is used in an entirely different sense in Great Britain and parts of the Commonwealth, to indicate a budding university that has not yet achieved sufficient stability and reputation to deserve complete autonomy, and that awards degrees through another institution.

regard as desirable, even if not immediately accessible. Drawn by emulation on the one side and pushed by accrediting agencies on the other, an increasing number of terminal colleges hire Ph.D.s from the leading graduate schools even though they fear the impact of men who may not be happy or complacent at a terminal college, and who may also make others less happy or complacent. As faculty recruiting becomes more national and less parochial, even colleges that might prefer staff from the old parish are forced to look elsewhere if they are to grow. New and better-trained faculty recruits in turn help propel the institution toward the recruitment of students on the basis of academic ability, with diminished reference to traditional considerations.[23]

Virtually all terminal colleges want to hire faculty of the kind now hired by the university colleges. Whether or not these faculty come out of the subculture to which a college has traditionally been tied is secondary. In most cases the terminal colleges also want to recruit students entirely on the basis of academic ability. They would prefer to ignore traditional considerations like geography, religion, ethnicity, and class. Specialization by sex and occupational intention is also somewhat less common among undergraduate colleges than it once was. Even administrators and trustees seem to be more often chosen according to the criteria of achievement, competence, and judgment that prevail in established national institutions, than according to the criteria of the special-interest group that initially founded the particular college.

One way to describe this change is in terms of changing reference groups. Special-interest colleges were established by laymen to serve a particular purpose, and were initially very committed to that purpose. The local college was local first and a college second; the Catholic college was Catholic first and a college second; the Negro college was Negro first and a college second, and so forth. But as time went on these disparate institutions took on lives and purposes of their own. Undergraduates thought of themselves less often as future women, Baptists, or teachers and more often simply as students, having a common interest with students in all sorts of other places called colleges rather than with girls, Baptists, or teachers who were not students. Similar changes have taken place at the faculty level. Even the college president today often thinks of himself less as the president of a college in San Jose, a college catering to the rich, or a college for Irish Catholics than as the president of an academically first-rate, second-rate, or third-rate college. Such a man's reference group is no longer the traditional clientele and patrons of his

[23] For a further description of this process of emulation see Riesman, "The Academic Procession." The major partial exception to this generalization is the two-year college discussed in Chapter XI.

institution or the trustees who still speak for them, but the presidents of other colleges, many of which had historically different origins and aims. The result is convergence of aims, methods, and probably results.

That these developments make both terminal and university colleges more useful to other established national institutions can hardly be doubted. They make higher education look like a fairly effective instrument for meritocratic sorting and grading of the future employees. They probably also help promote and disseminate values and skills useful in the maintenance of established institutions. The university colleges and their emulators usually try, for example, to help their students transcend whatever subculture they are born and raised in, and move them out into a slightly more cosmopolitan world. In part this is a matter of exposing students to heterogeneous classmates—heterogeneous, that is, by traditional demographic criteria, even though often quite homogeneous in terms of academic aptitudes. In part it is a matter of exposing students to professors who know something of a larger world than the one the students have encountered, and who may, if they are wise or charming, lure their students into it. In part it is a matter of giving the students books to read. In part it is a matter of giving young people with a yen for mobility the diplomatic passport they need to cross the borders of their racial, religious, economic, sexual, or generational parish.[24]

These efforts at emancipation are, it is true, necessarily limited in scope. Some colleges manage to bring together students and faculty of diverse class backgrounds, but this diversity almost never extends to class aspirations. Wherever they come from, college students by and large plan to end up in the upper-middle classes if they can, and they meet professors who have succeeded in doing just this.[25] Similarly, while some colleges bring together students from different regional backgrounds, few mix them with more than token foreigners, and even fewer create an atmosphere that appreciably curtails nationalistic biases. Then too, while many colleges attract a substantial number of students older than the undergraduate norm, and all employ professors who run the full age range, few are successful in establishing really close cross-generational contacts or in counteracting

[24] In Greek, a "diploma" was literally a doubled-over piece of paper and hence a letter of recommendation. A "diplomat" was one who carried a diploma. Today it could well be argued that the diplomats who serve as go-betweens for America's many subcultures and who hold the country together are the diploma holders from these subcultures.

[25] A small but interesting minority of students, often from the upper social strata, profess aspirations for downward mobility, often identifying with Negroes as the American equivalent of the proletariat and meeting on the way down Negroes and others on the way up. This minority is also using its college experience to achieve its own version of mobility out of the prevailing and despised majority culture into a subculture felt to be more authentic and less achievement-oriented.

the mutual chauvinism of young and old vis à vis one another. Nor can any college do much about the parochialism that comes from having lived only in the twentieth century. It is true that the formal curriculum tries to overcome all these limitations, but the number of students who can be significantly affected by books has always been fairly small, especially when the message of the book is re-enforced neither by human contact nor by daily experience.

These almost inescapable limitations are in most cases supplemented by self-imposed ones, often inherited from the special-interest group that founded a particular college. Local colleges, for example, often deliberately exclude students from outside their state or even their city. While many Catholic colleges and universities are deliberately seeking out non-Catholic teachers and ideas in order to become more ecumenical, others still feel they should hire only Catholics and also occasionally screen reading lists with an eye to orthodoxy. Upper-middle class colleges sometimes make no effort to provide scholarships for students from poorer families. White colleges often make life intolerable for black students, and Negro colleges often do likewise for white faculty. Professional schools frequently cling to a narrow view of their students' future responsibilities, and sometimes resist affiliation with a multipurpose university. Single sex colleges, while increasingly on the defensive in considering coeducation, occasionally cling to their exclusiveness, if not with pride then with the inertia of indifference.

Just as some small businesses continue to earn high returns in the interstices of a corporate economy, and local governments take on new responsibilities despite the parallel increase in federal power, so too the old nineteenth-century system of special-purpose colleges endures despite the rise of the national university system and the magnetic appeal of the university college model. Yet while local car dealers may survive and flourish, the future of the automobile industry is determined in Detroit, New York, and Washington. So too in higher education, while the old special-interest colleges and the energies they embody may give the present much of its flavor, they do little to shape the future. The model for the future is the university college, and the result is likely to be a continuing trend toward meritocracy.

II. *The War between the Generations*

Academic Age-grading Yesterday and Today

One way to determine the central purposes of an institution is to ask whether a given function could be eliminated without changing its name. An institution that does not facilitate social mobility, that has no connection with any occupational subculture, and that does nothing to perpetuate localism, sectarianism, sex polarities, or ethnic separatism can still be called a college. But an institution that does not bring together people called teachers with other people called students is not called a college but something else.[1] The confrontation between teachers and students is, in turn, usually a confrontation between those who are in some sense mature and those who are less so. The central purpose of a college can thus be defined as socialization. In nine cases out of ten a college pits the old against the young and becomes both a battlefield and a negotiating table in the ceaseless war between the generations.[2]

The character of any intergenerational confrontation obviously depends in part on the age of the participants. This is by no means uniform, either from one era to another or from one institution to another. During the eighteenth and nineteenth centuries many students presented themselves for admission to college during early adolescence—though Cotton Mather was unusual in graduating from Harvard at fifteen. Other students came to college only in their early twenties, after a local minister had decided that they might be suitable for ordination and had encouraged them to apply. All these applicants were at least semiliterate as a result of instruction by their parents, a local clergyman, a traveling schoolmaster or some other adult, and many had had some years of formal elementary schooling. But very few had had any secondary schooling, formal or informal.

---

[1] There are a few minor exceptions to this as to all such rules. The medieval term "collegium" was applied to groups of adults who had collegial relationships with one another, and the usage has survived down to the present time in cases such as the "College of Cardinals" and the "College of Physicians and Surgeons."

[2] Again, there are a few exceptions. Some colleges are strictly technical and have students who are by most standards as mature as their teachers. At the National War College, for example, the students are often older than the instructors.

As the nineteenth century progressed, free public elementary schools became quite widespread, and college applicants increasingly had the benefit of eight years in such institutions. But public high schools remained relatively scarce until the very end of the century, and students who wanted to continue beyond elementary school usually had to enroll away from home. Some enrolled in private academies, but others went directly into the "preparatory departments" of places that called themselves colleges. In some cases these were in fact exclusively preparatory institutions, offering no college-level work whatever. In other cases they offered only introductory college-level work. In still other cases they offered a regular college course, but enrolled the majority of their students in precollege programs.[3]

Given this mixing of different levels of instruction and different age groups within institutions, the distinction between secondary and college level instruction was extremely hard to draw. Few observers even bothered to try, and many institutions capitalized on the confusion by playing fast and loose with both nomenclature and promises. Places that were in fact academies frequently called themselves colleges, just as places that are colleges today often call themselves universities. Similarly, places that had small collegiate departments often invested a disproportionate amount of their time, energy, and hope in them, at the expense of their larger and more intellectually defensible preparatory departments, just as universities today often sacrifice their undergraduates for the sake of a few mediocre graduate students.

Under these circumstances it is hardly surprising that both academic instruction and social life in most nineteenth-century colleges often resembled a modern boarding school of the "Pencey Prep" variety more than a modern university. The nineteenth-century college was in many ways a logical extension of the nineteenth-century family. Colleges tended to be small, financially shaky, and extremely

[3] Bowman shows that even at the end of the nineteenth century nearly half the students in land-grant colleges were in preparatory rather than collegiate programs. More generally, a comparison of college with secondary enrollment statistics before 1914 makes clear that most college students could not have completed secondary school. In 1870 the U. S. Office of Education reported 7,064 male high school graduates, while in 1874 it reported 9,593 male B.A.s. In 1890 the high schools gave diplomas to 18,549 men, while in 1894 the colleges reported awarding 17,917 B.A.s to men. In 1914 male college graduates outnumbered 1910 high school graduates two-to-one, but colleges still reported total male enrollment greater than the total number of male high school graduates during the previous four years. This imbalance was not eliminated until after World War I. Pre-1914 enrollment reports should therefore be used very cautiously. See *Historical Statistics,* Series H 330, and 1965 Digest, tables 37 and 53. USOE estimates of B.A.s for these years are presumably inflated by counting M.D.s and LL.B.s as first degrees. Some men took a B.A. first and were thus counted twice, giving a misleadingly high estimate of the proportion of the age grade finishing college.

authoritarian. The life of the mind was not unknown, but neither was it usually central. The curriculum was largely prescribed, and the pedagogy consisted mainly of daily assignments and recitations. Extracurricular life was also closely regulated, and an enormous amount of energy seems to have gone into keeping unruly students from misbehaving. Corporal punishment was common, and the students often responded with violent rioting. While students undoubtedly had great influence on one another both socially and intellectually, their lives were circumscribed and the youth culture had nothing like the autonomy of its modern counterpart.[4]

The spread of free high schools during the late nineteenth and early twentieth centuries changed all this. The demand for private secondary education had always been modest, and once a free alternative became widely available the academies found themselves on the financial ropes. In the public sector, too, state "universities" and land-grant "colleges" which had mainly been residential secondary schools were forced to seek a new clientele. Yet the free local high school, while it killed the college preparatory departments, also created a substantial cohort of young men and women with twelve years of precollege training, some of whom wanted still more education. The new formula for institutional survival was therefore clear —though not necessarily easy to follow. All over the country institutions discontinued their preparatory departments and tried to become full-fledged colleges. Some failed to do this and went under. Some made it.

While the establishment of free local secondary schools brought a measure of uniformity to collegiate age-grading, the substantive distinction between "secondary" and "higher" education remained ambiguous for a time. By World War I, however, reformers at the Carnegie Foundation for the Advancement of Teaching and in the accrediting agencies had imposed a measure of uniformity in this area as well. Since then this country has been firmly committed to the idea that a place called a college should admit only students with twelve years of preparation.[5]

[4] It is true that foreign visitors thought American youth in or out of college both unregimented and unruly, but outside of the debating and literary societies they lacked the protective institutions which today force adult manipulators to become more subtle and generally more permissive, in ways *The Lonely Crowd* sought to describe.

[5] There is, of course, still great variation in how these twelve years are divided. Some communities have elementary and high schools, divided either 8–4 or 6–6. Others have elementary, junior high, and senior high schools, divided either 6–2–4 or 6–3–3, and a few are now moving to a 4–4–4 division. There is also enormous variation in what students actually learn in these twelve years—variation that the present efforts toward national assessment seek to document.

Colleges also adopted a somewhat more uniform approach to graduation requirements during this same period. We do not fully understand how America became committed to a four-year undergraduate curriculum as against the three-year English cycle. Many nineteenth-century colleges had tried other variations, especially in professional schools. By World War I, however, most colleges had come to feel that a B.A. or B.S. should take at least four years.[6] This did not always mean four years of sequential study in a single subject, or even in a single college. Professional schools of law, for example, usually required three years of study. But they offset this apparent lapse from academic rigor by requiring that their applicants do several years of undergraduate liberal arts work before starting law school. The net result was that it was very difficult to earn any sort of college degree in less than sixteen years after entering first grade. While unusually capable students were sometimes accelerated, this was never systematized.

The cumulative result of these changes was to fix the minimum age for both college entrance and graduation quite rigidly. At the same time, the spread of free local schools and the passage of child labor laws also made the maximum age more uniform. Almost all competent, diligent students began to climb the lower rungs of the educational ladder at the standard pace, for there were fewer plausible way stations and sidings to detain them. As a result, almost everyone who is interested in attending college today finishes high school before he reaches nineteen. Not all these potential collegians go directly to college, however. Many take time out to work, often for several years. Thus while almost all college entrants are at least seventeen, about a third are nineteen or more.[7] Similarly, while the "normal" pattern of college attendance is an uninterrupted four-year stint, a very substantial proportion of those who enter college take time off at some point, and therefore take five or more years to

[6] The Associate in Arts degree given by junior colleges after two years has never achieved real status or recognition from either students or adults. It is still seen as a step on the way to the B.A.

[7] In 1959 the Census Bureau found that 42 per cent of the men and 32 per cent of the women enrolled as freshmen had not graduated from high school the previous year; see Cowhig and Nam, table 3. Nearly half of these apparent delayers may, however, have been part-time students or repeaters who had been in college continuously since high school graduation. Of all high school graduates who did not go directly to college, the National Science Foundation estimated that in the middle 1950s a seventh went later. This meant that only about 20 per cent of all college freshmen delayed entry. The proportion was about 27 per cent for males and 9 per cent for females; see *The Duration*, p. 21. For data on the ages of college freshmen in March 1960, see 1960 *Census*, I, 1, table 168. It should be remembered that the ordinary freshman was six months older at the time of the Census than when he entered.

graduate.[8] The cumulative result is that while almost all college seniors are at least twenty-one, about half are twenty-three or more.[9]
Whether delays in entrance and graduation are more or less common
than a generation or two ago, we do not know.

Aside from the dramatic but transient effects of the GI Bill, the
only organized effort to alter the undergraduate age distribution in
recent years has been the unsuccessful venture associated with the
name of Robert Hutchins.[10] Convinced that the American high school
was filled with make-work, Hutchins opened the College of the
University of Chicago to able students who had completed only tenth
grade. Later the Ford Foundation induced a number of other colleges to try the same experiment. Although careful follow-ups
showed that exercising this option had harmed almost none of those
who chose it and had benefited many, the pattern never spread. One
of the main problems was the lack of cooperation from most high
schools. Few high school principals or teachers were ready to believe
that their students would be better off in college. Even if they did
believe it, they had a selfish interest in holding onto the talented
youngsters whom they had counted on to be student council presidents, yearbook editors, and the like during their senior year. In
addition, many parents were reluctant to let their children leave home
so young. This reluctance was especially strong when the student was
headed for the urban wickedness of Chicago. But even when more
protective and isolated colleges offered early admission there was no
flood of applicants.

It could be argued that Hutchins' mistake was trying to take students after tenth grade instead of ninth. Many school systems divide
secondary education into junior and senior high school and carry

[8] Perhaps a third of those who earn degrees interrupt their course of study in
some way, either by dropping out entirely for a time or by enrolling only part
time; see Summerskill.

[9] 1960 *Census*, I, 1, table 168. Data are for March 1960. Compare James Davis,
Great Aspirations, table 1.1b, which shows that only 30 per cent of those receiving B.A.s in June 1961 were twenty-three or more. The difference may be in part
accounted for by the fact that Davis drew his sample exclusively from *June*
B.A.s. About a quarter of all B.A.s are awarded in September and January, and
the recipients may be appreciably older than those earning degrees in June. In
addition, Davis excluded from his sample some marginal institutions which
Census respondents presumably regarded as colleges. The median age at these
marginal institutions may have been above average. Then too, not all those who
told the Census they were fourth-year college students took degrees that year.
This would have been especially true of those enrolled part time. If the part-time
students were also older, the median age of those actually taking degrees might
be less than that of all seniors, and Davis' sample may be more representative
than the Census reports make it seem. For evidence consonant with the Census
findings, see Laura Sharpe's study of the Class of 1958, reported in *Two Years*.

[10] The junior college movement might also be thought to fall into this category.
For reasons discussed in more detail in Chapter XI, we think it does not.

junior high school through ninth grade. Had students completing junior high been offered a "collegiate" option, more might conceivably have been interested. Avowedly secondary-level boarding schools have, after all, been attracting a growing number of ninth- and tenth-grade applicants, and they do not even shorten the over-all educational cycle, much less offer instruction that is manifestly superior to the better suburban high schools. If colleges and universities had gone into direct competition with these boarding schools, as they did a century ago with their preparatory departments, and if they had promised to cut two or three years out of the educational cycle, they might conceivably have found a market.

Yet we doubt it. Most successful boarding schools seem relatively safe and cloistered to the parents who patronize them. They tend to be located in New England towns that look like Norman Rockwell covers, and to regulate their students' lives very tightly. They are, moreover, only rarely coeducational. Indeed, that is one of their primary appeals, for many parents find the apparent sexual precocity of the local public high school alarming. Unlike cloistered prep schools, colleges seem anything but safe to most parents. This is especially true of parents who are being invited to expose their fifteen- or sixteen-year-old daughters to predatory older males. (It is probably no accident that the abolition of preparatory departments at colleges and universities came at about the same time as the advent of coeducation —though the old preparatory departments differed from the Hutchins scheme in that many of their students, while untutored, were over eighteen and less likely to be objects of parental anxiety.) Parental fear of precocious sex is obviously reduced when the college in question is not coeducational. But the rules governing freshmen at even the most protective girls' college are necessarily geared to some conception of what is appropriate for eighteen-year-olds, and parents may think these rules excessively permissive for sixteen-year-olds. (It is interesting and perhaps revealing that sexual relations between faculty and students, while a standard theme of novels and legend at both boarding schools and colleges, do not seem to be a matter of much parental concern in either setting. Parents seem to trust adults too much and children too little.)

Sex is not, however, the only source of anxiety about sending "school age" children away to college. Many parents—and many adolescents —fear that a freshman of fifteen or sixteen will have a hard time getting along with classmates several years older even if they are of the same sex. This seldom turns out to be a serious problem, but it is easy to see why people used to the incredibly rigid age-grading of American elementary and secondary schools would be worried about it. Many parents are also nervous about exposing their children to the presumptively sophisticated faculty and reading lists that they assume college implies. Influenced by psychoanalytic theories, they may fear the consequences of young people's becoming excessively intellectual "too soon." For some, intellectual precocity implies maladjustment or worse, and events like the Leopold-Loeb case are cited as proof that too much reading at an impressionable age can be disastrous. Preparatory schools are expected to take this into account and be safely bland—though the better ones often disappoint this hope.

Yet over the long haul the Hutchins scheme may nonetheless have a future. Perhaps the experiment failed principally because it came a generation too early. Not only has parental concern about college admission risen since the early 1950s but fear of intellectual precocity has diminished in many circles. Today many parents would feel guilty about denying one of their children a chance to go to a top college, even if they had doubts about whether the child was emotionally ready. It is true, of course, that any student who is offered early admission is also likely to be admitted two years later. If parents realize this they may feel it safe to wait. On the other hand, adolescents are in general more sophisticated and mature than they were a generation ago and are winning more and more freedom during their high school years. If this continues some parents may conclude that keeping a child at home offers only the illusion of supervision, support, and safety. In that case they may feel there is nothing to be lost by sending them away. Indeed, there may be something to be gained, for the frustrated parent may be able to forget or repress the fact that the child is almost certainly doing things the parent would rather not know about. The parent is also free to blame the college if the child gets into trouble. If such luxuries can be rationalized in terms of giving the child greater intellectual opportunities, early college entrance may eventually become quite popular. At the moment, however, there is no apparent trend in this direction.

While the age distribution of the *undergraduate* population has probably not shifted much since World War I, there has been an increase in the *over-all* student age distribution on many campuses. This is because there has been a slow increase in the proportion of graduate students, particularly since 1950.[11] Something like a third of all undergraduates now attend universities that also enroll large numbers of graduate students—though they are not always in the same classrooms.[12] The proportion is almost certainly rising. These

[11] For sources of data on this point see the discussion in footnotes 17 and 20 of Chapter I. The ratio of graduate to undergraduate students in the arts and sciences is in many respects more important than the over-all ratio, and it is here that the change has been greatest.

[12] Estimated from *Opening Fall Enrollment* (1964), and 1965 *Digest*, table 55.

graduate students represent a much wider age range than the undergraduates, and include many students who have worked for a number
of years at responsible jobs. They tend to be married, to have some
kind of part-time job on or off the campus while they are enrolled
as graduate students, and in general to be defined as adults rather
than adolescents. Their presence—especially that of the graduate
students in arts and sciences—has created a context for generational
conflict and accommodation quite different from what prevailed almost everywhere a generation ago and still prevails on many exclusively undergraduate campuses.

The Role of Student Subcultures

Among the many myths that afflict contemporary thinking about
American colleges, none is more persistent than the one that maintains that in the good old days, when colleges were small, faculty and
students had intimate personal contacts on a day-to-day basis. This
myth has several sources. One is the assumption that because the
faculty were not busy with research or consultation they had time
and energy for their students. A second reason for the myth is the
general American tendency, perhaps the human tendency, to assume
that if things are presently bad, they were once better, rather than
realizing that they are likely to be considered bad precisely *because*
they are getting better.

Whatever its origins, the myth does not square with the facts. Even
a cursory reading of academic history makes clear that eighteenth-
and nineteenth-century colleges, while small enough, were neither
harmonious nor intimate. The students were continually struggling
with the faculty, whom they almost all regarded as the enemy. The
faculty reciprocated in kind, devoting itself mainly to the enforcement
of academic and social rules, often of the most trivial sort. Just as
there was a somewhat autonomous juvenile culture in many of the
large families chronicled in Victorian novels, so college students were
never entirely defeated in their struggles with proctors and presidents.
Yet like peasant revolts or ghetto riots, their protests had little direction or lasting organization.

That conflicts inhibited faculty-student communication about non-
disciplinary issues is not surprising. As we suggested at the beginning
of this chapter, colleges have always been institutions through which
the old attempt to impose their values and attitudes on the young.
They therefore take over from parents the tension-filled and affect-
laden tasks of socialization. This was particularly difficult in a frontier
society where many parents were fearful lest their descendants revert

to the cultural level of the ever-visible Indians. Such parents clung with special passion to both large and small features of their inherited tradition, in part because they could see it crumbling in the face of new circumstances and feared they would soon have nothing recognizable left. These parents and their clerical spokesmen saw colleges as a device for protecting their precarious ties to an Eastern or even European past. Colleges were therefore expected to resist all compromise with the interests and predilections of the young—and, indeed, with the future generally. There could not but be conflict in such institutions, just as there could not but be conflict (however well repressed) in such families.

This conflict was intensified by the fact that most colleges also took over from the adult intelligentsia the task of transmitting some version of High Culture to the semicivilized young. Adult versions of High Culture have never had the same authority in America as in countries like France and Japan, and this is probably true of adult culture in the broad sense as well. Nonetheless, nineteenth-century American educators believed in the value of what they had to teach and sought to impose it on the young, whether the young enjoyed it or not. They seldom succeeded very well, but the mere attempt was often enough to produce continuing guerrilla resistance.

This resistance was often quite successful in small matters, though less so in large ones. The students were very closely regulated on paper, but they gained strength from numbers and were often quite successful in resisting the intent (and often even the substance) of college rules. The young man who would otherwise have had to stay on the family farm or go to work under the watchful eye of an office supervisor therefore found a limited kind of freedom in college, despite adult intentions. He had co-conspirators in breaking the rules and resisting academic demands. While such resistance could be punished by expulsion, this was not always an effective threat in an age where records seldom followed a man from one place to the next.

So while colleges were designed to familiarize the young with the best that had been thought and said by their elders, to give them a sense of continuity between their own problems and those of previous generations, and thus hopefully to spare them learning everything again by trial and error, they sometimes had precisely the opposite effect. Even when the college was in no sense a university, and its faculty was fully committed to transmitting the conventional wisdom rather than questioning or expanding it, the autonomy of the student culture could make the college a de facto instrument of cultural change. Whether it wished to or not, a college could become the crucible in which the younger generation shaped its distinctive values and acquired a sense of separate identity, rather than one in which the young were shaped by those who had gone before and acquired their predecessors' sense of history and purpose.

The extent to which a college separated the young from their elders depended in part on the degree of cultural homogeneity among students, faculty, and administrators. Colleges whose personnel came from similar backgrounds were usually less subversive than those that for one reason or another mixed dissimilar students and faculty. Yet even relatively homogeneous colleges could be the locus of generational conflict and evolution within a given subculture.

The lack of intimacy and harmony between young and old is, then, hardly a twentieth-century novelty. Nor are youthful efforts to meet adult pressure by sabotage and selective inattention a uniquely modern phenomenon. Nonetheless, we are convinced that nineteenth-century conflicts between the generations differed from today's in some important respects. Nineteenth-century young people seldom challenged the legitimacy of their elders' authority. They merely claimed that it had been abused in a particular case, defying it without creating any theory that something else should be put in its place. Even the riots that marked nineteenth-century college life were, as already suggested, more like peasant revolts against tyranny than like revolutionary movements. In the twentieth century, on the other hand, the increasing separatism of teen-age culture and the massing together in high schools and colleges of very large numbers of young people of identical age and social condition have gradually led to a new atmosphere, in which the basic legitimacy of adult authority has been increasingly called into question.

By the 1960s this challenge reached substantial and highly visible proportions. One by-product was the establishment of the Free Universities. Most of the books and topics of the Free Universities—other than propaganda and support for drug experimentation—can be found at major metropolitan universities in the regular curriculum. The distinctive features of these ephemeral institutions have been a deep distrust of those "over thirty" and a rejection of the kinds of cumulative, sequential learning adults normally insist on. They have been initiated and in good part staffed by the unlicensed and relatively inexperienced young. These manifestations of student power sometimes allow young people to learn when they have forbidden themselves to learn from adults. But for many fiercely anti-academic students, even the Free Universities seem pedantic. These students believe that what matters is untutored and wholly spontaneous feeling and McLuhanite media mixtures rather than books. Limited from above by academic inventiveness in adult universities and from below by widespread adolescent hostility to formal learning under any auspices, the Free University approach to education "of the young, by

the young, for the young" has been left with a small following. It is
more important for its symbolic role in justifying student discontent
than for any contribution to either pedagogic or political radicalism.

Generational conflict is an enormous topic, and we will touch on
only a few of its ramifications here. We will not, for example, discuss
experiments in cooperative learning ensconced within universities, like
the Experimental College at San Francisco State or the cooperative
student-led seminars at Monteith College of Wayne State University.
Neither will we deal with another and opposite kind of special-interest
college catering to a specific age group: the adult college. The YMCA
started several of these, and of course many regular colleges conduct
"evening schools," which are de facto adult colleges, segregated from
the adolescent college in terms of both student grouping and faculty
prestige. (Teaching adults in evening school has never been as well
paid or as respectable as teaching late adolescents—a fact which should
be pondered by those who see adolescents as a deprived class.) Instead we will focus on two specific changes in the character of higher
education that help give the collegiate manifestations of generational
conflict their present character. The first is the professionalization of
the teaching staff. The second is the changing position of the undergraduate years in the over-all maturational cycle.

There was a time, as we have said, when most college instructors
saw themselves, however reluctantly, as policemen whose job was to
keep recalcitrant and benighted undergraduates in line, exacting a
certain amount of work and imposing a measure of discipline. These
men were more often trained as clergymen than scholars, though some
saw themselves as both. They found it natural to justify their work
more in terms of improving the social and moral character of the
young than of their intellectual attainment. This cast them in a quasi-
parental role.

Today's college faculty seldom sees itself this way. Professors at the
better universities and university colleges are usually scholars or at
least pseudo-scholars and have much less emotional investment in
their students' social and moral development than did professors a
century ago.[13] Today's scholars are still willing to monitor the academic lives of the young, at least by proxy, insisting that students take
certain courses, pass certain examinations, and so forth. But few have
any interest in dominating the non-academic lives of the young—in
shaping what is today only rarely referred to as the students' moral
character. In part this is because they think the role of moral tutor

[13] For an acute description of the way in which research and science gradually
supplanted morality and religion as the prime values of academic life during the
last decades of the nineteenth century and the first few decades of the twentieth,
see Veysey, esp. pp. 140–41.

(or worse, policeman) would interfere with their ability to work with students on academic matters.[14] In part it is because, while they often disapprove of hedonism and athleticism and shower sarcasm on young people who indulge such heresies, they do not care enough to invent or supervise alternatives. Many professors and administrators are also less certain than they once were as to what students *ought* to be or become, and are reluctant to go to the mat with the young over principles in which they themselves only half believe. Then, too, even those professors and administrators who are individually sure of their ground and opposed to permissiveness in their personal dealings with the young sometimes find that it is politically expedient to avoid collective regulation of student behavior. If the adult community is divided on these matters, as it often is, any effort to impose adult standards on the young inevitably deepens and intensifies divisions within the faculty and administration. So it often turns out that the wisest course is to avoid the issue. The easiest way to do this is to deny the need for any rules in a controversial area, leaving it to the students' discretion.

The result of all this is that many faculty and some administrators develop a Veblenian ideal. They want undergraduates to act like graduate apprentices, both socially and intellectually, and when a particular undergraduate deviates from this norm they tend to say that he "doesn't belong at a university." Since only a minority of undergraduates have either the talent or the motivation to act like apprentice scholars, many professors disclaim responsibility for the majority, urge more selective admission, and hope for the best. They view the faculty and its apprentices as the "heart of the university," and the still uncommitted undergraduates as an expendable penumbra. The easiest way to ensure that the penumbra does not interfere with the main business of the university is to let its members go their own way relatively undisturbed, hoping that they will educate one another or pick up something in the library or from lectures.

There are, of course, exceptions. Some faculty, perhaps especially in the humanities, are more eager to have their students adopt a particular cultural style than to become imitative and not very capable scholars. Others, especially in the social sciences, look to students to carry out political mandates, either in alliance with them or in compensation for their defections.[15] Some who have become profes-

---

[14] It is interesting in this connection to examine the history of control over student discipline. At Harvard during the nineteenth century this was handled by the full faculty and occupied most faculty meeting time. Eventually patience wore thin, and it was turned over to a committee, but this committee remained responsible to the full faculty. At Berkeley, on the other hand, the Academic Senate decided before World War II that it wanted nothing to do with student discipline and handed the whole problem to the administration.

[15] See Gusfield and Riesman, "Academic Standards."

sors in recent years see themselves as ever-young, hedonistic, and hip, and revel in the more anti-intellectual manifestations of student rebelliousness even when it is directed at themselves. Even in a scholarly faculty some are ambivalent about their own scholarship and nurture other and contrasting qualities in the young. Transference obviously enters all these cross-generational transactions. There are even a few deviant academicians who are willing to participate at the adolescent level in both the make-believe and the reality of student life. Such men are sometimes frivolous but often dedicated. On the more academic campuses they sometimes protect the young from becoming too adult too soon. The danger is that they will also re-enforce the incompetent amateurism and the self-indulgent or self-pitying protective cults by which young people so often counteract adult expectations.

Nonetheless, the character of most faculties *has* changed, not only over the past hundred years but even over the past thirty. Until World War II even senior scholars at leading universities did a good deal of what they defined as scut work: teaching small groups of lower-level students, reading papers and examinations, and the like. Their labors were supplemented by aging but unscholarly instructors and assistant professors, who were not given tenure, status, or high salaries but were kept around precisely because there were lots of routine teaching jobs to be done and they were willing to do them. Today, however, few well-known scholars teach more than six hours a week, and in leading universities many bargain for less. Even fewer read undergraduate examinations and papers. At the same time the American Association of University Professors and other faculty groups have pushed through "up or out" rules on faculty promotion, so that the permanent assistant professor is now practically unknown at leading universities. The routine problems of mass higher education have therefore fallen by default to graduate students. These students have assumed the role of shop stewards, mediating between the highly professionalized faculty who run the curriculum and the still amateur undergraduates who pursue it. Graduate teaching assistants handle quiz sections, read examinations, listen to complaints, and generally protect the professors from overexposure to the ignorant.[16]

[16] The impact on all this of increasingly generous fellowships and research assistantships varies from field to field. In the natural sciences most graduate students have no economic need to teach. This means that routine teaching chores of the traditional sort may simply not be performed. Exams, for example, may be multiple choice and machine scored; papers may be eliminated; and laboratory work may be supervised by advanced undergraduates. Moreover, even outside the natural sciences the competition for graduate students' services is so stiff in the more esoteric fields that many cannot be dragooned into teaching assistantships. A good ABD (All But Dissertation) student in some fields can earn as much as

The changing needs and expectations of the adults on college and university campuses are one side of the equation that defines faculty-student relations; the other side is the changing needs and expectations of the entering students. Today's students are quite different from those who entered college a generation or two ago. They have lived in a very different sort of adolescent subculture before matriculating, and college occupies a different place in their over-all life cycle. There was a time in the not-so-distant past when a middle-class high school boy could goof off in class or get in trouble on his block with almost complete confidence that his misadventures would not be held against him. If he decided to go straight he could do so simply by applying to a reputable college. If his parents could pay the tuition his other failings would usually be forgotten. No more. Today's high school student is told that his future position in life depends on getting good professional training, that this depends on his getting into a good college, and that this in turn depends on his performing well in high school. A misstep in high school may, in other words, count against him forever. (Or so the myth says. In reality America still offers a great many second chances, as we shall see in the next chapter.) This does not, of course, mean that high school boys always *act* as if they will be held permanently answerable for the mistakes they made in high school or as if they will get permanent credit for their triumphs. But high school girls often act this way, and even boys are more inclined to do so than in the past, at least with regard to their work.[17] This is especially true in the East, where gradations of college prestige are finer and fear of not making the right college is correspondingly enhanced.

The effect of such assumptions is difficult to chart, but they appear to hasten a kind of maturity. High school students seem to feel that they are more on their own and that their fate depends more on what they do and less on what their parents do for them. Success seems to depend on what they have in their heads, not what kinds of property their parents have in the bank. Partly as a result, many children feel less obligation than they once did to maintain strong ties with their parents or to conform to their parents' standards. Some begin relating almost exclusively to their peers by the time they are twelve or thirteen. They also become involved with the opposite sex earlier

---

$10,000 a year as an assistant professor in a small college near his university, often with a lighter load than he would have had as a teaching assistant at the institution where he is taking his Ph.D. If, as is often the case, his appurtenances include a wife, two or three children, pets, a summer place, and so forth, the salary advantage of teaching in such a college will more than offset the frequent drabness of the students.

[17] For a discussion of the complex pressures discussed here and their differential effects on boys and girls in the sixth grade of a suburban school, see Maccoby.

than their parents did, partly because physical maturity comes sooner, partly because post-Freudian parents are ambivalent in their opposition to adolescent sexuality; also perhaps because the greater flexibility of sexual identities has heightened anxiety about the possibility of being homosexual and has thus made it more important to prove one's heterosexuality.

Breaking out of the family circle has always left the young uncertain where their loyalties lay and what limits still restricted their behavior. They have therefore tended to get involved in all sorts of quasi-familial groups which aroused at least temporary faith in something larger than themselves. The residential college, with its fraternities, football games, and general emphasis on school spirit, was once such a group. Today the suburban high school often plays this role, at least among the middle classes, just as the junior high school is now the scene for many early adolescent dramas once associated with high school. Thus by the time today's young people reach college some have already been through the family break and are ready for a more mature role. Whether one looks at the books they have read, their attitudes toward the opposite sex, their allergy to Mickey Mouse extracurricular (or curricular) make-work, or their general coolness, today's entering freshmen seem older than those of the 1920s and 1930s. Class, ethnic, rural-urban, and other differences exist here, but have been little charted. We believe that the mass media—especially television—have a large role in the earlier maturation of the young, making them sophisticated cynics about advertising (although also diligent consumers) almost before they can read, and exposing them to adult fare that would once have been kept out of reach or read under the covers late at night.[18]

At the same time certain kinds of responsibility come later and later. While young people still hold various kinds of temporary jobs during adolescence, they find it hard to embark on a career in the traditional sense before they reach twenty-two. The most interesting work usually requires professional training beyond the B.A. and often is not begun in earnest until twenty-five or more. This means not only that the young are denied the kinds of responsibility that go with many jobs, but that they often depend on their families for money until at least twenty-one and often even later.

Thus while adolescence begins earlier, it also continues longer. Students must begin making good records sooner, yet these records

[18] One set of studies in California suggests that adolescents who do not attend college (after applying) go through some of the same changes as their age-mates who are attending college; see the discussion in McCullers and Plant. The studies directed by Dr. Plant cover only a fraction of the problem but suggest its magnitude.

bring tangible results later and later. This combination of precocity and enforced dependency encourages students to create a make-believe world in which it is "as if" they were grown up. To achieve this they must organize their own lives, define their own limits, set their own ideals, and deny the authority and legitimacy of the adult world which they cannot join.

As in all class struggles, the actors in the war between the generations often take positions contrary to what an outside analyst would regard as their class interest. Just as the civil rights movement had to fight Negro apathy as well as white supremacy for many years, and depended in many ways on white liberals for both money and legitimacy, so too students who oppose adult discrimination and segregation have found that they are a minority among their age-mates and that both their political success and their internal morale depend on finding adult supporters. (Their political successes on college campuses seem to depend mainly on the tacit support of the faculty; their morale depends more on overt support from graduate students and from non-students of that age.)

The attitudes of the scholarly faculty, and the ways in which these encourage unscholarly students to create a counter-reality, have already been touched on. Feeling guilty about their neglect of unscholarly undergraduates, some professors talk about the importance of students' taking responsibility for their own education and about the impossibility of anyone else's doing the job for them. The faculty justify their neglect of the students by pointing to the students' neglect of them. Some precocious and sophisticated students welcome such talk, arguing that students are indeed mature and responsible, and that the university should recognize this and treat them accordingly. The net result is often that both sides conspire to encapsulate the undergraduates in their own world.

It is important to stress the mutuality of this relationship. Students, for example, often complain about lack of faculty-student contact and tell horror stories about professors who have office hours once a month in an ill-publicized place. But the professors rightly counter by noting that few students come to whatever hours they keep, and that those who do come usually argue about grades. Similarly, students complain that they have no unofficial, personal contact with their nominal mentors. Professors respond by pointing out that when they ask students to their homes many make excuses and the rest seem uncomfortable and eager to go. While we think this latter observation underestimates the significance of such encounters to some students, it is certainly true that they seldom provoke significant communication, much less rapport. What the students really need is a sense that an adult takes them seriously, and indeed that they have some kind of power over adults which at least partially offsets the power adults obviously have over them. In order to be taken seriously and exercise power they must, despite their youth, contribute in some way to the adult world. The academic enterprise in which professors are engaged seldom excites them, and when it does they seldom find any way to contribute to it, even at the margins. They feel irrelevant and expendable and as far as most scholars are concerned, they are.

This is not absolutely necessary. Imaginative faculty members, especially those working in the less fully organized and less sequential fields, have often been able to bring undergraduates to the frontiers of knowledge quite quickly and give them the feeling that they too could contribute. This has until recently been possible in microbiology, for example, and is still possible in sociology and psychology. It is evidently more difficult in most branches of economics or physics. Whether it is attempted seems to depend in part on what faculty members feel they stand to gain from success. In university colleges that have no graduate students, scholarly professors have long made do with undergraduate research assistants and have organized seminars for advanced undergraduates, which in a big university would usually be confined to graduate students. Where graduate students and indeed post-doctoral fellows are available as subordinates and colleagues, the greater effort needed to bring along undergraduates seems less necessary and less common. Nonetheless, it seems clear that the possibility exists, at least for a minority of students. When we look, for example, at the work published by undergraduates at the University of Kansas in the annual volume sponsored by that institution, or at the work published by Harvard undergraduates in the volumes of papers done for the second author's undergraduate course, it seems to us that the authors deserve to be taken seriously as colleagues by even the most distinguished scholars. So, too, if one looks at undergraduate journals, such as Reed College's *Journal of the Social Sciences* or the journals published by several of the Harvard Houses, the academic quality of the work is very impressive. This suggests that when undergraduates feel they cannot play a useful or responsible role in the adult work of their campus, this is not necessarily because they lack preparation but often because they lack the self-confidence and encouragement they would need to undertake a serious piece of research.

The central problem here is probably not so much one of age as of the relationship between professionals and amateurs. The academic profession, like almost all others, has been very reluctant to admit even the possibility that amateurs could make significant contributions. Such an admission would imply that all its training and certification machinery were superfluous and perhaps even that those who had fought their way through had wasted their time. Euphoric but untalented amateurs can, moreover, often do considerable damage—though this is far less of a danger in academic life than in, say, medicine or engineering. Whatever the merits of the case, however, the academic profession is at least as elitist and exclusive as the American professional norm. This makes it in some ways very unsuited to the socialization of young people, who are by definition outside the charmed circle. While some students nonetheless identify with their professors, the majority cannot afford to take the professorial model too seriously, for they have no reason to think they could approximate it if they tried.[19]

Whatever the reasons, and they are obviously many, the fact remains that most students feel they cannot compete with their professors and cannot relate to them in any other way either. So they retreat into their own world. Traditionally this was a world of football and fraternities—though it seems clear that there were always also a great many individual isolates for whom these communal rituals were either unattractive, inaccessible, or both. Today, however, students are increasingly anti-organizational in outlook, searching for spontaneity, informality, and freedom from restraint on more and more fronts. This means not only that they reject the adult world of big business and bureaucracies, but that they also reject its traditional juvenile counterpart, the formally organized extracurriculum. They fall back on smaller and more fluid groupings and activities. This pattern of life may well further increase the number of isolates, since those who have difficulty connecting with other people now have fewer institutional devices for making this either easy or inevitable. One important result of this new undergraduate style has been to make relations between the sexes far more important. This is partly because there are fewer competing outlets for sociability and fewer demands on leisure time, and partly because resistance to organizational life is related to a demand for honesty and openness that can be met, if at all, only in extremely close relationships. The appeal of sexual intimacy is obviously compounded by the extent of adult opposition and by the fact that it becomes a symbol of being grown up. The decline of the double standard has also made sex more important to undergraduates, for male undergraduates no longer have to depend on lower-class partners and therefore find it easier to blend sex with sociability and even study. The availability of coeds has not only driven the old campus prostitutes out of business but has encouraged protomarital

[19] Again, this may be a special problem at independent colleges where there are no graduate students. At universities, the graduate students suggest how the ascent from "lowly" undergraduate to professorial grandeur might take place in manageable steps; at independent colleges there are no such bridges.

relationships which consume far more time and emotional energy than was once common. These relationships occupy such a central place in many undergraduates' lives that they are no longer willing to endure the inconveniences and humiliations adults have traditionally imposed on premarital sex. There are few campuses on which the rules surrounding relations between the sexes are not under attack, as both irritating and hypocritical.

When one turns from the external forces which drive students to seek a self-contained subculture to the internal forces which give this subculture strength to resist adult pressure, the role of the graduate student assumes considerable importance. There was a time when undergraduates were almost as remote from graduate students as from professors. Undergraduates often came from more affluent families than graduate students on the same campus, and they were almost always less committed to intellectual values. The graduate students, in turn, felt that undergraduates were a frivolous lot, and had little or nothing to do with them. Today, however, undergraduates are more mature and more thoughtful, and the gap seems narrow at some points. It is true that graduate students in such professional schools as law and medicine still keep pretty much to themselves, for they have no institutional contact with undergraduates and have already identified to some extent with their future professions.[20] Graduate students in the arts and sciences, on the other hand, often seem somewhat less professionalized. While many of them make strenuous efforts to emulate their professors rather than undergraduates, others become double agents, maintaining ties with their past as well as their future. These dissident graduate students can become the leaders and legitimizers of undergraduate discontent—a phenomenon well documented at Berkeley in recent years but increasingly common elsewhere too. (At Stanford, for instance, a bearded graduate student was head of the student government in 1965–66, and similar developments are taking place on other campuses.)

The mere existence of this sort of graduate student has an effect on the self-conception of some undergraduates. Graduate students are not yet quite adults, but they have many of the adult prerogatives to which undergraduates aspire: somewhat responsible jobs, reasonably satisfactory incomes which do not depend on parents, the right to live where and how they please, sexual liberty, and fairly long academic tethers. They are, moreover, committed to this way of life for a more or less indefinite period, which they are often in no hurry to end. A graduate student may therefore look to his juniors—and sometimes to himself—like a perpetual student in the Latin American

---

[20] The frequent involvement of law students in Young Republican, Young Democratic, and other political groups is an exception.

tradition. For the undergraduate who finds himself unable to identify with any of the career alternatives he knows about, the life of the graduate student may seem a lesser evil—avoiding a difficult choice, preserving a measure of youthful non-commitment, and yet not exacting the full price usually demanded of those who remain dependent on their elders. Such identification is even possible at those university colleges where no graduate students are actually .enrolled but where large numbers of undergraduates nonetheless assume they will eventually do graduate work.

Graduate students of this kind, along with the undergraduates who identify in whole or in part with them, form a semistable occupational group. Unlike those undergraduates and professional students who expect to be on campus for a fixed period and then depart for something better, these students see no immediate prospect of changing their status.[21] They are therefore far more interested than other students in trying to improve their present circumstances. Most students have what might be called a white-collar mentality. They assume that if they conform to their superiors' demands they will be rewarded and will rise to a new role in the world. The dissident minority, on the other hand, has what might be called a blue-collar mentality. This outlook excludes promotion as remote or unlikely, and focuses on improving the conditions associated with the group's present work.[22] While this dissident cadre is small, it includes many of the most competent and articulate students.

Looking at undergraduate subcultures in historical perspective, we are inclined to predict that the dissident minority will continue to grow. It is a by-product of the extension of adolescence, both back into what was once childhood and forward into what was once adulthood. Such extension is likely to continue. Psychologically if not chronologically, college therefore comes later in the over-all life cycle, and its role in loco parentis is increasingly subject to challenge.

If stern administrators formed a united front and refused to yield, they might perhaps hold the line against this challenge. But unity is hardly likely. Given the growing logistical difficulties of enforcing rules made in loco parentis, the continental example of doing without

[21] The draft has, of course, been a major factor for some in prolonging student status, especially since the Vietnam war became a political issue. The elimination of graduate student deferments should change the pattern somewhat, but probably not dramatically.

[22] As John Finley Scott has noted, many of these students are in the humanities, where lush professorships are relatively scarce and "promotion" may mean leaving the comforts of Cambridge or Berkeley for nine hours a week of teaching at a state college. Some others are in fields like physics and math where jobs are many but standards of success so clear and so exalted that even able students often fear they will fail. They preserve their student status as a way of postponing a definitive test.

them, and the increasing moral and emotional doubts of the administrators and faculty who must make most of these rules, it seems likely that undergraduates who demand an end to the doctrine will slowly get their way on most campuses. A generation hence most undergraduates will probably be treated like today's graduate students, both socially and academically.

There are colleges, public and private, where undergraduates' impatience for such changes threatens the very survival of the institution, by arousing the ire of powerful adults who regard student pranks as funny but cannot laugh off student solemnity. We have talked to students on such campuses who say that if the college authorities would frankly say that the rules existed to protect the college from community reprisal, they would cooperate; what they say they cannot abide is being told that the rules are for their own good. Whether most would in fact cooperate we are not sure. Some among the current student generation are in revolt against all authority and obsessively test all limits. Clothes are a constraint; razors are a constraint; courses and examinations are constraints; intervisitation hours are a constraint; refined language is a constraint. This revolt is supported by developments in the arts and also in the bohemias of the world—developments that are readily visible to undergraduates. It is a revolt that has also won a measure of support in the courts. On many campuses the rebels can also count on the tolerance of their fellow students, who fear to be thought square or chaste or fearful or finks. In this situation there may be some students who will inhibit themselves in order to save the institution, but there are likely to be others who relish the prospect of the institution's succumbing to community disapproval, thus revealing the community's nastiness for all to see.

Nonetheless, despite some students' refusal to present a clean-cut face to the public, it seems certain that the colleges that now feel threatened will survive and probable that they will prosper. The real question is therefore how the increasing autonomy of many undergraduate subcultures will affect the individual participants' long-term growth and development—and thus how it will affect the larger society. We find it hard to imagine, for example, that students who spend four (sometimes ten) years in the more alienated Berkeley subcultures will ever slip easily into the established adult institutions within which the middle classes now earn their living. So, too, four years in Cambridge can develop a set of assumptions and habits rather poorly suited to the occupations for which Harvard has traditionally prepared its alumni. Some of these alumni may be permanently out of tune with the world of work.

In examining this question one must distinguish between students whose estrangement from adult life is so complete that they withdraw into passivity and privatism (often nourished by drugs) and students who, while alienated from the adult society they observe around them, still have enough hope for the future to make an active effort at political change.[23] The activists may seem almost wholly committed to anti-organizational ideologies and behavior, but they can often change their views quite suddenly, especially if institutions they had defined as hopelessly rigid and square take them seriously, adopt their rhetoric, and toy with their program. The relations between some radicals and the federal poverty program illustrate this. But even the hippies who have no political program may find a place in the corporate state if they have technical competence. Thus one finds industries employing computer programmers whose dress and demeanor remain aggressively bohemian and who often continue to live in colonies of like-minded souls on the fringe of some ethnic or academic ghetto. Technical writing and the academic profession itself absorb others of the same species. The continuing shortage of men with technical skills may force other less adaptable and less progressive industries to emulate the data processors.

It could be argued, however, that as students acquire more freedom their world may become more like that of adults—as, for example, the world of graduate students in some ways already is. One of the distinguishing features of student life is that its participants are allowed to make mistakes without paying too heavy a price. They can, in other words, be somewhat irresponsible. If students do not do their work they may get a bad grade, and if they get enough bad grades they may be fired; but the amount of absenteeism, indolence, and sheer incompetence permitted students is far greater than that permitted almost any other sort of worker.[24] Similarly, if a student gets arrested for smoking marijuana his parents will usually go to bat for him, find lawyers, pay bail, and the like. Not only that, but the civil authorities are likely to be relatively lenient, chalking up his failings to youthful excess rather than moral turpitude. Radicals and idealists often deplore all this, saying that students should have no greater privileges than other members of society. Yet if this were

[23] See Keniston, "The Sources" for a more detailed discussion of some of these themes, see also his *The Uncommitted.*

[24] By setting the passing grade at 60 or 70 per cent instead of the 95 per cent or more required on most "real" jobs, colleges can offer students more interesting and difficult challenges than most employers dare offer. "Real" jobs are therefore almost certain to bore most workers, for they must be overqualified and unchallenged in order to ensure that they won't make too many mistakes. (There are exceptions here, especially in organizations with no competition or no choice of employees. The Army, which has competition only in wartime and never enough money to pick and choose among applicants, seems to set "passing" even lower than most colleges.)

really to happen students would probably become far more cautious in their outlook, taking fewer risks and supporting fewer radical causes, both moral and political. There would remain many exceptions who utterly reject careerism, as can be seen even among the usually more discreet students who plan professional careers. Medical students are a case in point; their work is "real" in the sense that failures count heavily against them. Such professional students are generally far more conservative in dress and outlook than undergraduates in the social sciences or graduate students in arts and sciences.

Observing such students we are inclined to believe that other students' sympathy for deviant ideas and life styles is in good part a transitional phenomenon—a by-product of their currently ambiguous status as neither quite children nor quite adults. If so, a clear commitment to treating students as adults in all off-the-job respects might reduce the level of discontent. Or it might, on the other hand, exacerbate discontent by dramatizing the tension between off-the-job freedom and on-the-job subordination, as has happened in some cases with graduate students. It might be argued that this contrast causes relatively little trouble in other enterprises, where workers do what they are told on the job but enjoy full citizenship after hours. This is, however, only partly true. First, workers *don't* do what they are told in many cases, and it would be small consolation to educators to think that if they abandoned all efforts in loco parentis they would still have as much trouble with students as employers have with unions. Educators' sights are, perhaps foolishly, set higher. Second, workers' limited willingness to do what they are told depends on being paid. Students, on the other hand, are presumed to be working for their own good—although the students' readiness to strike or boycott classes implies that students themselves do not always see it this way. Rather, some see their labor as benefiting others and withhold it to coerce those others. Under such circumstances insubordination seems inevitable once the general principle of adult authority is abandoned.

The Adult Backlash and the "Safe" Colleges

The customs and concerns of student subcultures vary enormously, but all are in one way or another at odds with the adult subcultures from which they spring. The growing autonomy of such subcultures has therefore been greeted with less than universal enthusiasm by responsible adults. Fearful parents believe that if they let their children immerse themselves in one of these subcultures, the children may never outgrow it. This fear flourishes especially among parents who have not themselves been to college. Not having been undergraduates themselves, these parents have not had the experience of passing through this particular phase and slipping into the post-collegiate adult world. This may make them exaggerate the difficulty of the transition and underestimate the probability that it will eventually take place. But even college-educated parents worry about whether their children will prove as resilient as they themselves did. They worry doubly when they see that the distance between many student subcultures and adult society is wider than it was a generation ago. We ourselves, while less anxious about these matters than most parents and professors, are not sure that such fears are unfounded.

Parental worries are, it is true, full of ambiguities. Parents and other adults usually conform to the achievement ethic of the highly organized society in which they work, but many are also attracted by more spontaneous, hedonistic, impractical, and preindustrial possibilities. As David Matza has pointed out, this means that there is a kind of secret sharing between many adults and those adolescent subcultures that defy adult ambition, taste, and sobriety.[25] Adults may patronize teen-agers whose immaturity finds symbolic expression in panty raids, but only the most puritanical are alarmed by them. When frivolity turns to defiance, however, adult responses change correspondingly. Even those who view themselves as liberals are frequently upset by long hair, marijuana and LSD, miscegenation, and seemingly unpatriotic anti-militarism. There is, in other words, some point at which almost every parent wants to draw the line, even though not every parent dares to try.

When parents do try to draw the line and set standards, they are seldom entirely successful, but they are often partially so. All over America there are children who want to eschew adolescence and move with maximum safety and minimal delay into some kind of adult world. A number of otherwise undistinguished colleges have been able to attract substantial numbers of students by catering to these hopes and fears. These "safe" colleges fall into two categories: the closely regulated residential colleges, most of which are church-controlled, and the commuter colleges, most of which are publicly controlled.

We will discuss the church colleges in more detail in chapters VIII and IX. Here it need only be noted that church colleges are in most cases colleges first and church-related second. They feel obliged to meet at least some of the standards of academic excellence established in secular colleges, and this means they must compete for academically competent faculty. To do this many church colleges have recently raised their charges faster than their traditional clientele

[25] See Matza. See also the writing of Bennett Berger concerning youth cultures. Talcott Parsons and S. N. Eisenstadt view these matters in somewhat different perspective, arguing that the young are licensed to deviate from adults norms for a few years in order to tie them to non-fraternal achievement norms securely later on. See Eisenstadt's *From Generation to Generation.*

has raised its income. This has reduced the number of devout families that feel they can afford to enroll. Yet the drive for high quality faculty means that in many cases the colleges want to expand. This is by no means impossible, since the demand for high prestige non-sectarian education has been growing faster than the supply. The church colleges are therefore constantly tempted to abandon their traditional pious constituency and try to compete with places like Haverford, Bowdoin, Carleton, and Beloit. Even colleges that have not self-consciously decided to do this may be pushed in that direction simply because relatively sophisticated students who cannot get into these elite colleges now go to traditionally more orthodox ones. In due course these dissidents reach the critical mass at which they can create a partially self-contained subculture. Once established, this subculture can proselytize and can at least sporadically evoke rebellious impulses in a wide range of apparently contented students. The existence of such a subculture is also likely to frighten away the more repressed high school students and their parents, who fear corruption by all too tempting friends. So while the church colleges are still much closer than leading secular universities to their Victorian ancestors, many are considerably more emancipated from the past than their clientele, and many are also eager to widen their lead.

Even where the college authorities remain very conservative, their capacity to control the student culture is extremely limited in a residential setting. Undergraduates are too numerous to be constantly monitored. Relatively few faculty even at church colleges have a taste for this. So the youth culture tends to take hold and go its own way, even though it is seldom as unbridled as at a residential university. Many parents of limited means and views have therefore felt obliged to look elsewhere for a safer (and cheaper) route to the B.A. Many seem to have found it in public commuter colleges, especially public junior colleges.

The apparent safeness of the commuter college derives from the fact that students spend almost all their campus time in class. This gives adult faculty an almost completely effective veto over what students do while on the campus. As soon as the students leave the controlled classroom environment they normally leave the campus too, unless they are so unfortunate as to have a schedule with a dead hour or two between classes. Once they leave the campus they usually head for home or for a job. In either case they are likely to be interacting mainly with people substantially older or younger than themselves and their classmates. A distinctive student culture is therefore unlikely to develop.

There are, however, exceptions to this rule. Not all students at commuter colleges live with their parents. Some get married.[26] Married students usually set up their own households, often in apartments near the commuter college which one or both of them attends. Even those who do not marry are likely to find both reasons and resources to move out of their parents' home as they grow older.[27] Regardless of whether the owners are single or married, apartments of this kind tend to become the nucleus of an unsupervised and independent student culture which embraces single as well as married commuters.[28] Commuters of this sort often create a semiresidential, entirely unofficial student community around their university. Such a community will center near the campus if cheap housing is available nearby, as it is for example at NYU and Wayne State. At a place like UCLA or San Francisco State, on the other hand, there is little suitable housing nearby, and the commuter who does not live with his parents tends to merge with whatever incipient bohemia his city sustains. The result may be a Left Bank pattern of student life more in the European than in the Anglo-American tradition. Under these circumstances the very absence of dormitories may paradoxically encourage the creation of a student subculture more independent, more embracing, and more at odds with adult attitudes and values than a dormitory-based subculture would usually be. While such bohemianism almost never appeals to more than a small minority of the students enrolled at non-residential institutions, it can exercise a certain subtle but pervasive influence on a larger fraction. By frightening adults, moreover, it can polarize conflict with the college authorities and thus win more converts to the anti-adult cause—as the activist non-dormitory students have periodically done at Berkeley.

Almost any institution with graduate students is likely to spin off such a subculture as one of its by-products, and in large cities even the four-year commuter colleges often acquire some such penumbra. Two-year colleges, on the other hand, tend to be relatively immune.

[26] The 1960 Census, PC (2)-5A (School Enrollment), table 9, shows that less than 2 per cent of all college men under 19 are married, compared to 9 per cent of those aged 20 and 21, 30 per cent of the juniors and seniors aged 22–24, and 35 per cent of graduate students aged 22–24. The proportions are somewhat lower for women, presumably because women are more likely to drop out of college when they marry.

[27] The 1960 Census, loc. cit., shows that among unmarried men not living in college dormitories 79 per cent of those 19 or under, 64 per cent of those aged 20 or 21, and 54 per cent of those aged 22 to 24 were living with parents or relatives.

[28] An illuminating variant is provided at Oakland University outside Detroit, which began as a commuter branch of Michigan State University and has recently begun building dormitories. These attract students who have more sophistication and probably more money than most commuters. The dormitory students then sometimes form alliances with commuters to use the commuters' parents' homes for weekend parties, escaping a "dry" campus with few amenities.

While the public ones often have a fair number of older students who are not living with their parents, these are seldom promising candidates for student leadership or taste-making. Many are working full time. Many others have children and the sobriety that usually comes with them. While some are friendly with other students of their own age at a more advanced level, others spend their time mainly with high school chums who never went to college at all, have worked for some years, and now see themselves as part of the adult world. As a result, the public two-year college usually conforms quite closely to the archetypal commuter pattern discussed earlier, in which students see one another mainly in classrooms and hence mainly under adult supervision. When one combines this with a faculty that is seldom drawn from leading graduate schools and includes relatively few intellectual or social eccentrics, it is easy to see why two-year colleges have attracted a growing proportion of those who want the advantages of advanced certification and (perhaps) training without exposure to the dangers or distractions of the youth culture.[29]

Some community college advocates look forward to the day when virtually all high school seniors will go to a junior college, regardless of aptitude, income, or career plans. These prophets expect that today's colleges will gradually cut back or abandon their freshman and sophomore years, recruiting students from junior college just as they now do from high school. Under these circumstances senior colleges would probably de-emphasize the B.A. and enroll most students in three- or four-year Master's degree programs.[30] The net result would be to alter the present 6–6–4–Plus (or 8–4–4–Plus) sequence of American education, making it 6–6–2–Plus (or 8–4–2–Plus).

Such a development would resolve the present ambiguous status of undergraduate education, making the 13th and 14th grades more clearly an upward extension of high school general education and the 15th and 16th grades more clearly a downward extension of graduate professional training. The 13th and 14th grades would be taught by men and women recruited from much the same pool as high school teachers. They would not be expected to have Ph.D.s or to do scholarly research. Some would be graduate students at universities. Others would be alumni of the burgeoning M.A. programs at former teachers colleges. By freeing up the scholars who now devote some of their time to teaching freshmen and sophomores, this kind of reorganization would ensure a more adequate supply of Ph.D.s to teach juniors and seniors. These men would mostly be scholars first

[29] Concerning the many other reasons for these colleges' appeal, see the discussion in Chapter XI. What is in the text needs to be qualified for those community colleges that have actively recruited non-white students. It does not take many black students to lead a protest demanding still more black students. Such demands can usually count on substantial support from black students and faculty.

[30] See, e.g. Eurich.

and teachers second, and would make no pretense of offering their students non-professional education. Their colleges would also presumably abandon the last pretense of acting in loco parentis, while the junior colleges would continue in this role, or at least in active collaboration with parents who retained this role.

Enrolling all high school graduates in "comprehensive" junior colleges would postpone the college admission trauma two additional years. Instead of making the first irrevocable choice of their lives at seventeen, most middle-class youngsters would make it at nineteen. And instead of beginning to ready themselves for this choice at fourteen, most young people might well procrastinate until eighteen. If all students could enter the local junior college regardless of how badly they did in high school, and if none could enter a more prestigious college regardless of how well they did in high school, academic competition in high school would presumably lose much of its present intensity and significance.[31] The junior colleges would supplant the high schools as first-round sorting and screening institutions in the job market. Only when students reached junior college would they begin to feel that they were playing for keeps, that their successes might really count for and their failures against them in later life. Only then would they be forced to expose themselves to impersonal adult judgments from whose consequences neither their peers nor their parents could protect them. There is always a minority of students who enjoy extending themselves beyond adult or peer demand, and often in opposition to the restriction of effort peers at least demand. They find challenges in an academic program that their fellows take casually or cynically.

Those who find the current precocity of the young alarming might greet such delays with enthusiasm. There would, however, be serious problems. Tomorrow's high schools could well become like today's junior high schools. They would probably have increasing difficulty recruiting competent male teachers, since many of the men who now teach high school would be drawn into the junior colleges. The male students' tendency to equate learning and effeminacy would thus continue even longer than it now does. In addition, the high schools would be deprived of their main claim to seriousness, namely, their role in preparing students for their first quasi-adult choices, both among colleges and among jobs.

The main problem would, however, be the prolongation of youthful dependency. Many young people live at home too long even today. The universalization of junior college would make this even more common. Instead of striking out on their own both geographically and intellectually at eighteen, most students would have to wait until

[31] For a more extended discussion of this possibility see our chapter on California in *The Academic Enterprise* (forthcoming).

twenty. The gradual extension of adolescence has already produced a variety of problems that America cannot handle satisfactorily; universal junior college would make the situation appreciably worse.

For better or worse, however, junior colleges are unlikely to become universal. While highly rationalized state planning agencies may create a few new colleges like Florida Atlantic, which begins in the junior year and caters to junior college alumni, existing colleges and universities are unlikely to drop their freshman and sophomore years so long as they keep attracting competent applicants. For one thing, universities often make a financial profit on freshmen and sophomores. This is used to subsidize upperclassmen and graduate students. Even if they do not provide a short-run profit, the freshmen and sophomores often justify themselves over the long haul, for it is the four undergraduate years rather than the graduate years that seem to evoke the loyalty and generosity of alumni. Then, too, colleges are in stiff competition with one another for able students, and a college that admits freshmen and sophomores has an enormous competitive advantage over one that tells prospective applicants to wait two years. We doubt that many colleges will relinquish this advantage voluntarily.[32] And as long as universities and university colleges keep admitting high school graduates, we expect high school graduates will keep applying. We see no prospect of junior colleges competing successfully for students who have the money, ability, and drive to make it at a selective brand-name institution.

There is, however, more reason to expect the junior colleges to become the major vehicle for educating the less affluent, the less adept, and the less ambitious students, who are the great majority. This has happened in California, and it could easily happen elsewhere. This development seems especially likely in states where the adult backlash against student emancipation is strongest. In California, for example, adult reaction against youthful rebellion at Berkeley has led to some redirection of resources to less dangerous institutions. Legislative decisions to equalize certain kinds of expenditure between Berkeley and UCLA have been partly motivated by such considerations. Governor Reagan's tuition proposals worked in this same direction, for he sought to establish higher tuition at the University than at the state colleges, and asked for none at the junior colleges. This would push more students into relatively trouble-free local commuter colleges.

Despite these political pressures, however, we do not see how adults can indefinitely contain the generational revolt. In the long

[32] The only way we can imagine this happening would be for a cartel of elite private colleges to abolish the freshman and sophomore years. This might give the new pattern enough status to make it attractive to able students.

run, undergraduates are almost certain to win increasing autonomy. The adults officially charged with supervision have little more chance of success than a colonial administration confronted with a determined guerrilla movement. It is true that the dissident students are only a small minority on most campuses, as the administration constantly emphasizes. But the young "troublemakers" swim in a sea of relatively tolerant fellow travelers, many of whom will protect student rights against the adult administration even if they themselves feel little impulse to exercise such rights. While there are also many conservative students sympathetic to adult values, they tend to be apathetic and cannot be counted on to play an active role in defending the status quo against youthful defiance. Likewise, while there are many adult faculty nominally allied with the administration, their commitment to acting in loco parentis is ambivalent and the administration cannot count on them in a crisis—as it found to its sorrow at Berkeley.

All metaphors can, of course, be pushed too far. We do not expect the generational revolt to achieve victory in the same sense that the Algerian revolt did. Neither legislators nor trustees are ready to haul down the banner of adult responsibility and turn over the regulation of student affairs to the students themselves. Student government is regarded as a charade at most colleges, comparable in intention to the native governments established by colonial powers everywhere. It cannot command the respect of the increasingly restless natives because its authority depends entirely on the backing of the "foreign" administration, and the natives therefore want to deal directly with those who have power. Student governments cannot raise money unless the college administration enforces the students' right to tax their fellow students, and they cannot police their decisions without help from the administration. Since administration support will inevitably be conditional, will frequently be tested by militants, and will sporadically be refused, the young are seldom likely to take the business seriously.

Indeed, the idea of self-government in communities whose members all expect to be gone in a couple of years may well be unworkable. Lacking a deep stake in the future of the community as a whole, students naturally have a disproportionate interest in protecting their civil liberties as against meeting their civic responsibilities. Use of the word responsibility usually elicits a look of disgust from student activists, who have heard it invoked in all sorts of irrelevant ways (e.g. with respect to student sexual mores, where responsibility, while real enough, is almost entirely a private rather than a public issue). But the abuse of a political conception by administrators looking for ways to justify positions taken for moralistic or public relations reasons does not invalidate the conception itself. Self-government can work only if a substantial fraction of the community in question has a stake in its future and is willing to give up time, convenience, and a measure of personal freedom to promote the general welfare. We have not the slightest doubt that undergraduates are willing and able to do this under the right circumstances. Haverford, with its yeast of concerned Quakers, and a small, hand-picked student body, has in the past done it. But it is far from clear that a college can do this as long as most students take an instrumental view of higher education, see their college mainly as a place they must induce to give them a degree, and are already looking forward to moving on.

Instead of trying to establish student governments with full control over student affairs, a more practical and to our minds more constructive approach may be to give students a larger but never exclusive voice in the full range of college affairs. This approach has been carried quite far at Antioch College, and it has in the past worked quite well there. By giving students minority representation on all sorts of college committees, Antioch recognizes that they have a stake in many issues from which student government elsewhere is wholly excluded—decisions about hiring and retaining faculty and about the college budget, for example. The Antioch approach also recognizes the equally important truth that adults have a great stake in what students tend to regard as exclusively student affairs. The adults must, after all, live with students and their habits year after year whereas the students can and do move on when they weary of the manners and mores of their fellows. And the adults must also live with the next generation of students, attracted by the activities of an earlier generation, whereas the students whose doings helped recruit the next generation become alumni, whose stake in what happens at their alma mater is far less than the faculty's.

One difficulty with the Antioch formula, as with student government in its traditional form, is that students in larger, heterogeneous institutions seldom feel much sense of community with one another. Thus the presence of a few students on a policy-making or disciplinary committee may do relatively little to legitimize it in other students' eyes, especially if the students on the committee are thought to be "professional student government types" or administration stooges. The problem is analogous to that of legitimizing government in the ghetto, where lower-class Negroes have no leaders they trust. Black faces in high places may help a little, but to most poor Negroes the black faces they see on television belong to a different breed. So too with students in many big universities and some small colleges. A student on a committee of big shots becomes by definition one of "them," not one of "us." Nor can the problem be wholly solved by electing the representatives in question, for many students feel that anyone who exercises power is by definition one of "them" and not "us." Under these circumstances legitimacy is extremely difficult to achieve.

One partial and increasingly common answer may be to fall back on the residual legitimacy of local government. Colleges can, for example, either let students find their own housing or turn their dormitories over to private enterprises. They can then wash their hands of responsibility for students' personal behavior and leave the policing of sex, liquor, and drugs to the local constabulary. But this deals with only a small fraction of the potential problems, many of which involve issues for which the college cannot so readily disclaim responsibility. The use of college facilities for political purposes, for example, which sparked the Free Speech disturbances at Berkeley, is not an issue a college can ignore. The college must either permit it, restrict it, or prohibit it entirely, and it must then answer for its position to the public. So too with the choice of faculty members and many other matters.

Unable to enforce their will themselves and unable to find student "finks" who can or will do it for them, some college administrators are inevitably tempted to abandon the struggle. If, as we expect, social change continues to accelerate, the gap between generations will grow wider, and conflict will intensify. The impulse to throw up one's hands is likely to become widespread. Eager to be loved or at least not abused by the young, many deans are likely to consider retrenching to the position they now take vis-à-vis graduate students. But even where administrators find this sort of retreat appealing, their external constituencies are unlikely to accept it in the near future. It is, after all, an abdication of one of the college's traditional functions. And although earlier maturity and greater general permissiveness make the policing of undergraduate life more difficult, some faculty and administrators realize that relaxing adult controls subjects students to more pressure from their peers to experiment with drugs, sex, and defiance. Adult attempts to regulate and restrict undergraduate life are therefore likely to continue in a desultory way for many years to come, bringing periodic attacks on the students' sense of maturity and dignity. But as in guerrilla warfare, the occupying powers may win all the battles while gradually losing the war. The problem is at bottom one of legitimacy, and the claims of adults on undergraduates seem to achieve this less and less.

Nonetheless, the metaphor of guerrilla warfare and colonial liberation suggests another side to our prophecy. It is one thing for undergraduates to win the same actual rights as other adults; it is quite another thing to win the freedom they *imagine* goes with adult status. The waning of formal adult control over the social aspects of undergraduate life is unlikely to be accompanied by comparable waning of control over undergraduate work. Today's graduate students are nominally free, but they are actually very much constrained by the fact that adults control their future status in society. This will probably still be the case with tomorrow's undergraduates. Generational revolt, in other words, will probably bring the appearance of victory, but it will also lead to neo-colonialism, for the young can no more afford to go their own way independent of adults than Ghana or Cuba can get on without help from at least some of the Great Powers.

III. *Social Stratification and Mass Higher Education*

Education versus Certification

In the previous chapter we described the confrontation between old and young as the central feature of college life. Insofar as colleges are devoted to education this description is accurate enough, but many would argue that education is not a college's primary function. The crucial raison d'etre of the American college, the sine qua non of its survival and current importance, may not be education but certification. Virtually every college course culminates in an examination and a grade, and virtually all college curricula lead to some sort of diploma or degree. A college that does not sort and label its students in this way evidently cannot find a clientele—at least we know of none that has done so over any considerable period of time.[1] A "college" that does not offer any instruction, on the other hand, can still find a market for its degrees, and a substantial number of these diploma mills do in fact exist.

In part, no doubt, this is a function of student attitudes. The majority of those who enter college are plainly more concerned with accumulating credits and acquiring licenses than with learning any particular skill while enrolled. They are mostly eager to take "advanced placement" and other examinations that yield credits and hasten their degree without teaching them anything, whereas they are mostly reluctant to do academic work for which they receive no official recognition or reward. Yet it would be misleading to assume that the emphasis on certification derives exclusively from students. There are only a handful of colleges that make even nominal efforts to eliminate grades as the prime incentive for academic work, and we know of no college that refrains from making judgments about the relative ability and competence of the students whose education it has attempted. A few offbeat colleges such as Reed and Sarah Lawrence try to de-emphasize grades as learning incentives by not telling students how they stand on such a simple scale. Even these colleges, however, keep records that enable them to tell graduate

[1] Mark Hopkins College in Vermont still refuses to offer a degree, but it was founded in 1964.

schools and employers how a given student ranked on a more or less linear scale of academic merit. The ironic result may be that students in these enlightened colleges are even more anxious and competitive than those in conventional institutions. The students know, after all, that faculty ratings will determine whether or not certain options are open to them as alumni; yet they have no reliable way of knowing what these ratings are. Thus even those who are doing well enough to get where they want to go may not feel free to relax.

An ideal grading system might work in precisely the opposite way from Reed and Sarah Lawrence. Students could take examinations and be given grades indicating how well the instructor thought they had done. These grades would, however, be privileged communications, which no teacher could divulge either to the college administration or to outsiders. Graduate schools and employers would have to rely on other indices of competence and on other people to make their judgments for them. The result would be to maximize candor and cooperation in teacher-student relationships while minimizing duplicity and authority. Such a system would also greatly accentuate the importance of Graduate Record and other standardized examinations.

There is no necessary reason for America to entrust both the education and the certification of the young to the same institutions. In Britain, for example, the two functions are frequently separated. Education is in the hands of schools and universities, but certification depends in good part on national examinations, which schoolmen help write but do not wholly control or administer. Even at the university level many of those who instruct the young have little or no role in judging them. An Oxford or Cambridge don, for example, prepares his students for university-wide examinations rather than for his own. Conversely, the University of London gives examinations and degrees to many "external" students to whom it has offered no instruction whatever.

In America, however, efforts to divorce education from certification have been few. Hutchins made such an attempt at Chicago, enunciating the hope that the College would admit anyone who was academically ready and would graduate anyone who could pass the examinations, regardless of how long or short his struggle to achieve the necessary competence. The College would also offer instruction for those who needed it, but that was a separate matter. This dream, however, was never fully realized, and today it has been largely abandoned even in principle. Swarthmore has attempted a somewhat different stratagem, more akin to the Oxbridge pattern. During the last two years honors students are taught by Swarthmore professors but not graded. At the end of their senior year they are examined and certified by outsiders. A Swarthmore student is thus engaged in a collaboration with his teacher to impress the outsider, instead of being an adversary trying to outwit his teacher. (He cannot, however, take his examinations or receive his degree without also meeting a variety of procedural requirements established by his own teachers.)

In most colleges there is not even this degree of separation between education and certification. The two are inextricably and deliberately intertwined, each function being modified in some ways to facilitate the other. Certification requirements are constantly adjusted in order to ensure satisfactory socialization. The main consideration in setting many examinations, for example, is the necessity of passing students who have done the assigned work diligently, even if they have not mastered the fundamentals of the subject. The result is, for example, an English Literature examination that asks students to identify characters and quotations from the books they are supposed to have read, or to regurgitate ideas presented in lectures. Conversely, some professors will fail a student who has been lackadaisical in doing weekly assignments, even though he ends up knowing more physics or economics and doing better on his exam than his more diligent classmates. The professor will then justify such punishment by arguing that students must be "taught to work." And no matter what considerations determine the questions on examinations or the relative weight given quizzes, papers, and exams, the most important thing learned in college may not be physics or history but the importance of credentials and the art of acquiring them.

Ambiguities like this account for part of the furor aroused by the spread of standardized aptitude tests. Such tests reward able but indolent students and penalize the inept but diligent. They thus undermine teachers' and school administrators' hold over their students. By emphasizing the luck of the genetic draw, the tests also puncture the myth that the young can expect to achieve success as adults simply by working hard and doing what they are told. The traditional procedure of certifying the young entirely on the basis of grades on tests set by individual teachers gave this myth both plausibility and substance. Individual teachers can and often do give tests that measure only whether work has been done rather than whether anything has been learned. The Educational Testing Service has a harder time giving such a test, since the work assigned in different schools is so various. This creates almost irresistible pressure for ETS to measure either aptitude or knowledge that can be defended as intrinsically valuable. School teachers can also give good grades to students who have made a good impression in class but have done poorly on quizzes and tests, and can thus improve both the student's class rank and his college chances. ETS has no such device for rewarding poise, politeness, and the like. Thus stressing teacher rather than ETS judgments encourages the young to believe in salvation by diligence and helps keep the unruly in line. The use of "impersonal" national tests, on the other hand, frees the young from the control of those adults they see day by day, and makes the future depend more on the students' intrinsic qualities.[2]

Important as the interplay between education and certification may be, however, it will not be our main focus in this chapter. Rather, we will be primarily concerned with the interplay between academic certification, on whatever basis, and the larger system of occupational, economic, social, and cultural stratification. We will, in other words, be concerned with the role of higher education in social mobility and stability.

Social Stratification in America

Until relatively recently most Americans were allergic to discussions of social class, at least in their own country. In part this was because they assumed social classes were by definition hereditary. Admitting the existence of hereditary classes would obviously undermine the idea that America was meritocratic, rewarding diligence and competence irrespective of ancestry. But the desire to believe that America was a classless society had other roots too. The New World's great achievement was said to be its respect for regional, religious, and ethnic variety, for women as well as men, for the young as well as the old, for manual as well as cerebral work, for the culture of the populace as well as the culture of the palace. American diversity was thus portrayed as a product of egalitarian pluralism rather than invidious hierarchies. Talk of social classes seemed to deny all this, implying that America, like Europe, had a single national system of stratification.

There were, of course, skeptics. Many nineteenth-century observers noted, for example, that the elimination of traditional social hierarchies had forced Americans to rely on the one universal surviving measure

---

[2] Those who oppose national tests almost never articulate their objections in these terms. They merely say that the tests do not measure important human qualities with which educators are (or should be) concerned. How reliance on school or college grades to measure competence will ensure the measurement of these qualities is seldom specified, but it is probably a fair inference that the anti-testers assume that teachers grade somewhat subjectively, whereas they know the Educational Testing Service does not. (Some conveniently forget that teachers also grade and that these grades are critical in college admissions and other sifting processes.) Needless to say, there are many other sorts of objections to national tests too, especially the fear that teachers will teach only for the national tests.

of power and prestige: money. Cash was by no means evenly distributed in pre-industrial America, and those who had less than their share almost always envied those who had more, while those who had more reciprocated by looking down on those who had less. In this respect, then, America was never really a classless society. Wealth and poverty may have depended on individual merit more than on ancestry, but few denied that they were a source of inequality, just as in Europe.

Despite all the talk about "respect for honest labor," moreover, Americans were stratified in terms of their jobs as well as their incomes. So long as the majority of men lived on farms, manual labor was nearly universal. Nonetheless, there were probably very few young men, even in pre-industrial America, who would not have chosen a job that required them to use only their head over a job that required them to use only their back. During the nineteenth and twentieth centuries urbanization, industrialization, and the increasingly complex division of labor both intensified and complicated these concerns. Not only was there a division between blue-collar and white-collar workers but further divisions arose within these two broad classifications. Some white-collar workers, such as plant managers and higher government officials, exercised a good deal of power over other people; others, such as self-employed professionals and businessmen, had less direct power over others but more control over their own lives. Clerical and sales workers usually had neither. Just as those with less money envied those with more, while those with more felt superior to those with less, so too with power. The result was another system of stratification, based on occupation, parallel to the system based on income.[3]

As a general rule the economic and occupational hierarchies reenforce one another. Most jobs of high prestige and power also pay well, and most jobs that pay well give their holder both prestige and power. Those with "upper-middle" jobs are therefore likely to have "upper-middle" incomes and those with "lower" incomes are likely to have "lower" jobs. In the discussion that follows we will therefore collapse economic and occupational class into a single concept, which we will call social class. When we speak of the upper-middle class, for example, we will mean families headed by someone with a professional or managerial job, usually making at least twice as much as the average American family. When we speak of the lower-middle class we will mean families headed by clerical or sales workers or small businessmen, usually earning fairly close to the median national

[3] For a summary of the way people rate various jobs, see National Opinion Research Center, "Jobs and Occupations." On the stability over time of occupational ratings, see Hodge, Siegel, and Rossi.

income. When we speak of the working class we will mean families headed by a blue-collar worker, again with incomes close to the national average. When we speak of the lower class we will mean families whose head is frequently unemployed and often a woman, with average incomes around half the national average.

It is important to emphasize that these categories are indicative rather than exhaustive; many Americans fit perfectly in none of them but instead combine the attributes of several. One reason for this is that the broad occupational categories on which such classifications necessarily depend are by no means perfectly descriptive. There is no question that the most powerful and prestigious jobs in America are almost all "professional" or "managerial," for example, but these two categories also include many people whose work gives them neither power nor prestige. The Census category "managers, officials, and proprietors" includes self-employed peanut vendors and newsboys as well as the President of the United States, while the category "professional, technical, and kindred" includes stripteasers and baseball umpires as well as Wall Street lawyers and atomic physicists. An additional complication is that occupational power and prestige do not always correlate perfectly with income even in principle. A federal judge, for example, has more power and prestige than almost any attorney, but he usually makes less money on the bench than he would in private practice. The result is that some men prefer to remain attorneys even when offered a judgeship, while others will make enormous efforts to become a judge. Similarly, clergymen usually have more power and prestige than undertakers serving the same parishioners, but usually make considerably less money. This kind of dissonance is atypical but hardly unique.

Under these circumstances it is not surprising to find that many of those who hold nominally professional or managerial jobs do not have incomes anything like double the national average. In 1960, for example, about 10 per cent of all male workers held professional jobs, and another 10 per cent held managerial jobs. Within this crudely defined "top fifth" of the occupational distribution, only 46 per cent also had incomes which put them in the top fifth of the economic distribution.[4] A more detailed and therefore more sensitive selection of those in the top fifth of the occupational distribution would undoubtedly increase the proportion falling in the economic elite, but it would by no means make the two synonymous.[5]

Another way to describe this lack of congruence between the two

[4] 1960 *Census*, I, 1, table 208.
[5] There is considerable sociological literature on those individuals whose status in various hierarchies is not congruent. See, e.g. Lenski, "Status Inconsistency." See also his "Status Crystallization."

distributions is to start with an economic elite and look at its occupational distribution. Table I shows the occupations of the heads
of the richest twentieth of all American families in 1959.

TABLE I
OCCUPATIONAL DISTRIBUTION OF HEADS OF FAMILIES
WITH INCOMES OVER $15,000 IN 1959

Occupation		
Self-employed Professional	12	
Salaried Professional	14	
Self-employed Businessman	15	64
Salaried Businessman	23	
Clerical or Sales Worker	14	
Blue-Collar Worker	16	
Farmer	3	36
Unknown	3	
Total	100	

SOURCE: 1960 *Census*, I, 1, table 230. In 1959 5.1 per cent of all families reported
incomes of over $15,000. The distribution for unrelated individuals was considerably
lower. It could be argued that the relevant distribution is that of the jobs of the best-paid
individual male workers, rather than that of the heads of affluent families, but the 1960
Census, I, 1, table 208, shows that the two are almost identical.

While the majority of those with "upper" incomes have "upper" jobs,
there are plainly a lot of deviant cases. This is equally true of those
with "upper-middle," "lower-middle," and even "lower" incomes.

Despite these difficulties we know of no way to analyze the
character and impact of higher education in America without talking
about social stratification and class. Indeed, we have felt obliged to
use these conceptions to describe not only contemporary America but
also eighteenth- and nineteenth-century America. We have even used
them to describe America a generation or two hence, on the assumption that social stratification, while perhaps not an absolutely necessary feature of industrial societies, is found in all extant or readily
foreseeable societies.

To say that social classes are universal does not mean that they are
everywhere and always the same. We must therefore say something
about the changing size of social classes. For some this is merely a
matter of definition. One can, for example, define the "upper-middle
class" as the richest and most powerful fifth of the population. It is
obviously impossible for an upper-middle class defined in this way
to grow proportionately larger or smaller over time. Conversely, one

might define those whose jobs put them in the bottom fifth of the occupational distribution as a lower class. The size of such a lower class obviously cannot be reduced by full employment, an anti-poverty program, or anything else. Thus while this sort of definition may capture a good deal of the truth about life in a competitive society, it has the disadvantage of ignoring change even if it takes place.

Other people therefore define class in absolute terms, saying that anyone who can afford two cars is in the middle class, or that anyone who has a non-manual job is in the middle class, or some such thing. This sort of definition obviously makes the size of classes very responsive to technological innovations. During the past sixty years, for example, productivity has more than doubled.[6] If one had defined the "lower class" in absolute terms in 1909, say, as any family with $750 a year or less, the term would have subsumed half the population. If this same absolute standard were used in 1966 (with inflation taken into account), it would embrace only about one family in eight.[7]

This sort of definition helps us to understand society better than the strictly relative one just discussed. But what does it mean to say that the "lower class" has now shrunk to a quarter its size in 1909? It seems fairly clear that such a proposition greatly exaggerates the character and rate of social and cultural change. The real incomes of the poorest fifth of the American population today, for example, approximate those of the second fifth during the 1930s.[8] Yet this does not necessarily mean that the poorest fifth of the American population resembles the second fifth during the 1930s in other important respects. The fact of being at the bottom seems to be at least as important as absolute purchasing power in defining families' life styles. Families in the poorest fifth of the population today may have twice the income their grandparents had, but they have so much less than today's typical family that they still *feel* very poor. Competitive subjective feelings aside, the economic and social arrangements of an industrial society tend to presume a certain level of affluence, and this is always more than the poorest families have. When the median income was $750, for example, public transportation was essential for the majority of the population and was available to it. Today, on the other hand, 80 per cent of all families can afford an automobile. Public

<hr>

[6] The increase in real per capita GNP between 1909 and 1966 was between 150 and 175 per cent. See Denison for estimates of GNP trends from 1909 to 1957. See *The Economic Report of the President,* for estimates from 1929 to 1966.
[7] Extrapolated from sources cited in previous and subsequent footnotes and from Ogburn, p. 380.
[8] 1965 *Statistical Abstract,* table 465.

transportation has therefore deteriorated, and the minority that still cannot afford a car is relatively worse off than before.

Similar ambiguities mark the history of the occupational distribution. The occupational structure is constantly being upgraded. The typical job today requires more brainpower and less muscle than it did a century ago, and this trend is likely to continue, despite some gloomy contrary predictions about the effects of automation. In 1900, for example, 42 per cent of all men worked on farms; by 1960 it was 9 per cent. Similarly, one man in seven was an unskilled laborer in 1900; by 1960 it was one in fourteen. Conversely, the proportion of men doing what the Census calls professional work has risen from one in thirty to one in nine since 1900, most of the increase coming since 1940. The proportion classified as "managers, officials and proprietors" has risen from one in fifteen to one in nine, and the rise would be even greater if one looked solely at managers and officials and excluded small businessmen.[9] But this does not tell us whether the typical worker has more or less control over his own job situation than in the past, or whether modern economic institutions diffuse power or concentrate it.

It is very hard to quantify the distribution of power in the occupational structure.[10] Sociologists can measure the movement of workers from manual to non-manual jobs, from farm to city, and from job to job. Some have concluded that since the fastest growing groups are those that have traditionally exercised the most power over society, there is more "room at the top" today than in the past.

This conclusion is, however, probably premature. There were more people in jobs traditionally defined as "professional" and "managerial" in 1960 than in 1900, and fewer people chopping cotton or digging ditches. But changes of this kind do not necessarily mean any basic change in the distribution of power, prestige, or even self-respect. A janitor is still at the bottom of the heap even if he throws the switch on an oil furnace instead of stoking a coal furnace, and a farmowner's son is still in the middle of the heap if he becomes a school teacher, even though this means he has nominally risen into the "professional class."[11]

[9] See Folger and Nam, "Trends," p. 36.

[10] This is not to say that sociologists have made no contribution to our understanding of occupational power and its use. C. Wright Mills, Floyd Hunter, and many others have studied the subject. But their work tells us more about how power is used than about how much of it is associated with particular sorts of jobs. We have no simple index of the power associated with various jobs comparable to the indices of income and prestige commonly used by social scientists to rank occupations. For an excellent analysis of these latter see Blau and Duncan, pp. 117 ff., and also the sources cited there and in footnote 3, p. 65.

[11] On the relative prestige of farmers and teachers see, e.g. National Opinion Research Center, "Jobs and Occupations."

Noting all this, some observers have jumped to the opposite conclusion. Economists, for example, have noted the declining number of
small businesses, both farm and non-farm, and the increasing con-
centration of corporate power as a result of mergers. Some radicals
have taken this as prima facie evidence that power is today concentrated in fewer hands than a generation or two ago. At first glance
this implies that there is less and less room at the top. Actual ownership of large corporations has, however, grown more diverse as their
domination of the economy has increased. Ownership, moreover, may
be less important than radicals assume. It is far from clear, for example, that the owner of a corner grocery store has more power vis-à-vis
his creditors, suppliers, and customers than the salaried manager of a
supermarket. Nor is it obvious that a nineteenth-century farmer had
more freedom of action in his confrontations with the weather, the
railroads, the banks, and the market than his teacher grandson in his
confrontations with school principals, boards of education, parents,
and students.

Under these circumstances we cannot assume that the relative size
of various social classes is changing just because the over-all standard
of living and the over-all level of occupational competence are rising.
Instead, we must regard the size of social classes as a researchable
question, albeit one to which definitive answers are never likely to be
available. One way to investigate this question is to define a social
class as a group exercising certain specified kinds of power relative
to others or consuming a fixed share of the nation's goods and services.
We can then ask how the proportion of the population in each of these
groups is changing over time. We might, for example, define the upper
class as that group that controlled 51 per cent of the common stock
of all American corporations, and we might then see whether this
group constituted 1 per cent of the population or 5 per cent, or 20
per cent, at any particular moment in history. Similarly, we might
define the lower class as a group that consumed the bottom tenth of
the nation's goods and services. By examining Table II we could then
estimate that this group shrank from about 34 per cent of the population in 1929 to about 30 per cent in 1947 and then expanded to perhaps 31 or 32 per cent in 1962. (The definitions are, of course, only
illustrative.)

The only readily available measure of changes in the power or
influence associated with a given job is pay. Despite the exceptions
noted earlier, jobs that give the incumbent what is usually called
responsibility tend to pay well, while menial jobs usually pay badly.
Hence if the amount of room at the top of the occupational structure
were increasing we would expect more people to be sharing in the
slice of the pie traditionally reserved for the elite. Conversely, if the

number of marginal or expendable jobs were diminishing, we would expect to find fewer people dividing the (much smaller) slice of pie traditionally available for society's castoffs.

In point of fact, however, Table II indicates that there has been no significant change in the distribution of income since 1945. This makes it hard to believe that there has been much change in the distribution of occupational power and prestige. The whole labor force has been upgraded, but the relative position of various strata has evidently changed very little. There is, however, evidence that the share of all income going to the top 5 per cent of all families declined considerably during both the Depression and World War II. This suggests that these two upheavals may well have altered the occupational structure in significant ways, even though redistribution of workers among job categories was no more dramatic in these years than later. Although no good data are available on the over-all income distribution before 1929, tax returns from the well-to-do suggest that their share of the pie changed very little between 1913 and 1929.[12] This being the case, the safest working assumption is probably that there was little change in the over-all distribution during those years.

TABLE II

SHARE OF ALL INCOME GOING TO TOP 5 PER CENT
AND TO EACH FIFTH OF ALL AMERICAN FAMILIES
AND INDIVIDUALS 1929–1962

Year	Top 5 Per Cent	Next 15 Per Cent	Second Fifth	Third Fifth	Fourth Fifth	Bottom Fifth	Total
1929	30.0	24.4	19.3	13.8	— 12.5 —		100.0
1935–36	26.5	25.2	20.9	14.1	9.2	4.1	100.0
1941	24.0	24.8	22.3	15.3	9.5	4.1	100.0
1947	20.9	25.1	22.0	16.0	11.0	5.0	100.0
1957	20.2	25.3	22.4	16.3	11.1	4.7	100.0
1962	19.6	25.9	22.7	16.3	10.9	4.6	100.0

SOURCE: Miller, *Income Distribution*, p. 21. The data are from the series prepared by the Office of Business Economics. Miller also presents data from the Current Population Survey for years since 1947. Although the CPS data suggest that both the richest five per cent and the poorest 20 per cent are somewhat worse off than the above figures indicate, the differences are small and stability since 1947 is equally apparent. More recent data based on the CPS are shown in *Current Population Reports*, Series P-60, No. 51, January 12, 1967. These data suggest a slight decline in the proportion of income going to the top 5 per cent between 1961 and 1965, but the over-all pattern of postwar stability remains.

[12] See Kuznets. For a somewhat different set of figures and a very different interpretation, see Kolko.

What does this imply about social class in America? It seems clear that technological change and improvements in human skills have increased the productivity of the labor force, and that the increase in productivity has led to rising living standards for virtually all Americans. While some occupational groups have not gained as much as others, occupations with lagging wages have been mostly shrinking in size. Both old and new workers have gravitated toward occupations in which wages were rising fairly rapidly. The net result is that the distribution of goods and services has remained relatively constant despite the rise in absolute living standards. It should be noted, however, that if both the rich and the poor increase their income at about the same rate over the years, the absolute gap between them will necessarily grow. Between 1947 and 1962, for example, 80th percentile income was always between 4.0 and 4.5 times as much as 20th percentile income. But the absolute gap grew from $4,650 to $6,988 (1962 dollars).[13] Still, if the income distribution is taken as a crude index of the distribution of occupational skills, responsibilities, and prestige, it also seems fair to conclude that these latter have not been redistributed to any significant extent since 1945. In that case it also follows that the relative size of various social classes has remained essentially unchanged for the past twenty years. Nor is there much prospect of change in the near future.[14]

The importance of this conclusion cannot be overemphasized, for it shapes our over-all analysis of the relationship between social class and higher education. If, for example, the size of various classes is taken as fixed, social mobility must be treated as a two-way street. Upward mobility will be possible only if vacancies occur in higher strata for some reason. One reason for such vacancies is that the upper strata are less fertile than society as a whole and do not reproduce themselves. This used to be a major factor in American patterns of mobility, but fertility differentials between classes seem to have gradually narrowed over the years.[15] If there is to be appreciable upward

[13] Miller, *Income Distribution,* table 1–8. The actual effects of these changes clearly depend in part on changes in the relative price of the goods consumed by the rich and by the poor—a problem not taken into account in summary cost-of-living indexes.

[14] The reader will note that since we have defined social class as having only two basic determinants, namely power and income, and since we have also used the latter to measure the former, we have ended up putting enormous weight on a single measure. Although this can be defended on the ground that the measure in question is not a statistical artifact but has real objective and subjective importance to the individuals whose positions we are assessing, we still regret we have no good way to cross-check the inferences we have drawn from income trends.

[15] 1965 *Statistical Abstract,* table 55. It should be noted that virtually all groups more than reproduce themselves in the narrow sense of averaging more

mobility, then, room at the top must be created by downward mobility among the sons and daughters of the elite. This is not easy to arrange. Indeed, it is not even easy to contemplate, which is one reason why America's ideologists are so committed to the idea that the amount of room at the top is expanding rather than stable. Yet nobody believes it is expanding enough to accommodate *all* the upwardly mobile plus *all* those brought up on top. That is why the elite, while it may give lip-service to the idea of equalizing opportunity, also makes enormous efforts to ensure that the opportunities available to its children are in fact more than equal to those available to the rest of the population.

Nonetheless, there has been a good deal of social mobility in America. Suppose, for example, that we imagine two alternatives occupational systems. In one there is no mobility whatever: everyone inherits his parents' position. In the other there is perfect mobility: children from prosperous, well-placed families have no more chance of ending up in their parents' position than children born in the slums. Every country plainly falls somewhere between these two poles. America (probably like most industrial societies) falls closer to the equality model than to the hereditary model.[16] In interpreting this fact it is important to bear in mind that the genes affecting both physical and mental competence are probably not randomly distributed across classes. Success in America has always depended to some extent on intelligence, and intelligence is to some extent hereditary. While clever parents tend to have children duller than themselves, and dull parents tend to have children cleverer than themselves, the clever parents' children are not typically as dull as the national average, nor are the dull parents' children typically as clever as the average. This means that even a strictly meritocratic system for allocating class positions would probably put a slightly larger number of advantaged than disadvantaged children in the elite.[17] Uneven distribution of talent cannot account for more than a fraction of all occupational inheritance in America, but it probably does account for some of it.

Like the size of social classes, the rate of social mobility does not seem to be changing much, if at all. A man's chances of occupying the same relative place on the totem pole that his father occupied

---

than 2 children per family. But if, say, the upper-middle class included 15 out of every 100 people, and if they produced only 15 children while the remaining 85 people produced 105 children, then the top 15 per cent of the next generation would have to include at least 3 children from outside the elite of the previous generation.

[16] For a statistical demonstration of this point, see Jackson and Crockett.

[17] For a discussion of the evidence on this point, see Eckland, "Genetics."

have not changed significantly in the past forty years, and there is no good reason to suppose they changed much in earlier times.[18]

Cultural Stratification in America

Up to this point we have been talking about social classes in economic terms, defining men primarily as producers and consumers of goods and services. One can, however, define class as a broadly cultural rather than a narrowly socioeconomic phenomenon.

When Lloyd Warner and his colleagues first began arguing for the existence of cultural classes in the 1930s, most readers' initial reactions were hostile. Warner's findings conflicted with the mythology of egalitarian pluralism even more sharply than studies of income distribution and occupational hierarchy. It was not that Americans denied the existence of diverse subcultures, but most people wanted very much to believe that this diversity was only marginally related to differences in wealth and power.[19] In part, no doubt, public resistance to such arguments was a legacy of nineteenth-century America, in which subcultural differences may well have been rather loosely associated with wealth and power, at least west of the Appalachians. So long as most men's fathers had been farmers, High Culture remained at a definite discount and even formal education was often rejected in favor of the school of hard knocks. By the 1930s, however, the situation had changed. It took the conventional wisdom a while to encompass the new reality, but this too has now been largely accomplished. Students, for example, are no longer surprised by Warner's view of small-town America as socially and culturally stratified. On the contrary, they have picked up his views and terms without even having read him, and now casually put their parents down by charging them with middle-class prejudices. Newspaper columnists hold forth in the same vein about the characteristics of lower-class subcultures, and civil rights leaders rail against what they usually take to be an upper-class "power structure."

Nonetheless, cultural classes are clearly less hierarchical than social

[18] The best data on social mobility is that presented by Blau and Duncan in *The American Occupational Structure.* They find a simple correlation between the occupational status of fathers and sons of .34 for those born 1897–1906 and .37 for those born 1927–36. This means that if a father ranked in the 84th percentile of the occupational distribution, his son had typically fallen to the 64th percentile.

[19] The issue is nicely embodied in the well-known Hemingway-Fitzgerald dialogue, in which Fitzgerald is said to have commented that, "The rich are different from us," to which Hemingway replied, "Yes, they have more money." In the 1920s most Americans wanted to believe Hemingway's version; today Fitzgerald's is more accepted.

classes. The time is largely past when the uneducated considered themselves superior to those with book learning, but the deference paid to expertise, sophistication, and culture is still considerably less than in most countries. It is still very difficult, for example, to win political support for subsidies to symphonies, art, ballet, and other manifestations of upper-class taste. Nor does the nouveau riche seem as embarrassed by having unfashionable tastes and views as he would be in most European countries. Nonetheless, we would argue that, perhaps partly as a result of mass education, American subcultures are more hierarchical than they used to be and that the "lower" cultural strata increasingly defer to the "higher." This means that even those who do not themselves have upper-middle class customs or share upper-middle class concerns nonetheless tend to accept their legitimacy and even their superiority. (The typical voter, for instance, does not care for chamber music himself, but he may nonetheless be impressed by it and may have thought better of President Kennedy because he had Casals play at the White House.) One result is that upward socioeconomic mobility is increasingly likely to mean cultural mobility as well.

This tendency toward congruence between social and cultural classes has led some sociologists to collapse the two into a single conglomerate conception. At times we too will do this. There are, however, dangers in this approach. For one thing, it is by no means self-evident that the relationship between social and cultural classes is fixed. What are today described as "middle-class values," for example, may tomorrow be found waning among the middle classes but spreading among the working classes. Thus the fact that the upper-middle class (in terms of income and occupation) is of relatively fixed size does not necessarily mean that what have traditionally been regarded as upper-middle class cultural values are permanently confined to a fixed proportion of population. Some of the values traditionally associated with middle-class status could, for example, depend in large part on absolute living standards rather than relative status, and could be diffused to new groups in the same way that vacuum cleaners and football were. Under these circumstances it is useful to make a tentative distinction between social and cultural classes, and to treat their relationship as a problem for investigation rather than as a given.

Such an investigation is not, however, a simple matter, and this chapter can only suggest some of the possibilities. There are, as we have indicated, serious difficulties in assessing the distribution of power between various job holders and consequent difficulties in discussing changes in the size of occupational classes. Yet these difficulties are trivial compared to those we encounter when we try to define cultural classes and to describe their relative size at different points in time. For one thing, the subjective meaning of many behavioral indices (e.g. having a savings account or reading *Time* magazine) varies over time. Some changes in lower-strata behavior (e.g. smaller families) which might be taken to indicate a spread of traditional upper-strata values might also be attributed to external factors (e.g. the decline in infant mortality among the poor). Other changes (e.g. the spread of vacations) may reflect general increases in affluence rather than the diffusion of upper-strata values, for the impulse to take a vacation may always have been present among all strata. Still other changes (e.g. attitudes toward premarital sex) may involve not diffusion but historical evolution (so that the traditionally restrictive middle class may now be more permissive than much of the working class if not of the lower class). And even if the meaning of such changes were more clear, it would be hard to summarize them in any over-all measure of change in the size of various strata. Certainly that is a task beyond the scope of this book.

The impulse to quantify is, however, hard to resist. Just as we earlier took income as a crude measure of occupational power, so we will take educational attainment as a crude index of cultural class. In doing this we do not mean to imply a *causal* relationship between schooling and cultural level. While schooling may be an instrument for changing men's values, and more especially for disseminating the attitudes and skills that characterize the upper-middle class, evidence for this is by no means definitive.[20] Instead, the relationship between schooling and cultural class may often work the other way. Young people's ultimate cultural class may be almost entirely determined by factors such as genetic ability, family structure, social connections, and so forth. Schools and colleges may simply be a sifting device for separating those whose talents and inclinations will land them in one cultural class from those whose talents and inclinations will land them in another. We will have more to say about this question later on. The important point here is that, whatever the cause-effect relationship, there seems to be a strong *correlation* between educational attainment and cultural class.

On this basis, what can we say about the relative size of various cultural classes? To begin with, it must be said that data on the level and distribution of education before the 1930s are no more reliable than data on incomes before then. Table III gives two estimates of

[20] For a review of research regarding the impact of college on student values, see Jacob. He concluded that most colleges had very little effect on their students. For two critical reviews of these studies and Jacob's conclusions, see Riesman, "Review of the Jacob Report," and Barton.

the proportion of various age groups completing high school and college, one based on the decennial Census, the other on the biennial institutional surveys by the U. S. Office of Education. Unfortunately there is serious disagreement between these two sources, at least for the cadres born before 1915.

TABLE III

PER CENT OF ALL INDIVIDUALS BORN IN GIVEN YEARS FINISHING HIGH SCHOOL AND COLLEGE: 1855–1944

Years of Birth	Per Cent Finishing High School		Per Cent Finishing Four Years College	
	CENSUS	USOE	CENSUS	USOE
1855–1859	—	—	—	1.1
1860–1864	11.5	2.5	2.3	—
1865–1869	13.1	—	2.6	1.3
1870–1874	14.2	3.5	2.9	—
1875–1879	16.4	—	3.3	1.7
1880–1884	17.1	6.4	3.4	—
1885–1889	18.5	—	3.8	2.0
1890–1894	20.7	8.8	4.1	—
1895–1899	24.6	—	5.0	2.7
1900–1904	28.5	16.8	6.1	—
1905–1909	34.9	—	7.3	5.8
1910–1914	40.6	29.0	7.4	—
1915–1919	43.4	—	8.1	8.1
1920–1924	54.7	50.8	9.5	—
1925–1929	55.8	—	10.9	—
1930–1934	60.5	59.0	11.0	14.1
1935–1939	63.6	61.1	—	18.2
1940–1944	—	65.1	—	20.0

SOURCES: The Census estimates for those born prior to 1890 are derived from the 1940 Census, as summarized in Folger and Nam, *The Education,* table A. 11. The estimates for those born subsequent to 1890 are derived from the 1960 *Census,* I, 1, table 173. Those who report having completed four years of college include some who do not report having earned a degree. To obtain estimates of college degree holders, the figures for those born 1885–94 should be reduced by 20 per cent, for those born 1895–1904 by 21 per cent, for those born 1905–14 by 15 per cent, for those born 1915–24 by 11 per cent, and for those born 1925–34 by 10 per cent. These discount rates are estimated from Schwartz, table 1.2, and the 1960 *Census,* I, 1, table 173. No data are available for estimating the proportion of those who completed four years of college before the turn of the century without earning a degree, but the discrepancy might conceivably be even higher. If so, this might account for part of the difference between Census and USOE estimates for that era. For further analysis of the reliability of these census estimates see Orr and Nam.

The U.S. Office of Education estimates are taken from the 1965 *Digest,* tables 37, 53, and 74. They are based on institutional reports of degrees awarded divided by Census estimates of the total age group. We assumed that the median age at high school graduation was seventeen, since USOE makes this assumption, and that the median age at college graduation was twenty-two, since the NORC survey of 1961 B.A.s showed this to be the case (see James Davis, *Great Aspirations*, table 1.1). These estimates are for a single year—usually the fourth in the five-year period. (Given the steady rise in attainment, this should make USOE estimates very slightly higher than Census estimates for the whole five-year period.) Institutional reports to USOE might be suspected of incompleteness, especially in the early years, but every ten years the Census also collected enrollment statistics that were in substantial agreement with the USOE figures. USOE estimates of Bachelors' degrees awarded in a given year also include professional degrees such as the M.D. and LL.B., most of which now go to men who earned B.A.s in an earlier year. This means that the USOE estimates of first degrees exceed the actual percentage earning such a degree by an appreciable fraction. Karel, table 2, gives a series based on USOE data which excludes some of these professional degrees. The gap between his series and the Census is even greater than in the above table.

The discrepancy between these two statistical series is discussed by Jaffe and Adams, who give reasons for preferring Census to USOE estimates. While they make a strong case against the reliability of USOE data, an equally strong case can be made against the Census data. Both series are internally contradictory. As noted in footnote 3 of Chapter II, the USOE data show more male college students than high school graduates during the nineteenth century. But the Census data for those born before World War I also show more years of school completed by the over-all population than would be expected on the basis of Census estimates of school enrollment during the relevant years. But see also Nam, "Some Comparisons."

Individuals born before World War I reported receiving far more education than institutions reported giving in this period. Since then the discrepancy has narrowed. This means that institutional reports show a more rapid rate of growth in both high school and college graduation than do individual reports. The discrepancy in growth rates is particularly striking at the high school level, where Census data suggest that the proportion of the population graduating from high school rose by a factor of five between 1880 and 1940, while the USOE data suggest that it rose by a factor of twenty. On the whole we have more confidence in the Census statistics than in those supplied by USOE, but we cannot emphasize too strongly that neither series should be taken very seriously.

Table III gives many readers an impression of steady increase in both high school and college enrollment. The increase was, however, far from even. Chart I shows that despite growth in enrollment at higher levels there was very little change in median attainment between the Civil War and World War I. The typical youngster got between eight and nine years of school. There was a sharp increase in median attainment during the 1920s and 1930s to about twelve years.[21] Since World War II median attainment has risen relatively slowly.

[21] Much of the increase in attainment during the 1920s and 1930s was the result of more regular progress through school rather than of more protracted

Despite the difficulty of estimating educational attainment for different groups and periods, one thing is clear: the level has risen. This raises the thorny question whether general increases in attainment have affected the relative size of various cultural classes. If, for example, one were to define anyone who had finished high school as culturally lower-middle class, and anyone who had finished college as culturally upper-middle class, both classes would obviously be getting bigger. The lowest cultural strata would be shrinking correspondingly. This procedure would clearly be justified if schooling were a primary cause of cultural characteristics. If we knew that the many observable differences between the college-educated and the high-school-educated were a direct consequence of attending college, we could feel fairly confident that the proportion of the population with traditional upper-middle class habits and values had risen in tandem with college enrollment. If, on the other hand, differences between the college-educated and the high-school-educated result largely from the more favored social background, greater intelligence, or more enterprising temperament of those who attend college, then increases in college enrollment may not contribute much to the diffusion of upper-middle class culture, but may simply place the collegiate imprimatur on hitherto marginal groups.

Our own prejudices suggest that relatively few of the differences between the extensively educated and the briefly educated are caused directly by education per se. Many of the differences seem rather to result from selective withdrawal and ejection from the system. We would argue, in other words, that the differences between college graduates and high school dropouts are only occasionally caused by exposure to high school and college. Mostly these differences are the result of the fact that, let us say, intelligent but docile youngsters find schooling relatively congenial and therefore stay enrolled, while the less intelligent and more rebellious find it intolerable and therefore withdraw.

If this assumption is correct, what does it imply about the relationship between the absolute educational attainment of a given generation and the size of cultural classes in that generation? If schools' and colleges' standards of selection were relatively stable over time, an increase in the proportion of young people earning degrees would clearly indicate an increase in the proportion who had the traditional

---

schooling. The 1960 *Census,* I, 1, table 166, shows that between 1920 and 1960 the median school leaving age rose only two years, from sixteen to eighteen. The relevant age groups show a four-year increase in attainment during this same period (1960 *Census,* I, 1, table 173). This suggests that regular attendance and automatic promotion were crucial ingredients of the apparent change.

CHART I

MEDIAN YEARS OF SCHOOL COMPLETED
BY THOSE TURNING 17 BETWEEN 1880 AND 1955

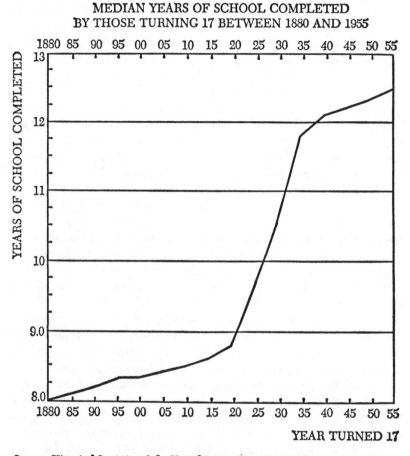

Source: *Historical Statistics of the United States*, Series H 395-406,
and 1960 *Census*, I, 1, table 173.

upper-middle class virtues, such as verbal fluency, perseverance, and ability to defer gratification. This might have nothing to do with the colleges per se and might be a result of urbanization, technological change, child-rearing practices, and the mass media, or other influences; but it could still be measured by changes in absolute levels of attainment, even if it was not *caused* by them. If, on the other hand, schools and colleges have had no absolute standards, but have mostly graduated anyone willing to go through the motions of acquiring education, rising enrollment may not really indicate growth of the more sophisticated cultural strata or shrinkage of the more benighted strata. Instead, it may simply imply steady devaluation of the academic currency, so that today's B.A. has the same cultural meaning as 1920's high school diploma.

American educational institutions have not generally set many absolute requirements for entrance or graduation. The increase in high school graduation, for example, has been accomplished in good part by automatic promotion and by the creation of "general" or "basic" curricula, which demand almost nothing of the student but persistence and docility. At the same time, however, the level of expectation in the academic curriculum has generally risen—as the spread of advanced placement courses, new science courses, and the like indicates. Whether the net result has been an increase or decrease in average competence we do not know; in either case, however, we suspect that the range of difference among high school graduates has grown. At the college level there has been, at least until recently, less social and political pressure to accommodate everyone, and the maintenance of traditional upper-middle class norms has been more general and more successful. Indeed, the level of competence required for a B.A. has probably risen at the same time that the number earning it has.

All this takes absolute levels of attainment as an index of cultural position. In order to give a more complete view one must, however, also look at an individual's standing relative to others of his generation. In 1900, for example, a man who completed high school was a member of his generation's educational elite. Most high school graduates of that era probably accepted most of the middle-class norms of their time—though we know of no data on this point. In 1967, on the other hand, about 75 per cent of all young people were finishing high school. Secondary schools were willing to keep all but the most uncooperative students, even if they were not able to live up to middle-class expectations, and high teen-age unemployment made even rebellious youngsters stick around, simply because there were few attractive alternatives.

If, then, we are interested in the changing size of cultural classes, we must look not just at absolute levels of schooling but at the distribution of schooling to various strata in different eras. We must ask whether the cultural elite and the cultural dropouts are getting closer together or further apart. Table IV estimates the distribution of schooling for three different generations. At first glance this distribution looks much more equitable than the distribution of income shown in Table II.

TABLE IV

PERCENTAGE SHARES OF TOTAL YEARS OF SCHOOLING OBTAINED BY BEST- AND WORST-EDUCATED TWENTIETHS AND THIRDS OF U. S. MALES: 1875–1934

Year of Birth	Top 20th	Bottom 20th	Top 3rd	Middle 3rd	Bottom 3rd	Total
1930–34	8	1	43	35	22	100
1910–14	9	1	46	34	20	100
1875–85*	12	†	53	34	13	100

* Includes all those alive and over seventy-five in 1960.

† Less than 0.5 per cent.

SOURCE: Folger and Nam, *The Education*, p. 162. Computations by Anderson, "Inequalities," p. 547, based on the 1950 and 1940 Census, yielded slightly different totals but showed the same trend, as did our own calculations dividing the population into fifths instead of thirds. The method of calculation is to aggregate the total number of years of schooling reported by the entire age grade to the Census Bureau, divide the population in twentieths, thirds, or whatever, and then aggregate the total number of years of schooling received by those in a given twentieth or third. Unfortunately, USOE data are not collected in such a way as to allow this computation, and it is therefore impossible to determine whether the same trends would show up if USOE enrollment figures were more accurate than Census figures. Judging by the ratio of college to high school graduates shown in Table III, however, the USOE distribution for those born before 1920 would be more equitable than the Census distribution, and the apparent trend toward equality would be negligible. Indeed, the USOE figures could even be used to argue that the distribution of schooling had grown *less* equitable over the years. We are, however, skeptical about the validity of the early USOE figures and in any case they are too incomplete to sustain any major conclusions about trends in distribution.

This may, however, be an illusion. For one thing, the table omits women. More important, a year of school does not have the same value under all conditions. The typical suburban school spends more than the typical rural one, and the typical college spends more than the typical elementary school. The allocation of educational *resources* between various segments of population seems to be almost as inequitable as the income distribution.[22] On the other hand, there is

[22] Our calculations on this point are very tentative. We hypothesized that those ending up in the best educated twentieth attended institutions that spent 20 per cent more than the national average in any given year; that those ending up in the best educated third attended institutions spending 10 per cent more than the national average; that those ending up in the worst educated third attended institutions spending 10 per cent less than the national average; and that those ending up in the worst educated twentieth attended institutions spending 20 per cent less than the national average. We further hypothesized that the cost of a year of high school was 1.5 times a year of elementary school; that the cost of a year of college was three times a year of elementary school; and the cost of a year of graduate school was ten times a year of elementary school. Finally, we hypothesized that men reporting five or more years of higher education in the 1960 Census averaged 6.0 years. If all these hypotheses were true, the best

strong reason to doubt that there is anywhere nearly as much variation in what students end up knowing or being as in the amounts
spent on their education. A year of graduate school may cost ten
times more than a year of elementary school, but the increase in a
man's intellectual competence or his future income associated with an
extra year of graduate school is nothing like ten times as much as the
increase associated with an extra year of elementary school.[23] Thus
while Table IV may underestimate the extent of inequities in the
distribution of schooling, a table showing the distribution of educational expenditures would probably overestimate these inequities, or
at least their results.

Whatever the absolute degree of inequity, it may be less important
than the trend. Table IV shows that if we imputed equal value to all
years of schooling, regardless of what was spent on them, the trend
was toward a more equal distribution. This would be even more true
if we were to look at the distribution of days of schooling instead of
years, for variations in the length of the school year and in regularity
of attendance have dropped sharply in recent times. It should also be
borne in mind, however, that, just as with incomes, the rise in absolute
attainment from one generation to another means that it takes a
very considerable redistribution to prevent the absolute gap between
the best and worst educated from growing. The absolute gap between
the best and worst educated thirds, for example, widened from 5.8
to 7.0 years between the 1910–14 generation and the 1930–34 generation, even though the distribution of schooling had grown more
equitable.[24]

Nor does the trend in the distribution of educational resources
necessarily parallel the trend in the distribution of years of school. It
is true that differences in expenditure among regions and jurisdictions are narrowing, so that eight years of elementary schooling or
four years of high school have more nearly the same value for everyone. But a year of higher education is much more expensive than a

---

educated five percent of 45–49-year-old men in 1960 had absorbed 23 per cent
of all educational expenditures on their age group, the best educated 33 per cent
had absorbed 53 per cent, the worst educated 33 per cent had absorbed 17 per
cent, and the worst educated 5 per cent had absorbed 0.5 per cent. Since these
figures rest on a set of unproven assumptions, they should only be regarded as
illustrative.

[23] On income, see 1960 *Census*, PC(2)-5B (*Educational Attainment*), table
6. The *causal* relation between education and income is obviously less than
the statistical *association*, and the latter can reasonably be regarded as an upper
limit for the former.

[24] Calculated from 1960 *Census*, I, 1, table 173. The median attainment of
men born 1910–14 was 13.1 years for the top third and 7.3 years for the bottom.
For men born 1930–34 the medians were 15.3 years and 8.3 years for the top
and bottom thirds. Means show the same trend as medians.

year of either elementary or secondary education. As a result, a one-year variation in the amount of college a man gets will affect the distribution of educational resources as much as a two- or three-year variation in the number of years of elementary or secondary school.[25] Our best guess is that the distribution of educational resources has changed relatively little in recent years.[26]

If the level of educational attainment is rising, while the distribution of educational resources remains relatively stable, what about inter-generational mobility? Are children from poorly educated families more or less likely to end up with a poor education today than in the past? If we judge cultural class by how long an individual has been in school, are upward and downward cultural mobility becoming more or less common? The best available data suggest that a man's chances of altering his father's position in the educational hierarchy were about the same in the 1950s as in the 1920s. The picture is complicated by the fact that high school completion has become less class-related over the past generation, while college entrance and graduation have not. This inevitably means that for those who finish high school, class is becoming more of a factor in college entrance and graduation. Nonetheless, the over-all picture is one of stability.[27]

On the basis of the evidence on educational attainment just re-

[25] If e.g. A gets four years of elementary education and B gets eight, B has gotten 100 per cent more years of schooling than A and has absorbed about 100 per cent more resources. If A's grandson gets 12 years of education while B's grandson gets 18 years, B's family advantage has been reduced from 100 per cent to 50 per cent and the distribution of years of school has grown more equitable. Yet if we assume that a year of high school costs 1.5 times as much as a year of elementary school, that a year of college costs three times as much, and that a year of graduate school costs ten times as much, B's grandson will consume 228 per cent more resources than A's grandson. Thus while a change of this sort would make the distribution shown in Table IV look more equitable than before, it would make a distribution based on resource allocation look less equitable.

[26] We have made crude trend estimates on the assumptions outlined in the previous footnotes. Since these assumptions were illustrative rather than empirical, and the results are quite sensitive to minor changes in some of the parameters, we have relatively little confidence in the results. The most that can be said is that the evidence for greater equity in the distribution of school days and school years cannot in itself be regarded as proving a similar trend in the distribution of school funds.

[27] The basic data on educational attainment are reported in Bureau of the Census, *Current Population Reports* (1964). Further analyses are found in Blau and Duncan and in Spady. Blau and Duncan, p. 178, report simple correlations between fathers' and sons' educational attainment for sons born 1897–1906, 1907–16, 1917–26, and 1927–36. These average around 0.40 ± 0.03 and show no trend over time. Spady has shown in correspondence that the rate of inter-generational turnover in the upper educational quartile fell from 59 to 51 per cent during this period, but our own calculations using his data show virtually no change in the rate of intergenerational turnover in the upper educational sixth. Additional evidence on these points will be presented later in this chapter.

viewed, it seems clear that cultural stratification follows many of the same patterns as social stratification:

1. The over-all level of educational attainment seems to be rising, just as the over-all income level is. The over-all level of cultural sophistication is probably also rising, though not at anything like the same rate as the standard of living.

2. The distribution of years of schooling is more equitable than the distribution of income, and unlike the income distribution is moving toward greater equity. The absolute attainment gap between the well educated and the poorly educated is growing, however, just as the absolute income gap between rich and poor is growing.

3. The distribution of educational resources, like the distribution of income, does not seem to be getting notably more or less egalitarian. What this implies for the distribution of intellectual competence is debatable, however, just as it is debatable whether a stable distribution of income indicates a stable distribution of occupational power and responsibility.

4. The rate of intergenerational mobility between cultural classes seems to resemble the rate of social mobility, in that both are quite high and neither has changed dramatically over time.

Under these circumstances we must ask to what extent social and cultural classes correspond to one another. While there is considerable overlap, it is by no means complete. Those with "upper-middle" educations are by no means always "upper-middle" in occupation or income, and those with "lower" incomes and occupations are not always "lower" in educational attainment. In 1960, for example, 18 per cent of all working men over twenty-five had completed at least one year of college. Only 45 per cent of this educational elite were in the best paid fifth of the male work force; one in four was earning less than the national median. At the other end of the educational scale 24 per cent of all male workers had not completed elementary school. Yet 21 per cent of these semiliterates were earning more than the national median, and 5 per cent were in the best paid fifth of the labor force.[28]

Neither is the relationship between education and occupation as tight as many people suppose. It is true that in 1960 some 76 per cent of all men over twenty-five in "professional, technical, and kindred" occupations reported a year or more of college, and about half held B.A.s. But only 35 per cent of all male managers, officials, and proprietors had ever been to college, and only 15 per cent held B.A.s. Even if we exclude proprietors and include only salaried managers and officials, only 45 per cent had finished a year of college.

[28] 1960 *Census*, I, 1, table 223.

Putting this the other way round, a man over twenty-five who had finished a year of college in 1960 had three chances in five of holding a professional or managerial job, but he also had one chance in six of holding a clerical or sales job and one chance in six of holding a blue-collar job.[29]

While these relationships are all relatively loose, they are obviously not inconsequential. This becomes especially clear if instead of looking at the relationship between only two of these hierarchies we look at all three together. Taking men between twenty-five and thirty-four in 1960, for example, and then focusing on those in *both* the best-paid fifth of the income distribution *and* the most prestigious fifth of the occupational distribution, we find that 68 per cent are also in the best educated fifth of the male population.[30] This suggests a considerable overlap in America's economic, occupational, and cultural elites.

The most interesting point about all these relationships may not, however, be their absolute level but their trend. The over-all relationship between education and occupational status has not changed much over the years, though earning a B.A. may be growing more important than it once was and a high school diploma less so.[31] The relationship between education and income also seems to be fairly stable.[32] The relationship between educational attainment and social mobility seems to be both modest and stable.[33]

Loose as these relationships may be, their existence and persistence bring us back to the problem we raised earlier, namely the character of the relationship between social and cultural class. Viewed from the top the problem seems simple. There seem to be plenty of opportunities for those with appropriate skills, habits, and attitudes; the "problem" is the shortage of qualified men for available top-level jobs. The educational system is constantly criticized for not turning out enough

[29] 1960 *Census*, PC(2)-5B (*Educational Attainment*), tables 8 and 9.

[30] Estimated from 1960 *Census*, I, 1, tables 173, 204, 279, and PC(2)-5A (*School Enrollment*), table 9.

[31] Different methods of analysis yield different conclusions on the relationship between education and occupation. For evidence that the relationship is slightly tighter for young men than for older ones, see Blau and Duncan, pp. 177 ff. For contrary evidence see Folger and Nam's comparison of 1940, 1950, and 1960 Census data in "Trends." Their data show a small decline, especially between 1950 and 1960, in the relationship between educational attainment and occupational status. For evidence of a decline in the relation between occupation and pre-college education, offset by an increase in the relation between college graduation and occupation, see Davis' analysis of 1950 and 1959 Census data in "Higher Education."

[32] Miller, *Income Distribution*, pp. 156 ff.

[33] On the relatively weak relationship between education and social mobility, see Anderson, "A Skeptical Note." The formulae and data given in Blau and Duncan, pp. 178 and 195, show that the simple correlation between educational mobility and occupational mobility was 0.321 for men born 1897–1906 and 0.315 for men born 1927–36.

men competent to fill these slots. Those at the top mostly assume that it is the difficulty of expanding their own cultural class that poses the crucial obstacle to both social progress and individual mobility. Hence their support for more and presumably better education.

Viewed from the bottom, on the other hand, the situation looks very different. Employers demand all sorts of seemingly irrelevant qualifications from applicants, and many fear that even if they meet these requirements they will not be allowed to climb very far. From the bottom, then, the main obstacle to upward mobility often appears to be the limited amount of room at the top, not their own cultural characteristics.

The changes required of a lower-class or working-class child for success in school and upward mobility are almost always painful—though the amount of pain depends on his character as well as the sort of lower- or working-class family he comes from. Even if the child takes the school and the larger society at face value and assumes that he will in fact be allowed to move into a relatively privileged position if he conforms to the demands made on him, he may well decide that the prize is not worth the price. Certainly the child who disbelieves the promise will be reluctant to change. And whether the child believes the promise almost certainly depends in part on whether it is really true. If he has relatives who have gotten ahead through diligence and competence—as most white American children now do—and if he sees older children in his neighborhood moving up and out, he may seriously consider emulating them. If, on the other hand, he sees young people who toe the line doing no better or even worse than those who thumb their noses, and if his circumstances also make nose-thumbing the most viscerally satisfying response to school, that is likely to be his choice. To the extent that this is true, the schools' ability to change the young and to diffuse traditionally middle-class values to the lower social strata depends on the actual availability of attractive opportunities. The relative size of cultural classes is, in other words, at least partly and perhaps largely dependent on the relative size of social classes.

All this suggests a partial answer to another question we raised earlier, namely how much of the difference between the uneducated and the educated should be attributed directly to school experiences and how much to other factors such as upbringing, intelligence, personality, and so forth. A good portion of the apparent impact of schooling is, we would suggest, anticipatory socialization. Sending a bright child to school, in other words, is like telling him he has a rich maiden aunt and will eventually inherit a fortune. The aunt and her money have no direct effect on the child's life or growth. But the *idea* of the money—even if it is non-existent—may have a considerable effect, for the child may feel he has special opportunities and responsibilities. So too with schooling. What actually happens from day to day in a school or college may have relatively little effect on the students—though it certainly has *some* effect. But a good student's knowledge that he can go to college and that a college degree will be a passport to a good job and a comfortable standard of living may have a significant effect on him. He may even adopt the attitudes and acquire the skills he thinks he will need in the world he expects to enter. The fact that he may not really be able to enter this world may be irrelevant at this stage, just as the actual terms of his aunt's will are.

This becomes critically important when we consider the possible impact on the over-all social structure of equalizing educational opportunities and/or results. Suppose, to take an extreme example, that all students stayed in school precisely the same length of time. Employers interested in getting the most fully socialized and most adaptable students would then presumably rely on school grades to separate sheep from goats. Students would come to anticipate this, and would therefore be able to tell quite early what kinds of jobs and living standards were open to them. Most of those who got poor grades would sense that adults already viewed them as prospective failures and would probably begin to protect themselves psychologically from this eventuality by adopting something very like the current lower-class cultural style. Most of those who were going to have important jobs and live well would, on the other hand, sense that adults thought well of them and would adapt themselves to the real or imagined requirements of future success. Such differentiation would occur even if all students attended the same schools for the same length of time, took the same courses with the same teachers, and so forth.

This fantasy suggests that the effects of schooling may depend as much on how well the student feels he is doing as on how long he stays enrolled. The apparent correlation between educational attainment and adult values may, in other words, be at least partially due to the fact that attainment is a surrogate for competitive success, first in school itself and later in adult life. To the degree that this is so, neither expansion of schools and colleges nor increases in the average length of schooling nor even increases in the average academic competence of the population will have much effect on the cultural characteristics of the adult population, for they will not affect people's sense of their own success or failure relative to others around them. These self-perceptions will be affected only by changes in the distribution of wealth and power among adults. As we have seen, this distribution does not seem to be changing much at present. In this context the primary importance of schools and colleges is not that they are changing the over-all quality of life, but that to some extent they determine which particular individuals will enjoy the good life and which ones will not.

Yet this is not quite the whole story. For one thing, while students tend to compare themselves to their age-mates and adapt their personalities to what they see, they also compare themselves to their parents and respond to this. If students feel they know more and are doing better than their parents did, this may give them self-confidence and a general sense of well-being even when their relative position vis-à-vis their age-mates is identical to that of their parents. In addition, it seems likely that schools and colleges do have *some* direct effect on the habits and values of those who pass through them, independent of the later fate of these youngsters. This is probably especially true in the younger grades, where students have foggier ideas about what is in fact likely to become of them and are more willing to accept the school as a world in itself to which they either can or cannot adapt.

Finally it must be noted that there is a variety of other educational institutions such as television and churches working to change the customs and concerns of the American people. These are not certifying agencies in the way schools are, and their effects are even harder to measure than the effects of schooling, at least if measurement is in terms of years completed or dollars earned. While the impact of television, religion, and so forth is also to some extent limited and mediated by the social class of the viewer, it is by no means clear to what extent this is so.

Despite these uncertainties it seems safe to conclude that the recent stability of the income distribution indicates a high degree of stability in the size of social classes and that stability in the size of social classes means considerable stability in the size of cultural classes. There may nonetheless be *some* changes on the latter front. These changes are extremely difficult to describe in single summary measures comparable to income, but over the years fragmentary evidence from opinion surveys, consumer research, and the like have given us the impression that the number of people with what have traditionally been called middle-class attitudes and tastes was slowly increasing. Yet even here the most conspicuous fact is that the enormous rise in the standard of living over the past two decades has brought relatively few of the changes in basic values that the prophets of affluence predicted, and that those changes that have come are in most cases of relatively modest magnitude.

Under these circumstances, we feel justified in assuming that social and cultural classes are for many purposes not only stable in size but identical. Even when they are not, the interaction between the two hierarchies is so complex that it is often impossible to separate them. At times we will therefore use a single composite concept of class. We trust that the context will make clear when we are talking about class in this all-embracing way and when we are referring specifically to either social or cultural classes.

The Emergence of Mass Higher Education

The men who founded colonial colleges were almost all part of what we would now call the upper-middle class. They expected their colleges to turn out alumni like themselves, and in this way to sustain the quasi-European social order they were trying to recreate in the New World. Yet while the colonial colleges were clearly intended to perpetuate the established social system, they were by no means unequivocally committed to perpetuating the privileges of particular families. Many donors certainly expected the new colleges to educate mostly children from respectable families such as their own, enabling these children to step easily into their fathers' shoes and setting them off from the all too numerous progeny of the lower classes. But the shrewder colonists, including many members of the gentry, evidently also saw that bourgeois European families were not coming to the New World in large numbers, and that people from "unsuitable" backgrounds were therefore going to have to play important religious, political, and social roles. If the established order was to survive—if colonial churches, courts, and drawing rooms were to retain the civilized English manner—the colonial elite had to find ways of co-opting untutored youngsters from unwashed families. The colonial college was one possible instrument for doing this. At the same time that it taught the children of the rich what they would need to know in order to feel (and be) superior to the poor, it also provided some poor boys with an ersatz family, prepared them for polite society, and put some of them in touch with power and opportunity.

Or so the theory went. As a practical matter the colonial colleges seem to have devoted a fairly small share of their meager endowments to scholarships.[34] Most gifts evidently went to pay debts and build buildings, thus subsidizing the rich as well as the poor. Such Anatole France equity meant that most poor boys had a very difficult

[34] Harvard, e.g., devoted only 7 per cent of its expenditures to scholarships between 1638 and 1762, according to Humphrey Doermann. Frederick Rudolph has, however, pointed out to us that since many colleges gave their students credit and many debts were never paid, this was a covert scholarship program of substantial proportions which is not usually reckoned as such.

time attending college, even when they had the ability and preparation to do so. How many actually went, however, is hard to document.

Yet the basic fact about the colonial colleges was that even the children of the colonial elite seldom attended them. It has been estimated that there were three thousand living college graduates in the colonies in 1776, or about one adult male in two hundred.[35] It seems unlikely that more than one boy in fifty was entering college in the 1770s, and most of these entrants probably did not graduate. This means that college graduation must have been exceptional even for the son of a minister, magistrate, merchant, or large landholder. The sons of farmers, craftsmen, and laborers must have come to college only under quite extraordinary circumstances.

Once recognized, the limited role of the colonial college is easy to explain. Only a few colonial towns had a school that could prepare young people for college. Most applicants had to rely on self-instruction or on private tutoring. Once prepared, the would-be undergraduate had to find money to support himself while in college. Even if these problems were solved, the case for attending college was still moot. Neither the subjects taught in college nor the degrees awarded there had much negotiable value in adult society. A poor boy who wanted to escape his parents' station in life was likely to go to college only if he hoped to become a minister or had a strong intellectual bent.

In the decades after the Revolution the overwhelming majority of colleges remained committed to what might for lack of a better term be called the neoclassical curriculum: a hodgepodge of miscellaneous information and skills largely oriented toward ancient languages but leavened with modern philosophy, both natural and moral. The colleges saw their task as much in terms of developing useful habits and values as in terms of imparting useful knowledge. Not only were they often preoccupied with character to the exclusion of substance, but they usually idealized a character-type best suited to an Eastern drawing room or parish house. This pattern was almost as characteristic of the Western colleges as of the Eastern, of the rural colleges as of the urban, and of the poor colleges as of the rich.

The spirit of Jacksonian democracy was hostile to the colleges' genteel vision of adult life, and enrollment therefore fell in many places during that era and remained static in others.[36] Since the public was evidently willing to let the classical liberal arts college perish with other remnants of the old order, educational reformers naturally tried to establish new kinds of colleges with broader popular

[35] Eells.
[36] See Veysey, p. 4, and the sources cited there.

appeal. Reform was usually linked in one way or another to the ideology of work. Some educators tried putting their students to work on college farms or at other manual jobs, hoping that this would both balance the college budget and overcome the popular conviction that college life was idle and therefore sinful. Colleges that stressed work as a form of character-building, however, found that most of their potential applicants preferred the regular labor market. Some therefore tried to link themselves to work in a different way, inventing "practical" curricula which allegedly prepared students for desirable adult occupations. By the time of the Civil War there were special-purpose colleges preparing young men for law, medicine, civil engineering, the military, and the clergy. The first normal schools had also been founded to train elementary school teachers, although these were still secondary-level institutions. The liberal arts program, which had earlier served as preparation for the ministry and in Europe still served as preparation for the higher civil service, seemed to have vocational value only to prospective secondary school and college teachers.

Then as now, the proponents of "practical" education argued that their curriculum was more democratic than the liberal arts, since it dealt directly with the career needs which inevitably preoccupied the impoverished majority of the population. A liberal arts college, they admitted, might make sense for the man who had inherited money, or who had enough personal and family connections so that he could afford to postpone thinking about his career until he reached his twenties. But for a young man with no skills, no contacts, and no wealthy ancestors, liberal education was a frivolous luxury. Such a student's most urgent problem was to choose a career and get on with it. Later, if he was successful, he might have time to acquire some Culture.

Whether the early occupationally oriented colleges actually attracted more upwardly mobile men than their liberal arts rivals we cannot say for sure. The failure of over-all enrollment to grow significantly, despite rapid growth in the total population, makes it seem most unlikely that the new occupational programs attracted many students from new groups to higher education. Histories of specific schools of law, medicine, theology, and engineering also suggest that many suffered from shortages of applicants perhaps even more acute than at the liberal arts colleges. Apparently the only people who wanted higher education in this era were the genteel middle classes, and they mostly wanted the traditional, socially approved product.

The slow development of graduate professional training and the rise of the research-oriented university after the Civil War did not at first alter this situation much. There was considerable growth in enrollment, but this was mainly because women began entering college in large numbers.[37] This being so, we suspect that the changes that took place in American higher education before World War I did not involve much democratization in the normal sense of that term. Rather, we would argue that they were primarily a response to the changing character of the upper-middle class—to increasing professionalization and the enhanced value of specialized expertise as against polite learning.

The colleges' inability to broaden their class appeal significantly can perhaps be explained partly in terms of their failure to come to terms with the business class and business ethos which dominated the country during the pre-1914 years. Yet the colleges did not fail for want of effort in this direction. College presidents often sensed that their institutions could not survive on faith alone, nor even by preparing the sons of the rich to discuss Plotinus in polite society. Colleges needed the political, financial, and social support of the new captains of industry, and they tried very hard to get it. Dozens of newly rich tycoons were added to boards of trustees, and there was a great deal of talk about this or that college's role in forming the next generation of business leaders. Nevertheless, the result was never very satisfactory. The businessmen did not understand the colleges (as Thorstein Veblen made bitterly clear in *The Higher Learning in America*) and neither did the colleges understand the businessmen.[38] The public evidently sensed this mutual antagonism and reacted accordingly. Those who wanted to pursue the main chance, who dreamed of success in simple financial terms, saw no reason to attend college. For the young man with no connections a college degree could look like a ticket to the drafting room rather than the board room. Some, of course, saw the former as a first step to the latter, but most still preferred to go directly to work and take their chances in face-to-face competition for promotion. Only the second- and third-generation rich, who expected to preside over already established corporate empires, habitually turned to the colleges for sociointellectual preparation.

After World War I both America and its colleges changed dramatically. The economic, political, and social institutions that had emerged after the Civil War became increasingly stable and established. Both within and around them power came to depend less on entrepreneurial imagination, zeal, and ruthlessness, and more on professional

[37] See *Historical Statistics*, Series H 321 and 331. See also Table III of this chapter and the relevant Census sources cited there.

[38] Veysey, p. 4, notes that the two most prominent donors of the post-Civil War period, Ezra Cornell and Johns Hopkins, were Quakers. In the 1890s more tycoons began to support higher education, but even then it was only the more conscientious capitalists like Rockefeller who became big givers.

expertise, personal adaptability, and packaging. The managerial revolution was not proclaimed until the 1930s, but bureaucratization and
the routinization of growth were already well along in some industries
by then. The proportion of the affluent population engaged in professional as against managerial work also rose slowly, and the value of
higher education rose correspondingly. At the same time, higher education was making new and more successful efforts to come to terms
with the business ethos and the over-all spirit of the time. Team sports,
Greek letter societies, and other extracurricular activities, having
achieved importance at a few colleges before 1914, came into their
nationally glamorized own in the twenties. More and more people saw
college as a place to meet "the right people." Since success in business
(and indeed in American life) was widely believed to depend on
"contacts," colleges came to seem relevant in a way they previously
had not. This trend was exploited by many educators. New business
curricula were established for students who found the traditional
academic fare indigestible, and corporations began to consider college graduates as potential junior management material. Conversely,
the idea of a non-college man's either starting at the bottom and
working up, or going into business for himself and expanding, seemed
less realistic. The Depression compounded doubts about such possibilities, giving millions of young men the feeling that it was better
to acquire credentials and work for a big, safe organization than
to gamble in the open market.

Colleges were also becoming more accessible. High school graduation became more commonplace, and this not only created a much
bigger pool of potential college applicants but also meant that those
who wanted to be more educated than the majority *had* to go to
college. Urbanization also continued apace, and this meant more families lived within commuting distance of both a college and a college-
oriented high school. Then too, incomes were rising faster than college
costs in both the public and the private sectors—though the proportion
of young men entering college rose rapidly not just during the comparatively prosperous twenties but during the thirties as well.[39]

The upshot of these developments was that by 1940 about one
youngster in six was entering college, and about one in twelve was
graduating.[40] The upward trend continued after World War II, at first
apparently aided by the GI Bill, but continuing unchecked even after

[39] For a more detailed discussion of cost: income ratios, see pp. 107 ff.
[40] As Table III showed, USOE and Census estimates of college graduation
rates are so different for earlier periods that it is hard to draw any firm conclusions about trends from them. The estimates converge for 1940 and remain
fairly close for later periods. Census data and USOE data give somewhat
divergent estimates of college attrition, but an over-all estimate of about 50 per
cent seems justified.

the veterans thinned out. By the mid-1960s more than two young men in every five were entering some sort of college, and more than one in five was graduating. The proportions were about 25 per cent lower for women.

When we first looked at these trends we assumed, like most other observers, that rapid growth in enrollment was largely a consequence of increased lower-middle and working-class access to and interest in college. In point of fact, however, this does not appear to be the case. The increase in enrollment among upper-middle class children seems to have been even greater than among lower-middle and working-class children.

There are several different ways of looking at class differentials in college enrollment. The simplest is to examine the chances that a given high school graduate will enter college, and then to see how much this is affected by his cultural background in any given decade. If, for example, we look at men who graduated from high school between 1915 and 1925, we find that the rate of college entrance ranged from 43 per cent among those whose fathers had not finished elementary school to 64 per cent among those whose fathers had entered college. If we then look at men who graduated from high school between 1945 and 1955, we find that the spread had widened. Only 31 per cent of the sons of elementary dropouts were going to college, compared to 84 per cent of the sons of college entrants.

If we look at a college freshman's chances of completing four years, we find a similar widening of the gap between the advantaged and the disadvantaged. In the years 1915–25 freshmen from poorly educated families were actually *more* likely to earn degrees than freshmen from well-educated families. (Perhaps the boys from well-educated families were more likely to have come for a good time, more likely to be disappointed, and more likely to feel they could drop out and pursue a successful business career. The upwardly mobile boys were presumably more carefully pre-selected in high school. Also, their hopes for a good job depended more on entering a profession, so perhaps they felt more obliged to stick it out.) Among those born thirty years later, on the other hand, freshmen with well-educated fathers were almost 50 per cent more likely to stay the full four years than freshmen with poorly educated fathers.

This approach to class influences is revealing in some ways but misleading in others. This is because it takes no account of the considerable democratization of the high schools that took place during the same period. The high school seniors of 1915–25 were a considerably more elite group than those of 1945–55, and it is perhaps not surprising that their chances of going to college were less influenced by class than they are today. This being so, it is important to look at changes not only in the college chances of high school seniors but in the college chances of all members of a given age group. When we do this we find that the over-all influence of a father's education on his son's has changed very little. If we look, for example, at those whose fathers had less than eight years of schooling we find that they had about 8 chances in 100 of entering college in 1915–25, compared to 14 in 100 thirty years later. If we then turn to those whose fathers had entered college, we find that their chances of entering college were 47 in 100 in 1915–25, compared to 78 in 100 thirty years later. The increase, in other words, was roughly proportionate. The picture was gloomier with regard to college graduation, however, because of the reversal of attrition patterns already noted. The sons of elementary school dropouts increased their college graduation rate only 20 per cent (from 5 to 6 per cent) between the 1920s and the 1950s, while the sons of college entrants almost doubled their graduation rate (from 28 to 52 per cent).[41]

In some ways the most startling fact to emerge from the historical data, and the one that fits least well with the conventional wisdom about higher education, is that until relatively recently even the sons of college-educated parents were not very likely to go to college. Men who completed a year or more of college in the late nineteenth century sent less than half their sons to college in the early twentieth century, and only a little more than a quarter of their sons graduated. This meant there was lots of room for growth in upper-middle class enrollment rates. This growth was probably concentrated among the less academically competent middle-class students, almost all of whom now go to college. The rise in enrollment of middle-class mediocrities evidently offset the parallel rise among able lower-class students.

Today, however, there is little room left for further increases in upper-middle class enrollment. Virtually all the sons of college graduates today at least enter college, and 80 per cent of the sons of college entrants do likewise.[42] It follows that further increases in the proportion of people entering college will now have to come mainly from the lower cultural strata. If children from uneducated homes cannot close the gap between themselves and children from well-educated

[41] All the above data is derived from the 1962 Current Population Survey analyzed in Spady. The above method of presentation can be criticized on the grounds that the son of an elementary school graduate came from a relatively more deprived family after World War II than World War I, while the son of a college entrant came from a relatively less elite family. Calculations based on attainment quartiles instead of absolute levels yield similar results, however, as indicated in the previous section. Comparison of data collected by Roper, pp. 142–43, on those entering college in 1949 with those collected by Astin, Panos, and Creager, "National Norms," on those entering in 1966 support the CPS data.

[42] Estimated from Astin, Panos, and Creager, "National Norms," and 1960 *Census*, I, 1, table 173. See also Spady.

families, the proportion of the age grade entering college will level off. If, on the other hand, we look at college graduation rather than entrance, there is still considerable room for growth among all strata. Given the current tendency to siphon first-generation collegians into colleges with high attrition and second-generation collegians into colleges with low attrition, the over-all attainment gap between children from different cultural backgrounds may well continue to widen for some time to come. The same would probably also be true if we had trend data on graduate school recruitment patterns, but we do not.

Higher Education as a Social Sieve

Like all stratified societies, America must engage in a constant struggle to prevent its elite from decaying into an hereditary aristocracy. In principle even the elite itself supports this goal. There is no vocal opposition to keeping American society open, to encouraging the poor-but-able to get ahead, or to equality of opportunity. Nevertheless, well-to-do parents also have an understandable impulse to make sure that their children will enjoy the same privileges that they do. While such parents hope their children will earn their privileges in fair competition, the parental commitment to fairness seldom takes precedence over family loyalty. If a middle-class child cannot win out on merit alone, his parents will try to obtain some sort of special treatment for him. Many of these exceptions to meritocratic principles have been institutionalized and have acquired legitimacy even in the eyes of poorer people who do not benefit from them. The fact that a man can pass on his business to his children, for example, is taken for granted by almost everyone, both rich and poor—although inheritance taxes place some limitations on this process. Nor do many people rail against the fact that a child whose father can pay tuition has a better chance of getting to an elite college than does a child who needs a scholarship. Yet when all such exceptions to meritocratic principles are taken together, they provide upper- and upper-middle class children with enormous advantages over other people's children. The elite, in other words, gets what Everett Hughes calls "equality plus." Nor are the reasons for this hard to discover. There seems to be a tacit consensus among all classes that downward social mobility is more painful than the frustration of upward aspirations. Devices for preventing downward mobility, or at least preventing too great or conspicuous a fall, are therefore widely accepted.

Yet in a society where the elite grows no faster than the rest of the population, and where fertility differentials are relatively moderate, devices for preventing or limiting downward mobility also necessarily limit upward mobility. If a business firm is both willing and able to hire all the incompetent friends and relatives of its managers and owners, it will have few jobs left for the talented children of its clerks and janitors. If a profession allows the inept sons of its practitioners to earn licenses and take over their fathers' lucrative practices, outsiders without connections will be left with a very small potential clientele and little incentive to spend years getting licensed. It is in this context that education becomes critically important. In principle it is the great leveler, treating everyone alike, judging everyone by universalistic meritocratic standards, and providing those who meet these standards with passports to success.

When we first began working on the relationship of higher education to social class, we assumed (like almost everyone to whom we talked) that education was playing an ever-larger role in determining social position. The empirical research cited in footnotes 31–33 is, however, ambiguous. The correlation between educational attainment and occupational status may be increasing, but if so the increase is quite slow. Whatever the real trend, however, there has clearly been a trend toward more popular *awareness* of the connection between education and adult success. Both rich and poor. parents today assume that the social escalator begins in the first-grade classroom and progresses through other classrooms for many years before emerging into the "real" world. Almost all parents today want their children to get an extensive education.[43] Indeed, modern parents show the same preoccupation with their children's higher education that an earlier generation showed with dowries and trust funds. They view diplomas as a peculiarly valuable sort of property and describe education as insurance against unemployment or as something on which a man can trade in the job market. Even parents who have themselves managed to get on without higher education generally feel that times are changing and that their children need credentials. Since teachers say the same thing, children have little ground for doubting it.

Few ambitious youngsters, rich or poor, today quit school to advance their careers.[44] A boy may personally feel that he is learning nothing

[43] Evidence on this point can be found in public opinion polls conducted by George Gallup, Louis Harris, and Elmo Roper. The escalation in educational aspirations over the years is quite remarkable—far outstripping actual increases in attainment.

[44] One possible exception to this generalization is the Negro who lives (or plans to live) in the North. Hanoch, table VIII, shows that a Northern Negro who discounted his probable future earnings at anywhere between 2 and 12 per cent would find it unprofitable to enter college unless he also expected to go to

in the classroom and that he would learn more from "practical" experience. This feeling may be re-enforced by knowing that his father, or at least some of his father's friends and relatives, started work young, learned on the job, and rose through the ranks. But his family, his teachers, the mass media, and every other opinion-forming agency all tell him that this is no longer possible. Even dropouts usually accept this judgment. Whether they are lower-class boys who leave high school because "it just isn't worth it," lower-middle class girls who leave college to get married, or upper-middle class men who leave graduate school to work in the civil rights movement, those who quit the classroom assume their decision will hurt their career prospects. They justify it, proudly or sadly, on other grounds.

Census reports suggest that the dropouts may be more defensive than they need to be. A significant fraction of those who fail to attend college seem to do quite well both occupationally and economically. This is particularly true of those who enter business. The odds against success have, it is true, always been greater for dropouts than for those with extensive education, but the advantage of the educated over the uneducated appears to be increasing very slowly. What is changing, however, is the relative importance of different *kinds* of academic credentials. There was a time when a high school diploma sufficed to give a man the inside track on most non-manual jobs. Today this is no longer so.[45] So too, there is some evidence that the economic value of a college degree may be rising, while that of a high school diploma may be relatively smaller than it once was.[46]

The foregoing comments suggest that one of the central functions of higher education—along with providing jobs for scholars—is to control

---

graduate school. The jobs open to Northern Negroes with college experience, in other words, are not enough better than those open to Northern Negro high school graduates to offset the loss of earnings which normally results from college enrollment. But very few dropouts have read Hanoch's thesis, and few defend their choice on economic grounds. The situation may, moreover, have changed since 1960, when Hanoch's Census data were collected.

[45] For an estimate of the small but significant increase in the occupational value of a B.A. between 1950 and 1959, see James Davis, "Higher Education."

[46] Miller, "Annual and Lifetime Income," shows little change in the over-all pattern of income distribution between high school and college graduates from 1939 to 1959. The high school graduates gained on collegians from 1939 to 1949, then slipped back from 1949 to 1959. The gap in lifetime earnings, while greater in absolute terms because of general income rises, also remained fairly stable in relative terms. But Miller's analysis in *Income Distribution,* table VI-2, suggests that this stability could be more apparent than real. College graduation became considerably more important for the young between 1950 and 1960, while older college graduates got a disproportionately small share of the fruits of economic growth. This is a puzzling finding, since the supply of young college graduates was expanding at an unprecedented rate during this period, whereas the supply of older graduates was fixed.

access to the upper-middle social strata. Since demand for upper-middle class jobs and living standards far exceeds the supply, colleges must (in Erving Goffman's terminology) cool out large numbers of youngsters whose ambitions exceed their ability.[47] Not only that—these individuals must be eliminated in such a way as to preserve at least the appearance of fairness to all social strata. Since college diplomas are a key to future power and affluence, they cannot simply be sold at auction to the highest bidders or automatically conferred on the sons of previous alumni. Instead, the distribution system must be in keeping with traditional American mythology, which portrays America as a land of opportunity with unlimited room at the top. The mythology also dictates that failure never be ascribable to what is called "the system" but must rather seem to derive from individual skill, character, or luck.

Higher education seems very well suited to this role, for it is in principle almost infinitely expansive. There does not seem to be anything inherent in the system that limits the number who can earn degrees—if they "have what it takes." At the same time, most young people find academic work both difficult and disagreeable. Many will revise their career goals downward to escape it. They do not even have to be flunked out of college and told never to return. If they are regularly told that they are doing poor work, and if others continually excel in a competition on which colleges place enormous emphasis, an appreciable fraction of the losers will quit the game voluntarily. (Some, of course, merely slip into the "soft" academic options, like business and education. But even these require a certain amount of perseverance and academic drudgery to complete.) Both the dropout and his college can then portray his departure as a matter of personal choice. Even if he feels frustrated later and is resentful about the doors that remain closed to him, his anger is likely to be directed against himself rather than against "the system."

Reliance on colleges to preselect the upper-middle class obviously eliminates most youngsters born into lower-strata families, since they have "the wrong attitudes" for academic success. But it should be remembered that colleges also eliminate a substantial fraction of the youngsters born into the upper-middle class, not primarily because they have the wrong attitudes but rather because they lack academic competence and dislike feeling like failures year after year. The Class of 1961, for example, represented the best educated sixth of its generation. If we look at the education of this elite's fathers, we find that 39 per cent came from the best-educated sixth of their parent's genera-

[47] For a discussion of this problem with special reference to public junior colleges, see Burton Clark, "The 'Cooling Out' Function." See also Goffman.

tion, 18 per cent came from the second sixth, 15 per cent from the third sixth, and 27 per cent from the bottom half.[48]

These figures, however, understate the actual advantage of being born into a well-educated family. The best-educated parents have somewhat fewer children than average, so that if all other things were equal they would produce less than a sixth of the children who end up in the educational elite of the next generation. We do not have precise estimates of fertility differentials among fathers who produced children just before World War II, so we cannot compare our figures on the Class of 1961 to the "expected" distribution if parental education had no effect on college chances but only on fertility. We do, however, have data on men born between 1927 and 1936, most of whom attended college during the 1950s, which allow us to deal with this problem.[49] We find that 39.4 per cent of the men who ended up in the best-educated sixth of this generation were among the most advantaged sixth at birth, as judged by their father's education. Thirty years earlier the amount of educational inheritance was microscopically greater. Among men born between 1897 and 1906, the best-educated sixth includes not only college graduates but college dropouts, as well as some men who had merely finished high school. We find that 37.8 per cent of this elite was born into the most advantaged sixth of its generation; the rest rose into it. Or to put it the other way, the rate of turnover in the educational elite (defined as the best-educated sixth) fell from 62.2 per cent for men born between 1897 and 1906 to 60.6 per cent for those born between 1927 and 1936.[50]

In weighing the significance of these figures it is important to bear in mind that even if educational opportunity were completely equal and attainment depended entirely on innate ability, we would expect *some* correlation between the educational attainment of fathers and sons. This is because well-educated fathers tend to be somewhat more intelligent than poorly educated fathers. Part of this difference is ge-

[48] James Davis, *Great Aspirations*, table 1.2c, and 1960 *Census*, I, 1, table 173. We have assumed that the typical father of a 1961 B.A. was 50.

[49] Bureau of the Census, *Current Population Reports* (1964), and Spady. We are indebted to Dr. Spady for help in analyzing these data.

[50] The rate of turnover would be somewhat lower if we included women in the analysis. It would also be somewhat lower if we used an index of paternal privilege based on occupation and income as well as education. If we do this, however, we also ought to measure filial privilege in terms of occupation as well as education. Since some of the advantaged sons who get a lot of education do not get good jobs, use of an occupational index would probably raise the rate of turnover in the elite to around 60 per cent again. The simple correlation of father's occupation with son's averages 0.35 for these two groups, while the simple correlation of father's education with son's averages 0.41, and the simple correlation of father's occupation with son's education averages 0.40. See Blau and Duncan, p. 178.

netic, and a man normally passes part of his genetic advantage along to his children. Assuming equality of opportunity, children would translate their inherited genetic advantage into high educational attainment, even if their parents could not provide them any special environmental advantages. A corresponding cycle of genetic deprivation presumably exists among poorly educated families. This being so, we must expect the best-educated sixth of any generation to include a disproportionately large number of individuals whose fathers were also in the best-educated sixth, and a disproportionately small number whose fathers were in the worst-educated sixth.[51] We have no basis for estimating the likely magnitude of these genetic effects, though we assume they are probably small.

Given the present state of genetic and sociological knowledge we cannot say with certainty how much intergenerational turnover would be expected in a "pure" meritocratic system. We can, however, say with considerable confidence that there would be more turnover than at present. Table V shows the influence of both academic aptitude and social background on a high school graduate's chances of getting to college. The table makes it clear that aptitude plays a larger role than class in determining who goes to college, but it is not *much* larger.[52]

Having said all this about the degree of cultural mobility in America, we must still ask to what extent cultural mobility implies social mobility. Society does not, after all, always automatically accept academicians' verdicts even on intellectual questions; when the verdict is being passed on one's children its acceptance is even less likely. Upper-middle class parents can and often do resist educators' efforts to relegate their sons and daughters to mediocre jobs and modest incomes. Those with connections in the business world, for example, can often find a sinecure for their dropout son in which he can

[51] For further discussion see Eckland, "Genetics and Sociology."

[52] The importance of aptitude as against class can be illustrated as follows: Take a high school boy in the lowest quintile both academically and socially. His college chances are 10 in 100. Now consider whether his chances would be more improved by rising one quintile in aptitude or in class background. If he rises one quintile in aptitude his chances are 14 in 100. If he rises one quintile in class background his chances are only 13 in 100. Applying this method more generally, we can judge the relative impact of aptitude and class by reading along the diagonals from lower left to upper right. This shows that an increase of one quintile in aptitude is always more of an asset than an increase of one quintile in class, with one exception: for low aptitude students, especially girls, a jump from the upper-middle to the top social bracket is worth more than a jump of one quintile in aptitude. The meaning of this can be oversimplified to say that having a college-educated parent is more important than the difference between an IQ of 100 and 110. Yet even here a jump into the top ability quintile does more for a child's college chances than does a jump into the top social quintile. For a regression analysis of similar data, see Nam and Cowhig, figure 1.

TABLE V

PER CENT OF HIGH SCHOOL GRADUATES GOING TO COLLEGE THE FOLLOWING YEAR, BY ACADEMIC APTITUDE, SOCIOECONOMIC BACKGROUND, AND SEX, 1960

Academic Aptitude		Socioeconomic Status				
	Low	Lower-Middle	Middle	Upper-Middle	High	All
MALES						
Low	10	13	15	25	4c	14
Lower-Middle	14	23	30	35	57	27
Middle	30	35	46	54	67	46
Upper-Middle	44	51	59	69	83	63
Upper	69	73	81	86	91	85
All	24	40	53	65	81	49
FEMALES						
Low	9	9	10	16	41	11
Lower-Middle	9	10	16	24	54	18
Middle	12	18	25	40	63	30
Upper-Middle	24	35	41	58	78	49
Upper	52	61	66	80	90	76
All	15	24	32	51	75	35

SOURCE: Project Talent 1960 High School Senior Sample, as reported in Folger. Data have been adjusted for non-respondent bias, but not for students who delay college entry. These latter are mostly lower status men, so that the long-term class bias of the system is slightly less than the table indicates. The socioeconomic measures were more diverse than those we have discussed, including many cultural indices, and were cumulated in a single scale. The quintiles for both socioeconomic status and ability are of equal size in the overall age grade but not among high school graduates. The cell sizes are quite unequal, because aptitude is not evenly distributed between social classes.

maintain both social respectability and reasonable income; indeed, he can sometimes do very well for himself, for sometimes he has valuable talents that school and college repressed or at least ignored.[53]

Conversely, those who maintain or even improve on their parents' educational status may not do the same in occupational or economic terms. Some children from elite families "overreact" to their education and move in directions that, while often involving more education than their parents had, provide less income and occupational power. The college that manages to get the son of a corporation executive excited about medieval history, for example, may induce him to acquire considerably more education than his father; but once

[53] For evidence that high status dropouts from the University of Illinois are more likely to find good jobs than low status dropouts, even though this is not the case among Illinois B.A.s, see Eckland, "Academic Ability." For more general evidence, see Blau and Duncan, p. 170.

he gets his Ph.D. he will have less power, less money, and hence will be socially downwardly mobile.[54] Similarly, the banker's daughter who goes to a good college and marries a composer will leave her parents' spacious home for a smaller one, making room for another girl from less favored circumstances to marry the father's successor in office.

Nonetheless, the striking fact about America, at least to us, is not the extent of these dissonances between social and cultural class but the extent to which the verdict of academicians on the young is accepted by men who have little apparent sympathy for academic values. Corporations, for example, evidently need a way to avoid hiring the office manager's dimwitted nephew without causing offense. They also need a preselection device that will help them pick out the more diligent, adaptable, and competent applicants from among the majority who have no inside connections. College degrees serve both these purposes, for college is a kind of protracted aptitude test for measuring certain aspects of both intelligence and character. The measurements are, it is true, very selective and very crude, and employers who put great faith in them are almost always disappointed. They continue in use only because other devices for predicting job performance are in most cases even less reliable and more cumbersome. On-the-job performance seems best predicted by previous on-the-job performance, when that can be observed. But companies do not want to hire large numbers of prospective managers, try them out on a mass scale, and then sack the majority, for incompetents get in the way and cause problems even if they are only around for a few months, and sacking them also causes morale problems.

When one turns to the question of why the rich and powerful have not monopolized college places, several factors must be taken into account. First there is the fact that some of the men who have run colleges have had sternly moral, self-denying temperaments. They have really believed that if their children or their friends' children could not measure up they should not get special treatment. Their capacity for self-deception about what constituted special treatment has, as we shall see, been considerable, but it has not been unlimited. One of the most important limits, especially in recent years, has derived from faculty pressure for strictly meritocratic selection. Faculty opposition has often been a decisive factor in reducing favoritism toward alumni (though not faculty) sons and daughters, and has sometimes pushed the administration into raising more scholarships for poor but talented

---

[54] We should make clear that while such mobility is downward in terms of both popular opinion and our formal schema for stratification, it is not usually seen this way by those who experience it. We make no value judgment here; indeed, both the authors are downwardly mobile in these terms, though not in their own.

applicants and doing more to solicit such applicants. Together these influences have kept a number of elite colleges fairly open to students from all classes and conditions.

Yet if the openness of higher education depended exclusively on the self-denying morality of the elite, the rate of turnover in that elite would undoubtedly be far lower than it is. The real key to this turnover lies rather in America's willingness to let those excluded from established institutions go into business for themselves. Even when the men who controlled a leading college were not willing to open it on equal terms to the academically talented children of the poor, they had neither the political power nor (in most cases) the ideological conviction to block creation of competitive colleges that would serve such students. The initiative for such ventures, has, it is true, usually come from people who would be classified as upper-middle class—if only because anyone who sets up a college is by definition upper-middle class. But these initiators and leaders, unlike those of older and more eminent institutions, have often held their position by dint of the fact that they served the interests of lower-middle and working-class parishioners or voters. The old Catholic commuter college, the municipal "street car" college, the rural teachers college turned state college, and the two-year "community college" have all played this role to some extent—though they have also been havens for the less competent children of the affluent and well educated.[55] While the alumni and trustees of older and more distinguished institutions have seldom welcomed such competition, and have sometimes fought against it quite actively, they have in due course acquiesced.

This acquiescence requires an explanation, however, especially when contrasted with the situation in Great Britain. Britain has not allowed independent entrepreneurs, either public or private, to establish new colleges and universities. Such enterprises have been allowed only under the auspices of the state and of longer established universities. New kinds of institutions with unorthodox goals or standards have been rare. In America, on the other hand, central authority has been weaker and more distrusted. Not only that—the mythology of unlimited room at the top and universal opportunity has supported the assumption that there is an unlimited need for college graduates, regardless of competence or social background.[56] The expansion of what were deemed mediocre colleges has therefore seldom

[55] For evidence on the relative importance of these two groups in various sorts of colleges see Astin, Panos, and Creager, "National Norms" and their "Supplementary National Norms."

[56] There have been occasional prophecies that supply would outstrip demand, especially during the 1930s and 1940s. These have, however, been largely and happily ignored.

seemed a direct threat to the upper-middle class colleges. Whether the upper-middle class was right in its relatively benign view is another question. The establishment of new sorts of colleges has probably led to a higher rate of both upward and downward mobility than would otherwise have prevailed, and has in this sense threatened established privilege. At the same time, however, these new institutions have, by opening certain callings to the less privileged, played an indispensable role in the over-all economic growth of the country and perhaps also a modest role in the maintenance of the established social and political order. It is reasonably clear, for example, that much of America's prosperity has been built on an agricultural revolution without parallel elsewhere in the world, and that this revolution owes a good deal to the land-grant colleges and especially their extension services. Agricultural research and missionary work have never attracted a significant number of men from educated or affluent families, nor from established exclusive colleges. Had there been no land-grant colleges to open such careers to upwardly mobile farm boys, history might have been quite different. While the rate of turnover in the upper-middle class might have been marginally lower, the rate of economic growth and hence the living standard of the upper-middle class would also have been lower. Even from a narrowly upper-middle class viewpoint, then, the existence of colleges for poor boys with semirespectable ambitions has probably been an advantage. A similar argument could be made with regard to engineering, which like agriculture has mainly attracted first-generation collegians. While engineers have in some cases displaced corporation executives from more socially advantaged backgrounds who lacked technical training, and have in this sense been a threat to inherited privilege, they have also helped increase the efficiency and profits of the corporations in question, and this has boosted both the living standards and the personal power of the old elite.

When we turn from economic to political questions the role of the special-interest college serving the upwardly mobile is less clear. It can be argued, for example, that such colleges have helped co-opt talented outsiders who might otherwise have been driven into opposition to established social institutions and arrangements. But it can equally well be argued that such colleges helped equip outsiders with sufficient competence and expertise to oppose and hence alter the system that excluded them, and that the absence of revolutionary movements in America derives from other sources. Certainly there is no historical evidence from other countries that educating selected members of the lower strata is the best way to defuse revolutionary demands. On the contrary, educated outsiders could easily be described as the enzymes without which revolution is almost impossible. The real political importance of educating such individuals may not have been the prevention of revolution or radical reform but preserving the internal viability of established institutions. The management of large corporate and governmental empires, for example, requires an ability to deal with extremely diverse personalities and social species. Without such peacemakers, mediators, and synthesizers at the top, large organizations tend to degenerate into mutually antagonistic fiefdoms working entirely at cross-purposes, making no effort to serve the external world. The survival of a given institution, and ultimately the survival of the whole system, depend on finding and promoting individuals who will prevent this. Yet they are relatively rare—perhaps especially so in homogeneous upper-middle class suburbs. Many of these individuals have been upwardly mobile youngsters from lower-middle class or small town families, and many come to the top by way of non-elite colleges. Whether they would have found their way into positions of power without such colleges is problematic, just as it is problematic whether the over-all American system could have won its present degree of popular support if such managers had not been found.

Colleges versus the Upwardly Mobile: Pricing

While lack of money is by no means the most serious problem confronting children from the lower strata seeking high-level education and certification, it is the most commonly discussed, the most easily analyzed, and the most readily eliminated. It is therefore important to say something about trends in the relation between family incomes and college charges.

The costs of higher education are of several kinds. The most obvious is the cost of instruction. By this we mean all institutional expenditures except those for externally financed research, dormitories, dining halls, parking lots, bookstores, football stadiums, and other self-liquidating or profit-making enterprises. Student tuition usually covers only part of these costs; the rest is made up from legislative appropriations and private gifts. While the proportion of instructional expenditure covered by tuition charges has been relatively stable on a nationwide basis over the past half century, hovering between a quarter and a third, this has not been true at many of the more selective institutions. It is therefore important to look at the problem of over-all instructional costs separately from the problem of tuition per se.

A second cost associated with higher education is immediate loss of income. A student who attends college is not, it is true, automatically barred from working. Perhaps as many as a quarter of all students work full time while attending college (usually part time) and many others work part time or in the summer. Full-time employees are, however, considerably less likely than other students to earn their degrees. Many are enrolled at two-year colleges, and most are taking only one or two courses. For the great majority of students the realistic choice is still between pursuing a degree on a more or less full-time basis and pursuing a career on this basis. They must therefore weigh the economic value of a diploma against an immediate loss of income. Some parents and children conclude that the sacrifice is not worth it. Unfortunately, we have no good data on wage trends among academically able late adolescents, and so we cannot say much about the historical trend of what economists would call opportunity costs. Enrollment increases during the Depression suggest, however, that widespread unemployment makes college seem more attractive. While few families could afford to spend much on their children's education during the thirties, and many badly needed extra income, their children could seldom find paying jobs. Under those circumstances college evidently made sense to some who would not have chosen it in the twenties. (In addition, the Depression very clearly illustrated the advantages of having a degree, for college graduates in bureaucratic, white-collar jobs suffered relatively less than other sorts of workers.) Whether a lag in adolescent wages has the same effect as actual unemployment we do not know.[57]

But even if data were assembled that measured the changing opportunity costs of higher education and compared them to the changing adult income differentials associated with it, these might not be the most relevant statistics for evaluating the economic obstacles to upward social mobility. The typical family with a child finishing high school today is used to supporting the child from its own income, without significant help from the child. Unless the family is very poor, or has no mature male breadwinner at its head, it is not likely to feel an urgent need to convert its teenage children into earners. Even the child, while often eager for pocket money, a car, new clothes, and so forth, seldom thinks he (or she) needs as much money as a full-time job would provide. It is true that once the child has taken a job, and both the child and the parents have gotten used to spending the proceeds, their feelings will change. Once this happens it is indeed necessary to reckon income foregone as an obstacle to further education. But for those young people who have not entered the labor

[57] On the effect of unemployment on precollege attrition, see Beverly Duncan.

force the major obstacle to college entrance is not lost wages but the necessity of finding substantially more cash than in the previous year to pay tuition and subsistence expenses.

By "subsistence expenses" we mean the cost of room, board, books, medical care, clothing, birth control pills, skiing weekends, automobile insurance, and all other out-of-pocket expenses except tuition and fees.[58] These costs, unlike those for instruction, fall almost entirely on the student and his family rather than on taxpayers or philanthropists.[59] Few parents borrow to meet them, though the proportion seems to be rising. The relation of subsistence costs to current family income is therefore of critical importance in determining who will go to college.

There was a time when the cost of subsistence was the major financial obstacle to most students' obtaining higher education. That time has, however, largely passed. The standard of amenity in many college dormitories and dining halls has risen, but not so fast as family incomes. Running dormitories and dining halls at a large profit to help subsidize instruction is also less common, partly because more scrupulous bookkeeping and auditing make this practice harder to conceal from watchful students. As a result, the constant dollar cost of college room and board increased about 25 per cent between 1928 and 1964, while the constant dollar income of the median American family increased more than 100 per cent. This meant that the proportion of families which could afford to support a child in college more than

[58] The distinction between instructional and subsistence costs is obviously somewhat arbitrary. We would argue, for example, that spending $500 per student to get commuters to live away from home usually has more pedagogic impact than spending $500 per student to improve faculty salaries or expand the library. Yet the former expenditure would be defined as increasing subsistence costs, the latter as increasing instructional costs. Similarly, part of the increase in dormitory rents over the years reflects attempts to give students more study space and more privacy, in the hope that this would encourage them to learn more. And much of the increase in student expenditure on books represents an increase in academic demands. All these shifts show up on the subsistence rather than the instructional side of our ledger. Nonetheless, the distinction seems to us a useful compromise between the logic of pedagogy and the categories in which accountants report expenditures for higher education.

[59] Some colleges subsidize their dormitories and dining halls in a modest way by building them with alumni gifts and then not amortizing them out of student fees. Many others make a considerable profit on dormitories and dining halls, which they use to cover deficits in the instructional budget. Some colleges subsidize the subsistence costs of needy students through scholarships, though this is relatively rare. See Nash, Nash, and Goldstein. Their table 3.3 shows that in no group of colleges studied did the mean value of scholarships awarded exceed mean tuition. An educated guess based on this table would be that one American undergraduate in forty received scholarship assistance in excess of his tuition fees. None of these practices except perhaps profit taking on dormitories has changed enough over the years to have a significant effect on trends in the ratio of subsistence costs to family incomes.

110

THE ACADEMIC REVOLUTION

tripled between 1928 and 1964. There is every reason to assume comparable trends before 1928, and also in the future.[60]

Urbanization has also done a great deal to increase the number of families that can afford to keep a child in college. The proportion of families living within commuting distance of a college, and especially a public college, is rising, both because more public commuter colleges are being opened and because more people are moving to big urban-suburban areas which have long had them. Living at home cuts subsistence costs by an average of about a third.[61] Urbanization also means that students are better located for seeking part-time jobs. This probably means that parents pay a smaller share of their children's subsistence costs than they once did, though we have inadequate historical data on this point.[62] The over-all result is that subsistence presents a serious problem to far fewer families than it did a generation or two ago.

When we turn from subsistence to instructional costs a very different picture emerges. From 1910 to 1950, par capita GNP rose faster than

[60] Data on student subsistence outlays were taken from Lansing, Lorimer, and Moriguchi, pp. 20–22. The median outlay was $1,550 in 1959. Deducting a median outlay of $350 for tuition we are left with $1,200 subsistence. Data on college room and board fees were taken from A Fact Book (1965), table 263. (The ACE has collected data on room and board fees at 132 probably unrepresentative institutions since 1928. The median charge at these institutions in 1964 exceeded the median charge at institutions reporting to the U. S. Office of Education in the same year by 25 per cent. But the trend in charges at these institutions has probably been fairly typical.) The ratio between room and board charges and over-all student subsistence outlays in 1960 was calculated and was assumed to have been constant over time. This indicated that living away from home would have cost a student (in 1964 dollars) about $1,335 in 1964 and $1,070 in 1928. In 1964 the College Scholarship Service judged that a family of four could spend $1,335 if it had an income of $9,500, and that it could spend $1,070 if it had an income of $8,300. (College Scholarship Service, Manual, chart 1.) The CSS assumed, in other words, that ability to pay for college increased faster than income in the upper income brackets. If we assumed, contrary to CSS and common sense, that ability to pay college costs rose only in proportion to income, we would have to count every family with over $7,600 (1964 dollars) in 1928 as able to pay a child's subsistence at college in that year. Incomes for 1964 were taken from Bureau of the Census, Current Population Reports, (1967). Incomes for 1928 were estimated from Miller, Income Distribution, table 1–6. In 1964, 26 per cent of all families had incomes of over $9,500. In 1928, 7 per cent had incomes over $8,300 and 9 per cent had incomes over $7,600. Since half of all students obviously subsisted on less than the median, and since we have no way of estimating the minimum feasible expenditure on subsistence, either while living at home or while living away, nor of estimating the proportion of families so located as to send a child to a college within commuting distance, the absolute percentages are meaningless. But the trend is not.

[61] Lansing, Lorimer, and Moriguchi, table 4.

[62] Patricia Salter West reports that the proportion of college graduates who worked their way through rose from 1914 to 1947; see "Social Mobility." A comparison of Havemann and West, p. 19, with Cowhig and Nam, pp. 4–5, suggests that this trend has continued. The data in Cowhig and Nam are, however, somewhat out of line with those in Lansing, Lorimer, and Moriguchi, p. 21.

college expenditures per student. Since 1950 the trend has reversed with colleges' expenditure per student rising faster than per capita GNP.[63] This means that the increase in national affluence is no longer sufficiently rapid to cover the increase in academic expenditures, quite aside from the fact that more students are going to college. If we extrapolated current trends sufficiently far into the future, the entire GNP would be devoted to higher education. This is plainly impossible: hence the much discussed "crisis in college finance."[64]

The reasons for this change are far from clear. It is often argued, for example, that the dramatic increases in expenditure since the mid-fifties have been necessary to "make up" for the "lag" in instructional expenditures during the 1930s and 1940s. This theory has considerable merit when applied to faculty salaries, which constitute a major share of instructional costs. Academic salaries did lag during the 1930s and 1940s, and even today's affluent academicians appear no better off relative to the general population than their predecessors in 1900 or 1929. (It should be remembered, however, that academicians are a much larger group relative to the general population than they were in 1900 or 1929, that mass higher education has somewhat narrowed the educational gap between the general population and the academic profession, and that this would lead one to expect over-all income levels to have risen more than academic ones. Such a trend was visible during the 1940s, but it did not continue in the 1950s or 1960s.) Academic salaries are, however, only part of over-all instructional expenditures, and the other parts never lagged significantly. On the contrary, instructional expenditure per student has risen faster than the general price level in every decade of this century except the 1940s, and even then the lag was only a few percentage points.

It seems clear that the basic reason for this inflation of academic costs has been a steady rise in the level of amenity expected (indeed

[63] We have no statistics on instructional expenditures before 1929–30, but official figures indicate that institutional *income* per student rose about 23 per cent in constant dollars between 1909 and 1929. Real per capita GNP seems to have risen between 30 and 40 per cent during this period. After 1929–30 figures are available on instructional expenditure per student and show that between 1929–30 and 1949–50 it increased about 23 per cent in real terms. Real per capita GNP rose 30 per cent between 1929 and 1949. Between 1949–50 and 1963–64 the real increase in instructional expenditure per student was 79 per cent. Real per capita GNP increased about 34 per cent during this period. For statistics on educational income, expenditures, and enrollment, see 1965 *Digest*, tables 53, 78, 81, and 83. For estimates of per capita GNP before 1929, see Denison, p. 21; for estimates since 1929, see *Economic Report of the President*, Tables B-2 and B-19.

[64] A similar tendency of expenditures to rise faster than per capita GNP can be found in a few other fields, notably scientific research and medical care. These fields face comparable "crises."

demanded) by college professors and administrators and to a lesser extent by students. Faculty members may not have improved their incomes relative to the general population over the past half-century, but many have gained private offices, secretarial help, much lighter teaching loads, graduate assistants to grade papers, and such other perquisites. These improvements have been made with the best intentions. Colleges always believe they can do a better job if they spend more money. Not only that, but almost every college feels that it can provide a better education *dollar for dollar* if it has a larger budget. This is probably an illusion in many cases, but there is no way to prove it so. If a college pays its top professors $20,000 per year, it can always argue that it would get better men if it paid $25,000. And who is to say these men would not be 30 or 40 per cent better, thus justifying the 25 per cent increase in expenditure? Similarly, if the library has 100,000 volumes, it would obviously be better if it had 200,000; if it has 1,000,000 books, it would obviously be better if it had 2,000,000. As in every enterprise, then, there are constant internal pressures to spend more, more, and still more.

Confronted with such pressures, boards of trustees and administrators have no rational grounds for either acceding or resisting. There are no balance sheets that show the rate of marginal return for an additional dollar invested in faculty salaries or libraries. Nor are there any generally accepted social or economic theories for what over-all national level of expenditure on higher education makes sense.[65] America spent $1,200 per student on instruction in 1964. Did we get equally good results for the $1,000 we spent a few years earlier? Or would we have gotten 50 per cent more if we had spent $1,600 or $1,800? No one knows. Expenditures are therefore determined by political and administrative bargaining, in which presumptive rates of return play a negligible role. Institutions try to raise as much money as they can (or in the case of tuition charges, as much as they dare) each year, simply taking it for granted that they can put such money to better use than any other competing enterprise. The idea that there is a rational limit to what America should spend on higher education is almost never discussed, either publicly or privately.

There is, of course, nothing remarkable about the fact that America's college educators and trustees think they could use more money to public advantage. The men who run every enterprise think this. They can hardly afford to think anything else; if they did, their morale would deteriorate and the more idealistic would go into other lines of work. The remarkable thing about American colleges is not

---

[65] For a discussion of some of these problems see Danière, *Higher Education*; see also his "Cost-Benefit Analysis."

their uncritical impulse to consume an ever-larger share of the national income but their capacity to persuade the public that this impulse should be humored. This phenomenon requires an explanation, especially since the present course of academic development depends on its continuation.

One popular theory is that recent expenditure increases reflect the rapid rise in middle- and working-class incomes. Once incomes rise above subsistence the discretionary funds available for all sorts of luxuries, from higher education to vacations, increase even faster than total income. Hence the 30 per cent increase in per capita disposable income between 1949–50 and 1963–64 brought an increase of more than 30 per cent in discretionary spending. Even assuming that a fixed percentage of discretionary income went for college, we would expect a rise of more than 30 per cent in tuition expenditures. This theory is quite plausible on its face. But if it were correct, per student instructional expenditures would have risen faster than parental incomes throughout the twentieth century, not just since 1950. The rise in discretionary income has, after all, been a continuing American phenomenon, interrupted only briefly during the 1930s. It can hardly account for a rate of increase in expenditure that is unique to the second half of the twentieth century.

A second popular explanation of rising expenditures is "the Ph.D. shortage." This shortage seems, however, to have been greatly exaggerated. Recent studies show that, while the ratio of college faculty to students has declined from about 1:12 to about 1:15, this has been accompanied by an increase in the proportion of Ph.D.s on college faculties.[66] It could be argued that rapid improvements in the standard of academic life were the sine qua non of this increase. Perhaps if instructional expenditures per student had not risen faster than the cost of most other things, the number of people embarking on Ph.D. programs might have lagged, the proportion dropping out might have increased, and the proportion taking non-academic jobs might have been higher. Yet none of these variables appears to be particularly responsive to market conditions, and it is therefore by no means apparent that a Ph.D. shortage would have developed even if academic salaries had continued to lag during the 1950s and 1960s.

So why the myth of a shortage? First, widely publicized but poorly worked out projections during the 1950s suggested a shortage. Second, while the proportion of professors with Ph.D.s rose, it never rose as fast as most deans and department chairmen wished it would. The academic profession wanted college faculties composed exclusively of Ph.D.s, and by this standard there was an acute shortage, since only about half actually had such degrees. Third, there was a real

[66] Cartter, "The Supply," p. 27.

shortage of first-rate scholars capable of conducting externally financed research projects. Competition for such men bid up their salaries in a quite spectacular way, and this affected the over-all pattern of faculty compensation.

But even if there were a "Ph.D. shortage"—and there *has* been a slight decline in the ratio of faculty Ph.D.s to undergraduates—we must ask why philanthropists, legislators, and parents were willing to finance competition between colleges for this scarce resource. The Ph.D. ratio was, after all, allowed to fall at some institutions. Why not more? Less satisfactorily certified instructors might have turned out worse educated alumni, but how was this danger made real or important to skeptical parents, alumni, or legislators? Or, to put it more precisely, why did these men show such an unprecedented lack of skepticism about educators' demands and claims?

Two factors seem to us crucial, and both are cultural rather than strictly economic. The first was the increasingly visible role of academic research in shaping both technology and social policy. Legislators, philanthropists, and publicists were more persuaded than ever before that productive scholars were a national asset—quite aside from whether they taught undergraduates anything. Money poured into the universities to support such scholars in the same way and for some of the same reasons that it had earlier poured into the Church to support monastic orders. The second factor was growing public concern with the quality of higher education for the young. As the over-all number of B.A.s rose, the psychological importance of quality differentiation within this cadre rose correspondingly. More legislators were anxious that their state have a first-rank public university rather than a second-rank one, for the mere existence of the university no longer seemed much of an achievement. Similarly, more parents were concerned with *where* their children went to college, for a degree in itself no longer seemed unusual. Both legislators and parents were evidently willing to pay for the slightly more valuable certification of an academically reputable institution.[67]

These shifts in public attitudes probably derive in part from demographic changes. Public willingness to pay for higher education depends primarily on the priorities of middle-aged men and women. These people's priorities in turn reflect their earlier educational attain-

---

[67] We know of no satisfactory study of the economic value of attending a "good" college. Havemann and West give income data on the alumni of various colleges, but they have no controls for the social background or ability of entrants. André Danière has made calculations based on the 1963 incomes of members of the Class of 1958 from various colleges, but income at age twenty-seven is not necessarily a good predictor of income at age forty-seven, and while he has been able to control some of the other relevant variables, others are more elusive. Danière's unpublished data are derived from the National Science Foundation study of the Class of 1958 reported in Sharpe, *Five Years*.

ment more than any other single factor.[68] The median attainment of forty-five- to fifty-year-olds rose less than one year between 1914 and 1949—the period when expenditure per student on higher education was lagging. Between 1950 and 1967, when expenditures accelerated, median attainment in this age group rose by three years.[69]

Middle-class demands for more and better higher education have created a variety of problems for upwardly mobile students with limited funds. There have been substantial increases in private philanthropic support for higher education, but these have not kept pace with enrollment and account for an even smaller proportion of over-all instructional expenditures. There have been even more substantial increases in tax subsidies, but not substantial enough to cover the whole increase in expenditures, especially in the private sector. Tuition charges to students therefore still have to cover about a third of instructional expenditure, as they have for some years past. The burden of these charges is greater in the private sector and is increasing faster than in the public, because the relative lag in philanthropic support has been greater than the lag in tax support. But even in the public sector tuition has risen faster than per capita disposable income since 1950. Neither trend shows any sign of reversing itself.[70]

When we look at the over-all picture, then, we see two contradictory trends. On the one hand the cost of subsistence has been declining relative to income; on the other hand the cost of instruction has been rising relative to income, offsetting some of the gains on the subsistence front. What is the cumulative effect?

Until the early 1950s the combined price of subsistence and tuition rose considerably more slowly than family incomes. This meant that a substantially larger proportion of the population could afford to attend college in 1952 than at any previous time. This was true of both public and private colleges, for both commuting and residential students. After 1952, and more especially after 1956, this encouraging trend slowed and in some cases stopped entirely. Median pre-tax real family incomes rose about 20 per cent between 1956 and 1964; 80th percentile incomes rose 28 per cent; per capita disposable income rose 15 per cent. The total cost (in constant dollars) of going away to a public college in one's home state rose about 15 per cent. For those concerned with social access and mobility, however, the cost of going away to college is perhaps less relevant than the cost of commuting, for this is the only option many lower strata students even consider.

---

[68] For evidence that parents' willingness to spend on a child's higher education depends on their education more than on their income, see Lansing, Lorimer, and Moriguchi, pp. 27–36.

[69] See Chart I, page 80.

[70] For data on tuition trends see *A Fact Book* and 1965 *Digest*, table 83. On income trends see *Economic Report of the President*, tables B-16 and B-17.

Since subsistence constitutes a smaller proportion and tuition a larger proportion of outlay for commuters than for residential students, the recent pattern of rapid increases in tuition offset by lagging subsistence expenses has hit the commuter much harder than the more prosperous residential student. If we made the extreme assumption that most low income urban families consider sending a child to college only if he can commute, and the further assumption that these families expect to handle the child's subsistence costs as they have for the previous seventeen years, we would conclude that the crucial determinant of access was the ratio of tuition to median family income. Between 1956 and 1964 real private tuition rose three times as fast as median income (60 as against 20 per cent) while public tuition rose almost twice as fast (37 as against 20 per cent).[71]

Does this mean that the proportion of the population that can afford to finance its children's higher education is declining? Almost certainly not. Yet the question cannot be definitively answered, because there are no generally accepted definitions of what families at different income levels can actually afford. Empirical research suggests that some very poor families are willing to make extraordinary sacrifices for their children's undergraduate education, while other affluent families are unwilling to spend very much.[72] If all families were willing to make the sacrifices that some now make, virtually everyone could afford to attend college somewhere. If, on the other hand, all families were as niggardly as some now are, virtually nobody could afford to attend. Under these circumstances we can hardly expect consensus about how fast families should increase their college expenditures.

The only systematic effort to answer this question seems to have been the one made by the College Scholarship Service—a private organization that advises a number of selective private colleges on how much scholarship assistance students need.[73] The CSS formula is prescriptive rather than descriptive. It embodies the judgment of a group of private colleges as to the proportion of various families' incomes they are entitled to pre-empt for their own use. The formula is rather like the one used for computing income tax, except that it is more progressive. The rich pay more while the poor pay less. Such a formula implies that family expenditures should rise much faster than family incomes. Between 1956 and 1964, for example, the median

[71] On income trends see *Economic Report of the President*, tables B-16 and B-17, and Bureau of the Census, *Current Population Reports* (1967), table C. Estimates of college costs were derived from the *Fact Book*, and the *Economic Report*, table B-42. We assumed that the room and board charges reported in the *Fact Book* represented 60 per cent of total subsistence expenses for resident students in both 1956 and 1964.

[72] Lansing, Lorimer, and Moriguchi.

[73] College Scholarship Service, *Manual*.

family's real pretax income rose 20 per cent while its anticipated contribution rose 52 per cent. Eightieth percentile income rose about 28 per cent during this period, and according to CSS this increased such a family's college obligation by 56 per cent.[74] If one accepts these formulae as reasonable, one finds that ability to pay has increased faster than tuition even in the past decade.[75] Considering that the sponsors of CSS mostly come from colleges that are raising tuition very rapidly, it would be surprising if the formulae showed anything else.

Even if one rejects the CSS formula as the handiwork of greedy educators eager to divert an ever-larger share of the national income to their own use (and it is certainly far more than that), it is still difficult to argue that the cost of higher education is the principal reason why lower strata children fail to earn B.A.s. A study by the Bureau of the Census in 1960 found, for example, that variations in parental income could explain less than 10 per cent of the variance in college enrollment rates among high school seniors.[76] This finding is supported by Table V, which compares parental income distributions at various sorts of colleges to the distribution for all families with heads between forty-five and fifty-four. Another sort of evidence indicating the limited importance of family finances in determining who goes to college comes from a 1959 Census study which showed that 45 per cent of the men and 30 per cent of the women

[74] Computed from College Scholarship Service, *Manual,* table A, for a family of four with no special financial obligations. The median family in 1964, with $6,600, was expected to find $700 for higher education. The 8oth percentile family, with $11,000, was expected to find $1,800.

[75] Using CSS formulae, e.g., we estimate that in 1956 about 8 per cent of all families of four could afford to send a child away to the typical private college. By 1964 the formula showed this had risen to about 10 per cent. The upward trend in ability to meet public residential college costs was even more dramatic, from about 17 per cent to about 24 per cent of all families. These percentages should *not* be read as indicating, let us say, that "76 per cent of all families could not afford to send a child to college in 1964." At most, they mean that 76 per cent of all families of *four* could not afford to pay the *full* cost of sending a child to the *average* public *residential* college in 1964. Many less affluent families were able to pay enough of the cost so that with the help of scholarships, loans, and jobs their children could go to college. In addition, half of all colleges cost less than the median, and were therefore accessible to lower strata students. The percentages cited are also subject to error because (1) the typical family has more than two children; (2) the typical family with college-age children is at the peak of its earning trajectory and earns appreciably more than the national average; and (3) because the estimate of subsistence costs is subject to a considerable margin of error, especially since it was computed for the *average* student rather than for one just scraping through. *Considering all these difficulties, these percentages should be viewed only as illustrating trends, not as indicating who can afford to go where to college.*

[76] Nam and Cowhig, table 16. The correlation between parental income and whether a student went to college was 0.29 with no other variables controlled; this figure must be squared to get an estimate of explained variance.

TABLE VI

INCOME DISTRIBUTION OF FAMILIES AND UNRELATED
INDIVIDUALS WITH PRINCIPAL EARNER BETWEEN FORTY-
FIVE AND FIFTY-FOUR IN 1965, AND OF FAMILIES WITH
CHILDREN ENTERING COLLEGE, FALL 1966

Income	All Families	All College Families	Public Four-Year Colleges	Private Universities
Less than $4,000	15.5	6.6	10.0	3.3
$4,000 to $5,999	14.6	12.9	17.8	7.3
$6,000 to $7,999	17.9	17.3	20.8	11.9
$8,000 to $9,999	15.6	16.9	18.3	13.6
$10,000 to $14,999	24.0	25.2	22.0	25.0
$15,000 to $24,000	9.8	14.0	8.7	20.9
$25,000 and over	2.7	7.1	2.5	17.9
Total	100.1	100.0	100.1	99.9

SOURCES: Bureau of the Census, *Current Population Reports,* 1967; Astin, Panos, and Creager, "Supplementary National Norms." The public four-year colleges have the lowest income distribution of the nine categories for which data are presented in Astin *et al.*'s study—lower, it should be noted, than the public two-year colleges. The private universities have the highest income distribution. (Supplementary data for Negro colleges shows that the parental income distribution at these colleges is much lower than that cited above, but so too is the income distribution for Negroes as a group.) It should be noted that the income distribution for the general population would be slightly higher if only families and not unrelated individuals were included. Such data was not available for 1965, however. On the other hand, exclusion of older and younger family heads raises it higher than may be realistic. Both errors are small and probably offset one another. A more serious problem is the known tendency of students to under-estimate their parents' income. André Danière has suggested, e.g. on the basis of comparisons between student reports and other data from parents with children entering college, that the number of college families with incomes over $13,000 may be as high as 39 per cent, instead of the 29 per cent which can be inter-polated from the above data. A formula for correcting student estimates of family income is badly needed.

enrolled in college said they got no support from home.[77] While most of these students were undoubtedly part-time, married, enrolled in graduate school, or exaggerating their independence, a study of full-time unmarried undergraduates in the same year found that 13 per cent of their parents reported spending less than $50 a year to support the child in question.[78] While some of these self-supporting students had scholarships, of which there are only a limited number, many did not. And while some had the good fortune to live near a cheap commuter college, others had moved there in order to get an education. It seems clear, in short, that if a student is reasonably

[77] Cowhig and Nam, table A.
[78] Lansing, Lorimer, and Moriguchi, p. 5.

talented and wholly committed he can get through college no matter how little money his parents have. This is even more true today than it was in 1959, for federal scholarships, loans, and subsidized jobs have become available to large numbers of students.

If substantial numbers of students were getting through college without help from home, why weren't more students doing so? In part, no doubt, the answer is that getting through college on one's own is influenced by whether one lives near a public commuter college, whether one can enroll part-time, and other external circumstances which apply to some students but not others. Equally important, however, is the fact that getting through college without help from home requires more interest in college than most students feel, and perhaps more ability too. An apathetic youngster who hates words and books may go to college when all his friends are going, when his parents foot the bill, and when collegiate social life seems comparatively familiar and congenial. He is hardly likely to go if few of his friends go, if college life strikes him as being different from anything he has experienced to date, and if he is going to have to work long hours after school and live in penury to make it. Money, in short, is seldom an insuperable problem when taken in isolation, but it may be decisive for the student who is ambivalent anyway.[79]

Similar conclusions seem warranted when we turn from the influence of money on college entrance to its influence on college completion and on obtaining a graduate degree. A variety of studies have shown that substantial numbers of students say they quit college because they are short of money.[80] Yet these same studies generally fail to find a correlation between parental income and a college freshman's chances of earning a degree.[81] These two findings are

[79] For this reason considerable caution is required when interpreting surveys that purport to show that lack of money has kept large numbers of students from college. Between 15 and 20 per cent of the nation's high school graduates say they are not going to college because they lack money (see Cowhig and Nam, p. 9, also the data collected by Project Talent, reported in Sanders and Palmer, table XXVI). This percentage is much higher than the correlation between parental income and college attendance would lead us to expect, implying that "lack of money" is a more subjective than objective condition. What one boy sees as insufficient money another boy sees as a down payment on his education which he can augment by borrowing, working, and hoping.

[80] The most recent and comprehensive data is that reported by Panos and Astin, "They Went to College." Table II of this report shows about 23 per cent of all students blame their withdrawal from the college they first entered on money problems. For a bibliography of other literature on this subject see Summerskill.

[81] Panos and Astin, "They Went to College," evidently did not obtain data on parental income, but they did find that parental occupation had virtually no relation to completing four years of college. These findings are supported by Eckland's "Social Class," a study of the University of Illinois, which showed a moderate relationship between class background and college graduation, but no relation between graduation and parental income taken in isolation.

probably not contradictory. We know that dropouts, while coming from homes as affluent as graduates, have worse educated parents than graduates.[82] We also know that at any given income level well-educated parents are much more willing to spend money on children in college than are poorly educated parents.[83] Hence while dropping out is probably not related to parental income, it probably *is* related in some cases to parental parsimony. Students who drop out are probably getting slightly less financial help from home, even though their parents have no less money.

A similar pattern probably also affects students' own efforts to solve their money problems. If a student finds himself short of money he can respond in several different ways. One is to borrow and/or take a part-time job. Another is to drop out. The student who drops out is perfectly correct in saying that he did so for lack of money. But outsiders, noting that many other students got through under similar circumstances, are equally correct in saying that the student in question dropped out for lack of commitment. It seems plausible—indeed inevitable—that parents with professional jobs and higher degrees make their children feel that staying in college is worth almost any sacrifice, since dropping out permanently will probably mean downward mobility. Conversely, those whose parents are poorly educated make their children feel that dropping out, while unfortunate, is not necessarily a disaster. Hence a schoolteacher's son or a clergyman's daughter will probably borrow if necessary to get through, whereas a steelworker's child with the same money from home may not. It should also be borne in mind, however, that some students who could have solved their money problems almost certainly give lack of money as a socially acceptable rationalization for a decision whose real roots they prefer not to discuss.[84] Thus the actual proportion of dropouts for whom money is a serious problem is probably less than it seems.

When we turn from college survival to graduate school entry and survival, the influence of parental support is less clear. Many affluent parents do not support their children in graduate school. Society does not expect this in the same way it expects them to support undergraduate children. Indeed, many children, eager to assert their independence, want no part of further parental support. Yet we know that a student's chances of entering some sort of graduate school are

[82] Panos and Astin, "They Went to College." See also Eckland, "Social Class," on the reasons why many studies of single institutions fail to confirm this finding. See also Spady, for evidence that this is a fairly recent development.

[83] Lansing, Lorimer, and Moriguchi.

[84] For evidence that upwardly mobile students experience more social stress in college—or at least in an upper-middle class residential college with an active fraternity system, see Ellis and Lane.

at least moderately related to his class background. This is particularly true of medical schools and law schools, which have made rather inadequate efforts to provide scholarships, work opportunities, and the like and have not publicized even what they do offer sufficiently for most poor boys to think they have a chance of getting help. In contrast to the situation during the college years, parental income has almost as much influence as parental occupation or education on who goes on and who does not.[85] Still, the cause-effect relationship is equivocal. While an appreciable fraction of college seniors say they are not going to graduate school for lack of money, virtually none of these same students apply for scholarships.[86] Given the fact that an appreciable fraction of those who said they had financial problems had fairly affluent parents,[87] and the further fact that the decision not to apply for financial help probably indicates either ambivalence about continuing or pessimism about whether one's record is good enough to get help, it seems fair to conclude that financial obstacles per se are of marginal importance in blocking the upwardly mobile in their pursuit of graduate degrees.

All in all, then, we are inclined to be skeptical about theories that emphasize the high cost of attending college as the major obstacle, and to look for other explanations of the relationship between class background and attainment.

Colleges versus the Upwardly Mobile: Tests

Until relatively recently most educators saw tests as a democratizing rather than an aristocratizing influence. They assumed that academic ability was far more evenly distributed than social status or economic power, and that if the educational system could dole out rewards on

[85] James Davis, *Great Aspirations*, table 3.17a, shows that among 1961 B.A.s 29 per cent of those from families earning less than $5,000 planned to go to graduate school next fall, 52 per cent planned to go "later," and 19 per cent planned never to go. For those whose families earned $20,000 and up, 40 per cent planned to go next fall, 31 per cent later, and 29 per cent never.

[86] James Davis, *Great Aspirations*, table 3.4, shows that 12 per cent of the Class of 1961 claimed finances were the major reason they were not going on to graduate school next fall, and 24 per cent said finances played some part. Yet Davis estimates (p. 78) that if all those who applied for scholarships had gotten them, the rate of enrollment in graduate school the next fall would only have risen 1 per cent. Laura Sharpe, "Five Years," table 25, shows a similar pattern of reports from members of the Class of 1958 five years after graduating. Her table 5 shows that financial problems were by far the most important reason given both for dropping out of graduate school and for going only part time (a pattern associated with much lower rates of degree completion). Yet her table 41 shows that very few of those who applied for money were refused.

[87] On the class background of those reporting financial problems, see James Davis, *Great Aspirations*, table 3.19.

the basis of academic performance it would be a major avenue of social mobility. The typical debate over college admission policy therefore found conservatives arguing that academic competence was not everything; that the sons of alumni had a "claim" on their college; that it was important to have "well-rounded" boys who had a potential for "leadership" (criteria that usually seemed to produce an entering class full of not necessarily interesting but usually well-bred Anglo-Saxon youngsters from middle-class families); and that the college should not simply admit students "by the numbers." Liberals, on the other hand, usually saw these arguments as manifestations of snobbery and urged that the college seek out the ablest students it could find, wherever they might come from. They defended this position partly by urging the importance of "equal opportunity," social mixing, and the like, but mainly by arguing that since the college was "really" an academic institution, it had no business judging its members by any standard other than their on-the-job competence. They found a happy coincidence, in other words, between their desire to professionalize the college and their desire to democratize it.

In recent years the liberals have increasingly won this battle, though there are still plenty of exceptions and holdouts.[88] Not only are students increasingly selected on the basis of probable performance in college, but more active efforts are being made to recruit promising students from all conditions of life. For reasons already discussed, it is also easier for most parents to finance their children's higher education. Yet this triumph of meritocratic values, far from democratizing the colleges, seems, as we indicated in the fourth section, to have been accompanied by a slight trend in the opposite direction. It has also been accompanied by a rising crescendo of protest, especially from the civil rights movement and others who believe in a more egalitarian society, against the use of tests to select students and allocate academic resources.

The more naïve of these critics have fastened on the most visible aspect of testing, namely standarized multiple-choice tests which purport to measure "aptitude" or even "IQ." But these, as we indicated at the beginning of this chapter, are only the tip of the iceberg. Most tests are made up and administered by teachers rather than by the Educational Testing Service, most are scored by hand rather than

[88] Anyone who believes that freshmen are chosen entirely on the basis of scholastic aptitude tests should look at the College Entrance Examination Board's *Manual of Freshman Class Profiles*, which shows the proportion of students in various ability groups rejected by different colleges. It is clear that high Scholastic Aptitude Test scores, while important, are not enough to gain admission to most colleges. Even when SAT scores and high school rank are taken together, they only explain part of the variation in a student's college chances.

by machine, and most purport to measure mastery of a particular subject rather than general academic aptitude. The results of these tests are called "grades" rather than "scores," but they appear to be at least as unfavorable to lower-class pupils as the standard aptitude tests and have at least as serious consequences for such students' careers.

The importance of looking at the question of tests as a unified whole can therefore hardly be overemphasized. Aptitude tests do not, as was once thought, measure genetic ability. They measure the extent to which a student has developed his ability, be it great or small, and absorbed or mastered certain skills psychologists and educators think important.[89] That, indeed, is precisely why they are so useful. For colleges are much like schools, and the student who was adept at picking up what was expected of him in school is a good bet to do the same in college, while a student who did not pick up such skills in school is not very likely to do so in college either. The predictive power of aptitude tests is admittedly limited by the fact that they tell relatively little about a student's habits and attitudes— about whether he is persistent or easily frustrated, whether he is competitive or easy-going, whether he is diligent or indolent. But these traits—or at least those of them that are likely to affect college performance—*can* be partially measured by high school performance. As a result, admissions offices place considerable emphasis on high school grades, which usually predict college grades better than aptitude tests do. But the important point to bear in mind is that the function of *both* aptitude tests *and* high school grades in college

[89] There has been a good deal of discussion over the years of the need for a "culture-free" ability test. Such a test is virtually inconceivable, but more important, it would be virtually useless if it existed. Life is not culture-free, and tests restricted to those aspects of life that *are* culture-free would measure little of importance. The point can be illustrated by the following example. Suppose we took a conventional test of academic aptitude and scored it separately for various subcultures. Suppose we then standardized the scores for each subculture so that there were no differences in group averages. Both Negroes and whites, e.g. would be assigned median IQs of 100; two-thirds of both groups would be assigned scores between 85 and 115; and so forth. The same could be done for urban and rural children, for rich and poor children, and so on. When a child took the test his raw score would then be translated into a standard score, with the formula varying with his race, parental income, geographic origin, or whatever. The result would be a "culture-free" system for ranking students from various backgrounds without making invidious group comparisons. The only defect of this procedure is that the results are of no use in comparing individuals from different subcultures unless the formula by which the tests have been standardized is known. In that case everyone would immediately restandardize them so as to allow group comparisons and eliminate the appearance of cultural neutrality. The point, of course, is that a test that suggests that youngsters from poor families are as competent as youngsters from affluent families is misleading and of little value to anyone. There are, indeed, some realms in which poor children are as competent as rich ones, but they are not mostly realms that play a major part in academic or professional competence.

admission is merely to predict college grades, and that in this role they do a moderately good job.[90] This is particularly true in extreme cases: a student who has aptitude scores conspicuously lower than his college classmates is quite unlikely to survive in competition with them.

When used in this way there is no evidence that reliance on either high school grades or aptitude tests discriminates against the poor. A student with poor grades or poor aptitude scores is likely to do about equally badly in college whether he comes from a poor home or a rich one.[91] The predictors, in other words, are no more "middle class" in their emphases than the colleges themselves.

This does not, of course, mean we must fatalistically accept the verdict of either tests or grades. Federally sponsored Upward Bound programs have, for example, demonstrated that apparently unpromising youngsters from disadvantaged backgrounds can improve their test scores dramatically when exposed to intensive academic "therapy" in settings that differ radically from the typical public school. There is some reason to think, however, that when such students are sent back to conventional academic settings they again withdraw from the game. What these programs may prove, in other words, is that a different academic program could reach many students untouched by the present one. But if this is the message, it does not argue against the relevance of aptitude tests to the present academic system, but only against the assumption that there are no alternatives to the present academic system.

Yet it would be naïve to assume that these alternatives would necessarily be any less class-biased than the present system. On the contrary, one of our strongest impressions in discussing current efforts to provide intensive and challenging precollege programs with their sponsors is that such programs might well work even better with underachieving middle-class students than with comparable lower-class ones. Indeed, they might work best of all with students now doing well in school. This implies that if schools were reorganized along the lines that the initiators of Upward Bound programs envision, middle-class students who do well on existing tests might gain even more than lower-class students who do badly on existing tests.

90 For a summary of the literature on the effectiveness of such predictive devices, see Fishman and Pasanella. The multiple correlation of high school grades and aptitude scores with college grades usually runs between 0.5 and 0.6, which means that these two predictors can account for about a third of the variation in students' college grades. This is not very good, but it is much better than any other known forecasting device. The correlation can be substantially improved if prediction is based on previous experience with the graduates of a particular high school at a particular college.

91 For some fragmentary evidence on this point see Eckland, "Social Class." For additional evidence, see Cleary.

Those who look askance at testing should not, then, rest their case on the simple notion that tests are "unfair to the poor." Life is unfair to the poor. Tests merely measure the results. Urban middle-class life in general and professional work in particular seem to nourish potentially academic skills and interests in parents, while lower-class life does the opposite. Parents who have such skills and interests pass them along to their children in a multitude of ways, from reading storybooks and playing complex verbal games to including their children in adult conversations. They also make an effort to put their children into stimulating schools. They often move to suburbs with presumably superior schools or send their children to private schools. Parents in the lower social strata, on the other hand, while often as outwardly anxious as upper-middle class parents to see their children do well in school, seldom have either the time, the money, or the personal skills to help their children in comparable ways. Most children born in poor homes grow up with limited vocabularies, limited contact with adults, and limited contact with intellectually stimulating teachers or classmates. They have no privacy, no quiet, no possibility of concentrating on any problem without interruption, be it homework or building blocks. As time goes on they fall increasingly behind their upper-middle class fellows, suffering intellectual damage which is both cumulative and progressively harder to remedy.[92]

The cumulative impact of all this is quite staggering. If we simply divide families into two social strata, white collar and blue collar, we find that high school seniors from white-collar families are four times more likely to score in the top than the bottom decile on a national aptitude test, while blue-collar families are twice as likely to score in the bottom as in the top decile.[93] The discrepancies would be even greater if we contrasted professional children to the children of unskilled laborers, and greater yet if we classified students by parental education instead of occupation. (They would be less, though, if we divided students on the basis of parental income.) If we combine several different measures of social and cultural class, such as whether

[92] The widening of achievement differences between first and twelfth grades may or may not be due to differences in the quality of schools. Coleman *et al.*, pp. 220–74, demonstrate that the percentile rank of Negroes in the over-all national distribution on achievement tests changes very little over twelve years in most school systems. The typical Negro fourth grader is in the bottom third of his class and is one year behind the white norm. He is still in the bottom third in the twelfth grade, but by twelfth grade this means he is three years behind. His relative position is basically unchanged, but both his absolute attainment and his absolute lag have increased—a familiar pattern.

[93] John C. Flanagan *et al.*, *The American High School Student*, table 5-11. We have included children whose parents are farmers and children who don't know their father's occupation with those reporting blue-collar backgrounds—a procedure justified by their other responses.

there is a television set in the house, whether the student has his own room and desk, the number of books and household appliances his family own, parental education, occupation, income, and so forth, we can explain as much as 28 per cent of the variance in students' aptitude test scores.[94] The pattern is not very different if one looks at high school grades instead of aptitude scores.

Confronted with these facts the colleges have simply accepted them. Selective colleges have, it is true, had a variety of small (though highly publicized) programs admitting "promising" youngsters with poor grades, poor test scores, poor disciplinary records, or all three. These students are usually given intensive academic survival training. Such ventures, essentially similar in conception to the federally sponsored Upward Bound programs, have many of the same virtues and vices as psychoanalysis. First, there are only a few men with the talent, commitment, and time to run such remedial programs successfully. Thus only a small minority can ever hope to benefit. Second, students get into such programs only if they have done something to convince somebody that their apparent lack of promise is deceptive. Again, only a small minority is likely to show such promise. Third, such programs seldom reach more than a fraction of those exposed to them, and are thus subject to endless criticism by skeptics who point to the many inevitable failures. Fourth, such programs, being of limited duration and coming late in life, can almost never undo more than a fraction of the damage done by earlier neglect. Their alumni, while sometimes helped in important ways and enabled to cope with the demands of higher education, will still be scarred by their pasts. (This does not mean that helping them is a waste of time. We are all scarred in one way or another, and those who emerge from a wretched childhood may become, whether by way of Upward Bound or psychoanalysis, more alive and more useful citizens than those whose upbringing leaves them comfortably bland.)

Such programs are, however, no more likely than psychoanalysis to bring a radical change in the lives of large numbers of sufferers. Preventive measures offer the only hope of that. Equally important, the limitations on remedial programs that we have mentioned mean that colleges are unlikely to expand or extend them very far, because it is not in their institutional interest to do so. On the contrary, the

[94] Flanagan *et al., One Year Follow-Up Studies*, appendix E. The multiple correlation of twenty-five family background variables with scores on various tests ranged from 0.53 for the information test through 0.48 for reading comprehension, and 0.46 for mathematical ability to 0.24 for word memory and visualization. These correlations must be squared to estimate the per cent of variance explained by the items in question. Contrary to what one might think, correlations of this sort produce discrepancies of representation in the top and bottom ability deciles even greater than those associated with occupation and reported in the text.

institutional interest of colleges pushes them relentlessly in the opposite direction, encouraging them to seek the ablest and most easily educable students rather than the neediest and most recalcitrant ones. Those who hope to change this should at least understand the reasons.

A college's justification for almost all increases in its academic expenditure is the improvement of instruction. Spending more will mean wiser, happier, or more erudite alumni. Otherwise, why "waste" the money? Such claims are, however, often quite hard to support. A college that seeks to endow a new chair in Oriental History, for example, cannot easily show that students will learn more from studying the Ming Dynasty than they now do from studying medieval England. (Indeed, the college often cannot even make this claim, lest the medievalists become agitated.) In any case, concern for the students is seldom the compelling reason for seeking the chair. Rather, the college wants such a chair to enhance its academic reputation vis-à-vis other colleges, and to make local faculty feel their institution is "with it." Yet the college is also a prisoner of its own rhetoric. If it spends more money than most of its rivals, those who are asked to pay cannot be candidly told their money is simply to boost faculty morale. They must be told that the extra outlay brings better pedagogic results. To "prove" that this is so, the college must turn out more distinguished alumni than its rivals. One way to do this might be to enroll ordinary students and then make them distinguished by devoting extraordinary resources and skill to their education. But the outcome of such efforts is seldom sufficiently spectacular to impress potential financial supporters. It is therefore necessary to recruit students who are extraordinary to begin with. Such students then educate themselves and each other. The faculty need only lecture them occasionally, give them reading lists of edifying books, and set a reasonably good example as cultured, disciplined adults. Since able students enjoy kindred spirits, they develop a measure of loyalty to any college that is composed mainly of other able students. This loyalty usually survives even if the faculty and administration are distant and dull. As alumni, these students become walking testimonials to their alma mater, both because of what they say directly about it and because of what their talents seem to say indirectly about it. Their existence seems to justify both earlier expenditures and current pleas for still more money.

For the university whose primary concern is to assemble, support, and pamper a faculty of gifted scholars, academically able students have another advantage. There was a time when an appreciable number of professors identified with their genteel patrons and preferred suave, well-bred, or even athletic students to clever ones. But that time seems to have passed. Today's faculty seek their own professional identities as scholars, and only rarely want to live vicariously through their students. Only a few of today's scholars are missionaries, either to the upper or the lower classes. Most prefer talking to the already converted. They like students who share at least some of their values and interests, not students who regard academic work as a chore to be gotten through in order to get a job. A college that insists on retaining individuals or subcultures that challenge the academic ethos is likely to have some difficulty recruiting a scholarly faculty. In order to do so at all it will usually have to pay more than its more exclusive competitors would. Low admissions requirements may thus drive expenses up in the short run as well as making it harder to raise money over the long haul.

Thus far we have been assuming that every institution's primary interest is in attracting better faculty and turning out more distinguished alumni. From the institution's viewpoint this is basically accurate. But society's interest is rather different. From society's viewpoint the merit of an undergraduate college depends on the amount of "value added" to its human product during the undergraduate years. If we accept this goal, the logic of student selection and expenditure ought to change radically. It is undoubtedly true that a dollar spent educating a genius adds more to the sum total of human competence than a dollar spent educating a fool. Hence if American colleges confronted a wholly uneducated population, and were exclusively concerned with advancing the over-all achievement of that population without regard to its internal homogeneity or cohesiveness, they would start with the ablest students and let the dullards languish. But this is not the situation. Virtually all America's most promising students already go to college.[95] Once they enter college very substantial sums are usually spent on their education. Meanwhile many less promising students are not attending college at all, or are attending colleges that spend very little on instruction. The question, therefore, is not whether a dollar spent on a talented undergraduate has more effect than a dollar spent on a mediocre undergraduate, but whether the 3,000th dollar spent on a talented undergraduate has more effect than the first (or perhaps the 500th) dollar spent on a mediocre one. Does an Ivy League college that spends $20 a day on able undergraduates really achieve five times as much as an overgrown teachers' college which spends $4 a day on less gifted young people? Does it make more sense to augment Cal Tech's budget by another $600 per student, increasing its resources by perhaps 10 per

[95] Flanagan et al., The American High School Student, table 11-1, shows that 97 per cent of those scoring in the top 1 per cent of their age group and 90 per cent of those scoring in the top 10 per cent go directly to college the year after graduating.

cent, or to augment Los Angeles State's budget by $600 per student, increasing its resources by 100 per cent?

The answers to cost-benefit queries of this sort obviously depend on the criteria used for measuring value added. But we know of no college or group of colleges that has yet attempted to answer such questions according to *any* criterion. The only investigation we know along these lines is one conducted for the U. S. Office of Education by André Danière, using alumni income as the measure of output.[96] His findings, while anything but definitive, suggest that an extra dollar spent in a high-cost institution will typically do far less to enhance students' future earnings than an extra dollar spent in a low-cost institution. This appears especially true for talented students, but seems to hold for all aptitude groups. If this is true, the implication is clear. Resources going to colleges with very expensive instructional programs for talented students are being misallocated. The payoff would be higher if these colleges admitted more students and spread their resources thinner. This would probably be equally true if we considered intellectual, attitudinal, or sociopolitical measures of college output.

Whatever empirical research may show, there can be little question that the public believes itself better served by quantity than quality in higher education. Legislative bodies have constantly sought to establish colleges that would give large numbers of relatively un-selected students a cheap program of instruction. The colleges, however, have seldom been very cooperative in such ventures. Once established they have been upwardly mobile, becoming progressively less expansive and more expensive relative to national norms. Legis-latures and private groups have therefore had to keep founding new colleges to provide cheaper programs for less promising students.

The reasons for this are relatively clear. Colleges are primarily interested in creating a more satisfactory and equable campus at-mosphere, not in serving a large, remote, and often ungrateful ab-straction called "society." In any case, they are ready to assume that what's good for Old Siwash is good for the country. And what seems good for Old Siwash is determined not by the transient adolescents who constitute the student body (or would constitute it if they were admitted) nor by the vocal alumni but by the tenured adults who give their lives to the place. Those colleges that allow students a significant official or unofficial role in setting priorities usually do so

[96] "Cost-Benefit Analysis," table 1.26. Like almost all economic analyses of education, Danière's assumes that there is a one-to-one relationship between what happens to a man after he leaves college and what happens to him in college. The only control variable used was student aptitude. This means that the analysis almost certainly overstates the effect of all sorts of colleges on income. Whether it also distorts the relative effect of different kinds of colleges is less clear.

because the students in question share most of the academic norms of the adults.

This may seem a harsh judgment, but the evidence for it strikes us as persuasive. Despite the hopes of some of the best admissions officers, few colleges evaluate applicants in terms of what the college might do for the student. Almost all colleges with which we are familiar ask, implicitly if not explicitly, what the student is likely to do for the college. College faculties have invented no devices for measuring growth during college, much less for predicting which students will grow most on which sort of campus. This is no accident. Colleges do not really care much about student growth in this sense. Rather, they are concerned with students' absolute levels of future attainment. They may be interested in growth if the candidate in question looks like a "diamond in the rough," who might end up at or near the top in some field, but not otherwise. A student who enters college in the 10th percentile of his generation and rises as a result of heroic faculty effort to the 25th percentile may represent more value added than one who rises from the 90th to 95th percentile, but he does not represent as much of a public relations asset nor as large an alumni contribution.

For this reason we think it highly unlikely that America's colleges will voluntarily invest substantial resources in remedial programs for the academically unpromising, even if it can be demonstrated that the ultimate payoff from such programs is greater than from conventional programs for advantaged students. The payoff, however great, does not go to the institution but to society, and the financing will therefore have to come from society rather than from the institutions. And society, while certain to put up *some* money for such ventures, is unlikely to be lavish. Nor would cost-benefit analyses of the kind already referred to be likely to provide an argument for lavishness. Low-cost programs for middle-aptitude students are a better investment in many cases than high-cost programs for high-aptitude students, but high-cost programs for low-aptitude students are much harder to justify. A dollar spent at Cal Tech or Harvard may well do more to increase the GNP than a dollar spent on Upward Bound, even though it does less than a dollar spent at Los Angeles State. (The justification for Upward Bound and similar ventures is not its effect on the GNP but its effect on the social and political life of the nation.)

It this is correct, intensive remedial programs aimed at high school students with poor grades or poor test scores are unlikely to grow enough to have a substantial impact on the pattern of student recruitment and selection. Significant increases in social mobility via higher education will therefore have to come about in other ways. The most promising would be to concentrate on students who have less intransigent problems: students who have done relatively well in high school, who have done relatively well on tests of academic aptitude, and who would have a relatively good chance of completing a typical low-cost college course if they decided to give it a try. These are the students who may now enter a sleepy church college, a former teachers college, or a public junior college, but who are more likely not to go to college at all.

Recent preoccupation with the more extreme reaches of poverty has to some extent blinded reformers to the existence of such students, but they are legion. There are not, it is true, very many students in the top ability groups who do not go to college. Even among students with very poorly educated fathers, for example, 87 per cent of the boys and 78 per cent of the girls who scored in the top decile on national aptitude tests went straight to college after finishing high school.[97] This was only about 8 per cent lower than for the population as a whole. But if the reader looks back at Table V on page 103 he will find that among those from the bottom half of the social ladder less than half the men and a third of the women in the second ability quintile went to college in 1960. While some of these students certainly had poor high school grades, and some would have needed intensive help or a radically new sort of college to get them on their feet academically, many would not.[98] It is among these students that there is currently most room for missionary work, assuming anyone can be interested in such unglamorous potential converts. It is the high schools' inability or unwillingness to encourage these students to attend college that accounts for the increasing importance of class background in determining which high school seniors go to college.[99] The upper-middle class child of moderate ability is today pushed into college no matter what; his working-class or lower-class age-mate is unlikely to go unless he has done well in high school, learns quite easily, and has come to regard books and classrooms as part of his turf.

Similar considerations continue to operate once students have entered college. Freshmen from well-educated professional families are more likely to stay the full four years than freshmen with comparable high school grades and test scores from the lower social

[97] Flanagan et al., The American High School Student, table 11-1.

[98] For evidence on the extent to which students with high scores who do not go to college have poor school grades, see Flanagan et al., The American High School Student, table 11-12.

[99] Although the trend data shown in Spady show only that cultural class background as measured by father's education has more influence than it used to, it seems reasonable to assume that social class background as measured by father's occupation and income also does so.

strata.[100] They are also slightly more likely to go on to graduate school.[101]

Having said all this about the reasons for the testing and certification system and its results, we must still ask whether there have been any changes in this system over the past forty years that help explain the increasing importance of class background in determining which high school graduates go to college, and which college entrants graduate. The academic obstacles to entering certain elite colleges have clearly risen, and the same is true of many graduate professional schools. Yet we can find no evidence that the academic obstacles to attending college in general are any greater than a generation or two ago. For every state university that has raised its entrance requirements there are two new state colleges open to virtually all comers on roughly the same basis that the state university previously was. For every Reed or MIT requiring its applicants to be in the top 1 or 2 per cent of their age group, there are two new junior colleges with no requirements whatever.

Nor can we see any reason to suppose that measures of academic competence are more class-biased than in the past. It is true that private colleges now place more emphasis on aptitude scores and less on achievement scores than they did, but this hardly seems likely to have worked against the poor. On the contrary, it was precisely to reduce the advantage of rich and well-prepared prep school boys that subject-matter tests were played down.

It could be that the cultural gap between the upper and lower strata is widening, and that for this reason both test scores and grades are more highly correlated with class than they used to be. This hypothesis seems, however, to fly in the face of almost everyone's impressionistic conclusions. The virtual end of immigration has reduced the proportion of foreign-born parents who worried about their children's going to college because it meant "losing" them. It is true that migration from the farm still produces a large number of Negroes and whites unable to cope with urban life, and that these groups in some ways resemble immigrants of an earlier day. But it must be borne in mind that these families existed in 1925 as well as 1965. While they are more visible in the city than on the farm, they have the same statistical impact on college enrollment patterns that they always had. And while their hegira to the city may have been disastrous in some respects, it has clearly increased the proportion doing well on aptitude tests and going to college.[102] Thus while we

[100] See Panos and Astin, "They Went to College," and Eckland, "Social Class."

[101] James Davis, *Great Aspirations*, table 3.18.

[102] On urban-rural differences in test scores and college *aspirations*, see Coleman *et al.*, chap. 3. On differences in college *enrollment*, see Cowhig and Nam. See also the work of Sewell and his collaborators, e.g., "Community" and the sources cited there.

know no long-term-trend data on class differences in academic ability, we doubt that they have widened.

Colleges versus the Upwardly Mobile: Motivation

Coming of age in America can be a race for the top. It is seldom a sprint, however, in which victory goes to the naturally gifted or enthusiastic. It is a marathon, in which victory goes to those who train the longest and care the most.[103] And it is here that the upper-middle class child has the crucial advantages. He is trained for the contest from birth, and more often than not he is convinced that losing it will mean metaphorical if not literal death.

For the lower-class or working-class child, going to college is a step up in the world, a way of improving on the conditions in which he or she was raised. It may be desirable but it is hardly indispensable. A child who has endured seventeen years in Harlem knows he can endure another fifty, and a child whose father is a steelworker knows that such a life, while hardly what he might wish, is at least a conceivable and tolerable alternative. Such a youngster may be under considerable verbal pressure from home to do better than his parents did, and in particular to do well at school and go to college. Yet even this is by no means universal. Substantial numbers of lower strata families seem to be relatively content for their children to occupy a similar position, and even those who would like to see their children "get ahead" sometimes see no connection between this and going to college.[104] Even those children whose parents do want them to go to college often sense that if they fail to live up to this hope their parents may be disappointed but will rarely be heartbroken. Life will go on as before, perhaps with a few recriminations but probably nothing more. (There are, of course, upwardly mobile youngsters with a passion to escape their origins, but they are the exception.)

For the upper-middle class child, on the other hand, the pressure to go to college and earn a degree is of a completely different kind. Here we are dealing not with an aspiration but an expectation. Today's college-educated parents simply take it for granted that their children will go to college. To do anything else would be to step onto the down escalator that leads to a poor job, low income, the wrong friends, and a generally unacceptable way of life. Downward mobility, as we suggested earlier, holds far greater terrors than the mere

[103] For a discussion of this theme, see Turner, "Sponsored and Contest Mobility."

[104] On indifference or opposition to college aspirations among lower strata parents, see, e.g. Kahl and also Hyman.

frustration of upward mobility. Both parents and children will struggle to keep what they have far more fiercely than most outsiders will struggle to occupy the same ground.

This basic difference in motivation between the potentially mobile and the already arrived seems to us to explain far more of the variation in college entrance and graduation rates than theories that emphasize economic or cultural obstacles to mobility. Those who examine the problem too often forget that most children, regardless of class, find schoolwork difficult and unpleasant. They have no taste for irregular verbs, quadratic equations, the five principal products of Venezuela, or the five reasons for the end of the Middle Ages. Things might be rather different if schools were run differently, but even then we suspect the proportion who found study exciting or even satisfying would be limited. Those to whom schoolwork comes easily may acquire a taste for it, especially if they find other things more difficult and if they value the adult approval they can win this way. They may therefore do well and go on to college no matter what their background. But those who find schoolwork fairly difficult, which means the great majority even among the upper-middle class, keep at it only so long as the price of quitting seems even higher than the price of staying on. And as we have indicated, children from the lower strata are likely to feel they have passed the point of diminishing returns much earlier than children from the upper strata. The street cleaner's son who hates schoolwork can take a job, go on living at home, keep dating his girl friend, and hope for the best. The doctor's son who decides not to go to college will end up with an ulcer if he stays at home and allows his parents to make him feel guilty. So he goes to college—somewhere, somehow—and more often than not he even manages to graduate.

Yet important as these motivational differences may be, they do not seem to go very far toward explaining the *increase* in class influence on high school seniors' chances of college entrance and graduation. Little as they may like schoolwork, the majority of youngsters from all but the very lowest social strata now finish high school, and this trend has reduced the influence of class on high school graduation chances. Why, then, has the gap been widening at the college level? The natural and obvious answer is that college is expensive, but we have seen that the cost of attending a public college has not increased as fast as family income. In addition, public commuter colleges have become more widely available.

The problem can be viewed equally well from the top. Why is it that if we look at the sons of college graduates who finished high school between 1915 and 1925 we find that 40 per cent of them went directly to work without entering college, whereas if we look at sons of college graduates born thirty years later we find that only 10 per cent felt free not to enter college?[105] If downward mobility holds such terrors today, why was it not equally terrifying a generation back? Again, the "common sense" answer is that failure to earn a college degree was less certain to ensure downward mobility a generation ago than today. Yet as we have seen, the relative economic value of a college degree has not changed much since 1940. Yet the increase in the influence of parental education on college chances has been quite marked since then. And while there may have been some increase in the relation between college graduation and holding a prestigious or satisfying job, this too is unclear.

The numbers involved in this sort of inquiry are extremely tricky, and all sorts of hypotheses can be elaborated to explain them. After considering a good many alternatives we have concluded that the most plausible hypothesis—for which we have no statistical evidence—is that changes in the class composition of high schools, both public and private, during the past generation have led to differential changes in their impact on children from different sorts of families. The same may be true at the college level.

Since World War I there has been a steady increase in the proportion of lower-strata youngsters entering and completing high school. At least in the big cities, this influx has been accompanied by a middle-class flight to urban Catholic and suburban public schools, leaving many urban public high schools with almost uniformly working-class or lower-class students. These high schools manage to keep substantial numbers of their entrants on the premises through the twelfth grade, and in this way help narrow class differences in high school graduation rates. But they do not prepare many of their students academically for even the least selective colleges, nor does anything in their atmosphere encourage students to think college would be enjoyable. At the other end of the spectrum, the number of suburban high schools with overwhelmingly middle-class enrollments and precollege atmospheres is growing steadily. Class segregation, in short, seems to be more common at the secondary level than it once was, and this may lie behind widening class differences in high school seniors' college chances.[106]

A similar line of reasoning might also explain changes in the

[105] Bureau of the Census, *Current Population Reports* (1964), table IV.

[106] There is considerable evidence that high schools' class composition influences whether a given senior will apply to college. See, e.g. Rogoff; Wilson; Michael; Ralph Turner, *The Social Context*. For a contrary and in many ways persuasive view, however, see Sewell and Armer. See also the heated exchange between Turner, Michael, Sewell, and Armer. Sewell and Armer argue on the basis of Wisconsin data that the character of a high school has little influence on individual students' decisions to go or not to go to college.

pattern of college attrition. It could well be that the college system has become more stratified by class over the past generation, both because of the widening cost differential between private and public institutions and because of the growth within the public sector of state colleges and junior colleges as alternatives to the state university. If this is true, and if the class composition of a college has any effect on individual decisions to drop out, this might help explain why the disadvantaged are more likely to drop out today than a generation ago, while the advantaged are less so.[107]

Toward a More Open Society: Financial Reform

The previous sections have described three sorts of obstacles to upward mobility through higher education: costs, tests, and lack of interest and/or commitment. We now turn to some proposed reforms in these areas, asking in each case whether they would bring substantial increases in the mobility rate.

Students' money problems are probably the least important of the three and the most easily resolved. It would be relatively simple for a country as rich as America to pay all students subsistence and tuition allowances. It would not, however, be cheap. There were about six million students in American colleges and universities in 1966–67. They were charged almost $3 billion, or $500 apiece, for tuition. If we allow another $40 per week for subsistence during the thirty-eight non-summer weeks, we get a total cost of $2,000 per student, or a total of $12 billion. Even by American standards that is a good deal of money. Furthermore, if the government took over responsibility for financing higher education, enrollment would rise slightly—at least that is one of the primary arguments for such a program. Barring Draconian restrictions, tuition would also skyrocket. Even assuming this could be prevented without destroying the colleges' autonomy, and assuming no student transferred to a more expensive college, such an effort to transfer all present and potential private expenditures on college tuition and subsistence to the public treasury would still have meant quadrupling tax support of higher education in 1966–67.

[107] We have not been able to find any good statistical measure of changes in the extent of class segregation within higher education. Some suggestive evidence on the situation in the 1920s can be found in Reynolds, pp. 14–17. Recent data can be found in Astin, Panos, and Creager, "National Norms." Estimating the overall extent of class segregation from these sources would, however, be very risky. Nor do we know of any evidence as to whether a college's class composition affects a given student's chances of earning a degree. Still, barring data to the contrary it seems reasonable to assume that institutions such as junior colleges, in which most students drop out, create a climate in which it is relatively easier to do this than it would be in a selective private college where most students graduate.

Such a program has a certain superficial appeal, especially since it looks like a logical upward extension of public schooling. It differs from public schooling today in at least one respect, however. Whereas virtually everyone benefits from public schools, only a minority benefit directly from colleges. Not only are colleges used by a minority, but they are mainly used by an affluent minority which is probably better able to absorb the cost than the average taxpayer. A scheme of the kind we have just outlined might even have a regressive effect on income distribution. It might, that is, reduce upper-middle class expenditures on college more than it increased upper-middle class taxes, while increasing lower-class taxes more than it reduced lower-class expenditures.[108] Whatever its effect on income distribution, such a program seems politically inconceivable in the foreseeable future.

Two possible modifications of this proposal do, however, deserve more serious attention. First, a program of subsistence and tuition grants which included a means test would cost less, achieve more per dollar spent, and have a more benign effect on income distribution. The federal government now has a small program of Educational Opportunity Grants modeled along these lines. Unfortunately, political support for this sort of program seems to be limited to the more liberal Northern Democrats. The driving force behind public support of higher education has always been middle-class parents eager to send their children to college at less than cost. A program that provides no subsidies for such parents and instead increases the number of working-class and lower-class students who can compete with middle-class children for scarce college places has about as much political appeal as the negative income tax. Those whose interests it would serve have traditionally regarded higher education as a low priority item—probably with good reason, though this may be changing among Negroes.

A second variant on the financial theme is the scheme recently put forward by the Panel on Educational Research and Development of the President's Science Advisory Committee. This calls for the creation of a federally sponsored but self-financing Educational Opportunity Bank which would lend, rather than give, students as much money as they needed for subsistence and tuition at the college of their choice. Repayment would, however, be contingent on subsequent earnings as well as on the amount borrowed, so that no student would have to fear being saddled with a debt he could not pay.[109]

[108] Estimating the effect of tax subsidies for higher education on the living standards of various classes requires a number of debatable assumptions. Our best guess is that they have very little redistributive effect either way. For further discussion, see Jencks, "Social Stratification and Higher Education."

[109] This idea is not original, having been urged at various times and in various forms by such economists as Charles Killingsworth, Allan Cartter, William Vickrey, and Seymour Harris. It has been strongly opposed by some state universities, which want institutional grants. These do not expose their recipients to what economists lovingly refer to as "the discipline of the market."

Yet given the present political climate, even this relatively modest scheme is likely to get a cool reception in Congress. There may be some expansion of federally subsidized loans and part-time jobs, but many needy students are too ambivalent about higher education in the first place to enroll if these are their only sources of funds.

Under these circumstances individual institutions might be expected to take responsibility for giving needy students the same opportunities as affluent ones. Yet very few make serious effort to do this. Most simply make pious speeches about opening the gates of opportunity to all, and then subsidize all students they admit almost equally, regardless of need, by the simple device of keeping tuition below costs. For most poor boys this hardly provides enough help to matter. The typical private college could easily do better. It is true that most private colleges have very little endowment. But they do usually manage to raise appreciable sums over the years for bricks and mortar. Having done this they could amortize the buildings out of tuition receipts and use the resulting surplus for scholarships. Instead, most colleges simply keep tuition artificially low and tell themselves and the world that they would gladly give more scholarships if only they had more money. Most public colleges are equally egalitarian, using their tax subsidies to keep down tuition for everyone while making almost no effort to help needy students meet their subsistence expenses.

The alternative is obvious, and some institutions have pursued it. A college that wants to maximize social mobility can increase its charges until it has sufficient revenue to provide all needy applicants whatever financial help they need to get through. When it has done this such a college usually finds that most of its applicants still come from prosperous families, so bankruptcy is no threat. Yet we know fewer than a dozen colleges that follow such a policy. With the exception of the federal military academies, they are all private (e.g. Amherst and Berea). We would guess that perhaps fifty others, also private, come fairly close to this ideal, offering packages of scholarships, loans, and jobs large enough so that recipients can make ends meet, and setting standards for such help only slightly higher than their over-all admission standard.

Derelict as the majority of institutions may be in this area, the striking fact is that the more scholarships a college offers the richer its students are likely to be. (Berea is an exception.) Perhaps this proves that if a college gets a lot of rich students it raises tuition so high that even its middle-class applicants need (and therefore monopolize) help. Or perhaps it proves that colleges are generous to needy applicants only so long as they do not have very many of them. Or perhaps it proves that high tuition, while providing the income needed to finance a big scholarship program, scares away the very students who should benefit, and leads them to apply to cheaper colleges where they get less help and have higher out-of-pocket expenses. Or perhaps it is simply that institutions with strong Puritan heritages struggle to establish both high academic standards and generous scholarship programs, and the former attract rich students.

Observing this paradox some public-college men have concluded the best way to increase the number of college students from the lower social strata is to keep tuition down. Whatever its economic consequences, they argue, such a policy is at least visible and helps convince high school students they have a chance. Yet we can find little evidence that the market is even this rational. If, for example, we rank institutions by expenditure per student, we find that there is a very considerable relation between expenditures and parental incomes. But within any given expenditure group, tuition seems to have almost no effect on the parental incomes of the students who enroll. The rich, in other words, go to the affluent, prestigious, "quality" institutions, regardless of price. A good state university attracts them in about the same proportions as a reputable private college. Conversely, low income families send their children to poorer, less selective, less prestigious colleges, again regardless of price. A mediocre private junior college gets about as many students from poorer than average homes as a mediocre public junior college.[110]

Under these circumstances one can perhaps cling to the belief that money is the root of all problems, but not to the belief that it will cure this particular problem. Indeed, we are inclined to suspect that the main importance of money to most students today is symbolic. We have frequently been astonished to hear students explain that they decided to attend one college rather than another because they "got a better offer" from it. In most cases this turns out to mean that the college where they finally went offered them $100 or $200 more scholarship help than the others they were considering. Or it may mean they were offered a scholarship at one place whereas they would have had to take a $500 loan at another. These same students may later mention that the college they picked actually charges more tuition than the one they rejected, so that the difference in actual outlay is nil. Even if this is not the case, we are talking about differences of a few hundred dollars in an outlay that will add up to many thousands. Confronted with such logic, which in any long-term economic sense is plainly mad, we can only conclude that students are like shoppers trying to decide between two makes of automobile about

[110] On income distribution at various sorts of institutions, see Danière, "Cost Benefit Analysis," table 1.23. For comparisons of public and private junior colleges see Astin, Panos, and Creager, "National Norms."

which they really know nothing. They make elaborate calculations of where they will get the best bargain—not because the price difference matters, but because they feel their shrewdness is being tested and they don't want to be taken. Or perhaps a better comparison is with the professor who moves from one college to another for a $1,000 raise. He does not move because he needs the extra money; it will barely cover moving expenses. He moves because the extra money symbolizes extra status, and because his earlier college's refusal to match the rival offer seems to prove that his new suitor has a better appreciation of his merits.

Only in this context can one begin to understand why most colleges, despite considerable criticism from professionals in the financial aid business, continue to offer lots of small scholarships that cannot possibly be of real use to a poor boy instead of a few big ones that might make the difference between attending college and not attending. The small scholarships are not meant to help the needy; they are offered to middle-class students whom the college wants to recruit and who it fears will go elsewhere if they don't receive some token of the college's esteem. If legislators made more money available for such courting rites, the colleges might woo more boys who needed large-scale help. But this is not by and large their current practice.[111] Neither is their failure to offer more big scholarships the main reason lower-strata youngsters are so scarce on most campuses. Their withdrawal from the academic race usually rests on other considerations, as a look at attrition in free public high schools indicates.

Toward a More Open Society: Academic Reform

A second popular approach to increasing upward mobility is to alter the academic standards for college admission and graduation. This tactic seems to us even less likely than massive financial aid to bring significant improvements in the circulation rate. We say this with considerable regret, for we believe that traditional academic standards need to be modified for intellectual reasons discussed in subsequent chapters. We would therefore like to believe such changes would also increase social mobility. But we can see no evidence to support this hope.

Broadly speaking there are two things that can be done with academic standards. One is to change the "passing" grade on an existing test or set of tests. The other is to devise new tests which

[111] For a revealing survey of these practices see Nash, Nash, and Goldstein.

measure different things. We will take these alternatives up separately.

The genesis of the current round of questions about academic standards was the "discovery" in the early 1960s that there were virtually no Negroes in most supposedly integrated colleges. Once the civil rights movement, student activists, and conscientious administrators had made an issue of this, college admissions officers scurried off to predominantly Negro high schools looking for choice prospects. Within a year or two they were back with the news that there were very few brilliant, eager Negroes waiting in the wings. If selective colleges were to have more than a handful of black faces it was clear they would have to take students with lower aptitude scores and/or high school grades than their prospective white classmates. It was also clear, or soon became so, that unless these Negroes got special help they would have considerable difficulty keeping up with better prepared white classmates. An appreciable number of colleges took a small number of such students. The results varied. In some colleges, where the presumptively unqualified students got a lot of academic and extracurricular support, a substantial fraction survived. In others the mortality was very high. Armed with the results of a few such experiments, however, some civil rights militants began demanding wholesale reductions in admissions requirements, on the grounds that these requirements were little more than a screen for perpetuating white supremacy.

In a sense this is true, at least if "white supremacy" is taken to mean "bourgeois supremacy" or something similar. But wholesale reduction of college entrance requirements, unlike the selective reductions made up to now, would hardly achieve the revolution the militants want. Such changes would open the colleges in question to middle-class children of middling ability as well as poor children of middling ability. And there are more of the former than the latter. Indeed, by making it easier for the middle classes to get the credentials they need to hang onto power and privilege, a general reduction of college admissions requirements might easily *reduce* the mobility rate. Once meritocratic criteria were eliminated, insiders among the older generation would find it easier to make sure their children stayed in, while outsiders would have less basis for demanding access.

The reason for this can perhaps be best understood by considering what happened to American high schools. High schools once served somewhat the same function colleges now do, separating the more talented, diligent, and pliable from the less so. But as high school graduation became nearly universal the occupational value of diplomas diminished steadily. No employer was impressed by a credential every applicant could produce: it was like a birth certificate. The same cycle will be repeated when everyone graduates from college. Americans as a group might conceivably be wiser, more civilized, or more productive if they all went to college, but some would still be more competent than others. Not only that—employers would be anxious to discover which college graduates were more competent and which less so, and would give the best jobs to the former. If college degrees no longer distinguished the adept from the inept, some other equally crude litmus test, such as college grades or graduate degrees, would be used. Raising or lowering the academic cutoff point for college admission or graduation would, then, probably have no effect whatever on the mobility rate, because society would find other academic yardsticks to serve the purpose B.A.s now serve.

If manipulating cutoff points on existing tests will not improve the competitive position of the lower classes, what about devising new tests on which they might do better? In principle this approach is feasible, but it is fraught with practical difficulties. It is not enough, after all, simply to de-emphasize verbal ability and abstract reasoning; it is necessary to supplant these legacies of Gutenberg and Newton with some new set of educational and cultural ideals. These must be chosen so as to ensure the steady improvement in material conditions for which the present middle classes rightly claim credit, and yet must at the same time be such that the lower classes come closer to having their fair share of them. It is a rather tough order for a Sunday afternoon.

Various expedients have been tried. One is to emphasize athletic ability. This has enabled an appreciable number of otherwise unqualified boys from impoverished homes to complete college, and has given them access to the income if not always the life style of the upper-middle classes. Unfortunately, however, athletes like composers command a premium only if they rank at the very top of the ability distribution. Not only that—a social system built on athletic prowess has a number of problems, including increasing the discrimination against girls. A large-scale assault on academic standards requires something better.

A variety of other possibilities has been tried out over the years. For example, by building commuter colleges in some places but not others, America has made upward mobility somewhat dependent on where a child happens to live when he reaches eighteen. A lower-middle class youngster from a town with a commuter college has about the same college chances as an upper-middle class youngster from a town with no college nearby. The efficacy of this device for randomizing access to education is, however, temporary. The middle classes in deprived areas soon catch on and build their own colleges, restoring their basic advantage. Another possibility has been to make skin color per se a criterion for selection. This has always been widespread. For years many colleges favored whites over blacks. Now many favor blacks over whites. The latter practice obviously increases mobility rates to some small extent. The same general objective could be achieved by deliberately favoring applicants from working-class or lower-class background regardless of race, as the Russians and Chinese have to some extent done, and as Berea College does in a different way. This has the disadvantage of being expensive, since it requires a lot of scholarship money. If done on a large scale it is also likely to be unpopular, for it means prejudicing the applications of alumni sons, sons of legislators' friends, and so forth.

As the examples illustrate, criteria that conspicuously favor the mobile or potentially mobile outsider over the already arrived insider are easy to imagine but probably impossible to implement on a large scale. Indeed, we would state it as a general principle that no criterion for selecting an elite is likely to gain widespread acceptance in modern America if its primary or most obvious purpose is to increase mobility. Those who want to alter present standards will have to find other more compelling arguments, which are at least superficially connected with the well-being of society as a whole. It might be argued, for example, that colleges should put more emphasis on mathematical than verbal aptitude, since America needs more scientifically trained men to sustain economic growth, the arms race, and so forth. A shift in emphasis from verbal to numerical skills might in theory bring the incidental benefit of reducing the middle classes' advantage over the lower classes. In practice, it would have no such effect, since mathematical ability is as highly correlated with class as is verbal ability. But whatever the effect of such changes on mobility, that could not be the primary rationale. Rather, change would have to be justified in terms of *national* needs or the *general* welfare.

It is not impossible to imagine other changes in selection standards. It seems fairly clear that abstract reasoning and verbal skills are of paramount importance for only a small proportion of tomorrow's (or today's) workers, voters, mothers, etc. Big bureaucracies, for example, desperately need managers who can keep a large number of diverse personalities working in harmony. They find it much harder to get such men than, for example, lawyers who can rationalize and defend these managers' actions in terms of a predetermined code. One reason such managers are in short supply is that the high school senior who is good at getting people to do what he wants and at keeping them from each other's throats cannot get through college on that account. If he does not get through college he often cannot get the kind of job where his talents would be useful. One could therefore argue that America needed colleges where personal skills of this sort were valued more than verbal facility, and where students of this sort consequently felt comfortable and competent. This, in a sense, was what the old fraternity-dominated collegiate campus sought to achieve —though, lacking constructive adult support or direction, it seldom came very close to what we would like to see such a college attempt. In any case, a modern university or university college with a professionalized faculty cannot be persuaded to let such a student through unless he shows at least moderate competence in the usual academic field events. New sorts of colleges would have to be founded to teach such skills, new faculty found who valued them, and new species of alumni thus turned out. Similar efforts could also be made to establish colleges that cultivated entrepreneurial energy and confidence, creative and artistic imagination, and perhaps even moral vision, compassion, and solidarity. (Some women's colleges, especially a few Catholic ones, do strain in these directions, though their commitment to hiring faculties composed of Ph.D.s limits how far they can move from conventional academic standards of excellence.)

Yet desirable as such colleges might be on social, economic, political, and humane grounds, they would not necessarily increase the rate of social mobility; they might equally well decrease it. It is true that non-academic skills are distributed through the class structure in somewhat different ways than academic ones.[112] But there is no reason to assume that just because they are *differently* distributed they must be *more equitably* distributed. They could well be less so. This would be particularly likely if the non-academic skills to be measured and rewarded were chosen (as they almost inevitably would be) by upper-middle class educators, with an eye to the further development of a society already shaped by present upper-middle class skills and values.

This point can be put more graphically by looking at the few existing offbeat colleges that have de-emphasized academic competence in favor of other virtues. The Sarah Lawrences and Goddards and even the Wheatons[113] do not attract any significant number of upwardly mobile students who could not otherwise have broken into established institutions. They mainly attract upper-middle class students who are in some way at war with established institutions. If these colleges were abolished most of their students would go to more conventionally academic places. A few, however, might not try to get

[112] For evidence that even within the academic repertory some skills are more class-related than others, see Flanagan *et al., One Year Follow-Up Studies,* appendix E.

[113] We speak here of Wheaton in Illinois, not Wheaton in Massachusetts. For a discerning portrait of this enclave of Midwestern fundamentalism, see Hilberry and Keeton.

a B.A. at all, or would drop out after a year or two. For these students the offbeat college that values non-academic competence is an important "back door" entrée into their parents' social stratum—though very few of the students in question see it that way. Without such a college some of these students would eventually be downwardly mobile. With it, they may still be downwardly mobile to a limited extent, especially in their first years out of college, but in the long haul most will remain within the charmed circle. Far from increasing the rate of social mobility, then, anti-academic colleges may unwittingly help reduce it, by helping the children of the elite cling to their privileges and reducing the amount of room at the top for the upwardly mobile. Encouraging more traditional colleges to diversify their criteria of competence might have the same effect.

If this seems an idle fantasy, consider the case of the public junior college. These colleges are in many respects the embodiment of what advocates of social mobility should want. They seldom cost any more to attend than high school, and they seldom have significant admissions requirements. They offer a variety of curricula, including some designed for the academically unpromising student. The results are shown in Table VII, which gives the chances that a high school senior in a given ability quartile and a given socioeconomic quartile will enter a junior college the following fall.

TABLE VII

PROBABILITY THAT A HIGH SCHOOL SENIOR IN A GIVEN ABILITY AND SOCIOECONOMIC QUARTILE WILL ENTER JUNIOR COLLEGE THE FALL AFTER GRADUATION

Socioeconomic Quartile	Ability Quartile			
	Bottom	Third	Second	Top
MEN				
Lowest	.04	.06	.06	.13
Third	.05	.07	.11	.07
Second	.08	.09	.10	.08
Highest	.12	.16	.11	.05
WOMEN				
Lowest	.01	.05	.08	.08
Third	.06	.04	.09	.08
Second	.04	.06	.08	.08
Highest	.17	.10	.17	.05

SOURCE: Flanagan *et al., One Year Follow-Up Studies,* table 5–1. The data are for all junior colleges, but 80 per cent of all junior college entrants are at public institutions, and the income distributions are not markedly different at the two sorts of institutions. (Astin, Panos, and Creager, "National Norms.")

Contrary to popular mythology, it does not mainly seem to be the poor who go to junior colleges. The highest rates of enrollment are found among the affluent but academically inept. This is particularly clear if one compares Table VII to Table V. The two-year colleges are doing slightly more than their typical four-year counterparts to encourage social mobility, but their effect is by no means unequivocal.

The same can be said of new curricula within established universities. In general it is true that "non-academic" programs (e.g. business, education, engineering) get more than their share of upwardly mobile students. This is not, however, because they cultivate special aptitudes found primarily in the lower social strata. The skills required to do well in these programs are often as academic as those required to master Hittite grammar. (Physical education is an exception.) Tests that predict performance in physics seem, with some marginal exceptions, to predict performance in engineering equally well (or equally badly, depending on one's standards). The same is true of psychology and education, or of history and business. There are differences in temperament but not in the basic skills needed. In some cases the "non-academic" programs attract the upwardly mobile because they are easy: business and education have this appeal. But engineering is extremely competitive and works its students very hard. One reason all these programs appeal to first-generation collegians is that they seem to lead directly to a job—and jobs are understandably very much on the minds of the upwardly mobile. Beyond this, however, it would be hard to prove that the cause of social mobility and fluidity had been better served by education schools than by engineering schools, or by low academic standards than by high ones. Meritocratic standards, whatever their nature, seem to ensure a certain amount of mobility but no more.

Mobility or Equality?

If neither financial aid nor de-emphasizing academic competence promises much change in the outcome of competition between the advantaged and the disadvantaged, what does? One answer is that reform must come in the area where the previous section located the major cause of current disparity: the subjective attitudes of the competitors rather than the objective characteristics of the competition. Reformers must somehow deal with the fact that, popular mythology to the contrary notwithstanding, the poor outsider is not usually "hungrier" than the rich insider and is not usually willing to make greater sacrifices to achieve the same objective. On the contrary, it is the children of the upper-middle classes who are most likely to be "hooked" on power and privilege, or at least on the kind of work that leads to privilege, and who are most willing to do what must be done to feed this addiction.

Schools and colleges do sometimes make an effort to alter this pattern. A suburban school, for example, will sometimes try to persuade an upper-middle class family not to push its subnormal son toward college, and will try to counsel the child into a less demanding career. But parents usually take such advice very badly, and many schools are reluctant even to offer it. At the opposite end of the spectrum teachers and counselors usually make some effort to push their most talented students into college preparatory curricula and then into college itself, even if the child comes from a family where this is not expected.

Yet it seems clear that none of these efforts to prod from the outside has much effect: even dull children of the upper-middle class usually go to college anyway, and the adept children of the lower class, unless notably athletic or brilliant, still drop out in large numbers. In part, no doubt, this reflects the fact that the school itself is often half-hearted in its devotion to academic values. A well-spoken middle-class child who "just can't learn" still seems "nice" to his teacher, while a more sullen and less controlled working-class child who does equally good work may seem like a "troublemaker."[114] So the former is pushed into a program that will allow him to attend an unselective college, while the latter is given a hard time, made even more rebellious, and often eventually pushed out on the street. These non-academic standards of merit almost inevitably tend to favor the middle-class student over the upwardly mobile, though we have occasionally seen the opposite sort of bias too.

Yet the heart of the problem is not, we think, in the educational system. So long as the distribution of power and privilege among adults remains radically unequal, and so long as some children are raised by adults at the bottom while others are raised by adults at the top, the children will more often than not turn out unequal. In part this may be because parents with time, money, and the respect of their fellows can do a better job raising their children than the parents who lack those things. But the real point is that children raised in different circumstances necessarily have different hopes, expectations, and compulsions. We suspect that these differences account for more of the class variation in college chances than all other differences combined.

Such differences can be eradicated. America could commit itself, for example, to a kibbutz-like system of child rearing, in which all children would be raised communally and biological ancestry would

114 For evidence that somewhat similar non-academic biases are also at work in colleges, see Junius Davis.

count for relatively little. In its most extreme form such a system could virtually equalize life chances, making every child's future dependent on his genes. We do not think, however, that such a proposal would win much popular support in America, even among those whose children would presumably benefit. Rightly or wrongly, most Americans are convinced that children need to have someone around who is unconditionally and passionately devoted to them, someone who will love them not in the collective way that a good preschool teacher loves her charges but in the individual way that parents love their children. The experience of the kibbutzim suggests that this premise is probably oversimple and perhaps wrong, but it is not likely to be abandoned for that reason.

Failing such radical measures, what can we realistically hope to do? We suggested earlier that the rate of intergenerational turnover in the best-educated sixth of American men had fallen over the past generation from 62.2 to 60.6 per cent. This is hardly a significant difference. Yet the past generation has seen quite significant changes both in the relationship of college costs to incomes and in the devices colleges use to attract and select students. This suggests that mobility rates are not greatly affected by these variables. Reforms of the kind we have discussed—in college financing, school atmosphere, and the like—might conceivably raise the turnover rate in the educational elite to 65 per cent but even that is problematic.

Nor are we convinced that efforts to go beyond these modest limits would be particularly desirable unless they were accompanied by more fundamental changes in the character of American society. If adult wealth and power remain as unequally distributed as they now are, and if child rearing remains family based, increasing the rate of social mobility substantially above its present level could be a formula for misery. A mobile, fluid society in which men move up and down is simultaneously a competitive, insecure, and invidious society. The more we have of the one, the more we will have of the other.

This truth is often forgotten—nowhere more often, indeed, than in higher education. But it is fundamental. If, for example, colleges attracted as many applicants from the lower strata as they now do from the upper strata, the admissions scramble would become even more hectic than it is. There would be no more room at the top of the academic system, because the amount of room at the top is by definition limited. The "best" colleges are "best" precisely because they are competitive and exclusive. If they got more applicants they would not expand appreciably to accommodate demand, for that would jeopardize their elite standing. They would raise standards even further than they have already done, making it even harder for those who now apply (including the already upwardly mobile) to get in. Most professors would no doubt welcome such a development, on the ground that it was another step toward "a really first-rate student body." Corporate recruiters and professional schools would probably also be pleased, since it would facilitate their efforts to sift and screen talent. But if we were right at the outset when we suggested that downward mobility is usually more painful than blocked upward mobility, such a change might not do much for the sum total of human happiness.

Suppose, for example, that Yale must choose between two applicants. One is an obviously gifted boy from the wrong side of the tracks in Bridgeport. The other is a competent but unremarkable youngster whose father went to Yale and now practices medicine in New York. All right-thinking people assume that Yale should choose the first boy over the second. We agree. Nonetheless, this decision almost certainly causes more individual misery than the alternative. If the Bridgeport boy is refused a place at Yale and goes to the University of Connecticut (where he still has a fair chance of discovering a new world) or even to the University of Bridgeport (where this is conceivable if less likely), he will be disappointed but seldom shattered. The University of Connecticut is a smaller step up than Yale, but it may in fact more nearly fit his temperament if not his talents. The New Yorker who fails to make Yale and winds up at the University of Connecticut, on the other hand, will very likely feel himself branded a failure. Connecticut may suit his talent, but probably not his temperament. The verdict will seem doubly harsh for being just. The rejected Bridgeport boy can blame his fate on snobbery and feel it is not his fault but "the system." The New Yorker has no such defense.

In stressing the price of meritocracy we are not arguing for its abandonment. Efforts to accommodate the upwardly mobile have always been a crucial ingredient in economic growth. While it is in one sense true that the relative amount of room at the top is fixed so long as the distribution of wealth and influence is fixed, it is also true that the absolute amount of room is not fixed. Efforts to expand the amount of room at the top may come to nothing in relative terms, but they ensure that the absolute size of the system will keep growing. Incomes are constantly rising, unskilled jobs are being replaced by more skilled ones, and all this makes people feel they are better off even if their relative position is unchanged. In good part these changes take place because talented individuals insist on carving out new niches for themselves. The old elite is paid off—its income keeps rising and its influence declines slowly if at all—but upwardly mobile individuals create new parallel elites that share in the ever-larger pie. In a sense this means that the old elites are downwardly mobile, for their relative position is no longer unchallenged. But it is precisely their effort to maintain their old status, while somehow accommodating the more gifted and insistent outsiders, which forces expansion all along the line. If opportunities for upward mobility and the fear of downward mobility diminish, this kind of pressure for expanding and upgrading the over-all system diminishes correspondingly. Indeed, expansion may slow down or stop altogether. Contrary to what many people think, growth is not automatic; it is strenuous and sometimes painful. It is much easier for those who are already well off just to let things go on as they are. Complacent elites that feel their position secure tend to do just that. It is the hot breath of the upwardly mobile that keeps them running—though conscience plays a role too.

Nonetheless, there is a point of diminishing returns beyond which the advantages of meritocracy and mobility to society as a whole may no longer offset their disadvantages to individuals who fail to meet the test. We know no way of telling when a given society has reached that point. Viewed from the top there is always a shortage of talent, and hence an argument for encouraging still more youngsters to compete for elite jobs and life styles, even though no more can make it than in the past. From the bottom, too, there always seems to be a shortage of opportunity, and hence a reason for being even more ruthless in weeding out incompetents who owe their privileges mainly to their ancestry. Both views are correct, and one of the great virtues of meritocratic competition is that it fuses them is such a way as to keep the system as a whole expanding. Nonetheless, there seems to be something basically perverse and sadistic in trying to make society any more competitive and status conscious than it already is. If, to revert to our earlier example, there are talented boys who do not want to go to Yale and mediocre ones who do, is any useful purpose really served by recruiting the former and excluding the latter? It is one thing to say that men who want a given thing that is in short supply should be judged on their merits in deciding who gets it. It is something else to say that the demand for such goodies (and insofar as B.A.s are certificates of competitive rank, they are among them) should be deliberately intensified.

What all this suggests is that further efforts to increase mobility may be not only fruitless but undesirable. What America most needs is not more mobility but more equality. So long as American life is premised on dramatic inequalities of wealth and power, no system for allocating social roles will be very satisfactory. Genes may be somewhat better than parental status, but damning a man for having a low IQ is not in the end much better than damning him for having a black skin or a working-class accent. Furthermore, unless discrepancies in parental influence and life styles are reduced, the possibility of increasing mobility is in fact remote. Only if the elite knew that downward mobility could not involve falling very far would it be willing to tolerate the probability that its children would do less well than itself. And only if its influence were relatively limited could it be forced to tolerate such developments.

Whether education makes people more or less equal has not been much debated in recent years, though Jefferson and other pre-industrial political philosophers were much concerned with it. Yet it is in some ways the central political question posed by the academic revolution. Our tentative answer to it is that elites based on knowledge are likely to be somewhat larger, somewhat less exclusive, somewhat less powerful, and somewhat more responsible than elites based on property. And while the accumulators of property probably work as hard as the accumulators of knowledge in the first upwardly mobile generation, the children and grandchildren of property are less likely to keep at it than the children of expertise. Still, all this seems to be a difference of degree, not of kind. If, for example, we revert to income distribution as a measure of equality, it seems clear that the spread of education has not brought anything like a revolution. Yet it could be argued that the modest redistribution of income away from the top 5 per cent and toward the middle classes, that took place during the Depression and World War II was in some way casually related to the enormous jump in the median educational attainment of the young during the 1920s and 1930s. Conversely, it could be claimed that the stability of income distribution since World War II reflected the relatively slow rise in median attainment since then. If this hypothesis were correct—and we must emphasize that we are rather skeptical—it would provide a strong argument for attempts to make higher education as nearly universal as secondary education became a generation ago.[115]

Whatever the effects of education on the social structure, we find very little evidence that colleges are committed to reducing the intellectual inequalities among men and some evidence that they tend to increase them. A relatively small number of established institutions dominate American society, and colleges are understandably concerned with educating the men who seem likely to control these institutions. They may educate others because they cannot get their hands on the future elite, because they are not entirely sure who the future elite will be, or because it is politically expedient to mix students who will control established institutions with students who will merely work for and around them. But despite all these com-

[115] Another approach to measuring the effects of education on income distribution is to look at the distribution *within* groups of any given attainment. A few random calculations suggest that the income distribution among college graduates is considerably more equitable than among elementary school dropouts. What this means is by no means entirely clear.

plications and the ideological noise that accompanies them, the basic
fact is that future leaders are likely to get more attention than future
followers. Americans are virtually unanimous that potential doctors,
for example, both need and deserve more expensive education than
potential hospital orderlies (or even potential nurses); that prospective corporation executives require more expensive education than
prospective assembly line foremen; and that future legislators ought
to get a more expensive education than future voters. Nor is there any
real opposition from the academic profession itself, which has rarely
had the public schools' bias against ability grouping, honors programs,
and other devices for giving promising students special attention.
(Neither has the academic profession shared the school teachers' commitment to equality within its own ranks; professors rarely oppose
merit pay, for instance, whereas school teachers mostly do.)

Not even the critics of higher education seem to oppose this pattern
of recognizing and accentuating inequality. There are, it is true, some
who advocate a redistribution of educational resources. But their aim
is almost always to increase social mobility rather than to make
America a more classless society. They have no objection to spending
more on future doctors than on future orderlies. They simply object
to a system that spends more on the sons of *past* doctors than on the
sons of *past* orderlies. If given a "fair chance," they say, more children from poor families would be able to rise into the next generation's elite. They also argue that it is dangerous to try to decide too
early who has the ability to become a doctor. If resources are concentrated on those who show promise of joining the future elite while
they are still young, the much discussed "late bloomer" will never
bloom at all. But by accepting the basic premise that people with a
bright future need a better education than those with a dim future,
such critics also accept the present degree of stratification in society
and end up in arguments over statistical correlations and cost-benefit
ratios.[116]

The more radical critics of higher education seem equally uncon-
cerned about inequities in the distribution of educational effort. Many
are so allergic to the form and content of American education that
they believe in the moral superiority of dropouts. For them, the
young man who stays in school longest and gets the most intensive
training is the most victimized rather than the most favored member
of his generation. From this perspective the problem is not that

[116] Cost-benefit analysis need not, of course, support the status quo in all its
aspects. See Danière, "Cost-Benefit Analysis." But an economic analysis of educational "outputs" which assumes that present income differentials represent real
differences in productivity and which allocates educational resources on this
premise can hardly be expected to imply the need for radical changes in income
differentials.

"good" students get more and better education than "poor" ones, but that the good students seem to have a monopoly on the good jobs, while the poor students are condemned to poor jobs and low incomes. While radical critics would almost all like to see a more egalitarian society, they usually propose to achieve it by ignoring differences in individual competence rather than by reducing them.[117]

Our own guess is that universal higher education will diminish the economic or social differences among classes a little but not much. It must be remembered, however, that the universalization of college is also an attempt to spread what have traditionally been thought of as upper-middle class customs and concerns to people whose rank in the economic and occupational spectrum will remain lower-middle. In a superficial sense this effort is plainly succeeding. Even with far from universal higher education, many of those who have not been to college feel defensive and try to adopt the collegiate style. How deep this adaptation goes is problematic, however. We suggested at the outset that a great deal of what happens to undergraduates is anticipatory socialization. If a student realizes that he is not going to find a place in the upper-middle range of the social spectum, his assimilation of upper-middle culture may slow down or stop altogether. Furthermore, even if most students keep assimilating what we have called upper-middle class attitudes in college, they will retain mainly those that their adult life re-enforces. A college graduate whose income remains below the national average, for example, and whose occupational status makes him feel inferior to the majority of Americans, is likely to have great difficulty maintaining the kind of self-confidence and self-respect that often seem to undergird upper-middle class ideals. If that is the case, it may be theoretically impossible for many aspects of upper-middle class behavior to spread to the whole society. Those on or near the bottom may, simply by dint of their position and regardless of education, need their own special style to protect them from the consequences of their situation.

Another reason for doubt about universal higher education's chances of spreading upper-middle class values is the growth of predominantly lower-middle and working-class commuter colleges which seem to do comparatively little to alter the habits and attitudes students bring to them. These colleges enroll many of their students only part time; they create almost no social community outside the classroom; and they encourage students to regard higher learning as a commodity,

[117] There are exceptions: men who care enough to work with any student because he is there, often out of some religious commitment, and other men whose idiosyncratic values lead them to concentrate their efforts on students who are athletic, charming, wealthy, pretty, or whatever. But the student who counted on any of these things to get him attention or help would usually be disappointed.

acquired in the same impersonal ways as groceries or lingerie. In some of these colleges, especially the two-year ones, the faculty does not even try to change the customs and concerns of its students, and the students themselves come without expecting such a change to take place. Together, such students and teachers may conspire to make college no more than a continuation of secondary school. Academic standards may be higher, "homework" assignments may be longer, but the basic pattern of authority and passivity can remain unchanged. Such a college may (and should) transmit technical skills and thus help its students move into professional jobs, and it may in this way also encourage them to move into a new subculture. But only in this indirect sense is it likely to affect students' view of themselves or of society. As the demand for higher education becomes more widespread and the tax burden climbs, politicians will be increasingly tempted to channel as many students as possible into these presumptively (though not always actually) cheap public commuter colleges.

This means that universal higher education, while in some ways helping to blur class differences, may also legitimize and freeze them by giving all sorts of youngsters the outward parity of the B.A. Our over-all feeling is that homogenization is proceeding faster than differentiation, but this is a very tentative and impressionistic judgment. Our feeling rests primarily on our sense that at the faculty level all but the junior colleges are caught up in the academic revolution. Yet the relative similarity of adult objectives at different colleges may not matter as much as we think. The student culture is a prism giving faculty pressures different meanings from one campus to another. From a student's viewpoint a public commuter college is a very different milieu from a private residential college, and the fact that the faculty say the same sorts of things may be relatively unimportant compared to the fact that most of a student's classmates hear what the faculty say in different ways on different campuses. We think that colleges have more in common than their constituencies do, and tend to make their constituencies more alike, but this would be hard to prove quantitatively.[118]

Be that as it may, it is at least clear that universal higher education and the academic revolution will not contribute to the emergence of an egalitarian, classless society in the same relatively clear-cut way that they contribute to the emergence of a non-sectarian, ethnically homogenized, nationally organized, and in some ways sexually undifferentiated one. The next few chapters will take up these themes.

[118] For a review of literature that draws this conclusion among others, see Jacob.

IV. *Nationalism versus Localism*

With the possible exception of sectarian fission, geographic isolation has probably been the most common reason for founding a new college in America. Ever since colonial times states and cities have been unhappy about depending on colleges located beyond their physical and cultural boundaries. All states and many cities have therefore set up their own institutions "responsive to local conditions." Local boosters can thus be viewed as a special-interest group, analogous to the professions, the income groups, the sex groupings, the denominations, and the ethnic groups that founded most of America's other colleges. Like most of these other special-interest groups, moreover, localists have found that the rise of meritocratic national institutions has somewhat undercut their initial cultural and ideological base, making localities somewhat more like one another and making mobility between localities more common. The localists have also found that instead of remaining responsive to local conditions their colleges have in many cases been taken over by academicians with no local roots or commitments. Many local colleges have thus become national and even international in outlook, losing touch with those who founded them. For all these reasons we have been tempted to treat the local college as just another legacy of nineteenth-century pluralism, analogous to the teachers college, the women's college, or the church college, and doomed to extinction as the academic profession with its anti-local outlook tightens its hold on higher education.

Yet for a variety of reasons this seems somewhat premature. It is true, for example, that the number of young men and women attending college outside their home state has risen steadily over the years. But the number attending college within their home state has risen at almost exactly the same rate, so that the proportion of students attending college outside their home state remains remarkably stable.[1] Similarly, most private colleges are becoming more na-

[1] In 1934, about 2.5 youngsters in 100 attended college outside their home state. In 1963, it was about 7 in 100. But in 1934 only about 12 per cent of all young people entered college, whereas in 1963 it was about 37 per cent. Of those who go to college, about 1 in 5 has attended college outside his home state since World War I. (Data on total enrollment are from the 1960 *Census*, I, 1, table 68. Data on migration were supplied by the U. S. Office of Education.)

tional in their recruitment of faculty and students and in their financial support. But private colleges enroll a diminishing proportion of all students. The growth of higher education is concentrated in colleges under state and municipal control, and these colleges still recruit students mainly from their own geographically delimited tax jurisdiction. Two-year municipal colleges, which enroll a growing proportion of all students, often even recruit their faculty locally. Localism, in short, is not dead. Nor does the increasing dependence of all colleges on federal tax subsidies seem likely to kill it, especially since continued urbanization is making local commuter colleges accessible to more students. The cumulative result is that both nationalization and localization are proceeding simultaneously.

The Early Localists

Geographic considerations were critically important to the establishment of new colleges in the colonial era. While the founders of Harvard College were eager to preserve their posterity from the Anglicanism of Cambridge and Oxford and from what they regarded as the generally lax morals of those towns, the settlers who subsequently sent their children to Harvard probably cared less about such matters. Many would presumably have sent their children to Oxford or Cambridge had these institutions been on the right side of the Atlantic; they chose Harvard because the journey was cheaper and safer, and it cost less to maintain a son in Massachusetts than in England. While doctrinal considerations were never altogether irrelevant, they were probably of secondary importance to Harvard's early survival and growth.

A mixture of sectarian and geographic considerations influenced the founding of other colonial colleges too. While William and Mary was Anglican in contrast to Harvard's Congregationalism, its main appeal was its location within a few days' ride of most Virginia plantations. Some of the Connecticut settlers who established Yale wanted to create an orthodox alternative to Harvard's increasingly liberal views and a small-town alternative to life near the fleshpots of Boston, but some merely wanted to have a college that would be more accessible than Harvard. This pattern was repeated throughout the English colonies. The primacy of geographic considerations is underlined by the fact that each Northern colony had one college, but despite sectarian feuds in every colony, only New Jersey had two colleges.

Although the Revolution led to a measure of political unification among the colonies, efforts by George Washington and others to establish a national university in the District of Columbia came to nothing. One major obstacle appears to have been the opposition of sectarian interests, none of which could expect to control the proposed institution, and all of which opposed a non-sectarian one. Yet these same attitudes did not prevent the establishment of nominally non-sectarian local colleges, beginning with the University of Pennsylvania and continuing after the Revolution throughout the South and Midwest. This suggests that the decisive obstacle to creating a national university was not the hostility of sectarian interests but the preference of local spokesmen for local institutions. Even those men who cut a national swath and helped form the national government were for the most part committed to what they called a federal rather than a national system. They were no more enthusiastic about a national university than about any other central institution. There were a few patrician families in the South that were dissatisfied with local opportunities and sent their sons north to Princeton or even Yale, but they were evidently not sufficiently numerous to create an avowedly national college for their sons. Similarly, there were settlers in the Midwest eager to shore up their ties with the seemingly cosmopolitan Seaboard by sending their sons "back East" to college. But these men (frequently clergymen) were for the most part loyal to their particular alma mater, not to any larger vision of national as against local higher education. They talked often about nation-building, patriotism, and shaping the American character, but they usually saw this as a missionary or imperial task, symbolized by Yale's sending its alumni to the Midwest to spread light and learning. The idea that Yale, or any other college, ought instead to recruit beyond the Alleghenies and be a melting pot for accommodating and reorienting students with diverse local and regional identifications seems to have come later.

So instead of a national system of higher education, America got a Balkanized pattern that made even the decentralized and polycentric German approach look orderly and monolithic. Each new American state felt impelled to assert its own autarchy and establish its own college. This tendency was encouraged by Congress's setting aside federal land to support a college in each new state. Later the Morrill Act (1862) provided that each state set up its own separate institution.[2] So far as we can discover nobody even considered the possibility that several states should be required to collaborate in establishing land-grant colleges—though it was clear that many states were too small to support a college of what we would now regard as efficient

[2] For a discussion of the role of federal land grants in the establishment of state colleges before the Morrill Act, see Rivlin, pp. 9-14.

size. Nor did the establishment of separate colleges in each state exhaust the claims of localism. There were also geographic divisions *within* every state, and even before the Morrill Act most states had not one but half a dozen colleges (though usually only one under state control).

Localism was to some extent merely a function of the difficulty, danger, and expense of travel. But in most instances it also involved sectarian, ethnic, and economic differences in viewpoint. Since this was an era when there were nearly as many would-be college presidents and would-be college towns as would-be college students, new institutions exploited all these differences and potential conflicts to attract students from their too-numerous competitors. Local boosters might want a college primarily because it would be built on a piece of land they wanted to sell, or because it would bring it outside money in the same way that a prison, a county courthouse, a railroad junction, or a paper mill would, but they eventually discovered that students would come only if the college had other virtues also. Thus propagandists played on local and regional patriotism, work opportunities, easy credit, low travel costs, and any other selling points they could devise.[3]

One persistent theme in these appeals to state and local loyalty was the dialectic between "Eastern" and "Western" values. The men who went into the Midwest to found colleges were missionaries in spirit if not always in name. They saw themselves as civilizing the wilderness, bringing the benefits of Eastern and especially New England culture to the newly settled communities. At times this impulse was directly linked with the dissemination of a particular brand of Christianity; at times it was non-sectarian and reflected a commitment to the humanistic classical tradition. In either case it led to the establishment of Eastern-style colleges.

Some of the settlers, on the other hand, did not want their children "Easternized," disliked what they regarded as Eastern snobbery, and distrusted the Old World morality, culture, and politics that they thought the Eastern colleges propagated. While generally hostile to the Eastern curriculum and outlook, however, Westerners took a long time to invent a substitute. As a result, most of them forewent college entirely during the nineteenth century. The minority who did patronize colleges wanted higher education primarily in order to help them get on in one of the more traditional polite occupations, such as the ministry, the law, medicine, or perhaps banking. College was not, however, a prerequisite for any of these careers in the West. Perhaps

---

[3] For a discussion of local boosterism and its relation to college founding, see Boorstin, chap. 20.

what Western parents really wanted was a college that would enable their sons to deal on equal terms with Easterners. Presumably
such parents were sufficiently the products of Eastern values to assume
that this meant mastering an Eastern curriculum. Be that as it may,
the handful of innovative educators who tried to develop alternatives
to the classical curriculum in the West got nowhere. It was not until
after the Civil War, when the classical curriculum began to give way
even in the East, that its opponents in the West began to find students
eager for an alternative.[4]

This does not mean that there were no variations in the pattern of
higher education from East to West or North to South before the Civil
War. But the most important geographic differences among colleges
at that time were probably based not on regional ideology but on the
urban-rural split within states. A college like Harvard, for example,
was identified in the minds of many families with the "advanced"
views of the Boston Brahmins. It attracted students from small towns
and farms all over Massachusetts (and to some extent from all over
the country) who thought they would prefer an urbane atmosphere
to the suffocating orthodoxy of their own locality. On the other hand,
it repelled believers in traditional theology and the old rural virtues,
including many Bostonians. Such families turned to rural colleges,
such as Amherst and Williams, even when they themselves were
committed to urban life. The same dichotomy appears to have arisen
in Pennsylvania with the urban University of Pennsylvania playing
a role analogous to Harvard's. Dickinson, Franklin, and later La-
fayette and Lehigh got students not just because their physical location was convenient and accessible to certain rural and small-
town families but because their location symbolized a style of life
many families in Philadelphia thought desirable for their children,
even if they themselves had to some extent given it up. Similar considerations helped make colleges like Dartmouth and Hamilton popular even outside their own states.

Yet these were the exceptional cases. The typical pre-Civil War
college, urban or rural, was quite unknown fifty miles from its campus.
When it flourished (or, more commonly, when it merely survived)
this was not usually because it stood for a unique set of objectives,
but because the founders had had the good judgment to locate the
college in an area that proved prosperous, in which a few rich benefactors came its way, and in which tuition-paying students were relatively numerous. With local ties so important, most colleges found
it difficult to "specialize" along sectarian, ethnic, class, or pedagogical

[4] For a discussion of the initial rise of scientific studies in the East before the
Civil War and the later development of scientifically based occupational curricula
in the land-grant colleges both East and West, see Rudolph, chaps. 11 and 12.

lines. If the neighboring area was overwhelmingly Congregational, German, agricultural, or conservative, the college reflected this fact. But if the area was heterogeneous, the college usually felt obliged to be likewise. Only a handful of colleges were sufficiently famous to define their clientele primarily in non-geographic terms.

The Rise of National Professions

In the years after the Civil War both businesses and professions became more national, and a number of local colleges added nationally oriented graduate schools to serve these callings. The local orientation of some undergraduate colleges was consequently attenuated, though seldom eliminated.

The importance of professionalism in undermining localism is suggested by the fact that the first truly national institution of higher education was the Military Academy founded at West Point in 1802. Congressional appointments gave it a degree of "geographic distribution" unequalled even today outside the service academies. The events of 1860–61 showed that this system was not in itself enough to create a national profession, for at that time the first loyalty of most Southern officers proved to be to their native states rather than to national institutions. But those who, like Robert E. Lee, had shared the experience of West Point with Northerners, rather than attending the Virginia Military Institute or The Citadel in South Carolina, seem to have found it very difficult to support state against nation.

In the last quarter of the nineteenth century a number of nonmilitary professions began to develop on a national rather than local basis. This was most conspicuously true of the academic profession, which was national and even international from the very start. Until the late nineteenth century there had hardly been an academic profession at all; once it came into existence, however, its stress on research made it inevitably cosmopolitan rather than local in outlook. As colleges became universities and began to attract and encourage creative scholars, certain faculties acquired national reputations for competence in particular fields. Places like Hopkins, Clark, Harvard, Columbia, Chicago, and later Michigan, Wisconsin, Minnesota, and California were recognized as providing training for the future college professor that was qualitatively different from that available in local institutions. Idealistic young men came to these universities because they promised to open intellectual windows that would otherwise stay closed. In addition, it became increasingly common for a local institution, impressed by the professional reputation of these universities, to hire their Ph.D.s in preference to its own B.A.s This further encouraged local boys with academic aspirations to spend at least a few years at a nationally known university.

In due course, future doctors and engineers were also subject to similar pressures. Once institutions like Johns Hopkins and MIT developed national reputations, they attracted intellectually ambitious young men who wanted to do what nobody had yet done or yet knew how to do. In due course, moreover, their graduates began to win preference in competition for certain kinds of work, so that attending a place like Hopkins or MIT became advantageous for the most pragmatic careerist as well as the idealists. Even in law, a largely locally oriented profession, Harvard and a few other places established national reputations that attracted students who did not come from nearby or plan to practice there. The cumulative result was the creation over half a century of a national market for both graduate students and faculty.[5] It is true that this market does not embrace *all* institutions or *all* graduate students. There are still a number of students, notably school teachers, who attend a local college and then do some graduate work at a similar place. The institutions that serve these students are seldom universities in the sense of having "productive" faculties, or in the sense of having large Ph.D. programs. But they give a lot of M.A.s and sometimes also M.D.s and LL.B.s.

As universities begin to define their responsibilities in national terms, their need to accommodate themselves to local pressures diminishes. In due course this leads to a breakdown of economic ties with the surrounding community, which has an understandably limited interest in supporting abstruse research and training programs for students who come from all over and are unlikely to stay. Only nationally oriented philanthropists and the federal government have a logical reason to support the more esoteric professional specialties. (To be sure, the desire for visibility, local generosity, and individual whim has frequently led to local support for some "useless" academic specialty. Despite the general tone of this chapter, not all localism is provincial or narrow-minded, any more than nationalization always leads to disinterested patronage or a long-term perspective.)

In principle, national financing for the leading graduate schools

[5] In 1963 only 26 per cent of all graduate students said they were from out of state (20 per cent from other parts of the United States and 6 per cent from foreign countries). Thirty-four per cent of all students seeking graduate professional degrees said they were from out of state (32 per cent from other parts of the United States and 2 per cent from foreign countries). See *Residence*. These figures are misleading, however, for many graduate students, especially married ones, give their local apartment, not their parents' home, as their "permanent address." The number of graduate students whose parents live in other states is probably closer to a half than a quarter.

should perhaps have begun in the late nineteenth century, when their clienteles became national and they began to develop specializations that could be justified only as national rather than local services. But it did not happen this way. The Morrill Act was not expanded as it might have been to support programs in medicine, law, pure science, the arts, or corporate administration. And while a few philanthropists like Rockefeller put their money into setting up universities like Chicago and Johns Hopkins, this remained atypical. Instead, support for graduate professional programs continued to depend largely on state legislatures, nostalgic alumni, and tuition-paying students. Only since World War II have the federal government, a few big corporations, and national philanthropic ventures like the Ford Foundation begun to take major responsibility for financing national graduate schools.

Recent as this development is, however, almost all major universities have today recognized the federal government and the major foundations as the most promising potential sources of extra funds for graduate programs and research. This has inevitably accentuated the professional impulse to pursue exclusively meritocratic production-oriented policies, which impress leaders in national centers of power, rather than responding to the parochial claims of local politicians, donors, or vigilante groups.

Such changes have been less rapid and less dramatic at the undergraduate level. Although national graduate programs were almost always grafted onto local colleges, either public or private, the administrators of the new universities were long reluctant to attack localism head-on at the undergraduate level.[6] They have assumed that local financial support depended primarily on the orientation of the undergraduate program and have tried to keep this harmonious with local needs and expectations even while the graduate programs took on a radically different character. This has been particularly characteristic of the better state universities, which recruit most of their undergraduates from within their state while getting graduate students from everywhere.[7] In part this has been because the public universities have had fellowships and assistantships to support out-of-

[6] There were perhaps a few exceptions. Both Yale and Princeton outgrew their tiny native states early in the nineteenth century and both drew students not only from New York but from the South and West. This happened before they became universities in the modern sense. The same may have been true of some other colleges.

[7] In 1963, 34 per cent of all graduate students in public universities *said* they came from out of state, compared to 14 per cent of all undergraduates. These figures understate the real differences for reasons given in footnote 5, plus the fact that students at public universities have an interest in claiming to be local and thus paying lower tuition. See *Residence.*

state graduate students. In addition, some have waived out-of-state tuition or allowed graduate students to establish nominal residence in the state to avoid these fees. These incentives were not usually available for out-of-state undergraduates at public colleges. But the same pattern was repeated in private universities too. Locally oriented undergraduate programs provided recruits for the graduate school, alumni to support the university, teaching jobs for graduate students, tuition to help pay a scholarly faculty, and a link with the local community that was both politically and economically useful. This kind of symbiosis arose even at the three universities that originally hoped to resist it by operating as national graduate schools: Catholic, Clark, and Hopkins. Perhaps one could even trace the relative decline of these three institutions at the graduate level to financial problems stemming from their failure to develop strong undergraduate programs and reputations.

It was far easier to preserve localism at the undergraduate than at the graduate level, for college life was often expected to place more emphasis on social and cultural experience than on professional training. But there was continual interplay between the two levels, and this tended over the long run to create pressures of nationalization of undergraduate life. At first this process affected only the kinds of training offered undergraduates—training that reflected the diverse backgrounds of the faculty and took national rather than local needs as the common denominator. But what began in the nineteenth century as an effort to prepare alumni for life anywhere in the country ended up in many twentieth-century cases as an effort to recruit applicants from everywhere in the country. Especially since World War II a number of undergraduate colleges, some attached to national universities and some independent, have begun self-consciously to seek a national constituency. The number of undergraduate institutions that draw the majority of their students from outside their own region is, however, still modest. Probably no more than a hundred have well-developed national recruiting networks for non-athletes. Some others, especially those with distinctive ethnic or sectarian traditions or professional reputations, attract significant numbers of students from far away without systematic recruiting. Yet even colleges that get their students from nearby often get their faculty from all over and shape their students' ambitions so that they spread out across the country once they have their B.A.s. One might label colleges of this kind, which serve as switching points from local to national orbits, as seminational.

National recruiting of students was seldom designed to achieve geographic mixing per se. At the graduate level, the aim was rather to collect the ablest possible group of students, from whatever source. Only a few colleges, notably in the Ivy League, felt that a student from an underrepresented area would add something important to undergraduate life even if he was not brilliant, and that he should therefore be given preference over abler students from overrepresented areas. (This kind of thinking is much more common with regard to foreign students, which suggests something about the extent to which America now thinks of itself as a homogeneous part of a heterogeneous world.)

So long as national recruiting was a means rather than an end, the geographic distribution of students at national colleges remained quite spotty. Much depended on what kinds of excellence the recruiters went out looking for. Football and basketball coaches usually cast their nets wider and finer than admissions officers whose concerns were primarily social or academic. Certainly very few national colleges recruited in the South, or in rural areas outside the South, except in search of promising athletic material. Those colleges that have been primarily interested in scholars or well-rounded student leaders recruited mainly in the big cities and suburbs, especially in the Northeast, Midwest, and California. If they got students from elsewhere—and of course they often did—these usually applied unsolicited, or because of accidental contact with an alumnus or current student. Recently these same national colleges have also begun to seek out Negroes, and have sent recruiters for the first time into "low yield" black high schools where they are likely to find only one or two possible applicants. Low yield white high schools in, say, small-town Iowa or Georgia remain almost untouched. With limited resources it makes more sense to hit the schools where a substantial number of students may be interested, and these are mostly in or near large urban areas.

In the past generation something approaching a national market has developed for students who are in the top 1 per cent and to a lesser extent the top 5 per cent of their age grade academically, as well as for the smaller minority who are, say, in the top tenth of 1 per cent athletically, artistically, or charismatically. Instead of merely attending the nearest denominational institution, their parents' school (if any), or the state university, the most promising high school graduates are now often solicited from all directions. Recruiters and national publicity have made students in many places conscious of the fact that they might apply to MIT or Cal Tech, to Harvard or Stanford, to Oberlin or Haverford, to Michigan or Berkeley. Many colleges and universities send enticing brochures to all National Merit Scholarship winners and finalists; Michigan State University and Macalester College offer such people scholarships.[8] In general, the big scholarships go principally to outstanding scholars and athletes, and increasingly to a few outstanding Negroes, but the stir made by the recruitment of these individuals affects the rest of the college-bound population and even increases the size of that population. At the same time, one should not forget that the stir fails to touch many other students. The irrationality of the academic market place—its dependence on accidental contacts and miscellaneous reading—should be constantly borne in mind in weighing our account of the few stable and predictable elements we have found.

Non-Meritocratic Nationalization

In general, the colleges that have gone farthest in escaping localism are those whose claim to distinctiveness rests on their academic standing, their capacity to prepare students for top graduate professional schools, and their general reputation for training (or at least enrolling and certifying) future "leaders" in business, the professions, and recently government. Far fewer colleges have been able to rely on sectarianism, ethnicity, sex, or class as a basis for recruiting outside their own locales. Yet these exceptions add up to a considerable number when taken together, and so deserve some scrutiny.

At first glance it may seem puzzling that, having blocked the establishment of a non-sectarian national university, no post-Revolutionary group created a sectarian one. But none did. Every denomination seems to have accepted the inevitability of localism in its colleges even though some fought bitterly over the establishment of national seminaries. The denominations themselves were often split along geographic lines and were in some cases little more than federations of local clergymen. Each encouraged the would-be educators among its clergy to set up colleges wherever a clientele could be found—and in many places where they merely hoped the presence of a college would create a clientele. These colleges, in turn, gave the local or regional variant of their denomination additional legitimacy and autonomy vis à vis other groups of the same nominal persuasion.

The most significant exception to this general pattern was perhaps

<hr>

[8] David Ricks of Teachers College, Columbia University, in an unpublished paper describes the effect on him as a small-town high school senior in a Mountain state of winning a National Merit Scholarship. This altered his horizons completely and changed his life, making it legitimate for him to aspire to go beyond the local state college. It gave him a new confidence in himself, as well as an excuse for leaving behind his friends, who were going to the local college, to work, or into the army.

the Catholic Church, which founded Catholic University in 1889 as the first national sectarian institution. Even Catholic, however, was not designed to help parochial school graduates escape their parish, but to upgrade the professional skills of priests and nuns who taught in Catholic colleges. It was therefore national only at the graduate level. (Even at that level, its reputation among Catholics was in due course eclipsed by Notre Dame and the better Jesuit universities.)

Another exception to the general pattern of sectarian localism was Brigham Young, which, while largely Utah-based and oriented, drew together Mormons from all over the world. Some smaller sects have rejected localism simply because there are not enough of their faithful in any one place to support a college. Many Seventh Day Adventists, for example, while eager to keep their children as near home as possible, preferred sending them away to having them attend a local, non-Adventist college. The result was the creation in the late nineteenth century of a network of small regional institutions such as Atlantic Union and Pacific Union. These enabled the Adventists to avoid the multiplication of the equally tiny and even more local institutions that scattered the energies and resources of nineteenth-century Congregationalists, Presbyterians, Methodists, and Baptists. Perhaps this is because the Adventists were more confident than the better-established and less fervent sects that their faithful would travel several hundred miles to attend an appropriate sectarian college. Or perhaps it was because by the end of the nineteenth century Americans were beginning to feel that a place called a college had to meet certain minimal academic and physical standards, and it was therefore impossible to justify a college of less than a certain size, even on the grounds of convenience and orthodoxy. (Almost all the Adventist colleges today have at least five hundred students.) Yet respect for academic competence has not led the Adventists to emulate the Catholics or Mormons in establishing a national university to compete with comparable secular institutions. No doubt this is partly because Adventists are, or feel, too poor to send their children a thousand miles to college. The regional network puts the majority of Adventist families within less than a day's drive of one of their colleges, and often makes coming home for weekends feasible.

Among ethnic minorities, too, localism has carried considerable weight. A few Negro colleges like Fisk draw from all over the country, but most do not. The Irish, Polish, and French-Canadian brands of Catholic college have also usually been local. Yeshiva is national, but its appeal is really to the sectarianism of Orthodox Jewry rather than to the ethnic loyalty of Jews in general. Brandeis is also national, but then it is only ambivalently Jewish.

Among colleges catering to a particular social class, those with aristocratic pretensions have usually been more national and also international in their recruitment than those catering especially to lower-income families. In part this has been because the comparatively well off are more likely to feel that they can afford to travel some distance for the "right" college. In part it is because such families know more about colleges in general and are less likely to assume that the nearest is as good as any other. Then, too, low-income students usually work part time when attending a college, and jobs are often easier to find in one's own home town. The less affluent students are also more likely to attend publicly subsidized institutions that discourage non-locals from applying. Conversely, colleges with an upper-class outlook have seldom been able to recruit enough "suitable" students locally, and have had to mix the children of disparate elites to fill their classrooms.

We have already mentioned that Yale and Harvard and presumably other Northern colleges attracted some Southerners before the Civil War. This was probably more because of their social than their intellectual traditions. After 1861, most Southerners stopped coming North. But their places were taken by Midwestern students whose fathers were reaping the profits of industrial and commercial expansion and wanted their sons' education to establish them as equals of the emerging East Coast elite. This elite, while in some ways parochial, seldom had deep local roots or loyalties. It moved with comparative ease between the various capitals of Seaboard gentility and sent its children to a handful of Eastern liberal arts colleges, many of which were later to become known as Ivy League institutions. The institutions in question thus got a measure of geographic distribution at the undergraduate level even before their faculties acquired much national reputation.

Academic elitism has, however, increasingly supplanted social (and athletic) elitism as a basis for national recruiting. There are fewer and fewer nationally known colleges that retain modest admissions requirements. (Parsons College in Iowa is an ambiguous exception.) A student with low grades and low test scores must, in most cases, attend a locally oriented college, which has few scholars on its faculty, prepares few of its students for graduate work, and provides comparatively limited access to established national institutions. (This varies from state to state. State universities with distinguished faculties tend to have fairly high admissions requirements, but this is not universally so, especially among the Big Ten schools.) Families that have always lived and worked in a local milieu accept the appropriateness of these local colleges for their children, and some even prefer them to a national institution. But families that are part of the upper-middle class usually realize that attending an unknown local college is a first step toward downward social mobility for their children. Knowing this, those with academically inept children search desperately for colleges with a national reputation that will take (and keep) average or below-average students. Almost without exception, however, colleges that acquire any such reputation parlay it into higher admissions standards and more emphasis on academic achievement. A college like Kalamazoo, for example, having developed a first-rate program for exposing its Midwestern students to alien ideas and influences (through overseas programs, non-Western studies, and the like), soon developed a national reputation and began attracting students from New York and other Eastern states.

This process has gone further in women's than in men's colleges. A number of Easter women's colleges were founded in the second half of the nineteenth century as female counterparts to the upper-class men's colleges. Like their brother institutions, they drew students not from their immediate area but from the great Eastern cities and their new suburbs. But the feminists who played such an important role in founding and staffing these colleges were seldom content with social elitism. They were committed to academic excellence, and they recruited faculty and students accordingly. Like their male counterparts, these colleges have today placed themselves beyond the academic reach of a large part of the national elite. As this happened, the daughters of the elite began to apply to what were previously local or regional women's colleges—places like Wheaton in Massachusetts or Hollins in Virginia. In due course, however, the "second-choice" or "spill-over" institutions have been able to raise their academic standards to nearly the level of the "Heavenly Seven." More and more of them are open only to the unusually bright. The duller daughters of wealthy, nationally oriented families are therefore under increasing pressure to join their brothers in state and local institutions—or private junior colleges of some national repute. But whereas this would quite clearly be a downward step for the men, a well-connected family can still hope that its daughters will recoup the damage by marrying well.

Politics, Taxes, and Localism

We suggested in the second section of this chapter that the major force working against localism has been professionalism. The academic profession wants students who can perform competently in scientific and scholarly exercises, and students want institutions whose academic reputations will help their professional careers no matter where they decide to work. Since professionalism of all sorts is very much in the ascendant, one might expect localism to be in retreat. Yet as we indicated at the outset, it is not entirely clear that this is the case. One reason is that the increasing acceptance of college as an indispensable part of professional training has led to larger public subsidies. At the undergraduate level these subsidies have come mostly from state and local governments and have gone to state and locally controlled institutions. For both fiscal and ideological reasons these jurisdictions have not been eager to attract outsiders to their colleges. Neither have they been eager to subsidize natives of their own jurisdiction who want to go elsewhere to college. As a result, the growth of state and local tax support has to some extent re-enforced localism at the undergraduate level.

Legislative efforts to keep colleges and universities local probably reflect fiscal pressures more than principled parochialism. As budget requests for higher education have climbed, state legislators have searched ever more carefully for items they could both understand and confidently dismiss as superfluous. Subsidies for students from other tax jurisdictions have been an ideal target. At the same time, students leaving their own tax jurisdiction have never been sufficiently well organized to lobby for scholarship support, even though their departure reduces costs at local public institutions. The result has been a steady rise in out-of-state and out-of-town tuition fees, and a corresponding increase in the financial advantage of attending a local institution.[9] This advantage has been only partially offset by increases in family income.

Given the rise in out-of-state tuition one might expect state and local institutions to be growing more provincial in their recruiting patterns. Historical evidence to support such a presumption is, however, thin. In 1963 the public institutions as a group drew 11 per cent of their undergraduates from outside their states.[10] Twenty-nine years earlier they drew 9 per cent of their students from out of state.[11] The shift, such as it is, seems to be toward greater cosmopolitanism. In many publicly controlled Midwestern universities, for example, there is a growing cadre of Easterners. These émigrés are often Jewish, and usually identified by locals as coming from "New York." They tend to be urbane in outlook, hostile to the fraternity-sorority system and big-time athletics, and in control of one or more student publications. Some are in flight from Eastern provincialism and in search of what they think of as the more democratic and egalitarian ethos of the West, but the majority come because the in-

[9] For statistics on out-of-state tuition at a sample of public colleges over the past forty years see A Fact Book, tables 261 and 262. In 1928, out-of-state tuition averaged 167 per cent of in-state. In 1964, it averaged 235 per cent.

[10] Residence.

[11] Kelly and Patterson.

stitution in question combines a distinguished faculty with comparatively low tuition and relatively modest admissions requirements. Many come from families whose education and income might, in an earlier era, have led them to send their children to private institutions. But tuition has climbed so fast since the mid-1950s that some of these parents no longer feel they can afford private tuition without scholarship aid. If their children have been insufficiently diligent or adaptable in high school to qualify for scholarships, or if their parents are too proud to let them apply, they turn to the public sector. Comparing Eastern public institutions to leading private institutions in the same area, they find the former wanting. Western institutions, on the other hand, have no firm place in the Eastern pecking order, and can be invested with a variety of hypothetical virtues. This is particularly true of the better-known state universities, whose national reputations as centers of research and graduate training lend an aura of potential excitement to what are often rather drab undergraduate programs.

It seems likely that this kind of cultural diffusion will continue for some time. Out-of-state tuition at leading public universities, while rising fast, will almost certainly remain substantially lower than tuition at the better private institutions, and will therefore appeal to a significant number of Eastern middle-class families looking for academic bargains. As both out-of-state and private tuition rises, however, Eastern parents will put more and more pressure on their own legislatures to develop first-rate public universities within their home states. Indeed, this has already begun to happen in some Eastern states where ethnic, religious, and class conflict had traditionally worked against public institutions. Two of the most important traditional centers of private higher education, Massachusetts and New York, are today committed to spending substantial amounts on public universities. At least in New York, these will try to rival the Big Ten in both size and academic distinction. Should these institutions attain academic eminence while keeping tuition comparatively low, many Easterners will see less reason to head west. If, for example, it costs a New Yorker $500 a year more to go to the University of Indiana than to Stony Brook, and if the two have comparable academic status, only the most embittered enemies of Eastern "snobbery" and the most enthusiastic advocates of geographic mixing will continue to leave New York for Indiana.

Even if out-of-state students do keep applying to the better public institutions, there is constant danger that they will be refused admission. Many big public universities have in recent years been raising their admissions requirements for out-of-staters, arguing that there are insufficient places for all the local students who apply. Others have established quotas for out-of-state students. College administrators usually argue against such concessions to local feeling on the ground that the outsiders lend a more cosmopolitan tone to the campus. This position is, however, difficult to sustain if, as often happens, the aliens become leaders of anti-administration ferment or play a visible role in whatever activities are enraging the local legislature at the moment. Yet even when "outsiders" are excluded from the student body, they continue to penetrate the faculties of the better state institutions, and in some measure "corrupt" the local students. The result is that the undergraduate programs of most state universities fall into what we have called the seminational pattern.

Regional Variations

There have inevitably been great variations in the way in which these general patterns affected particular parts of the country. In some states and cities there is enormous local pride in either public or private institutions, while in others many natives assume that local institutions are almost by definition inferior and that it is worth the price to send a child out of state. Some states have been politically able to create quite good public institutions, and the existence of such institutions naturally reduces the likelihood that local residents will forage outside the state. The over-all level of demand for higher education has also varied by region, as has the competence of those who go to college. This has affected the chances that students in particular areas would have enough like-minded classmates to sustain locally either the academic and professional specialties that interested them or a social and cultural style they found congenial. Variations in both the density of population and the demand for higher education have affected the possibility of organizing higher education around commuter colleges, and this in turn has made a difference in students' readiness to look beyond local horizons.

Northern New England seems quite content to remain an academically underdeveloped area. Perhaps this is because the existence of so many private, small, and often experimental colleges gives residents and legislators an impression of academic abundance. In practice, however, colleges like Bennington, Goddard, Marlboro, Middlebury, Dartmouth, Colby, and Bowdoin draw most of their students from Massachusetts, Connecticut, and New Work rather than from their immediate neighborhoods. The same is true of the University of Vermont, which while now fully public was for many years a private liberal arts college with publicly supported agriculture and engineering schools. Half its students still come from out of state, despite admissions standards and tuition charges higher than many private institutions. Vermont undergraduates also follow the private pattern by majoring in liberal arts far more than in occupational specialties. Maine and New Hampshire have more conventional public universities, but neither ranks very high in academic prestige compared with either state universities elsewhere or the general New England standard. As a result, the student from Vermont, New Hampshire, or Maine who wants to attend a major-league university usually looks outside his state. Despite the fact that 40 per cent of the students from these states go elsewhere, however, none has a substantial scholarship program to open this option to its poorer residents. Unlike California, there is no public feeling that every student has a *right*, regardless of means, to attend a suitable institution. As the cost of attending out-of-state institutions climbs, and more middle-class families feel the pinch, all this may change. Indeed, it is already changing, at least in quantitative terms, through expansion of state universities and former teachers colleges. Whether these will become distinguished institutions on a par with the best public institutions elsewhere is, however, still problematic.

Northern New England is not unique in its view that higher education is mainly for those who can pay for it, nor in its indifference to whether students attend college within the state or outside it. Massachusetts, Connecticut, New Jersey, Pennsylvania, and Maryland have somewhat similar traditions. Yet rising costs and admissions requirements at private colleges in these states, including Catholic ones, are producing new middle-class pressure to improve the relevant public institutions. This has meant both expansion of state universities and, more important, conversion of teachers' colleges into multipurpose state colleges, mainly serving commuters. It has not meant significant state scholarship programs for students who want to leave the state or attend its private institutions. Several states have token scholarship programs, but even the largest of these, in New York and Rhode Island, reach far fewer students than do public institutions within the same state.

Outside the Northeast, local patriotism has usually been stronger and willingness to leave one's native state correspondingly less common. In part, no doubt, this reflects the triumph of public over private control in most of the South and West. The eclipse of old sectarian colleges by the land-grant institutions in the late nineteenth century was more complete in the South and Midwest than in the East. The state university taught "practical" subjects of a kind small-town Midwesterners thought their children needed, while the well-known out-of-state colleges seemed to be relevant to a job market that existed only on the Eastern Seaboard. In the East, on the other hand, warfare between Catholic and Protestant and between the elite and the upwardly mobile prevented public higher education from winning widespread support. This left the field largely to private colleges whose appeal was religious, ethnic, or class-based rather than geographic.

Yet this is not an adequate explanation of the support given public higher education in states like Michigan, Minnesota, Wisconsin, Illinois, Indiana, California, North Carolina, and Texas. Like medieval cathedrals, public universities in these states seem to have become symbols of communal solidarity, a focus of civic pride, and a tribute to faith in ideas that transcend the here and now. The state legislature is often dominated by men who share this faith—men who are "anticlerical" in the sense that they fear their university is not in good hands but who are nonetheless committed to their "church." There are, indeed, some states where half the legislature attended the state university, especially its law school. We have already mentioned the hostility in these states to outsiders who cause trouble in "our" university. One sometimes meets a corresponding feeling that a good local citizen has an obligation to attend "our" institutions and not "theirs." In this context, moreoever, "theirs" can mean not only an Eastern college but nearby private colleges as well, as least if the private college has a national reputation and clientele. As a result of their symbolic role as the embodiment of local democracy, state universities have generally obtained more adequate appropriations than other equally useful public enterprises, such as public health, elementary education, and the like.

Once a state has made a commitment to public higher education, it seems to perpetuate itself even in conditions that would not have favored it initially. As urbanization spread from the Northeast to the Midwest and Pacific Coast, it did not bring a reversion to the privately dominated academic system, but led to an expansion of public universities and to the transformation of teachers colleges into a network of multipurpose state colleges. This made it far easier and more natural to attend a local public institution in the Midwest or in California than in the East. It also put the private sector in the Midwest and California under pressure to seek a national constituency. While places like Cal Tech, Stanford, and Oberlin have done this with great success, others (including even the University of Chicago's undergraduate college) have had trouble.

In the South and in the Rocky Mountains, where the tax base is smaller, employers' demands for college graduates more limited, and the proportion of competent potential college applicants in the general population apparently lower, both public and private institutions have been less distinguished.[12] The alliance between self-interested farmers and enlightened business and professional men on which public universities often depend for appropriations is not usually very strong in these areas. Only a few of these states, such as Colorado, North Carolina, and Texas, have even tried to create universities that would rank with the best in other areas, and even they have been ambivalent.

Given the inadequacy of most Southern state institutions, one might have expected upper-middle class Southerners to emulate the custom in the Northeast, sending their children to private institutions. Some have in fact done just this, turning to Duke, Vanderbilt, Tulane, and Emory, as well as to private women's colleges such as Randolph-Macon, Sweet Briar, and Hollins. A few have even turned to Northern colleges like Princeton. But the majority of Southern families, including many that have both the money and the social contacts to take these alternatives seriously, have been content or even proud to send their children to the state university. In part this may be because local pride persuades them that the university is better than it is. This is perhaps especially true in states like Virginia where the public institutions are private in spirit if not in law. In large measure, however, the Southern elite's commitment to its state universities seems based not on an overestimate of their academic standing but on indifference to it. The families in question usually distrust the academic profession, fear that attending a big-league Northern institution would attenuate the "Southern" values they have tried to inculcate, and believe that the life of the mind is not the most important part of

[12] On regional variations in high school seniors' ability, see Coleman *et al.* The effect of such variations on the relative competence of college students in different regions is difficult to assess, especially if one happens to be interested in the competence of students coming from the region rather than the competence of those who go to college in that region. One source of evidence, admittedly open to a variety of criticisms, is the failure rate on the 1966 Selective Service College Qualification Test. The Selective Service System reports these rates as follows:

Area	Percentage Failing
New England (Conn., Mass., Me., N.H., R.I., Vt.)	7
Middle Atlantic (N.J., N.Y., Pa.)	9
East North Central (Ill., Ind., Mich., Ohio, Wisc.)	12
Pacific (Cal., Ore., Wash.)	13
West North Central (Iowa, Kan., Minn., Mo., N.D., Neb., S.D.)	16
South Atlantic (D.C., Del., Fla., Ga., Md., N.C., S.C., Va., W. Va.)	22
Mountain (Ariz., Col., Idaho, Mont., Nev., N.M., Utah, Wyo.)	22
Non-Contiguous (Alaska, C.Z., Guam, Hawaii, P.R., V.I.)	28
West South Central (Ark., La., Okla., Texas)	32
East South Central (Ala., Ky., Miss., Tenn.)	47

college anyway. While this attitude may be changing, it is probably not changing fast enough to offset the growing financial cost of attending a nationally known college in another state.

While a few Southern institutions, such as Duke, Vanderbilt, North Carolina, and the University of Virginia, have some appeal for non-Southerners, outside prejudice against the region seems durable and in most though not all cases understandable. As a result, even the better Southern institutions tend to think in regional terms. Emory, for example, wants to be "the Harvard of the South," an ambition that probably pays too much deference to both Harvard and the South. (One exception to the general pattern of Southern isolation is the enrollment of Northern Negroes in Southern Negro colleges, discussed in more detail in Chapter X.)

Within the over-all Southern pattern, Florida and Texas are exceptional cases deserving some attention. The University of Texas is a wealthy and dynamic institution, which has in recent years managed to hire a number of distinguished professors from Northern universities. Like many other Texans, its members suffer from feelings of both grandeur and inferiority. Local officials and other influentials have never quite made up their minds whether to accept national academic norms or simply to follow the dictates of passionate local prejudice. There has been continuing warfare between the state legislature and the university administration on this score. Drawing as it does from a state which is really a small empire, combining Southern and Western attitudes and individuals, the university has a comparatively heterogeneous undergraduate body, including enclaves of almost every sort. Yet it has not attracted a significant number of out-of-state students, and in this it resembles other academically distinguished Texas institutions. Rice University, for example, with an enormous endowment and a scientifically reputable faculty, has not succeeded in widening its net to include more than a few students from outside the Southwest.

Florida is a different kind of exception, for it has no university comparable to Texas or Rice. Indeed, the University of Florida in Gainesville is probably unique in being the only state university in the country that has less academic standing than a newer (formerly all feminine) institution, Florida State in Tallahassee. Gainesville is still the place for the fraternity-football-fun culture that appeals to many Floridians. Florida has experienced a tremendous population boom, and has developed a pattern of education in many respects similar to California's. Junior colleges are springing up on every side, and a variety of new, experimental institutions in both the public and private sectors, such as New College, Nova University, Florida Presbyterian, and Florida Atlantic. It remains to be seen whether Florida, with its much smaller economic base and its lack of distinguished universities, will become as educationally self-contained as California.

Although the total numbers involved are smaller and the race question obviously less important, the academic systems of the Rocky Mountain states are in some respects similar to those of the South. As in the South, the tax base is usually small, and it would require enormous effort to support a state university with a large and distinguished faculty, adequate libraries and laboratories, and the other amenities taken for granted in the public universities of the Midwest and Pacific Coast. As in the South, the cultural tradition does not encourage making such efforts. Anti-intellectualism is widespread in almost all the Mountain states, the right wing is strong, and the struggle to maintain academic freedom is continuous, even though less publicized than in Mississippi. Nevertheless, these institutions have traditionally been somewhat less provincial than their Southern counterparts. For one thing, while there are even fewer Mountain than Southern institutions with national reputations, the proportion of students from outside the region is higher than in any other section of the country, including New England.[13] (Despite all we have said about the academic revolution, the great outdoors and proverbial Western "friendliness" still have tremendous appeal to many students.) Although we have not been able to gather data on this, we also have the impression that Rocky Mountain institutions are more likely than their Southern counterparts to recruit professors who grew up outside the region. While Southern politics have in the past been monolithic, chiefly on the issue of race (and not always there) with great diversity on economic and cultural issues, many liberal faculty members hesitated to send their children to Southern public schools where they would be exposed to anti-Negro attitudes. In contrast, the Rocky Mountain states, though often centers of John Birch Society activity, have had visibly strong liberal blocs. As a result, a college faculty has been less likely to feel overwhelmed by its environment, less likely to try to blend into the spectacular landscape, and more likely to feel it could and should maintain its ties with the national academic community. The faculty is likely to feel under collective attack, but isolation is not so complete. The faculty to whom we have talked often complain, however, that they cannot get the majority of students to work very hard or to take academic concerns very seriously. Students and the public are apparently united in the feeling that attendance at a state institution is a matter of right, imposing no particular intellectual obligations. Still, we would guess than until recently an open-minded and curious student was more likely to glimpse the existence of a larger and more cosmopolitan adult world at a university like Wyoming or New

[13] *Residence.*

Mexico than at Alabama or Louisiana State. Today this may no longer be true, for the successes of the civil rights movement in the early 1960s have opened many Southern universities to dissent on this issue, and consequently to dissent on many others as well. There is a degree of freedom and openness on some Southern campuses that would have been unimaginable a decade ago and is in some ways greater than in the Mountain states today. (The exception here is the University of New Mexico, which profits from spaciousness, nearby defense installations, the attraction of Spanish and Indian traditions, and a liberal climate.) At the same time popular overregard for local institutions and disregard for national academic respectability persist in both Southern and Mountain states and keep down the number of undergraduates leaving to study elsewhere. We have the undocumented impression, however, that once they receive their B.A.s, Mountain state students are somewhat more likely than Southerners to move beyond their regional orbits.

The drive for local self-sufficiency has gone farthest on the Pacific Coast. California in particular has created an educational system that caters to virtually every taste and produces a lower rate of emigration than any other major state in the country. Conversely, California is so far from other major centers of population that among non-Californians only a student with a highly developed feeling for the nuances of academic prestige and differentiation is likely to feel that it is worth going "all the way" to a California college. As a result, while California enrolls 13 per cent of the nation's students, it gets only 5 per cent of the migrants. These out-of-state students are concentrated in a few institutions: Stanford and Cal Tech, the Claremont Colleges, Mills, Berkeley, and the graduate programs at UCLA. Most of the rest of the California colleges are as local as CCNY. This may affect the character of their student bodies less than it would in other states, for most of these colleges recruit faculty from all over, and even their "native" students have often grown up elsewhere.

Localism, Pluralism, and Meritocracy

Taking the nation as a whole, it can be said that graduate education in both public and private institutions has been almost wholly nationalized in terms of style, and to quite a large extent even in logistical terms. Undergraduate education presents a more mixed picture, with nationalization having gone quite far in those states that rely primarily on private institutions, somewhat less far in those that depend on public ones. Having said this, however, it is not easy to decide how much cultural weight to give the persistence of localism as a logistical fact in undergraduate life. Ours is an era of national rather than regional or local consciousness. The mass media purvey the same pictures of reality to all Americans everywhere, and the academic profession tends to re-enforce this as do many other institutions. But should we therefore discount regional and local variations as a basis for classifying Americans?

In answer this question two issues must be distinguished. First, there is the question of whether regions and localities differ from one another in significant ways. On this score there can be little doubt that they do. Even casual scrutiny of national opinion polls or market research shows such differences. Southerners, while similar to Midwesterners in many respects, have quite different attitudes and tastes in some; Far Westerners are also different, although in all these matters social class, ethnicity, and education tell more than region does about differences and similarities. Can we assume, for example, that a middle-aged German Catholic dairy farmer from upstate New York is significantly different from one in Wisconsin or even Texas? Can we expect that a young Methodist school teacher raised in a small-town Vermont grocer's family will be appreciably different from a Methodist school teacher raised in a small-town Oregon grocer's family? These are not impossible questions to answer, but we know of no good empirical data regarding them.[14]

Whatever the facts of the matter, two points do seem reasonably clear. First, regional differences seem to be of diminishing over-all importance in American life, at least if the character of national politics is taken as an indicator. Second, regional differences taken in isolation are much less important than other sorts of differences described in this book, such as age, class, sex, race, and religion. The University of Wisconsin and the University of North Carolina, for example, are certainly different from one another, but they are nowhere nearly as different from one another as both are from the other institutions in their respective states. What this implies is that the differences *within* regions and localities are far greater than the differences *between* them. It also implies that virtually no college is in fact able to cater to anything like the full range of differences within a locality much less a region. Even a college with acute regional consciousness, like Berea in eastern Kentucky, defines its Appalachian clientele in such a way as to embrace only a portion of the cultural

[14] One good potential source of such data for the present purpose is the material on student attitudes collected by Alexander Astin and his colleagues at the American Council on Education. Regional differences are reported in Astin, Panos, and Creager, "Supplementary National Norms." This data is presented in terms of over-all norms for students *in college* in a given region, not for students *brought up* in a given region. The data could, however, be analyzed from the perspective outlined in the text, looking at individual students and controlling other demographic variables to get at the residual regional influence.

varieties found within its geographic area. The same thing is even clearer with state universities, which always accept and usually welcome some division of labor between themselves and other colleges serving their state.

This proposition has a converse, which is that if people are alike in other important respects, mere diversity of geographic origins will not produce much diversity in their outlook or aspirations. It is important to leaven Harvard with non-Bostonians, in other words, only if recruiting in New York City brings Jews as well as Gentiles, if recruiting in Utah brings small-town students as well as suburbanites, and if recruiting in the South brings fundamentalists as well as liberal Protestants. When geographic distribution does not bring these things —when, for example, Princeton recruits upper-middle class Protestant suburbanites from outside Baltimore, Chicago, and San Francisco as well as New York, or when Notre Dame recruits the children of white-collar Irish Catholics from all over the country rather than just from Indiana—the result is a very modest increase in diversity. Student ideology to the contrary notwithstanding, no college can ever be fully cosmopolitan in the sense of appealing to every element in the American population and encouraging every sort of person and outlook to mix on its campus.

A national recruiting network can, actually be used to restrict cultural diversity as well as to increase it. A college that feels it needs to grow may reach out to other areas for students who are basically like the ones it already has instead of altering its policies to accommodate new kinds of local talent. This is clearest in the sectarian colleges and the upper-middle class colleges, but it is also true of those that prepare for a particular profession or group of professions. Harvard, for example, spread its recruiting net across the country during the 1930s partly in order to get more students who had the aptitude and interest to go on to graduate school. Once such students began to apply in large numbers it felt free to reject the less able and ambitious local boys on whom it had previously depended. Similarly, most state university faculties would like to get more students from out of state because they have found these students brighter than the average applicant, not because they value outsiders per se. If the faculty had its way the result would be a student body with a narrower range of test scores and occupational ambitions, and probably a student body drawn from more uniformly upper-middle class background, though this last would not be deliberate.

No college can ever be fully cosmopolitan in the sense of appealing to every element in the American population and encouraging every sort of person and outlook to mix on its campus. Every college must differentiate itself in some way, carving out a particular image and constituency. Of the possibilities discussed in this book, localism is in some ways the least restrictive. The college that serves everyone in a particular geographic area is likely to have a wider variety of personalities and styles on its campus than the college that serves only Catholics, only Negroes, or only the poor. It may even be more diverse in some important respects than a university college that gets only the academically gifted, though this is certainly debatable. Localism can in this way open up extraordinary educational possibilities, of the kind traditionally emphasized in paeans to the comprehensive high school and the land-grant college. Yet educators have never been as good at exploiting these opportunities as at describing them. In practice, the very pluralism of a local college (as of a local high school) often prevents it from serving any particular group very well. It often becomes large and amorphous rather than small and coherent, doing a little of this and a little of that but not much of anything.

Perhaps partly in response to this danger, more and more local colleges have begun to specialize along academic as well as geographic lines. California, for example, has developed a three-tier system of state universities, state colleges, and municipal junior colleges. Such a system represents a retreat from "pure" localism in the sense that none of the institutions in question really seeks to cater to *all* those who happen to live nearby. At the same time, none except the graduate departments of the university habitually reaches beyond the boundaries of the state to find more suitable students. The result is a compromise in which student bodies are typically more economically and academically diverse than in a "national" college, but less so than in the old-style state university, which accepted every high school graduate and taught everything from ceramics to archaeology.

This retreat from pure localism is very much in the American tradition, which has placed great emphasis on voluntary association and relatively little on communal loyalties. Yet it is not without its price. Voluntary association is a fine principle for those with whom others are eager to associate; it is a disaster for those whom others instinctively avoid. America as a whole never really established a national network of local or state colleges open to everyone in their area, as it did with secondary schools. But many individual states did so. As a result, everyone in those states had a college he could call his own. He had an initial claim on this college, regardless of how it felt about him. Under this system nobody was simply expendable, and nobody could fall through the cracks without being noticed. It is true that professors at most public colleges did a good deal to nullify the "open door" policy by flunking out students who did not meet the faculty's standards of competence, and by only making a serious effort to educate a small minority of students with rather special gifts. Still, the principle that men had a right to education was important even when it was not honored in practice.

To the extent that legislatures abandon the idea that mere residence in an area conveys the right to a higher education in its colleges, more students will probably find themselves academically surplus. If public colleges accept only those local students they want, this will improve these students' chances of being taken seriously and of learning something of value, but it will also increase the number of students who cannot find any campus that wants them. Giving public institutions the right to choose their clientele instead of being chosen by it thus undermines the one great argument for locally based higher education. The virtue of a geographically based system is that it ensures that everyone will have somewhere to turn and usually puts every college under political pressure to do something for those who turn to it. Yet this system has not actually produced much good education for the academically inept, and it is probably foolish to shed too many tears over its passing. Indeed, it may be that the present division of labor among public institutions will do more to ensure that somebody tries to educate the academically unwanted than did the traditional system of sending everyone to the state university and then sending half of them back home by the end of the academic year.

Localism and Commuting

Up to this point we have been discussing the influence of geographic factors on the recruitment of students and faculty. But localism affects not only the mix of various kinds of students and teachers on a campus, but the *way* these individuals mix. There would, in other words, be differences between a truly national and a truly local college even if the students and faculty at each were identical, for students who attend college near home tend to be more exposed to continuing parental influence than those who go far away. At one extreme is the local junior college, almost all of whose students live with their families. At the other extreme is the national university, almost all of whose students come from so far away that they return home only on vacations. Somewhere in the middle lies the college with a statewide or comparable watershed, very few of whose students live with their families but many of whom may return home on weekends. Somewhere in between, too, lie the urban universities discussed in Chapter II, many of whose students come from nearby but nonetheless live in their own apartments rather than with their parents. We have no good figures on the numbers of institutions falling into each of these categories, but the Census has collected data on the living arrangements of individual students. These show that about 40 per cent of all freshmen live at home, but that the proportion falls to about 23 per cent by the senior year.[15] The way in which faculty and students spend their days and nights is not, of course, determined solely by the distance between the campus and their homes. There are some colleges that create a campus life sufficiently exciting for students to want to stay around on weekends, even if they live near enough to go home. There are others that, while assuming that students will live with their parents, manage to keep most of their undergraduates on campus during most of their waking hours. Nevertheless, it is generally true that a strictly local college will also be a commuter college in a constricting sense, with students exposed to one another and to the faculty for only a few hours each day.

When this happens the religious, ethnic, economic, and academic heterogeneity that often goes with localism is not likely to have much effect. The college may draw the daughters of local businessmen as well as of local plumbers, and may even mix them in the same class, but as soon as the bell rings they will go their separate ways. Catholics and Protestants may study the same version of Reformation history together, but they will seldom have occasion to talk about it—or even about more neutral topics.

The commuter not only sees less of his classmates but more of his parents, siblings, and former high school chums. One of the functions of a residential college is to emancipate the young from the inevitable limitations of their home and neighborhood before it is too late. Late adolescents are given a chance not only to think about questions their parents feel are unimportant or even dangerous, but to live their lives and choose their friends without worrying daily about their parents' reactions. This kind of freedom, however limited by the colleges' tendency to stand in loco parentis on some matters and by the students' lack of interest in escaping their past, is very important. It not only encourages collective emancipation of each generation from its elders, but facilitates the upward (and downward) social and intellectual mobility of individual students. Residential colleges, perhaps even more than elementary and secondary schools, have helped transform some of the sons and daughters of the blue- and white-collar classes into professional and managerial leaders with a

[15] 1960 Census, PC(2)-5A (School Enrollment), table 9. It is not clear to what extent the shift represents higher attrition among commuters and to what extent it represents individual students' moving out of their parents' homes. Perhaps half the freshmen commuters are at two-year colleges.

comparatively cosmopolitan outlook. We doubt that a commuter college can do this with equal success. Even a superb academic program is unlikely to move most students very far if they return every night to home and mother.[16]

To many families, as we indicated in Chapter II, the fact that a commuter college fails to touch important aspects of its students' lives is a virtue. Parents who have not themselves been to college are likely to view undergraduate extracurricular life with suspicion rather than nostalgia. They may feel that if their children are heavily influenced by their age-mates they will turn to frivolity and loose living, while if they take their professors too seriously the result may be radicalism or an unremunerative intellectualism. Such parents may not want their children "emancipated," either socially or intellectually, and may be extremely reluctant to send them away to a college that seems likely to infect its students with the values of either the academic profession or established institutions generally. Many students, however rebellious against parental supervision, have these same fears, inhibitions, and ambivalences. Under these circumstances there is a positive demand for colleges organized along the safe and familiar lines of a secondary school, as against colleges whose residential character clearly implies that the students will be expected to adopt new manners and ideas.

Nevertheless, the main reason why so many parents and students choose commuter colleges is probably not that they are "safe" but that they cost less. It is true that commuting sometimes means buying and maintaining a car—an expendable luxury for a student who lives on campus. But living at home is cheaper than living in a dormitory or fraternity, or even living with classmates in an off-campus apartment. Taking one's meals at home is also cheaper than eating college food. There are a number of other savings, from laundry to vacation transportation. The savings seem especially great if, as is often the case, the parents have gotten used to feeding and housing their children at home, and assume unconsciously that this really costs nothing at all. On that assumption they reckon that a child's going away to college saves them nothing, while adding perhaps $1,000 a year to the cost of his higher education. It is hardly surprising that many encourage their children to commute, even when they dislike the idea on educational, psychological, or social grounds. Because it is hard to measure what a student gains from getting away from home, it is hard to get anyone to pay for it. Very few states, for example, subsidize dormitories and dining halls at public institutions, even

[16] For further discussion see our descriptions of Boston College, the University of Massachusetts in Boston, and San Francisco State College in *The Academic Enterprise*, forthcoming.

though all subsidize tuition. Nor will the academic profession formally recognize the advantages of living away from home. We suspect, for example, that students who spend three years at a residential college usually grow as much intellectually and emotionally as students who spend four years commuting. But no college gives any more credit for a term spent in residence than for a term living at home.

In some respects this is perhaps surprising. One might expect the academic profession to look on commuter colleges as thoroughly undesirable institutions, which weaken the faculty's hold on the students and re-enforce home attitudes, which most faculty see themselves fighting. Yet this stance is by no means universal, and even those who take it are unlikely to be aggressive about it. Asked their opinion, most professors will say that a residential college is preferable to a commuter college. But they seldom give such a choice very high priority in their own institution. New departments, new graduate programs, better qualified faculty, and other improvements in the formal curriculum almost always take precedence in their minds over building dormitories. In part this is because many professors have no realistic sense of what their students' families are like or of what living at home may mean to a student's intellectual development. More important, however, is the fact that the benefits of curricular improvements are thought to be more tangible than the benefits of dormitories. The habit of mind that equates education with attending lectures, covering reading lists, writing exams, and accumulating grades and credits is as firmly entrenched in the academic profession as among the students. The professional ethic dictates that "performance" is what really counts and that "what the students do outside the classroom is their own business." The dedicated professional scholar would be appalled by the idea of giving a student credit for spending his "leisure" on campus rather than at home, just as he would be appalled by a proposal to give tenure for hanging around the faculty club and making good conversation. Such scholars sometimes tell incoming freshmen that what happens outside the classroom is as important as what happens inside. But these same scholars bitterly oppose efforts to translate these sentiments into a system of grading. For others the difference between a commuter college and a residential college is mostly a matter of snob appeal, not substance. Those who resist this whole approach, notably the non-scientists at residential liberal arts colleges in the Northeast and Midwest, are very much on the defensive and tend to be hostile to many other aspects of academic professionalism.

The upshot of these competing prejudices is difficult to predict. As the nation becomes more urban and surburban and as the proportion of students attending college rises, it will become possible to build colleges of reasonable size within commuting distance of an ever-larger proportion of homes. In California, where urbanization (or perhaps we should say suburbanization) and affluence have been most felt, more than nine students out of ten have at least a junior college within commuting distance. Elsewhere, new two-year commuter colleges are springing up by the dozen each year. Many of the teachers colleges now being turned into multipurpose state colleges are also expected to serve the particular community in which they are located rather than the whole state. The cumulative result is likely to be that within a generation the great majority of American high school graduates will be able to attend at least a two-year and often a four-year college without leaving home.

At the same time, the nation is becoming richer, more sophisticated, and more conscious of the subtler nuances of academic prestige. Family incomes and student earning power are rising faster than the cost of living away from home, and this is likely to continue. The number of high school seniors from prosperous college-educated families is increasing steadily, and most of these families are both willing and able to pay for residential education. Unless the junior college movement succeeds in completely transforming the pattern of American college-going, the residential colleges are therefore likely to keep their near monopoly on second-generation collegians. This will probably force the more ambitious commuter colleges to apply for federal loans to build dormitories—as, indeed, many are already doing. They will then try to fill these dormitories by building statewide or national rather than local reputations.

Geographic Dispersion and Community Development

It seems safe to predict that the tension between localism and nationalism, which has pervaded academic history in the past, will continue unabated for the foreseeable future. The character of this tension is, however, changing. In the nineteenth century the drive of every state and community for its own college could be seen as part of a more general quest for cultural and logistical autarchy. Like ex-colonial nations today, nineteenth-century American jurisdictions wanted institutions they could call their own even when they had no money to hire faculty, no secondary schools to prepare students, and no cultural or economic opportunities suited to the kind of alumni they hoped to turn out. They wanted colleges partly because of pride, partly because they distrusted "foreigners" (with "the East" playing somewhat the same demonic role in nineteenth-century America as the ex-colonial powers and the United States play in Africa today), and partly because they knew that more people would get higher education if it were available locally than if they had to go away to get it.

Nor were these concerns misplaced. On those occasions when American parents in small towns and rural areas did send their children off to the larger and better-known colleges, the children were often awakened to the existence and seductions of a more cosmopolitan America. Instead of wanting to return home and become pillars of the community in which they had been raised, these students frequently headed for (or in some cases merely stayed in) the larger and more prosperous cities. Founding a local college was therefore a way of keeping the best young people "down on the farm" or at least, "down in Jonesville." But even local colleges (or local high schools, for that matter) sometimes contaminated their students with alien ideas, for their curricula were almost always imported rather than home grown. Those students who took the classical curriculum or its up-to-date equivalent seriously were unlikely to feel comfortable with the intellectual and career limitations of small-town or rural life. For this minority local colleges became steppingstones on the way to the big city, defeating the hopes of their founders. Still, most local graduates probably stayed near home. If they did this and if they had also acquired any erudition or understanding of non-local ideas in college, this presumably helped narrow the gap between local life and the metropolis. The multiplication of local colleges may, indeed, have been a significant factor in preventing America from following the highly centralized cultural and economic pattern of England and France, where the desiccation of the provinces and the hegemony of the metropolis are constant topics of complaint.[17]

The seekers of autarchy were probably right in expecting local colleges to lure more young people into the classroom than national or even regional colleges would have done. By reassuring parents that they would not necessarily "lose" those of their children who went to college, and by providing a visible symbol to the children of this possibility, local institutions today encourage a rate of attendance far higher than that in areas where going to college means going away to a distant and unknown community. There is every reason to assume that this was even more true in the nineteenth century. Nonetheless, while localism probably increased total enrollment, it kept enrollment at each individual institution low. This was often disastrous. The typical college during the early nineteenth century seems to have had perhaps a hundred students and half a dozen professors, and even

[17] For a contrary view of nineteenth-century higher education, stressing the operation of Gresham's law in nineteenth-century academic work and the dissipation of resources on small marginal institutions, see Hofstadter and Metzger, pp. 209–22.

late in the century these numbers had only doubled or trebled. As a result most colleges were hard-pressed to cover the new branches of knowledge emerging in Europe even if they wanted to do so. The students, too, while often challenged at first by their classmates, were likely to become socially and intellectually inbred over four years.

An economist might also argue that the multiplication of small, local institutions was foolish, because it kept costs high and quality low. From a national viewpoint, which assumes that resources devoted to colleges have other potentially productive uses, this argument has weight. But from the educators' viewpoint it is probably misleading. There is no reason to assume that the money devoted to small, local colleges would have been equally available to support larger and presumably superior regional or national ones. The record strongly suggests that colleges got most of their support through local, face-to-face relationships. Localism, then, may have been the only way to induce a comparatively underdeveloped nation to support something as apparently superfluous as higher learning. In an era when almost all other aspects of American life were locally rooted, there was no alternative.

Today the character of America's national-local dialectic has changed. No small or medium-sized community can any longer expect to be culturally or logistically self-sufficient. State and local prosperity now depends more on "attracting" industry (i.e. branches of national corporations), less on nurturing native enterprises. This means that state and local colleges, instead of existing solely to develop indigenous talent for local tasks, become one of the amenities with which the state or town seeks to establish its national reputation as a "progressive," "forward-looking" place appealing to outsiders. To serve this purpose a college must play to an adult rather than juvenile audience, and it must play according to whatever rules seem nationally relevant. None of this is entirely new. Nineteenth-century local boosters also saw their colleges as devices for putting their town on the map and attracting new residents if not new branch offices. Perhaps the real change is in the ways the local boosters now pursue their aims. There is less emphasis on the college as a place where new arrivals can send their children, more on the services it renders directly to adults, by dint of raising the cultural tone, providing consultants to industry, and so forth. Even when such services are very limited, the idea that local prosperity depends on "decisions made in New York," along with the idea that these decisions may somehow be affected by the character of state or local colleges, helps local educators rationalize changes in their colleges that local parents and bigwigs might once have opposed more confidently.

Even among those institutions that serve an overwhelmingly local clientele, there has been a change in style. During the nineteenth century, localism usually meant keeping undergraduate behavior in line with local mores, not developing a locally relevant curriculum. Today, localism often does extend in a certain sense to the curriculum, with the choice (though seldom the content) of training programs being geared to the demands of local corporations, school systems, governmental agencies, and so forth. Such locally oriented programs may even be found at the graduate level, and may include research and consulting as well as teaching. This is an important component in the growth of what we have called the seminational university. Lacking large-scale federal research support or substantial funds of its own, such a university cannot compete for the abler and more mobile professors and students, for these would almost all rather be at a national institution. But it can attract individuals whose work (or husbands' work) ties them to the local community, and who want to teach or study part time. In 1963 a fifth of all undergraduates and a substantially larger proportion of graduate students were studying part time. Almost all of the part-time undergraduates and many of the part-time graduate students were employed full time. In this same year, a third of all faculty above the rank of Teaching Assistant were employed part time.[18] Most of these part-time faculty were also employed full time in nearby industries, law firms, governmental agencies, or else were women with young children. The rest were attending graduate school part time at a nearby university. Among this latter group, some were teaching in a local college because it happened to be near the national graduate school of their choice, but others were studying in a local graduate school because it happened to be near a college where they had found a teaching job. It is our impression that seminational universities are far more likely than their fully national counterparts to welcome students of all ages, and to arrange programs of study sufficiently flexible to suit those whose obligations and identities are centered elsewhere.

In addition to serving students of all ages who have to be in a particular area, the typical seminational university also recruits graduate students from its own and nearby undergraduate colleges. There is a good deal of variation in the extent to which such universities try to hold their best B.A.s, as well as variation among departments within a university. Most departments want to get full-time graduate students and are tempted to recruit their own undergraduates in preference to local housewives, school teachers, and civil servants. Those faculty who have studied at national institutions are, however, also eager to

[18] The part-timers did less than 14 per cent of the instruction. 1965 *Digest*, table 64.

impress their former mentors (and themselves) with the quality of their undergraduates. To do this they must send their best seniors on to the top universities instead of keeping them at home. They are also concerned for their students' development and believe that they would benefit from exposure to more eminent faculty, more talented fellow students, and a more cosmopolitan atmosphere than the home institution can provide. Having come from such a world themselves, they know the difference.

The typical program of a local university is heavily weighted toward Masters' degrees, especially in fields like education and the sciences. It may also have a law school, which until recently would have had as many night as day students, although at present night law students are a declining industry. Such an institution is not likely to give many doctorates, although it may have a substantial number of students who are working on a doctorate (often in Education) at a rate of perhaps one course a year. The paucity of full-time advanced graduate students is, however, seldom a matter of deliberate choice. The typical local university would expand its doctoral programs if only it could. It sees doctoral students as a way to get more scholarly faculty and thus more outside research funds. Its ambitions along these lines may get considerable support from enlightened local civic leaders, who see a good graduate program as a selling point in efforts to attract outside business, as a potential nucleus for a research oriented industrial complex, and recently, as the sine qua non of successful competition for federal research installations. (These latter, with annual budgets sometimes running into hundreds of millions of dollars, have become a major piece of federal pork. They have traditionally been located near national universities. But congressional politics, in combination with certain federal officials' desire to transform particularly promising local universities into national ones, have recently intensified the pressure for more equitable geographic distribution. In this context a seminational university may be of decisive importance in some site selections. Even if it is not, local boosters may think it will be.)

The decline of local autarchy has affected not only the attitudes of local boosters and trustees toward their colleges but the attitudes of parents and students as well. Ambitious individuals who want to move in national rather than local orbits must increasingly meet the standards of a national comporation or profession rather than the standards of their local community. In addition, those who want to use their college years for a non-vocational moratorium need to escape their community in order to free themselves from both their past and perhaps their future. Parents who understand this usually want their children to leave home sometime during adolescence. In the East this may mean sending a child away to boarding school. Most parents, however, postpone the break until the end of high school. At that age, the professional and managerial classes usually encourage children to enter a national college. There are regional differences in this respect, with more such pressure in the East than in the West and South, more in big cities than in smaller communities, and so on. And in addition, there are all kinds of irrationalities and accidents in the choice of college, which means that many students who "should" be at a national college aren't. Nevertheless, students who remain at local colleges tend either to be slow-witted or to come from homes where established national institutions are not viewed as the employers of choice. There are also some extremely bright underachievers who are unwilling to enter what they call the national college rat race and who may end up at a local college as a last resort, but they are exceptional.

An able and ambitious student from a parochial home may, however, discover the existence and lure of the larger world even if his parents reject it. This may happen in high school, in which case he will try to go away to college. Or it may happen after a year or two at his local college. He may then try to transfer, or he may in due course apply to a national graduate school. Some seminational colleges see such aspirations as the litmus test of their own success and regard students who go to work for a local company or school as symbols of the institution's lack of impact. But other outwardly similar colleges make relatively little effort to encourage anyone to "go on." Still others want both to send students on to national universities and to develop programs of their own for local students.

An institution's character obviously depends in good part on which of these missions it chooses to emphasize. In a seminational college that sees itself as a feeder to national graduate schools there is likely to be considerable faculty emphasis on transmitting the national academic style. This is particularly true of the undergraduate colleges of the better state universities, which get most of their students from a single state but are conducted by a national faculty and attached to a national graduate school. Such a college is national in aspiration, even if not in recruitment. In the undergraduate college of a seminational university, on the other hand, the psychological pressure on students to shed local prejudices may be much less. Those local colleges that continue to stress training for local jobs tend to remain pillars of local mores, not subverters of them. Yet even this has to be qualified, depending on what sorts of local jobs are being trained for and what the local balance is between different commercial and industrial styles. Thus local teachers, policemen, and other minor civil servants may be "local" precisely in the sense of Robert Merton's original distinction between locals and cosmopolitans, while those men who go to work for local department stores or light industry may become more cosmopolitan in terms of what they are willing to spend on schools for their children, how late they stay up, and how much they drink at the country club.[19] Not all the stay-at-homes will remain local psychologically, and what happens to them in college may have small bearing on what paths they eventually take.

Age and Sponsorship in Nationalization

Most of what we have written up to this point has suggested our preference for national as against local values and life styles. Perhaps this preference is no more than a projection of our own personal prejudices, but we would defend it on more general grounds. There is, it is true, much to be said on behalf of community, of rootedness, and of living out one's life in a relatively stable, predictable environment. But these desiderata can be had only at a price, and most twentieth-century Americans have not been willing to pay it. Despite their nostalgia and ambivalence, the fact is that Americans have chosen over and over to uproot themselves and move on in search of a better life. Between 1955 and 1960, for example, half the population moved to another house. Sometimes, of course, the house was in the same community as its predecessor, but more than a sixth of the population moved to another county during this five-year period, which almost always meant that whatever local ties they had had were broken. The most mobile group was in its late teens in 1955 and early twenties in 1960.[20] Many, of course, were uneducated—for example, Southern Negroes moving to Northern cities. But a disproportionately large number were college graduates. We have found no good statistics on the point, but we would guess that today's college graduates are more likely than not to leave their native state before they die. Whatever the exact statistics, higher education must take account of geographic mobility. A college can hardly defend preparing its students for life in a particular geographically defined subculture if they will in fact live elsewhere. In this context the question is no longer *whether* a student should be introduced to a cosmopolitan world, but *when* and *how* this introduction should take place.

If people are sooner or later going to make a transition from local to national orbits, then it will in most cases be easier to make it sooner

[19] One of the many questions we have not been able to investigate is the role of in-service training programs in nationalizing the young. The Army may do this for some high school dropouts or graduates, IBM for some college dropouts or graduates.

[20] See 1960 *Census*, I, 1, table 164.

rather than later.[21] The young are generally more flexible and adaptable than their elders. Surely they are more likely to flourish in a mobile, nationalized society if they have been educated for it than if they have been protected from it throughout their formal schooling.

There have been times and places when the transition from localism to a more cosmopolitan style was expected to come relatively early. Two generations ago established national institutions were mostly Eastern-based and recruited from leading Eastern colleges. These in turn relied on prep schools to prepare most of their students. If parents wanted their children to work for a Wall Street law firm or brokerage house, in other words, they were likely to feel obliged to send them away to a prep school in early adolescence. As the national colleges acquired more scholarly faculties, however, and as the proportion of their students going directly to work declined, these faculties became increasingly dissatisfied with this sytem. They noted that while the prep school students who had left home early arrived at college with better academic preparation and more cultural sophistication, they were not usually willing to commit themselves to the values of the faculty. By the end of their four years in college the prep school alumni are often doing less satisfactory work than students recruited from local high schools. During the past generation most national colleges have therefore cut back the proportion of their students from boarding schools. While this has not reduced the absolute number of students who leave home in early adolescence, the number has probably not grown as fast as the number leaving home later.

A similar logic might eventually transform recruitment to the national graduate schools. These schools now get a large proportion of their students from the national colleges and from the seminational colleges associated with leading state universities. Many graduate schools, especially in the arts and sciences, still place considerable emphasis on an applicant's having been to such a college, both because they think it ensures good academic preparation and because it provides a moderately efficient preselection device for eliminating probable "lemons." Applicants from obscure local colleges are often at a considerable disadvantage. Systematic research might, however, show that good undergraduate preparation, while affecting perform-

---

[21] We ourselves do not know how to answer the question how soon is too soon? Readers of Stephen Spender's *The Backward Son,* a more or less autobiographical novel about a British prep school (that is, a residential elementary school), will be apt to think that he went away too soon, unless they also ask whether his family would have been any better for him than his school. A secure, unthreatened childhood is undoubtedly an advantage in coping with later, less predictable environments. Erik Erikson's *Childhood and Society* suggests some of the phasing that might be involved here, without setting chronological time zones that would not in any event fit all individual cases.

ance in the first year or two of graduate work, makes comparatively little long-term difference in a prospective professional man's life. Aptitude and motivation might, in other words, prove as important in picking graduate students as in picking undergraduates, and previous training might prove as unimportant. If this were to be the case—and we know of no systematic research on the point—the national graduate schools might eventually respond in much the same way that the national colleges did, stressing Graduate Record aptitude scores more than the quality of instruction offered at the applicant's undergraduate college, and sending scouts to obscure colleges.

The strongest opposition to such a recruiting policy seems to come from the graduate departments of arts and sciences, and especially from those in private universities. Men who spend time teaching undergraduates inevitably have an emotional investment in the idea that their labors produce permanent results, at least among their best students. It would take an avalanche of statistical evidence to persuade most professors that a bright, highly motivated undergraduate really lost nothing of permanent consequence by attending a college where none of his professors did research or even kept up with other people's research. Even those who were persuaded that poor undergraduate training made little long-run difference would, moreover, tend to prefer students from national colleges, simply because in the short-run such students can be put straight to work as research assistants. Those from less high-powered colleges often need a year or two of courses covering the basic tools and concepts of the discipline in question before they are useful to their professors. Some graduate departments in some fields are willing to make this extra effort for graduates of Negro colleges, but this is by no means universal.

In the great public universities the undergraduate programs usually engage less professorial energy. This means that the faculty has less investment in the idea that it matters where an applicant did his undergraduate work. The faculty in these institutions is habituated to accepting undergraduate transfers from obscure colleges and seeing them do as well as students who entered as freshmen, and it is also used to accepting graduate students from the state's less prestigious colleges. It has learned to assume that its students are ill-prepared, and to judge them on the basis of how quickly they pick up professional skills and values once they enroll.

Professors in those graduate professional schools that do not have an undergraduate counterpart tend to be less concerned with where an applicant went to college. Both public and private schools of medicine and law, for example, are inclined to look at undergraduate academic work primarily as an aptitude test, to be weighed in the same spirit as an applicant's scores on appropriate multiple-choice tests. Whether the applicant has attended a cosmopolitan or provincial institution is usually important only insofar as it influences the admissions committee's judgment about a given student's "real" aptitudes. In part this is because most medical schools and almost all law schools place great emphasis on grades and have great faith in what these show. Equipped with this simple definition of who is worth admitting and who is not, they have found it both natural and easy to investigate the relationship between a student's success and the quality of his undergraduate college, his scores on aptitude tests, and other factors. When it turns out that students with high scores on the Law School Aptitude Test do well in law school even though they came from "bad" colleges, while students with low scores do poorly in law school even though they come from "good" colleges, the effect on admissions policy is fairly immediate. This is particularly true because the law professors, unlike their colleagues in arts and sciences, have relatively little professional contact with professors at any undergraduate college, good or bad, and are therefore not especially impressed by the letters of recommendation an average student from a good college can sometimes assemble. In the arts and sciences, on the other hand, where graduate students are judged by rather amorphous standards, prediction of graduate school "success" is inevitably more difficult. This allows graduate admissions committees to indulge their prejudices more, and makes them pay more attention to a student who is highly recommended by a friend or by a celebrity at a well-known college. Such selection procedures catch a number of promising students who would fall through an IBM net, but of course they miss many others whose flair has not been apparent to their college teachers.

Given these variations in graduate school admissions policies, and given the understandable uncertainty of the general population about these policies, it seems likely that the transition from local to national orbits will continue to come at different ages for different sorts of people. Some will go to national boarding schools in early adolescence. Some will wait until seventeen and go to a national college. Some will wait until twenty-one, attending a local college and then getting onto the national ladder by way of graduate school or a junior executive training program. Some will wait even longer, attending a local graduate school but then landing a job with an established national institution after finishing their formal education. National enterprises, especially business corporations, will continue to prefer employees schooled in national colleges and universities, but their over-all need for manpower will also continue to outstrip the supply from such colleges. Many big corporations have found in recent years that they get relatively few takers at the well-known university colleges where they have traditionally recruited, for most of the alumni of these colleges now enter the professions. Some corporations have therefore shifted the focus of their recruiting to more provincial terminal colleges. This means that even those who make the local-to-national transition late will find doors open if they approach them with moderately good credentials and seem to have the skills and manner their prospective peers value.

The preservation of such alternative trajectories is highly desirable. It reduces the importance of any one choice point, and keeps second chances available. This is good for the student, who is under less psychological pressure. It is also good for the employer, since one-shot selection systems are very inefficient, certifying a lot of mediocrity and rejecting a lot of talent. Keeping the "national option" open as long as possible also helps shift responsibility for the choice away from the family and toward the child. If, for example, the recruitment to national institutions were to depend largely on attending a national boarding school, this would in effect make it depend on having a family which sponsored the child's mobility. Early adolescents are "sent" to boarding school. They themselves only rarely have a voice in the matter. Late adolescents "go" to college, with the relative weight of their choice and their parents' varying from one family to another. If the choice is postponed from thirteen to seventeen, then, the family will still play some role, but an ambitious youngster will be able to exercise considerable independent influence. If an Iowa boy decided to go to Yale, for example, and if he can get in, his family may go along with his decision, even though it would not have been their own. If the national option is again opened up at twenty-one, his freedom is even greater. Even the boy whose parents vetoed Yale College will not be in a position to veto a Berkeley Ph.D. program or a Harvard LL.B., if that is what their son wants. (After sixteen years in local institutions, of course, it is not *likely* to be what he wants; but at least the option is there for the persistent.)

Looking ahead, we would guess that the number of young people choosing the national option at each age level will increase slowly but steadily for the foreseeable future. The demand for admission to national institutions will therefore rise steadily, and some currently seminational or local institutions will be able to "go national" if they wish. Except where there is strong legislative pressure to maintain local ties (i.e. in the undergraduate colleges of state universities), colleges and universities which have a chance to recruit nationally will almost all exercise this option. Another partial exception may come from denominational colleges, especially Protestant ones, which are under strong pressure from religious-ethnic communities to maintain openings for "their" young people. The faculty in such colleges will, it is true, usually want to recruit the ablest young people. But these may mostly come from nearby, because only those who live nearby will regard the college as a first choice. Those who apply from a distance are frequently those who were rejected by a more selective and better known national or seminational college, and come because somebody persuaded them to list this particular local church college as a safe third or fourth choice. (A striking and paradoxical example of this latter phenomenon is Rice University, which is the first choice of many of the ablest high school graduates in its region but is elsewhere regarded as a second choice for those who cannot get into Cal Tech or MIT. If it picks students solely on the basis of academic promise, then, it is likely to get mostly Texans for some time.)

At the same time, however, local colleges will also flourish as never before. These colleges represent a transitional steppingstone for some local boys, who end up in national graduate schools or working for national institutions. They also represent an effort by local boosters to accommodate national values and pressures through partial incorporation. They seek to give the young the skills they need to live in an increasingly nationalized economy, but without exposing them to any more alien cultural influences than necessary and without encouraging them to leave the community of their birth. The increasing centralization and mobility of American society will make such colleges more rather than less important. These colleges accommodate children who would not in an earlier generation have gone to college at all, and give them the flavor of the world beyond their parish without usually creating an addiction to it.

Taking these two trends together, we would guess that individual colleges would tend to become more national. At any given institution, be it relatively local or relatively national today, the proportion of both faculty and students from out of state will tend to rise over the years. At the same time, the fastest growth in enrollment is likely to take place at what are now the most local colleges, especially the public two-year colleges. The paradoxical result is likely to be that while the majority of individual institutions will become more national, the system as a whole will not. Instead, nationalization and localism will both spread in tandem, just as they have for the past two generations. This reflects the fact that in domestic politics, if not in foreign affairs, America remains a federal rather than a centralized society. The states continue to grow in power, in expenditure, and probably in quality of government, even though more and more people expect the federal government to solve problems which overleap state boundaries, state resources, and state competence. While localism understandably sees itself on the defensive almost everywhere, its power to delay, sabotage, and veto national measures remains large.

Yet localism need not be an entirely regressive force. Insofar as localism simply stands for ignorance of the world beyond the physical horizon and suspicion of new ideas brought by outsiders, it is obviously a negative influence and can never have a creative role either in education or anywhere else. But as we suggested earlier, localism and regionalism can have a positive side. Localism can imply communal solidarity and a commitment to other people simply because they are there rather than because they have wealth, brains, or some other set of special virtues. Analogously, a local college can be one which takes its constituency as a given, in the same way and for the same reasons that a politician must, and tries to make what it can of this. Instead of trying to gerrymander the district or find a new and more suitable clientele, it works with those who happen to be there. This commitment may be justified by religion, sentiment, inertia, or other factors, but it is valuable no matter what its source. It is not, however, a commitment with much appeal to most academicians, for even more than most professionals they believe in the voluntaristic principle that they must choose their clients as well as having their clients choose them. Nonetheless, it is a principle which has done a great deal for America at the elementary school level and something at the secondary level. It may have untapped possibilities at the college level too.

The trouble is that even nominally local colleges seldom take this principle seriously. Here and there one finds a college like Berea which sees its mission as working with a particular group rather than moving beyond that group. But Berea is almost unique in the private sector for having such an orientation. Political pressures ensure that most public colleges give these ideals lip service, but public college faculties only rarely take them seriously. Localism may define who will be admitted—though even this is now rare in state universities—but academic professionalism then takes over and defines who will be educated, who will be strung along, and who will be pushed out. Local politicians and parents seem quite acquiescent in the face of such treatment. Here and there one finds political opposition to the academicians' version of meritocracy, and sporadic insistence that some attempt be made to educate those whom the profession has deemed uneducable. Such ideas have played some role in the shaping of some of the two-year community colleges discussed in Chapter XI. In general, however, it seems clear that localism is not currently forcing academicians to broaden their traditional definitions of who could or should be educated. Here and there, it is true, local pressure had led to the employment of new sorts of educators with somewhat non-academic standards of merit. The locals may insist, for example, that sanitary engineering or cosmetology are worth mastering, despite the academicians' scorn for them. Yet these very examples illustrate the depressing fact that local opposition to academic definitions of what is worth knowing and who can be taught it usually depends on some sort of national validation. By playing one profession or sub-profession off against another, local leaders may force the academicians to admit subjects and instructors who are not strictly respectable. But without some such "outside" support the claims of communal solidarity seem too weak to exercise much independent effect. Far from ensuring that everyone will be counted in, therefore, most local colleges serve as devices for helping the ablest local youngsters to separate themselves out. The local colleges give able youngsters the credentials they need to move into the middle and upper reaches of a society based on voluntary association, and leave the less gifted or energetic to find some other basis for survival in such a society.

V. The Professional Schools

Professionalism and Its Consequences

In almost any discussion of American higher education, whether with professors, students, or the general public, somebody is likely to put forward the idea that the nation's colleges have been corrupted by vocationalism. In the good old days, it will be argued, colleges were pure and undefiled seats of learning. Students came to get a liberal education, not a degree in accounting, mortuary science, or X-ray technology. The professors, in turn, were interested in broadening the minds of the young, not advancing themselves through government contracts, business consulting, or publication poundage.

Like other pastoral idylls, this myth serves all sorts of polemical purposes, good and bad. But it is a myth nonetheless. There was no golden age in American higher education. Young men of college age worried about their future careers in the colonial era just as they do today, and this affected both the kind of men who came to college and the kind of things they did once they arrived. During the colonial era people usually went to college because they hoped to become clergymen; today they go because they hope to become doctors, lawyers, teachers, business executives, and the like. While this is an important change, and has affected the character of higher education, it does not imply either a rise or a decline in vocationalism. The same is true of the faculty. In colonial colleges the younger instructors were often aspiring ministers waiting for a promising pulpit to come their way; today they are more often aspiring scholars, teaching because this is a good way to finance their professional training. In colonial colleges the older teachers were sometimes failed clergymen; today they are sometimes failed scholars and scientists. This does not mean that nothing has changed in higher education since the seventeenth century. But it does mean that purity of motive and single-mindedness of purpose have never been characteristic of American colleges, and that the question has always been *how* an institution mixed the academic with the vocational, not *whether* it did so.

One reason for so many liberal arts professors' nostalgia for some hypothetical prevocational era is that they have lost their monopoly on undergraduate instruction. Substantial numbers of undergraduates

are today enrolled in avowedly professional schools. They are studying subjects they and their professors hope will be useful to them
in their work after graduating. This makes some liberal arts professors
feel that their influence over the young has declined. But this is almost certainly wrong. Relatively few of the students enrolled in
undergraduate professional schools today would have enrolled in liberal arts programs a generation or two ago. They would have gone
directly from high school to work. The fact that they now come to
the college campus and yet shun the liberal arts may make liberal
arts professors more aware that they have a limited following, since
it puts them physically closer to their potential critics. Yet these
young people's parents, most of whom did not go to college at all,
were almost all even more indifferent or hostile to the liberal arts
than their children are.

The point can be made statistically too. The proportion of all
undergraduates studying the liberal arts and pure sciences has declined over the past hundred years—though it has not declined much
since World War II. But because so many more people are going
to college, the proportion of the whole age grade taking degrees in
the liberal arts has risen steadily over the past hundred years, and
especially since World War II. There is hardly a field of study that
does not today have more (and better) students than it did a generation ago, though there are inevitably some fields whose *relative*
position has declined.

The growth of the liberal arts is partly a matter of more young
people going to college, but that is not the whole story. One of the
most important changes over the past century, and one that largely
offset the rapid spread of professional schooling in the late nineteenth and early twentieth centuries, was the growth in enrollment of
women. While some of these coeds simply wanted to earn a teaching
license, and others simply wanted to find a husband, they were in
general more open to the humane aspects of undergraduate education
than men were. Certainly they provided the liberal arts professors
with larger audiences than they ever had before. Professors have not,
it is true, usually welcomed the feminization of their subject. But this
says a good deal about the professors' commitment to a higher vocationalism of their own, which judges a student's merit by whether he
will go on in the field and discounts women because they usually
will not.

Another important reason for the popularity of the liberal arts is the
fact that they have long been, and continue to be, regarded as suitable
undergraduate preparation for those callings that delay professional
training until graduate school. Thus as graduate professional enrollment rises, undergraduate liberal arts enrollment does likewise. It is

true that the liberal arts have themselves been somewhat professional-ized, so that students often study chemistry or economics with an eye to advancing their career rather than satisfying their curiosity or ad-vancing their wisdom. But this process owes at least as much to the professionalization of the faculty as to changes in students' motiva-tions.

Even where there has been a shift in enrollment into avowedly professional subjects, it is not clear that this has always led to a parallel shift in student attitudes or values. We have the impression, for ex-ample, that the best seminaries today get students who are less job-oriented than their eighteenth-century counterpart who enrolled in a classical liberal arts course along with non-clerics. Many of today's seminarians hardly think of themselves as having a career at all. Yet there are also less eminent places where future clergymen are as wor-ried about the future and as likely to see what they were taught through the glasses of pseudopracticality as any eighteenth-century aspirant. Similarly, it may be that the fraternity boy who came to college in the 1920s to make friends for a later career was different from his modern counterpart because in those days he often majored in economics or political science whereas today he is somewhat more likely to major in business. But we suspect that the academic change has made far more difference to the faculty than to the students, and that the latter learned very little in either program.

Still these are impressionistic judgments, and others may differ on the basis of experience or prejudice. This chapter will not attempt to resolve the issue but will instead take up another and to our mind more interesting question, namely how the professional schools fit into the over-all system of higher education.

We have neither the knowledge nor the space for a comprehensive discussion of professionalism in America. We must, however, make clear that we use the term in a rather special sense. Unlike many people, we do not regard an occupation as a profession simply be-cause it requires advanced training or expert knowledge. We use the term only to describe an occupation that is relatively colleague-oriented rather than client-oriented. Professionalization in our lexicon therefore implies a shift in values, in which the practitioner becomes less concerned with the opinion of laymen (including such outward signs of their approval as a large practice and a big income) and becomes more concerned with the opinion of his fellow practitioners (which may, of course, lead to a large practice and a big income, but may also lead to a professorship or a judgeship). More specifically, as Everett Hughes has emphasized, professionalization means that the practitioners seek the exclusive right to name and judge one

another's mistakes.[1] Military officers are in this sense highly professionalized even though they have relatively little esoteric knowledge.
Commercial artists are less professionalized, though they have more
specialized expertise. In addition, professionalization often involves
winning the right to charge the client for services rendered in accord
with the standards established by one's colleagues, even if the client
receives no satisfaction or benefit. One prerequisite to these developments is the establishment of a clear line between professionals and
non-professionals—a line usually enforced by the power of the state
through some sort of certification or licensing. Yet while they often rely
on the state to enforce their will, most professions arrange the certification process so that they themselves have the decisive voice in
who gains entry into the occupation and who does not. This is often
done by establishing control over formal professional training and
making this prerequisite to certification. As this description makes
clear, a profession is akin to a guild or even a club.[2]

Intensive professionalization is a relatively recent phenomenon, at
least in America. Using the criteria outlined in the previous para-
graph, for example, it is doubtful whether any American occupational
group was really professionalized in pre-Civil War America—though a
few practitioners in some fields probably were. Certainly no group
was professionalized to anything like the same extent as many today.

The historical causes of professionalization are unclear.[3] It is often
attributed to the increasingly specialized division of labor, the explosion of knowledge, and the rising demand for expertise in the management of a highly technical and highly bureaucratized society. But it is
not evident what is cause and what is effect in these relationships.
In religion, for example, there has long been an enormous body of
esoteric theological knowledge available to those who wished to master it. It would be hard to argue that the objective need for such
knowledge is any greater today than in the past. Yet almost all Protestant denominations today insist that their ministers have some
years of specialized professional training whereas in the eighteenth
century the Protestants educated their clergymen alongside laymen,
giving them very little specialized knowledge. The same thing is true
of the law. There has always been a large body of esoteric legal
knowledge available to those who wished to pursue it. But in the
eighteenth century most men picked this up through apprenticeship, or made it up as they went along. The lay Justice of the

[1] Our whole understanding of professionalism is deeply indebted to Hughes. See
especially his *Men and Their Work*.
[2] For a useful discussion of these themes, see Greenwood.
[3] For an early analysis, see Carr-Saunders and Wilson.

Peace was not thought to need specialized training. Today, on the other hand, attending a law school is deemed indispensable not just for practicing lawyers and judges but for all sorts of quasi-legal work. The rising demand for legal expertise may well reflect changes in the organization of legal practice (e.g. the rise of large law firms) more than it reflects changed social needs.

In teaching, on the other hand, it would be hard to demonstrate that even today there is any body of knowledge about pedagogy that can be transmitted from old-timers to apprentices. Yet enormous efforts have been made to professionalize teaching and to ensure that all recruits will go through the motions of acquiring whatever expertise there is. The same pattern is found to a lesser extent in business, where the desire for professional training predated the existence of a body of knowledge needed by practitioners.

Even in fields where there has clearly been an explosion of knowledge, the causal relationship between this explosion and professionalization is not easy to demonstrate. Medical research in the late nineteenth and early twentieth centuries does seem to have helped bring about the reform of American medicine, and that reform certainly involved greater professionalization. (Licensing requirements were tightened, self-regulation intensified, and "quacks" driven out of practice—and as Everett Hughes has noted, the very concept of quackery boils down to the charge that a man is doing better at pleasing his patients than at pleasing his colleagues.) In engineering, on the other hand, there was a comparable increase in scientific knowledge, but no comparable degree of professionalization. As the amount of expertise available grew, formal training became more common, more extensive, and more intensive. But engineers are still almost wholly at the disposal of their employers, and make little collective effort to set the terms of the relationship. The line separating engineers from nonengineers is blurred, and other hallmarks of professionalism are also missing. (The fact that most engineers want to move into management, and many do so, is a symptom of this.[4]) The engineer, indeed, may be rather like the commercial artist: a man who has esoteric knowledge and expertise but who has not used this to construct a protective guild with its own ethic. This probably reflects the fact that both engineers and commercial artists are usually employed by a large corporation rather than by individual clients, and are therefore in a weak bargaining position. The relationship between esoteric knowledge and professionalism is, then, problematic. Our feeling is that professionalization depends relatively little on the intellectual demands of a line of work and much more on its social setting,

4 For evidence on this score see Goldner and Ritti.

economic arrangements, and the like. It seems to be easier to professionalize groups sufficiently small, powerful, visible, or all three, to form an in-group in terms of both communication and policing quackery and trespass. There may simply be too many engineers and too many school teachers in comparison with the more manageable numbers of doctors, dentists, lawyers, and architects. Yet this last instance again suggests the difficulties of generalizing, for many builders are de facto architects and hard to police. Historical accidents also play a role. Engineering in America started with the military and grew with the railroads and steamboats, and this history of dependence on big organizations may help explain the lack of professionalization even today.[5] If doctors in this country had been employed in the early nineteenth century primarily by the Army, the states, and big hospitals, it might have been much harder to professionalize them. One must also look at the respective power positions of the excluding and the excluded: male physicians could drive out midwives in the United States, as Irish immigrants could drive out Negro caterers and skilled workmen, but architects are not strong enough to drive out contractors, who often make more money and have more political ties than architects.

Nor should one overstate the degree of professionalization even in the recognized professions. When one looks at the actual rather than the ideal picture of medical practice, as Dr. Osler Peterson did some years ago in North Carolina, one finds disparities of the pre-Flexner Report sort.[6] And the practicing solo lawyer, as described for example by Jerome Carlin, may be merely an insurance agent, bail bondsman, or petty fixer, only slightly more schooled than his nonprofessional rival.[7] Such a man has only nominal linkages to the world of the national law schools and the big professionalized firms. Whatever the trajectory of particular fields, however, there can be no question that professionalization is one of the distinctive phenomena of the past hundred years, and especially of the years since 1941.[8]

Furthermore, while the development of advanced occupational training programs and of expertise may not be sufficient conditions for professionalization, they do seem to be necessary ones. There are no professions of consequence that do not operate their own train-

[5] See Calhoun.

[6] See Peterson, Anderson, Spain, and Greenberg.

[7] See Carlin.

[8] The proportion of the labor force classified by the Census Bureau as "Professional, Technical, and Kindred" rose from 3.4 per cent in 1900 to 4.8 per cent in 1940 to 10.8 per cent in 1960. It is expected to reach 14 per cent by 1975. This is the fastest growing of all major occupational categories. See Folger and Nam, "Trends," p. 26. While not all those classified in this group are "professionals" in our special sense of the term, an examination of the detailed Census categories shows that most are at least partially so.

ing programs, and there are very few professions in which these programs do not seek the legitimacy that comes from offering degrees and affiilation with a college or university.

Yet even this phenomenon is difficult to explain. Common sense suggests, for example, that professions require professional schools because competent practice of the profession requires certain kinds of specialized knowledge and theoretical understanding. These are presumably taught most efficiently in professional schools rather than through apprenticeship or trial and error. Yet it is by no means easy to adduce empirical evidence in support of this seemingly self-evident presumption. On the contrary, the available evidence suggests that what seems to be self-evident may well be quite untrue.

It seems reasonable to suppose, for example, that the professors in a professional school have a fairly good idea what they are trying to teach. It also seems reasonable to assume that there is some relationship between the grades they give their students and their success in teaching whatever it is that they try to teach. It therefore seems reasonable to anticipate a relationship between the grades a student gets in professional school and his subsequent success in the profession itself. Yet a recent review of the literature on this subject shows that the relationship between course grades and occupational success is in fact very low, often approaching zero.[9] This review covers studies of students trained in business, engineering, medicine, school teaching, and scientific research. The studies used criteria of occupational success ranging from income and professional reputation to employer ratings and on-the-job observation by colleagues. There are a number of unsolved methodological problems in such research, but they are mostly problems that, if solved, would further reduce the already low correlation between academic and later achievement.[10] The fact that

[9] Hoyt.

[10] Even if there were no *causal* relationship between mastery of academic subject matter and subsequent achievement, we would expect the brighter and more diligent individuals to do relatively well in school, simply because school constitutes a challenge, and they presumably have the equipment to rise to it. We would also expect these individuals to do relatively well in the world of work, for similar reasons. This would produce a statistical correlation between grades and job success even if there were no causal link. In addition, even if there were no causal relationship between the learning measured by grades and success, we would expect students with good grades to be given certain advantages not open to others, simply because so many employers *presume* a relation between grades and occupational potential. On the other hand, it is true that neither the measures of college grades nor the measures of occupational performance used in most of these studies are very reliable. This tends to reduce observed correlations by increasing random variations. We doubt, however, that this sort of distortion is any greater than the distortion in the opposite direction introduced by not controlling for intelligence, diligence, and other personal characteristics, which affect both grades and later achievement.

the correlations are low despite these methodological difficulties suggests that there may be almost no causal relationship between learning what is taught in professional school and doing well as a professional practitioner.

Yet this plainly cannot be entirely true. For those who complete medical school and become doctors, for example, medical school grades may have little relationship to later professional competence.[11] But there is surely a difference in the probable level of medical competence of those who complete medical school and those who do not enter. The medical student must learn *something* in the course of this professional training, even if his professors are unable to measure it very well. Indeed, the low correlation between grades and later success may show only that professors cannot measure their own success in teaching whatever they seek to teach, rather than showing that what they teach is irrelevant to job performance.

This leads to another hypothesis, namely that the function of a professional school is not primarily to teach a narrowly defined set of skills of the kind measured by examinations, but to define a set of general criteria that recruits to the profession ought to meet and to screen out those who do not measure up. The novice is supposed to display a certain amount of diligence and the right mixture of assertiveness and docility, to accept the basic values and assumptions of the professional subculture, and to master the rudiments of the professional vocabulary. If he does this he gets through the course of study; otherwise he does not. Whether he actually learns the details of anatomy, court procedure, or sewer design may indeed be irrelevant, or nearly so, since if he gains entry to the profession he can fill in the gaps in his technical knowledge later. The primary role of the professional school may thus be socialization, not training.[12]

On the basis of what we have said so far, it is clear that professionalism is on the rise rather than on the wane, and that it is one of the basic trends that will shape higher education in the future. In this respect it resembles generational conflict and social mobility. This chapter, however, will not deal with this trend. Rather, it will treat professional schools as special-interest institutions and will analyze the impact of the academic revolution on them. We will say something

[11] For evidence on this point see Hoyt, pp. 25–30, and the sources cited there.

[12] Perhaps the best account of the fact that the professional school is one career and the profession itself another is found in the pioneering study of the University of Kansas Medical School: Becker, Geer, Hughes, and Strauss. In this account, the idealism of the premed is converted into the casing of the academic joint of the medical student, who realizes that if he is to make it as a doctor he has to finish medical school first of all. His ability to accomplish this testifies to a certain amount of diligence and a certain level of morale.

about how various professional schools got founded, how they evolved, and how they usually ended up either becoming multipurpose universities or affiliating in some way with such universities. In order to illustrate these processes we will look briefly at six species of professional schools: seminaries, medical schools, military academies, engineering schools, teachers colleges, and graduate academic departments. We will not attempt to discuss in any detail the professions for which these institutions offer preparation, but will simply try to illustrate some of the general patterns of evolution that seem to characterize all sorts of professional schools.

Seminaries

America's colonial colleges were expected to provide educated leaders for all callings. But those concerned with religion felt the need for education considerably more urgently than those concerned with the law, commerce, farming, or other kinds of work. The colonists viewed the ministry as *the* learned profession, and some churches were willing to pay quite well in order to get a minister whose erudition they could respect. There was no such premium on learning elsewhere. The result was that most colonial college alumni became ministers. Conversely, when the colonists set out to found a college to preserve and propagate learning, they naturally turned to clergymen to administer and staff it. The boards of these colleges were almost all clerical; the president was almost invariably an ordained minister; the instructors were usually young alumni awaiting a call to a pulpit. Under these circumstances it is hardly surprising to discover that the colleges required subjects like Greek and rhetoric whose primary relevance was to a clerical career. (While these subjects could also be defended as relevant to the general education of prospective legislators or shipowners, that was surely rationalization. Advanced courses in chemistry or economic statistics can today be similarly defended as part of a liberal education, but everyone knows that they are really taught because future chemists and economists will need them—and because present chemists and economists like to teach them.) And so, while it is clear that the colonial college was more than a seminary, it is also clear that it served as a seminary for many of its students. Had there been no shortage of literate preachers most of the colonies probably would not have founded colleges, and had a B.A. not been an asset in seeking a pulpit, few of the colleges would have been able to attract enough students to survive. In the South, indeed, where theology and clerical learning were less valued, William and Mary was the only college that took root.

Even when the majority of a college's alumni became clergymen, the fact that a minority did not do so had an important effect on both the colleges and the clergy. Educating prospective clergy and laity together prevented a college from going very far in catering to the specialized needs of future ministers. A general purpose college could not, for example, introduce a subject unless there was *some* theoretical ground for arguing that it was relevant to non-clergymen. In theory colleges could have offered students a choice of studies, but this was rare. Colonial colleges were small enough to teach all students at a given level in a single class, and dividing them into several classes would have made more work for the already burdened faculty.

The colleges' insistence on treating future clergymen and non-clergymen alike also meant that the future clergymen acquired no special expertise not available to their college-educated parishioners. The clergy were therefore in a poor position to claim special wisdom or understanding, even in theological disputes. The result must have been to strengthen the position of the laity, and especially educated laymen's feeling that they were competent to pass judgment on their minister, hiring and firing him as they saw fit. The idea of educating the laity, in other words, was closely related to a kind of anti-clerical bias among Calvinists and their heirs. (Since most college graduates became ministers, there must have been more college-educated ministers than laymen. Even in Congregational New England, then, the local minister must more often than not have been the only college graduate in his community. But this was not the case in the larger towns, which presumably set a pattern of lay-clerical relations that others followed.)

The first separate theological seminary was founded in 1784 by the Dutch Reformed Church, adjacent to its undergraduate college in New Jersey. During the nineteenth century other denominations set up seminaries either linked to liberal arts colleges or separate. These new seminaries would not have been financially possible in the impoverished colonies. Their rise also reflected a feeling among laymen that a clergyman *ought* to have some kind of esoteric knowledge, over and above classical languages, familiarity with the Bible, and the traditional course in Moral Philosophy given by the clerical president of most liberal arts colleges. This feeling was probably exacerbated by the growth of secular knowledge, and especially by Darwinism, which put the clergy on the defensive and called for countervailing expertise, however irrelevant. The rise of separate seminaries also reflected what we would describe as a greater degree of professionalization in the Protestant clergy. Ministers were increasingly involved in disputes with one another over subjects about which their parishioners knew and cared very little. In part, no doubt, this was a by-product of improved communication among clergymen. In part it may have been related to popular apathy about organized religion, which may have encouraged ministers to talk mainly to colleagues who were still committed. Whatever the reasons, esoteric theological debates seem to have multiplied in number and fervor during the nineteenth century, and the spread of theological seminaries was probably a partial response to this. No denomination or even sect apparently felt it could long maintain its competitive position without theologians to carry its banner and define its strategy.[13] (The Catholics had always held this view. The Catholic clergy was never responsible to the laity and has always been educated in separate seminaries when this was practical.)[14]

Yet while the nineteenth centry saw a growing effort to professionalize the clergy and give them separate specialized training, there were continuing economic difficulties. Many Catholic priests, for example, opened institutions they hoped would serve exclusively to recruit and train additional priests. But in order to keep these institutions solvent they sometimes had to take in non-clerical students and diversify their curriculum. Making a virtue of necessity they then tended to redefine their institutional mission as the education of the laity, relegating the preparation of priests to a somewhat subordinate role. This pattern was also found in some Protestant denominations.

The evolution of seminaries into liberal arts colleges was not always a matter of economic necessity, however. In some cases the seminaries

[13] The foregoing sentences encapsulate a long and complicated history. A fuller account would have to take cognizance of the fervent proselytizing of newer sects, such as the Mormons, whose biblical and textual polemics put Protestant ministers on the defensive, much as the pedantry of the radical right can put unprepared liberals on the defensive. (For discussion of this theme see Bitton.) Moreover, even if a sect began with Populist or evangelical zeal and an anti-intellectual bias, holding the second generation might require a more educated ministry with the social and intellectual accomplishments appropriate to more affluent parishioners—a kind of creeping intellectualism, which has led the Quakers just recently to begin their first seminary. The dialectic between being saved by fervent faith and by careful words is an old story, played out in America in the competition among sects and in the social mobility of what came to be called denominations.

[14] The training of a Catholic priest takes a tremendously long time compared to the Protestant norm. Despite the sporadic shortage of vocations, the Church has made no concessions on this front. The isolation of the seminaries and especially of the scholasticates is, however, beginning to diminish, for the more advanced orders and dioceses now feel that a rural seminary, which is a combination of oasis and prison, is likely to produce an excessively unworldly and unprepared priesthood. On the whole subject of Catholic recruitment and training of priests, see Fichter.

established liberal arts divisions as preparatory or remedial programs
to bridge the gap between their students' inadequate elementary education and the demands of higher theology. Such preparatory programs had a way of growing faster than the seminaries to which they
were supposedly adjuncts, for they attracted many students who were
not firmly or even tentatively committed to a clerical career but
simply wanted a general education. While some of these students no
doubt "got religion" after enrolling in the preseminary program, most
did not. The eventual result was sometimes the creation of a separate
liberal arts college larger than the seminary itself.

  Like other collegiate institutions, nineteenth-century seminaries had
to have very flexible admissions requirements, especially if they had
no preparatory department to bring poorly prepared applicants up
to snuff. But the spread of free secondary education in the late nineteenth and early twentieth centuries enabled them to require at least
a high school diploma, and most took advantage of this opportunity.
This effort at upward mobility was, moreover, only a beginning. As
higher education became increasingly common after World War II,
the seminaries took another step up and began requiring a B.A. for
admission. Today most theological schools are graduate level institutions. This gives them a more mature and more sophisticated student
body, which requires less parietal supervision even when it is more
intellectually rebellious. It also allows more efficient preselection,
since applicants have had their academic ability tested in undergraduate courses quite comparable to those they will have to pass
in the seminar.[15] Requiring a B.A. also raises the status of both the
seminary and its faculty, not to mention that of the denomination itself.[16]

  Nonetheless there are still a few holdouts. Some fundamentalists
continue to reject the idea that religion depends on the kind of
knowledge that is enhanced by formal study. Convinced that even the
unlettered can communicate directly with God, tell right from wrong,
and be saved without recourse to abstractions, these sects tend to be
led by preachers with no formal training. Yet even these groups usually place considerable weight on ability to read and interpret the
Bible, and many of their preachers have spent a year or two in some
sort of Bible college. These colleges usually require no more than a

  [15] We have no statistical evidence for the proposition that college grades
predict graduate school grades better than high school grades predict college
grades, but faculty admissions committees usually think so. A student with
poor grades and good test scores has a better chance of getting into a selective
college than into a selective graduate school.
  [16] We do not mean to exaggerate the rate of change in educational requirements. Among clergymen trained in the 1920s, half completed at least a year
of graduate work. Among those trained in the 1930s two-thirds made this
claim. 1960 Census, PC(2)-5B (Educational Attainment), table 9.

high school diploma of their recruits, and sometimes not even that. Few keep their students for four years.[17]

There are also regular seminaries that still accept high school graduates for a four-year Bachelor's degree. This is particularly common in the South, especially in Negro colleges where few prospective clergymen can scrape up enough cash to finance both undergraduate and graduate study. By making religious studies available as an undergraduate option, these colleges tend to "hook" those who are considering a religious career and make it difficult for them to change their minds. If a candidate's sense of vocation is fragile and he is required to delay entry until he earns his B.A., more lucrative and worldly alternatives often begin to appeal to him. If, on the other hand, he starts specializing at eighteen, he may feel so committed to his four-year investment in theology that he cannot give up his clerical plans even if he loses his faith. This desire to rope in likely prospects is presumably one reason why the Catholic Church maintains separate undergraduate colleges for those who have made a religious commitment. But the Catholics insist that all prospective priests also do four years of work beyond the B.A.

What we have seen so far is a pattern of institutional evolution in which multipurpose institutions have sometimes developed seminaries as specialized subdivisions (e.g. Harvard and Yale), in which seminaries have sometimes developed liberal arts divisions (e.g. Drew and Dubuque), and in which seminaries have sometimes been founded and remained separate institutions (e.g. Episcopal Theological School and Andover-Newton Seminary). In recent years, however, still another pattern had manifested itself, in which a long-established and traditionally independent seminary has sought affiliation with a university, often a non-sectarian one. The reasons for this are several. Most theological seminaries are small and cannot afford to maintain the large libraries, diverse faculty, and other expensive facilities now presumed to be necessary for graduate study in a scholarly subject. This problem is compounded by the fact that seminaries have traditionally charged low tuition, have had few rich alumni to endow them, and have been ineligible for public subsidies. Union Theological Seminary, to take an early example, therefore found it expedient to establish a variety of links with nearby Columbia University, both to gain access to Columbia's facilities and staff and to give its degrees in certain fields slightly greater academic standing. The advantages of such an arrangement for Columbia are less clear, but presumably a theological affiliation helps protect the University against charges of godlessness and helps appease trustees who are

---

[17] Of those who reported their principal occupation as clergymen in 1960, about a sixth had never entered college. Many other poorly educated individuals preach part time but hold a full-time non-clerical job.

worried about the University's failure to teach morality and wisdom. Having a "token" seminary in tow is in this respect rather like admitting a handful of "token" Negroes, who quiet the conscience and whose presence can be emphasized when hostile questions are asked by critics. Similar considerations may also encourage a university to devote substantial resources to a seminary. When, for example, President Nathan Pusey of Harvard decided to launch his first major fund drive in behalf of the Divinity School, he acted primarily out of personal conviction, but his decision had a benign political effect too. While it antagonized the many faculty who thought religion in rather bad taste, it also consolidated alumni support by assuring them that Harvard was not quite the center of godless radicalism that its critics claimed.[18] Even some faculty have been reconciled, recognizing that the Divinity School has recruited distinguished theological scholars who can hold their own in the company of historians and philosophers. Columbia administrators may well have felt that Reinhold Niebuhr, Martin Buber, and Jacob Taubes were more exciting and creative scholars than many in the humanities departments.

All of this suggests that the historical linkage between professional training for clergymen and other occupational groups still has considerable institutional and political logic behind it, at least in the private sector. While the seminaries are in some ways becoming more specialized (since they now presuppose a liberal arts education instead of trying to provide one), they seem to be getting less rather than more isolated. They gravitate toward multipurpose universities for both institutional and intellectual reasons. While this tendency is not nearly so marked as among medical and law schools, the fact that it is found at all in theological institutions is significant.

Medical Schools

Although the early colonial colleges were in many respects seminaries, the first separately organized professional schools in America appear to have been colleges of medicine. The University of Pennsylvania early espoused the practical spirit of Franklin and other leading Philadelphians and established a medical faculty in 1765. Kings College (now Columbia University) followed suit in 1767. (It may or may not have been an accident that the University of Pennsylvania was the only non-denominational college in the colonies, and that Kings regarded itself as interdenominational if not quite non-denominational.)

[18] In recent years many divinity schools have become centers of intellectual, existential, and political ferment, more concerned with training campus ministers and professors of religion than clergymen and parish priests; some students who would once have entered philosophy and more recently sociology or psychology now find a freer intellectual home in the divinity school.

These and similar ventures were not, however, an unmitigated success. There was a tradition dating back to the Middle Ages that medicine was a suitable subject for university instruction, but very little was actually known about human health, and it was far from clear that men who had enrolled in a college of medicine were better doctors than those who had learned their trade by apprenticeship, or indeed simply by trial and error. Thus while there was a desperate need for doctors in eighteenth-century America, there was no great rush to enroll in medical colleges.

There was probably no significant improvement in the quality of medicine taught or practiced in America during most of the nineteenth century. It has been said that even in 1900 the odds were less than even that a random patient with a random disease encountering a random doctor would benefit from the experience. Yet nineteenth-century Americans could no more afford to believe this than Navahos or Zulus could, and medicine men flourished. As patients grew richer, moreover, the practice of medicine became increasingly profitable. This had several consequences. First, a number of young men with scientific interests decided that the easiest way to support themselves would be to practice medicine. Second, the number of doctors in major cities became quite large, and medical societies sprang up. (These were often scientific discussion groups of a very general sort, devoting time to evolution, phrenology, and electromagnetism as well as medicine.) These groups of local physicians often established proprietary hospital-based medical schools in which they taught aspiring doctors. In other cases local physicians took over a college-linked medical school and used it as a base from which to build their practices and reputations. In neither case, was the medical school physically or intellectually connected to the rest of higher education.

Looking at American medical education in 1890, many observers concluded that it was hopelessly unscientific and ineffective. Within a generation, however, the entire situation was transformed. The revolution began with the founding of the Johns Hopkins Medical School in 1893, as part of a predominantly graduate university much influenced by German models. It continued with the reform of other university-affiliated medical schools, such as Harvard and Pennsylvania, which also became graduate-level institutions and shared the Hopkins idea of scientific medicine and research. The successes of this approach were quite spectacular, and it was not long before educated people everywhere came to believe that this was the only sound model for medical training. When Abraham Flexner issued his famous Report in 1910, the majority of America's medical schools were still little more than diploma mills. Within a few years, however, half the existing institutions had closed. The remainder almost all moved toward the Hopkins model of a science-based, graduate level, research and training institution.[19] Only a handful of medical schools survive that do not conform to this model, and they are under constant pressure.

This revolution was made possible by a radical change in the kinds of men who wanted to become doctors. During the nineteenth century medicine had been a relatively ordinary profession, attracting some able, ambitious men but also a large fraction of opportunists and charlatans. The rise of scientific medicine had the sudden effect of making medicine *the* profession for able, altruistic young men, including those with money. It thus became possible to enforce far more rigorous training requirements than in the nineteenth century. Today a few other professions have managed to catch up, and medicine has lost some of its old scientific and humane appeal. The chemists and biologists who teach undergraduate premeds persuade some of their ablest students that medicine is not really science at all, while the muckrakers (ably assisted by the AMA) persuade them that, far from being selfless altruists, the majority of doctors are complacent cynics driving around in Cadillacs. The medical schools report that they get slightly fewer first-rate applicants than they did a decade or two back.[20] The leading colleges in turn report that their ablest students are increasingly likely to prefer a Ph.D. to an M.D.[21] Still the medical schools' success in upgrading both themselves and the practice of medicine remains a model for many other occupational groups.

One striking element in this success story has been the re-establishment of the historic relationship between medical education and the

[19] The statement in the text collapses all the fierce arguments, not quite dead yet, about full-time versus clinical professors of medicine. See, e.g. Fleming and also Riesman, Sr. There are still some part-time medical faculty who espouse a "patient-centered" and clinical model as against a research-centered one, even though also insisting on the importance of intensive training in the preclinical sciences in the first part of the medical curriculum. They want medicine to remain an art while also becoming a science.

[20] The actual picture is rather complex. Scores on medical aptitude tests keep rising, but the proportion of students with A averages seems to have declined slightly. This suggests that it is harder to get an A today than in the past. Future chemists and biologists now need A's to get into the graduate schools of their choice, so they work as hard as premeds. That was rarer a generation ago.

[21] An apparently increasing number of medical students at research-oriented schools such as Harvard continue on for the Ph.D. after completing their internship. Their insistence on the double degree represents partly career vacillation, partly the bifurcated nature of medical education, and partly insurance in case they turn out not to be spectacular and original scientists. In some cases, perhaps, the decision to get a Ph.D. represents a way of escaping a career imposed by parents—a kind of return of the repressed. This seems especially plausible in medical families or among upper-middle class Jews where medicine is still seen as *the* career and an M.D. as *the* degree. More recently, some major medical schools have reflected the still incipient shift away from the natural sciences and research toward active involvement, particularly in urban problems. Many idealistic medical students think they want a new kind of patient-oriented medicine and prefer direct service to people, especially poor people, to oblique service via research.

universities. As we have said, such a relationship existed during the Middle Ages but was allowed to lapse because it did not prove intellectually fruitful and was not monetarily useful to physicians. Once the relevance of modern science to medical practice became clear, however, the link between medical education and the university revived. Today all but about ten of America's hundred-odd medical schools are university-affiliated. For many years, it is true, this affiliation remained more juridical than operational. Medical schools have often been located some distance from the main campus of the university with which they were affiliated. Sometimes, as in the cases of Cornell and Illinois, they have even been in different cities. Their faculties have been composed largely of M.D.s, with only a sprinkling of Ph.D.s. There has been relatively little collaboration between professors of medicine and professors in the "pure" sciences, either in research or in teaching. Noting this, we must ask why affiliation became so nearly universal.

On the university's side, attaching the institution's name to a medical school has several advantages. To begin with, it helps establish the institution's claim to be a "real" university. An institution like Princeton, for example, which has a first-rank graduate school of arts and sciences but no medical school or law school, is still widely regarded as a slightly overgrown liberal arts college. Having a medical school also helps establish the institution's over-all commitment to "hard," "practical" subjects, as against the "soft," "irrelevant" humanities. This is a considerable asset in fund raising, not just for the medical school itself but for the university as a whole. It can also be an asset in recruiting undergraduate students, especially since some students suffer from the (usually quite exaggerated) idea that they will find it easier to get into, say, Tufts Medical School if they have been to Tufts as an undergraduate. These premeds, in turn, set an example of seriousness and competence that most colleges value, even though it is often associated with a rather narrow practicality and even anti-intellectualism. Finally, and perhaps most important, having a medical school helps give a university the appearance of public utility, offsetting the widespread assumption that universities are purely self-serving and parasitic. On the other hand, medical schools are fabulously expensive public-relations gimmicks.

The medical schools' motives for affiliating with universities are less clear. In the early years of the century university affiliation was perhaps a symbol of commitment to the modern, scientific brand of medicine, and a way of making clear that the school was not a profit-making proprietary institution. University affiliation also gave a medical school some immunity from smaller-minded pressures and prejudices of the local medical society. University affiliation ensured, for example, that most of a medical school's trustees would be lawyers, bankers, and industrialists chosen for their value to the university as a whole. These men had usually attended a liberal arts college, earned a B.A., and come in later years to think they knew a good deal about how such institutions should be run. But they had not attended medical school, and the M.D. who served as dean of the medical school could usually get his way with them. If the medical school remained independent, on the other hand, its board was likely to include a lot of physicians, many of whom felt the same confidence that they knew how a medical school should be run that the university trustees felt about its undergraduate college.

Almost all medical schools have affiliated with universities; none has itself become a general purpose university, as seminaries, engineering colleges, and teachers colleges have often done. One reason for this is that the medical schools established their position as graduate rather than undergraduate institutions at the same time the modern university came into existence. This meant that so far as students were concerned the interaction between medicine and the academic disciplines had to be sequential rather than simultaneous. The doctors did not have to hire English professors to teach their students to write, or chemists to teach them "scientific method," for they could and did expect medical students to master these subjects as undergraduates. Without these "outsiders" around to act as irritants, the medical schools were content to remain relatively self-contained. Their faculties were composed almost exclusively of men trained in medical schools rather than graduate science departments, and these men had little impulse to remake the medical school into a university.

Another factor preventing the evolution of medical schools into multipurpose institutions was the high status of doctors. Unlike engineers, for example, doctors felt almost no need to seek legitimation through acceptance by the traditional academic disciplines. Hence there was little pressure to teach academic subjects to medical students even when they had not mastered these subjects as undergraduates. A semicivilized doctor was, after all, still a doctor, and if he did not know Homer from Hoover or even Einstein from Eisenstein, he could still feel competent and respected.

In recent years, however, the increasing prestige of the academic professionals has begun to exert an influence on the medical schools, perhaps partly because today's professor of medicine may see himself more as a scientist with ties to other scientists and less as a physician linked to fellow practitioners outside the university. Whatever the reasons, the better medical schools are beginning to bring in nonmedical scientists in large numbers. This means not only molecular biologists and biochemists but sociologists, psychologists, and economists. The result is that some medical school faculties are becoming more like regular university faculties. The University of California's San Francisco campus, for example, has branched out in a variety of paramedical dirctions, and were it not for physical limitations might well become the nucleus of a regular university campus. The Rockefeller Institute (now University) has evolved in a somewhat similar way. In most cases, however, the link-up between academic and medical research has been handled by affiliation rather than expansion.

As the Rockefeller example suggests, one reason for the special character of medical schools has been their special relationship to sources of big money. Medicine became an approved object of philanthropy at about the same time that big foundations under relatively disinterested management came into existence. The foundations were often willing to put money into academic and scientific aspects of medicine that the majority of practitioners or even clinical professors would not have supported. More recently this same pattern has been repeated on an even grander scale under the auspices of the National Institutes of Health. The fact that most congressmen have a relative who died of cancer or is in a mental hospital makes NIH relatively affluent. The NIH management has used this affluence to channel money not only into medicine itself but into a multitude of marginally related and relatively impoverished academic disciplines. Some of this money has gone directly to the academic departments of universities, but some has been channeled through medical schools and has helped build up groups of ecologists, geneticists, psychologists, and so forth on medical faculties.

In addition to its scientific claims, another apparently important element in the professionalization of medicine and the high status of the medical school has been the delay of entry into the profession. It takes little longer to train a doctor than to train an engineer, but the doctors have managed to prevent men from starting until they reach twenty-two, whereas the engineers mostly begin at eighteen. Delay has several advantages. First, it probably allows the medical schools to make a somewhat more judicious choice among applicants than undergraduate professional schools can. About half the students who say they want to become either engineers or doctors at age seventeen abandon this plan within four years, but the would-be engineers have often consumed a good deal of the engineering faculty's time and energy, whereas the would-be medical students have not burdened the medical faulty at all.[22] Those whose medical ambition persists, and who gain admission to medical school, almost all earn M.D.s. Most stay in some branch of medicine throughout their lives. Delayed admission has the additional advantage that the medical schools can ask

[22] For data on career changes among undergraduates see James Davis, *Undergraduate Career Decisions*, table 2.5.

somewhat more of their students. Graduate medical students can be worked even harder than undergraduate engineers, and probably learn more in less time.[23] Since medical education is fabulously expensive under the best circumstances, this kind of efficiency is of considerable importance. (Whether the savings from cramming more work into fewer years offset the cost of cutting every doctor's working life by four years—an average of about 10 per cent—is seldom asked.)

Another important element in the medical success story has been social exclusion. Medicine and law are the two occupations with the lowest proportions of recruits from lower-status families.[24] In part this is because they are among the few fields that look respectable to children from affluent, cosmopolitan families, so they are relatively overchosen by the sons of the well-to-do. But medicine is also known as a field that takes many years to enter, and therefore seems particularly inaccessible to those who cannot count on family support.[25] In addition, the medical schools have traditionally offered relatively little financial support and few opportunities for part-time employment.

All this suggests a more general point about the transformation of American medicine, namely that the medical schools have probably played a far larger part in medical history than seminaries, military academies, teachers colleges, law schools, or business schools have in the history of their respective professions. This is partly because medical research has produced much more dramatic results than research in most other professional specialties and has thus given the medical professors higher status vis-à-vis practitioners than is common in other professions. This is relatively obvious in the cases of the clergy, businessmen, lawyer, and teachers, for all of whom research is relatively inconsequential, at least in the short run. Research has been at least as central in engineering as in medicine, however, and yet the role of the engineering professor has been smaller. Perhaps this is because much of the research that has shaped the practice of modern engineering has been done by industrial scientists rather than by professors. In medicine, on the other hand, the non-teaching hospitals have seldom been major research centers, and certainly the solo

[23] Whether what they learn is what they need to know to practice medicine is another question. See Becker, Geer, Hughes, and Strauss. For a less astringent sociological account of medical education, see Merton, Reader, and Kendall.

[24] James Davis, *Undergraduate Career Decisions*, table 2.19.

[25] It is, however, interesting that Davis finds no special tendency to abandon medical plans among undergraduates from low-status families. This means either that students from low-income families have sized up the difficulty of becoming a doctor even before they arrive at college, which seems unlikely in the light of the general lack of realism in freshmen career choices, or else that high-status premeds are being scared away in disproportionately large numbers for other reasons.

practitioner has done little to advance his profession. The medical schools have therefore become the primary centers of innovation, if only by default. Once physicians recognized this, the medical schools acquired considerable leverage over the whole profession.

A related reason for the importance of the medical schools has perhaps been their relative hospitality to reformers and dissenters within the medical profession. Like many professional schools, they have seen themselves as struggling against the frequently lax and even dangerous practices of the profession at large. They have provided a haven for those who were out of favor with the county medical society, whether because they had advanced views on a particular controversial question of medical practice or because they thought the over-all organization of American medicine left much to be desired. While such reformers and innovators are by definition a minority at any given moment, they nonetheless exercise some long-term influence. This has been particularly true in the past few years, as the role of the federal government in medical financing has grown. For both political and personal reasons, the federal government has found it easier to work with leading medical researchers and educators than with the AMA. This has produced growing reliance on the medical schools as the major federal instrument for raising the quality and improving the distribution of American medicine.[26]

Military Academies

Unlike theology and medicine, the military never found a place in the medieval universities. Martial virtues like physical strength, courage, discipline, and steadiness of nerve were not generally thought to flourish in academic settings. Conversely, scholars concerned with formal, abstract, communicable knowledge seldom thought they had much to say to men of arms. Military leadership was widely regarded as a profession, for reasons we have already discussed, but it was emphatically not regarded as a learned profession, and would have rejected such an appellation had it been offered. And so while the military frequently thought it desirable to train prospective officers in special academies or colleges, these were never associated with universities or with other professional schools.

This European tradition of separatism was continued in America after the Revolution. The newly independent nation moved quite quickly to set up its own military academy, but this enterprise had no

[26] We are indebted to unpublished research by Theodore Marmor concerning the relationships between organized medicine and the federal government.

connection whatever with the rapidly multiplying liberal arts colleges of the same era. When West Point opened in 1802 it was the first college in America to emphasize technical subjects, and for a quarter century it had no competitors. Annapolis, too, had a technical bias, albeit of a somewhat different sort. And both institutions, while sharing the interest of their liberal arts rivals in character development, had a distinctive vision of the kind of character they wanted to develop. (Or so one assumes. When we read accounts of nineteenth-century college life, however, the clerical emphasis on discipline and manners sometimes seems little different from what we would expect of a West Point Superintendent.)

With the rise of the modern university at the end of the nineteenth century the chasm separating military from academic professionalism began to narrow at some points The universities, and especially the land-grant colleges, accepted the importance and legitimacy of the scientific and technical subjects on which the military placed such emphasis. During the twentieth century the universities became the major mechanism for advancing knowledge about a number of different subjects with military implications, and World War II forced the military establishment to recognize this fact. After World War II the Department of Defense made concerted efforts to build (or maintain) bridges between itself and the academic profession.

These bridges have by no means made the military into a learned profession in the sense that law, medicine, or engineering is, nor have they won military science a generally accepted place in the university.[27] The armed services continue to judge officers in the same way that corporations judge executives and school systems judge educators: according to their capacity to exercise authority over others rather than according to their capacity to give others expert advice. The exercise of authority is an art the university has not found ways to teach effectively. Nonetheless, military officers are increasingly dependent on the technical advice others give them. This being so, it has seemed important for future officers to learn what advice to heed and what to ignore. The character of these efforts deserves some attention, for it illustrates in extreme form a set of responses to the academic revolution that also characterizes more recently professional fields like education and business.

One military answer to the academic revolution has been to develop a set of quasi-academic educational institutions for military officers, which parallel the university without quite duplicating it. A military officer can study almost any subject from civil engineering or business

27 On the question of what makes military officers "professionals," see Huntington, The Soldier, chap. 1.

management to international relations or Swahili under military auspices. Indeed, the Defense Department allocates between 5 and 10 per cent of its budget to various kinds of education and training, much of it at the graduate level. While these programs have not always followed the same ideological lines as their analogues in universities, they have usually had the same formal content and have been quite adequate in strictly technical terms. Some, like the language programs, have been technically outstanding.[28]

Just as in civilian institutions, however, innovation at the graduate level has had a delayed and restricted impact on undergraduate education. West Point and Annapolis have been quite slow to emulate their civilian counterparts by broadening their curricula and placing more emphasis on general education and non-technical subjects. The Air Force Academy, starting late with a clear slate, has been somewhat more progressive but is still a long way from Swarthmore or even MIT. (The non-federal military institutions, like the Virginia Military Institute and The Citadel in South Carolina, have more diverse programs, but then they now send most of their alumni into non-military careers.) As at other hitherto specialized institutions, diversification and liberalization have been encouraged by an increase in the proportion of military academy alumni who go on to do graduate work in other subjects and by the university trained faculty who were hired to teach non-military subjects. These faculty have sought to duplicate the programs, and to some extent the atmosphere, they met in their own graduate training, and this has set off a ferment within the military academies to which no immediate end is likely. The more progressive military professionals, sensing that the "McNamara Revolution" and other civilian incursions result from the philistinism and technical limitations of traditionally trained officers, tend to support such ferment. Many hope that transforming the military academies will transform the next generation of junior officers, producing a breed that can compete with civilian "whiz kids".[29]

While waiting for that day, however, the progressives have also sent many West Point and Annapolis graduates back to study at civilian universities.[30] This kind of study has given the military its own experts and pseudoexperts, to deal with—or work against—the civilian professionals hired by defense contractors and the Secretary of Defense. Yet these civilian-trained officers are often distrusted by their less-educated military colleagues, precisely because they seem so

28 On the development and character of military education of this type see Harold Clark, and Masland and Radway.

29 On this subject see Huntington, "Power."

30 For explicit comment on the relationship between liberalization and the spread of graduate study among military officers, see Bennett.

civilianized. Officers with higher degrees have not often risen to the very top—at least not yet. Instead, men with diplomas and expertise more often than not stay in subordinate positions, just as in business, giving advice to others with supposedly better judgment. "Judgment," being largely unmeasurable, tends to be imputed to those who have had "experience," and experience, in the military as in business, means commanding large numbers of individuals, showing a talent for adjudicating their squabbles, keeping one's superiors happy, and avoiding disastrous trouble. The road to the top is therefore still thought to be through field command. For this, it seems, no suitable schooling has ever been devised. The traditionalists maintain that the old spit-and-polish emphasis of the military academies served such a purpose, but it has never been clear how. Progressives argue that the disciplinary style of the academies, while perhaps suitable for selecting and indoctrinating second lieutenants who will throw their lives away when told to do so, is irrelevant for choosing or training future generals, who will have to make decisions on their own rather than being told what to do. But if spit and polish goes, the traditionalists ask, what will take its place? Berkeley?

The military mystique is a puzzling thing and varies from service to service. Like the Catholic Church, military men have been convinced that the esprit de corps necessary for leadership and membership requires some kind of separatism, even when this is logistically and technically awkward. Not only that, but this separatism has been thought to depend in good part on the initial solidarity and commitment created at a military academy.[31] The regular college graduate in the military has been seen as in some way deficient, even when he has shared the far more protracted separatism of life on a military post or even in combat. Few regular academic institutions mark their alumni so clearly as a military academy. (Medical schools are perhaps in the same class.) Certain extracurricular activities, notably athletic ones, seem to breed this sort of esprit, but an academic department does so only under extraordinary circumstances.

The discussion up to this point has been wholly concerned with the academization of the military. Equally important, however, have been the efforts to militarize the university. Perhaps the most obvious example of this is the development of Reserve Officer Training Corps programs on many university campuses. In some ways these ROTC programs have the same relationship to the service academies that university education departments have to state teachers colleges, or university business colleges have to independent business colleges. Yet there are also decisive differences. While the ROTC programs turn out more new officers each year than the service academies, these

[31] On this and other aspects of military professionalism see Janowitz.

officers do not usually make their careers in the military. Even when they do, they are not noticeably more sophisticated or more competent than the West Point and Annapolis men; quite the contrary. Thus, instead of constituting the elite of their profession, as university-trained educators and businessmen tend to do, the ROTC men tend to be regarded as semiprofessional transients. Not only has ROTC been a military stepchild; it has also had a very marginal position in the universities. The status of the military officers who teach military science is almost everywhere even lower than that of the professors of education and business, and universities have never allowed students to major in ROTC. All in all, this particular marriage has proved quite unsatisfactory to all concerned.

The military has, however, made other more successful efforts to co-opt civilian universities to its purposes. It has contracted directly with many universities to conduct research, both open and secret, whose results were thought potentially applicable to war. Some of these research projects, like the Los Alamos and Livermore projects of the University of California, have only the most tangential relationship to the university of which they are a part; others have been closely tied to a particular department and the work of its faculty and students. Perhaps more important than these direct efforts to co-opt segments of the academic profession, however, has been the effort to buy up university alumni. This has been done mainly by contracting with private industry to perform a multitude of military jobs. Industry has in turn hired thousands of university graduates and put them to work on the military's projects. By allowing these men to maintain non-military professional identities (e.g., as economists or engineers), the defense contracting system has co-opted many who would not have been willing to remain in uniform or under military discipline for more than a few years. In a sense, the contract system has been an alternative to ROTC, and a highly successful one. It has allowed the Army to employ university trained experts without trying to impose the special ethic of military professionalism on them. Yet this kind of compromise, which transfers many important decisions from military to civilian hands, has also contributed to the defensiveness of the military professionals, even while it magnified the powers of the over-all military system.

Engineering Schools

We have already indicated that West Point, founded in 1802, was the first technical school in America and for some years the only one. In 1824, however, Rensselaer was founded as a civilian technical school in Troy, New York, and it soon became the leading center of applied science in the country. By the late 1840s science also began to make inroads on established institutions. Yale and Harvard both established scientific schools at this time. During the 1850s other colleges followed suit, so that by the time of the Civil War there were something like a dozen colleges that would train future bridge builders, railroad designers, and even in some cases experimental farmers.

With the exception of West Point, Rensselaer, and the Michigan State College of Agriculture, all these technical programs were attached to older liberal arts colleges. It was seldom a happy relationship. The liberal arts colleges went out of their way to make clear that applied science was a very inferior subject, suitable for inferior students. At both Harvard and Yale, for example, the scientific schools had lower admissions requirements, shorter courses of study, and different degrees from the liberal arts. At Yale the scientific students were even segregated from their classmates in chapel.

The animosity, moreover, was mutual. The scientists mostly regarded the traditional liberal arts curriculum as uninteresting, impractical, undemanding, and effete. Indeed, one of the more puzzling questions about the evolution of higher education during this era is why a marriage of the liberal arts and applied science was even attempted. Considering all that we know about the general pattern of American higher education, we would have expected the applied scientists to go into business for themselves. Yet they did so only when they got ample private support, as in the case of Rensselaer, or state support as in Michigan.

The passage of the Morrill Act in 1862 gave applied science a great boost—probably more of a boost than it was intellectually prepared to absorb. Every state received federal land to support a college (or colleges) of agriculture and the "mechanic arts." The immediate result was to establish more than three dozen small teaching and research centers—probably more than an undereducated, underpopulated nation should have tried to develop.[32] In some cases the money went to established scientific schools, such as Yale's. In some cases new private institutions like MIT and Cornell persuaded state legislatures to assign them the money. In some cases established public institutions with no previous interest in applied science managed to corral the money, as in Wisconsin. More often, however, as in Indiana and Iowa, the legislature decided that it would be safer to establish a new institution devoted entirely to agriculture and engineering rather than entrusting the money to humanists who had hitherto shown only con-

[32] By 1961 there were sixty-nine land-grant institutions in fifty states. The excess of institutions over states was caused largely by the establishment of separate land-grant colleges for Negroes in the South, but also by the separation of agricultural and engineering colleges in a few states.

tempt for such studies. In those states where there had previously been no public university, the Morrill Act often helped bring one into existence, as in Illinois and Maryland. But in states like Colorado and Kansas the split between business and farming interests on the one hand and the humanists on the other was so deep that both a traditional liberal arts college and a separate land-grant college were set up after 1862.[33]

Logical as such divisions may have been, they seldom endured. To begin with, the A & M colleges turned immediately to more traditional academic institutions for faculty. Sometimes they hired European-trained scientists, sometimes American ones; sometimes these men had an interest in the problems of farmers and engineers, sometimes not. But almost nowhere did the new colleges emulate the colleges of medicine, law, and theology, which sought out leading practitioners and made them professors. Perhaps this was because the founders of the A & M colleges were not impressed by the competence of the men who were building bridges and raising hogs in their state, or perhaps it was because successful builders and farmers were doing too well financially in their regular work to be recruited as professors. Geographic problems were certainly one consideration, for while the medical and law schools tended to be urban and so to get part-time faculty from among their cities' many paracititioners, the A & M colleges were rural and had to rely on full-time faculty. This made it much harder to get affluent practitioners on the cheap.

Whatever the reasons, the A & M colleges mostly appointed men who had attended traditional colleges and universities, even though they had not usually studied traditional subjects. This faculty found itself in constant battle with its students over how practical the curriculum should be. Some of the agricultural colleges, such as Michigan, Massachusetts, and Cornell, developed an early enthusiasm for applied chemistry imported from Germany. These studies did not, however, always produce immediate results that impressed the legislature. Equally serious, they often diverted their students to scientific instead of farming careers, arousing the ire of rural parents who had expected their sons to return home after college.

The engineering professors felt that their students needed to know math and physics, and in due course they hired mathematicians and physicists to teach these subjects rather than doing it themselves. In part this was because they did not want to be bothered, in part because they thought specialists would do a better job even with introductory courses, and in part because they thought such men would raise the over-all status of the institution, making it more of a

[33] On the development of these colleges see Nevins. See also Rudolph, chaps. 11 and 12.

real college. The agriculture professors wanted to hire biologists, chemists, and statisticians for similar reasons, and could even justify rural sociologists and agricultural economists with the argument that their work might help the hard-pressed farmers of the state. The cumulative result was that in addition to the pure scientists who had been smuggled directly into the applied science departments, the A & M colleges came to have a number of other scientists and scholars on their faculties, some of whom did not even pretend to have any special commitment to farming or industry. These men were eager to recruit freshmen engineers and agriculturists to their own academic specialty, and they struggled to establish their own departmental majors for their converts. The result was a gradual growth in the number of students, instructors, courses, and research projects in pure science.

A similar but less rapid growth took place outside the sciences. The new A & M colleges almost all suffered from an inferiority complex vis à vis the older and better established (though seldom *much* better established) liberal arts colleges. They were always susceptible to the argument that their alumni were "the leaders of tomorrow" and therefore needed "more than a technical education." For a long time this rhetoric had only minimal consequences, often amounting to little more than freshman English and a course in American history. But in recent years the first two years of undergraduate work have been increasingly devoted to non-technical subjects. These subjects have been taught by professionals trained in literature, history, economics, and the like. Like the natural scientists, the social scientists and humanists have recruited for their own disciplines, fought for the right to offer advanced courses and majors, and struggled against efforts to confine their role to what they contemptuously called "service courses" for engineers and "ag" majors.

The faculty has not been the only source of pressure for diversification and liberalization of the A & M curriculum. Students have also played a role. Not all the students who came to the A & M colleges had firm commitments to engineering or agriculture. Many, indeed, had no firm commitments at all. They came because the college was cheap, near home, without the aristocratic pretensions of the state university, and an alternative to working for their fathers on the family farm or in the family drugstore. Even when these students arrived believing they wanted to become highway engineers or county agents, this idea was subject to change without notice, like almost all ideas held by seventeen-year-olds. The result was a modest but continual student demand for more diversified offerings to accommodate those who changed (or merely discovered) their minds.

While the A & M colleges could have dealt with this demand by telling the malcontents to transfer to the state university, these malcontents were often the most talented students, and in any case their demand for more diverse offerings had considerable support from professors in the relevant disciplines. Indeed, even the applied science faculty often supported such proposals, on the ground that having an advanced program in physics or economics or even literature would raise the status of the whole institution in the eyes of outsiders. Ambitious administrators, needless to say, had the same interest.

Once diversification begins, its momentum tends to accelerate steadily. So long as a college trains men mainly for engineering and agriculture, its upward mobility is limited by the kinds of young people who are interested in such callings, and by the amount of time and energy recruits to these callings are willing to devote to formal education. No engineering school can, after all, be better than the best students attracted to engineering. It can be only a little better than the best employers of engineers want it to be. If it gets too far ahead of the pack its alumni will look like "troublemakers," its reputation will suffer, and the quality of its applicants will decline. Engineering schools can, of course, exercise some collective influence over the character of both recruitment aand working conditions, but this influence is both slow and modest. Once a college develops a more pluralistic vision of its purposes, however, its upward mobility is no longer tied to the development of any one adult calling. It can pick and choose among the occupations for which it prepares, as well as among men interested in a given occupation. Once an A & M college develops this sort of freedom, it is likely to expand those of its programs that prepare students for high-status callings, while making less effort to build up programs in areas that have relatively low adult standing. In this, of course, it resembles virtually all other sorts of colleges.

Nor has diversification been confined to the A & M colleges. Other leading technical institutions have moved in the same direction, and for many of the same reasons. MIT, for example, started out as a technical school and got a share of Massachusetts' land-grant money, but it early developed distinguished departments in the pure physical sciences. More recently it has branched out into a number of other related and not-so-related disciplines, from economics to linguistics, as well as moving into new sorts of professional training such as corporate administration. Carnegie Tech has recently pioneered in training business executives to use computers for managerial purposes. Cal Tech, having long played a leading role in physics and chemistry, is now seeking to build up its non-scientific departments.

It is easy to be cynical about such developments and subsume them, all under a pejorative rubric like "empire building." One can, however, equally well reverse the metaphor and describe diversification as a form of "anti-colonialism." Most technical colleges are today realistic enough to see that the academic profession sets the terms of trade in intercollegiate relations, and that so long as they lack "pure" academic departments of their own they will tend to lose their most talented students and faculty to the more "developed" universities. Having strong academic departments of one's own thus turns out to be rather like having heavy industry in an underdeveloped country; it may be inefficient from the disinterested viewpoint of outsiders, but it is usually necessary to win one's due in a world where rewards go mainly to the visibly powerful. This international metaphor also helps explain why established state universities so often oppose the efforts made by the A & M colleges to build up their academic programs. A state university, like all "advanced" societies, tends to be convinced that an A & M college could not manage anything as difficult as a regular academic program for able students, and that this should be left in the competent hands of the duly qualified. That this policy would help perpetuate the superior social and economic position of the university vis-à-vis the "cow college" is rarely mentioned but also rarely forgotten.

Whatever the rights and wrongs of the matter, most of the A & M colleges have today become full-fledged state universities, and have changed their names to reflect this fact. In Iowa the former A & M college has achieved virtual parity with the state's former liberal arts college, and in several other states, such as Michigan, the gap has narrowed considerably over the years. In states that have only one public medical school or law school, however, these are still almost always affiliated with the former liberal arts college. A law school helps the former liberal arts college maintain a political advantage in the state legislature, which is likely to be something of an alumni meeting for the state university's law school. In most respects, however, the majority of the A & M colleges have become programmatically indistinguishable from other public universities, even though their competitive position is still usually second.

The A & M colleges' drift toward the ubiquitous university model has not, however, been an exclusively one-way affair. The universities that evolved from liberal arts colleges have also adopted many features of the A & M colleges—though without abandoning their sense of superiority. Universities like Michigan, Iowa (in Iowa City), and Kansas, for example, have set up engineering schools in competition with their land-grants rivals. Indeed, Indiana is the only major state university we know that has not done this. Agriculture, on the other hand, has remained a monopoly of the original land-grant colleges, perhaps partly because it has always suffered from a shortage of students even when its research contributions were most dramatic and valuable, and perhaps also because it has been more heavily dependent than engineering on Morrill Act subsidies and has not been financially viable except at colleges designated to receive these federal funds.

The integration of engineering into the larger pattern of university education has been accompanied by the usual efforts to delay both entry and graduation. Until relatively recently the study of engineering began in freshman year and ended four years later with a B.A.[34] But the proportion of engineering students going on to do graduate work is now rising, and a graduate degree is now a prerequisite for employment in many of the choicer jobs. This has made it somewhat easier for the more progressive engineering professors to rationalize giving up control over part of their students' time during the first two years, arguing that those who don't get all the know-how they need by the time they get their B.A. can go on for a Master's. Thus while engineering has by no means become a predominantly graduate profession, it is beginning to show the same tendency to upward mobility that long ago affected theology, medicine, and law.

This tendency has met considerable resistance from prospective engineers, most of whom are first-generation collegians who tend to view college in very narrowly vocational terms and to be aggressively hostile to liberal arts subjects, learning for its own sake, and other presumed by-products of snobbery. Their prejudices have been reenforced by the corporations that employ engineers. It is true that these organizations constantly talk about the need for men with broad backgrounds and advanced degrees. But they continue to pay very attractive starting wages to men who have neither. Many students therefore conclude that there is no real reason to worry about mastering what they regard as "all that cultural BS." Nor do they see any pressing reason to obtain a graduate degree—as they would, for example, if they were entering college teaching and knew that the market for B.A.s was very weak while the market for Ph.D.s was very strong.

So long as the majority of engineering B.A.s and B.S.s go directly to work, most professors of engineering will remain reluctant to delay the start of an engineering major until the junior year, as the reformers urge. One compromise has been the five-year B.S. in engineering, in which the first two years are devoted to general education, the last three to technical training. The problem here is that those who have to

34 The National Science Foundation's 1963 survey of the Class of 1958 showed that 31 per cent of the engineering majors had attended graduate school at some time during their first five years out of college. This was the lowest percentage for males in any undergraduate major except business and pharmacy. See Sharpe, "Five Years."

spend five years in college would rather have an M.S. than a B.S. to show for their troubles. Over the long haul the colleges will almost certainly have to yield to this demand, perhaps offering a six-year M.S. program. Some, indeed, are already moving this way.

Yet even if the engineering faculty can be assured enough time to teach its students what it thinks they need to know, it may still be skeptical about delaying entry. It is true that older students seem more serious, often work harder, and can therefore be taught more in less time. Engineering professors nonetheless often share their students' disdain for general education, regarding it as airy and irrelevant. They rightly suspect that professors in the humanities and social sciences will not make freshmen and sophomores work as hard as engineering professors would. Some therefore fear that if students spend their first two years in soft, dilettantish courses they will never acquire the habit of hard work, or will at least enter engineering in their junior year without it. Yet these fears are increasingly offset by anxiety about the status of engineers in the larger society, and particularly by awareness that large portions of the national elite regard engineers as competent but unsophisticated boors. More and more engineering professors therefore want their students to make themselves intellectually presentable before becoming engineers.

What stands out most clearly in all this is the tendency of both the initially technical and the initially non-technical institutions to diversify their activities and try to become all things to all people. The A & M college could not resist the temptation to imitate the state university, and the state university could not resist the temptation to adopt the more popular A & M programs. These propensities have been encouraged by both institutions' inability to attract either students or faculty who are entirely committed to the institutions' goals. The institutions have therefore been under constant internal pressure to reshape themselves to suit the students and faculty whom they did attract. In a sense this is inefficient. Men who are unhappy should in theory move. But even in America men are never wholly mobile. They often become irrationally attracted to the particular institution where they happen to be. Even if they find local conditions stifling they do not want to pick themselves up and move to a more suitable environment. Instead, they want their present campus to adapt itself to their needs. Clear-cut divisions of labor (and hence of cultural styles) have therefore been hard to maintain over long periods of time.

Equally important to institutional evolution, however, has been the public's refusal to take specialization as given. During the late nineteenth century farmers and businessmen sometimes complained that the A & M colleges were too highfalutin' and were not turning out simple farmers and technicians. But this complaint is no longer common. Today when a state decides it wants a second full-fledged public university, as almost all the more populous states now do, the legislature invariably assumes that the A & M colleges can be readily adapted to this purpose. Almost nobody argues that the training of agronomists or engineers will suffer as a result, nor do many people fear that training in the other professions will be handicapped by a land-grant college's earlier commitment to agriculture and engineering. On the contrary, there is a perhaps irrational and certainly very American assumption that mixing everyone together in a single big institution is more efficient, more productive, and more democratic than separatism.

Teachers Colleges

Although the colonial colleges were not founded primarily to train teachers for elementary or secondary schools, they played this among many other roles. School teaching was not a prestigious or lucrative profession during the colonial era, and almost no sensible man would have chosen it over the ministry. Most parents assumed that any literate fellow could teach school, and saw no reason to pay college graduates well for what non-college men would do for less. Still, not every college graduate could find a pulpit, and some ended up teaching by default. The more fortunate found jobs in one of the larger towns, where primary schooling was offered on a fairly regular basis. Others ended up as itinerants, teaching in a succession of small towns.

This haphazard pattern of recruitment into school teaching continued down to the 1830s. By that time educational reformers like Horace Mann were convinced that if universal schooling of reasonable quality was to become an American reality, a larger and more dependable flow of teachers was necessary. The established liberal arts colleges did not seem the appropriate vehicle for providing this flow. In the first place they were still open only to men, and it seemed clear that an adequate supply of cheap teachers would have to depend mainly on women. In the second place most of the colleges of the time were sectarian establishments, for which public subsidies were increasingly hard to raise. In the third place the better colleges of the time insisted on more than an elementary education from their applicants, and even the worst ones pretended to do so. To require such lengthy preparation of prospective "schoolmarms" seemed wasteful and would have excluded many whose services were badly wanted. The need was rather to develop a publicly financed training institution that would recruit women at the end of eight years of elementary school, give them semiprofessional training, and send them back to the elementary schools as teachers. This need was met by a new institution: the state normal school. The normal school movement began in Massachusetts during the late 1830s under Mann's leadership. It spread to other states during the 1840s and 1850s, and by the end of the nineteenth century there were several hundred of these institutions spread across the country.

The effort to professionalize school teaching had other sides as well. There was an intellectual effort to create a science of pedagogy and to train teachers in its use. This movement gathered strength during the late nineteenth century and won a place within the emergent universities. By World War I most major universities had established separate schools of education, and in many cases these had grown to considerable size. These schools served a variety of purposes. They were expected to provide a modicum of pedagogic training for students majoring in academic subjects who wanted to become high school teachers. They also competed with the normal schools by offering prospective elementary teachers a chance to earn (and perhaps also marry) a B.A. while majoring in education. They often offered advanced work for present and future school administrators. And perhaps most important for our purposes, they trained many of the men who became professors in normal schools. Knowing this last fact, the reader should not be surprised to discover that the normal schools showed a persistent tendency to become more like universities.

Yet the mimetic tendency of the normal schools, as of most other institutions, depended on other factors as well. There was, to begin with, the disruption of their traditional ecological position caused by the spread of free local high schools. The high schools cut into the normal schools' traditional clientele by offering girls a chance for secondary education while living at home. Not only that—they threatened the normal schools' share of the elementary teaching market, for high school graduates were as old and as competent as the normal schools' traditional alumnae and had almost as much reason to believe they could teach the Three R's. The high schools were, however, an opportunity as well as a threat. The very abundance of female high school graduates that threatened the normal school's position as a secondary institution helped it to raise its admissions requirements and to become a college. One by one the old normal schools began requiring a high school diploma for admission, and in due course they also began requiring four years of academic work for graduation. Their new status was confirmed when they won permission to award B.A.s, and was given symbolic legitimacy by altering the institution's name from "state normal school" to "state teachers college."

Such developments were, however, only the beginning. Once the normal schools had become colleges they felt even more obliged than before to hire university men with doctorates, and this meant increasing dependence on university graduate programs in education. The Ed.D.s who emerged from these programs often had little idea what academic research was about, much less how to do it, but they did have a fairly clear idea how the academic pecking order was organized and what constituted respectability in the university world. Naturally they wanted the same perquisites as their former mentors at the universities.

Once an institution had earned the right to award B.A.s the next major evolutionary step was usually to expand from elementary into secondary education. This meant offering academic majors in subjects usually taught in high school, and this in turn meant recruiting professors with Ph.D.s in these subjects. It also meant admitting male students in large numbers for the first time. The shift into secondary education was usually accompanied by the arrival on campus of students whose primary interest was not becoming a teacher but rather earning a B.A. with minimal academic, cultural, and financial strain. While few of these entering students knew from the start that they would not become teachers, many made this decision at some point in their college careers, and many others did so after graduating. In due course this situation was accepted and legitimized by allowing students to take B.A.s without meeting state requirements for teacher certification.

At this point an important change took place, for the evolution of the college no longer depended on the evolution of the teaching profession. Instead of trying to attract better students into teaching the college could move ahead by attaching itself to more prestigious callings. Like the A & M colleges, which found themselves in a similar situation, it usually took advantage of this opportunity. One by one the state teachers colleges have added occupational programs in new areas to cater to those who were not headed for teaching.[35] They have also added graduate programs, first in education, then in other areas as well. This transformation has been symbolized by another change of name, from "state teachers college" to "state college" or even "state university."

By and large the older and better established colleges and universities opposed the transformation of the former teachers colleges just as they earlier opposed the transformation of the former A & M colleges. But their opposition has been weakened by their own

[35] We cannot resist the suspicion that this diversification has somewhat reduced the number of would-be teachers by opening up more attractive opportunities to local boys at local colleges. The educationists used to have the only statewide recruiting network for respectable white-collar work; no longer.

evident incapacity to find places for all the students who want higher education or to turn out enough alumni to satisfy the demand for B.A.s. The former teachers colleges have had an unbeatable combination of advantages in satisfying these needs. On the one hand they have had a tradition of very low tuition—usually even lower than the state university. On the other hand they have been geographically dispersed so that students could often commute and in any case stay near home. And to cap it all they have not been encumbered by a tradition of academic selectivity or any assumptions about what a student had to know to deserve a B.A., so they could give even quite dull students degrees without too much faculty protest.

From the legislative viewpoint, then, the former normal schools were even more attractive vehicles for expanding public higher education than were the former A&M colleges. And even more than in the A&M colleges, the evolutionary process we have described was often accelerated by a legislature that wanted more full-fledged multipurpose campuses to accommodate the ever-rising tide of applicants. The typical pattern was one in which a few of the more "advanced" teacher training institutions began to outgrow their traditional role, campaigned for a new status, and helped foment a climate of opinion in which a statewide need for more college places was recognized. Then the legislature typically responded by reorganizing *all* the teacher training institutions, including some that were not really "ready." Or at least the legislature conducted such reorganizations on paper. In practice the change often takes a full generation to accomplish.[36] Thus many of the places now called state colleges or universities still have more Ed.D.s than Ph.D.s on the faculty, more girls than boys in the student body, and more docility and low-level vocationalism everywhere than one would find in better-established institutions.

But while the majority of the new state colleges are still unequal to the responsibilities recently thrust upon them, further changes are already in the making. Teaching, like engineering, is trying to become a graduate rather than an undergraduate profession. The drift can be seen both at the bottom and at the top of the program. At the bottom, more and more teacher-training programs delay entry until the junior year, insisting that students spend their first two years pursuing a general education. At the top, more and more wealthy states require new teachers, especially secondary school teachers, to have at least a year of graduate education beyond the B.A. This latter innovation is often instigated and almost always supported by the

[36] For further illustration of these and other aspects of the evolution of a normal school into a university see our study of San Francisco State College, in Sanford.

universities, old and new, for it creates more demand for graduate work. It also encourages students to major in an academic discipline as undergraduates, cramming their work in education into a fifth intensive year leading to a Master of Arts in Teaching degree. While relatively few colleges have abolished undergraduate majors in education, the trend is clear.[37]

Strangely enough, this development seems to be going even faster than in engineering. There are several plausible reasons for this. First, education professors are probably more eager to expose their students to the liberal arts than are engineering professors. Educationists have never had the same self-confident contempt for the humanities and social sciences that engineers have had. They have not been able to put down the liberal arts as being vague or "soft," nor as having a slack grade curve, for their own courses have been even more subject to such criticisms. And while they have sometimes argued that liberal arts courses were irrelevant for future teachers, this argument has never made much rhetorical headway in the face of the fact that most future teachers are expected to teach some version of these same liberal arts subjects to their students. The most the educationists have been able to say in response to the academicians' claims for their disciplines is that they are too narrow, too specialized, and insufficiently sensitive to student interest and motivation. This attitude has made education faculties sympathetic to interdisciplinary general education programs. Education professors have often welcomed proposals that future teachers spend their first two years in general education. In the long run they hoped this would raise the competence and status of teaching, and even in the short run they expected it to bring more careful selection of prospective teachers, since the education department could reject applicants who did poorly in the first two years.

Another reason why education has moved somewhat faster than engineering to become a graduate profession may be that the employment market for teachers is more nearly monopolistic. If a small group of educationists in the state universities and state colleges decide that they want to put teachers through five years of higher education rather than four, and if they persuade a few key figures in the state's educational establishment and in the legislature that this is economically feasible and pedagogically desirable, the change can be brought about by changing state certification requirements. Once the legislature has acted, the student with only four years of higher education can get only a temporary teaching license and has a quite low salary ceiling. This is true even if the teacher's immediate su-

---

[37] For discussions of current trends in teacher education, see e.g. Conant, and Koerner.

periors think him extremely competent and would willingly pay him more than most men with higher degrees. In engineering, on the other hand, there are no effective legislative mechanisms for raising professional standards. Engineering professors may feel that every engineer should have five or six years of higher education, but they cannot easily enforce their view so long as substantial numbers of corporations go on hiring men with only four years of training. If engineers with B.S.s prove competent, private corporations can promote them despite their lack of credentials, in a way that school systems cannot promote comparable teachers. The result is that the initial qualifications demanded of engineers are probably somewhat more closely related to actual job requirements than is the case in education. The market for engineers is much harder to manipulate, for either good or bad ends. It is also hard to avoid the conclusion that the leaders of teacher education have played a large and not entirely selfless role in managing the market for their alumni, helping create a demand for more extensively trained teachers instead of a demand for more competent classroom performance.[38]

Graduate Schools of Arts and Sciences

Although scholars popped up from time to time in pre-Civil War America, they never constituted a distinct profession.[39] A man with a passion for research in the natural sciences or history could not make his living from such work, and unless he inherited or married money he had to pursue a career of some other sort. A would-be scientist, for example, was likely to become a doctor, or perhaps a government surveyor. A would-be historian was likely to become a clergyman, a writer and lecturer, or perhaps a college teacher. If he became a teacher, however, his scholarly talents and interests would have to remain a part-time avocation, just as they would if he became a

[38] We are not arguing that training and actual competence are unrelated, although this may well be true. We are arguing only that the correlation between training and performance is at best very low, and that the best way to get competent performers would be to observe and evaluate first-year teachers in the classroom rather than raising certification requirements and hoping for the best. For a more extensive discussion, see Lieberman, *Education* and *The Future*.

[39] A note on nomenclature may be helpful. We occasionally use the term "scholar" broadly, to cover anyone engaged in advancing the frontiers of any field of knowledge. In this section, however, we will include only men in the humanities, social sciences, and natural sciences, excluding those in applied fields like engineering, law, medicine, and business. At times we will use the term more narrowly still, including only men working in the humanities and the social sciences. When we use the term in this last sense we will usually juxtapose it to the term "scientists." The context should make our meaning clear.

preacher. His primary responsibilities would be pedagogic and disciplinary, and it would be for competence in these activities (especially discipline) that he would be hired, paid, and retained. Competence in scholarship might even be a liability, first because it would suggest that he was not devoting his full energies to the students for whose education he was responsible, and second because it might lead him into conflict with received ideas about the substance—or worse yet the form—of the curriculum.

There were a number of early efforts to change this situation by establishing universities that would hire scholars and try to advance knowledge as well as transmitting it. Thomas Jefferson's plans for the University of Virginia embodied this kind of thinking, and a decade later the plans for New York University did the same. But neither scheme bore the intended fruit. Reformers within established institutions, like the classicist George Ticknor at Harvard in the 1820s and President Henry Tappan at Michigan in the 1850s, were also frustrated. At the outbreak of the Civil War America had very few productive scholars anywhere, and only a minority of these was probably employed in colleges. Virtually none, either in a college or anywhere else, was employed *primarily* as a scholar or scientist.

A generation later all this had changed. Beginning slowly in the 1870s and then gathering force during the 1880s and 1890s, institutions began to develop that were universities in practice as well as nomenclature.[40] These institutions played two related but distinct roles in shaping the academic profession. They provided employment for men who did research and provided substantial rewards to those who did it well.[41] They judged quality largely by asking other men with comparable training and interests what they thought of the work, rather than by asking laymen. In addition they also created a supply of professional scholars by establishing graduate programs that trained and certified men for every field in which professorships existed. The fact that the university became not only the producer but the consumer of academic professionals makes an analysis of the subject particularly complex and also explains some of the professions' more unusual features.

One source of confusion is the scholars' habit of making a sharp distinction between a graduate department and a professional school. A Ph.D. program in history or botany, scholars usually say, is not

[40] For an excellent account of this process see Veysey. See also Storr, *The Beginnings.*

[41] Although most colleges paid miserable wages at this time, a few leading professors made $5,000 or more a year by 1914. Since the cost of living about trebled between 1914 and 1967, and real incomes about doubled, the equivalent salary in 1967 would be about $30,000. Such salaries are not unknown, but neither are they common, even in leading institutions.

"practical" or "applied." Its aim is not to help men do what is useful
but to help them learn what is true. And so, it is argued, a graduate
department is not like a professional school, and a Ph.D. is not like
an M.D. or an LL.B. These arguments, it seems to us, reflect the fact
that academic departments are primarily interested in training men
for employment within their own ranks, or at least in other similar
departments, rather than training men for employment elsewhere.
They are therefore freer to define their own objectives and freer
from the "corrupting" influence of worldly problems that demand
immediate solutions. This does not, however, make a history or botany
department less of a professional school. On the contrary, if one
defines a profession as a group that claims the right to regulate itself,
determining its own methods and judging its own members, academicians might be judged the most professionalized of all occupational
groups.

Unlike a doctor or lawyer, an able scholar does not have to
persuade non-professional customers to respect his expertise; his "customers" are other scholars. Of course he needs non-professional financial support, but he gets this in ways that give the non-professionals only minimal power to direct or even evaluate his work. His
two principal sources of funds are teaching and research grants.
Teaching means working with young people who do not themselves
usually pay for the services they supposedly receive, and who cannot usually affect their professors' incomes directly by taking their
trade elsewhere.[42] Research grants come mostly from large bureaucratic organizations. While such a bureaucracy may adopt the over-
all priorities of laymen rather than professionals, it usually hires academicians to work out the details of its relationships with the academic
profession. This means that decisions about how research will be done,
who will get to do it, and even (on a de facto basis) what the research will really be about, are made by members of the guild—though
not always by those with the highest professional status in the guild.

For all these reasons we regard graduate departments in the
sciences and humanities as professional schools. Having said this,
however, we must immediately add that the character of these pro-

[42] Departments do compete for majors in order to be able to hire more teaching
assistants and to expand the departmental offerings, as well as for less practical
reasons of status. But the very point of this competition is to free the senior or
more favored professors for work in their own specialty with their own cadre of
graduate students, and to enable them to reduce their teaching loads in terms of
both coverage and of hours. The department, in other words, does its best to
insulate individual professors from the effects of unpopularity. No university we
know penalizes professors economically if students fail to enroll in their courses,
nor does any we know pay men extra if they attract more than their share
of students and thus do more than their share of the work.

fessional schools is in many ways ambiguous. The most important and frequently discussed of these ambiguities is whether Ph.D. programs are intended to train men to teach or to do research. The answer, of course, is that they are intended to do both. But they combine these objectives in a paradoxical way. The *training* offered in a graduate department is almost exclusively for research; yet the *certification* they provide, in the form of a Ph.D., is often more important if one plans to teach than if one plans to do research.

The typical graduate student is taught the frame of reference and vocabulary of those who do research in his discipline. This, it is hoped, will enable him to read and understand their scholarly work. His ability to do this is measured in papers and examinations and recorded in grades. He is then told to go out and do similar work himself in the form of a dissertation, and is given a Ph.D. if he does a moderately competent job. A man who wants to do academic research usually benefits from such training, and he certainly finds it easier to land a research job if he has had it. But it is important to remember that, unlike most other professions, scholarship does not *require* its practitioners to have had formal training or to meet certification requirements. Many research organizations hire men without Ph.D.s or even M.A.s in any relevant field. If such men do good work they can usually advance within the organization without being seriously handicapped by their lack of credentials. Certainly few argue *in principle* that research jobs should be open only to Ph.D.s, as they argue that medicine should only be open to M.D.s or law to LL.B.s. The test, at least in theory, is competence rather than certification. An untrained researcher can also publish his findings. A scholarly reviewer may say petulantly that "this book should never have been published," but few would support legislation designed to prevent non-Ph.D.s from getting their ideas into print, or even legislation requiring that books in given fields be approved by Ph.D.s in that field before publication, "so as to prevent the spread of misinformation." The closest the academic disciplines come to this is to referee publications in some journals and by some university presses. This is hardly a major step toward monopoly, since other publications are open to those who are rejected by the professional journals and university presses. Scholarship, then, is not a closed profession in the sense that medicine or law is. The rewards of openness have been evident in the contributions made by men who have switched fields (moving in recent years from physics into biology, or from economics into sociology) or who have been autodidacts.[43]

[43] On this whole subject see Hughes, especially his discussion of the difference between a profession and a learned society.

When one turns from scholarship to teaching, the relationship of training to certification is reversed. The typical graduate school offers no formal training in the art of teaching. Its professors make no effort to develop or codify a body of knowledge about what works in the classroom and what does not. They do not even try to provide clinical training by giving their graduate students classes to teach and then supervising their work. A graduate student can, if he has a research assistantship or a fat fellowship, usually get his Ph.D. without doing any teaching whatever. Even if he resorts to teaching as a way of making ends meet, he can be almost completely incompetent without his department's knowing it. And even if his professors know he is an incompetent teacher, they would never refuse him a Ph.D. on that ground alone.[44]

All this is well known to colleges hiring teachers. Yet almost all these colleges insist that their teachers have M.A.s and preferably Ph.D.s. In some cases publicly controlled junior colleges and teachers colleges are legally forbidden to employ teachers without graduate training. Even where there are no legal requirements, regional accreditation agencies look askance at institutions whose older professors lack the Ph.D. And withholding accreditation can mean the loss of certain government subsidies as well as the loss of some applicants.

Colleges have several reasons for insisting that prospective teachers have had graduate training. Many have persuaded themselves that they want to move upward academically and that they care about research, even if in practice they do not. Some departments in such colleges then persuade prospective faculty that they will have an opportunity to do research. The department may even believe this, though the promises tend to become more guarded after the man's arrival. But even in colleges where such aspirations are dormant, the belief may prevail that a man trained at Chicago or Ohio State or Columbia will know his stuff and will be able to connect local undergraduates with ideas they will need if they go on to graduate school. These colleges know that once they have hired a professor their chance to evaluate him as a teacher will be rather limited. A

[44] The Ford Foundation's recent decision to make major grants to a number of leading universities for the reform of their graduate programs is in part aimed at this problem. The Foundation hopes to ensure that graduate students get some supervised teaching experience during their graduate years. It also hopes to establish a fellowship program that will ensure that students move through their academic training at a more rapid rate and can predict with somewhat more confidence how long it will take them to earn a Ph.D. (Academic training is today unique among the professions in that there is no realistic way to predict how long it will take to get a degree.) It should also be emphasized that institutions differ widely in the extent to which the senior faculty care about teaching and in the extent to which this rubs off on the graduate students.

new man's colleagues will make informal judgments about whether he knows his subject, but they will only rarely visit his classes, scrutinize his reading lists, read the examinations his students write after taking his courses, or make systematic efforts to see what his students thought of him. In some cases this is because the man's colleagues do not really care whether he is a good teacher, so long as he shows scholarly promise—or, if he is over thirty-five, performance. But in other cases faculty reluctance to evaluate teaching derives from genuine uncertainty about how this should be done—and how reliable the results would be. Some professors will even argue that such evaluations somehow constitute an invasion of privacy and a violation of academic freedom. Knowing all this about their own practices, colleges tend to seek *advance* assurance that the men they hire are competent. Graduate training and degrees may not provide much proof of this, but they seem better than nothing.[45]

The fact that universities will hire non-Ph.D.s to work in a research institute but not as regular members of the teaching faculty has a second explanation as well. Holding a Ph.D. certifies a pattern of competencies that is more likely to be relevant to a teaching department than to a task-oriented research enterprise. An academic department wants its members to talk a common language and have at least a nodding acquaintance with the various branches of knowledge that fall within its administrative purview. It wants men who can and will give courses covering some of the subjects the department has defined as falling within its range of responsibility, not men who will wander into other fields and leave the departmental work load to their colleagues. There is a fairly well worked out national consensus about what a physics or political science or English literature Ph.D. ought to know, and this coincides roughly with the fields covered

[45] There are, it is true, other ways of judging prospective candidates, but most are less than satisfactory. There is no Federal Trade Commission to police letters of recommendation and they therefore tend to be as euphoric as other forms of product promotion. Men can be brought for visits or asked to give a lecture without being made to feel they are on trial, and this is sometimes helpful. Yet it is also expensive and time-consuming. Not only that, but in our limited observation the combination of social awkwardness and professional deference often means that these encounters give a very misleading impression to all involved. Ph.D.s are, moreover, in such enormous demand that many colleges are reluctant to seem too guarded in their approach to them, lest they decide the college does not really want them and opt for another institution which is more willing to make a quick commitment. The result is that in many cases a preoccupied department chairman hires a man he has never seen in action or only heard read a ten-minute paper to an audience at a professional meeting. Or, if the appointment is at a higher level, the committee involved will often judge the candidate almost entirely on the basis of his reputation and credentials. (The British system of advertising academic openings and requesting formal applications avoids some of these pitfalls, though there too actual decisions are often made on the basis of brief personal encounters and recommendations of varying reliability.)

by undergraduate departmental offerings.[46] A man with a Ph.D. in, say, economics is therefore likely to be able to teach the kind of courses economics departments want taught, and to talk the language other economists talk.

Research enterprises have different exigencies. Their clients' problems may be real or imaginary, but in neither case are they likely to fall into neat departmental categories. The organization is therefore more likely to be engaged in what is known as interdisciplinary inquiry, and for this it needs men with special combinations of skills such as sociology and psychiatry, or chemistry and systems management. The combinations are, constantly changing and graduate departments make only modest efforts to keep up. A man may therefore have a set of interests and skills that are quite relevant to a research organization's agenda, but may find that he cannot pursue these interests easily in graduate school. He may therefore drop out of graduate school—not because he is incompetent but because he is impatient and tired of working in a framework that seems irrelevant to him. Many problem-oriented research organizations realize this and make tempting offers to men who have not finished their degrees. Universities are less likely to do this, for they want teachers socialized in more conventional ways. (Indeed, it can generally be said that the rules of the teaching game are much more conservative than those of the research game, and that there is still a feeling that students must be protected from mistakes or omissions in a way that readers of books or even research reports need not be.)

A second sort of ambiguity in the character of the graduate school is its relationship to the nation's intellectual and cultural life. This is not the place to explore such a complex issue in detail, but it is useful to distinguish between the academic and the intellectual. We have used the term "academic" to describe a professional guild and its activities. An academic question is therefore one raised by some lacuna or ambiguity in the data or interpretations of a world-wide discipline. It is a question asked by one's colleagues or on their behalf and answered primarily as a service to these colleagues. The term "intellectual" refers to an amateur role. Many people assume an intellectual role occasionally, and some do so almost constantly, but few make a living from it. Intellectual questions grow out of reflection on experience, are asked by all sorts and conditions of men, and are

---

[46] This assertion may seem unwarranted to academic readers aware of bitter controversy in their own field—between behaviorists and theorist-historians in political science, for example, or between New Critics and literary historians in English departments. But major splits of this sort are relatively few in number, and even "protestant" graduate departments usually share enough with the "catholic" ones for their Ph.D.s to fit fairly easily into a standard undergraduate program.

answered, insofar as they can be answered, in ways that make sense to such men. In an academic argument the participants are supposed to have professional detachment and to collaborate in the search for a generally acceptable answer. Moral and political questions that cannot be resolved by research and do not yield to cooperative investigation are almost by definition outside the academic orbit. The protagonists of an intellectual argument, on the other hand, are expected to be "interested parties." Heated debate is respectable for intellectuals, since the outcome of their argument is expected to have personal as well as professional consequences.

Our distinction between the academic and the intellectual should not be viewed as a device for classifying particular questions or particular methods of getting answers. It is rather a device for classifying the motives that induce men to ask questions, with academic questions being asked for primarily professional reasons and intellectual questions being asked for primarily personal ones. It is true that motives are always mixed. Men find their personal interests absorbed and redirected by their profession, just as the professions are continually reshaped by the kind of personalities they recruit. In the best cases intellectual inquiry and academic discipline achieve a creative symbiosis. One consequence is that the most creative men in different fields often resemble each other more than they resemble the more regular academic members of their own field. Some physicists, mathematicians, and biologists may feel an intense, almost religious and poetic sensitivity about their theoretical work. Yet so personal and affect-laden an approach is certainly atypical in most of the natural sciences, where very little is discovered that has personal significance or consequences for the inquirer. It is almost equally rare in the "hard" social sciences, like economics, and in the "hard" humanities, like linguistics. It is perhaps somewhat more common in "soft" fields like literature, history, political science, clinical psychology, and the like, but even in these areas only an exceptional scholar would say that his life style—or even his voting behavior—could conceivably be altered by his research findings.[47] To some students this means that almost all academic inquiry is irrelevant and inconsequential. More neutrally, it means that almost all academic inquiry is highly professionalized. Lawyers and doctors, after all, also try to treat their clients' problems as technical rather than personal challenges and try to avoid

[47] Tracing the relation between intellectual inquiry and academic discipline as fields grow and create their own constituencies would be an interesting contribution to intellectual history. For example, one can find clinical psychologists today, like many psychoanalysts, who have discovered a good and lucrative field and who share few if any of the intense exploratory interests of the creators of the field. For a discussion of some of these themes see Hofstadter.

taking cases (like those of relatives) that have personal consequences for them.

Having said all this about the special character of the academic profession, we return to the major theme of this chapter, namely, the evolution of professional schools. It would be convenient to be able to make a simple dichotomy between graduate professional schools on the one hand and undergraduate liberal arts colleges on the other, and to say that the former were academic and the latter intellectual. But this has never been the case.

The nineteenth-century liberal arts college had almost no connection with the main intellectual currents of its time, and its curriculum was by no stretch of the imagination responsive to the kind of question that troubled its more curious students.[48] It was rather a degenerate survival from an earlier era, whose program reflected partly the professional needs of aspiring clergymen and partly the culture of eighteenth-century gentlemen. Nor is today's university college usually an intellectual institution in our sense of that term. It is, rather, a downward extension of the various graduate professional schools for which it prepares, and more especially of the academic graduate schools. While some professors and some departments, especially in the humanities and social sciences, may attempt to provide instruction that will be interesting and relevant to students who do not plan to "go on in the field," this is atypical. The more orthodox and prestigious pattern is to offer a pre-graduate major aimed almost exclusively at future professionals. This major is deliberately made sufficiently disciplined and difficult so that dilettantes will stay away. This is clearest in the natural sciences, but is also increasingly common in the social sciences and humanities.

In the light of all we have said about the general tendency to delay entry into the professions, academicians' continuing interest in undergraduate instruction may be surprising. The usual pattern, as already indicated, has been for professions to establish themselves on the highest academic rung they could, so as to get more mature and more carefully selected students. Scholarship followed this pattern of establishing itself as a predominantly graduate profession in the last quarter of the nineteenth century, even earlier than medicine or law. Unlike doctors and lawyers, however, scholars did not stop offering undergraduate education when they went into graduate work, nor have they done so since. While a few of the newer academic specialties have been content to remain largely graduate subjects, the traditional disciplines all offer extensive undergraduate programs.

[48] For a particularly mordant view of the situation, see *The Education of Henry Adams*.

The reasons for this are complicated, especially in view of the fact that many of the most eminent academicians prefer to teach graduate students, and for much the same reasons that professors of medicine do. Preliminary reports of a study of the academic profession by Talcott Parsons and Gerald Platt suggest, however, that the great majority of academicians, in both the most and the least eminent institutions, *say* that they want to teach undergraduates.[49] In some cases the commitment to undergraduate teaching reflects a fear that if the discipline became an exclusively graduate subject it would not get enough recruits. But this is by no means a widespread preoccupation. Many scholars, indeed, feel they already have too many recruits and would like to make their field more exclusive. In some cases undergraduate programs are justified on the ground that maximum productivity in the discipline (e.g. physics) comes in the middle or late twenties, so that unless students begin to study the subject in their middle teens they may not be ready to do original work when their creative potential is at its peak. Correspondingly, when creative potential declines, and "elderly" professors of physics are "retired" at thirty-five, they may not have the talent or inclination for academic administration. Some of them will prefer to teach undergraduates, even though they may no longer be able to lead them quite to the ever-receding frontier of research. In most cases, however, academicians' enthusiasm for undergraduate teaching is something that comes only in small doses. Given their choice, most professors would probably teach an undergraduate course now and then, but they would prefer it not to interfere with their "real" work.

None of these reasons for maintaining undergraduate academic programs is, however, probably decisive. The crucial fact is that undergraduate instruction provides jobs for members of the academic profession. If the teaching of undergraduates were turned over to other sorts of instructors—and it should be remembered that there is no organized and powerful group eager to take over—scholars in many disciplines would have a hard time making a living. Some, of course, could become teachers of graduate students, but this is by its nature a minority calling within any profession.[50] Some could work

[49] The forthcoming study of British academic men by A. H. Halsey and Martin Trow shows, however, that they are much more undergraduate-oriented than the American norm.

[50] Assuming that the faculty:student ratio in an exclusively graduate department were one to ten; that five of these ten students dropped out without taking a doctorate, and that the remaining five take an average of five years to earn their degrees, each professor would turn out one Ph.D. a year. If each professor taught for an average of thirty years after earning his own Ph.D., then the graduate schools would have jobs for only one out of each thirty Ph.D.s they produced.

for industry and government, especially in the natural sciences. But in the social sciences and especially the humanities, most scholars can earn a living only by teaching undergraduates.

This fact finds expression in institutional politics on a day-to-day basis. The easiest way for most departments to justify adding new professors in new specialties is to increase their undergraduate enrollment. A department could afford to abandon its undergraduate program only if it had ample grants, contracts, or endowments to support its professors. Very few departments are in this position, though most would like to be. To the extent that they are, their professors tend to withdraw from undergraduate teaching. As the resources available to support academic research grow, this withdrawal becomes more common and its organizational implications more obvious. Over the next generation it seems likely that many more academic specialists with outside research grants will regroup themselves in exclusively graduate departments or in university-based research institutes, leaving the bulk of undergraduate education to professors in less affluent specialties.

Yet we make such a prediction with considerable hesitation, for while it seems both economically and professionally logical, history is replete with similar prophecies that came to nothing. The men who organized professional academic training at the graduate level in the last quarter of the nineteenth century were in many if not most cases convinced that it should be quite separate from undergraduate education. The early plans for Johns Hopkins University, Clark University, and Catholic University all called for exclusively graduate instruction. Other institutions, such as Chicago and Columbia, sought to maintain an undergraduate college but also to have a separate graduate school with its own faculty. Yet all such efforts to erect a wall of separation between graduate academic training and undergraduate liberal arts training have failed. The exclusively graduate universities have admitted undergraduates, and the bifurcated universities have for the most part moved toward a unification of graduate and undergraduate faculties.

This unification is partly a result of the graduate faculty's positive desire to teach undergraduates, partly of its aversion to letting non-academicians do so. The idea that undergraduate teaching jobs are going to non-professionals seems to be ideologically offensive to graduate faculty, and they will even take on the irksome task themselves to avoid this outcome. There is a certain protectiveness in this attitude, which has its well-meaning as well as tariff-like aspects. The academic equivalent of senatorial courtesy forces professors to tolerate the heterodoxy and even the destructiveness vis-à-vis students of those with scholarly credentials, but the line can be held against those who, lacking these credentials, may "spoil" students for further work in the field. There is also a desire to have students committed early to a discipline, not only out of a missionary impulse to spread enlightenment but also out of a feeling that the early committers may have higher ability than the late committers, for whom the field may be a second-choice calling. (Whether this is actually so is doubtful. It depends very much on the particular field and perhaps on the particular institution.)

The fate of general education since World War II, discussed in more detail in Chapter XI, suggest that these attitudes are still very much alive. For a variety of reasons most colleges have been unhappy about letting students start majoring in a single discipline during the first two years. Partly this is because early commitment would be unfair to the many disciplines that are not represented in the high school curriculum, and that therefore need time to let students feel them out. Partly it is because early commitment would mean a lot of switching, which is administratively complex and perhaps wasteful. Partly it is because men in each discipline want their students to know something about others. The first two years must therefore be devoted to exploratory and introductory work. This means the college must offer something that has been commonly called general education: a program aimed at freshmen and sophomores who are not yet committed to any one field. Academicians tend to look down on such courses as dilettantish, and it is hard to get department members to staff them. But attempts to hire new kinds of faculty with new sorts of training to run them have gotten almost nowhere. Only a handful of institutions will give a man a permanent job teaching such courses. Elsewhere faculty are drawn on a part-time basis from the regular departments. This reflects the department's desire to create additional job slots for prospective colleagues, its eagerness to proselytize among freshmen and sophomores for majors, and its professional distaste for the amateurism it associated with general education. There are some departments so affluent or so complacent that such considerations play a minimal part, but these tend to be in scientific fields where early recruitment seems important on other grounds.

Taking all this into account it seems likely that, while the more eminent faculty and the more affluent subdisciplines may withdraw from undergraduate instruction, there will not be a mass exodus. On the contrary, so long as undergraduates study anything that resembles the established academic disciplines, the established departments will probably seek to control it. The departments will then staff the courses in question with scholars if these can be found and protoscholars if they cannot. The graduate schools are therefore by far the most important shapers of undergraduate education. It is, indeed, only a small exaggeration to say that undergraduate education in most universities and university colleges is simply a cut-rate, mass-produced version of graduate education. Most currently popular efforts at the reform of undergraduate education are simply attempts to narrow the gap, by giving undergraduates more seminars with senior faculty, more reading courses where they can set their own intellectual agendas, more research experience, and more original papers to write. In saying this we do not mean to deny the merit of these reforms. They have the great advantage of not patronizing undergraduates and of taking account of their increasing precocity and superior preparation. In the elite university colleges such reforms may even mean that a senior honors thesis if often not a cut-rate doctoral dissertation but a more lively monograph than most such dissertations. Nonetheless, there is a real problem—the one we keep recurring to in this book—namely the scarcity and inadequacy of other models. The graduate school model is valuable enough at its best for a few undergraduates to pursue, but it is certainly no answer for all the many different types and levels of undergraduates now found in American colleges.

The refusal of the graduate academic departments to give up their hold on undergraduate education is only one of several respects in which they differ from the other professional schools examined earlier. They have also shown remarkably little propensity to diversify their activities. The division of academic labor established at the end of the nineteenth century and formalized into departments, learned societies, and journals has persisted almost unchanged down to the present day. Departments have been slow to look to their neighbors for new ideas and agendas, and when they have, they usually assimilated ideas rather than men. Thus when political science began to incorporate the behavioral approach of political sociology, this rarely meant adding Ph.D.s in sociology to political science departments. Still less have academic departments sought to enrich their fare by hiring men with non-academic training or experience, in the way that medical schools have added non-doctors, engineering schools non-engineers, business schools non-businessmen, and so forth. There are virtually no politicians in political science departments and very few lawyers. Psychology departments hire very few psychiatrists and no clergymen or novelists; engineers do not get job offers from physics departments. The balance of trade has been overwhelmingly the other way. (That is to say, the medical schools hire Ph.D.s in biology, but the biology departments almost never hire M.D.s; the seminaries hire Ph.D.s in philosophy, but philosophy departments hire no D.D.s in theology.) We are not suggesting that practitioners can easily be converted into teachers, any more and perhaps less than "pure" researchers with Ph.D.s are easily converted into teachers. Both groups need induction into the art, which is not mastered simply by intuition or by exposure as an undergraduate or graduate consumer.

But the resistance of academicians to the pedagogic potential of practitioners—and, indeed, to the potential of experienced teachers from other professions—also rests to a large degree on the belief that while pure academic work constantly fertilizes applied fields, the reverse process is relatively rare. This view would, we think, be hard to sustain historically. Pasteur is not the only chemist whose stimulus came partly from practical problems, nor Freud the only psychologist, nor applied anthropologists the only social scientists who find a fruitful dialectic between the problems society defines and those their discipline defines. Yet it is undoubtedly easier for the academician to relate his work to other work in his discipline, which can be bitten off in manageable chunks, than to problems presented by the undigested "outside" world, which can be overwhelming and disorienting.[51]

Another reason why academic professional schools deviate from the usual professional pattern is that they have always been graduate-level institutions, relatively immune to the temptations and pressures that derive from undergraduates' chronic uncertainty about their career plans. The eighteenth-century seminary college, the nineteenth-century A & M college, and the twentieth-century teachers college all recruited undergraduates whose goals were more amorphous than the prescribed curriculum. Once these students came, the college often felt obliged to do something for them, even if that something had not been envisaged by the founders. Such pressures are much weaker at the graduate level. Medical schools get relatively few students who then decide they do not want to become doctors. Those who enter graduate departments in the natural sciences are also likely to become scientists, even if they don't get the Ph.D. for which they had hoped. Uncertain and uncommitted B.A.s do enter law schools and the graduate departments of social science and humanities, but little effort is made to accommodate them if they decide they made a mistake. A law student may not expect to practice law, but he is expected to master the regular law curriculum. If he does not want to do this he will normally be encouraged to drop out and try something else.[52] The same has been true in the academic disciplines. Very little effort

[51] For a remarkable discussion of the relationship between the pure and applied in the natural sciences, see Price. The literature on this topic is enormous, and this is only a beginning.

[52] Yale Law School is a partial exception to this rule, trying to make room for students who are only half committed to it. The University of Southern California and the State University of Iowa law schools have been moving in a similar direction, and at Harvard Law School there are some efforts in this direction, though at the time of writing the curriculum remains geared to the practitioner.

has been made to design new graduate programs to hold the many students—including some of the most brilliant—who find they do not want to follow the kind of careers for which a Ph.D. program is presumptively designed. One large group of these consists of returned Peace Corps Volunteers who would like to do graduate work in the social sciences with the aim of working eventually in the less-developed parts of the United States or in the new nations, whether as teachers, researchers, or private and governmental policy-makers. There are very few if any programs geared to their experience abroad and to the particular bent of their potential academic interests.

Another important reason why the graduate academic departments have not diversified internally is that they have almost all been associated from the start with pluralistic universities. The political scientist who thought his department had a lot to learn from sociology could not argue that his department should hire a sociologist, for there were already plenty in the sociology department. Still less could he argue that his department should give a course in sociology, for that was already somebody else's turf. Most of the leading academic departments have, indeed, been part of a university that had a full panoply of professional schools, and this has meant that an academician in search of new colleagues could find them without trying to broaden his department. Thus the molecular biologist could build ad hoc bridges to the medical school, or the historian to the law school, without trying to formalize them by forcing his departmental colleagues to be equally open.

Despite the relative clarity with which they perceive their purposes and define their programs—a clarity that is almost certainly illusory—the academic graduate schools are the primary force for growth within the modern university. Their enrollments have been rising at a fantastic rate, in comparison to both population and undergraduate enrollment. Their status is also rising. Both in their own minds and in the minds of the other professional schools, they occupy a position somewhat comparable to that of theology in the medieval university. Other professional schools justify themselves (and their budgets) in terms of external problems and needs. The graduate academic departments are for the most part autotelic. They resent even being asked whether they produce significant benefits to society beyond the edification of their own members, and mark down the questioner as an anti-intellectual. To suggest that the advancement of a particular academic discipline is not synonymous with the advancement of the human condition is regarded as myopic. Perhaps, considering the affluence of American taxpayers and the relatively ample supply of talented, well-educated college graduates, it really is.

An Overview

We have discussed six major species of professional schools. These
are not the six most important professional species in terms of numbers
or influence. Such a ranking would have to omit seminaries and
military academies while including law and business schools. Still less
is our list exhaustive. We have said nothing about schools of architecture, art, music, social work, librarianship, pharmacy, or dentistry,
to name a few. Nor have we said anything about two-year "semiprofessional" programs in the junior colleges. Our six species of professional schooling do, however, illustrate most of the evolutionary
patterns found in the institutions we have ignored.

The first of these patterns is the one in which professionalization is
accompanied by tightening the ties between a particular occupational
group and its schools. This relationship seems to be only partly a
matter of intellectual necessity. A profession, as we suggested at the
outset, is a subculture that shares certain values and attitudes, that
feels itself separate and superior to the laity, and that is prepared to
enforce its claims. Professional schooling is crucial to developing these
attitudes—perhaps even more crucial than to the mere transmission
of knowledge. One consequence of this is that the reformers in any
given profession are disproportionately concentrated in its training
institutions. The men who founded seminaries were usually trying to
produce better clergymen, the men who founded military academies
were dissatisfied with mere "gentlemen officers," the men who
founded normal schools wanted an end to incompetent teachers, and
so forth. The reformist impulse usually abates somewhat once the professional schools are going concerns, but at any given moment the
quality of practice taught at a professional school is likely to be higher
than that actually carried on by the alumni of that school. Indeed the
exalted image of a profession provided by its better schools may first
help it attract better recruits than it deserves and then help sustain
these men in the face of its often sordid and tedious reality.[53] The
importance of professional schools has, it is true, varied from one
calling to another. The consultative professions like the clergy, medicine, law, engineering, and academic research seem to depend on
formal schooling to socialize their novices more than do the manage-

[53] The speeches of Justice Holmes about the calling of the law are eloquent
examples of this, highly self-conscious about the disparity between ideal and
reality. Medical teachers like Osler and Welch or law teachers like Ames,
Llewellyn, and Freund managed to transfer their own charisma to their subject
for many students. As with other American dreams, practitioners whose experience did not live up to the billing often blamed only themselves.

rial-bureaucratic professions like business and schoolteaching. Nonetheless, the general trend has been for schooling to become more important for all professions, whatever their character.

A second major theme of the previous sections has been the professional schools' tendency either to affiliate with a multipurpose
university or to expand into one. Such changes have often involved
upward social mobility. One result of this has often been to de-
emphasize the school's initial occupational commitments in much the
same way that state colleges de-emphasized localism as time went
on, or church colleges abandoned their initial ethnic and sectarian
ties, or lower-middle and working-class colleges moved beyond their
initial class loyalties to seek talent of all sorts.

The professional schools' tendency to herd together and merge into
ever-larger units is in some ways analogous to comparable mergers
and consolidations in the business world. The results are by no means
easy to appraise in either case. The affiliation of professional schools
with universities probably encourages those who educate future professionals to take a more academic and less practical view of what
their students need to know. Proximity, be it physical or administrative, seems to make professional schools more aware of one another
and less concerned about the professions to which they are linked.
As they look across the street instead of into their students' futures,
they become more concerned with the "broad" academic and quasi-
academic skills they all value in common, less concerned with the
"narrow" professional skills that set them apart from one another and
from the university as a whole. (The choice of adjectives like "broad"
and "narrow" to describe these alternatives is, of course, an academician's choice, not a practitioner's.)

As a general rule it is probably fair to say that professional schools
cultivate a narrower range of talents than the professions themselves
reward, but that they cultivate these talents more deeply. The leading
national law schools, for example, are more academic (though less
legalistic) than the law firms and government agencies for which
they prepare. They encourage the speculative and inquisitive side of
their students' interests, and reward intellectual skills more than legal
practice itself usually does. But they pay almost no attention to their
students' non-intellectual development, even though this will be critically important to most students' subsequent career achievement.
There is, it is true, often some effort to train students to think quickly
on their feet and to talk well, but there is little emphasis on these
skills in selecting among applicants. Such "courtroom" skills are in
any case important for only a small proportion of practitioners. More
relevant, perhaps, would be attempts to cultivate students' perceptive-
ness about one another and about strangers. Success or failure in the

law frequently depends, for example, on sizing up a client, witness, or opponent quickly and accurately. It is this that often distinguishes the shrewd and the wise attorneys from the bumblers. Yet no law school teaches these skills, if indeed they can be taught, nor do law schools often try to determine if a given student has such skill before recommending him for a job. A lawyer is also, to take another example, likely to need the personal skills of a mediator; his training, however, is in the skills of an adversary or an analyst, and it is usually for these that he is primarily judged.

While we suspect this sort of divergence between professional training and professional practice is greater when training takes place in a university context than when it takes place in an independent professional school, we certainly could not prove this. Even in unaffiliated professional schools professors normally assume that their own skills and values are the most important ones for their students to acquire. Engineering professors, for example, are usually interested in turning out men with skills appropriate to teachers of engineering; they simply take it for granted that these skills will also be appropriate to the practice of engineering. In many cases, of course, they are right. But in many cases they are probably wrong. The typical engineer is more concerned with advancing himself in the company that employs him than with solving the technical problems his professors trained him to solve. His company is likely to share his concern, valuing him more if he can "take responsibility" than if he is merely a "first-rate engineer." Both he and his employer, in other words, may have somewhat unprofessional standards of competence and success. What both the young engineer and his employer really want, beyond a minimal level of technical skill, is often a set of human skills, which few engineering professors have and even fewer try to teach. Engineering faculties are not, for example, interested in how a manager resolves conflict among his subordinates, how he placates his neurotic boss, or how he decides when to delegate responsibility, when to take it, and when to pass the buck up the line. Indifference to such issues is, we suspect, as great in independent technical schools as in the engineering departments of universities. The only difference is that an engineering student at a university can, if he wishes, usually find a course or two in the school of business administration where problems of this sort are taken seriously. Even there, however, the quest is often for an "academic" answer, which can be copied into a notebook and memorized for future use. Some of the better business schools, on the other hand, have moved away from this style, emphasizing the case method and steering the student away from formula-based responses. Some business schools also try to give their students "clinical" experience which will make them more self-conscious and skeptical about their instinctive reactions and "solutions." Yet this approach is often hard to defend in a university setting, where it looks unscientific.

A third major theme of our discussion has been the way in which the professional schools sift and screen potential apprentices. We have repeatedly argued that this sorting and certifying is considerably more important than what the schools actually try to teach. Just as it is easier to change the character of a college by changing the admissions requirements than by changing the curriculum, so too it is easier to change a profession by recruiting new sorts of apprentices than by changing the rules of the apprenticeship. Professional schools have their students for only a few years, and they can do only so much with whatever raw material they get. But to the extent that they are overapplied and can select their raw material according to some preconceived plan, they can influence the profession they serve decisively. They exercise this influence first by setting the age at which students enter a profession, second by setting qualifications for entrants, and third by selecting a minority of students for special rewards (e.g. law review) that make subsequent occupational success much more likely.

Almost every professional program seems to want to establish itself as a graduate specialty. This enhances the status of the program and those who teach in it, and it also makes the profession as a whole more exclusive and prestigious. This kind of upward mobility among institutions means that more and more students must do sixteen years of academic work before even starting their professional training. This inevitably affects the character of recruitment to the professions, eliminating most of those who find academic work difficult or acutely distasteful. On the other hand, delaying the start of professional training makes it easier for an academically competent but occupationally ambivalent student to delay his career choice. There are, it is true, a few professions that must ordinarily be chosen very early, and a number of others where a decision must usually be made by the end of sophomore year. There are, moreover, all kinds of psychological pressures for early commitment to a particular calling, even if the calling in question has no undergraduate prerequisites whatever. Nonetheless, the fact remains that a student with a good academic record can postpone a career decision until he is twenty-one and still find a graduate professional school in most fields that will take him. On the other hand, a student who dislikes academic work and compiles an unpromising transcript finds himself in serious trouble if he suddenly gets interested in a particular field during his senior year or later. Thus while it is almost certainly a myth that the young must choose their careers earlier today than in the past, it is probably true that they must display some sort of competence earlier than used to be necessary.

When we shift our attention from the age of screening to the criteria used, the role of the professional schools in sorting the young is subject to even more obvious criticism. Like other sorts of colleges, professional schools assume that applicants who they think will make good students will also make good alumni. This assumption is perhaps slightly more likely to be accurate in a professional school than in a liberal arts college, but not much more. The low correlation between performance in professional school and performance on the job, referred to at the outset, makes this kind of selection very questionable. The same criticism must also be leveled against the way in which professional schools certify their students. There is very little persuasive evidence that students who flunk courses in professional schools would be incompetent practitioners if allowed to graduate, or that those who do very well and have "crown prince" jobs offered to them as a result will live up to their apparent promise. It seems clear, for example, that men who would have difficulty getting through any law school often have successful legal practices. Some are good go-betweens, lobbyists, or personal counselors, even though their grasp of the law is mainly intuitive and far from reliable. Such men can, of course, do a lot of damage. But so can technically more competent men who lack their personal finesse. The problem, as always, is that the profession requires either supermen who can do everything or a division of labor. The law schools often presuppose the former and ignore the necessity for the latter.

The world of work may not be a pyramid, then, in which large numbers of young people start at the bottom and try to scramble up a steep and steadily narrower slope toward a necessarily exclusive pinnacle of talent and power. The right metaphor may rather be a factory surrounded by a wall. The gates through the wall are watched by educators, who admit would-be workers only if they perform certain exercises that the educators think good for character, or at least think reliable signs of good character. Like most gatekeepers, these educators are an independent lot, keeping their own hours, making their own judgments, consulting occasionally with one another but almost never with the management inside the walls. They turn away some people whom the management would admit if asked, and they let in others who were neither invited nor wanted.

The dangers implicit in such a system are obvious enough, but they should not be exaggerated. For one thing, there are many gates, and a man turned away at one can fairly easily apply at another. Since the gatekeepers' standards vary, most people who persevere can get through somewhere. Then too the walls on either side of these gates are low and poorly watched. Almost anyone turned away can, with a little extra effort, find a secluded spot where he can scramble over unhindered. Once inside, his right to be there will rarely be challenged. Such arrangements obviously leave a lot to be desired. It is therefore tempting to make the educators involved scapegoats whenever there are serious problems within. But this is almost certainly unfair. If the educators listened more carefully to the management and admitted only those who were wanted and needed, the situation might well be worse, not better.

VI. Class Interests and the "Public-Private" Controversy

The Bifurcation of Higher Education

The distinction between a public and a private college was of no special importance during the first two centuries of American higher education. Then, after the Civil War, it became one of the central issues and divisions within the emerging academic system. Today, with the near-triumph of academic professionalism and the development of what Clark Kerr calls federal-grant universities, the distinction seems once again to be losing some of its importance. In the first section of this chapter we will briefly summarize this evolutionary process. The following sections will take up certain enduring differences between the two species of colleges. We will conclude with a brief discussion of class segregation and the probable effects of the steady decline of the private sector.

The colonial college was neither "public" nor "private" in the modern sense. It was seen as a public trust, subject to state regulation. Chartered by the state, its board of trustees often included public officials ex officio, and sometimes other public appointees. On a year-to-year basis the colonial college was usually expected to balance its books without tax assistance, but when it needed a new building or had other special expenses it often appealed successfully for legislative help. Its activities and solvency were viewed as public rather than private questions, yet it was not an arm of the state in the same sense that a modern state university is. Its position was in some ways analogous to that of a modern private university vis à vis the federal government: dependent, but not wholly so; responsive, but not wholly so.

After 1787 the colonial system of higher education was gradually undermined. Two developments were particularly important. First, sectarian controversies led to the disestablishment of state churches and to the adoption of new state constitutions which barred tax support of sectarian institutions. Even where constitutional prohibitions were not enacted, politicians began to find it inexpedient to give money to colleges that were strongly identified with a single denomination, for this was an era when most specific denominations had more enemies than friends. Second, the Dartmouth College case barred legislative intervention in the affairs of what were consequently defined as private colleges. This meant that American legislatures could not reform sectarian colleges that refused to move with the times in the way the British Parliament repeatedly reformed Oxford and Cambridge during the nineteenth century. Lacking ultimate control over these institutions, legislators were evidently reluctant to invest large sums in them.

These developments encouraged many legislatures to establish their own non-sectarian public colleges, controlled by state-appointed trustees and explicitly subject to legislative supervision.[1] At first, however, these new public colleges were pedagogically very similar to their private, sectarian counterparts. The trusteees appointed by state governments were seldom significantly different from the trustees appointed by private bodies, and as a species they had few distinctive educational ideas. They hired the same sorts of men as presidents, and the presidents hired the same sorts of faculty as in the private sector. The result was that public colleges embodied much the same genteel tradition as their private rivals. The Jacksonian voter looked on both species with equal distaste, and state legislators were almost as reluctant to vote tax assistance to public as to private institutions. In his discussion of mid-nineteenth-century higher education Frederick Rudolph lists a number of symptoms of the growing divorce between colleges and the public.[2] Whereas the federal government had set aside land to support higher education in new states during the late eighteenth and early nineteenth centuries, the Treasury distribution of 1837 went for such things as common schools, roads, and banks. In 1842 the Georgia legislature, which had been the first in America to charter a state-operated college, cut off support for its stepchild. And in 1845 a Virginia newspaper summed up the spirit of the time by asking, "Cannot the annual appropriation of fifteen thousand dollars to the University be more profitably expended for the great cause of education [i.e. for the common schools] than in instructing from 100 to 150 youths, all of whom have the means of finishing their course through their own resources?" Such questions evidently received no satisfactory answers, and public support for higher education languished throughout America. The new public institutions did, it is true, usually fare slightly better than their private rivals in bids for state assistance, but their position was still precarious, as the University of Georgia's vicissitudes illustrate. Certainly legislative support was almost nowhere sufficient for public colleges to offer significantly better or cheaper programs than their private

[1] On this subject see Tewksbury, pp. 142–54.
[2] Rudolph, chap. 10.

competitors. Nor did legislative control give these colleges a distinctive character or purpose.

After the Civil War public demand for an alternative to the classical collegiate system became increasingly insistent. Educators in the public sector responded somewhat differently from those in the private one, and the two began to diverge in significant ways. Progressives in both camps exploited the findings of Old World science, both were influenced by the Germanic image of the professor as a productive scholar, and both sought to enlarge their potential clientlele by making the college an avenue to occupational success. But private institutions typically tried to preserve the old collegiate model at the undergraduate level, while confining the new professionalism to graduate studies. Public colleges, on the other hand, frequently saw professionalism as a substitute for the genteel tradition rather than just a supplement to it. They went somewhat further than the private sector in developing terminal occupational curricula for undergraduates and placed somewhat less emphasis on undergraduate liberal arts courses, either as an end in themselves or as preprofessional training.

This divergence was an almost inevitable by-product of the political economy of higher education. Public institutions were primarily concerned with establishing programs that would win the support of state legislators. Private colleges, on the other hand, were more interested in winning the approval of the millionaires whose wealth derived from the emergent national corporations. While both sectors showed considerable ingenuity in turning their resources to purposes legislators and philanthropists had not envisaged, both were to some extent influenced by their benefactors' prejudices. We will discuss the effect of this first in the private sector, then in the public one.

The market for the private colleges' traditional product had been declining slowly even before the Civil War. In the decades after 1865 industrialization created a new world in which neither the old liberal arts college nor its alumni had much place. By the end of the nineteenth century many astute private college presidents had come to understand that their survival depended on linking themselves in some way to the industrial revolution. At the very least they had to tap the enormous new private fortunes being accumulated in mining, manufacturing, transportation, merchandising, real estate, banking, and the like. And this seemed to require a pedagogy that would somehow prepare men for life in such milieus.

The new captains of industry were a mixed crew. Some felt that not only history but all forms of higher learning were bunk. Others, while not militantly anti-intellectual, preferred to spend their money on yachts, art, religion, or orphanages rather than colleges. Still others, while ready to support higher education, believed in old-time religion and hence in old-time colleges. (In this, as in many other things, John D. Rockefeller seems to have been an exception; he remained a Baptist and yet was prepared to back William Rainey Harper's academic progressivism—partly because Harper was also a Baptist.) But there were also wealthy men who believed in science and social progress. Charismatic educators like White, Eliot, Gilman, and Harper were able to persuade a number of these men that universities were the key to progress.

They did not always do this in a simple or direct way. Laurence Veysey has shown, for example, that Eliot's emphasis on individualism, the elective system, and competitive excellence led Harvard to an eventual emphasis on research that was not present in Eliot's original plan and was not especially stressed in his efforts to win support for Harvard. Conversely, men like David Starr Jordan at Stanford and G. Stanley Hall at Clark were relatively unsuccessful when they tried to sell the idea of a research-oriented university in its pure form. What one sees at work here is not a direct coincidence of views between the great academic entrepreneurs and their industrial counterparts, but rather a similarity of temperament or at least a symbiosis between complementary temperaments. This allowed the academic entrepreneurs to coax money from business tycoons for purposes the latter often only half understood, and might well have disapproved if they had understood better. It was thus less a matter of the industrial barons personally insisting that pastoral colleges be turned into "knowledge factories" than of their feeling a natural kinship with the men of large vision who thought this necessary.[3] It was in this sense that the academic revolution was a by-product of the industrial one.

The tie-up was, however, a protracted and sporadic process. A few self-made men gave appreciable sums to universities, but many were bitterly critical. Yet even the critics sent their sons to college. Thus when industrial wealth trickled down to the second generation it was much more college-oriented than in the first. Not only that, but at least in the East the rich tended to send their children to colleges with some academic reputation. Since the rich also tended to move "back East" once their fortunes were established, the more academically reputable colleges began to attract an appreciable number of children from extremely wealthy homes. This meant that colleges that were at least partially committed to meritocratic professional values had a better-than-average chance of acquiring alumni with second-generation money. And even when children from wealthy families went to colleges that placed morality and orthodoxy ahead

[3] For a fascinating account of one such relationship, namely that between the elder Rockefeller and William Rainey Harper, see Storr, *Harper's University*.

of intellectual competence and erudition, they often went on to business or professional careers that made them think their alma mater needed to update its program. When the college approached them for a substantial gift, they often made it clear that they were interested in supporting some sort of innovation, especially efforts to make the college more scientifically and professionally oriented. Their money often went for a new science building, a professorship in engineering, law, or medicine, or some other step toward becoming either a university or a university college. (On the other hand, some of the most forward-looking industrialists turned quite nostalgic when giving their money away, evidently hoping to preserve through philanthropy the very culture that they were destroying through technology.)

Variations in the growth of different kinds of private colleges and of different programs within private colleges can, then, be partly explained by the fact that private gifts came mainly from men who had created or maintained their wealth by mastering new technical and organizational problems. Their money was a factor in the struggle of progressive minorities against conservative majorities on many private campuses. It enabled imaginative administrators to move in new directions when only a few of their faculty (usually including the abler ones) supported them.[4] Furthermore, even when such money was not actually available, the hope of obtaining it made the university or university college model attractive to many administrators and faculty. Finally, even those colleges that had no hope of obtaining large contributions from the professional and managerial class usually wanted their alumni to join this class and organized their curriculum accordingly.

The interplay between business wealth and private higher education was not, however, without its ambiguities. The brassy business culture that dominated America from 1865 to 1929 was far from uniformly sympathetic to academic professionalism. Students who came to college to kill a few years before returning home to join their father's bank or shoe factory, or who sought a B.A. in order to gain entrée to a comfortable job in a brokerage, saw little reason to submit to professional discipline, be it academic or otherwise. Such students often worked out covert mutual security treaties with the less professionalized faculty. Indolent students were offered minimal assignments and easy examinations, and in return they kept up enrollment in un-

---

[4] Faculty members and students at modern universities have such an anti-administration bias that they find it difficult to realize that most of the improvements in American colleges have been initiated by former faculty turned administrators, often over strong faculty protest. During the era under discussion most reformers were concerned with making their institution more attractive to professional scholars, and were opposed by faculty who believed in an older ethos. More recently, administrators have led many efforts to go beyond professionalism.

scholarly professors' courses. This gave the old-style liberal arts professors (and the old-style liberal arts colleges) a clientele and a raison d'être, while leaving the terminal students time and energy for non-curricular life.

This compromise was, however, inherently unstable. Those liberal arts colleges that added graduate programs found their newly acquired scholarly faculty contemptuous of less professional colleagues and made enormous efforts to prevent any more non-scholars from getting appointments. It was usually a generation or two before they succeeded in this, but by 1939 the best private universities had committed themselves to hiring only scholars as professors. These professors, in turn, sought to restructure the liberal arts as professional specialties. They usually saw undergraduate liberal arts courses primarily as preparation for graduate work in the same field, secondarily as a preprofessional socialization for fields like law and medicine which had no undergradute counterparts, and only incidentally as preparation for adult life.

Nor was the triumph of professionalism confined to the universities. After World War II many of the better private colleges, while too poor or too proud to become universities, began turning themselves into university colleges whose primary purpose was to recruit and prepare students for graduate schooling on other campuses. Even those private colleges that continued to send students directly into the job market often dreamed of becoming university colleges and acted to some extent as if they already had. They were more reluctant than public institutions to establish terminal occupational curricula at the undergraduate level, regarding this both as a loss of face vis à vis other private colleges and as an admission to themselves that their students were uneducable in now-conventional academic terms.

There were, of course, plenty of private colleges that could not live up to these "pure" ideals. Many offered undergraduate engineering programs in order to attract able, hard-working, upwardly mobile students. Almost all felt obliged to offer enough undergraduate education courses for their B.A.s to get certified as teachers. Almost all also offered chemistry majors that could lead to corporate employment as well as graduate school. In addition, some of the less prosperous and socially prestigious private colleges, especially those that attracted mainly urban, first-generation collegians, yielded to economic and social pressure and offered undergraduate occupational majors in fields like business, education, nursing, and home economics. (Business and education are usually taught in large lectures, and tend to cost very little per student. Many private colleges make a profit on students in these fields and use it to subsidize more expensive and prestigious subjects such as physics.)

Despite all the exceptions, however, the dominant ideal in the private sector was that students should do liberal arts work as undergraduates, postponing occupational training until they entered a graduate school or took a corporate job. The ideals of the public sector were somewhat less clear and somewhat more realistic. The passage of the Morrill Act in 1862, while nowhere nearly so important as some observers have suggested, did symbolize the fact that political support for higher education depended on the development of new kinds of job-related education. It also symbolized the decline of sectarian veto groups to a point where Congress could vote with impunity for "godless" non-sectarian colleges. The forces that made the Morrill Act possible at the national level also affected those state and municipal colleges that did not benefit directly from Morrill Act funds. In one state after another, educators in public institutions sought to develop practical curricula which would win legislative support. After a number of false starts they began to succeed.[5]

Outside the Northeast, business and farm interests united behind the state universities and land-grant colleges. This was true even in states where private colleges were extremely numerous. Despite their numbers, neither the Midwestern nor the Southern private colleges were able to get tax money, nor were they able to prevent its going to their state-controlled rivals. By World War I a public university dominated higher education in almost every state outside the Northeast.

The fact that the Northeast followed a rather different pattern is often accounted for by pointing out that private colleges were already entrenched and used their political influence to impede the growth of their public competitors. This is true, but it is not a sufficient explanation. Private colleges were, after all, dominant in the Midwest too, albeit not so well established as Harvard and Yale. Our own interpretation is that religious and economic divisions ran deeper in the Northeast than elsewhere. Eastern legislators were therefore unable to unite around any one version of higher education that would serve their state's diverse interest groups. On the one side was usually the Irish Catholic clergy, convinced that cheap public colleges would lure immigrant children into perdition. On the other side were the Anglo-Saxon "first families," many of whom had attended Protestant colleges and most of whom saw no reason why such colleges could not provide for the future just as they had for the past. In states where both these groups were powerful, the extension of the common-school principle to higher education proved difficult, and publicly controlled colleges got very little support.

[5] For an excellent account of the problems, see Rudolph, chap. 12. See also Nevins.

Unable to rally round public institutions, education-conscious Northeastern legislators made some effort to continue their traditional support of private higher education. Vermont, Rhode Island, New York, New Jersey, Pennsylvania, and Maryland, for example, continued to subsidize the private sector until well into the twentieth century, and some of these states do so even today. These subsidies usually took the form of sporadic capital grants for buildings. But New York and Rhode Island emphasized scholarships for students attending private colleges. Initially, these may have been expected to increase enrollment in both the Catholic and Protestant colleges and help solve these colleges' financial problems by allowing them to raise tuition. But the number of scholarships was not increased anywhere near fast enough to open private higher education to appreciable numbers of middle- or low-income students. Nor did states like Maryland and Pennsylvania, which stressed capital grants instead of scholarships, make them on a large enough scale to influence the cost or quality of private programs significantly. So private tuition rose, and total enrollment tended to grow somewhat more slowly than in economically comparable states with large public sectors.

The bifurcation of higher education into public and private sectors was almost everywhere accompanied by some division of labor with regard to both the recruitment of students and the placement of alumni. Initially, the supporters of public colleges were primarily concerned with placement, and attacked the old-style colleges because they prepared students for only a few genteel occupations. (They also attacked private colleges for recruiting only the children of the idle rich, but this was largely demagoguery. Had it been a serious concern, the reformers would have supported state scholarship programs to help poor boys attend private colleges. In practice, they opposed such programs on the grounds that the private colleges taught very little worth knowing and were bastions of snobbery and privilege.) Most of the reformers recognized, however, that if colleges were to prepare students for ungenteel callings such as farming and engineering, they would not only have to offer new programs of instruction but attract new sorts of students. They therefore made an effort to keep both prices and admissions requirements at public colleges somewhat lower than in the private sector. Until recently, however, these efforts had a limited effect. Public admissions requirements were permissive, but so were private ones in all but a handful of leading colleges. The major cost of attending college was subsistence, and this did not vary much by sector. Even tuition differentials were modest. The major source of variation in students' college choices during the first half of the twentieth century was therefore the fact that public institutions seemed to promise a somewhat different kind of education from private ones, leading to a rather different (though overlapping) set of careers.

We have already suggested that this division was rooted in different sources of support for public and private colleges. The regular legislative appropriation was both the carrot and the stick with which laymen persuaded public educators to do their will. Starting with a profound (and to our minds largely justified) distrust of the traditional curriculum and the men who venerated it, legislators used their annual review of academic budgets to redirect the collegiate tradition in radically new channels. They were comparatively generous with money to train experts in agriculture, engineering, veterinary medicine, home economics, and other practical fields. The classics, philosophy, and other traditional subjects got less money and less sympathy. Not only did legislators have a bias in favor of what they thought useful, but they also had a bias in favor of saving time and money. Few saw any reason why students should spend four years studying the liberal arts before starting their professional work. They preferred starting professional training at the undergraduate level, dispensing with irrelevant preliminaries, and saving both the state and the student money.

There were, it is true, exceptions. After the Flexner Report of 1910, medical reformers began a protracted drive to increase the amount of undergraduate work required for admission to medical schools. Some state legislators resisted such pressures, seeing no reason why applicants shouldn't continue to enter medical school directly from high school. But once the bulk of the profession united in support of this particular kind of exclusiveness, few legislators cared enough to fight. College professors, too, persuaded the public that a man had to have graduate training before he could teach competently, and legislatures in many states accepted the necessity of providing appropriate Ph.D. programs. In general, however, the public sector tended to put more resources into undergraduate than graduate professional programs. Nor was the proportion of liberal arts students going on to graduate school as large in any public institution as in the leading private ones.

While fiscal review was a legislature's most important lever for pushing its colleges in new directions, it was not the only one. Legislatures also determined admissions requirements at public institutions, either directly or indirectly, and they were almost always lower than the faculty liked. While the faculty often struck back by flunking out a substantial proproportion of its involuntary apprentices, this seldom produced a student body as able or committed as the faculty wanted. Public liberal arts faculties were therefore always on the lookout for ways to escape responsibility for the mediocre students by whom they felt surrounded. Since they could not eliminate them entirely, they were somewhat more sympathetic than their private colleagues to proposals for undergraduate programs in business, education, and the like. They expected these programs to siphon off large numbers of dull students whose only interest was getting certified for subsequent employment. Yet, while this made it easier to raise standards in the liberal arts departments, it also reduced the college's over-all academic reputation. Able high school students who hoped to go to a leading professional school often assumed that they ought to go first to a private college that sent an appreciable proportion of its alumni to graduate school, rather than to a cheaper (and sometimes better) public university where graduate plans were atypical. Mediocre students, on the other hand, frequently concluded that they would find it easier to manage at a public institution with a lot of academic soft spots, even though they could have afforded to go to an expensive private college. Seeing all this, public liberal arts faculties tended to have mixed feelings about undergraduate occupational programs. In general, ideology and snobbery triumphed over the conflicting claims of self-interest, and the liberal arts professors were hostile to these innovations. But since they had less power than their private colleagues, their hostility was not only more ambivalent but less relevant.

Dependence on regular legislative appropriations affected the style as well as the structure of the public sector. Public accountability, for example, almost inevitably led to bureaucratization. Elaborate administrative machinery had to be set up to ensure that no embarrassing mistakes were made, especially in the expenditure of public funds. The private sector, being far less accountable, could leave many more choices to individual discretion. This meant taking more risks, covering up more abuses, and earning more flexibility in return.

Accountability also influenced the time perspective of public college administrators. In the long run a public college and its trustees might be answerable to the people, but in the short run it was mainly subject to the whims of a few clearly identifiable individuals such as the governor and a few key legislators. These men were often influenced by what they took to be popular opinion, but on a day-to-day basis they had the last word. A private college, on the other hand, while theoretically accountable to a narrower constituency, had more freedom to define this constituency in its own terms. The president and trustees of a private college might know, for example, that the college's future depended on attracting a few extremely large gifts. But they seldom knew exactly where these gifts were likely to come from, and so they could not tailor the college program to potential donors' prejudices as easily as their public counterparts could. Under these circumstances private colleges could and sometimes did convince themselves that the surest way to get rich in the long run was to do what they wanted to do anyway. This could be rationalized both as the best way of contributing to long-term social welfare and as the best way of establishing a sound reputation. Whether private colleges therefore served the general welfare better than public colleges remains problematic.

The cumulative result of these developments was that by World War II American higher education could be crudely and oversimply characterized as having responded to the scientific and organizational revolutions in two distinct ways. The public sector had subordinated the old liberal arts rhetoric to a new vocabulary which stressed job training and social progress. It was devoting the bulk of its resources to terminal undergraduate curricula geared to the real and imagined needs of employers. Its graduate programs were, with a few important exceptions, upward extensions of these undergraduate curricula. The private sector, on the other hand, had clung somewhat more tenaciously to the old liberal arts, reorganizing them in such a way as to make them mainly pregraduate subjects.

Broadly speaking these differences could be attributed to differences in the sources of support of public and private institutions. Public institutions relied primarily on tax subsidies, and therefore had an interest in serving as many different kinds of students as possible and creating the broadest possible sympathy for their claims on the public purse. Private non-sectarian institutions which relied heavily on individual gifts were concerned less with the number of their supporters than with their affluence. This pushed them in an elitist direction, making them appeal primarily to the children of the upper-middle and upper classes and secondarily to able youngsters who seemed likely to join these classes as adults. The private church colleges relied mainly on tuition and secondarily on subventions, both of which required broad middle-class support. The result was often a curricular compromise between the public and the non-sectarian private pattern. (As always, we are talking here about tendencies rather than rules. The tendencies were, moreover, mainly visible in extreme cases, with enormous overlap in the middle.)

In the years since World War II the stylistic and programmatic differences between the public and private sectors have become even more blurred than before. Just as earlier divergences were partly due to different sources of support, so today's convergence derives in part from increasingly similar financial arrangements. Both public and private universities now get substantial portions of their budgets from the federal government. While this money has been concentrated on research and professional training, it has had important indirect effects on undergraduate education. The academic profession has been able to exercise far more control over federal funds than it ever did over state or private ones. Federal money has therefore promoted the academic revolution in both the public and the private sector. Federal funds have, for example, enabled the better state universities to expand their research and graduate programs at much the same pace as private universities. The traditional hostility of state legislators toward research, and their traditional bias in favor of undergraduate rather than graduate professionalism, are increasingly irrelevant when Washington is willing to pay. Furthermore, many young state legislators have been impressed by the results of federally financed research and of graduate education, so that they are willing to spend state money on such items if no federal money is to be had. Legislators remain more skeptical than professors about the value of undergraduate liberal education, and seem less willing to postpone professional training to the graduate level. Still, they are certainly more responsive to such ideas than they once were. In part, no doubt, this change reflects their middle-class constituents' increased willingness to keep their children in the classroom beyond the B.A. In part it reflects an expanding tax base, which makes not only federal but state support for protracted education more natural. In part it reflects greater lay deference to academicians and academic opinion—a deference stemming to some extent from the federally financed affluence and worldliness of leading professors.

Federal money has not transformed all higher education. Research funds have been concentrated in a few dozen leading universities. Most of the rest has gone to another two-hundred-odd universities and university colleges. The eighteen hundred less distinguished public and private institutions have gotten almost nothing beyond an occasional matching grant for a new building and some money for student loans, work-study programs, and small scholarships for the desperately poor. Thus while public and private universities are becoming very much alike, public and private terminal colleges still look in different directions for support. Private terminal colleges depend mainly on tuition, while public ones depend mainly on taxes, and this means the private terminal college still has a bias toward students who can pay their way, and more later, while the public terminal college has a bias toward numbers and voters.

But while publicly controlled institutions remain quite different from private ones in some marginal ways, their fundamental social purposes and organization seem remarkably similar. Both public and private colleges accept the national norms of the academic profession about what should be taught and how. Only a handful of subjects are still taught principally in one sector (biblical studies and agriculture come to mind). Despite radicals' anxieties, we have found little evidence that the intellectual content of a given course is significantly affected by the type of control or the source of support. (The church colleges are an occasional exception to this rule.) While the over-all curriculum is still quite different in a terminal and a pregraduate institution, both sequences are found in both sectors. Some politicians and some trustees still think that they (rather than the faculty) should decide what is to be taught, under what circumstances, and to whom. Such men are, however, rarer than a generation ago, and their influence at universities and university colleges is sporadic and marginal even when it is widely publicized and bitterly resented. Both the trustees and other non-academic influences often play a larger role at terminal colleges. Yet this only underlines our conviction that the crucial division in modern higher education is not between public and private colleges but between terminal undergraduate institutions and the universities and university colleges.

We indicated at the outset that we did not think colleges were primarily shaped by the boards that formally controlled them, since they were much more alike than their boards. Still less do we believe that the character of colleges depends on who appoints and regulates the board. Colleges are shaped by many interest groups. A few exercise their influence through representation on the board, but most do not. The differences between public and private colleges seem to us to derive not from their boards of control but from their sources of financial support. To the extent that these sources become more alike, the colleges will do likewise. Indeed, we are tempted to go further and suggest that budgetary support and review are the *only* forms of public control that make much sense. Publicly elected or appointed boards of trustees seem in many ways to cause more trouble than they are worth. Suppose, for example, that nineteenth-century legislatures had done as Congress did in the twentieth century, contracting with established private institutions to perform particular services and not setting up new institutions of their own. A few moved tentatively in this direction, for example, by turning over land-grant money to private colleges. It would be hard to show that the farmers of New York suffered from having Cornell administer the state agriculture school, or that Massachusetts got less for the Morrill Act money it put into MIT than for what it put into the University of Massachusetts. If this approach had been followed on a larger scale, on all the many fronts where public action was needed, perhaps no publicly administered universities would have been needed. A great deal of controversy generated by state boards of regents and trustees might have been avoided without any serious loss to the public interest. Certainly the federal government, which proceeded in this way, has had far less turbulent relations with higher education than most states have had. It could be argued that it has also achieved more of its objectives at less cost. Yet this is speculation, and it is important to remember that private boards of trustees have also been embroiled in many destructive controversies with their colleges over both budgetary and other matters.

In any event, the most conspicuous fact of the current period is that the objectives and methods of the public and private sectors are increasingly similar. It is true that the results remain different, but the main reason for this seems to be that the two sectors work with rather dissimilar raw material. Despite a great deal of overlap, the class background, academic aptitude, and occupational ambitions of students in the two sectors remain rather different. Among freshmen entering private universities in 1966, for example, nearly two out of every five came from families with incomes over $20,000 compared to a little better than one in five at public universities. The imbalance was even greater at four-year colleges. Private ones got about 29 per cent of their students from families with $20,000 and up, while public ones got 11 per cent. Parental incomes at public and private junior colleges, on the other hand, were quite similar. If one looks at the proportion of students whose fathers are college graduates, at the proportion who plan careers in medicine, law, or academic life, or at the proportion with outstanding high school grades, the imbalances between the public and private sector tend to be of about the same magnitude. The differences are much less dramatic, however, if one looks at the middle of the distribution instead of the extremes. Median parental income, for example, varied only about $2,000 between the private and public sectors in 1966.[6]

These differences between student bodies seem to depend partly on differences in cost. The next two sections of this chapter will therefore look at the question of cost in more detail. In the fourth section we will turn to the equally important influence of admissions policies. Finally, we will return to the question of residual variations in institutional purpose and institutional imagery, for these still have some effect on which students go where.

The Financing of Public and Private Colleges

Public instruction has been more heavily subsidized than private, and the imbalance has increased fairly steadily over the years. In

[6] All the above comparisons are calculated from Astin, Panos, and Creager, "National Norms."

1909–10 American colleges received $76 from endowment and annual gifts for every $100 they got from state and local governments. By 1963–64 they received only $35 from endowment and annual gifts for every $100 they got from state and local governments.[7]

The lag in subsidies for the private colleges has played an important part in the over-all development of the private sector. It is not a result of the graduated income tax or the alleged decline of great private fortunes. On the contrary, the private colleges' income from philanthropy rose four times as fast as GNP between 1910 and 1964. But until the 1950s private colleges allowed their enrollments to rise almost as fast as gifts. As a result, private colleges' real income *per student* from endowment and current gifts rose only about 66 per cent between 1910 and 1964. The public sector's real tax subsidy per student rose about 120 per cent in this same period.[8] The private colleges' failure to attract subsidies comparable to those going to public institutions led to a lag in private instructional expenditures. In 1919–20, the first year for which we have found data, the private sector received (and presumably spent) nearly 70 per cent more per student than the public sector. By 1929–30 the advantage was less than 50 per cent. In 1949–50 the public institutions spent as much per student as private ones did.[9] Despite its deteriorating competitive position, the private sector continued to try to compete with the public sector almost across the board. Since private gifts could not offset tax subsidies in most colleges, the typical college had to charge two or three times more tuition than its public competitors. But there were some private colleges, especially church-related ones, that kept their charges at about the same level as public institutions. They did this by paying faculty less, working them harder, and providing fewer amenities. Even so, many private colleges stayed afloat only because they were in major population centers, so that their students saved as much by living at home as they spent on extra tuition charges.

By the early 1950s, however, the handwriting was on the wall for the private colleges. It was clear that private subsidies were going to continue to lag behind public ones, and that private colleges were

[7] See 1965 *Digest*, tables 76 and 78. The ratio of private to state and local subsidies is not quite the same as the ratio of subsidies for the private sector to subsidies for the public sector. The private sector gets some state and local subsidies, and the public sector gets some private gifts. Today, however, these two complications offset each other. Private sources accounted for 23.0 per cent of all subsidies to higher education in 1963–64, and the private sector received 23.2 per cent of all subsidies (exclusive of federal research grants). Whether these ratios were equally neat in 1909–10 we do not know.

[8] 1965 *Digest*, tables 53 and 78. The figures are subject to some error for reasons described in the previous footnote.

[9] See *Biennial Survey of Education, 1828–30*, and *Biennial Survey of Education, 1949–50*.

therefore not going to be able to compete financially with their public rivals. It was also clear that many of the special interests that had been willing to pay extra for a private college tailored to their prejudices were losing their commitment to separatism. One by one the private colleges therefore worked out new strategies for survival. These, it turned out, were remarkably similar. Most of the private colleges decided not to try to maintain their traditional share of the middle-income, middle-ability student market. Instead, they began to seek out what they hoped would become a sociointellectual elite. They sought to attract these students by offering a manifestly superior product. This meant that their expenditure per student had once again to be raised well above their public competitors'. In order to do this several new departures were necessary.

To start, private colleges began limiting enrollment. The private sector's share of the market, which had hovered around 50 per cent from 1910 to 1950, started falling about 1 per cent annually. It was 36 per cent in 1964 and is expected to be about 20 per cent in 1980. Limiting enrollment had two important consequences. One, it raised the ability of the average student, making the private colleges relatively more attractive to both students and faculty, and probably indirectly raising the cash value of their degrees. Two, it meant that philanthropic income did not have to be spread so thin. Indeed, on a per student basis the private colleges' receipts from endowment and current gifts rose faster between 1950 and 1964 than did the public colleges' receipts from state and local governments.[10] Limiting enrollment, in other words, was enough in and of itself to arrest the earlier decline in quality (as measured by expenditure per student) of private relative to public instruction.

But the private colleges were not content merely to stop their competitive position from deteriorating further. Once they had decided to stress quality they found themselves engaged in a competitive struggle with one another in which there was no real ceiling to ambition. Competition was, of course, not new. But when competition was for enrollment, demography put a ceiling on what could be accomplished, and to some extent on what could be spent. When competition refocused on student ability and program quality, such limits on expenditure was less operative. So private colleges began raising tuition. For nearly thirty years private tuition had averaged between two and three times public tuition. Then between 1956 and 1964 it rose to about four times the public level. Or, to put it another way, having hovered around 12 per cent of median family income from 1928 to 1956, mean private tuition rose to 18 per cent of family in-

[10] See 1965 *Digest*, tables 51, 76, and 78.

come in the next eight years.[11] While lagging room-and-board charges plus expanded scholarships may nonetheless have prevented the private colleges from becoming more economically exclusive, this has not been their primary concern. Rather, they have wanted to increase their income per student, raise faculty salaries, cut teaching loads, provide better fringe benefits, build more ample facilities, and in general corner the "Buick and Cadillac" market. This was not, as private college spokesmen often suggest, simply a matter of "maintaining quality," either vis-à-vis past standards or vis-à-vis current public college standards. Rather, it was a matter of improving quality —getting a better ratio of talented to mediocre professors, providing more favorable conditions for teaching and research, and so forth. While private colleges have not been the only ones doing this (some leading state universities have also restricted enrollment and raised their tax receipts sharply), the private colleges have generally improved their position faster than public ones. In 1963–64 private college expenditures per student were 20 per cent higher than at public colleges, whereas they had been equal fourteen years earlier. This change did not, of course, restore the private colleges' pre-1939 advantage, which is probably gone forever. But it did mean that the majority of conspicuously able or affluent students looked first to the private sector.[12]

While endowment and gifts have not increased as fast as over-all expenditures, private philanthropy continues to play an important role in private college pricing. Ironically (though not particularly surprisingly) the best endowed institutions tend to charge the highest tuition. (Berea, Rice, and Tuskegee are among the famous exceptions.) Very few well-heeled colleges see their endowment as a way of making their product available at lower prices. Instead, they see endowment as a way of improving their product. Give an institution with room for one thousand students $1 million a year income from endowment and gifts, and it will not find one thousand needy students and give them a $1,000 education for nothing. Instead, it will conclude that it cannot possibly provide one thousand students with a good education for $1 million. It will convince itself that it

[11] See *A Fact Book* (1965), table 200, and 1965 *Statistical Abstract*, pp. 340–41, for data since 1928. The data on both tuition and incomes prior to 1928 are extremely unsatisfactory. One of the many enigmas of educational statistics is that tuition trends at the 132 colleges studied by the American Council on Education and trends in aggregate receipts from tuition, reported to USOE, have not paralleled each other over the years.

[12] For evidence on this point see the annual reports of the National Merit Scholarship Corporation on the college choices of award winners. See also Nichols, table 5. Of those scoring in the top 8 per cent of the NMSC test, about 65 per cent of the men and 62 per cent of the women named a private college as their first choice.

should spend at least $3 million (or $5 million, or $10 million—there is no ceiling on what academicians can imagine spending in the name of education). It will then need $2 million in tuition receipts to supplement its $1 million endowment income, and will seek one thousand students who can provide $2,000 apiece in tuition. If there are particularly deserving students who cannot afford $2,000 a year, it will raise tuition to $2,200 and use the surplus for scholarships to help the poor. This marketing strategy is usually successful. Upper-middle class buyers seem to recognize a good thing when they see it, and they will ante up $8,000 over four years in order to get an additional $4,000 in endowment subsidies. (While most families have only the vaguest idea what a college spends to equip one of its students with a B.A., they have fairly clear ideas which B.A.s are worth "more" and which are worth "less." These perceptions are fairly well correlated with what colleges actually spend. The well-endowed college can thus charge more because its degree is "worth more," while the impoverished college must usually charge less because its B.A. is less valued.) The net result is that, far from encouraging a college to lower its charges, new endowment makes it possible to raise them.

An institution with one thousand students and a philanthropic income of only $100,000 is, of course, as anxious to spend $3 million a year as its better endowed neighbors. But it knows that it cannot market a $3,000 product for $2,900 if its competitor down the road charges $2,000 for the same thing. Indeed, it cannot even market a $2,100 product for $2,000 if its competitors are marketing a $3,000 product for $2,000. Most families with $2,000 a year to burn on tuition will spend it only for "the best," and an institution can seldom establish this image if it spends much less than its neighbors. The well-endowed college seems to offer affluent families a better buy for the same money. A few comparatively impoverished colleges, such as Antioch, Bennington, Reed, and Sarah Lawrence, charge as much as better endowed colleges without offering a comparable subsidy. They do this by offering a highly specialized product, which their more affluent competitors think too risky to touch. Normally, however, poor institutions compete by selling a cut-rate product—perhaps a $1,100 product for $1,000 per year. This product appeals to families that feel they cannot afford $2,000 a year, or do not recognize they might get more, dollar for dollar, in the $2,000 than in the $1,000 price field.

As a practical matter, of course, the market for higher education is nothing like as rational as this discussion suggests. Expenditure per student is not the only determinant of academic quality; academic quality is not the only determinant of demand for admission to a college; and demand for admission is not the only determinant of what a college thinks it can get away with charging. Still, the economic logic we describe does seem to explain much of the variation in pricing, however indirectly. The logic is, moreover, circular. Colleges that offer an expensive education at a discount attract students from sophisticated, well-to-do families that can afford to enter this market.[13] These families are, in turn, a prime source of new endowment for the rich colleges. Not only that, but since most of their applicants come from affluent families, the wealthy colleges tend to feel that they can raise prices without losing able students. This cycle means that endowment mostly goes to subsidize rich children, while lower- and lower-middle class families have great difficulty entering what might be called the discount market unless their children are very bright and can get scholarships.

The importance of scholarships in the political economy of private higher education should not, however, be underestimated. Most college faculty want higher admissions standards and brighter students. Most college administrators share this ambition, for they know that able students will become able alumni. Able alumni will, in turn, tend to become rich or well-known alumni, essential if faculty demands for higher salaries, lighter teaching loads, better facilities and the like are to be met. (Administrators will, however, tend to be somewhat selective in their search for able students, admitting the son of a rich alumnus even if he is not especially talented.) This quest for able students provides one of the few internal checks on rising expenditures. At least in theory, raising tuition could eventually force a college to select its students mainly on the basis of family background rather than academic promise. In recent years, however, the shrewder private college administrators have largely eliminated this problem by enlarging their scholarship programs. These have reassured the faculty that obviously first-rate students will be able to matriculate even if they cannot pay much. As a result, the sky now seems to be the limit on tuition at wealthy private colleges.[14] Other private colleges follow a few hundred dollars behind, even though they lack comparable programs to help needy students.

The steady increase in the standard of amenity in most of the private sector has inevitably put pressure on the public sector for comparable improvements. Legislators have, however, been under-

---

[13] For evidence that here as elsewhere the rich get the bargains, see André Danière, "Cost-Benefit Analysis," table 1.23. Danière's data show that colleges that spend substantially more on instruction than they charge for tuition get rich students regardless of their absolute charges, while the poor are more often found in colleges that spend very little on instruction, even when these colleges are quite expensive.

[14] Of course the sky isn't the limit, as the recent spate of publicity about the financial problems of private colleges has indicated. See Doermann.

standably reluctant to appropriate the necessary funds. And neither legislators nor public-sector educators have been willing to emulate the private colleges in pushing up tuition faster than family incomes. Faculty and administrators at public institutions tend to assume, just as their private colleagues did a generation ago, that higher tuition will exclude many desirable students. (State legislators have never been willing to appropriate adequate funds for scholarships at public institutions.) This is not to say that public college men are exclusively concerned with the ability of their students. If they thought higher tuition would solve their over-all financial problem, they would probably favor it despite the possible consequences for recruitment. But they rightly suspect that if tuition receipts rise, tax subsidies will be allowed to lag correspondingly. They therefore see tuition as a substitute for higher taxes rather than as a supplement to them. (Strangely enough, almost nobody in the private sector makes the parallel argument that raising private tuition will provide the alumni and foundations with an excuse for giving less.)

As already indicated, these attitudes meant that public colleges' expenditure per student lagged behind private colleges' after 1950. This is a puzzling phenomenon, however, for almost all observers have assumed the private institutions were in fact lagging behind the public ones. One reason for this misconception *may* be that in 1950 the typical private university spent more per student than the typical public one, while the typical private church college probably spent more than the typical public teachers college. Today the private universities' lead seems to have narrowed, and the church colleges' lead, if it ever existed, appears to have evaporated entirely. How, then, can the private sector as a whole have gained on the public one? It would be quite difficult to gather statistical evidence that would answer this question definitely, but our guess is that the explanation lies in the differential growth of different sorts of institutions in the two sectors. Over-all expenditures in the private sector rose relatively rapidly because the high-cost universities and university colleges were growing at least as fast as the low-cost church colleges. Over-all expenditures in the public sector rose less rapidly because the high-cost public universities expanded less than the low-cost teachers colleges that became state colleges. Or to put it another way, the low-cost public colleges may have grown so fast that they made it look as if the public sector as a whole was lagging when in fact individual public institutions were mostly improving their competitive position.

Having said all this, however, the question remains why legislators who were unwilling to spend more than token sums on scholarships for needy students, and who were generally anxious to keep all public expenditures to a minimum, appropriated enormous sums for public universities. Why didn't they insist that the student beneficiaries and their families pay, as they were increasingly doing in the private sector? The answer must clearly be sought in the attitudes of the middle-class parents to whom legislators are responsive.

For many middle-income families taxes that support higher education are a bit like compulsory insurance. Instead of anxiously trying to save enough money each year to put their children through college, fearing that inflation may make their savings inadequate or that some accident may wipe them out, middle-income parents in states with good public institutions can pay their annual taxes and to some extent relax. This benefit is less important to the poor, who usually sense that it would take more than subsidies to get their children through college. It is also less important to the rich, who do not have to worry about financing even private higher education for their children.[15]

Tax subsidies for higher education have another psychological appeal as well. Like many other kinds of insurance, they represent a calculated risk as well as a compulsory savings plan. But unlike other forms of insurance, they benefit those who have had good luck rather than those who have had misfortunes. Everyone pays into the kitty. Then families whose children stay in school win; families whose children drop out lose. Taxation for higher education is thus punitive: it takes money from those parents whom society deems have done a poor job of raising their children, and it gives money to those who have instilled socially approved habits and aspirations. Most parents are optimistic about their ability to socialize their children in the ways they and society want and therefore assume they will benefit from such a system, if they think about it at all.

The politics of public higher education have inevitably reflected these attitudes, though seldom in a very direct fashion. For a long time state universities were the main recipients of legislative subsidies. Populist politicians made a habit of denouncing these universities as country clubs for the rich, maintained at the expense of the poor workingman. Even undemagogic labor lobbyists, while mildly favorable to public higher education, were usually more interested in other sorts of programs that benefited their membership more directly (including state aid for the public schools). The struggle for more generous university appropriations was therefore often led by

[15] Saving for the children's higher education seems to be quite unusual. Lansing, Lorimer, and Moriguchi, pp. 36 ff., report that less than half of all parents with children in college drew on savings to cover expenses, and that less than 30 per cent had saved specifically for college bills. If one were to look at the population as a whole, one would probably find that less than 15 per cent of all families saved for their children's education. Those who do save, moreover, often save only token sums. (On the other hand, there are some covert savings, such as payments on a house, which can be turned into collateral if a family wants to borrow to meet children's college expenses.)

Republican moderates—successful farmers who felt they owed something to the agriculture school, comfortable small-town business and professional men who had themselves attended the state university and expected their children to do so, and corporation executives who wanted a steady supply of junior management trainees. The university provided them and their friends with a good education at low cost, created at least the illusion of equal opportunity throughout the state, and had very little effect on the tax rate. It was in many respects the secular counterpart of an established church, exploiting the fiscal resources, admonitory instincts, and idealism that conservative legislators might otherwise have channeled into religion.

Today this is changing to some extent. The demand for higher education has become far more widespread. Urban (and now surburban) blue-collar families have begun to discover that a high school diploma is not enough for their children, and this has strengthened Democratic support for higher education. But such families often still assume that the state university is a remote, godless, Anglo-Saxon institution. Many feel they cannot afford to send their children to it, and many would not want to do so even if they could. A nearby state college or junior college is, however, a somewhat different story. Democratic politicians whose careers depend on such voters tend to support commuter colleges, even when they are cool to the state university.

Yet these are not simple matters. The Democrats may be the party of the many, while the Republicans are the party of the few, but the Democrats are also the party of profligacy, while the Republicans are the party of parsimony. Republicans worried about unnecessary public expenditure tend to find more they can quarrel with at state universities than at the relatively underprivileged state colleges and junior colleges. Their morality may therefore get the better of their class interests and may lead them to support the austere local commuter colleges against the flush residential university.

There are other ambiguities, too. In general the Republicans are opposed to all public expenditures, but they are less opposed to those that benefit the middle classes than to those that do not. This means that while they may want to curtail the budget across the board, higher education is seldom their first target. (Ronald Reagan's obsession with the University of California is in this respect exceptional. Reagan's attitude reflected Republican revulsion against the morality and politics of the University as much as it did concern with the University's impact on the state tax rate.) In many cases, indeed, it is the Democrats, with their commitment to a wide variety of other public programs, who find that they cannot do everything on a fixed budget and decide to skimp on higher education. The Republicans are more willing to shortchange the lower classes and therefore have more left for subsidizing middle-income groups such as those who send their children to college.

Admissions Requirements in the Public and Private Sectors

Until comparatively recently almost all colleges, both public and private, accepted the great majority of their applicants. This meant that admissions policies could have relatively little direct influence on the character of a college. Colleges did, it is true, exercise considerable indirect influence over who applied—through pricing policy, choice of location, sectarian links, establishment of informal contacts with various secondary schools, and other decisions about how to define and publicize the college. Once these decisions had had their effect, however, and a particular group of students had chosen the college, few colleges exercised much choice among their applicants.

Most colleges always had *some* admissions requirements, however, and these varied from the public to the private sector in ways that still have important consequences. Legislatures often saw public colleges and universities as part of the larger system of public education and tried to use admission to state institutions as a lever for improving local high schools. State accreditation of high schools was established partly to ensure that students coming to the state university would have appropriate preparation. If a high school lost its accreditation there was a possibility that its graduates would not get into the university—though we have the impression that this threat was more potential than real. The political quid pro quo for this was that if a local high school met accreditation requirements it acquired the power to decide for itself which local boys and girls would be admitted to the university. If an accredited high school gave a student a diploma, most state universities would admit him with no further questions. At one time an accredited high school was expected to demand a certain minimal level of competence before conferring its diploma. But this was often no more than a polite fiction, and as public pressure to reward perseverance grew, it ceased to be even that. By the 1930s virtually anyone willing to stay the course could get a high school diploma. This implied that anyone willing to finish a high school course would be admitted to most state universities, if he chose to go, and that was in fact the policy in most states.

The private sector, on the other hand, kept control over student selection in its own hands. At first this meant that each college devised its own tests of academic competence, administered them to prospective students, and accepted those whose performance it judged adequate. The difficulty with this system was that every college had a different test, and a school that prepared students well for one test often prepared poorly for another. This was a problem for both schools and students, but especially for the latter since a senior often found himself unprepared for the college he wanted to attend. So in 1909 the College Entrance Examination Board was organized to give a single set of comprehensive tests for applicants to all leading private colleges. The Board was controlled by the colleges collectively, but individual colleges retained complete freedom to use its test results as they saw fit. Most used them in the most minimal way, for they mostly had fewer applicants than they wanted and felt obliged to admit any applicant who had finished high school and even some who had not.

The net result was that while there were differences in academic ability between one campus and another, these differences do not seem to have followed public-private lines. It has been said, for example, that the average IQ at CCNY in the 1920s and 1930s was about the same as at Harvard, and we are inclined to believe it. The average at Berkeley may well have been higher than at Stanford, and the average at Michigan was probably not very different from Chicago. The private college students were probably somewhat better prepared than their counterparts at public institutions, since their parents had often sent them to private schools or moved to suburbs with good public schools. But good preparation did not mean that private college students did better work once admitted to college.

From the viewpoint of the faculty both the public and private admissions systems were inefficient, for both allowed large numbers of freshmen to matriculate who had neither the talent nor the interest to do what the faculty defined as college work. Unable to exclude these undesirables before they arrived, both public and private college faculties tended to be more or less consciously hostile toward them. The first year was often deliberately designed to "weed out the misfits." Freshmen and sophomores were in most cases presumed inept and indolent until they proved themselves otherwise, and often this attitude extended to all undergraduates. Even when it did not, upperclassmen often assumed that it did, since their perceptions of the faculty and of the college had usually been fixed early in their freshman year. It is therefore hardly surprising to discover that most colleges, both public and private, had extremely high dropout rates.

The past two decades have seen major changes in this situation. Returning veterans forced many colleges to choose between expansion and exclusion in 1945. Educators assumed demand would soon recede, and they were therefore reluctant to build new dormitories or hire new professors. They crowded some extra bodies in without expanding facilities or staff, but some, especially in the private sector, also became more selective. Having done this, they found that internal morale improved, faculty took students more seriously, students showed more interest, and life generally became more agreeable. When the GIs began to graduate, the colleges in question were reluctant to lower admissions requirements again. On the contrary, they sought ways of pushing them still higher. The rapid increase in college applications during the late 1950s and 1960s provided a basis for doing just this.

The increased emphasis on selectivity after the middle 1950s led to a change in the framework for discussing admissions policy. A generation ago most colleges spoke about their admissions requirements as if they were based on intrinsic standards of "what every freshman should know." This was manifestly untrue, in the sense that colleges adjusted their standards over time to take account of improvement or deterioration in their market position. Different colleges also had different standards at any given time, according to what they thought they could demand without going bankrupt. Nonetheless, people mostly talked as if a college set its standards and then admitted all applicants who met them. If this led to expansion, so much the better for everyone. To some extent the colleges even acted out this rhetoric. From 1919 to 1929, for example, applications rose almost as fast as from 1956 to 1966. Instead of curtailing enrollment and pushing up admissions requirements, the private colleges in the 1920s kept requirements fairly stable and expanded. It was in this context that students could speak of "passing" or "failing" their College Board exams (i.e. getting a score known to be acceptable or unacceptable to the college of their choice). Today admissions officers in the private sector talk a different language. Almost all private colleges of any standing treat the size of their freshman class as a given, determined by abstract considerations like "the need for a manageable community," "faculty resources," and other presumptively immutable considerations. Students are then ranked competitively, and enough are admitted to bring the class to the desired size. The idea of an absolute standard lingers only in enigmatic announcements like "Harvard College last year admitted only a fifth of all qualified applicants." ("Qualified" in this context means a student would not flunk out if admitted.)

These changes have been accompanied by changes in the yardsticks private colleges use to rank their applicants academically. Until World War II most private colleges evaluated applicants in terms of their mastery of standard secondary school subject matter. But experience with war veterans strengthened the hand of reformers who argued that formal preparation for college was less relevant in predicting college performance than motivation and native intelligence.

Educational research also helped raise serious questions about the traditional emphasis on mastery of particular subjects as a way of separating sheep from goats. Statistical studies showed that general verbal and mathematical ability tests predicted college grades better than did achievement tests in particular subjects. Related studies showed able graduates of poor high schools got better grades by their senior year in college than less adept graduates of good prep schools. For these and other reasons, almost all leading colleges rejected pleas (usually made in the hope of "reforming" public high schools) that they require mastery of more subject matter (e.g. four years of Latin or mathematics) for admission. Instead, they moved in the opposite direction, placing more emphasis on general aptitude tests and on rank in high school class, less on knowledge of specific subjects. Academic work prior to college came to be seen less as an end in itself and more as a litmus test of future academic performance. At the same time academic performance in college was coming to seem more important than it had, so that the various devices for judging academic promise played a larger role than they once had. Football talent, geniality, breeding, and other non-academic qualities were correspondingly de-emphasized.

The private sector has taken the lead since World War II in making admission academically competitive, but public colleges have moved in the same direction. The tradition of admitting large numbers to state universities and then flunking most of them out seems to be on the wane. Only a handful of state legislatures still clings to the principle that a high school diploma should entitle a student to enter the leading public university in his state. The nominal justification for this change has usually been lack of space at the university, but this explanation conceals more than it explains. Having barred unpromising students from the university, most legislatures have spent enormous sums establishing or expanding state colleges and junior colleges for the rejects. These are often said to be more economical than expanding the university, but the savings to the taxpayer are frequently marginal.[16] The savings to the student, through commuting, often seem greater, but we doubt if even this is usually decisive. The main reason for excluding mediocre students from state universities, it seems to us, is the increasing public acceptance of the idea that these universities, like their private counterparts, exist to serve able students headed for professional and to a lesser extent managerial careers. Exposure to high-price scholars is not deemed especially necessary for other undergraduates, who are thought equally well served by a less carefully selected faculty of "dedicated teachers." While no state university faculty has been able to make undergraduate

[16] See e.g. the cost estimates in A Master Plan, pp. 156–57.

admission as selective as graduate admission, many are moving in this direction and few are encountering strong political resistance.[17]

One reason for the relative absence of resistance is the fact that most state universities still accept the judgments of local high schools at their face value. That is to say, they set formal requirements in terms of high school courses and grades, and then admit any student whom the high school certifies as having met these requirements. The local authorities thus still have a large measure of freedom in deciding who will go to the state university, who to a state college, who to a junior college, and who nowhere. The reason for this is clearly political. Few state universities can afford to discriminate against the graduates of rural high schools, no matter how likely these students are to flunk out. Reliance on aptitude tests or other universalistic devices would give the highly competitive suburban high schools a much larger share of university places. Urbanization and reapportionment are reducing the political need to take rural schooling at face value, and standardized tests are more politically acceptable than they used to be as a basis for choosing state university students, but in most states localism still holds sway. Students whose high school records are only average can often get in by doing well on a standardized aptitude test, and this gives the graduate of a highly competitive suburban high school a somewhat better chance than his rural or slum-bred age-mate. Florida is one of the few states that has reversed this logic and set a minimum aptitude score below which even a good record in high school will not earn admission. But this too may become more common. The old principle of external certification has long since been rejected in most public professional schools, which are free to set their own standards in their own way, and it seems inevitable that public liberal arts colleges will eventually win the same privilege.

Those state universities that continue to accept high school grades at face value will inevitably continue to admit appreciable numbers of students whom the faculty doesn't want, including some who cannot survive the four-year course. The University of California, for instance, admits roughly the top eighth of California's high school graduates, mostly on the basis of grades. Yet the UC faculty treats these students with the same habitual disdain as much less selective universities such as Illinois, and UC has about the same rate of attrition as its less selective rivals. In part, no doubt, this is because a research-oriented faculty prefers to believe that its undergraduates are uneducable, since this assuages guilt feelings about neglecting them. But the fact is that many of the students admitted

[17] The University of Colorado under Quigg Newton was an exception. Newton's drive to make Colorado a "great" institution upset many parents and alumni who assumed their children would not be able to get in, and this contributed indirectly to his downfall in 1963.

to the University of California *are* almost uneducable *in traditional scholarly terms*. Perhaps this is partly because reliance on high school grades and credits forces the University to pick a rather different and less promising "top eighth" from the one a private college would choose on the basis of aptitude tests and subjective criteria.[18] Yet perhaps the only real difference between, say, UC and Stanford is not that UC lets the high schools rank students whereas Stanford makes its own judgments, but that UC is still trying in a half-hearted way to deal with the top 12 per cent whereas Stanford works with what it regards as the top 1 or 2 per cent.

This difference between UC and Stanford is, and will probably remain, characteristic of leading institutions in the two sectors. Public colleges have great difficulty committing substantial resources to any small group or problem, including the academically gifted. They depend on politicians for money, and they therefore constantly play the numbers game, spreading their resources and patronage wide rather than deep. They can, for example, gain little political advantage by spending $2,500 a year subsidizing both the tuition and subsistence of a would-be engineer from a desperately poor family if $1,200 a year in tuition subsidies to prospective engineers from middle-income families ensures a supply sufficient for industry's needs. Committing extra resources to the unusually gifted is as difficult as committing them to the unusually needy. Traditionally, tax support of high-cost programs for unusually able students has depended on the programs' having obvious spillover value to the rest of society, as was the case with agriculture or engineering. Expensive programs whose value was less obvious, such as doctoral study in the arts and sciences, have usually been funded in such a way as to conceal their high unit cost. This was often done by lumping together graduate and undergraduate instruction in the same subjects. In recent years university accountants have often insisted on bringing these differences out in the open, sometimes to the detriment of expensive programs and at times also to the disadvantage of gifted students. On the other hand, we suspect that the idea of spending extra money on especially promising college students is more politically acceptable today than it was a generation or two ago, perhaps partly because of Sputnik and the Cold War.

The logic of student selection in the private sector is rather different from that in the public sector. Private colleges normally seek a small group of enthusiastic donors, not a large group of passively sympathetic taxpayers. This group of donors must be mostly composed of alumni. A private college is therefore anxious to placate its alumni for the same reasons a public college is anxious to please

18 For an analysis of the Berkeley student body which sheds light on these problems, see Trow, "Notes on Undergraduate Teaching."

the voters. Alumni children are hard to reject, even if they are un-exciting prospects, and alumni political sentiment is seldom forgotten, even when it is flouted. Yet the fact remains that selective private colleges which reject a high proportion of alumni children usually get more money from their alumni than unselective colleges which accept almost all alumni children, just as selective public colleges usually get more money than unselective ones. This is certainly not a simple cause-effect relationship, however, but reflects the relative standing of various colleges and consequent variations in the degree of hauteur they can permit themselves in dealing with all sorts of groups.

Exaggerated or not, administrative anxieties have gradually yielded to the internal pressures for more rigorous selection. Academically inept or apathetic students are, after all, a chronic source of irritation to faculty members. An administration that has to deal with a hostile legislature may be afraid to eliminate the offending aliens, but an administration that has only alumni to deal with is quite likely to eliminate "misfits" as soon as it has enough competent students to put in their place. Mediocre students are also a threat to their fellow students, for they encourage the faculty to establish all sorts of defense mechanisms (like big lecture courses) and policing devices (like inane exams) which affect the able and committed as well as the inept and indolent. A college composed almost entirely of compe-tent, diligent students seems better able to talk about freshmen seminars, independent study, pass-fail courses, and the like.[19] If its students are good enough a college may even begin to act as if it had some responsibility for their successes and failures. Thus when a stu-dent at a selective private college flunks out, or even when he leaves under a disciplinary cloud, he is still regarded as "one of ours" and can usually return in a year or two. The college assumes he has what it takes to make a good alumnus; "otherwise we wouldn't have admitted him." If, on the other hand, a student flunks out of a relatively unselective public institution, he is often forced to go else-where for a second chance. His original institution assumes he was one of the people "we should never have admitted in the first place," and that it is well rid of him.

The differences between public and private admissions policies are not likely to disappear entirely in the foreseeable future. Many private colleges are today far more selective than any of their public competitors. The degree of difference between the public and private sectors can be roughly gauged by looking at the "selectivity index" James Cass and Max Birnbaum compiled on the basis of 1962 test

[19] This depends, however, on subjective as well as objective factors. Santa Cruz has adopted these innovations while Berkeley long insisted they were impractical, even though they have students of about the same aptitudes.

scores.[20] Text scores were not available for all colleges, especially not all public ones, but the more distinguished colleges were almost all included. Of the 60 most selective, only 1 (Harpur College in upstate New York) was publicly controlled. Of the next 100, 12 (Brooklyn College, the University of California, CCNY, the University of Massachusetts, the University of Michigan, Michigan State, Oakland University (also in Michigan), the University of New Hampshire, the University of North Carolina, Rutgers, the University of Vermont, and the University of Virginia) were publicly controlled. Thus only 13 of the 160 most selective colleges were public. It should be borne in mind, however, that these 13 were much larger than average.

College Imagery and Self-Imagery

Although cost and admissions requirements are today the two primary variables differentiating public from private colleges, popular mythology has an important second-level influence. In particular, low tuition and low admissions requirements are generally presumed to make public institutions more socially heterogeneous than private ones. (We have never seen any empirical evidence to support this proposition, but we are inclined to believe it is true.) This presumed heterogeneity has some independent influence on who applies, quite apart from cost and academic standards.

While some of the students at state universities come because they do not want to spend extra money for a private college, and others come because they can't get into an equally reputable private college, some are attracted precisely by the state university's heterogeneity. They want, or at least imagine they want, to meet "all kinds," even though once they arrive on campus they may go to enormous lengths to avoid actually doing so. (Fraternities and sororities are only the most formal of the many devices by which students escape the challenges of learning to cope with and enjoy radically different classmates.) Some lower-middle and working-class students who could get scholarships at private colleges also choose public ones because of their apparent pluralism. Especially west of the Mississippi, but often also in the Midwest and South, the most academically distinguished and socially prestigious institution in a state is likely to be its public university. The student who wanted to do better would often have to go to a private college "back East." This would put him too far from home to make the weekend visits both he and his parents expect will soften the blow of going away. More important, perhaps, going East would mean cutting himself off from local friends,

[20] Cass and Birnbaum, pp. 526–28.

both physically and psychologically. Going to a distant private college implies that local institutions are not good enough. This is a criticism of local manners and mores and in some cases of one's own family. It is hardly surprising that many students and their parents prefer to affirm family and community solidarity by attending the state university. If, as students usually believe, the state university includes all the subcultures that might appeal to them, going there also allows them to postpone choosing any one identity and life style. Going to a small, relatively homogeneous private college requires more choice between possible life styles, and many high school seniors want to avoid such choices.

The converse case, especially common in the East, is the family that feels almost any sacrifice is worth while to provide its children with private higher education. Such families may scrimp to send their children to mediocre private colleges even though better formal instruction is available at lower cost in the public sector. In most cases these families are paying to have their children educated under a particular set of rules or alongside a particular set of classmates. Parents may know, for example, that the faculty at the University of Colorado is better than at the University of Denver, and may nonetheless prefer Denver on the grounds that their daughters will be less likely to marry the wrong man at Denver, or that their sons are more likely to make friends who will be useful in later life. Or they may want their children to go to college only with other girls, only with Seventh Day Adventists, or only with whites. The private sector can cater to such feelings and prejudices while the public one generally cannot.[21]

Yet the number of families willing to pay for this kind of distinctiveness appears to be declining, certainly relative to the over-all demand for higher education and possibly in absolute terms as well. In part this is because the cultural differences between the sexes, between denominations, and perhaps even between social classes and races seem less salient than they once did. In part it is because such differences as endure are no longer thought legitimate bases for segregation either for oneself or for society.

The one form of distinctiveness that seems likely to have more rather than less appeal in the years ahead is academic. The private sector has two advantages in such competition. First, the public sector seems almost unable to support small independent university colleges that focus exclusively on teaching undergraduates. The University

<hr/>

[21] There are, as we shall see in Chapters VII and X, a few sex-segregated public colleges and a few racially segregated ones, but both sorts are growing rarer. Religious segregation is impossible in public institutions but some are dominated by one faith or another.

of California's Riverside campus, the State University of New York's Harpur College in Binghamton, and Michigan State's Oakland campus were all intended to be such places. Political pressure has forced Riverside to expand, adding graduate work and diversifying its offerings so as to become more like a conventional state university. Harpur is trying to retain its autonomy within the new state university campus at Binghamton, but its position is under considerable attack. Oakland is expanding, though as yet only marginally into graduate work, and hopes to create a group of relatively small subcolleges, each with its own cohesiveness and distinctiveness. This indicates that strong leadership can at least partially channel public pressure to become a "standard" university. Still, the academically distinguished college with no graduate school remains an essentially private phenomenon. There are no public Amhersts, Oberlins, or Reeds. Indeed, small distinguished institutions have to be private even if they do have graduate schools. There are no public Cal Techs or Princetons. The only small public institutions are those that cannot get more applicants.

The private sector's second asset in a market place that values academic distinctiveness is its power to be even more exclusive than the public sector. As we saw in the previous section, there are relatively few public institutions anything like as selective as the better-known private ones. Nor does any public institution send anywhere nearly as many of its B.A.s on to graduate school as do the leading private colleges. There are, it is true, some undergraduate departments, honors programs, and professional schools (as well as many graduate schools and departments within public universities) that are as selective and nearly as self-contained as the top private colleges. But these are seldom visible to high school seniors or their parents, who know the reputation of an entire institution rather than of its subdivisions. Under these circumstances it seems likely that both students and families who are impressed by academic distinction and by the occupational successes that tend to be associated with it will continue to opt for the private sector. They will, however, be interested in only a small part of the private spectrum—the highly selective institutions that enroll perhaps a quarter of all private college students.

Yet even the academically selective private colleges will be in trouble if the price differential between them and their public rivals continues to widen. Between 1956 and 1964 the tuition gap between the typical private college and its typical public rival grew from $500 to $1,000.[22] Private tuition increased fastest at the academically selective colleges, for these grew used to affluence in the days when endowment covered a large share of costs and responded to lags

[22] *A Fact Book*, table 263.

in endowment by pushing up tuition even faster than poorer colleges. It seems obvious that at some point the premium for academic reputability will become so great that the proportion of families willing to pay it will begin to decline. The more distinguished private colleges are beginning to worry about reaching that point, but they have not yet reached it.

The real crisis in private higher education today is among those private institutions that cannot boast any more academic distinction than nearby public universities. These colleges are caught in a vicious circle. Most have little to offer that public colleges do not offer at a lower price, except smallness, protectiveness, and sometimes piety. So they cannot raise tuition much above the public level and cannot get enough resources to offer a more appealing program than their public rivals.[23] And so ad infinitum. Over the long haul these colleges have very bleak prospects. The big urban ones will probably become state institutions. This has already happened to the University of Houston, the University of Kansas City, the University of Buffalo, the University of Pittsburgh, and Temple University in Philadelphia. It will probably happen to several dozen others in the next decade. A few other big urban universities, such as New York University, will probably make it into the elite group that competes with the public sector on the basis of quality. Small rural private colleges with no particular claim to distinction are in an even worse way. Most are still church-affiliated and unwilling to consider public control as a way of getting public subsidies. Even when they are not church-affiliated, they may be unwilling to trade public regulation for public money. Or if they are, state planners may not be especially interested in taking them over, for they are usually poorly located, poorly staffed, and generally unpromising nuclei for developing a big public campus.

Under these circumstances many would argue that the colleges in question should simply be allowed to wither and ultimately die, as so many others have done before them. We do not share this view. Despite many reservations we believe the free market can usually regulate higher education better than legislators can. We therefore believe that any college that gets applicants should also get a fair share of available resources. Today this does not happen. Legislatures subsidize public colleges no matter how bad they are; privately controlled colleges get subsidized only if they are good enough to attract private philanthropy on a large scale. This means privately controlled colleges are competing on very unequal terms. The student who

---

[23] There are a variety of groups such as the Council for Assistance to Small Colleges that try to mobilize private philanthropy behind these colleges, sometimes on no more substantial grounds than that they are private and that it is bad for big government to run everything. On the whole, however, the take from such fund-raising is modest.

chooses a marginal private college must pay almost the full cost of his education. The student who chooses a marginal public college pays only a small fraction of the cost. We can see no virtue in such an arrangement. Insofar as possible, subsidies should be allocated on a per-student basis, regardless of control. In order to maximize the independence of the private sector these subsidies should go directly to the student, and be recouped by the institutions through higher tuition.

This does not mean that there should be *no* institutional grants, nor that market decisions are *always* the wisest. If all state subsidies today took the form of scholarships and subsidized loans, we would no doubt be urging institutional grants to socially useful programs that were underenrolled. But that is not the situation, nor is there any foreseeable danger that student tastes will play too large a role in determining institutional priorities.

The first section of this chapter argued that the public and private sectors had increasingly similar objectives and methods, and that the major differences between them today reflected differences between the students who chose one sector as against the other. In this section we have qualified that generalization by suggesting that the public sector is unable to support independent university colleges and has great difficulty supporting colleges with small homogeneous student bodies. These forms of distinctiveness are not important to most students, but it does seem to us that they should be preserved for those who value them. We say this because, although the bias generally expressed in this book is toward the cosmopolitan and heterogeneous, we want students to have the option of postponing or even avoiding pressures to expand their horizons.

Furthermore, if public subsidies were equally available to all sorts of institutions, some under private control might well be able to do a better job than public ones in achieving conventional objectives, such as mass education at moderate cost. One of the great strengths of American higher education has been its lack of regulation. It has been possible—though certainly never easy—for innovators and entrepreneurs to go into business for themselves. While most have failed, some have thrived. It would be unfortunate if America were to abandon this open system for a closed one in which nobody could establish or maintain a college unless he was either directly sponsored and controlled by the state, or else began with the enormous private resources needed to compete with top state institutions in terms of academic reputation.

VII. *Feminism, Masculinism, and Coeducation*

The Rise of Coeducation

Although Oberlin admitted women in 1837, and Elmira Female College was founded in 1855, American higher education remained a virtually all-male affair until after the Civil War.[1] Not only were women thought generally incapable of intellectual self-discipline and rigor, but the attempt to impose it on them was thought debilitating to both mind and body. (This may not have been wholly delusory, given the character of nineteenth-century academic life.) The men who controlled job opportunities had no interest in hiring women in any but menial roles, and men looking for wives were also unlikely to be impressed by a girl's educational qualifications.[2] The lack of advanced educational opportunity for women was thus paralleled by lack of incentive.

It is hard to say what effect the absence of women had on pre-Civil War colleges. These colleges certainly gave short shrift to many of the presumptively feminine virtues, such as warmth, compassion, sensitivity to other people, and even aesthetic sensibility. But the same could be said of all nineteenth-century America. It was a very "masculine" time, in which the virtues of the frontier and the market place seemed more glamorous than those of the hearth. Nonetheless, the arid pedantry and tyrannical discipline of most nineteenth-century colleges probably would have been more difficult to maintain if coeducation had become common earlier.

After the Civil War the attack on sex segregation and exclusion in higher education accelerated very rapidly. This attack was, of course, part of a broader feminist movement, which affected almost every aspect of American life. This movement had much in common with other "minority" struggles against "majority" oppression. Male prej-

---

[1] It is interesting to note, however, that the U. S. Office of Education's first survey of higher education reported that women had received 1,378 of the 9,371 Bachelor's awarded in 1870; see *Historical Statistics*, Series H 330–332. We suspect that many of the 1,378 women in question received degrees from academies that were more nearly secondary schools than colleges.

[2] One partial exception to this rule was the public school movement, which hired women to "keep school" and established secondary-level normal schools to train them. Here economy triumphed over ideology.

udice and protectiveness were the enemy, but success depended on finding liberal male allies to serve as a fifth column in the seats of power. This was not always easy. While most men had little to lose from female emancipation in any direct and self-interested sense, many certainly *felt* they had something to lose in a larger psychological sense. Feminism was one of the many nineteenth-century movements Joseph Gusfield has termed symbolic crusades, and both its advocates and opponents often saw it as a threat to a traditional pattern of life. The fury of male opposition was thus akin to that of modern squares who see the hippies as a threat to the American way of life, even though the hippies' decision to opt out actually serves the interests of those scrambling for scarce places at the top of the occupational and social pyramids. Yet like other minorities the feminists often found that their worst enemies were not men, relatively few of whom felt personally threatened by female emancipation even when they opposed it for traditionalistic reasons. The most dangerous opposition often came from other women, who interpreted the feminists' program as an indictment of the kind of femininity they themselves had adopted. Docile subordinate "Uncle Toms" of this variety still play a major role in the war between the sexes.

Another important similarity between feminism and other minority revolts was the feminists' tendency to accept virtually all the assumptions and aspirations of their oppressors, with the single exception of anti-feminism. Thus the leaders of the feminist movement were strikingly masculine in outlook and manner and often asserted their "independence" by adopting hitherto male clothing, speech, and the like. They struggled to gain entry into male careers and male social life. In a more general sense, their aim was to establish their right to deny the difference between the sexes when they chose.

The necessity of winning male allies and the tendency to emulate male models had important consequences for the higher education of women. The feminists' primary objective was to open traditionally male institutions to women. Since men controlled the nation's economic resources, "piggy-backing" on male colleges was a more promising approach to finance than setting up new colleges exclusively for women. And since men still defined what was academically respectable and what was not, integration also provided much the best guarantee of true equality. This strategy was re-enforced by the fact that sexual segregation proved economically ruinous in many small school districts, and was therefore generally (though never quite universally) rejected at the elementary and secondary level. This set a pattern that residential higher education found it natural, if not quite necessary, to follow. By the end of the nineteenth century most public colleges and universities had opened their doors to women, even in states where women still did not have the vote. In the Midwest and Far West, moreover, even the private colleges had mostly gone coed.

The equalization of educational opportunity did not, of course, bring overnight equality between the sexes, any more than the waning of racial segregation has brought parity between the races. Even today many families feel protective about daughters and want to keep them near home, whereas sons, who are likely to be in more open conflict with their parents, are often encouraged to go away. Most American families still feel it is more important for their sons to get a college degree than for their daughters to do so. Their sons will need it to earn a living, whereas their daughters may be able to marry a college man without having gone to college themselves.[3] The occupational world still shows a strong bias against women.[4] Many jobs are open only to men, and in many others a woman has a chance of being considered only if she is clearly superior to the male alternatives. Perhaps more important, the world of work is organized along lines that inevitably favor men. Few employers have made any effort to create job descriptions sufficiently flexible to accommodate mothers of pre-adolescent children, and few professions have tried to establish career trajectories that would allow a woman to curtail her work for a few years without completely losing touch with her field and her colleagues.[5]

Under these circumstances it is hardly surprising that neither parents nor educators typically take women's higher education as seriously as men's. Nor is it surprising that women should attend college less often than men, despite increasing equality of nominal opportunity. Women constituted about 56 per cent of all secondary school graduates in 1870, 60 per cent in 1900, 55 per cent in 1930, and 51 per cent in 1964. They have slightly higher secondary school grades

[3] Negroes are the main exception to this rule. Negro women are more likely to go to college than their brothers. Among other things this reflects the fact that at least until recently they have had a better chance than their brothers of getting a professional job once they earned a degree. Negro women are also more likely than white ones to be the main support of their family. And while girls of any color are likely to do better in high school than their male classmates, the gap is wider among Negroes than whites, for a variety of cultural as well as economic reasons.

[4] One of us once asked the dean of a leading dental school who was complaining about the poor quality of male applicants why he did not recruit women, who could make excellent dentists for children and who could maintain such a practice on a part-time basis. He replied that his school would like very much to have more women, but could not recruit them without endangering its tenuous hold on the men it attracted. Similar arguments are, of course, made in behalf of racial exclusion.

[5] For discussion of the kinds of changes necessary to provide women with a more equal place, see Rossi, pp. 98–143.

and do slightly better on standardized tests than male high school graduates. Yet they are significantly less likely to go to college, and if they do go they are likely to go to a cheaper college nearer home.[6] During the last quarter of the nineteenth century women constituted a little less than a fifth of all college graduates. This rose to about two-fifths by 1929, but has leveled off since then.[7] In 1964 the typical woman was about three-quarters as likely to get a higher education as the typical man.[8] Women with B.A.s are only a little less likely than men to *enter* graduate school, but they are less than half as likely as similarly qualified men to earn a graduate degree.[9]

To some extent these statistics reflect discrimination against women in college admission. Except at Negro colleges, very few admissions officers allow their female:male ratio to rise above 50:50. The public ones are almost always nominally committed to admitting freshmen on a sex-blind basis, but even they may establish covert barriers by building too few dormitories for women. Private institutions are often quite open about discrimination, establishing sex quotas quite independently of the number or talent of each group of applicants. Nonetheless, we doubt that eliminating discrimination (e.g. by putting admission to Harvard and Radcliffe on the same competitive basis, or providing "compensatory" scholarships for poor girls whose parents won't make sacrifices to send them to the state university) would have much effect on the over-all statistics. The most it might do is

[6] Komarovsky, 1954. See also the Project Talent data cited in Chapter III. On enrollment ratios in secondary school, see 1965 *Digest*, table 37.

[7] Although the ratio of men to women is about the same today as in 1930, it has oscillated somewhat in the interim. The proportion of women rose slowly during the Depression, continuing the historic trend, then fell during the GI Bill era. The proportion of women entrants stabilized around 40 per cent after 1950, but the proportion of women B.A.s continued to fall until 1958. Since then, women have recovered their pre-1939 position among graduates as well as entrants. See *A Fact Book*, p. 70, and 1965 *Digest*, table 52.

[8] This meant that women constituted 43 per cent of all college entrants and graduates, men 57 per cent. Although women drop out of college at the same rate as men, this is not true when one holds income and academic aptitude constant. A girl of a given family income or aptitude is slightly more likely to drop out than a comparable man. See Panos and Astin, "Attrition."

[9] Sharpe, "Five Years," table 1, shows that among members of the Class of 1958, 61 per cent of the men and 53 per cent of the women enrolled in graduate courses between 1958 and 1963. If one looks only at those who enrolled *for a degree*, however, the difference between the sexes is more marked: 41 per cent of the men compared to 22 per cent of the women with B.A.s had started a graduate degree program. If one looks only at those who *earned* degrees, the sex difference is greater still: 28 per cent of the men had earned graduate degrees compared to 13 per cent of the women. Sharpe's sample shows women earning a slightly lower proportion of all Master's degrees than do the 1965 *Digest*, table 73, and *A Fact Book*, table 71, but the differences are not large. All these sources suggest that women with B.A.s are less than half as likely as men to earn a graduate degree, despite the fact that they have better undergraduate records on the average. About half the women earn their graduate degrees in education.

enable a few girls to go to better colleges than they now do, and hopefully get an education more nearly equal to their talent. Even without such improvements the striking thing about American higher education is how little discrimination there usually is against women, at least compared to the rest of society. It is something of a tribute to scholars' persistent belief in liberal education as an end in itself that many still "waste" time on girls who become "mere" housewives. (To some extent the relatively favorable position of women simply reflects scholars' reluctance to apply *any* non-academic criterion in selecting students. Yet this cannot be the whole explanation, for these same men are quite capable of self-conscious discrimination against women applying to graduate school.) Similarly, the power of egalitarian rhetoric (and the women's vote) is illustrated by legislators' readiness to spend billions of dollars educating women, very few of whom will make a direct contribution to the tax base comparable to the taxpayers' investment in them (It is probably true, however, that legislatures spend more per male student than per female, because there are more men in expensive vocational fields like medicine and engineering.)

Still, the triumph of coeducation has not obliterated either the persistent differences between the sexes or the persistent myths of difference, which simultaneously enhance and obscure the reality. As a result, women are by no means universally integrated with men even inside nominally coeducational institutions. Academically, the men tend to study the more quantitative subjects, such as science and engineering, while women are concentrated in seemingly qualitative fields of psychology, sociology, and the humanities. There is a further division along occupational lines, with men going into areas like economics, law, and business while women turn to education, nursing, and home economics.[10]

In the social sphere, too, segregation has been at least partially preserved. Most coeducational colleges have separate deans of men and women. They justify this partly on the grounds that students would find it hard to discuss personal problems with somebody of the opposite sex, but it is notable that college psychiatric services make no comparable effort to segregate their clientele. The real reason for separating students by sex seems to be that the dean of women is expected to look (and often act) like a maternal disciplinarian, keeping college girls in line in a way that is not thought necessary for men. Women are almost always subject to tighter rules than men,

[10] Home economics began as a prehousewife course, but it has increasingly become a kind of female engineering, requiring considerable scientific training and turning out dietitians, institutional managers, and the like. The heads of home economics departments are now often men, though male students are still rare.

and violations are usually taken more seriously. (Several state universities, for example, have a policy that if girls are out after hours their parents must be notified immediately.)

Residential segregation has also been almost universal in coeducational colleges, though off-campus housing has usually been integrated and a few mixed dormitories are now being built. The most culturally elaborated version of such segregation has been the fraternity-sorority system, which arose in the late nineteenth century at about the time coeducation became common and has begun to decline only in the last decade. The "Greek" system may, indeed, have been as much a response to the problem of segregating and organizing relations between the sexes as to that of the relations between classes and ethnic groups, though the two are obviously related. (John Finley Scott has shown how sororities systematically dissuade girls from choosing the "wrong" husband, or indeed from choosing any husband at all during their first college years.[11](Sororities differ in this respect from fraternities, which exercise far less control over their members. In part this is because the "mistakes" boys can make seem less serious to adults: they cannot get themselves pregnant, and if they marry a low-status girl, they confer their own status on her. In part, however, the fraternities' failure to control their members as tightly as sororities control theirs reflects the generally lower interpersonal resonance found in small male groups, which makes them less effective instruments of social control. It also reflects the failure of the rah-rah national fraternities to control their local chapters, some of which sporadically see the assertion of independence as a test of their masculinity and as a way of expressing their distaste for adult-imposed restrictions on their membership. Nonetheless, the fraternity-sorority system has served in a general way to preserve nineteenth-century definitions of proper sexual roles, keeping them considerably more polarized than the twentieth-century avant garde has thought necessary or desirable. The recent decline of the Greek system at predominantly upper-middle class colleges and universities seems in turn to reflect upper-middle class rejection of stylized sexual distinctions and agendas. Fraternities and sororities seem to be doing quite well, on the other hand, at colleges catering primarily to first-generation collegians—though even there undergraduates' increasing tendency to pair off in protomarital relationships leads a good many to drop their membership after an initial year or two.

The decline of fraternities and sororities is a symptom of a more general drift away from sex segregation and differentiation among the upper-middle classes. The past decade has even seen the rise of a hippy masculine counterpart to the old feminist movement. This

[11] See Scott.

subculture encourages men to indulge in traditionally "feminine" activities, ranging from the arts to long hair to tears. Yet many men are still worried about homosexuality, and most are as reluctant to abandon the symbols of sexual separatism as the female majority was a century ago.

The slowly increasing similarity between the attitudes and behavior permitted men and women has obviously not eliminated all the basic differences between them, nor is it likely to do so. Educational research still constantly shows that sex is one of the most important factors differentiating students' hopes and performance at all levels. The feminist lobby argues that these differences, like apparent differences between ethnic groups, merely reflect the prevailing cultural barriers. Clearly they are right that cultural conditioning can alter the polarities. Nevertheless, the biological differences do, in our judgment, tend to predispose the two sexes to somewhat different psychological attitudes, such as a greater receptivity in women and a greater performance orientation in men.[12]

But while the modal responses of men and women will probably remain quite different, the *range* of permissible responses for each sex may continue to widen, and the two distributions may increasingly overlap. The average woman is unlikely ever to be as career-oriented as the average man, and the average man is unlikely ever to be as emotionally expressive as the average woman. But America may be sufficiently pluralistic and tolerant for some women to pursue careers with the same passion that men do, for these women to be accepted in their jobs on the same basis as men, and for them not to feel guilty about it. Conversely, men may eventually feel largely free of the exigencies of the occupational world, quite willing to be economically dependent if they can find others willing to support them, and eager to live the emotionally less fettered life available to many women. This latter development is more remote, but its beginnings can be seen in many bohemias, both on and off campus.

Some might argue that this pluralistic dream also requires the preservation of at least a few traditional masculine subcultures, where those who cling to an older ethos can find comfort and a sense of sexual superiority. Perhaps this is true. Yet no principle can be pushed to its logical conclusion without crushing all other principles, and none can be applied except in a particular historical context. The pluralistic argument for preserving all-male colleges is uncomfortably similar to the pluralistic argument for preserving all-white colleges, and we are far from enthusiastic about it. The all-male college would be relatively

[12] For psychoanalytic and psychological discussion of these matters, see Erikson, McClelland, and Fromm. For an anthropological view stressing the extent to which sex differences are shaped by culture, see Mead.

easy to defend if it emerged from a world in which women were
established as fully equal to men. But it does not. It is therefore likely
to be a witting or unwitting device for preserving tacit assumptions of
male superiority—assumptions for which women must eventually pay.
So, indeed, must men. We are generally skeptical about the claim
that oppressors suffer as much from their prejudices as the oppressed,
especially when they never see their victims face to face. But we do
feel reasonably confident that men pay a price for arrogance vis-à-vis
women. Since they almost always commit a part of their lives into a
woman's hands anyway, their tendency to crush these women means
crushing a part of themselves. This may not hurt them as much as it
hurts the woman involved, but it does cost something. Thus while we
are not against segregation of the sexes under all circumstances, we
are against it when it helps preserve sexual arrogance. Historical and
social context are critically important here. The reader will see later
that we do not find the arguments against women's colleges as
persuasive as the arguments against men's colleges. This is a wholly
contextual judgment. If America were now a matriarchy (as some
paranoid men seem to fear it is becoming) we would regard women's
colleges as a menace and men's colleges as a possibly justified
defense.[13]

Whatever their merits, however, men's colleges persist, especially in
the Northeast but also to a lesser extent in the South. These colleges
are almost all private, and about half of them are Catholic. They enroll
about 5 per cent of America's male undergraduates.[14] We know of no
men's colleges founded in recent years except the Air Force Academy,
but then relatively few private colleges of any sort are being founded.
Existing men's colleges show some tendency to become coeducational,
but the rate of integration until very recently has been glacial. The percentage of men attending men's colleges is probably declining, but
mainly because the percentage in the private sector as a whole is
declining.

Princeton is the only first-rank university whose graduate schools
take virtually no women on principle, and even it makes a few
exceptions. But many graduate schools and departments are strongly
prejudiced against women applicants and end up with a largely male
student body. Most graduate schools expect women who apply to
graduate schools of law, medicine, or even the arts and sciences to

[13] Since black America is in some respects more of a matriarchy than white,
a stronger case can perhaps be made for Negro men's colleges than for white
ones. Morehouse is, however, the only test case, though Lincoln in Pennsylvania
was all-male until recently.

[14] 1965 *Digest*, table 70, lists 20 public colleges for men, 57 private non-
sectarian ones, 38 Protestant ones, 131 Catholic ones, and 7 "others." For statistics
on first-time enrollment at Catholic and non-sectarian men's colleges, see Astin,
Panos, and Creager, "Supplementary National Norms."

stop working when they have children and not to return to a professionally respected role. Since this expectation is often realistic, it is hard to argue against the professional schools' misogynistic judgments. The professions may have very narrow assumptions about what kinds of work are valuable and what kinds are not, but this narrowness is not easy to rebut. Suppose, for example, that a man gets a Ph.D. and becomes a scholar at a leading university, while his equally talented wife gets a Ph.D. and teaches at a small women's college nearby. We would argue that the wife may well make more of a contribution to the general welfare through her teaching than her husband makes by writing for the *Publications of the Modern Language Association* or the *Physical Review*. In saying this we do not mean to prejudge the debate over teaching versus research, which must be looked at on a case-by-case basis. The problem is that graduate admissions committees *do* prejudge the debate, taking it for granted that a "serious scholar" who publishes is *automatically* doing more for the world than a more brilliant woman who "dissipates" her energies teaching irregularly at local colleges. We have noticed, however, that it is often precisely the part-time female practitioner who is most available for professional innovation, such as the medical and legal programs sponsored by the Office of Economic Opportunity. Men with families to support are less free to heed their consciences and imaginations when asked to work on such ventures.

In addition to these problems, there is the further difficulty that many women do not even finish their course of study and do not put their education to *any* obvious use.[15] Graduate professional schools tend to be even less nurturant than the undergraduate colleges from which many women come, and women are more likely than men to drop out. Yet even the woman who drops out and does nothing tangible with her education often makes an intangible contribution, both to society and to the graduate school in which she is briefly enrolled. The presence of women in graduate courses seems to us to have a small but significant effect on the attitude of the professors and the male students, and it is almost invariably a benign effect. Women seem less easily caught up in the gamesmanship of the academic profession and less easily inducted into its ritualistic excesses. Just as very few girls collect stamps, play chess, become science-fiction afficionados, or take up other hobbies, so, too, relatively few women become entranced with the apparatus of scholarship that

15 Sharpe, "Five Years," table 1, shows that among members of the Class of 1958 five years out of college, 69 per cent of the men who entered graduate degree programs had taken degrees, compared to 61 per cent of the women—a rather small difference. The proportion of terminal M.A.s was, however, substantially higher among women.

serves so many men as a substitute for thought. This indifference to academic games for their own sake can combine with passivity in the face of adult authority to produce rote learning and mechanical imitation as answers to external pressure. Yet it still seems to us that women are somewhat more likely than men to fuse their human and academic concerns, and that this makes the admission of women in more than token numbers an asset in a graduate school. Yet this may be precisely why many scholars want to keep women out.

When one turns from the graduate to the undergraduate scene, the persistence of all-male enclaves is both more common and harder to rationalize. A number of universities that admit women to their graduate departments (e.g. Yale, Johns Hopkins, Cal Tech, the University of Virginia, Georgetown) do not admit them to the undergraduate college. Others, like Tufts, the University of Pennsylvania, and the University of Richmond, have separate undergraduate colleges for women, which allow the men to segregate themselves in non-academic affairs. A variety of "coordinate college" relationships also exist, ranging from the near-integration of Harvard and Radcliffe (which have separate governing boards but a common faculty and largely integrated extracurricular activities) through the looser ties of Columbia and Barnard (which have adjacent campuses, separate faculties for lower division students and separate Boards of Trustees) to the almost complete separation of the University of Virginia and Mary Washington (which have a common board but are in different towns). A number of exclusively undergraduate liberal arts colleges have no women at all (e.g. Amherst, Claremont, Dartmouth, Holy Cross, Randolph-Macon). A number of technical institutions follow the same policy de facto.

The results seem to us usually unfortunate. Stag undergraduate institutions are prone to a kind of excess. Many are notable for athletic overemphasis and for a narrow Philistine pragmatism, whether in the engineering or business administration programs. (We have no prejudice against either of these fields, only against teaching them or anything else in a mindless, complacent way that rules out all alternatives as "soft" or unrealistic.) These stag institutions preserve earlier collegiate styles, like the Jazz Age pride in holding hard liquor one can still find at the University of Virginia, the teen-age muscularity only now disappearing at Princeton, or the John Wayne militarism of Texas A & M. There are still many women of all ages who find such delayed maturity charming, and who are as enamored of athletes and moneyed arrogance as are their male classmates. Nonetheless, it seems to us that girls are seldom quite as complacent as men about their college lives, if only because the dilemmas of being adult women are more obvious and less repressed. Girls also tend to be more socially conscious than men, in both the good and bad sense of that term. They are more aware of other people and more concerned with them at an earlier age. They become sociometrists when boys are still fooling around with machinery, guns, sports, and trading cards, and show a concern for moral and personal issues that many men feel obliged to repress lest they not seem tough enough or masterful enough. The presence of girls in classes gives humane and troubled undergraduate teachers a more responsive audience than they would have if all their students were men. The very docility of many girls also helps professors in the less competitive colleges create an atmosphere in which a modicum of work gets done.[16] We have been struck even in coeducational colleges by the extent to which men will come to class unprepared and then hold forth, counting on improvisation, luck, and gall to get through. In contrast, while male professors are fond of stories about coeds who do no work and count on private charm or tears to save the day, such girls seem to us atypical. In general, girls are likely to talk in class only when they have done the work and feel some confidence they are right.

Yet it is true that, by pre-empting the "safe" ground in this way, girls may sometimes push their male classmates into exaggerated know-nothing postures, which they hope will dramatize their masculinity and help them escape the danger of subordination to "feminine" facts and reading lists. In the more benighted colleges this stance often leads to overt anti-intellectualism among men, who measure themselves as athletes, lovers, and men of affairs rather than as scholars. Furthermore, just because the women students identify with the more humane undergraduate professors, the male students may reject these professors as sissies or fairies and eschew academic values even more than they would in a stag college. (At the latter a professor may be regarded as a kind of coach, especially if he actually plays this role in the afternoon or takes a keen interest in sports.) If this polarization goes far enough even the girls will be greatly affected. They remain more academically diligent than the boys but take care never to be too bright or too assertive, contradicting neither their boy friends nor their male professors.

In the better colleges, however, fear of being stupid is today even stronger than fear of being awkward or ugly. Most men therefore feel obliged to deal obliquely with the threat posed by girls' getting

16 During the nineteenth century, when the established men's colleges were debating coeducation most vigorously, one of the most popular arguments for admitting girls was the benign effect of their presence on the boys' social behavior. The men kept their incipient barbarism under wraps when women were around and had to work a little harder because women pushed up performance norms.

better grades than themselves. Their most characteristic response is to reject the terms on which women compete (and professors judge). Men do fewer assignments and spend less time on papers, writing off the girls who do these things and get A's as uncreative grinds. But, unlike their fathers, they try to persuade themselves they could get A's if they tried.

This kind of posturing takes place whether or not girls are physically present in the classroom; it is a response born of coeducational elementary and secondary schools, of predominantly women teachers, and of American culture generally. Yet we would argue that it is a response more likely to be overcome in coeducational than in all-male colleges. In mixed colleges the boys are more likely to learn that their attractiveness to girls is not really dependent on being radically different from them, but rather the reverse. This reassures them about exploring seemingly feminine behavior like doing assignments, getting excited about books, and developing aesthetic sensitivity. Such reassurance is probably harder to come by if girls are seen only on weekends and never in academic or extracurricular settings.

The Women's Colleges

While most of the major bulwarks of masculinism have today fallen to coeducation, their collapse was so slow in some parts of the country that advocates of women's education felt obliged to establish "separate but equal" colleges for their daughters.[17] Elmira was the first of these, but it was eclipsed in 1865 by Vassar. The 1870s saw Smith and Wellesley opened, and by the end of the 1880s all of today's leading northeastern women's colleges, now known as "the Seven Sisters," were in operation. Like other minority-group colleges, the Seven Sisters offered instruction almost identical to the leading Eastern men's colleges of the time. (Radcliffe, indeed, depended on the Harvard faculty from the start and made no effort to develop its own program.) But unlike most other minority-group institutions, the women's colleges found that, while they were hard pressed to compete for the most desirable instructors, they were able to get students just as talented and often more easily educable than those at the established institutions. As a result, Bryn Mawr and perhaps some of the other leading women's colleges set standards of undergraduate academic competence that no male college would match for many years.[18]

[17] For portraits of some of the early leaders of this movement, see Bernard.
[18] For a picture of an atypical Bryn Mawr graduate of this era, see Riesman, "Two Generations."

The early success of the feminist colleges in meeting male payrolls is so unlike the history of other minority-group colleges that it deserves additional comment. One factor was certainly the size of the female minority: women's colleges had a far broader base from which to start than did Catholic colleges, Negro colleges, public colleges, and so forth. Women were, moreover, a "minority" with the same parental backgrounds as the male "majority," and had never suffered the same degree of exclusion as most minorities. Not only was their upbringing in many cases more conducive to academic success than the upbringing of other minorities, but even in 1870 they were more likely to finish secondary school. The women's colleges thus began with a much larger pool of potentially able recruits than did other special-interest colleges. These recruits were, moreover, in some ways temperamentally better suited to academic work than was the male majority that had designed and dominated the system. Female students did not feel obliged to establish their sexual identity by rebelling against adult authority, and they were relatively willing to do large quantities of academic work in a fairly methodical way.[19]

In their early years the aggressively feminist colleges recruited predominantly female faculties, partly because it was hard to get men and partly because they felt an obligation to offer careers to their more scholarly alumnae. Once the first flush of female emancipation had worn off, however, and fear of spinsterhood had reasserted itself, the recruitment of women to academic careers began to fall off.[20] Discrimination against women on coeducational college faculties also became less obvious, so the women's colleges felt less of an obligation to discriminate in reverse. These colleges are also aware that college-age girls dislike spending all their time with other women, and they may see male faculty as a way of reducing the resemblance to a nunnery. Whatever the reason, the Seven Sisters and other women's colleges have increasingly male faculties and often male presidents as well. These faculties have conventional academic training and qualifications, and they offer curricula that differ in no important respect from those of comparable men's colleges.[21]

The Seven Sisters are not the only models for American women's colleges. In the South, academic competence and competition with

[19] For a discussion of these and other issues at Vassar in the 1950s, see Bushnell and Freedman.

[20] *Historical Statistics*, Series H 319, shows that the proportion of college faculty who were women rose steadily until the 1930s, reaching 30 per cent. It then began to decline slowly, and has now returned to its level around 1900, about 20 per cent. Most of these women are in low-ranking jobs and/or low-ranking institutions.

[21] One partial exception to this rule is the emphasis on the performing arts at Bennington, Sarah Lawrence, and some other women's colleges. Yet this innovation has now been copied at coed colleges like UCLA and San Francisco State.

men's colleges have been less emphasized, and the production of moderately cultured Southern womanhood more heavily stressed. A college like Winthrop in South Carolina (one of the few remaining public women's colleges) embodies this outlook, while Sweet Briar, Mary Baldwin, and Hollins struggle sporadically against it. Randolph-Macon Woman's College and Goucher seem more academically competitive and sympathetic to "Northern" norms, though the level of effort and of sophistication is lower than in the Seven Sisters, and social grace seems more cultivated. Yet even the most "feminine" of these colleges has done little to develop a distinctive curriculum, and it would be hard to show that their extracurricular traditions had a very different influence from those of coeducational Southern colleges. The same must, in general, be said of private junior colleges for women, such as Briarcliff (now going four-year), Pine Manor, and Bradford. It must also be said of most of the Catholic women's colleges, discussed in more detail in Chapter IX. A few of these seem more effective than any of their male rivals, but most are entirely undistinguished.

There have been a few experimental women's colleges, of which Bennington and Sarah Lawrence are the best known. These two were set up in the late 1920s and early 1930s after the Seven Sisters and similar ventures had proven that women could compete with men on men's terms. They sought to move undergraduates into new cultural areas that male colleges had traditionally shunned. In the humanities they emphasized artistic as well as academic competence, hiring composers as well as musicologists, novelists as well as literary scholars, dancers as well as historians. They also stressed the social rather than the scientific aspects of the social sciences, placing more emphasis on ethics and politics than on methodology. And in all areas they developed a pedagogy that stressed small rather than large groups, catering to girls' hunger for personal contact and support. The result was not, however, a group of alumnae conspicuously better adjusted to their adult feminine roles than the alumnae of more traditional colleges. Indeed, the sexual and political attitudes associated with these two colleges became the staple of a certain sort of cynical short story. While we would judge these experiments quite successful in comparison to, say, Vassar and Barnard, others were less enthusiastic. Perhaps the real question here is the extent to which an educational institution should cut its students down to fit the requirements of institutions at the next level. Is Putney a failure if its graduates often find Harvard and Radcliffe unsatisfactory? We would say not: the failure is the colleges', not the school's. Is Bennington a failure if some of its graduates are more experimental than their husbands and hence unhappy? Again we would say not. Reform, like revolution, has victims, but this is no argument against it. Probably the crucial questions are whether the victims of reform are more numerous over the long haul than the victims of the status quo would be, and whether the short-run victims know what they are getting into.

Less aggressively intellectual experiments have been tried in California. Lynn White, Jr., for example, aroused the fury of the feminists by writing a book called *Educating Our Daughters* in which he argued that women should study subjects like ceramics and not necessarily be expected to master the intricacies of a professionalized academic discipline. While he was never fully able to impose this vision on Mills College, of which he was president, Scripps developed somewhat along these lines. In Missouri, Stephens Junior College (now a four-year institution) had rather similar aims. In New England, Simmons College took a different tack, emphasizing vocational competence and turning out girls who could get on in female careers.[22] All these colleges had a common impulse to provide women with education that would be neither identical to that usually given men nor a watered-down version of it.

As a result of all these varied efforts there are now something like 275 independent women's colleges, of which about 200 are four-year institutions. Two-thirds of these 200 are Roman Catholic, most of the rest non-sectarian. The number seems to be growing steadily, but this is largely due to the multiplication of marginal Catholic colleges for women. (We know of no non-Catholic four-year college for women founded in recent years.[23]) With a few dozen exceptions, all women's colleges are relatively impoverished. Even the relatively affluent Seven Sisters are poor by comparison with their Ivy League counterparts. In principle, women's colleges should do fairly well from bequests, since women usually outlive their husbands and could then give to their own rather than their husbands' colleges. But tax laws encourage husbands to give away their money before they die, or to tie it up in trusts for their children, and sentiment often encourages a widow to memorialize her husband at his college rather than herself at her own. Men's colleges also benefit from the fact that their alumni are often business colleagues, and are therefore in a good position to put pressure on one another on behalf of alma mater, whereas women have less chance to exploit such fraternal solidarity.

Like other special-interest institutions, the women's colleges have remained largely dependent on the national (and predominantly male) graduate schools, both to define their objectives and to train

[22] For an extended discussion of Simmons, see the profile in Hilberry and Keeton.

[23] There is at least one partial exception. Pitzer College has been established as part of the Claremont group, partly to equalize the sex imbalance created by the presence of Claremont Men's College and Harvey Mudd's male engineers.

their faculty. Only one women's college, Bryn Mawr, has made a successful effort to establish doctoral instruction, and even Bryn Mawr
has achieved national distinction only in the humanities. The Bryn
Mawr graduate departments are, moreover, an effort to outdo men by
male standards rather than to establish distinctively feminine objectives
or methods. The graduate departments admit men as well as women,
and their Ph.D.s are presumed to be indistinguishable from others
given by coeducational universities.

Lacking legitimation from the graduate schools, efforts to establish
"feminine" curricula have seldom proved very durable. Indeed, the
very idea of such programs seems patronizing to the die-hard feminists
and ridiculous to the traditional masculinists. Just as the academic disciplines have no time for "Catholic biology" so, too, they give short
shrift to "women's mathematics" or "women's literature." In most
ways, this is fair enough. But there are special problems in persuading American women they can do mathematics, and special
possibilities open to the teacher of literature who has a class composed entirely of women. Sensitive teachers usually recognize and
respond to this, but nobody writes about it; there is no systematic
body of theory and experience to help a teacher deal with it;
and no effort is made to train teachers to recognize or solve these
problems. So long as women feel they are still less than fully equal,
they seem, in Diana Trilling's phrase, to insist on an education at
least as bad as that given men.

The feminist revolution is in this sense like the other "missed"
revolutions Paul Goodman speaks of, which are incomplete. Yet it has
gone far enough so that there is little value in further demonstrations
of the fact that women can beat men at the latter's game. What is
needed is rather the reverse: an attempt to restore the respectability
of the "feminine" virtues and to see what they might contribute to the
various academic disciplines. This would be most interesting not in
traditionally somewhat feminine fields like literature and the arts, but
in fields like the natural sciences and economics, which might benefit
from perspectives other than those of the aggressively virile.[24]

For this and other reasons there may still be some advantages to
educating women separately from men. Women worried about their
femininity are understandably fearful of seeming too bright or too
competent in direct competition with male classmates. Only the most
self-confident are really uninterested in men duller or less intellectual
than themselves; the majority are afraid to burn any bridges, no matter
how uncongenial. The result can be a kind of vicious circle in which
the men do no work because they know the girls will always have
done more, while the girls try to conceal what they know lest they

[24] For some further suggestions along this line, see Riesman, "Permissiveness."

embarrass the unprepared men. We have been struck at several women's colleges by the change in the tone of classes on Saturday mornings if girls bring along boys who are visiting them for the weekend. These male presences seem to inhibit discussion quite no-ticeably—though it may simply be that they create a "last day of school" atmosphere in which serious discussion inevitably lags. As this implies, docile and passive women sometimes clam up entirely when confronted with aggressive young men in a coeducational college, whereas they may discover some of their resources in a sexually sheltered setting.[25]

Yet the advantages of segregation for women are equivocal. Men are almost always vicariously present for girls, just as whites are for American Negroes, even if they are physically missing. Girls in women's colleges seem to worry as much about being really feminine as girls in coeducational colleges, and perhaps more. And getting seriously committed to an academic discipline seems to threaten their sense of femininity no matter where they are. A few certainly feel more inhibited in front of boys, but others seem to be liberated by the discovery that they can talk to boys in class on a non-sexual basis without losing their "after hours" appeal. Similarly, while some girls may flourish when they do not have to compete with boys, others evidently need the stimulus of male rebellion and aggressiveness. As a result, the academic case for sex segregation is moot.[26]

When one turns from the curriculum to the extracurriculum, many similar ambiguities arise. If one looks at girls working on college news-papers, for example, it could theoretically be argued that an exclusively female college forces girls to take charge and discover their talents, whereas a coed college encourages them to play subsidiary roles. Some women's college papers lend credence to this thesis (e.g. the Vassar *Miscellany* or Immaculate Heart *Comment*). In general, how-ever, the girls who run newspapers at women's colleges appear even less willing to be combative or entrepreneurial than those in coeduca-

[25] See Riesman, "Some Continuities." This essay, originally a lecture at Ben-nington College in 1956, makes a stronger case for sex segregation than either of us would be willing to make today. Donald R. Brown has argued the same case in the *Yale Daily News* of April 15, 1966. Proposing geographic but not curricular or extracurricular proximity, he writes: "In a certain sense, young women deserve the opportunity to compete with each other in order to develop their capacity for leadership rather than having constantly to compete with the cultural scale weighted against them as it is in the coeducational institutions. Male students in coed universities are in the position of running a race against cultural cripples, if you will." The relative handicaps under which women compete vary according to social class, region, ethnicity, and religion, so that it is hard to reach any general conclusion.

[26] This impression is supported by Astin, "Productivity," which shows that a woman's chances of earning a Ph.D. are not significantly influenced by whether she attends a women's or a coed college. The odds are, of course, low in either case.

tional colleges. They create papers that, instead of liberating their staffs from conventional definitions of femininity, seem to re-enforce them. On coeducational campuses, on the other hand, the newspaper is more often a mix of masculine and feminine staff, skills, and attitudes. Girls often rise to the top of these papers, and despite the pseudo-professionalism and front-page posing into which their male colleagues sometimes push them, they usually get a broader view of themselves and their powers than they would on a girls' college paper.

The dilemmas confronting women in extracurricular activities are, of course, mainly a reflection of larger dilemmas confronting all American women. Such dilemmas can and sometimes should be postponed by staying within the shelter of a single-sex college. But they cannot be avoided indefinitely, as women's college graduates quickly discover. The question is thus not *whether* to integrate but *when*. Our own view is that sex segregation is more likely to be helpful in junior or senior high school than in college. But there are doubtless exceptions, and we would hate to see women's colleges entirely eliminated just because they do not seem to suit the majority. The fact that these colleges cannot solve most of their girls' problems must not be taken as proof of their worthlessness, for coed colleges cannot do so either. So long as the tensions and ambiguities of adult womanhood remain unresolved and seemingly unresolvable, *no* college will be able to do very much. Certainly we have difficulty imagining any system of undergraduate education that would prepare girls for the full range of roles and problems they may encounter after graduating. That is one reason why women's colleges are inclined to focus their program on the minority that plans to attend graduate school and hopefully pursue an academic career. It is relatively easy to determine what a girl ought to know to succeed in graduate school and become like her professors. It is much harder to tell what she ought to know to succeed as a lover, mother, or sporadic career woman. But even if they knew how to train women for non-academic roles, most of the young scholars hired to teach at the more selective women's colleges would regard this as second best. They say over and over that their principal problem is to distract girls from single-minded pursuit of a husband. In his place they try to substitute a passion for books and scholarship, an interest in some sort of graduate study, and a career involving formal abstract thinking. While this is no longer presumed to be a permanent substitute for marriage, it almost certainly requires a postponement of childbearing.[27]

[27] A rich young mother could in principle have her children cared for by a nanny and remain almost as free for graduate study as a young married man who has to mow the lawn, cook, or baby-sit on occasion. But with very rare exceptions even wealthy young women refuse to use their means in this fashion,

These faculty hopes are fulfilled often enough at the leading women's colleges to make them self-sustaining. But even the less selective women's colleges, where very few girls do graduate work or have professional careers, show only limited interest in preparing their students directly for other futures. Like most second and third rank colleges, their eyes are on the first rank institutions and not on their students' problems. They assume that if only they could do what Bryn Mawr or Randolph-Macon or Manhattanville does, they would be more effective. Even when their agenda is not slavishly mimetic, moreover, they seldom have the imagination or resources to tackle the enormously difficult task of educating girls for living with people as well as paper.

At least one new women's college, Simon's Rock in the Berkshires, is focusing directly on this problem. It takes girls for the last two years of high school and the first two years of college—one more effort to follow Robert Hutchins' lead and change the prevailing academic timetable. By concentrating on the social sciences, taught in a humanistic way, it hopes to make young women conscious of the problems that face them because of their sex and also the opportunities for them in whatever mix of job, career, and matrimony they choose or fall into. As a relatively powerless group, women need more guidance than men in making their way in the somewhat alien, if often indulgent, academic and postacademic world. Such guidance now tends to vacillate between feminist confrontation and feminine acquiescence. But the problems are often subtler than these polarized alternatives suggest. Many women enter college with very little sense of which academic fields they might find exciting and which will be inhospitable. They are often convinced as a result of high school experience that science and mathematics are opaque to them, but even this judgment might prove reversible if an effort were made to penetrate the psychic obstacles to mastery of these "male" subjects. Many women with excellent college and even postgraduate educations also too readily assume that after an interruption for child-rearing they have lost their hold on "the literature" of their fields.[28] Yet while such problems deserve special attention, it is as easy to provide this in a coed college as in a segregated one.

---

regarding it as exploitative or neglectful not to care for their own infants and taking only the periodic respites allowed by baby-sitters and au pair girls. This is one of the many ways in which American young women are too democratic in spirit to exploit wealth and social position fully.

[28] Oakland University in Michigan has set up a Center for Continuing Education for women who want a chance to appraise their talents and reexamine their occupational potential. Sarah Lawrence College has a similar center, and no doubt there are others with which we are not familiar.

Taking all things into account, we are inclined to conclude that women's colleges are probably an anachronism. They try to separate women from men at a time when most women rightly want proximity. The reasons why women shun women's colleges are clear. The complete emancipation of women may or may not be desirable, but it certainly does not appear to be imminent. A woman's adult life is still in large measure shaped by her choice of a husband—and by her ability to persuade the husband she chooses to choose her. She is expected to go where his career takes him, regardless of how it affects hers; to have children, and in most cases to take considerable time off from her career to see them through their childhood; to adapt her leisure life to her husband's pocketbook and perhaps even to his tastes and career needs. Her husband may, for all practical purposes, marry his job or his golf rather than his spouse; she is almost always married to her husband in a far more complete sense. Most undergraduate girls realize this, and their hopes and fears for the future rightly reflect it. Such worries may be dysfunctional in the sense that they compound the problem, but they are hardly irrational. So long as they persist, undergraduate women will be male-oriented, and women's colleges will have a hard time competing with coed ones for students. There is no objective evidence that women's college alumnae are less likely to marry the right man; but most girls want to explore the possibilities during their undergraduate years, and most think this will be easier if men are around all the time.

Even the girl who wants to put the marriage question aside for four years is unlikely to find a women's college appealing. She may, for example, be interested in preparing for a profession. But she will usually expect to go to a coeducational graduate school to prepare for it, and she will only rarely see her professional ambitions in combative feminist terms. She will accept the fact that work is a man's world and will be interested in learning to accommodate and make her way in that world, not in challenging or changing it. Most women find it easier to come to terms with male dominance at an integrated college than at a segregated one.[29]

None of this means that Smith, Bryn Mawr, or Sarah Lawrence is about to go begging for applicants. The small private women's colleges

[29] Wrapped up in these attitudes is a certain degree of female self-hatred, which leads many women to say that they cannot stand women—a statement virtually no men would make about their own sex. (It is also notorious that women prefer male bosses.) Mary Haywood's "Were There but World Enough and Time . . . ," documents the low priority Radcliffe girls give same-sex friendships in contrast to the exigencies of premarital involvements and other career concerns. It should be added that as male college students become less boorish and boyish, many also become engrossed in cross-sex relations and limit their ties to same-sex "buddies."

with established academic and social credentials are, on the contrary, almost certain to be inundated with impressively qualified prospects. Girls will come despite the apparently growing gap between these colleges' faculties and the faculties of the big universities, just as they will come to the better small coeducational colleges despite similar faculty problems. Some will feel they have no satisfactory alternative. In the Northeast, Harvard-Radcliffe is the only "top drawer" university that admits women, and it admits very few. Swarthmore is the only small liberal arts college of comparable standing that admits women, and it takes even fewer. A girl can, of course, attend a slightly less prestigious coed university like Cornell, or a slightly less prestigious coed college like Bates, Middlebury, or Brandeis, or a Midwestern college like Oberlin, Kalamazoo, or Antioch. But faced with these choices, many girls, especially those from the East, will continue to accept sex segregation at the Seven Sisters, even though they would prefer not to if all other things were equal. Despite their success by these and other conventional indices, however, the elite women's colleges feel very much on the defensive. They lose many of their most promising prospects to Harvard-Radcliffe, Stanford, and even Cornell and Middlebury.

In good part, of course, the difficulties confronting the women's colleges are those of the private sector as a whole, and especially the private liberal arts college. But even within this context, the majority of the women's colleges seem to be in special difficulty. We have not been able to find any trend data on the proportion of women enrolling in women's colleges. But we have the strong impression that the proportion (probably less than 10 per cent)[30] is declining even faster than the proportion in the private sector as a whole. This does not mean that many women's colleges will fold, but it does mean they will grow much less rapidly than coeducational colleges and that they will exert a declining influence on coming generations.

[30] Estimated from Astin, Panos, and Creager, "Supplementary National Norms."

VIII. *Protestant Denominations and Their Colleges*

Protestant Denominationalism

It is perhaps a tribute to the present influence of academic professionalism that we have been able to postpone a discussion of the relations between America's Protestant denominations and higher education to this point. A century ago this would have been Chapter I of any book on American colleges. But while the Protestant clergy dominated American higher education from the founding of Harvard to the end of the Civil War, their role has diminished steadily since then and is today hardly consequential for the system as a whole, though it remains important in some colleges. A complete history of the academic revolution would have to chart this transition in detail, but we have not attempted this. The chapter that follows merely outlines some of the major reasons for the change, partly as a way of amplifying themes suggested earlier and partly to provide an historical context for a more extensive discussion of Catholic colleges in Chapter IX.

We are all prisoners of our language, and this is nowhere more obvious than in discussions of Protestantism. The vocabulary that divides Americans into "Protestants," "Catholics," and "Jews" seems to imply that Protestantism is a definable entity with some common institutional or theological core. Yet the obvious easily forgotten truth is that Protestantism is not one faith but many. Whereas Catholicism has continually sought to contain its differences within a single organization and theology, Protestants have tended to resolve their problem by fission. The effort to avoid compromise and retain both doctrinal and ritual purity has led one group of dissidents after another to break off from its parent church and go into business for itself. As their negative name implies, American Protestants share only a common memory of having protested against the errors of some older and better-established church. Even this is not such a bond as it first seems, for there is no single common enemy. Many of the major denominations were born in rebellion against Roman Catholicism, but others defined themselves in opposition to another Protestant group.

As a result, American Protestant denominations have never had much in common except their feeling of being distinct from Catholics and Jews. If one looks at income, occupation, educational attainment,

PROTESTANT DENOMINATIONS AND THEIR COLLEGES

family size, or other demographic variables, Protestant denominations are as different from one another as from American Catholicism or Judaism. The same thing is almost equally true of doctrinal beliefs.[1] The institutional forms of Protestantism also cover an enormous range. None believes the Pope infallible, and all believe in the special role of Jesus, but their unity does not go much beyond that. In part this diversity is a function of denominational separatism, but many Protestant denominations are very loosely organized internally, and some therefore contain a range of different beliefs and forms almost as great as that within Protestantism as a whole. Almost every variation in the fabric of American society has at one time or another compounded this diversity. Schismatic tendencies have drawn strength from ethnic separatism and assimilationism, from class differences and conflicts, from urban-rural and regional diversity, and from cultural and political splits.

Under these circumstances it is extraordinarily difficult to generalize about American Protestants. Indeed, even the foregoing generalization about diversity is subject to attack. Will Herberg's famous book *Protestant-Catholic-Jew* argued, for example, that the differences between Protestant denominations were no longer really important and that Protestants of all sorts were increasingly united by a common set of "non-sectarian" assumptions. (If this is taken to mean that religious differences are no longer as important to people as they once were, it is probably true, though we could not prove it. But that generalization applies not only to differences among Protestant denominations but to differences among Protestants, Catholics, and Jews, all of whom are shaped more by their common Americanism than by their separate faiths.) Certainly diversity has not prevented a continuing quest for ecumenical unity—though it has undoubtedly limited the effectiveness of such efforts. The doctrinal and organizational quarrels that led to the establishment of Protestant denominations have mostly lost their original salience with the passing of generations and even centuries, and very few Protestants can today give an accurate account of how their denomination differs from its rivals. This does not mean that there are no differences. But if most Protestants cannot identify them accurately, it is not surprising that many share Herberg's suspicion they are really all alike. This sentiment, in turn, gives rise to continuing efforts to merge separate denominations into larger groupings, or failing that, to encourage collaboration on projects of mutual interest. The National Council of Churches with its manifold commissions and agencies is the most prominent manifestation of this, but it is only the top of the iceberg. The major Protestant denominations may have

[1] On the diversity of Protestant beliefs regarding various points of traditional religious belief, see Glock and Stark.

devoted a good deal of effort to sectarian bickering, but they have also often been anxious to emphasize what they had in common and to play down their particularism and exculsiveness.

This tension between diversity and ecumenicism has been mirrored in Protestant higher education. Diversity led to the establishment of an inordinate number of separate colleges, but ecumenicism then led most of these colleges to emphasize their collegiate rather than their sectarian side, seeking faculty and students of all persuasions and becoming annually more like one another. The pages that follow will be mainly devoted to a more detailed description of these two tendencies. We will begin by discussing the religious, political, ethnic, class, and geographic sources of fission and diversity within Protestant higher education. Then we will turn to the economic, geographic, and professional pressures for unity which have gradually obscured the initial differences.

Diversity, Separatism, and the Founding of New Colleges

Most histories of higher education place considerable emphasis on the role of theological feuds in the birth of America's Protestant colleges. The Puritan founders of Harvard attracted students partly because they were more orthodox, at least in New England eyes, than the Anglican colleges at Oxford and Cambridge. Yale won the support of men like Cotton Mather and later Jonathan Edwards because it promised to stem the backsliding implicit in developments at Harvard. The Great Awakening led to the establishment of still more colleges, of which the Presbyterians' College of New Jersey (now Princeton) became the best known. The Baptist founders of Brown were also at odds with the Congregationalists who ran New England's other colleges (Harvard, Yale, and Dartmouth).

Similar schisms recurred throughout the nineteenth century. The founders of Williams and Amherst won support by promising an orthodox alternative to Harvard, which had appointed a Unitarian professor of divinity in 1805. Dissident clergymen played a decisive role in the establishment of literally hundreds of colleges before the Civil War. If the Congregationalists opened a college in a given area some Methodist or Presbyterian almost always saw this as a threat to the orthodoxy of the younger generation. If he could find a backer or two he was likely to open a competing college, ensuring that there would not be enough students at either institution to support a competent faculty or adequate facilities.

There were exceptions to this pattern. The Anglicans who founded the University of Pennsylvania, for example, were evidently anxious not to alienate Philadelphia's Quakers, and they made their new college officially non-sectarian. The Anglicans who founded Columbia after a bitter fight with the Presbyterians made a similar effort at compromise, including Presbyterians and others on Columbia's governing board. A similar pattern recurred in the nineteenth century. Union College, as its name implied, was the non-sectarian creation of an upstate New York coalition, and so were a number of the state colleges founded in the South and Midwest. Nonetheless, coalition was the exception rather than the rule in the founding of nineteenth-century colleges. In most cases, as we shall see, it was only after the college had opened its doors, acquired a life of its own, and confronted the problems of survival and growth, that the impulse to accommodate diverse denominations made its weight fully felt.

Doctrine and ideology played a diminishing role in the creation of new colleges after 1900. First the teaching faculty and then the administration were recruited from the ranks of the academic profession rather than from the ministry. This made denominational affiliation seem less and less important. The rise of the academic profession was accompanied by an apotheosis of "objective" research and teaching. This made it difficult to admit that doctrinal commitments had any effect on a college's program, and therefore difficult to claim that the curriculum at, say, a Presbyterian college was different from that at a Methodist one. A few new Protestant colleges, such as Bob Jones University in South Carolina, have been founded with the avowed intention of preserving and promulgating fundamentalist religious doctrine. A few others, notably Harding College in Arkansas, have been established to do the same for fundamentalist political doctrine. But most of the new Protestant colleges of the past half-century have claimed to teach the standard academic fare. This does not preclude requiring students to take courses on religion or philosophy *in addition* to "non-sectarian" chemistry or history, nor does it preclude emphasizing the role of religion in setting rules about extracurricular life. But new Protestant colleges have not, with a handful of fundamentalist exceptions, claimed that they were elaborating a comprehensive world view that involved rejecting or even reworking the kinds of knowledge being acquired by the rest of the academic profession though some saw the search for truth as a Christian mandate.

All this suggests that ideology and doctrine play a declining role in the establishment of new American colleges. This appearance may be somewhat illusory, however, for the foregoing account probably exaggerates the importance of ideology and doctrine even in the eighteenth and nineteenth centuries. In a great many cases what appears in the history books as a sectarian feud about some seemingly arcane theological issue was probably a convenient symbol and symptom of a cultural division between ethnic groups, between social classes, between urban and rural ways of life, or all three at once.

Ethnic variations never played as great a role within Protestantism as within Catholicism or Judaism, but they cannot be ignored on that account. The theological differences between the first three American colleges (Harvard, William and Mary, and Yale) were expressions of intramural Anglo-Saxon divisions, but the founders of the fourth, The College of New Jersey (now Princeton), were set apart by their Scottish ancestry as well as by their Presbyterianism. The Dutch founders of nearby Queens College (now Rutgers) were even more ethnically distinct, for they were set apart by language as well as religion. During the nineteenth century a number of other Protestant colleges gained strength from ethnic separatism, the most notable case being the many Lutheran colleges. These appealed to the children and grandchildren of German and Scandinavian immigrants in part because of their orthodoxy—though given the division within American Lutheranism this was often suspect. In some cases their appeal derived less from their religious commitments than from their being uncontaminated by students and teachers of English ancestry and pretensions.

As these examples illustrate, ethnic groups almost always clothed themselves in religious garb when they wanted to found a separate college. (The Negro colleges are the major exception to this rule, and we will postpone discussion of them until Chapter X.) Those Scots who did not hold with Presbyterianism do not seem to have regarded Princeton as "their" college, nor did Princeton regard such Scots as part of its natural constituency. Nor did those Dutch who rejected the Dutch Reformed Church flock to Rutgers. Germans showed no special interest in German Lutheran colleges unless they were Lutherans, and the same was true of Scandinavians. The reasons for this are reasonably clear.

Ethnic differences were subtle, diverse, and hard to define. When the nineteenth-century German-American population looked at itself, for example, it was hard put to find any single factor except language that distinguished it from the Anglo-American majority.[2] By the time German-Americans began sending appreciable numbers of children to college, even language differences had largely disappeared. In addition, ethnic differences were a matter of birth and early unbringing and could not be altered by rational adult choice. Given the wide-

[2] It is interesting to speculate on what would have happened to German-Americans if World War I, with its accompanying anti-German prejudice, had come a generation or two earlier. Our guess is that it would have produced more abiding unity.

spread commitment to a "land of opportunity" mythology, which denied that birth per se made a difference in a man's fate, it was natural to de-emphasize the effects of ethnicity and substitute an emphasis on religion, which was in principle subject to rational adult choice. Most ethnic minorities therefore played down their strictly ethnic distinctiveness and defined their differences with the American majority in religious terms. Those who found no religious expression for their separatism seldom maintained it for more than a generation or two. This made it almost impossible to provide a persuasive public rationale for a new college whose mission was defined in strictly ethnic terms. A college could not be conducted in German, or even teach German rather than English literature, without appearing un-American. But it could teach Lutheran rather than Anglican theology, and enforce Lutheran rather than Anglican morality, without seeming to oppose the assimilation of its students.

Yet the tincture of ethnicity has endured. A century after the establishment of Rutgers, President McCosh of Princeton could still refer to it as an "excellent college at New Brunswick, managed by a few Dutchmen."[3] And today, a century after their establishment, St. Olaf and Gustavus Adolphus Colleges in Minnesota are still widely identified as Norwegian and Swedish, respectively. In neither case is the management eager to define its clientele in narrowly ethnic terms, but the stereotypes have proved quite durable; in part because the management has made some effort to keep its transatlantic ties alive, even though it no longer conceives them as implying ethnic exclusiveness; in part perhaps because potential students and other outsiders are desperately eager for labels with which to pigeonhole seemingly similar institutions.

Still, as we have said, the striking fact is that except where Negroes were involved religious loyalties have invariably overriden ethnic ones in Protestant higher education. Perhaps one reason for this has been relatively rapid deracination of those ethnic groups that chose Protestant churches to define their identity. When Eisenhower ran for President, for example, nobody thought of him as "German-American" in the way that eight years later they would think of Kennedy as "Irish-American." Eisenhower was just plain American, despite the fact that his family belonged to the Brethren, a rural Protestant sect far less assimilated to modern American ways than Catholics of the Kennedy breed.[4] Similarly, when Daniel P. Moynihan and James Q. Wilson studied patronage in New York State between 1954 and

3 Rudolph, p. 255. Whether McCosh's description was accurate we do not know; our point is only that the ethnic stereotype was durable.
4 On this point see Riesman, "Some Informal Notes."

1958, they found that only Catholic and Jewish immigrant groups were treated as ethnically distinct, while the Protestants—including the only partly Protestant Germans—were treated as a homogeneous majority.[5] Yet perhaps this only underlines the puzzling character of assimilation, for if Catholicism were an obstacle to assimilation we should expect German Catholics to remain at least as distinct as, say, Irish Catholics, and to be less assimilated than German Protestants. We know no evidence that this has actually happened. Furthermore, we shall see in the next chapter that ethnicity has also played a relatively modest role in Catholic higher education, despite its importance in other aspects of Catholic life.

The nature of the dialectic between religion and ethnicity can also be illustrated by comparing Protestant to Jewish experience. It is a matter for argument whether the Jews constitute one ethnic group or several. German Jews, Spanish Jews, English Jews, and East European Jews were culturally quite different when they arrived in America, lacking even a common language. They were also divided religiously, with many German Jews bringing or adopting Reform while others usually found themselves more at home with Orthodox or Conservative Judaism. But all sorts of Jews felt relatively free to move around among these Jewish denominations, according to their temperament and hopes for their children, just as Protestants often shopped around among "their" denominations. Some also adopted a distinctively Jewish brand of secular radicalism. Each of the Jewish denominations founded its own college to train rabbis and Hebrew schoolteachers, but these remained tiny. Only the Orthodox followed the usual American pattern of expanding their institution for teachers and preachers into a general purpose undergraduate college: Yeshiva. And even Yeshiva attracts a rather small proportion of all Orthodox Jewish undergraduates. (It also attracts some non-Orthodox Jews, especially to its professional programs. But even the Albert Einstein College of Medicine, founded in a day when discrimination against Jews was taken for granted in Gentile medical schools, enrolls only about 5 per cent of all Jewish medical students.[6])

In general, Jews have preferred universities and colleges where they

[5] Moynihan and Wilson.

[6] Davis, *Great Aspirations*, table 1.2, shows that 8 per cent of all 1961 B.A.s were Jewish. In that year Yeshiva awarded about 0.05 per cent of all B.A.s in the United States or 0.6 per cent of all the B.A.s awarded to Jews. Greeley, *Religion and Career*, table 3.16, shows that 24 per cent of all B.A.s planning to enter medical school were Jewish. Einstein enrolls slightly more than 1 per cent of all medical students, or about 5 per cent of all Jewish medical students. Since we have no exact data on the proportion of Jewish students who are Orthodox, we cannot say with assurance what proportion of Orthodox students are at Yeshiva or Einstein.

were not a majority, or failing that where their majority was un-official, as at CCNY. The major exception, and one that perhaps proves the rule, has been Brandeis. A by-product of the wave of ethnic self-consciousness provoked by the Hitler massacres and the founding of Israel, Brandeis nevertheless chose a name that stressed its commitment to "American" rather than narrowly "Jewish" standards of greatness. Avowedly non-sectarian, it placed no special emphasis on either Jewish religion or the Jewish secular radical tradition. It aimed for precisely the same kind of academic and professional distinction as the leading Gentile universities.

The relationship between Brandeis and the Jews was thus rather like the relationship between the University of Tennessee and Ten-nesseans, or the University of Washington and Washingtonians. It was not that Brandeis was thought to be *different* from rival institutions, or that its boosters were attracted by unique programs tailored to their particular needs. For both donors and applicants, Brandeis' appeal was simply that it was "theirs." The donors were not usually from the assimilated German-Jewish families whose names appear on plaques at Harvard and Columbia. They were more likely to be second- or third-generation East European immigrants, whose millions would otherwise have built hospitals, bought Israeli bonds, or con-tributed to Jewish "civil defense." Yet it no more occurred to these donors that the Brandeis curriculum or pattern of student life should deviate from nationwide academic norms than that Mount Sinai Hospital should deviate from national medical standards. Brandeis was meant to be "separate but identical," a monument to Jewish ability to compete successfully in the non-Jewish world on "Ameri-can" rather than distinctively "Jewish" terms. Brandeis was to be distinctive in its clientele, but even here there was some ambivalence. Located two hundred miles from the major center of Jewish life in America, near the epicenter of Anglo-Saxon first family respect-ability, Brandeis appealed to some Jews precisely because it did not seem "too Jewish." The University did not recruit non-Jewish faculty members as such, but it was understandably proud of the many distinguished ones it got. Similarly, its graduate students repre-sented all faiths (though the majority probably had none). Its under-graduate body was more conspicuously Jewish, but even here Gen-tiles were both present and publicized. What, then, was its appeal? Many Jewish families evidently want a college that minimizes the danger that their children will marry Gentiles, while at the same time ensuring that they can enter a Gentile graduate school or land a job with a Gentile employer if they choose. For a Jewish family in the hinterlands, local institutions look like a poor bet on both counts. They usually have relatively low academic prestige, and also too few Jews to form a Hillel or sustain a self-enclosed dating system. Brandeis, on the other hand, seems to maximize both the chances of getting into a good professional school and the chances of meeting a "nice Jewish girl (or boy)." (Like other Northern institutions, however, Brandeis seems to have had limited appeal in the South, perhaps because Southern Jews are often more Southern than Jewish. Many find Northern Jews abrasive, cynical, and culturally alien.)

What stands out among the Jews as among the Protestants is the inability of even a relatively cohesive and very education-conscious ethnic group to create a distinctive pattern of higher education differing in any significant respect from all-American norms. Distinctiveness evidently requires a religious rationale, though as we shall see even that may not suffice over the long run.

Ethnic differences were not, of course, the only social source of sectarian schism. Just as immigrants from different European countries brought different churches with them, so too the natives of different parts of America joined different churches, which expressed their diverse life styles. To some extent this was a matter of regional diversity. When New England Congregationalist ministers fanned out across the Midwest in the nineteenth century, for example, they found the other new settlers relatively unreceptive to their austere version of Christianity. Some of these ministers founded colleges, but these too were imperfectly adapted to the ethos of the expansive hinterland in which they had been planted. Thus it is hardly surprising to discover that many of these Congregationalist colleges dropped their denominational label and ties. Nor is it surprising to discover that other denominations more attuned to Midwestern enthusiasms felt called upon to set up rival colleges to protect their faithful against the seemingly free-thinking Congregational colleges as well as their non-sectarian successors. Yet the Congregationalists and non-sectarian colleges also had a following, especially among those Midwesterners who felt nostalgic for the older Eastern ways they had left behind.

Rural-urban conflict within regions also helped fuel sectarian quarrels, both between denominations and within them. The founding of Williams and Amherst was, as we suggested in Chapter IV, in part a small-town protest against the free-thinking wickedness of Boston, and the founding of Hamilton and Dickinson in rural New York and Pennsylvania represented a somewhat similar protest against the hegemony of New York and Philadelphia. These differences, like the ethnic and regional ones already discussed, often found expression and achieved legitimacy in arguments about theology, ritual, and morality.

Both rural-urban and regional conflicts were bound up with class differences. The Midwesterners' antagonism to the East was in part antagonism to a self-proclaimed social and intellectual elite, and small-town hostility to the big city was in many cases a form of lower-middle class rejection of upper-middle class pretensions and attitudes. Like other forms of social tension, these conflicts were to some extent mirrored in the religious battles of their time. In the South, for example, the men who founded state-supported and avowedly non-sectarian colleges at the end of the eighteenth and early in the nineteenth centuries were trying, among other things, to bring together the future elite of their state on a single campus. They eschewed religious ties not because they opposed religion per se, which only a few did, but because a tie with one denomination seemed to alienate families from the others. This pattern was found not just in state-supported colleges but in elite private ones. Initially Methodist colleges like Vanderbilt and Duke, for example, became non-sectarian in practice, and at times even in theory, in order to avoid embroilment in such controversies. But most Southern denominational colleges made their appeal on exactly opposite grounds. Theirs were not to be colleges for the present or future elite but for the children of plain folks, eschewing the social snobberies and high living that were thought to characterize Charlottesville, Chapel Hill, or Ole Miss. The emphasis on piety and orthodoxy at many Southern Protestant colleges was thus in part a way of reassuring small-town preachers and storekeepers that their children would not be exposed to the corrupting influence of the idle rich, would not be infected by the alien customs of their state's elite families, and would not leave their small town homes for bigger cities. Such promises were too often and too easily broken for any college to make them explicitly, but for precisely this reason colleges made special efforts to publicize the religious symbols in which these promises were implicit.

These ideological, ethnic, geographic, and class schisms led to the establishment of small, struggling, highly competitive Protestant colleges in every corner of the country. We have no exact statistics on the number of such ventures, but our guess is that it was on the order of one thousand.[7]

[7] Tewksbury, p. 28, shows that about 80 per cent of the colleges founded before 1865 were defunct by 1929. Table VI, page 90, shows that 145 Protestant colleges founded before 1865 survived, which means that roughly 700 must have been started before then. Another 150 Protestant colleges founded after 1865 have survived, and even assuming the mortality rate for later foundations was only 50 per cent, this means another 300 attempts. The total, then, must be close to 1,000 for four-year colleges. There are also upward of 100 surviving Protestant seminaries, nearly that many surviving unaccredited Protestant colleges, and nearly 100 surviving Protestant junior colleges.

Natural Selection and Evolution among Denominational Colleges

Up to this point we have emphasized the theological, ethnic, geographic, and social diversity of the men who founded America's Protestant colleges. Yet when we look at these colleges today the striking fact is that despite the diversity of their origins they are quite alike in some fundamental respects. With a handful of exceptions they have been caught up in the academic revolution and have accepted the academic profession's views about what, how, and whom a college should teach. The influence of the Protestant clergy has diminished almost to the vanishing point in many of these colleges, and while a generalized piety and respect for traditional Protestant mores persist in many cases, this is equally true of many small-town teachers colleges with no church ties. The reasons for this change deserve at least brief description.

Prior to the Revolution, American colonists almost all took it for granted that colleges should be run by clergymen. This did not mean that colonial colleges were devoted exclusively to the propagation of revealed religion, nor that they were uniformly hostile to secular scholarship. There has always been a tension in Christian thinking between reason and revelation, and colonial colleges also vacillated between the two. Indeed, they often put more stress on reason and less on revelation than their sponsoring denominations would have liked.

Between the Revolution and the Civil War a number of leading Americans came to the conclusion that this tension should be resolved by making colleges entirely independent of any denomination or dogma and wholly committed to the rationalist tradition. While the majority of early nineteenth-century colleges held to traditional assumptions about the role of the clergy, a minority began recruiting lay trustees, presidents, and faculty. Some of the clergymen involved in higher education during this era also began to think of themselves as educators first and clerics second. Colleges became sufficiently numerous so that a clergyman with an academic bent could reasonably expect to make his career in education. Men could move from one college to another according to their judgment of where the main chance lay, rather than moving from a college to a pulpit and then back to a college as they had often done in earlier times. They therefore paid less and less attention to the sectarian disputes and pieties that often preoccupied their clerical colleagues. Thus both the laymen who played a growing role in nineteenth-century colleges and the clergymen who continued to exercise great influence became more professionalized. Their ideas about higher education came more and more from educators at other colleges, less and less from the denomination that officially sponsored their college.[8]

This change resulted partly from numerical expansion. Once there were enough college presidents and teachers to form self-contained reference groups, these groups were bound to exercise growing influence. The possibility of a career in teaching also changed everyone's view of the work. The consequent professionalization of college faculty, discussed in Chapter V, led to a change in recruiting standards. Academic work came to be seen as an independent activity, to be evaluated in its own terms rather than in terms set by a religious denomination. The eventual result was that professors were selected for their academic competence rather than for their theological views or moral probity.

This change was, of course, extremely gradual. Even in 1880 piety and orthodoxy probably still counted for more than erudition in landing a job at most colleges. But the spread of graduate training and certification in due course made it much easier for college presidents to make quick (if seldom very accurate) judgments about job applicants' competence. Orthodoxy and morality remained unpredictable. Today most Protestant colleges judge prospective faculty members principally in terms of academic reputation and personal compatibility. The idea that a college teacher should set a good moral example for his students lingers, but mainly as a rationalization for rejecting men whose behavior will clearly be a public relations problem. One almost never hears of a Protestant college's appointing anyone because of his positive moral virtues, or because his example would inspire his students to behave in a more Christian manner—though some are perhaps kept on for such reasons when no better man is in sight. And while a few Protestant colleges still insist that their professors accept certain major tenets of traditional Christian doctrine, this too is increasingly rare. Most nominally Protestant colleges would indeed be shocked by the idea that there was any special reason for them to hire Protestant rather than Catholic, Jewish, or Hindu physicists, or even philosophers, though many would be unhappy if *all* their philosophers were from outside the relevant denomination.

These changes in the character of the teaching staff have rippled outward in all directions. Students, for example, are today selected mainly on the basis of their ability to do the academic work set for them by the faculty rather than for their willingness to conform to the behavioral and doctrinal requirements of the denomination that sponsors the college. Today the majority of Protestant colleges prob-

[8] For an excellent description of this transition on one campus, see Le Duc.

ably do not even inquire about their applicants' religious convictions, and virtually none insists on student orthodoxy. Indeed, even religiously sanctioned restrictions on the behavior of students who are admitted have tended to go by the boards. Administrators have found it hard to justify imposing these restrictions on students whose families do not believe them necessary. They have also feared that restrictive rules would make the college unattractive to many if not most prospective students. The more enterprising college presidents have even feared lest regulations that suited only their own denomination might antagonize potential local donors of another denomination. If Baylor University wants Waco businessmen to support it as "their" local college, for example, it cannot conduct its affairs in a way that discourages local non-Baptists from applying.

Changes in the character of the faculty have also led to changes in the choice of administrators. As faculty members came to be Ph.D.s, trustees came to feel that college presidents should have these same credentials. Clergymen who lacked them had trouble winning the respect of their faculty and often seemed to be out of touch with what was going on in their institution. The changing conception of higher education also brought changes in the character of trustees themselves, who were increasingly chosen from the laity rather than the clergy.[9] These trustees were likely to take pride in their college as an academic institution, though one with a particular religious flavor. They were in many cases more concerned with its academic reputation relative to other colleges (which was relatively easy to determine in casual conversation) than with the moral or doctrinal views of its alumni (which were difficult to determine and by no means clearly related to anything the college itself had or had not done). Indeed, even the denominations themselves were changing, becoming better organized and more bureaucratic. This meant that most had special departments for dealing with their colleges, and staffed these departments with scholarly men sympathetic to the claims of secular learning and eager to link these with those of the church.

All these changes relate to the fact that colleges were gradually becoming more self-directed, establishing their own goals, their own career lines, their own standards of competence and folly, and their own system of rewards and punishments. In part this was a function of numbers, but that was not the whole story. There were also external pressures. Perhaps the most important of these stemmed from poverty.

The founders of Protestant colleges were often devout clergymen

[9] Even in the nineteenth century clergymen were not typically a majority on college governing boards. See Hofstadter and Metzger, p. 305.

concerned with preserving or propagating a particular orthodoxy. The men who came later were seldom so ideological. They almost always assumed that their first responsibility was to ensure the survival of the institution, at whatever cost to the founders' hopes. Survival was by no means easy in the nineteenth century. Very few people wanted to attend any sort of college. Those who did seldom wanted to travel very far. Those who traveled seldom did so in order to attend a college whose primary appeal was a particular sort of orthodoxy. This meant that sectarian specialization was almost impossible. A college that wanted to survive had to accept the fact that geography was the most powerful influence on young people's college choices. There were only a few colleges like Yale and Princeton that reached outside their locale; most others had to find a local clientele or perish. Unless they were located in a very large city, this meant that they had to appeal to a wide range of belief and disbelief. A narrowly sectarian institution that got only the children of the local faithful had a very poor chance of balancing its budget or outliving its first president.

The economic arguments for presenting a non-sectarian face to the public were obvious to some colleges even before they opened their doors, as the cases of Pennsylvania and Columbia illustrated, but they impressed themselves on many more as time went on. They provided one of the compelling reasons for replacing clerical with lay trustees. It was almost impossible to choose "non-sectarian" clergymen who would be equally acceptable to all denominations, whereas it was relatively easy to find a prosperous businessman or attorney who could fill this bland role. Similar arguments were used to justify lay presidents. The choice of a layman was a way of disengaging the college from the sectarian feuds of its time, and this often increased its popularity with the public, much of which was impatient with what it regarded as clerical nit-picking. In all of this there was, however, a great deal of double-talk and fudging, with a single college trying to hold its traditional devout clientele by pointing, let us say, to its clerical president and to compulsory chapel, while also trying to attract non-believers by pointing to its lay faculty and talking about liberty of conscience. Still, behind the double-talk the trend was almost always away from the clerical model.

Even if the college did not self-consciously mold itself so as to attract outsiders, it often got them willy-nilly. Methodists went to Presbyterian colleges in a nearby town rather than to a Methodist college farther away, and Presbyterians reversed the process. Both sets of colleges welcomed the other sort of student—first because they needed his tuition, and second because there was hope of converting him. Recruiting students of diverse faiths was, however, a potentially dangerous business. Initially the college often assumed it could do this without sacrificing the essentials of its ancestral faith. Non-believers were accepted but were expected to accept the college on its own terms. But such a policy contained the seeds of further change. Once non-believers were admitted they demanded religious liberty, and this was difficult to deny them in a country where the rhetoric of toleration rang so clear. So most colleges felt obliged to let students attend the church of their choice. They also watered down daily chapel so as not to offend any denomination very much. But this was only the beginning. Morning chapel might be doctrinally innocuous, but students suffering from boredom or simply anxious to sleep late were nonetheless willing to describe it as an outrage against their consciences. And while the administration and trustees usually knew this emotion was feigned, they still found it hard to muster positive arguments for devotion without specific content. It is also hard to play the keeper of another man's conscience in a country that is as strongly committed as America to the proposition that every man should keep his own. In the end, compulsory chapel has usually become voluntary —in part because efforts to make it innocuous have long since robbed it of its appeal even to the devout. Similar onslaughts have been made against other denominational legacies (e.g. bans on smoking and drinking). The success of such arguments rests mainly on the gradual spread of the belief that undergraduates should be treated as young adults rather than overgrown children, but the desire to attract and educate students of diverse backgrounds also plays an important part.

The other major external force working against the continued influence of the Protestant denominations on their colleges was the gradual professionalization of adult jobs. Employers' interest in technical competence as against good character or personal charm is easy to exaggerate, even in the 1960s, but it has certainly increased somewhat over the past hundred years. In some cases this has led Protestant liberal arts colleges to add professional schools, either at the graduate or at the undergraduate level. In other cases it has simply forced them to redefine their mission as liberal arts colleges, placing more emphasis on preparing alumni for some sort of graduate work and less on preparing them for "life." In both cases, however, it has undermined the position of those who argued that colleges should be primarily concerned with character building. Such demands were often given lip service in catalogues, and played some role in shaping the extracurricular life of many Protestant colleges long after they had been jettisoned from the curriculum. But once the academic professions are firmly in the curricular saddle, their views tend to infect the extracurriculum as well. Not even the most devout and humane Dean of Students can indefinitely resist a faculty of decisively secular views. Or if he does, his successor will be so chosen as to reduce future conflict—which usually means he will be less devout and more willing to go along with prevailing faculty views about student life. The students themselves can resist the faculty far more successfully, and they do. But if the faculty is committed to professionalism, it will flunk out students who refuse to make any concessions. Some of the more devout freshmen, offended by talk of evolution or cultural relativism, may withdraw voluntarily.

The net result of these changes in the internal dynamics and external pressures on Protestant colleges was that while most started out as narrowly sectarian establishments very few remained that way. In part this was probably a matter of natural selection. Colleges founded to preserve a particular kind of orthodoxy had a much lower life expectancy than colleges whose founders possessed a more expansive and more academic view of their role. Yet natural selection was not the whole story. Unlike organisms, colleges can change their gene pool in response to external pressures and can thus direct their own evolution in ways likely to ensure not only survival but comfort. Many Protestant colleges have done just this, starting with sectarian ties that were ill-adapted to market conditions and deciding (often unconsciously) as time went on to play these ties down and in some cases eventually eliminating them.

Over the past century several hundred formerly sectarian Protestant colleges have dropped their church ties and have become officially non-sectarian. This has been particularly characteristic of the predominantly Anglo-Saxon colleges, of the predominantly upper-middle class colleges, and of the predominantly "national" colleges drawing from suburban families. Today, while most leading private universities and university colleges can trace their origins to some Protestant denomination, very few can point to any significant current difference between themselves and those private institutions that have always been non-sectarian. Organizations like the National Council of Churches as well as individual denominations are constantly commissioning investigations aimed at defining a unique mission for those colleges which remain Protestant, but the very idea that such questions require research is a tribute to the triumph of academic over clerical values.

It is perhaps significant in this connection that Wesleyan in Connecticut and St. John's in Annapolis are almost the only secular colleges whose past is betrayed by their names. The Methodists named some of their other colleges after Wesley, and the Lutherans named some Concordia, but most Protestant boards, unlike their Catholic counterparts, followed Harvard, William and Mary, and Yale, in naming themselves for financial rather than spiritual patrons.

In a few now secular colleges (e.g. originally Quaker Swarthmore or originally Congregational Oberlin) the unusual level of concern with social and moral issues may be rooted in the religious past. In others, such as once-Presbyterian Princeton or once-Congregational Amherst, the Protestant tradition has provided conservatives with ammunition in the debates over such matters as compulsory chapel. In most, however, official religious influence is quite dead. This does not necessarily mean that individual religious commitment is declining or that faculty members or students are less interested in ultimate questions. It does, however, mean that both faculty and students today tend to regard religion as a private rather than a public matter. Attempts to build a community around commonality of faith and ritual have steadily lost appeal, even in those periods and on those campuses where the level of individual interest in religious issues seems to be rising. Religiously concerned individuals have increasingly depended on self-interrogation and individual action for justification, or have turned to voluntary organizations such as YMCAs, Wesley Foundations and Newman Societies for a partial community to which they could give as much or as little as the spirit of the moment dictated.

The Holdouts Face the Future

If one asked the presidents of Protestant colleges what they thought their most serious problem was, most would probably answer "money." Most would be right. Church colleges are today caught in a financial squeeze. Only a few have any endowment worth speaking of, or any prospect of getting it. Only a few get appreciable subventions from their church sponsors. Most rely almost entirely on tuition to make ends meet. The rapid rise in academic costs over the past decade has therefore forced them to push tuition up very fast—often faster and further than their traditional lower-middle class clientele was willing to match. As with other private colleges, the gap between Protestant colleges' tuition and that at public institutions has widened, and this has encouraged many students who might otherwise prefer a church-related college to settle for a public one instead.

The families that feel they can afford private higher education, as we have noted, come mostly from the urban and urbane upper-middle class, and most are interested in brand-name colleges of high academic reputation.[10] Given the prejudices of able faculty and students, a college must almost always be de facto non-sectarian to acquire such a reputation, and this usually leads to a change in its de jure status. The Protestant college that wants to compete in this market is unlikely to have much success unless it reinterprets its denominational commitments in largely secular terms or else gives them the flavor of snob appeal rather than piety.

Under these circumstances it is not surprising that enrollment in Protestant colleges, while not literally falling, has been lagging behind enrollment in most other sorts of institutions.[11] The typical Protestant college is not only poor but underapplied. Even when Protestant universities are included, the average enrollment is only twelve hundred.[12] If we looked exclusively at four-year Protestant colleges the average would almost certainly be less than a thousand. These colleges cannot compete academically with their non-sectarian rivals, nor is there any prospect of their competitive position improving in the foreseeable future. More likely it will deteriorate, for the Protestant colleges are not benefiting much from the glamour and affluence that accompany the academic revolution. They are in many cases no worse than the state colleges and community colleges in their area, but these latter get steadily increasing public subsidies, which save them from raising tuition as fast as their church-related competitors. The Protestant colleges therefore offer a progressively less attractive

[10] For a comparison of parental incomes at Protestant and other sorts of colleges, see Astin, Panos, and Creager, "National Norms." The income distributions at Catholic and Protestant colleges are almost identical, and fall between those at non-sectarian private institutions and non-sectarian public ones. For a comparison of the tuition charges at Protestant and other colleges see Nash, Nash, and Goldstein, table 3.3. Tuition in 1963 was the same at Protestant colleges and universities as at Catholic ones, averaging $800. Tuition at non-sectarian colleges and universities averaged $1,200, and that at public colleges and universities averaged $200–$250.

[11] Nash, Nash, and Goldstein, table 3.1, shows that Protestant colleges and universities enrolled 10 per cent of all students at four-year colleges in 1963. Taking junior colleges into account would probably reduce the figure to 9 per cent. Astin, Panos, and Creager, "National Norms," show that 85 per cent of the freshmen at four-year Protestant colleges were Protestants in 1966. Assuming this was also true at two-year Protestant colleges and at Protestant universities in 1963, about 7.5 per cent of all students were Protestants at Protestant institutions in 1963. Since Astin, Panos, and Creager found that 54 per cent of freshmen at all institutions were Protestants in 1966, and since religion is not a factor in attrition, about one Protestant in seven was attending a Protestant college. We have no good trend data on these proportions, but there has obviously been a considerable decline in the Protestant sector over the past fifty or hundred years, and there is no reason to suppose it has stopped, much less reversed. At present, Protestant colleges account for about a quarter of the private sector. Even in the unlikely event that this ratio is now constant, there has been and will probably continue to be a decline in the relative size of the private sector and hence in the size of the Protestant sector as well.

[12] Nash, Nash, and Goldstein, table 3.1.

bargain to money-conscious parents—though their very smallness will appeal to some who hope it bespeaks community and individual attention. Rising charges might be partially offset by a state or federal scholarship program that would help students pay private tuition, but as we have noted, such programs have so far been funded only at token levels. Not only that, but if, as often happens, such scholarships were available only to the academically able, most of the beneficiaries would choose private non-sectarian rather than private denominational colleges.

The survival of recognizably Protestant colleges therefore seems to depend on the survival within the larger society of Protestant enclaves whose members believe passionately in a way of life radically different from that of the majority, and who are both willing and able to pay for a brand of higher education that embodies their vision. Such enclaves still exist, but they are few in number.

Some of these enclaves are remnants of pre-industrial America. Their faith appears dependent on both physical and socioeconomic isolation, and they do not seem likely to survive the agricultural revolution now in its last stages. In several cases they are completely rural, like the Amish and Hutterites, and have opposed schooling in virtually all forms. But most Americans, rural or otherwise, have felt obliged to educate their young. This forced them to choose between sending their children to what they regarded as overly urbane and secular institutions or else establishing their own institutions and watching these become increasingly tainted. The Brethren, the Adventists, the Mennonites, and the Church of God have all set up their own colleges. This has meant making some intellectual and social compromises with the larger society, and particularly with the definitions of knowledge established in the leading graduate schools. Still, these colleges are very different from those tied to the more worldly Protestant denominations. In some of them local warfare still focuses on smoking rather than drinking, on dancing rather than dormitory hours, and on dogmatism in the classroom and in marking examinations. Some observers feel that the superficial differences between these and other American colleges do not run very deep, that the quainter rules are in fact constantly violated, and that the appearance of community solidarity is something of a sham. In some places this may be so. Perhaps some fundamentalist colleges in the South fit this description. But there are other colleges that do not. The young Mennonites who attend Bethel College in Kansas, for example, come with a set of values most American adolescents would regard as both absurdly ascetic and square. With the help of the college they appear to maintain these values, not only while at Bethel but after graduating. (Indeed, some of them have already "proven" their ability to keep the faith in an alien setting by attending non-Mennonite colleges for a year or two before returning to Bethel's more congenial and communal setting.) The time may come when such students will no longer exist, or when colleges like Bethel will no longer be able to preserve the outlook of such students while at the same time preparing them for the kinds of occupations to which they aspire. But that time is not yet.

A somewhat different pattern of sectarian survival is found in Utah, where the Latter-Day Saints flourish despite increasing urbanization and the encroachment of outside influences. The Saints are ascetic but not otherworldly, and they have never distrusted education in the way that many other fundamentalist sects do. Brigham Young once remarked that "God is intelligence," and subsequent generations of Mormons have given Utah the highest average level of educational attainment in the nation. The rate of college enrollment is also among the highest. Since Mormon incomes are usually modest, most of the college-goers attend public institutions. Some of the smaller public institutions are, indeed, de facto Mormon establishments. The University of Utah in Salt Lake City, however, enrolls substantial numbers of Gentiles as well as Saints, and is insufficiently devout and overly divided for many Mormon families. Those who do not want to send their children to a less prestigious institution, like Utah State in Logan, turn to Brigham Young University, a private Mormon institution that attracts the faithful from all over the world and now enrolls more than ten thousand students.

Despite academic upgrading, Brigham Young has not lost its sectarian character nor even been troubled by the kinds of public soul-searching that go on in the milieux tied to the National Council of Churches and in intellectual Catholic circles. Potential conflicts between religious and secular beliefs seem to have been handled largely by compartmentalization and avoidance of public debate. This has posed no problem in the natural sciences, which draw strength from the pragmatic, activist, "Western" culture of the Mormons. Mormon efforts in the humanities and the more humanistic social sciences have been more intense but less fruitful. Men of Mormon origin have done distinguished work in these fields, but they have not found it as easy to reconcile themselves with Mormon theology as their colleagues in the natural sciences have. Debate goes on over such matters in a quiet way at Brigham Young, but some young Mormons evidently find the atmosphere too close. The new intellectual Mormon magazine, *Dialogue*, is edited from Stanford, California, rather than Salt Lake City. Despite debate, despite steady growth, despite intense emphasis on professional competence, Brigham Young remains a familistic enterprise, characterized by both mutuality and self-help. A large pro-

portion of the male Saints come to college after several years of
missionary work either in America or overseas and have held posts
in the complex Mormon church system. This gives them both the
serious maturity of veterans and an apparently greater capacity to
tolerate conflict between their own commitments and those of outsiders. All in all, Brigham Young is probably as unlikely to be secularized as any Protestant college in America.

The other major grouping of holdouts against the onrush of post-
industrial society and the triumph of the academic revolution is the
radical right. We do not here want to argue the general question of
whether communism or anti-communism is "really" a religion. But we
would argue that until recently anti-communism played somewhat the
same role at a college like Pepperdine in Southern California that
traditional Protestant doctrine once played at many other Protestant
colleges. Indeed, it is hard to find a regular Protestant college that still
takes its theology as seriously as the anti-communist colleges do. Very
few Protestant colleges, for example, admit that the substance of what
they teach is influenced by ideological considerations.[13]

The interesting thing about anti-communist colleges is that they do
not appear to be surviving simply by exploiting a dying social tradition. Pepperdine, for example, is said to draw many students from
"post-industrial" families, whose heads work for established national
institutions and whose children were raised on television and auto-
mobiles. These families are evidently in revolt against what they take
to be the dominant ethos of their time, and their revolt is tied up with
nostalgia. Such people tend to marry one another, to socialize with
one another, to attend church with one another, and even to move
into suburbs with one another. Safe within Orange County, a conservative sect, and in some cases the John Birch Society, their ideology is
relatively immune to dissonant messages from the mass media, the top
management of the companies where they work, or the books their
children read in public schools. They see a college like Pepperdine
(which is changing, however, and turned down a large bequest left
on condition that it give an honorary degree to Dan Smoot) as another
pillar upholding their faith in a hostile world.

Yet enrollment statistics suggest that even in Orange County most
conservatives send their children not to Pepperdine but to public
institutions. In part this is because the state college at Fullerton and

[13] For a fascinating account of a partial exception, see the portrait of Wheaton
College in Illinois in Hilberry and Keeton. There are a few other exceptions,
such as Calvin College in Michigan and a number of Southern fundamentalist
colleges of which Bob Jones University in South Carolina is probably the best
known (On Bob Jones, see King.) Harding College, a Church of Christ college
in Searcy, Arkansas, has been a prolific promoter of anti-communist films and
other programs.

the various two-year community colleges are virtually tuition free. Equally important, however, is the fact that these public commuter colleges allow parents to keep their children at home and look after their ideological and moral development personally. Perhaps no residential college, no matter how conservative, can seem quite that safe. If Orange County is indicative, perhaps fundamentalists in other parts of the country, be they religious or political, will also shift over to cheap commuter colleges as these become available. If so, the future of small-town Protestant colleges committed to orthodoxy is bleak indeed.

What then will become of the Protestant colleges? Some will doubtless become non-sectarian and absorb the overflow of students looking for brand-name labels. Others will probably be driven to the wall and after much soul-searching will try to sell themselves to the state. A few may combine with other neighboring institutions, and a few others will doubtless close their doors. But the great majority will probably struggle on, just as they have for a century or more. Lacking the resources to build a clientele on the basis of academic distinction, the location to build it on the basis of physical convenience, the connections to build it on the basis of social snobbery, and the competence to build it on the basis of professional training, they will cling to their religious labels in order to escape complete anonymity. There are many students who are equally uncertain of their identity and strengths, and some of these will also make a religious commitment to escape being "only a number" at a big public institution. Thus the Protestant college will survive as a distinctive phenomenon, even though the shape of the future is in other hands. Indeed, it is precisely the fact that the future *is* in other hands that gives the Protestant colleges their appeal to those who are looking for an alternative. It is ironic indeed that ascetic Protestantism, which Max Weber and others saw as fueling the restless development of industrial America, should now seem to depend for survival on its ability to oppose the very world it helped create.

IX. Catholics and Their Colleges

Catholicism in America

Catholics have always been a religious minority in America, and until recently an impoverished one. When the Catholic aristocrat Alexis de Tocqueville visited America in 1831, for example, Catholics probably constituted only 2 or 3 per cent of the total population. Yet he concluded that American Catholicism was a more dynamic and coherent force than American Protestantism, and imagined a future in which America would be divided between Catholicism and more or less free-thinking Unitarianism. The Protestants who controlled the machinery of American government, commerce, and education were often acutely concerned about this possibility. By Tocqueville's time intra-Protestant divisions had led to the disestablishment of the colonial churches, and not more than 20 per cent of the norminally Protestant population seems to have attended church regularly.[1] At the same time, American like English Protestants had continuing fantasies about Roman plots to take over the government and establish Catholicism in a favored position, such as it had once enjoyed in England and still enjoyed in much of Europe and Latin America. These fears made local Protestant majorities even less tolerant of the Catholic minority than of deviant Protestant ones.

Despite these troubles Catholics kept coming to America in ever-larger numbers.[2] Not only that, but they began coming from countries which had hitherto contributed only token numbers of settlers. Instead of English Catholics seeking religious liberty, the Catholic influx became increasingly Irish and German during the middle part of the century. By the end of the century it was predominantly Italian and East European. These new migrants were perhaps less likely than their predecessors to be fleeing religious persecution, more likely to be seeking economic opportunities. Whatever their motives, they came

[1] Cf. Herberg, p. 48.
[2] See Power, pp. 25–26, for estimates of the Catholic population from 1770 to 1852. Comparing these estimates with Census data we conclude that until about 1800 less than 1 per cent of the American population was Catholic. By 1820 it was 2 per cent, by 1840 4 per cent, and by 1852 8 per cent. Today it is about 25 per cent.

to a country that was less and less a wilderness waiting to be conquered, more and more an established nation seeking unskilled foreign labor for enterprises already established by the "first families." Instead of becoming frontier settlers on an equal footing with Anglo-Saxons and everyone else, the new Catholics tended to stay in established cities. (The importance of this is suggested by contrasting the connotations of the terms "settler" and "immigrant.") Catholicism was thus a religion of the downtrodden and the oppressed. This was true not only because American Catholic families were occasional victims of religious persecution, but because they frequently bore the brunt of ethnic prejudice, and almost all began their American lives with acute economic disabilities.

The result was the creation of both institutional forms and a cultural style that tried to provide ideological, emotional, and sometimes political protection against the larger society. By the end of the nineteenth century Catholicism was probably the single most powerful church in America, but its influence was limited by the almost universal prejudice against it among non-Catholics.[3] This prejudice made it hard for Catholics to build political coalitions even when their interests coincided with those of other groups.

The character of the Church was also shaped by the fact that of all the ethnic groups claiming membership in it, the Irish were by far the most likely to assume religious vocations. This has sometimes been attributed to allegedly Jansenist Irish prudery, sometimes to the peculiar pattern of Irish land tenure, which encouraged late marriage, and sometimes to other factors. Whatever the cause, readiness to take orders seems to have been characteristic of the Old World Irish as well as the New. In America, however, the Irish differed from most other Catholic immigrants in that they arrived with a knowledge of English. As Philip Gleason has pointed out, this meant that preservation of their ethnic identity could not focus on the futile struggle to preserve the mother tongue; instead, it went largely into preserving the mother Church.[4] Mastery of English encouraged the Irish to become brokers between other Catholics and the Anglo-Protestant majority. They also organized these diverse ethnic minorities in opposition to the Anglo-Saxons. The Church was one instrument for doing this; urban political machines were another.[5]

Given the overwhelming domination of the clergy, and especially

[3] There was considerable regional variation in the extent of prejudice. In Baltimore, where Anglo-Saxons were often Catholic and dominated the Church for many years, anti-Catholic prejudice was minimal. St. Louis was also relatively free of this virus. Boston, on the other hand, suffered acutely from it.

[4] See Gleason.

[5] For more detailed discussion and documentation, see the chapter on the Irish in Glazer and Moynihan.

the hierarchy, by Irish-Americans, other Catholic ethnic groups inevitably tried to establish separate national parishes. So long as the
non-Irish group was composed mainly of men and women who did
not speak English, these parishes had to be tolerated, since there was
no other way to keep many immigrants in the fold. Nonetheless,
ethnic parishes clearly threatened to fragment the Church, and seemed
both to dilute its political power and to limit its organizational effectiveness. They also threatened the favored position of the Irish
Catholic leadership. Once the majority of immigrants had learned
English, such parishes were in most cases gradually eliminated.
(Ethnic parishes do, however, survive in some big cities. There are
more than one hundred in Chicago, for example.) The general decline
of ethnic subdivisions in the Church has left many Puerto Rican,
Italian, Polish, and other Catholics feeling less than completely at
home in what they still regard as an Irish Church. This is especially
common among those ethnic groups that came to America with strong
anti-clerical traditions. Many of these families maintain only nominal
contact with the Church.[6]

Having defeated the national parishes, the Irish leadership set out
to organize the Church along geographic lines. The Church maintained a wide range of para-governmental agencies to minister to the
educational, economic, and medical needs of the faithful, and these
were expected to embrace everyone in a particular area, regardless
of ethnic background, income, or other differences.[7] Every Catholic
in a parish was expected to attend the same church, contribute to the
same charities, send his children to the same school, and die in the
same hospital. This ideal did not preclude gerrymandering parish
boundaries so as to make particular jurisdictions more homogeneous,
either ethnically or economically. Nor did it preclude charging parishioners for attending a parochial school or going to a diocesan
hospital, thus excluding poorer Catholics. Nor, finally, did it preclude
observing the color line in the South, and the sex line almost everywhere. But the Catholic system probably produced more ethnic and
economic mixing than was common in Protestant institutions.

The existence of this enormous para-governmental apparatus has
occasionally created vested interests which led the Church to oppose
the expansion of competitive secular enterprises (e.g. federal aid to

[6] For evidence on ethnic and generational variations in participation in one
Catholic institution, the parochial school, see Greeley and Rossi, tables 2.14 and
2.15.
[7] It should be recalled that the Church developed some of these para-governmental activities before government-supported alternatives were available. This
was clearest with regard to assisting the poor, but applied to a large extent to
hospitals as well. It was not generally true in the field of education, where public
institutions usually preceded Catholic ones in a given area.

public schools). Since the Church has also tended to endorse paternalism and coercion in social and moral affairs, non-Catholics (and especially non-Catholic intellectuals) have tended to regard it as a conservative or even reactionary force in American life. While this view contains part of the truth, it also misses part of it.

In trying to locate the Church politically, one must begin by recognizing that the definitions of liberalism and conservatism that are taken for granted by those who follow national politics (and that underlie most discussions of the subject in this book) are not taken for granted by most other people. In general, the poor and uneducated in America favor big government, but show little interest in protecting individual rights. This makes them "liberal" on economic issues, "conservative" on civil liberties. Conversely, the old Protestant elites tend to oppose big government, but to favor protecting individual rights, so that they are "conservative" (though seldom vindictive) on economic issues and "liberal" on civil rights and liberties. These polarities often show up in local politics; it is primarily at the national level that one finds politicians slipping into what intellectuals would describe as a consistent set of positions: all "liberal" or all "conservative." Perhaps this is because national politicians' constituencies are defined geographically rather than economically, and they look for positions that will unite rather than divide their potential supporters. Spokesmen for urban areas tend to be "liberal" on both economic and civil liberties issues, while those from small-town and rural areas tend to be "conservative" on both.

In this context the historic position of the Catholic Church looks quite consistent and natural. The Church has been "liberal" on economic matters, "conservative" on social and moral issues. It has opposed both laissez-faire economics and laissez-faire morality, just as most liberal Protestant denominations outside the South increasingly support both, albeit with reservations. The Church's position has, in other words, been corporatist rather than individualist. This is consistent with the feudal tradition of noblesse oblige and mutual obligation, which still plays a large part in Vatican thinking and papal encyclicals. It is also consistent with the prejudices of the American working classes, from which the Church has drawn much of its leadership and membership.[8] It is inconsistent only with the pattern of contemporary national politics and the parallel assumptions of intellectuals, Catholic and otherwise, about the necessary relationships between various kinds of liberalism.

As the number and influence of Catholic intellectuals has grown,

---

[8] While the Church now claims a substantial upper-middle class membership which might be expected to support capitalism with the fervor born of self-interest, even this is somewhat modified by the fact that a relatively small fraction of this class came up through small business, where the doctrine according to Adam Smith is most fervently held.

however, internal pressure for "liberalizaton" of the Church has grown correspondingly. The Church is being asked to be less vigilant in trying to detect and suppress error among its faithful, to let individual priests and laymen make more decisions for themselves, to allow more diversity and dissent from established convention, and, in general, to welcome the cacophony traditionally associated with American Protestantism. Despite Vatican II, the hierarchy has thus far done relatively little to accommodate itself to these new pressures, but the future may bring more movement in this direction.

In some cases these differences within both the clergy and the laity have ethnic roots. The Irish middle classes, for example, have long displayed a mixture of prudery and propriety which seems less widespread among comparable families of Italian or German descent. This Irish phenomenon should not be confused with New England puritanism. It does not usually define smoking, drinking, dancing, or gambling as sinful. It does, however, often view such activities—and many other seemingly even less risky ones—as improper for young ladies. It is usually accompanied by a great deal of public piety, and loud attacks on "modern materialism." As among Protestant fundamentalists, such attacks on materialism are frequently accompanied by detailed descriptions of the new buildings the Church is putting up and the new bequests rolling into the treasury—all, no doubt, for the greater glory of God.

Catholic fundamentalism of this kind is often allied to anti-communism. Here again ethnic variations are important. Hungarian, Polish, and German Catholics may be anti-communist because of what has happened to their homelands—and sometimes to their relatives. The Irish, on the other hand, seem more often to be anti-communist because this is a useful club with which to beat the Anglo-American Establishment, made up of men like Acheson, Marshall, and Hiss. As Daniel P. Moynihan has suggested, anti-communism has given the Fordham men in the FBI a chance to get even with the Harvard men in the State Department and the White House. It has also, we suspect, given the Irish and many other "new" Americans a chance to show that, far from being foreigners, they are more jingoistic than self-proclaimed "real" Americans of earlier vintage.[9]

The role of ethnicity in this kind of Catholic fundamentalism should not, however, be exaggerated. The minority within the Church that opposed McCarthy, for example, was probably as likely to have Irish names as the majority that supported him, either passively or (in cases like Cardinal Cushing) actively. The fundamentalist mentality has been found not only in the East, where ethnic differences are still quite salient and are tied to immigrant versus "old stock" tensions,

[9] See Dohen.

but in Los Angeles where the laity came not from County Cork or Warsaw but from Chicago or Queens. (It should be noted, however, that the Southern California brand of Catholicism is in some ways even more "ethnic" than New York Catholicism, for part of the Los Angeles clergy is Irish "surplus," born and educated in the Old Country and exported to America only after ordination.) Nor should it be assumed that religious liberalism or political conservatism are related in any necessary way to Catholicism. An organization like the John Birch Society, for example, seems to unite all ethnic and religious groups in a common fantasy, and Catholics are no more likely than Protestants to join it.

It should be apparent, then, that while Catholicism can be described as an American subculture with certain dominant characteristics, it can also be viewed as a self-contained world, within which almost every other sort of American subculture finds embodiment and expression.[10] In some cases, indeed, subcultural differences are more dramatic within the Catholic context than within the larger society. (This seems true, for example, with regard to differences between men and women.[11]) It follows that an analysis of Catholic colleges and their constituencies must in practice be an analysis of many different species of Catholic colleges, some of which have relatively little in common.

Catholicism has, for example, managed to contain diverse social classes just as, since the Reformation, it has managed to contain many ideological and theological ones. In the face of the mass immigration that began in the 1840s, the old Catholic elite responded somewhat like the German and Spanish Jews who wanted to disassociate themselves from their East European co-religionists, or like the Negro professionals who were embarrassed by their lower-class cousins. While meeting religious obligations more onerous than those assumed by most comparable Protestants, many upper- and upper-middle class Catholics tended to take a narrow view of their membership in the Church. Not only were they Americans first and Catholics second, but they were often lawyers or businessmen first and Catholics second. Their children were seldom born in Catholic hospitals or educated

[10] The reader may find helpful certain demographic facts about today's American Catholics. They constitute 25 per cent of the total population. Catholics of Italian origin constitute 5 per cent of the total population, Irish 4.5 per cent, German 4.3 per cent, Polish 2.5 per cent, French-Canadian 2.5 per cent, East Europeans other than Polish 2.3 per cent, English 1.5 per cent, Spanish 1.3 per cent, and others 1.5 per cent. They are heavily concentrated in the Northeast and Midwest and in larger cities. The older generation is somewhat less affluent and less educated than Protestants of the same age, but the younger generation has caught up with Protestant norms in these respects. (Cf. Greeley and Rossi, chap. 2.)
[11] See Astin, Who Goes Where, p. 39.

in parochial schools—though they might go to an exclusive private Catholic school like Portsmouth Priory. In general, these Catholics saw their Catholicism as a personal and private matter rather than as a link with their all too numerous co-religionists.[12]

While the more sophisticated Catholics' ambivalence about their Church was inspired partly by disdain for their fellow parishioners, a more fundamental source of difficulty was probably the character of the American clergy. Some of the early Catholic clergy, particularly in Maryland, were men of cultivation. But after the great waves of Irish immigration this became exceptional. Relatively few educated Catholics seem to have encouraged their sons to take orders—or if they did, these sons did not respond. Religious life was a calling for the upwardly mobile, at least among males, and clerical attitudes therefore tended to have a good deal in common with those of the nouveaux riches.[13] Cardinal Cushing has said that not a single American bishop's father attended college, and while this is not literally true, his willingness to make such a claim with pride suggests an ideology that has affected not only the hierarchy but the parish priests.[14] As a result, while most sophisticated Catholics kept the faith in a formal sense, they tended to minimize rather than maximize their identification with the Church. Those in metropolitan areas might shop around for a church whose liturgy did not jar their sensibilities and a priest to whom their life style did not seem sinful, but they seldom became afficianados.

As long as the Church remained an overwhelmingly lower-middle and working-class organization, the estrangement of a handful of refined and sophisticated Catholics was hardly a matter of great concern. But Catholicism is no longer a predominantly immigrant church. Its members now occupy much the same range of occupations as Protestants, even though they are somewhat underrepresented in top business and professional jobs.[15] There are now substantial numbers of Catholics whose grandparents made a good deal of money, whose parents have been to good colleges, and who are themselves so far removed from the lace-curtain Irish world around which the Church has long revolved as to find it quaint. One of the most important

[12] These comments are not based on any systematic data but on personal acquaintance, irregular reading of the social pages of *The New York Times*, and other equally fragmentary sources. Some Catholic readers have argued to us that there really is no Catholic elite of the kind we describe. A study of the subject is badly needed.

[13] On the social origins of a sample of priests in 1950, see Fichter. While priests tend to be upwardly mobile, we have the impression that nuns are more often (though still not commonly) drawn from elite families.

[14] Donovan, "The American Catholic Hierarchy," shows that in 1957 one Catholic prelate in twenty had a college-educated father.

[15] Cf. Greeley and Rossi, pp. 28 ff.; Bogue, p. 703; Lipset and Bendix, p. 50.

questions confronting the Church, and especially the Catholic colleges, is whether these cosmopolitan Catholics will go the same way as their predecessors, remaining Catholic only in the sense that other Americans might remain Episcopalian, Presbyterian, or Congregationalist. The issue is especially salient for men, just as it is among Protestant denominations, for men's jobs tend to draw them into the established non-sectarian institutions of American life more irresistibly than women's civic causes, personal interests, or children do.

One question, then, is whether Catholicism will be able to assert its special claims on those who have reached the top of society; the converse question is how an increasingly affluent Church will relate to the enormous number of Catholics who are not only not members of the upper-middle class, but have no immediate hope of becoming so. This is not, it is true, a wholly new question. Even in the nineteenth century the really poor Catholic, especially the poor Catholic man, was seldom an active member of his Church.[16] Both Church loyalty and piety were more common among the lace-curtain than among the shanty Irish—though even the latter were more religious than their nominally Protestant counterparts. More recently, it has been the white-collar Italian or Polish American who proved a strong supporter of the faith, while poorer and newer immigrants, such as the Puerto Ricans, have been more sporadic communicants.[17] Such families tend to distrust the clergy, which is not only often Irish (whereas poor Catholics seldom are) but also seemingly complacent about having "arrived," and adroit at putting everything and everybody in their verbal places. Such families are likely to send their children to public rather than parochial schools, partly because the public schools are cheaper, but also because they frequently prefer them.[18] Similarly, the few children from such families who get to college are likely to go to public rather than Catholic institutions.[19]

The Catholic Church in general and Catholic education in particular have been vehicles for the Americanization and social betterment of an enormous immigrant population. Catholicism has been a religion for the upwardly mobile, promoting many of the ascetic and disciplined attitudes required for success in a highly organized society. Its beneficiaries have, however, moved forward at uneven rates, and relatively few have already arrived at their intended socioeconomic destination. Yet these few have produced children for whom upward

[16] For a description of the Irish poor in nineteenth-century Newburyport, see Thernstrom, and compare Lloyd Warner's Yankee City series on the same city.
[17] For evidence that religiosity increases with education and income, see Lenski, The Religious Factor. For evidence that this may be a function of the generally greater activity of the middle classes in all sorts of activities, see Goode.
[18] See Greeley and Rossi, p. 38.
[19] See Greeley, Religion and Career, chap. 5.

mobility is no longer a major issue, and these children have today become too visible and numerous to be ignored. They are not interested in the old ethnic, religious, or class wars, or in a Church whose main function is to help them fight on these fronts. Yet the Church cannot easily abandon such struggles, for the majority of its faithful has not arrived in any sense and still looks to the Church for help in the old ethnic and class battles. The Church is therefore undergoing a kind of identity crisis, whose ramifications are felt in higher education as everywhere else. This conflict has been variously described as one between liberals and conservatives, modernists and traditionalists, ecumenicism and sectarianism, urbanity and parochialism. Whatever the label, it is real and often bitter.

In many instances this conflict takes the outward form of generational warfare, such as that described in Chapter II. The younger generation of American Catholics, including the younger generation of Catholic priests and nuns, shares the general youthful impatience with tradition, established authority, and the alleged need to maintain order and dignity in the life of the Church. These young Catholics seldom yield to their anarchistic impulses to anything like the same extent as non-Catholics in organizations like the Student Non-Violent Coordinating Committee or Students for Democratic Society, but their mood is analogous. Given the historic character of the Catholic Church in America, which is unused to having its customs and concerns brought into question, it does not take anything like the same degree of rebellion and dissent to evoke anger and alarm. The generational war may, indeed, soon be even more intense within the Catholic Church than elsewhere, for while the demands of the young are still considerably less radical than the demands of some young non-Catholics (and ex-Catholics), the opposition of the old is more confident and more firmly grounded in tradition than is the case among most other older Americans. The Church may, therefore, have to move even faster than most American institutions if it is to retain the loyalty of its most talented and innovative spirits. Nor can it be sure that, even if it does move, this may not arouse greater expectations than it fulfills and thus increase rather than decrease discontent.

In this cultural and demographic context, Catholic colleges have two alternatives. One is to change relatively little, continuing to concentrate their resources on first-generation collegians from the Catholic ghetto, for whom a Catholic college is a way station on the road up. Even if this is theoretically desirable, however, Catholic colleges will have to ask whether it is still feasible now that public commuter colleges are offering the same opportunities at lower prices. The other alternative is for the Catholic colleges to emulate their better-known Protestant predecessors, turning their attention mainly to educating second- and third-generation collegians and to developing a Catholic intelligentsia. In order to do this, these colleges may have to stop being Catholic in any traditional sense. The Catholic upper-middle class may only be willing to enroll in large numbers if their colleges move from sectarian separatism to denominational secularism, just as the leading Protestant colleges did a hundred years ago. If the colleges do move in this direction, whether to attract better students, better faculty, or both, their ties to the Church will probably become as attenuated as those of the more academic Protestant colleges did. The claims of the academic professions are not, it must be remembered, any more nearly identical with those of Catholicism than with those of Protestantism. While individuals have often been able to compromise these conflicting claims satisfactorily, no American institution of higher learning has done so.

The Control of Catholic Colleges

Important as current internal schisms may be to American Catholicism, the outstanding fact about the Church is the extent to which, unlike Protestantism, it has been able to resolve its differences by compromise and syncretism rather than fission. Related to this has been the Church's ability to retain authority and control in clerical hands, rather than allowing every layman to become a law unto himself. The clergy has, moreover, remained a relatively disciplined, centrally organized and controlled body—even though, like General Motors, it has allowed its local managers a large measure of day-to-day autonomy. In general, the Church has organized most of its operations on a geographic basis, putting every activity in an area under the local bishop or parish priest. But higher education has been an exception to this pattern. While many of the first Catholic colleges were established by energetic bishops to serve a particular diocese, less than two dozen now operate on this basis. The rest of America's 260-odd Catholic colleges are operated by autonomous teaching orders, which are free to define their missions and clientele as they wish.[20] The result has been pluralism verging on anarchy, and a division of labor hardly less complex than among Protestant colleges.

Approximately seventy-five different Catholic orders today operate colleges in the United States. These orders have different national origins, different systems of organization and government, different

[20] No two enumerations of Catholic colleges arrive at the same total. Our figure is taken from the preliminary report of a recent National Catholic Education Association survey conducted by Charles Ford. In addition to 260 colleges primarily for laymen, there are something like 200 Catholic seminaries.

traditions, and often very dissimilar leaders. All are ultimately responsible to Rome, but until relatively recently communication has been slow and often deliberately imperfect, so that local colleges have had great autonomy. All orders accept a common body of doctrine and ritual, but here, too, there has been room for highly diverse interpretations. Thus, while differences among orders are not quite comparable to the differences among Protestant denominations, they are often much more significant than non-Catholics assume. These differences have certainly had many of the same effects on higher education as denominational differences among Protestants. Catholic colleges differ not only in the locality they serve, but in the sex, ethnic origins, social class, and occupational ambitions of their students, and in their academic standards, cultural styles, ideological commitments, and curricular emphases. This diversity has frequently been accompanied by intense competition for students, donors, and respectability. The American Church never tried to curb such competition by adopting a "master plan" for higher education comparable to those of the more progressive states. Nor, indeed, have individual teaching orders adopted such plans. The Jesuits, for example, run twenty-eight colleges without any national scheme for allocating resources, setting priorities, curbing institutional imperialism, or ensuring that unpopular needs are met.

One interesting attempt to impose order on a national scale was Catholic University, founded in Washington in 1889 by the American hierarchy to provide graduate training for priests and nuns from all the many teaching orders conducting colleges in America. Originally an exclusively graduate institution, it went through many of the same vicissitudes as the two secular graduate schools founded in the same era: Johns Hopkins and Clark. Like them it eventually reverted to the American norm and accepted undergraduates, eventually becoming a predominantly local institution at the undergraduate level. While it continues to train a substantial proportion of the religious taking graduate work in certain fields, it has suffered from involvement, on the conservative side, in the ideological warfare between Catholic liberals and conservatives. For this and other reasons many of the more progressive Catholic religious and laymen chose to do graduate work elsewhere. Here again, despite its authoritarian structure, the Church was unable to impose order.

Outsiders who view Catholicism as a conspiracy usually find the heterogeneity and chaos of Catholic higher education hard to credit. Even if they finally conclude that there is no national or international control center for Catholic colleges, they tend to assume that on the local level the bishop and his staff must exercise a large measure of supervision and authority. While this assumption is not without foundation, even the bishop's role tends to be exaggerated. A local bishop must authorize the founding of a college in his diocese. Once it is in business, however, it is usually legally controlled by a board drawn from the teaching order which conducts it. While the local bishop has certain kinds of spiritual authority over all the faithful in his diocese, including priests and nuns, he cannot intervene directly in the affairs of a college.[21] This does not, of course, prevent his exercising enormous indirect influence over nearby colleges if he has the time and inclination. Few teaching orders are willing to remain at swords' points with a local bishop for very long.[22]

One reason for cooperation is financial. Unlike some Protestant colleges, Catholic institutions almost never get direct subventions from the Church; thus they are not subject to direct annual review and reprisal. Nonetheless, a teaching order that does not want to depend wholly on tuition to cover costs must raise money from local Catholic businessmen, competing with Catholic hospitals, charities, schools, and the Church itself. An order that is at odds with the local bishop is unlikely to fare well in such competition. Then, too, Catholic colleges compete for able local students, and if a particular college is on the outs with the local priests or bishop its potential students can be steered to more compliant competitors.[23] On the other hand, Catholic colleges also have considerable power over local bishops. They are, for example, the principal source of lay teachers for the parochial schools. We have been told of uncooperative local bishops who were discreetly reminded that the parochial schools paid considerably less than public ones, that the college with which he was at odds had been making great efforts to cajole its alumnae into parochial-school teaching, and that conflict between him and the college might leave his schools shorthanded in the coming fall. Under these circumstances both bishops and the teaching orders almost always find it expedient to maintain at least the appearance of cooperation, and in most cases this appearance is quite genuine.

[21] One exception of growing importance is the liturgy. The bishop controls the liturgy used anywhere in his diocese, including that used by priests on college campuses. The present wave of experiment with new forms has centered on these campuses, and conflict with conservative prelates has grown more frequent as a result.

[22] Perhaps the most interesting case of conflict between a Catholic college and its bishop is Los Angeles, the bailiwick of America's most reactionary Catholic prelate, Francis Cardinal McIntyre. In the midst of his diocese is Immaculate Heart, one of the two or three most progressive Catholic women's colleges in the country.

[23] We have been told of this happening at Immaculate Heart, though it may not be as common as Catholic college administrators fear.

The preservation of outward unity between the Church and its colleges has depended in part on the fact that, diverse as Catholic colleges are, they have until recently almost all been entirely controlled by the religious. Unlike their Protestant counterparts, relatively few Catholic colleges have had laymen on their boards of control, even fewer have had lay presidents, and none had vested title to the college and its property in a lay board until 1967. Catholic laymen have served on advisory boards, but these have had no real power. Diocesan colleges have occasionally had appreciable numbers of laymen on their governing boards, but these have also included the local bishop, and his views are usually decisive. A few teaching orders have had laymen on their colleges' governing boards, but this has been exceptional and the laymen have always been a hesitant minority.

During 1966 and 1967, however, a rapid movement developed toward lay or mixed lay-clerical control. The President of Webster College left her Order (the unusually magnanimous Sisters of Loretto), observing that control of a college by the religious involved the Order and the Church in seeming to sponsor actions that might be heretical. She persuaded Rome to authorize turning the college over to a lay board, including both Catholics and non-Catholics. The Sisters of Loretto will remain on the faculty if they and the college both wish, but without exercising ultimate control. St. Louis University, always in recent years in the forefront of change, has added laymen to its governing board, including one as chairman. A number of other Jesuit colleges are following the same path, as is Notre Dame. Many other Catholic colleges are considering such moves, and it no longer seems fanciful to predict that their boards will eventually be as diverse as those of Protestant colleges.[24]

The logic leading to greater lay control over Catholic education is similar to the logic that led so many Protestant colleges in the same direction over the past century and a half. One of the reasons why Protestant colleges began adding laymen to their boards was that clergymen were frequently identified with one or another side of a sectarian squabble in which the college did not want to take sides. A layman was a "safe" choice, for his theological views were usually unknown and his bank account non-sectarian. Most Protestant colleges were under financial pressure to attract students from as wide a spectrum of Protestant belief and disbelief as possible, and a lay board played down the sectarian image of the college. Theological disputes among Catholic clerics have seldom reached the same in-

[24] For a survey of Catholic colleges' plans with regard to lay control, see McGrath and Dupont.

tensity as among nineteenth-century Protestants,[25] and have never involved appreciable numbers of Catholic laymen. Until lately no Catholic college had to worry about the effect on recruitment of appointing a "progressive" as against a "conservative" priest to its board.

Vatican II and its aftermath may, however, have altered this situation to some extent. Dissident religious are increasingly ready to air their views in public, and to recruit lay faculty to Catholic colleges for the purpose of expressing views not yet sanctioned by the official Church. Furthermore, laymen who would in an earlier day have left the Church and become anti-clerical are today inclined to feel that the Church is not so monolithic, that they can find outspoken clerical allies, that their place in the Church is tolerable, and that they should therefore fight from within. As these disputes are reported in *Commonweal, The National Catholic Reporter,* and other critical journals, sometimes including the Jesuits' *America,* lay faculty may well be recruited or fended off from a Catholic college by their sense of the composition of the board of trustees or the power of the top administration. In due course even students may be influenced by these considerations. Trustees drawn from the business world could then come to seem more neutral and hence less likely to scare anyone away.

The traditional outward unity of the clergy has also led to a gradual growth of anti-hierarchic feeling among dissidents, both lay and clerical, so that today most of those who believe in pluralism also believe in the complete elimination of clerical authority in higher education. There is also growing self-doubt within the teaching orders, which expresses itself in clerical admiration for secular academic achievements, and in an often aggressive effort to recruit students and faculty who meet secular standards of academic competence.[26] Such individuals may be "good Catholics," "bad Catholics," or perhaps best of all, non-Catholics. In order to attract them, the teaching orders want to prove that their colleges are in sympathy with the going secular standards of academic excellence and the professionally approved means of meeting these standards. A lay board symbolizes this. It also seems less intramural: a firm tie to the "real world" or at least

---

[25] See e.g. the attack on William Rainey Harper as an heretical Baptist sparked by President Augustus H. Strong of the Rochester Seminary, as described in Storr, *Harper's University.* Or compare the battles between Boston Congregationalists and Unitarians for control over Harvard during the early nineteenth century to the far more genteel struggles within Catholicism today.

[26] The term "secular" is, of course, full of ambiguities. Non-religious men often have idolatrous if worldly faiths, such as nationalism. But so do the religious. Many Catholics deny that there is a necessary conflict between secular scholarship and religious faith, seeing only a complex dialectic in which what is nominally secular actually serves to refine what is nominally religious. So long as secular scholarship remains a means to a religious end, this makes sense. But for most scholars it is an end in itself—a form of idolatry for which Catholic colleges have shown growing sympathy.

a break in the veil that clerical control is somehow felt to impose between the college and the world. In this context the fight for lay control is an aspect of the fight for relevance, which in the secular colleges takes the form of attacking the genteel or the excessively academic. While we ourselves are not sure that lay boards will necessarily introduce the college either to a wider reality or to the going standards of academic excellence any more quickly than clerical boards will, most prospective faculty and graduate students to whom we have talked assume they will. A clerical board is therefore an important symbolic tie to the old order, while adding laymen is widely, if often naïvely, interpreted as a progressive move.

A second important reason why Protestant colleges added laymen to their boards was financial. Businessmen who joined the board were expected to make greater efforts to raise money from their friends than businessmen who were merely members of the alumni association. Conversely, the alumni and other laymen were expected to give more generously to a college controlled by "sound" business and professional leaders than to one run by presumptively fuzzy-minded and financially naïve preachers.

Historically, this argument for a lay board has had less force in Catholic colleges. For one thing, Catholic businessmen had relatively little money to give their colleges. The principal subsidy available was from the teaching orders themselves, which provided their service free.[27] It was not only logical but inevitable that those who provided this subsidy and made such enormous sacrifices in behalf of a college should expect to control it. Today, however, the number of young men and women assuming vocations is not increasing at anything like the same rate as the number of Catholics entering college.[28] There are very few major Catholic colleges in which the

[27] This subsidy has never been calculated systematically by Catholic colleges. It is probably less than it first appears to be. It is said, for example, to cost $70,000 to train a Jesuit. If this investment were amortized over a teaching career, and the cost of subsistence were added, the total would not be much less than the salary paid a typical lay professor.

[28] This lag is principally the result of rapid increases in the proportion of young people entering college. This increase has been even more rapid among Catholics than for the total population. There has also been a decline in the proportion of young people taking up religious vocations. Clifford and Callahan report that in 1954 the ratio of priests to faithful was 1 to 660, that in 1964 it had declined to 1 to 785, and that in 1985 it could be expected to be 1 to 1,000. We have found no trend data on religious vocations among women, although in general nuns outnumber priests about three to one. There is little doubt that some orders of sisters are becoming more selective in accepting applicants, but we do not know whether the rejects turn to other less selective orders or remain in the laity. For a general discussion, see Fichter. There has also been some conspicuous and some less publicized relinquishing of orders, especially among the avant-garde impatient with the pace of change in the Church. "Kicking the habit" has become increasingly attractive partly because non-clerical careers in academic life or public service seem more accessible to young Catholic girls.

religious now outnumber the lay faculty, and on many campuses the
religious number less than 20 per cent of the total. Yet this is hardly
a new trend. The big jump in lay faculty began a hundred years ago.
After the Civil War 88 per cent of all Catholic college teachers were
in orders. By 1924 this percentage had been halved, and by 1934 it
was down to 38 per cent. It dropped from 38 to 30 per cent between
1934 and 1964, but this is hardly the basis for a revolution.[29] The
real change has been in the *status* of laymen in the Catholic college.
They are no longer seen as a necessary evil, no longer recruited
primarily from the alumni of the college, and no longer paid secondary school salaries for secondary school qualifications. Instead, they
are increasingly drawn from the same pool of M.A.s and Ph.D.s as
non-Catholic college faculty. As a result, the economics of Catholic
colleges increasingly resemble those of their Protestant counterparts.
Today's Catholic colleges want to keep their quality: price ratio
competitive with non-Catholic institutions and this means they must
raise far more money from wealthy Catholics than they did a generation ago.

There is no decisive evidence that boards of control with lay
minorities or majorities find it easier to raise money than boards
composed exclusively of clerics. Catholics seem less suspicious of the
financial acumen of their clergy than comparable Protestants, and
more willing to trust their money to clerics, so the shift may not be as
helpful as among Protestants. Still, Catholic colleges have had relatively little success raising money from laymen, and some new tack
is clearly needed. In 1964 no Catholic college or university ranked
among the thirty best endowed in the country, and only three
(Georgetown, Notre Dame, and St. Louis) ranked among the hundred best endowed. At the other end of the scale, nineteen out of
the thirty worst endowed private four-year colleges with moderately
competent student bodies in 1962 were Catholic.[30] While this lack of
lay support may reflect partly the dearth of wealthy Catholics willing
to give their money away, and partly the competition of other
Catholic enterprises, it may also be a result of the relative non-
involvement of Catholic laymen in the affairs of their colleges. It is
true that some Catholic colleges, perhaps especially those for women,
are most successful in raising money when they seem most cloistered
and least businesslike, for in this role their very appearance of weak-
ness is a lever for making prospective donors feel strong and consequently generous. There are, however, limits to what men will give
out of sympathy. Big gifts seem to depend on a sense of identification

[29] The data on lay:clerical ratios over the years are from Donovan, *The
Academic Man,* pp. 23–24.
[30] Astin and Holland.

and real or imagined self-interest. (St. Louis University has been relatively successful in exploiting these latter motives, appealing to the local patriotism of businessmen who have recently done well and have no "established" charities.) Whatever the facts of the matter, many Catholics *believe* that lay involvement in policy-making will make fund-raising easier, and this belief makes the involvement of laymen increasingly appealing.

Another major reason why the more enterprising Catholic teaching orders have been bringing laymen into the management of Catholic colleges has been a restless desire to free themselves from long-term commitments to particular institutions. Some orders now want flexibility to deploy themselves in whatever areas show greatest need at the moment, instead of being tied down to a particular college. Equally important, many of the younger religious are concerned with the effect on themselves and the Church of having a proprietary interest in a big, rich, and essentially secular enterprise, which may end up owning them rather than the other way around. Some want to move out of academic work into other less professionalized lines, like work with the urban poor. But even those who want to do academic work resist the idea of taking administrative as well as intellectual responsibility for it.

While the addition of laymen to the boards of Catholic colleges may produce modest changes in these colleges' policies and climates, we doubt that these changes will be as significant or as uniformly progressive as Catholic liberals, both clerical and lay, usually assume. The leading figures in the Catholic teaching orders are in many instances more sympathetic to the academic revolution than are lay Catholics of the type a college might appoint to its board of trustees.[31] Lay Catholic boards are, after all, no more likely to be composed of intellectuals than are non-Catholic boards. Most lay advisory boards are made up of wealthy real estate tycoons, hopefully influential political figures, loyal football promoters, and the like. The laymen appointed to governing boards during 1967 were for the most part of this same stripe, though there were conspicuous exceptions. These men are in many cases quite literally more Catholic than the Pope. They are frequently distressed by liturgical reform because they find it easier to ascribe magical powers to what they cannot understand than to what they can,[32] and many are equally distressed by

---

[31] Not all the laymen on Catholic college boards are Catholic. It seems safe to assume, however, that Protestant and Jewish representation will be kept at modest levels for the foreseeable future.

[32] Cf. DiRenzo, who suggests that some authoritarian laity accepted liturgical reform out of submissiveness rather than understanding, just because it came from Rome.

proposals to eliminate outmoded academic traditions in which they have been taught to have faith.

The clerics who serve on Catholic college boards have, on the other hand, usually had some experience on college faculties. Today a growing minority has been trained in an academic discipline as well as in theology, sometimes at a secular graduate school. This certainly does not mean that their first loyalty is to the academic profession rather than to their Church or order, nor does it mean that they will necessarily be innovators. But it seems to us that Catholic clerics are at least as likely as the typical Catholic layman to support the claims of the academic profession on Catholic colleges. Indeed, it might even be argued that academic innovation in a Catholic institution is easier under clerical than lay auspices, since no layman has the authority to force changes in long-established Catholic traditions.

This argument is, however, somewhat analogous to the argument that Negro colleges can move forward faster under white than Negro presidents, since whites can afford to be radical and can legitimize radical change in a way that Negroes cannot. This is true in the short run, but perhaps not in the long haul, for it exploits the basic psychological sickness instead of healing it. Just as Negroes need to learn they can do things on their own without white help, so Catholic laymen may have to learn to get on without clerical guidance. If lay Catholic deference to clerical opinion is really like Negro deference to whites, the Catholic colleges may have to go through a "lay power" phase in order to open the way for more satisfactory lay-clerical relations later on. Since Catholic laymen do not have the power to hire and fire priests, as many Protestants do, it may be doubly difficult to establish their power vis-à-vis the teaching orders, and also doubly important. The immediate results may be far from uniformly progressive, but perhaps only by taking this risk can the Catholic colleges turn out a new generation of alumni ready to run the colleges as the best clerics think they should be run.

Analogies with "black power" also cut the other way. There is a real need to bring the dominant group (in this case, the religious) into less sheltered contact with the formerly acquiescent (though often half-consciously resentful) laity. Today it is the Catholic laymen who can be "fired," by being excommunicated, and this basic definition of where power lies may be as bad for the clergy as it is for the laity.

Perhaps the most important change likely to come from adding laymen to governing boards is the selection of more lay presidents at Catholic colleges. Several diocesan colleges, such as the University of Dallas and Sacred Heart University in Bridgeport, already have lay presidents. So do Our Lady of the Lake in San Antonio and St.

Benedict's in Atchison, Kansas, both of which are conducted by teaching orders. Other orders have in the past tried having laymen run their colleges, and have found that it worked out rather badly. We gather that this was because real control continued to be in the hands of the religious, who filled all the places on the board. This meant that the religious on the faculty could circumvent the lay president's authority by appealing directly to fellow religious on the board. Under such circumstances the lay president became (or at least seemed to become) an errand boy with no real power. We have heard it said that lay presidents of diocesan colleges have had similar difficulties establishing their position vis-à-vis the local bishop and his staff. If a lay president came as a by-product of a self-perpetuating lay board, rather than one chosen by the bishop, presidential authority would be less open to question. Perhaps some Catholic parents would be reluctant to send their children to a college headed by a layman, and irate alumni might find it easier to intervene in the affairs of a college that had no clerical garb in which to take refuge. Still, the evolution of American Catholicism has now reached a point where such experiments are almost certain to be tried on a substantial scale.

The results are difficult to predict. There is much to be said for choosing both governing boards and presidents in such a way as to ensure that their first loyalty is to the college rather than to some outside group. Indeed, one of the reasons why religious heads of Catholic colleges have sometimes wanted laymen on their boards has been to free them from pressures from their order, which often has a number of irons in the fire and sometimes sacrifices the interests of a particular college to some other objective. The same argument applies to college presidents. If they come from a teaching order and know they may have to return to it in due course in another role, their loyalties are inevitably somewhat mixed (like a lay college president who is trying to become an ambassador or a Senator).[33] What is good for the Jesuits is not, after all, always good for Fordham or the University of San Francisco, and it does not help any college's morale to think that its chief executive places other interests before those of the institution.

Even a teaching order whose sole activity is to conduct a college (and there are many such), and whose interests are therefore virtually identical with the college, faces internal pressures in appointments to administrative jobs. There are great variations in clerical-lay relations from one college to another, depending on the ratio of religious to laymen and on the rule of the order. Some orders

[33] Greeley, Van Cleve, and Carroll discuss this problem sagely and meticulously in their book, *The Changing Catholic College.*

require their members to dine separately; others do not. Some orders confine their members to residence halls or other such buildings when they are not on the job; others allow their members to mix quite freely with laymen during non-business hours. In addition, there are variations in outlook within a given order. Younger Jesuits, for example, trained in secular graduate schools and committed to a discipline more than to a college, may feel they have more in common with young lay professors than with administrators and older faculty. Despite these variations, lay faculty have traditionally felt that they were second-class citizens, that they had no real influence on college policy, and that it was the religious, living on campus and meeting together for religious exercises, who controlled the institution.[34] This feeling may have relatively little basis in fact. Some college presidents, for instance, forbid members of the order to discuss college business with them in the residences. This, as William Jarrett has pointed out to us, is less an effort to preclude "kitchen cabinets" than to protect the president from unwanted criticism—a job performed during the day by secretaries. Whatever their purpose, such rules seldom quiet lay fears, however paranoid these may sometimes be.

Such fears cannot be ignored if Catholic colleges are to compete successfully for lay faculty. The only way to allay them may well be to give laymen both symbolic and real power in the administration of the college. Many of the better Catholic colleges have been appointing laymen to key committees, department chairmanships, and deanships for some years. This may or may not alleviate tension. Just as insurgent Negroes tend to assume that any Negro who works for a white board of directors is a fink and will sell out Negro interests when "whitey" gives the word, so lay faculty at Catholic colleges tend to assume that laymen who occupy apparently important jobs are "lay finks" fronting for clerics who have "real" power. Sometimes this is quite true. The laymen appointed to administrative jobs in Catholic colleges have in the past often—though certainly not always—been those who had proved their loyalty and docility. Furthermore, even when Catholic colleges pick lay administrators who have been critical of the status quo, this may not solve the problem. The clerical president may, for example, expect a given layman to talk back to him, representing his lay colleagues with candor and passion. But he often finds that the individual in question has very little taste for this. Many lay faculty are used to assuming that the religious are somehow more

[34] Donovan, *The Academic Man*, p. 183, shows that in the early 1960s lay-religious problems were the most important and consistent source of unhappiness among lay faculty of Catholic colleges, outstripping even complaints about salaries. See also Greeley, Van Cleve, and Carroll.

than merely human, and after forty years of deference have no combat skills.[35]

Under these circumstances a lay board and a lay president may be essential both to improve morale among lay faculty and to attract highly professionalized scholars who regard a clerically controlled college as out of the question. The only alternative we can see for an academically ambitious college would be to decentralize, giving faculty committees, lay department chairmen, and lay deans more autonomy, while sharply curtailing the powers of the board and president. This kind of democratization, while useful as a protection against the worst kinds of administrative despotism and incompetence, is probably inappropriate to an institution on the make, for it allows mediocrity to protect and perpetuate itself in a multitude of ways. It can be argued that all American institutions must remain on the make if they are not to stagnate, and hence that none can really afford the luxury of autonomous faculty baronies with their complacency and lack of initiative. Be that as it may, there are few if any Catholic colleges in which the academic revolution has progressed far enough for this kind of consolidation to be prudent.[36]

For this reason we are as skeptical about lay presidents as about lay boards. Lay presidents will almost certainly feel compelled to democratize their colleges to some extent. Democratization and lay power are likely to produce a competent but undistinguished imitation of secular higher education. While this may be what American Catholics now want, it is obviously not a prospect of much interest to outsiders looking for sources of creative initiative within the over-all academic system. In saying this we do not mean to imply that existing clerical boards or presidents are taking such initiatives. The more talented and energetic religious are believers in the academic revolution too, and their principal claim to distinction is that they can force the pace of change faster than the laity. Still, we would like to believe that the Church could make some creative contribution to American higher education beyond adding a few more conventional second- and third-rank campuses. This contribution will almost cer-

[35] One solution to this problem has been to appoint laymen who are not even Catholics. During 1966 Fordham appointed two Jews and a Negro to head its colleges of Education, the Performing Arts, and Social Work. Given their previous records in non-Catholic settings these men could not easily be viewed as stooges for the clerical president. But neither would they probably have been appointed by a non-clerical president, for without the full authority of the Jesuit Order behind him, a president who made such appointments might have faced a revolt by the increasingly insecure Catholic old guard.

[36] Greeley, Van Cleve, and Carroll offer persuasive, though not conclusive, evidence that the distinction or mediocrity of a Catholic college or university today depends more on the talent of its president than on any other single factor. This conclusion derives from comparisons of colleges within given orders, and of colleges with comparable resources.

tainly not come from academic professionals who happen to be Catholics; if it does not come from the religious with their divided sense of identity, it will not come at all.

One reason Catholic colleges have been able to get along without lay presidents has been the teaching orders' continuing ability to recruit young men and women of unusual entrepreneurial and administrative ability who could eventually fill this role. While the leading figures in the Catholic orders do not seem to us any more intellectually distinguished than their Protestant counterparts, some have a measure of personal authority and sociopolitical deftness that strikes us as unusual among Protestant ministers. The Jesuits are notable for their long period of preparation, and a wise provincial can see to it that a younger member of the Order gets the relevant training for complex administrative tasks. Teaching orders have been in a better position than the less disciplined Protestant ministries to persuade a scholar with administrative gifts that he should assume a college presidency, at least for a term. Yet some orders (notably the Jesuits) have taxed their resources of leadership more than any Protestant denomination by rotating able presidents out of office after a few years. This practice is becoming less common as orders become more realistic about the extraordinary difficulty of doing a good job as a college president and the waste involved in removing a competent man. Yet many orders still settle for men and women who lack the necessary financial, administrative, and scholarly talent.

Perhaps one reason why the best Catholic colleges have found better clerical leadership than their Protestant counterparts is that a generation ago the religious life still attracted a number of young Catholics with considerable entrepreneurial energy and organizational flair. We are not sure whether this is still common. The best young religious are very impressive intellectually and humanly—perhaps even more so than their predecessors. But they are becoming more like their Protestant counterparts; they do not seem to have the temperament of empire builders. Catholics of that sort may be getting scarcer, or they may just be eschewing the ministry, as their Protestant counterparts have done for generations. The breakdown of the Catholic ghetto, the rise of ecumenicism, and the opening of more secular opportunities for able lower-middle and working-class Catholics could all contribute to such a trend. On the other hand, the renewal under way in some orders may make the religious life more attractive to gifted young people despite (or because of) the self-doubts that some religious now feel freer to reveal. Whether these will include enough of Veblen's "captains of erudition" to lead the next generation's Catholic institutions we do not know. We have met a number of ex-seminarians in the Peace Corps and in domestic poverty programs who had rejected the prospects of becoming a curate in Chicago or a teacher in a Catholic college or high school. The plans now under way to remove at least some of the Jesuit scholasticates and seminaries from their present pastoral settings onto the campus of a big urban Catholic or secular university may somewhat reduce this sort of attrition, but it could also increase it by dramatizing the alternatives.

If complete lay control over Catholic colleges is established in the near future, it may not come from the transformation of existing colleges but from the establishment of new ones. Lay Catholics have shown considerable interest in this possibility, and some bishops are also said to be interested. A particularly promising variant of the idea has been the effort to establish a lay Catholic college in association with an existing secular university. This scheme has been obstructed by skeptical non-Catholic universities in some places, by the hierarchy in others, and by clerically controlled Catholic colleges working through the hierarchy almost everywhere, but it seems certain to be tried somewhere sooner or later.

The association of clerically controlled Catholic colleges with a predominantly secular university is already going forward. Immaculate Heart in Los Angeles is moving to Claremont and will join the Associated Colleges there, paving the way for its girls to take courses under non-Catholic faculty and to make non-Catholic friends. (A similar, though not identical, motivation presumably lies behind the recent announcement that Barat College will move from its comfortable Chicago suburb to Hyde Park on the edge of the Chicago ghetto. The desire to be near the University of Chicago and "where the action is" apparently outweighs the physical and social advantages of suburbia. Barat does not, however, have any plans for formal ties with the University of Chicago.) A similar departure has been tried at the University of Toronto, where Catholic students can take courses in theology, philosophy, and literature at clerically controlled St. Michael's College, but are encouraged to forage throughout the secular colleges of the University for instruction in other subjects, and indeed even for courses that parallel those offered by St. Michael's.

Professionalism: Clerical versus Lay Models

Like their non-Catholic counterparts, Catholic colleges are widely perceived as an entrée into the upper-middle class, and especially into professional and managerial employment. The real or imagined requirements of future employers therefore limit their choice of students, faculty, and program to some extent. Except for students planning religious vocations, most of whom are in seminaries rather than regular colleges, these requirements are much the same for both Catholics and non-Catholics. The result is that Catholic colleges feel they have only limited freedom to deviate from national norms regarding what a college graduate should know and what he should be like.

There are, however, important variations among Catholic colleges in this as in every other respect. At those universities that seek to prepare their students for professional and managerial careers requiring graduate work, the academic revolution is often well launched. At the other end of the spectrum, those women's colleges which expect their alumnae to become wives, mothers, office workers, and school teachers are as insulated from the claims of established institutions and the academic professions as any American college can be.

Many nineteenth-century Catholic colleges were founded with the hope of recruiting and training future priests.[37] Traditionally, the Church had educated the religious and the laity separately. But some of the nineteenth-century Catholic seminaries found this difficult. Like their Protestant rivals, some admitted students to their liberal arts programs who felt no religious vocation, simply to make ends meet. Some then developed a liberal arts program aimed primarily at laymen. Few, however, prepared students directly for non-religious callings. Even those institutions that established professional schools quite early, such as Georgetown, St. Louis, and Notre Dame, still placed their major emphasis on undergraduate liberal arts programs —programs that were in many cases even more rigorously classical than their Protestant and secular counterparts.[38]

We have no statistical measures of the proportion of nineteenth-century Catholic college graduates who took up callings within the Catholic community, but our guess is that it was high. Those who did not become priests were likely to become doctors catering to Catholic patients, lawyers serving Catholic clients in (hopefully) Catholic political and social contexts, contractors working for Catholic-run government agencies and the Church, and so on. Some Catholic college graduates moved in wider orbits, but most seem to have felt that this would require breaking with the distinctive traditions that had set American Catholics and their colleges apart from the Protestant majority.

Some independent professionals tried to build a clientele from both the Catholic and the larger non-Catholic world, without facing an

[37] For sketches of the origins of these colleges, see Power, appendix A.
[38] For a discussion of the differences between Catholic and non-Catholic programs of study in the nineteenth century, see Gleason. See also Power.

either/or choice, and some succeeded. Others, however, were re-
buffed by prejudice and either fell between the two camps or crept
back toward the Catholic one. Those careers that required employment and promotion within a large organization often left even less
room for compromise. A Catholic who wanted to follow a business
career either had to choose one of the few fields in which Catholic
entrepreneurs had a foothold, or else try to conform to the style and
outlook of the Protestants who controlled most of America's big corporations. Even if he did adapt, he often encountered a job ceiling imposed simply because he was Catholic. Similar problems sometimes
arose for Catholics considering an academic career: either they "went
secular," got a non-Catholic Ph.D., and played down their faith in
order to rise in the profession, or else they stayed in the Catholic orbit,
isolated from the profession and consigned to second-class citizenship
in clerically managed institutions. Many Catholic college graduates
were therefore reluctant to try to "pass." This may be one reason they
were underrepresented in academic and corporate jobs. Government
agencies, on the other hand, seem to have been more attractive to
Catholics than to non-Catholics. This presumably reflected the political strength of Catholics in many areas, and the young B.A.'s consequent assumption that he would receive equal or more than equal
treatment in public employment. Catholics also moved into the regulated private bureaucracies, such as insurance and the public utilities,
which provided quasi-governmental job security and relied on relatively impersonal standards of competence for promotion.

These patterns of job selection seem to have been characteristic of
the era between the Civil War and World War II. In the generation
since World War II, however, they have altered quite sharply. When
the National Opinion Research Center surveyed college seniors in
1961, the career choices of Catholics and non-Catholics differed only
marginally. Reversing the earlier inhibition, Catholics were somewhat
more likely than non-Catholics to enter business. They were also somewhat less likely to enter elementary and secondary education. But in
both cases the difference was quite modest.[39]

Efforts to accommodate changing Catholic occupational ambitions
have led to a large measure of secularization on many Catholic campuses. This is particularly evident at the graduate level, where Catholic universities must compete on the open market with non-Catholic
ones and must promise comparable professional skills and status.
While there is some parental and parochial pressure to attend a

[39] There were also only small measured differences in attitudes toward these
careers. See Greeley, *Religion and Career*, chap. 3. See also Bressler and
Westoff.

Catholic college as an undergraduate, there is very little effective pressure to stay on in a Catholic milieu for graduate and professional training.[40] Just as disinterested faculty members at a poor state university may warn their own students against staying on, so Catholic college faculty, both lay and clerical, often urge their abler students to go on to the best secular graduate schools, where they will meet stronger competition and more distinguished teachers than at any Catholic university. The students, too, often want to test themselves in a larger world and prove they can make it there. Many want to have the option of working outside the Catholic fold, and they see secular professional training as a device for keeping this door open.

Even those who do not care about such options (e.g. those already in religious orders) often prefer secular graduate schools. Those who expect to stay within the Catholic community are less likely than in the past to feel that this will allow them to challenge or ignore the professional standards of the larger American society. With this perspective, college students are inclined to choose between Catholic and non-Catholic graduate schools on the basis of the schools' secular professional standing rather than their religious affiliation. There are, of course, some students who prefer not to compete on the open market until later, or who hope that in one way or another they will be able to avoid competing at all. There are others who find that a particular Catholic graduate school is the only one to which they can gain admission, the only one within convenient distance of their home, or the only one whose tuition they can afford. But these are not the students Catholic graduate departments want to attract. They want to compete with secular departments in terms of faculty, facilities, program, and professional reputation, not location, price, or ease of admission.

Catholic graduate schools of arts and sciences have only developed to significant size in a few of the leading institutions. No Catholic university ranks among the top twenty in Ph.D.s awarded. Catholic University, Notre Dame, Fordham, and St. Louis are the only Catholic institutions among the top fifty producers of Ph.D.s.[41] Taken together, Catholic graduate departments turned out less than 3 per cent of all Ph.D.s during the early 1960s. This was a significant increase over the

---

[40] In 1963 Catholic institutions awarded 11 per cent of all B.A.s but only 8 per cent of the M.A.s, 7 per cent of the professional degrees, and 3 per cent of the Ph.D.s (*Summary of Catholic Education* [1963], and 1965 *Digest*). The NORC surveys reported by Greeley, *Religion and Career*, and Greeley, Van Cleve, and Carroll show that Catholics were both entering and completing graduate school at about the same rate as Protestants. Hence it seems clear that while many were taking B.A.s from Catholic colleges, these students very often moved to secular universities for graduate work.

[41] See Chase and Wensel, "Doctor's Degrees Awarded."

1950s, and even more so over earlier decades. Nevertheless, it still meant that the great majority of Catholic doctoral candidates were turning to non-Catholic graduate schools, and that even those prospective scholars who earned B.A.s in Catholic colleges usually went elsewhere for graduate work.[42]

Underdeveloped as they may be, the Catholic graduate schools are growing extremely rapidly. Many Catholic progressives deplore this development, arguing that the Catholic colleges should concentrate on undergraduate education and send their B.A.s to secular universities for advanced professional training. But we know no Catholic college in a position to build a graduate school that is not doing so, simply because graduate programs are an enormous asset in the competitive struggle for professionally reputable faculty. In most cases, Catholic graduate departments' aspirations are virtually indistinguishable from their secular rivals', partly because of their respect for secular achievements and partly because of the need to compete in a secular world. Less and less lip service is paid to the notion of Catholic biology, economics, or history. There are separate Catholic learned societies in some disciplines, such as sociology and psychology, but almost nobody imagines that these are substitutes for the corresponding secular societies. The American Catholic Sociological Society, for example, brings together Catholics and non-Catholics studying one or another aspect of Catholicism or of comparative religion from a non-sectarian academic viewpoint, rather than trying to create a new breed of sociologists who would study the full range of social phenomena from a distinctive Catholic viewpoint. A good many religious attend the meetings of this Society because of their specific institutional concerns, but the more professionalized sociologists among them also attend the nearly simultaneous meetings of the American Sociological Association.[43] Catholic institutions compose so large a world that they deserve special study by both Catholics and non-Catholics. But this is not the same thing as the unending search for a special Catholic angle of vision with which to approach the regular academic disciplines—disciplines that have been almost wholly organized and subdivided by secular schol-

[42] The NORC survey of 1961 B.A.s (Greeley, *Religion and Career*) in combination with USOE data on degrees suggests that about a tenth of the nation's Ph.D. candidates come from Catholic colleges. About a thirtieth of all Ph.D.s are awarded by Catholic universities. Thus, even if all Ph.D. candidates in Catholic universities came from Catholic colleges, only a third of the Catholic college B.A.s headed for Ph.D.s would be accounted for. The remaining two-thirds must be seeking Ph.D.s in non-Catholic graduate departments. Whether this rate of dispersion is higher or lower than in the past we do not know.

[43] The decision of the *American Catholic Sociological Review* to rename itself *Sociological Analysis* underlines the fact that at least in this discipline the quest for a separate identity is nearly dead. Cf. Mundy.

ars.[44] Many professors in Catholic colleges—and, indeed, some Catholic professors at secular colleges—see Catholic philosophy, or the Catholic view of history, as having a contribution to make to an academic discipline; and the textbooks used in Catholic colleges often have such an aim.[45] But these efforts strike us as peripheral rather than central to the activity of Catholic academic departments—a series of Catholic footnotes to a text drafted largely by secular scholars (some of whom happen to be Catholic).

The development of Catholic graduate programs has been somewhat uneven. The traditional focus of effort was the humanities. Yet this did not result in a flowering of humanistic Catholic scholarship comparable to that in Europe, nor in contributions to the disciplines of the kind that impress non-Catholic scholars. In the past generation, many Catholics have moved into the natural sciences, and a number of Catholic universities (notably Notre Dame) have developed respectable, if not distinguished, departments.[46] Today the leading Catholic universities have turned their attention to the social sciences —the area in which conflict between professional opinion and Church doctrine has been most common in recent times, and also the area most neglected by Catholic institutions over the years. Catholics are now entering all these areas in numbers roughly proportional to their place in the over-all population,[47] but whether this will bring comparable distinction to Catholic graduate departments is not easy to say.

Graduate programs in the arts and sciences are not the only ones that have accepted the supremacy of secular models without equaling them. The four Catholic medical schools (Georgetown in Washington, Loyola in Chicago, Marquette in Milwaukee, and St. Louis) are also much like their secular competitors, and none ranks among the national elite. All are Jesuit controlled, but none is staffed by Jesuits. At

[44] One index of the extent to which the disciplines have been shaped by secular scholars is the virtual absence of Catholic universities from lists of "leading" departments in various disciplines. See Cartter, *An Assessment;* he found only one Catholic department that ranked among the top twenty in its field. This was the Classics Department at Catholic University, which ranked nineteenth.

[45] Many Catholics also hope that Catholic theology and philosophy will somehow form students' intellectual and extracurricular loyalties, even if they do not influence the substance of the curriculum. For a compendium of such hopes, see McGannon, Cook, and Klubertanz.

[46] Federal reasearch grants, most of which are in quantitative fields, almost never go to Catholic institutions. In 1962, for example, no Catholic university ranked among the top seventy-five recipients. Of the four Catholic universities in the top hundred, three had medical schools which probably accounted for the bulk of their grants. See *The Federal Government and Education.* See also *Federal Support*, which suggests that the Catholic colleges' competitive position in research was, if anything, even worse in 1965 than in 1962. This study shows that even Notre Dame was not among the top hundred recipients of science grants and contracts.

[47] Greeley, *Religion and Career*, table 3.16.

Marquette, for example, there was only one Jesuit on the medical faculty when one of us visited in 1963. Seton Hall, which until recently operated a medical school, saw so little difference between its objectives and those of a secular institution that it arranged for the state of New Jersey to assume both administrative control and financial responsibility for it. This does not, of course, mean that Catholic medicine has been *socially* integrated with non-Catholic. Catholic hospitals are a major outlet for the energies of many nuns, and these hospitals form the network of medical sociability and referral for many Catholic doctors. Conversely, the exclusiveness and snobbery of the elite non-Catholic hospitals still makes it more difficult for Catholics than non-Catholic to move in, even if the Catholics attended non-Catholic medical schools. Our unsystematic sampling of Catholic undergraduates who want to be doctors suggests, however, that they are considerably more concerned with finding a place that will admit them and give them technically adequate training than with finding a place that is Catholic. They know that Catholic medicine differs from non-Catholic medicine in only a few minor particulars, such as its priorities in handling human reproduction. They also know that if they kill a patient they could have saved, it will be small consolation to those concerned, even if they are Catholic, that the doctor got his training at a Catholic university. So they want a medical school that can claim professional parity with the better secular institutions. About 6 per cent of all M.D.s come from nominally Catholic medical schools, whereas Greeley's data indicate that, as in arts and sciences, nearly 25 per cent of all medical students are Catholics. This suggests that about a quarter of would-be Catholic doctors are attending Catholic medical schools. Even those with Catholic college B.A.s choose secular medical schools more often than Catholic ones.

Similarly, while there may in theory be a distinctively Catholic way to run a law school, this possibility has scarcely been tested. Men from Catholic colleges are slightly more likely to choose legal careers than men from other colleges, but as we have already noted, they have traditionally aspired to the lower rather than to the upper reaches of the law—a local practice, a local civil service job, or the FBI, rather than a Wall Street or Washington firm. Most Catholic law schools have concentrated on the practical side of legal training—often on training trial lawyers. Some offer little more than a cram course for the state bar examination. At a few schools such as Notre Dame there are men interested in natural law and in legal philosophy, who believe that Catholic thought has something distinctive to contribute to the legal order. But most Catholic law schools are just as "secular" and narrowly vocational as their non-Catholic counterparts, and their professors are for the most part considerably less interested in the origin and nature of the law than men in such national law schools as Yale, Chicago, and Harvard. Furthermore, with the exception of Detroit, Georgetown, and Boston College they have shown little interest in what might be thought to be the more moral and Christian side of the law: the impact of the law on the poor, on family life, and so on.

Despite small differences in atmosphere, then, it can be said that the Catholic universities are generally very much like second- and third-level non-Catholic ones at the graduate level. They recruit students and faculty from much the same environment, compete with secular institutions for research funds and foundation support, and judge themselves successful or unsuccessful according to their standing in non-sectarian eyes. Most Catholic graduate programs are now eager to attract non-Catholics, as both students and faculty. Able non-Catholics have traditionally been reluctant to join Catholic faculties, fearing not only a loss in professional prestige and mobility but a loss of academic freedom and voice in institutional policy. But, as we have noted, leading Catholic universities are actively trying to allay these fears and are having considerable success.

These developments are relatively recent, and have not been universally applauded in the Catholic colleges. Sometimes a clerical administrator has pushed for academic professionalism, dragging along his faculty, both lay and clerical. At places as different as Georgetown and St. John's universities, on the other hand, the pattern has been reversed. Clerical administrators have underestimated pressure for modernization within their own faculty, giving ground too slowly and provoking a rebellion of unfulfilled expectations. Somewhat similar conflicts have arisen between Catholic schools of law and medicine and their alumni—especially those alumni who now teach part time at their alma mater. This old guard is almost always more conservative than the full-time professional educators. Nevertheless, professionalization and modernization continue, however unevenly.

The impact of graduate programs on the handful of Catholic institutions that have had the resources and desire to encourage them cannot be underestimated. None of these institutions has completed the academic revolution, but some are well down the road. Places like Notre Dame, Fordham, and Boston College more and more view their faculties as contributors to the national and international intellectual community, rather than merely as teachers of the young Catholics who happen to be on the campus. These institutions' graduate programs are on their way to becoming as important financially (and sometimes even numerically) as their undergraduate programs. A substantial proportion of these institutions' undergraduates usually go on to graduate school, and terminal undergraduate programs in fields like business, nursing, and education play a diminishing role.

Universities in the above sense are, however, still the exception on the Catholic scene. There are less than a dozen Catholic institutions that could conceivably be included under this rubric, and they enroll no more than 20–25 per cent of the students in Catholic institutions. The free-standing "university college" is even rarer in the Catholic sector. The Catholic male institutions we know that come closest to our definition of a university college are Holy Cross in Massachusetts and St. John's in Minnesota. While the faculty is quite uneven academically at Holy Cross, academic pressures are increasingly intense, and 80 per cent of the most recent graduating class went on to graduate or professional school, particularly the latter. Some of the better Catholic women's colleges are also moving toward the university college model, but the gap between their faculties and those of the leading Catholic universities is much greater than the gap between, say, Smith's faculty and Yale's.

Given the relative scarcity of Catholic universities and university colleges, it is important to consider the effect of occupational pressures on the two hundred or more terminal colleges that constitute the overwhelming majority of all Catholic institutions and enroll most of the students.[48] With a few conspicuous exceptions, Catholic colleges have resisted professionalization more at the undergraduate than at the graduate level. One illustration is engineering. While National Opinion Research Center data show that Catholics are as likely as non-Catholics to become engineers, the data also show that Catholics who want to become engineers mostly go to non-Catholic colleges. Only a handful of Catholic colleges have been willing to spend the money and make the inroads on their traditional undergraduate curriculum that engineering seems to require. While Catholic engineering programs are almost identical in tone and content to non-Catholic ones, their rarity tells something about both the psychology and the economics of Catholic undergraduate colleges.[49]

[48] In speaking of two hundred institutions we are ignoring the seminaries, which not only train priests for parish work but also provide members of teaching orders with at least part of their training for academic careers. Important as these institutions are, we do not know enough to discuss them. We are also ignoring the Catholic junior colleges, again out of ignorance. One interesting example of the latter is Marymount Junior College in Boca Raton, built next to the new upper-division state university, Florida Atlantic, in part with the thought that transfer students will go on to FAU. (This stands in contrast to the usual pattern, exemplified by a place like Marymount Junior College in Arlington, Virginia, whose graduates would be encouraged to attend a Catholic college such as the four-year Marymount in Tarrytown, New York.)

[49] Ethnicity may also be involved here. Glazer and Moynihan, p. 202, report that the majority of Italian boys graduating from CCNY take degrees as engineers, and we know that Italians are among the Catholics least likely to attend Catholic colleges (although there is an increasing number at Fordham and elsewhere). See also the discussion in Hassenger, chap. 5.

It used to be thought that there was some special affinity between Protestantism and the development of the natural sciences—just as there was, in Max Weber's thesis, between Protestantism and the spirit of modern capitalism. This impression was supported in America by the Wesleyan studies, which showed that men who achieved scientific distinction during the 1930s and 1940s came in disproportionate numbers from such Protestant or ex-Protestant colleges as Oberlin, Carleton, Grinnell, Hope, and Kalamazoo. Today, however, the NORC surveys show the average Catholic college turning out as many would-be scientists as the average non-Catholic college—though no Catholic college seems to rival the most productive secular institutions in this regard.[50] It is too soon to tell whether this shift will in due course lead to more Catholics becoming eminent scientists.

Catholic college B.A.s also underchoose schoolteaching as a career.[51] Two-thirds of all students in Catholic colleges come from parochial schools, and probably half have spent their entire elementary and secondary careers in such schools.[52] A girl who has never been in a public school may be hesitant about taking a job in one, especially if her parochial school (and perhaps even her college) imbued her with a feeling that the public schools were no place for a good Catholic. If, on the other hand, she thinks about becoming a lay teacher in a parochial school, she must face poor pay, subordination to nuns who often find subtle and not so subtle ways of putting her down, and a rigid job ceiling.

At least until very recently, most Catholic educators have acted as if public education were a predominantly Protestant affair. They have not built education departments that would contribute intellectually to the shaping of public school policy, nor have they sought to train a cadre of Catholics who would become leaders in the public schools. In part this has been because Catholic educators believed that the best way to train a teacher was to provide him (or more often her) with a good liberal arts education. As a result, Catholic departments of education have tended to provide minimal programs, aimed at meeting local certification requirements but not much more. Perhaps more

[50] See Greeley, *Religion and Career*, and Astin, "Productivity," p. 133. Dr. Astin has generously supplied us with the institutional data used in this article, which make clear that none of the Catholic institutions he studied attracted an outstandingly high proportion of future scholars.

[51] Greeley, *Religion and Career*, p. 80, shows that about 25 per cent of all Catholic college graduates plan to teach school, compared to 36 per cent of Protestant graduates. The differences are primarily the result of Catholic women's underchoosing elementary school teaching.

[52] Greeley, *Religion and Career*, p. 80, shows that almost a third of all Catholic college B.A.s are graduated from public schools. Data in Greeley and Rossi, table 2.2, suggests that about a quarter of those who have graduated from Catholic schools had also attended public schools at some point. This means half the Catholic college B.A.s have no public school experience.

important, the domination of Catholic schools by the religious has discouraged Catholic universities from building up large graduate programs for training lay school administrators. This has limited their ability to influence the development of public schools in their areas, even when many of their alumnae were becoming teachers in these schools.

While education remains a somewhat underdeveloped field of Catholic undergraduate interest, business and government have proven more attractive. The NORC data show that public administration is the most overchosen field among Catholic college graduates, with accounting and corporate administration not far behind.[53] A third of all 1961 B.A.s from Catholic colleges expected to work for big corporations, compared to a quarter of the graduates, Catholic and otherwise, of non-Catholic colleges.[54]

In response to such student plans, many Catholic colleges developed a "commerce course," now typically upgraded to the status of the business college. Such courses have seldom been any more relevant to the work students hoped to do than comparable programs at Protestant colleges. These programs grew mainly in response to student rather than employer needs. Their function was to teach a few minimal skills, or in some cases merely to certify that these were already present, and to give the student something he could do moderately competently in the years between high school and employment. This is still true today. The business college keeps the student off the street, awards him a B.A., and in this way gives him some confidence for the future. In many cases it also makes money, which is used to finance more esoteric studies.

Whatever their professional value, business colleges have to some extent served as conduits for bringing business values onto the Catholic campus. Their faculty frequently identify with the business world and use the rhetoric capitalism and free enterprise freely despite papal encyclicals regarding the pitfalls of such thinking. (This is not to say that professors in other Catholic faculties are generally out of sympathy with business values; on the contrary, one of the things that sometimes seems to distinguish the older generation of professors at Catholic colleges from their counterparts elsewhere is a lower degree of alienation from American life generally and established institutions in particular.) Yet in some respects separate business pro-

[53] Greeley and Rossi, table 3.16. The data are for Catholics from all sorts of colleges. There are no special tabulations on this point for Catholics from Catholic colleges.

[54] Greeley and Rossi, tables 3.17 and 5.3. Strangely, while Catholics overchoose public administration as a calling, the proportion of Catholics who expect to work for federal, state, or local governments (exclusive of schools) is almost the same as for Protestants and Jews (table 3.17).

grams, far from bringing business values to a campus, have had the opposite effect, vaccinating the bulk of a college against the claims of the corporate world for which a minority was headed. Neither clerical nor lay liberal arts instructors are eager to teach undergraduate business students, any more than most of them want to teach prospective school teachers. By segregating these students into separate colleges with their own faculty, administrators have allowed liberal arts professors to ignore prospective businessmen without even feeling guilty. Students of modest ability are often pushed into the accounting or business or commerce course as a way of keeping them in college—and keeping their tuition coming—without trying the patience of the more influential or stellar faculty.[55]

Taken together, the professions seem to have had much the same influence (and lack of influence) on Catholic as on non-Catholic higher education. The more academic and better organized professions have established enclaves of influence within the universities, at the graduate level if they could and at the undergraduate level if they could do no better. Yet both intellectual and institutional power in most Catholic colleges still centers in the departments grouped together as "liberal arts" or "arts and sciences." And Catholic faculty in these departments more and more resemble their colleagues at non-Catholic institutions. Their antennae are far better attuned to signals from these colleagues than to influences emanating from other organizations and professions, however wealthy and powerful. Such sensitivity varies among Catholic institutions just as it does among non-Catholic ones. The Jesuits, for example, seem more concerned than, say, the Christian Brothers or the Benedictines with the number of Woodrow Wilsons and National Science Foundation Fellowships their students win, the proportion going on to "top" graduate schools, and the reception given faculty publications by colleagues elsewhere. There is also great variation within orders, so that the Jesuit outlook at Boston College or Fordham is quite different from that at the University of Seattle or Spring Hill outside Mobile.

Yet even in those colleges where very few faculty write anything and where very few students are entering professions that require specialized preparation, the academic revolution makes itself felt. Clarke College in Dubuque, for example, has traditionally emphasized "character building" and "preparation for life" rather than professional training, and has provided its girls with a "feminine" program that gave a large place to the arts. Yet it is proud when one of its girls goes on for a Ph.D., and at least some of its faculty would like to see

[55] Hassenger, p. 158, has data on the Verbal and the Mathematical aptitude test scores of 1965 Notre Dame freshmen intending to major in various fields. Those planning to major in business administration score much the lowest.

the proportion increase. This does not mean that Clarke or other similar colleges will soon stop expecting the majority of their girls to become housewives—nor that we think they should. Those who expect to teach school may be pushed to become scholars instead if they have talent, but they will not be pushed very hard. Nevertheless, the range of questions raised at a college like Clarke is being broadened to include the natural and social sciences as well as the humanities. This has accentuated pressures to employ lay faculty, since the already short supply of religious has in the past been mostly trained in the traditional subjects, especially theology and philosophy.[56]

Lay faculty hired to teach the "new" subjects inevitably bring new values as well, and the younger religious, who are now likely to have studied modern languages, mathematics, sociology, history, or even the natural sciences, do the same. Many of these people, both religious and lay, have been trained in secular graduate schools.[57] The laymen typically know little or nothing about religion except what they may have learned in undergraduate courses on philosophy and theology. They have traditionally had comparatively little contact with the religious on their faculties, and what contact they did have involved little intellectual interchange. So they talked to one another and assumed their "colleagues" were not the religious but laymen teaching the same subject elsewhere.

When Catholic instructors have studied under the same scholars as non-Catholics, when they attend the same national meetings, and when they read the same journals, they are not likely to teach a subject such as American history very differently from non-Catholics. They may have different convictions on a few points where their faith or personal experience is salient, such as the character of the nineteenth-century public school system or the implications of John Kennedy's election in 1960, but for the most part they pass on a tradition defined by men whose religion, be it Catholic or otherwise, has had no apparent effect on their scholarship.

Perhaps the special influence of the Church and of the religious will be preserved in the distinctively "Catholic" subjects, notably philosophy and theology. Courses in these subjects have traditionally

[56] Julian Foster, a non-Catholic political scientist, has illustrated this in his portrait of the Jesuit's University of Santa Clara, with its "Ivy League" bias toward the humanities as against the newer social sciences. His essay also suggests some of the ways in which the newer subjects and the newer people can be and are partially assimilated.

[57] Donovan, *The Academic Man*, p. 78, found in 1960 that 81 per cent of Catholic college faculty had attended Catholic colleges, compared to about a third of the general Catholic adult population surveyed by NORC (Greeley and Rossi, table 7.9). Donovan found, however, that a third of the Catholic college faculty with M.A.s had them from non-Catholic institutions, while half those with Ph.D.s had them from non-Catholic universities.

been taught almost exclusively by priests and nuns, and have been required of all Catholic undergraduates. Students have traditionally responded with a mixture of bored indifference and hostile resentment. This reaction was not, so far as we can tell, sparked primarily by the dogmatic structure of the courses, nor even by the fact that they were required, but by the fact that they were highly abstract and seemed irrelevant to the social and vocational concerns of an earlier generation of Catholic college students. Such students were not worried by conflicts between their secular and religious beliefs; they were quite content to compartmentalize potentially contradictory ideas. The few instructors who asked them to integrate their ideas were either troubling, wearisome, or both.

Such students and such complaints are still widespread, but a growing minority is critical for different reasons. These new dissidents are interested in difficult philosophical problems, troubled by spiritual and moral conflicts, and eager to discuss the problems that bother them with elders whom they can respect. Their complaint is that most of those who teach philosophy and theology courses still act as if they were dealing with students who wanted a pat catechism to memorize, regurgitate, and forget.[58] Being uncertain and uncommitted, the new breed of Catholic students often resents what it takes (perhaps sometimes naïvely) to be the certainty and commitment of the religious. The last few years have, however, seen considerable ferment in some theology departments, especially among the young religious now coming out of the seminaries.[59] Gifted laymen are also becoming more interested in Catholic thought, and some colleges have used them to supplement religious instructors, particularly in philosophy courses. A number of Catholic colleges, such as Assumption and Fordham, have also hired non-Catholic clergymen to teach philosophy and/or theology. In addition, the increasing employment of non-Catholics in non-religious departments has sometimes enlivened religious discussion, since these non-Catholics are often much readier to ask basic questions of Catholic priests than the typical Catholic layman would be. Many of the best students and a few of their young teachers now want to explore all the intellectual alternatives, and this has brought changes in syllabuses as well as in personnel. Traditional reading lists have been expanded to include controversial modern Catholics, such as Fathers Teilhard, Kung, and Rahner. Many also include non-Catholics. All this has brought a resurgence of stu-

[58] Greeley, Van Cleve, and Carroll describe the still depressed condition of most Catholic theology and philosophy departments in bitter detail.

[59] The quarterly journal *Continuum*, sponsored by faculty at St. Xavier College in Chicago, has given voice to some of these moral and pedagogic concerns. The independent quarterly *Cross Currents* has done the same, discussing ethical and political questions in a frequently European Catholic perspective.

dent interest in theology on some campuses, and a parallel administrative willingness to relax the requirement that all students study theology. At Fordham the result has been an increase in the number of theology majors. If this trend spreads, so that large numbers of Catholic laymen begin emerging from college equipped to argue religion with their priests, American Catholicism may indeed undergo a revolution.

We can see in all such developments the general process Harold Lasswell has called "restriction through partial incorporation." Just as the Tory ruling classes in Britain brought able working-class and middle-class people into their own ranks, so too (and with even greater success) the Catholic Church has traditionally prolonged its life by partial incorporation of the non-Catholic world. Catholic conservatives have always seen this process as an assault on the purity of their doctrine and have asked where it would all end. So long as the Church endures the answer is that it will not end at all. Rather, as the liberals within the Church insist, there has always been and must continue to be a complicated dialectic between liberty of conscience and obedience, between faith and reason, between reinterpretation and heresy, between clerical and lay authority.

As a result, it sometimes seems as if what is distinctively Catholic rather than simply American must be found in interstitial matters of style and vocabulary. When we read the student papers at Catholic colleges and universities, for example, and compare them with the student press at secular institutions, what seems "Catholic" is often a particular set of terms ("prudence," "natural law," "right reason," "just authority").[60] This student journalism also often reveals a sharp polarization between a clever but brutal *National Review* style and a "softer" concern of the Catholic Action variety.

While lay professionals now largely shape the Catholic college curriculum, making it increasingly like that of a non-Catholic college, the same cannot so easily be said of the extracurriculum. Church colleges generally control their students' non-academic lives more than secular colleges do, and Catholic colleges are no exception. Student government, which is pretty much a fraud at all but the most "advanced" secular colleges, does not exist even on paper at many Catholic institutions. Student journalism has for the most part been closely supervised, although the number of exceptions is growing steadily. Fraternities and sororities have often been forbidden and almost always discouraged. The administration has thus limited the independ-

---

[60] Michael Novak has pointed out to us that these are not really "Catholic" words, but secular terms from another era, just as the nun's habit is not a "Catholic" costume but a secular medieval dress, which became distinctively Catholic only when styles changed.

ence and autonomy of the student culture on almost every front, although the trend is clearly toward liberalization.

At times, though, these limitations are more apparent than real, for while many colleges have very strict rules, some enforce them quite selectively. When Andrew Greeley toured Catholic colleges recently he was occasionally told that such rules were to prevent scandal. If a student got into trouble the college could always disclaim responsibility by saying the student was breaking a rule, even though it had made no effort to enforce that rule. Such spinsterish anxiety and hypocrisy sometimes derive from the religious order, sometimes from the lay community. In either case it is now subject to violent criticism by the more outspoken religious and lay reformers. (Again, this situation is hardly unique to Catholic colleges. Telling different stories to different audiences is evidently a universal necessity among college administrators—one of the many traits that makes them feel they have more in common with one another than with other people in their institutions.)

Perhaps the major impact of paternalistic policies is to discourage certain kinds of Catholics from applying to a particular college and to provide easy targets for the incipient snipers among those who come. Conversely, the possibilities opened up by a non-paternal approach are seldom seized by many, especially if the students are recruited mainly from local parochial schools. Most Catholic college students are evidently so habituated to the idea that adults in general and the religious in particular reward docility and conformity that they cannot believe their professors or administrators are really sympathetic to curiosity and rebellion. Even if they finally grasp this unsettling fact, they may feel betrayed and be unable to respond.

Judging by straw polls on student political preferences during the Goldwater campaign, by the relative rarity of civil rights and peace activities on Catholic campuses, and by our conversations with individual undergraduates, we have the impression that students at Catholic colleges are more conservative than those on nearby campuses to whom they might normally be compared. If one compares Boston College to Brandeis, Tufts, or Boston University, for example, or the University of San Francisco to San Francisco State College, Stanford, or Berkeley, or even Georgetown to George Washington, American University, and Howard, the Catholic institutions seem less rebellious and more complacent. If, on the other hand, one compares Catholic students to the whole country, including Southern Baptists and Mennonites, the verdict is less clear. These are not easy matters to judge, and there is a good deal of conflicting evidence.[61] Catholic college

[61] See, e.g. Greeley and Rossi, chap. 7.

attitudes are also undergoing fairly rapid change. When one of us analyzed interviews done with college seniors in 1955, some of the Notre Dame graduates showed an anti-communist fervor similar to Protestant fundamentalists. At that time Notre Dame's right-wing Law School Dean, Clarence Manion, undoubtedly spoke for these students, for some of the faculty, and for a large complacently patriotic segment of Catholic higher education.[62] Today Notre Dame has linked itself to social protest in Latin America, and many of its students and faculty are critical of the war in Vietnam—though the election of General Westmoreland as Notre Dame's 1967 Patriot of the Year shows the majority are emphatically not.

It is not inconceivable that the time might come when the American Catholic clergy, far from being Super-American, will find itself criticizing American life from an increasingly "un-American" perspective. Adhering as they do to a morality that in principle transcends nationalism, and to an organization in which Americans are still only minority stockholders, the Catholic religious may be among the stronger potential opponents of American ethnocentrism. Thus far their collective voice has been feeble, involving for example the condemnation of unjust wars in general but not in particular. Still, the seeds of a more radical alienation from modern nationalism have always been there, and they keep sprouting in unpredictable places.

In this context it may not be altogether unfortunate that the religious still preserve a substantial measure of influence over the extracurricular activities of Catholic college students—far greater, we have found, than their influence over the curriculum. In most residential colleges the priests or nuns live in the dormitories as counselors and advisers. They sometimes use this opportunity to offset what they see as unorthodox influences radiating from lay faculty. The laymen, living off campus with their families, usually have no equally effective way of making their weight felt in off hours. At many colleges the religious require students to participate in religious retreats and other exercises. These requirements are often fiercely attacked by faculty and student liberals who argue for voluntarism, and are equally fiercely defended by conservatives who think that these practices are the only thing that keeps the college really Catholic. Judging by Catholic students' experience at secular institutions, the conservatives are in some ways right. Voluntarism is correlated with less frequent attendance at mass and less devoutness on other quantitative indices.[63] Yet it does not follow that these overt signs of faith are

[62] Ironically, the very internationalism of the Catholic Church has brought to Catholic colleges a sizable sprinkling of fanatical if knowledgeable anti-communist refugees from Eastern Europe, China, Cuba, and so on.

[63] See Greeley, *Religion and Career*, chap. 5, and Trent.

indicative of otherworldliness or intellectual reflection: they may, as their critics charge, be substitutes for real religious self-examination. It seems to us that life on a Catholic campus, with its reassuring religious rituals and ethnic overtones, discourages some Catholic adolescents from the kind of search for unfamiliar insights that distinguishes the Catholic avant garde. Indeed, this is often deliberate. There are priests and nuns who, faced with Father Cavanaugh's question, "Where are the Catholic Oppenheimers and Einsteins?" would reply that it didn't matter so long as the students kept the faith and were saved. Indeed, they would say, if Catholic Oppenheimers and Einsteins can be bought only by allowing Catholic orthodoxy to go the same way as Jewish orthodoxy, they are not worth the price.[64] There is still a strong tradition of pastoral concern for the moral and personal well-being of students on Catholic campuses, and while we have little evidence that this concern has been efficacious, this does not detract from its strength. Such faculty, both clerical and lay, usually lead the opposition to faculty research-mindedness and student autonomy.

It is obviously difficult to determine to what extent attending a Catholic college leads to either religious observance or orthodoxy, and to what extent it merely follows from it. There is considerable evidence, both logical and empirical, that Catholics who choose Catholic colleges are predisposed to keep the faith, and that some of those who choose secular colleges are indifferent or hostile to the Church.[65] Constant exposure to priests and nuns also seems to encourage apathetic students to make the slight extra effort required to meet their religious payroll. Then, too, some of the religious lead lives whose serenity and grace seem to influence their students, especially girls. On many Catholic campuses one finds one or two priests or nuns who serve as catalysts for discussion and occasional action. Even the Jesuits, who strike outsiders as extremely worldly, have a contemplative and speculative side which may flourish in the informal life of a residential Catholic college. While such teachers reach very few students, the same is true on non-Catholic campuses. Certainly if one compares Catholic colleges not to Swarthmore or Berkeley but to the typical Protestant or ex-Protestant college, it is remarkable how often the Catholic institutions manage to produce at least a small minority of concerned and questing students, relatively

[64] Donovan, *The Academic Man*, p. 165, shows that Catholic college professors with B.A.s from non-Catholic colleges were twice as likely as those with B.A.s from Catholic colleges to publish. This finding, taken in conjunction with those of Greeley and Trent cited above, suggests that it is hard to maximize both piety and scholarship simultaneously. Donovan's other findings tend in the same direction. See also Greeley, "Religion and Academic Career Plans."

[65] See Greeley, *Religion and Career*, chap. 5; Donovan, *The Academic Man*, chap. 4; Greeley and Rossi, chap. 7.

immune to the bland all-Americanism and myopic pragmatism that characterize the collegiate majority on almost every campus, Catholic or otherwise.

Looking to the future, we are constantly tempted to write off the influence of the religious on both academic and non-academic life, and to assume that all Catholic colleges will eventually serve the same secular professional interests as non-Catholic institutions. But while such a prediction surely captures a large part of the truth, it may not be the whole of it. The professions, after all, need not be wholly secular. The Protestant colleges were secularized because the Protestant clergy lost out in competition with other professional interests, but the Catholic clergy may prove more resilient. The situation in Catholic higher education today, while in some ways similar to that in Protestant higher education a century ago, is by no means identical. On the one hand, the university model is no longer a dream but an omnipresent reality. The academic disciplines are now well organized and in some respects highly productive guilds. Their standards are therefore harder to resist than they were a century ago, when the Protestant clergy began its long retreat. On the other hand, Catholic priests and nuns are better equipped to maintain some sort of distinctive influence over their colleges than the Protestant clergy ever was. At some minimum level, which is subject to continuous fluctuation, the Catholic religious are united in a way Protestants never were. Bitter and seemingly irreconcilable ideological battles go on within religious communities and between them, in the diocesan clergy and in Rome. These occasionally lead individuals to leave the Church rather than to stand and fight another day. But the resilience of the Church is great, its openness apparently increasing, and the kind of endless schism and splintering that divided nineteenth-century Protestantism and lowered its attractiveness for many as a calling is less of a clear and present danger to Catholicism. The Catholic religious may not be able to work out a master plan for Catholic higher education, or to agree on a rational division of labor among the teaching orders, but such a division of labor does not seem entirely inconceivable. And while there may not be enough religious to staff the Catholic colleges fully, they are far more numerous than their Protestant predecessors: few Protestant undergraduate colleges of the past century drew even a third of their staff from the clergy, as the typical Catholic college still does. This is partly because Catholicism has been able to harness the energies of women in a way that Protestantism never did, but that is not the whole story.

Yet even if Catholic priests and nuns continue to play a large role in Catholic higher education, the academic revolution may still follow its familiar course. Many enterprising priests and nuns are already doing everything in their power to promote secularization of the same kind that lay professionals generally want. Indeed, for reasons indicated in the previous section, they may sometimes be able to promote it even more effectively than laymen. This being the case, one must ask what the special role of the religious in a Catholic college will be. If they do not maintain a monopoly on administration, and if their monopoly on theology and philosophy is to be broken, what unique role is left? Some would say none, and urge either that the religious get out of higher education entirely or else that they acquire secular training, accept secular academic standards, and teach secular subjects as best they can, bringing to bear whatever special wisdom their religious studies and discipline may give them. But in that case why should the religious work on Catholic rather than on secular campuses?

A small but growing minority among the religious has decided that there is *no* reason not to move onto secular campuses, and is doing just that.

This raises a larger question, namely, what should be distinctive about a Catholic college? It is not a question to which we have ever heard a satisfactory answer. In the short run such a question does not require an answer: the colleges are there, the students come, and that creates a need to which many religious respond. But in the long run there must be some sort of answer that satisfies the participants, and we have not heard one that seemed persuasive to the most rigorous. That is why we think the eventual triumph of lay professionalism is likely if not inevitable.

Defining a Clientele: Sex

The Catholic Church, like most other organizations, is controlled entirely by men. While it does not take the view that men have a monopoly on divine guidance (note, for example, the high proportion of female saints), it does grant men a monopoly on power within the Church. Women cannot become parish priests or rise into the hierarchy, nor have they any role in choosing those who do. In this, of course, Catholicism is not significantly different from other major Christian denominations. What sets it apart is rather the fact that, having excluded women from its management, it has nonetheless recruited enormous numbers of them into the religious life. Traditionally engaged in elementary schooling, nursing, charitable activities, and contemplation, American nuns have in the past sixty years entered higher education on a large scale, often competing directly with male teaching orders.

In medieval Europe some orders of sisters were little more than women's auxiliaries to male orders, but this is no longer common. The basic rules governing nuns are still made by men in Rome, but on a day-to-day basis each order has a large measure of autonomy. Today there are some four hundred orders of sisters in the United States, many of them "made in America." Most of these groups still devote themselves primarily to hospitals, parochial schools, and other good works, but about fifty conduct colleges.

There is sometimes cooperation but seldom much social or intellectual mixing of nuns and priests. The nuns are second-class citizens, and both they and the priests mostly accept this, viscerally if not intellectually, as right and proper.[66] Yet an outsider often senses a good deal of latent antagonism between nuns and priests, only partially concealed by the superficial sweetness that has been the nun's traditional defense against almost all difficulties. As with other second-class citizens, the nuns' outward docility may mask rebellion as well as obedience. Some are among the most conservative, self-deprecating and shy of American women; others are among the most spirited and outspoken.

Both the segregation of the sexes in religious orders and the hegemony of the male over the female have been reflected in higher education. Nineteenth-century Catholic colleges were founded by male orders exclusively for male students. (This was, of course, also true of Protestant colleges in the first half of the nineteenth century, though less so in the second.) While nuns opened a number of secondary schools for women, none at first offered college-level instruction or degrees. But the growth of public secondary education and the spread of non-Catholic higher education for women toward the end of the century inevitably affected Catholic girls as well. Fearing lest Catholic families send their daughters to secular colleges, and wanting to show that Catholic women need not be ignorant, several orders of sisters upgraded their secondary schools into colleges. The first was Notre Dame in Baltimore, which began offering higher education in 1896. After the turn of the century more and more orders of nuns began throwing their energies into higher education. Unlike their male counterparts, nuns were under relatively little pressure to help their students meet professional payrolls. They therefore felt no obligation to assemble large, specialized faculties, build expensive libraries and laboratories, or offer diversified curricula. On the contrary, many Catholic women's colleges made a virtue of their

[66] Another small category of second-class citizens is composed of orders of lay brothers, such as the Christian Brothers who run Manhattan College in New York and LaSalle College in Philadelphia. Unlike the most assertive and rebellious nuns, they do not seem inclined to challenge the authority of the priests.

smallness, and sometimes also of their scholarly limitations, by emphasizing the fact that they were both spiritually safe and "feminine." As a result, enterprising nuns were free to proliferate Catholic women's colleges at a fantastic rate. In 1965 the Office of Education reported the existence of 136 four-year and 42 two-year Catholic women's colleges.[67] By the way of contrast there were only 100 non-Catholic colleges exclusively for women.

While nuns created a plethora of undergraduate institutions for women, they made much less effort to accommodate Catholic women who wanted to do graduate work. In part this reflected awareness of their own intellectual limitations, in part their inability to raise the necessary money to run a university. Nonetheless, it left some ambitious Catholic girls with no choice but to do their professional work in a secular graduate school. This was not, however, a pattern the Church wanted to encourage. As a result, male teaching orders were persuaded reluctantly to admit Catholic girls to their professional schools at the graduate level. Today, the Canon Law ban on coeducation having been modified, most Catholic universities admit women to their graduate programs and most of the holdouts are considering it. Having admitted women to their graduate programs, many have also found it hard to justify excluding them from undergraduate programs. This has been especially rare in the Midwest and Far West, where non-Catholic colleges are almost all coeducational. In the Northeast, where sex segregation is still common in the private non-Catholic sector, the Catholics are also more traditional.

Four-year and two-year Catholic colleges have clung to sex segregation throughout the country. Only 32 of the 270 Catholic institutions that awarded no graduate degrees in 1963 were coeducational. (Among 1,187 non-Catholic colleges in the same category, 1,045 were coed.)[68] In part, this pattern of sex segregation reflects a feeling among many religious that mixing boys and girls may lead to trouble, and a paternalistic willingness to protect the laity from such temptations. In part it probably reflects some Catholic parents' eagerness to keep their children from marrying too young, and more generally to keep them out of trouble.[69] But the primary reason for it is the sex-

[67] *Education Directory*, p. 13.

[68] *Education Directory*. Perhaps 100 of these 270 Catholic "colleges" were seminaries.

[69] The pattern of delayed marriage among Catholic collegians is shown in Greeley, *Religion and Career*, table 2.1 This pattern may reflect Church taboos regarding birth control, which if followed are likely to force married students to leave school and support an unwanted family. Back in 1947, when *Time* surveyed a sample of living college graduates, only 52 per cent of the Catholic women were married, compared to 69 per cent of the Protestant women and 77 per cent of the Jewish ones. (See Havemann and West, p. 55.) We suspect this differential has shrunk since then.

segregated organization of the teaching orders, which creates strong internal pressures for perpetuating separate colleges for men and women.

Only a few male teaching orders have made room on their faculties for even the ablest sisters, though this trend is spreading. Conversely, few orders of sisters feel they can afford to let their most talented members take such jobs, which help the Church as a whole but do nothing for the often precarious order. An entrepreneurial nun is thus almost forced to spend her energies building up a women's college—or perhaps founding a new one. These women's colleges then become a powerful lobby against coeducation in colleges run by male orders. Thus when the Jesuits decided after some soul-searching to admit women to the undergraduate liberal arts program of the University of San Francisco, they were opposed (unsuccessfully) by the Religious of the Sacred Heart who run San Francisco College for Women (Lone Mountain) a few blocks away. This pattern has been repeated in many other cities and has slowed the advent of coeducation long after principled traditionalist objections lost their force. Catholic college girls seem as interested in marriage as non-Catholics, and every nun knows that her all-women's college will have a hard time competing against a nearby coed one. This is, of course, true of non-Catholic women's colleges too. But the Catholic women's college that fears for its future can appeal to the local bishop to keep a potential rival from going coed, while non-Catholic colleges have no such recourse.

Given the fact that nuns will continue to found new colleges, and that Catholic girls will continue to go to them, it has become clear to some that serious efforts should be made to improve these frequently stifling places.[70] In part, no doubt, this means bringing men onto their faculties—not because men are necessarily better teachers for either sex, but because there are so many more of them with the academic credentials that all colleges value. Catholic women's colleges could, of course, draw on housewives, but they usually want full-time professors with higher degrees and have conventional academic ideas

[70] It is not clear exactly what proportion of Catholic women are in Catholic women's colleges. Our best estimate is that about 24 per cent of all Catholic women are in Catholic women's colleges, 16 per cent in Catholic coed colleges, and 60 per cent in non-Catholic colleges. This is based on calculations described in more detail in footnote 78 below, which suggests that roughly a third of all Catholics are in Catholic colleges; on reports of the sex ratios for Catholics in both Catholic and non-Catholic colleges in Greeley, *Religion and Career*, table 5.1; and on National Catholic Welfare Conference reports on the proportion of degrees awarded by colleges run by male and female orders. Both the proportion of Catholic women in Catholic colleges and the proportion in Catholic women's colleges are probably falling, the former because of the growth of public competition and the latter because the big Catholic universities are admitting more women.

about who should teach what. There are not enough women, either religious or lay, who can fill these requirements. Nonetheless, the proportion of sisters on a Catholic women's college faculty is almost always higher than the proportion of priests at Catholic men's colleges, and the sisters are more likely to monopolize the key administrative jobs. As a result, efforts to help the Catholic women's colleges have had to focus primarily on the religious.

The Sister Formation Conference, founded in 1954 and virtually abolished as a national effort in 1964, was the most promising of these efforts. Led by an extraordinary group of nuns, the Conference set out to develop both the intellectual and moral resources of sisters in all orders. Through its Bulletin and through workshops and meetings the Conference gave innovators in dozens of colleges the courage and sense of direction to push ahead, and it also helped stir things up in many sleepy Mother Houses, just as Vatican II opened the windows of Catholicism generally. The Conference encouraged many orders of sisters to move away from their traditionally cloistered system of training young nuns. A number now go to regular Catholic colleges alongside lay students. Another offshoot of the Conference was Marillac College outside St. Louis, conducted by the Daughters of Charity of St. Vincent de Paul. Marillac is open to nuns from all orders. Its founders initially wanted to establish a program on a Catholic university campus, but when they could not find a Catholic university willing to take this on, they went into business on their own. Predicated on the plausible assumption that sisters are reluctant to talk freely in the presence of laymen, Marillac is open only to the religious. This approach has been widely criticized—within the Conference as well as outside.[71] The critics believe that the sisters would be better off in a less sheltered setting, and some even urge their dispersal to non-Catholic universities.

In complicated maneuverings we have never been able fully to unravel, the Conference was caught in the post-Johannine backlash, along with many other liberal Catholic ginger groups. As often happened in Church struggles prior to the emergence of freewheeling journals such as *The National Catholic Reporter*, the Conference was curtailed quietly and privately rather than dramatically and publicly. It was, indeed, not officially curtailed at all, but merely "reformed." Some of its originating figures are scattered. But its spirit lives, not only in a few local efforts but in the concern of many Catholic women's colleges with the issues it so forcefully raised.

[71] A brief breezy description of the arguments that swirl around Marillac can be found in Wakin. His book portrays St. Louis University, Catholic University, Notre Dame, Rosary, Rosary Hill, St. John's at Collegeville, and Marymount College in Virginia, each pretty much in its own terms.

Defining a Clientele: Geography

As we noted earlier, Catholic colleges are almost all run by national and international teaching orders rather than by local bishops, and they are free to solicit and accept students from wherever they please. A few have taken advantage of this freedom to establish national constituencies. Notre Dame helped put Catholic higher education (and, indeed, American Catholicism generally) on the map with its famous football teams, and it is now trying to do the same thing academically. It seeks students from all over who will help in this effort, and rejects local boys who will not, letting them attend other nearby Catholic colleges. At the graduate level Catholic University is also a national institution, appealing mainly to the more devout Catholics and especially to the religious. Georgetown has had considerable national appeal for Catholic undergraduates, and a number of other urban Jesuit universities such as Boston College, Fordham, and St. Louis have now built dormitories and are trying to move down this same road. Among the women's colleges, too, there have been a few whose social and academic prestige extended beyond their immediate area. Manhattanville in Westchester County and Trinity in the District of Columbia are the best-known instances, but a number of others also recruit from the national rather than the local upper-middle class.

National Catholic colleges are, however, exceptional. The typical Catholic college, like its typical public counterpart, has defined its constituency geographically and then tried to be all things (or at least most things) to the Catholics within its area. Like a public institution it has been reluctant to exclude the academically inept, the socially unrefined, or the financially pinched student. It has felt a measure of religious responsibility to these students, and it has also felt that exclusion of any sort would narrow its political and economic support within the diocese. In this respect Catholic colleges have differed to some degree from their more successful Protestant counterparts, which have tended to define their clientele in less geographic and more social or meritocratic terms.

Catholic localism was to some extent a by-product of poverty. Big-city Catholics have seldom felt they could afford to send their children away to college, and this meant that the Catholic system almost had to include a network of urban commuter colleges. The Jesuits took the lead in establishing such a network, but their efforts have been supplemented by a number of other orders.

In other cases, however, localism had no compelling economic justification. The Catholic like the non-Catholic system has developed not only "streetcar colleges" for the economically pinched but "suitcase colleges" for the psychologically pinched. These latter colleges have dormitories and cost as much as any other residential college, but they recruit most of their students from within a hundred miles of the campus. Students can thus take their laundry home on weekends and go on dating home town boys or girls. Some students choose these colleges because they are too timid (or their parents too protective) to go farther from home. Others are too ignorant to know that another Catholic college in another part of the country might be better for them. Yet their ignorance is partly a by-product of the character of the Catholic colleges themselves, very few of which have deserved or had national reputations. The typical high school student, Catholic or otherwise, will go to a distant college only if he believes he will find something special there. While we would argue that for many students a sharp break with family and peers is often an end in itself, justifying the choice of a remote college even if it has no other virtues, few parents or students see it that way. And except for remoteness from home and from neighborhood chums, very few Catholic colleges offer a prospective student an experience significantly different from what he could get in his own diocese. Even those colleges that do offer something special may not be known to students or teachers in the Catholic secondary schools, where the level of information about Catholic higher education is no greater than the level of information about non-sectarian colleges in the public schools.

Not only is the localism of Catholic higher education sometimes economically unnecessary—it may even be economically costly. There are, for example, six Catholic four-year colleges and two Catholic junior colleges in the state of Iowa. While several of the four-year colleges have appreciable numbers of commuters, all are predominantly residential. Since the Catholic population of Iowa is relatively modest (Iowa's Catholic high schools graduated fewer than 5,000 students in 1964), the existence of six competing residential liberal arts colleges almost guarantees that none will achieve distinction. The six four-year colleges now award almost 1,000 B.A.s a year between them, but individually this means their graduating classes average about 160. This would not necessarily be cause for alarm if the colleges in question were rich enough to provide diverse faculty and facilities for small student bodies. But they are not rich. The four-year colleges have more than 300,000 volumes in their collective libraries, but this leaves only 50,000 volumes in the typical campus library. The number of subdisciplines in which any one of these colleges can boast a faculty expert is similarly limited.

Fragmentation of effort is, of course, by no means confined to

Catholics. (There are also between fourteen and sixteen Protestant colleges in Iowa, depending on how one defines "Protestant.") Nonetheless, fission is somewhat harder to justify in a church that prides itself on unity than in a non-church that is really no more than a collection of separate denominations. The best that can be said for the Catholic college situation in Iowa is that having a lot of small campuses may allow more students to develop a greater feeling of confidence and competence than would be possible if all Iowa's Catholic colleges were consolidated into a single Catholic university of perhaps six thousand students. Consolidation might be better for the most enterprising and competent students, but somewhat worse for the shy, the slow, and the uncertain, who might be overwhelmed by competition and by professional standards they felt they had no chance of meeting.

While many Catholic educators doubt that small, isolated Catholic colleges can do an adequate job of education, new ones continue to be founded. A new Catholic women's college has, for example, recently opened in Bismarck, North Dakota. When one of us asked an enterprising and vivacious sister who had played a part in its creation why she thought it necessary, she reported that there were many Catholic girls in North Dakota, particularly farm girls, who thought Minnesota colleges like St. Catherine's and St. Theresa's impossibly far away. Some Catholics would argue that in that case she should have opened a Catholic junior college, which would have broadened rural and small-town horizons and encouraged the girls in question to transfer after two years. Others maintain that religious energy would be better invested in enlivening and enriching the Catholic community at North Dakota's state institutions. But in a system that has no master plans and no central policy-making body there will always be some entrepreneurs who reject these alternatives and found new colleges. Given their willingness to live in poverty, and given sufficient readiness among Catholic educators, parents, and students to assume that any Catholic college, however marginal, is better than any non-Catholic one, these ventures have a fair chance of staying afloat.

Defining a Clientele: Class

A class analysis of Catholic higher education, past and future, must begin with two basic sets of facts. First, there are the economic constraints and pressures that affect all private colleges in their competition with state and municipal ones, described in Chapter VI. Second, there are the social and intellectual constraints and pressures

peculiar to Catholic institutions, which affect their competitive position vis-à-vis private non-sectarian colleges and a few leading state
universities. The first set of forces mainly affects the college choices
of children from the Catholic lower and lower-middle classes. The
second set affects mainly the choices of the Catholic upper-middle
and upper classes.

We have no historical data on the proportion of Catholic children
from uneducated families attending college, but it must have been
higher than among comparable Protestant families. Otherwise the educational gap between Catholics and Protestants would be as wide
today as it was at the turn of the century, whereas in fact it has
entirely disappeared. The Catholics' ability to narrow this gap over
the years doubtless rested partly on their being concentrated in big
cities. The parochial school system may also have played a role.
Whether the Catholic colleges were an asset or a liability is, however,
more problematic. We have no data on the socioeconomic background
of Catholic college students in earlier times. But given what we know
about previous generations of students at colleges in general, and
about the current relationship of Catholic college recruitment to that
of colleges in general, it seems likely that the Catholic colleges always
got the majority of their students from white-collar rather than blue-
collar families. The same was, of course, true even of public colleges,
but these latter probably attracted more poor Catholics, partly because they were cheaper and partly because, being neither Irish nor
clerical, they appealed to many newer immigrants who found the
American Catholic establishment even more alien than the relatively
neutral public-Protestant establishment.[72] Yet despite their appeal to
many poor Catholics, public colleges were relatively rare in cities
with large Catholic populations. In part this reflected state legislators'
fear of urban wickedness, but in part it reflected the Catholic hierarchy's opposition to public institutions that competed directly with
Catholic ones. In this sense the existence of Catholic colleges reduced
the academic opportunities open to poor urban Catholics rather than
increasing them.

In recent years this pattern has changed somewhat. Tuition charges
at all private colleges, including Catholic ones, have risen faster than
room-and-board charges at public colleges. It is now usually more
expensive to commute to a Catholic college than to go away to a
public one. At the same time, state universities that have traditionally been in small towns are opening commuter campuses in the

[72] For evidence on the relative affluence of today's Catholic college students
see Astin, Panos, and Creager, "National Norms." For comparisons of Catholic
B.A.s from Catholic and non-Catholic colleges in 1961 see Greeley, *Religion and
Career*, table 5.1.

major urban centers of their states. As tax subsidies for state institutions rise, Catholic colleges find themselves at more and more of
an economic disadvantage. The problem is accentuated by the lag in
religious vocations, for this means the Catholic colleges must rely ever
more heavily on salaried lay professors and that their costs are thus
escalating at an unusually rapid rate.[73] Catholic colleges' tuition, like
private colleges' tuition generally, is climbing faster than the income
of their traditional clientele. The impact of this on recruitment is
particularly acute at the Catholic commuter colleges, for while these
colleges cost less than residential ones, the percentage increase in
their charges is relatively more rapid.[74] While working-class incomes
are also rising, working-class Catholics are not likely to want to spend
their hard-won wage increases sending their children to an expensive
Catholic college if a cheap public one is available in the same city—
especially if the public college is also attended mainly by other
Catholics. Few Catholic colleges have large scholarship programs.[75]
The major burden of educating the lower-income Catholic population
is therefore likely to fall increasingly on public institutions.

Since growth in college enrollment over the next generation is likely
to be concentrated in the less educated and less affluent classes,
Catholic colleges will almost inevitably get a declining share of total
Catholic enrollment. Historically, about a third of all the Catholics
who attended college seem to have done so at Catholic institutions.[76]
The proportion may have risen somewhat after World War II, especially as a result of the GI Bill, but our best estimate is that only
25 per cent of all Catholics in the Class of 1970 entered Catholic
colleges. By 1985 the proportion is expected to fall below 20 per cent.

[73] As we indicated earlier, the long-term savings to a college from having a
religious faculty may be less than they seem. Still, the costs of training,
retirement, and the like have usually been carried by the order rather than by
particular colleges, so from an institutional viewpoint religious faculty were
cheap. Many orders now charge their colleges for services rendered by their
members, thus clarifying the cost-accounting problem and reducing the economic
incentive to hire religious.

[74] Illustratively, if tuition were rising 10 per cent per annum while room and
board were rising 5 per cent and if tuition in a given year were $1,200 while
room and board was $800, the next year's increase in charges at a commuter
college would be $120, while the increase for a residential college would be $160.
This would be a 10 per cent increase for the commuter compared to an 8 per cent
increase for the resident.

[75] Catholic colleges give scholarships to a smaller proportion of their students
than either Protestant or private non-sectarian colleges, though the average size of
their awards is larger than at the Protestant colleges. Tuition charges average the
same as at Protestant colleges, less than at private non-sectarian ones. See Nash,
Nash, and Goldstein, table 3.3.

[76] Greeley and Rossi, table 7.2, report that in their random sample of adult
Catholics born between 1906 and 1940, 117 of the 367 college graduates reported attending a Catholic institution.

Since Catholics who attend non-Catholic colleges concentrate in public institutions, and these have high attrition rates, the proportion of Catholics taking B.A.s at Catholic colleges will probably remain higher than the proportion entering such colleges—perhaps 35 per cent in 1965 and 25 per cent in 1985.[77]

[77] The National Opinion Research Center survey of June 1961 B.A.s showed that 25 per cent were Catholics. (James Davis, *Great Aspirations,* table 1.2d.) Greeley's subsample from this survey was 27 per cent Catholic (Greeley, *Religion and Career,* table 2.1). Astin, Panos, and Creager, "National Norms," found that 28 per cent of all 1966 freshmen were Catholics. Panos and Astin have also found that over-all attrition between freshmen and senior year is the same for Catholics and non-Catholics (see their "Attrition").
Estimates of the distribution of Catholics between Catholic and non-Catholic colleges show less agreement. Greeley, *Religion and Career,* table 5.1, shows that 14 per cent of all June, 1961, B.A.s were Catholics from Catholic colleges, while 13 per cent were Catholics from non-Catholic colleges. This suggests that more than half of all Catholics were attending Catholic colleges. The National Catholic Welfare Conference's 1962 *Summary of Catholic Education,* on the other hand, reports total Catholic college B.A.s for 1961 equal to only 9.9 per cent of the Office of Education total for all colleges in the same year. Part of the discrepancy between this and Greeley's 14 per cent figure may be accounted for by the fact that non-Catholic colleges award more degrees in February and September. Thus Greeley's June sample probably included more Catholic college B.A.s than would a sample for the entire year.
Assuming that the NCWC-USOE estimate is correct, and that Catholic colleges awarded 9.9 per cent of all B.A.s in 1961, we must adjust this figure to exclude non-Catholics. Astin, Panos, and Creager, "National Norms," show that 8 per cent of the freshmen entering four-year Catholic college were non-Catholics. The figure for Catholic universities was presumably higher. If we assume that 9 per cent of all Catholic college B.A.s were non-Catholics, we are left with an estimate of 9.0 for the percentage of 1961 B.A.s awarded to Catholics at Catholic colleges.
At this point we have two choices. One is to assume that the 25–28 per cent figure given by Greeley and by Astin, Panos and Creager for Catholics' share of all degrees is correct. In that case about one Catholic in three gets his B.A. from a Catholic college. Another possibility is that Greeley's estimate of the number of Catholics getting B.A.s from non-Catholic colleges is correct, while our adjusted NCWC-USOE estimate of the number of Catholics getting B.A.s from Catholic colleges is correct. Greeley estimates that Catholics received 14.8 per cent of the B.A.s awarded by non-Catholic colleges in 1961. Since these colleges awarded 90 per cent of all B.A.s, this would mean that Catholics from non-Catholic colleges constituted 13.3 per cent of the over-all total, while Catholics from Catholic colleges constituted 9.0 per cent. Taken together these figures would mean that Catholics accounted for 22.3 per cent of all B.A.s rather than 25–28 per cent. They would also mean that Catholic colleges awarded 40 per cent of all the B.A.s going to Catholics, instead of 33 per cent.
Whatever the correct figure, it is clear that the proportion of B.A.s awarded by Catholic colleges is higher than the proportion of freshmen entering these colleges. Comparison of USOE with NCWC data for 1961 shows, e.g. that while Catholic colleges awarded 9.9 per cent of all B.A.s they enrolled only 8.4 per cent of all undergraduates. This presumably means that they enrolled less than 8 per cent of all freshmen in 1961. Assuming that a quarter of all freshmen were Catholics, the Catholic colleges enrolled less than a third of them. Our best guess is about 30 per cent. These enrollment statistics are, however, full of pitfalls. Working with USOE data for the fall of 1963, for example, Nash, Nash, and

Catholic colleges have recently been enrolling about a fifth of all students in the private sector, and that figure seems steady. The decline in their share of total enrollment has been part of the general decline in the size of the private sector relative to the public one. Catholics seem as willing as Protestants and Jews to enroll in state and municipal colleges if their social and economic circumstances push them in this direction.[78] Catholic colleges are likely to respond to this fact in the same way as other private colleges. Most will try to become elite institutions for a predominantly upper-middle class clientele that is willing to pay extra for the presumed virtues of private instruction and a private college B.A. Many—perhaps most—of the originally Protestant colleges have long since succumbed to such pressure.

The Catholic college which wants to compete with the public sector in terms of "quality," be it social or academic, faces a number of problems. Catholic colleges have not traditionally been either intellectually or socially exclusive. Most of their students have been drawn from the lower-middle class, just as many of the students at public institutions were. This might not be a problem if the Catholic upper-middle class were numerous and sure of its ground. Its children could then attend colleges like Notre Dame and Holy Cross and could create elite subcultures at odds with the dominant ethos of the campus, just as happened in the better state universities. But few Catholic colleges have encouraged this. For one thing, most Catholic colleges forbid or at any rate do not encourage fraternities or sororities, which have been one of the primary devices by which large state universities kept the social elite happy on a predominantly non-elite campus. The more sophisticated members of the Catholic upper-middle class have often shied away from sending their children to Catholic colleges, whose public piety and football orientation seemed unlikely to lead to the kind of adult life they wanted for their young.

Goldstein, table 3.1, report that Catholic colleges enrolled 9 per cent of all students, while USOE-NCWC comparisons for that year show 8 per cent.

Between 1961 and 1965 unpublished USOE statistics show that the Catholic colleges' share of total enrollment fell from 8.4 to 7.5 per cent. This meant that their share of freshmen enrollment must have been less than 7 per cent by the fall of 1966, when Astin, Panos, and Creager found that 28 per cent of all entering freshmen described themselves as Catholics. If 8 per cent of the freshmen at Catholic colleges were non-Catholics, the Catholic colleges enrolled less than 25 per cent of all Catholic freshmen. If this is correct, Callahan and Clifford's prediction that Catholic colleges will enroll only 20 per cent of all Catholic undergraduates in 1985 may prove high rather than low.

[78] Astin, Panos, and Creager, "National Norms," shows that 27 per cent of all freshmen at public institutions were Catholic, compared to 28 per cent of all freshmen everywhere. Catholics were underrepresented only at private non-Catholic colleges.

The same has been true of those Catholic children who wanted to escape the prim Catholic lower-middle class world in which they were raised. They have seen their opportunities in the same non-sectarian terms as non-Catholics did. They therefore wanted to acquire credentials that would open doors in established secular institutions, and they rightly opined that no Catholic college B.A. had quite the same magic as a B.A. from a leading non-sectarian private college. Even if there had been a Catholic college that was as good academically as the best non-Catholic ones (and there wasn't), the very fact of being Catholic and therefore presumptively parochial would have been a handicap. (The same would have been true of any college with what Americans regarded as a narrowly defined constituency.)

Today the number of young Catholics in this category is growing. The Catholic colleges, having served as a decompression chamber for those climbing out of the immigrant Catholic ghetto, have now been deprived of this traditional function by changes in what is left of that ghetto, by public competition, and by changes in the economics of higher education. If they are to survive they must define and seek out a new clientele, composed primarily of the sons and daughters of their own alumni. These children have in most respects already escaped the more obvious limitations of traditional parish Catholicism, and they no longer want or need the protection of a Catholic college against the competition of non-Catholic ideas and individuals. They will choose a Catholic college only if it is as socially and academically attractive as its non-Catholic competitors.

While we have little systematic data on the current college preferences of the ablest and most sophisticated young Catholics, the choices of National Merit Scholarship winners provide some evidence. During the late 1950s, 42 per cent of the Catholic men receiving NMSC awards chose Catholic colleges, while 48 per cent of the women did so.[79] These proportions were probably somewhat higher than the proportion of less gifted Catholics choosing Catholic colleges during these same years, but they hardly provide grounds for complacency among Catholic educators. Most Catholics, after all, opted out of the Catholic system because they could not afford it and felt obliged to attend cheap public institutions. While this may in some ways have loosened their ties to the Church, it did not necessarily indicate basic reservations about the adequacy of Catholic colleges.

[79] The NMSC does not collect religious data until after its winners have graduated from college. A follow-up is, however, available on winners in the years 1956–59. The data on college choices of Catholic winners was generously tabulated at our request by Dr. Robert C. Nichols of the National Merit Scholarship Corporation. It is worth noting that Catholic men were only about half as likely as non-Catholics to win NMSC awards during these years.

On the contrary, many Catholics in public colleges would have attended a Catholic one if they had had enough money and could have met the admissions standards.[80] The Merit Scholars *did* have enough money to attend Catholic colleges, and all met Catholic college admissions standards. Yet they *still* did not mostly turn to Catholic colleges. They left the Catholic sector for non-sectarian private colleges or leading state universities rather than for low-tuition public commuter colleges. If the Catholic colleges are to become a major force in American higher education they certainly cannot afford to lose their appeal to such students, for it is clear they cannot compete numerically with state-subsidized institutions for run-of-the-mill undergraduates.

The implications of public competition have not, however, been fully digested at most Catholic colleges any more than at most still-Protestant ones. Some Catholic colleges are now eager to become universities or university colleges appealing to top students, but others resist this sort of secular tendency as they have resisted so many others. The pace setter in the academic revolution as in many other aspects of Catholic collegiate development is the Society of Jesus. The Jesuits are by far the largest Catholic teaching order, conducting twenty-eight colleges in America. Almost all their colleges are located in major cities. These tend to be both the largest Catholic college in their metropolitan area and the most academically distinguished, though there are a few exceptions. St. John's on Long Island (conducted by the Vincentians) is larger than the Jesuits' Fordham in the Bronx, though it is hardly competitive in any other respect. The Vincentians' De Paul in Chicago is almost as large as the Jesuits' Loyola, and perhaps freer and more open as well. La Salle in Philadelphia, conducted by the Brothers of the Christian Schools, is larger than the Jesuits' St. Joseph's in the same city, though neither has any claim to academic eminence. Catholic University in Washington is almost as large as the Jesuits' Georgetown and in some departments more distinguished. The more typical pattern, however, is that of Boston and St. Louis, where the Jesuits' institutions (Boston College and St. Louis University) are not only the most academically respectable in their area but much the largest. While no Jesuit university faculty is as good as Notre Dame (conducted by the tiny Congregation of the Holy Cross), the other leading Catholic universities are all Jesuit. And while no Jesuit college probably does as much for its students as the best Catholic women's colleges, the latter are too small, too poor,

[80] We have no data to support this proposition except casual conversation. It is clear, however, that Catholics at Catholic colleges are richer than Catholics at non-Catholic colleges, and probably also brighter.

and too handicapped by the stigma of being run by and for women to have much impact on the larger Catholic system.

Always involved, often controversial, never monastic, the Jesuits have long been the Church's most worldly teaching order and the most responsive to new developments in the secular academic world. In Europe they were for this reason the tutors of the Catholic aristocracy. Perhaps they could have followed the same course in America, founding Catholic counterparts to Yale, Williams, and Oberlin, but they didn't. European Jesuits founded some of the American Jesuit colleges, but their successors were shaped by America as well as by their international order, and particularly by their experience as an ethnic and religious minority in an Anglo-Protestant milieu. They still saw *themselves* as an elite cadre, but they never concentrated their educational efforts on a corresponding *lay* elite. Perhaps this was because, unlike their intellectual counterparts in the Protestant clergy, American Jesuits have hardly ever been recruited from the Catholic upper classes, or felt at home with them. An American Catholic who became a Jesuit was almost always taking a step up in the world. This step seldom implied or allowed a complete shift in allegiances. The Jesuits have therefore usually sought students such as they themselves once were: bright and ambitious but not cultivated or affluent. (Given their subdivision into largely autonomous Provinces, the Jesuits might have had a hard time establishing socially and intellectually refined colleges even if they had wanted to. There were not enough suitable Catholic students to fill such a college in any single city, and probably not enough in any single Province. It would have had to be a national effort, and that would have been administratively difficult.)

In their own personal lives Jesuits have made time for contemplation and prayers, but their colleges have reflected the hard-driving, workmanlike qualities of the American professional classes and the no-nonsense austerity of the upwardly mobile. Indeed, the Jesuits' disciplined dedication, ability to master academic detail, and willingness to submit to anonymous verdicts (in the form of censorship) from fellow professionals all remind us of the older generation of American physicians. Their distaste for aestheticism, their lack of interest in most speculative theorizing, and their generally unshakable confidence that they are working for a good cause, also show a kinship with the medical profession. There have nonetheless been decisive differences. Jesuit "practicality" has been more explicitly shaped by theology and philosophy than its medical analogue. Then too American medical schools since Flexner have been academically and economically exclusive, while the Jesuit colleges have been rather the reverse.

On the academic front, the Jesuits have traditionally put more resources into expanding their faculties and facilities than into raising salaries or improving the program for existing students. While many Jesuit colleges have been unable to grow fast enough to accommodate all applicants, none has yet tried to become as selective as the leading secular colleges. In one sense this reflects the relative scarcity of brilliant applicants to Jesuit colleges; but if the Jesuits had kept their colleges smaller they might well have been able to establish much higher average levels of academic ability.

On the social front, Jesuit colleges have given dormitories lower priority than other budget items. With a handful of exceptions, such as Holy Cross and Spring Hill, they have therefore remained predominantly commuter colleges. Despite such "collegiate" symbols as the winning football teams of earlier eras and the neo-Gothic architecture that unfortunately survives into the present, the Jesuits' institutions have had trouble escaping the social taint of being "streetcar colleges."

The Jesuit colleges were also slow to raise their tuition charges, even though this traditionally meant paying their lay faculty second-class salaries and in most cases attracting second-rate men. The avowed reason for not raising tuition was the incapacity of many Catholic families to pay more. But this could have been dealt with by charging higher tuition only to the affluent and offering more scholarships to others. Low tuition reflected fear that rich Catholics would not pay "Ivy League" rates for a commuter college, either because they preferred a truly Ivy League college or because they preferred to spend their money on other things. In addition, priests who had taken vows of poverty may have been ambivalent about putting the financial squeeze on parents of limited means so as to pay high salaries to lay faculty. There have always been some priests who felt that if a layman could be lured or kept only by a fancy salary he was not really dedicated either to education or to the Catholic cause, and that it would be no loss if he went elsewhere.

The Jesuit colleges are now under considerable though very uneven pressure to alter this situation. For one thing, the Jesuits have been affected by the debate over the state of Catholic intellectual life.[81] There is a Jesuit Educational Association and a Conference of Presidents of Jesuit Colleges and Universities, and while these and similar communication networks have no real authority, they make Jesuits more self-conscious about the fact that none of their institutions ranks academically with leading secular institutions. Some are merely de-

---

[81] This debate, now more than a decade old, has produced a library of its own. Among the more significant early contributions were John Tracy Ellis, "American Catholics"; O'Dea, *American Catholic Dilemma;* Weigel, "American Catholic Intellectualism."

fensive about the fact that Protestants and Jews look down on Catholics intellectually, and want to show that Catholic colleges can win at physics as well as football. But others have a more personal sense of disquiet about the unreflective mindlessness of American Catholicism, wanting to change this because they themselves find it distasteful, not because others do.

There are, in addition, more narrowly institutional pressures on the Jesuit colleges to adopt a new style. It was one thing for the Jesuits to "lose" some sons of the old Catholic elite, whom no amount of ingenuity was likely to lure to a predominantly lower-middle class Irish Catholic college anyway; it is something else to lose the sons of one's own alumni. Today there is a growing body of college applicants whose fathers attended Jesuit colleges, got good professional or managerial jobs, moved to suburbia, want "only the best" for their children, and can afford to pay for it. Some of these fathers have an emotional tie to their alma mater, but others do not want their sons to attend a commuter college, which seems tied to the ghetto past rather than the affluent, ecumenical future. Even in families where the father would be pleased if his son went to such a college, the son may have been raised in such a way that he finds this prospect unattractive. He often wants a college that will remove him physically and psychologically from home and that will ensure him entrée in both Catholic and non-Catholic circles. While very few of these students inquire about the scholarly reputation of the faculty at the colleges they are considering, a number do ask if its B.A. will serve as a ticket to a "good" graduate school. And in a more general sense, many more prospective applicants from good suburban schools and college-oriented families are influenced by grapevine judgments about "quality," which derive at least indirectly from the reputation of various colleges' faculties.

Like other professors, the typical Jesuit prefers students who come to college with a fair amount of cultural sophistication, who are at home with books and abstract ideas, who score high on verbal aptitude tests, and who can figure out the "right" answers to complex questions. (The otherworldly priest who cares mainly for his students' souls is increasingly rare on Catholic faculties.) Few Jesuits want students who are really critical, rebellious, or abrasive, but then neither do most secular scholars want such students, despite sporadic protestations to the contrary. The Jesuits talk a great deal about teaching students to think, and the heavy doses of theology and philosophy seem to provide a good deal of training in the formal manipulation of abstract ideas. They seem less interested in teaching students to observe as well as reason, which may be one reason for the scarcity of good social

scientists on Jesuit faculties. Most of the Jesuit colleges are still seeking the same sorts of applicants as the medical schools and the military academies: all-American boys, sober, hard-working, intelligent,
responsible, untroubled, able to learn quickly within a framework
defined by others. Such students are expected to show only enough
inclination to apostasy to make clear that their faith is more than a
matter of inadvertence.

But these are also the students most eagerly sought by the majority
of non-sectarian private colleges. In order to get them, the Jesuits must
not only make their colleges more attractive than nearby public institutions but more attractive than, say, Wellesley or Claremont. This
is not easy, though a variety of efforts are being made. Low interest
federal loans for dormitories have enabled a number of Jesuit colleges to become more residential at little cost. Applications have
risen faster than either capital gifts or available faculty, making it
easy to justify raising tuition and letting lower-income Catholics attend the expanding urban public colleges. Rising applications have
also encouraged the Jesuits to raise academic requirements for admission. While this has by no means been thought of as a device for
excluding first-generation collegians, high standards do tend to have
this effect.

Despite these gradual changes in orientation, however, the Jesuits
have yet to create a college that would be attractive on non-religious
grounds to the sons of the Catholic social and intellectual elite. Boston
College does not compete in the same intellectual or social league
with Harvard, nor is Holy Cross a Catholic Amherst. Fordham cannot
offer anything like the advantages of Columbia, nor can Loyola compete with the University of Chicago. Even in an area like St. Louis,
where the secular institutions have had a less distinguished tradition
and the Jesuits have in recent years moved forward very rapidly under an extraordinary president, St. Louis University has caught up
with its nearby non-sectarian rival, Washington University, on only a
few fronts. The District of Columbia is probably the only major city
in the country where the Catholic institutions are academically as
good or better than their non-Catholic rivals. Georgetown, being the
oldest Catholic university as well as one of the richest, has attracted
the sons of some Catholic "first families" and has developed ties with
the Foreign Service and other prestige-bearing professions. Since
Washington also has Catholic University, some of whose graduate
programs are adequate if not distinguished, the city probably has
as many competent Catholic faculty and students as any in America.
Even so, the standing of its Catholic institutions reflects not only
their achievements but the mediocrity of their non-Catholic rivals.

Elsewhere, the Catholic youngster who wants "the best" in traditional academic and professional terms usually finds he cannot get this in the Catholic sector, and he makes his choice accordingly. While his parents may rightly say that the local Catholic college is "better than it was in my day," few will consciously sacrifice their children's careers in the name of religious orthodoxy.

Aside from the Jesuit universities, the only Catholic institution that has much prospect of attracting the sons of the Catholic elite is Notre Dame. Notre Dame has had a residential tradition, but it has never sought to remain small or exclusive. Today, under a president who wants to compete with the Big Ten academically as well as athletically, Notre Dame is making enormous efforts to upgrade its faculty, to break new ground in research (both connected and unconnected with the Church), and to win government grants and contracts. It has made special efforts to lure both Catholic and non-Catholic liberals and to establish close ties with Catholic social action programs in Latin America. By hiring "controversial" professors like Samuel Shapiro (whose departure from Michigan State's Oakland branch was clouded by charges that he was a Castro sympathizer) and James Silver (who was driven out of the University of Mississippi by racists), it has sought to reassure both insiders and outsiders about its commitment to academic freedom. It has also sought to move into the social sciences and the arts in a way that few other Catholic men's colleges have done. Notre Dame has more National Merit Scholars than any other Catholic college; it now has an exchange program with nearby St. Mary's College; yet many sensitive and cosmopolitan sons of the Catholic social and intellectual elites think it an old-fashioned, staid college where one can pray for football victories. Reflecting the past more than the present, a Notre Dame diploma still does not impress non-Catholics in positions of power in the way that a Yale or Stanford one does.

Nor have the smaller Catholic men's colleges managed to become elite institutions. The Benedictines have shared the widespread American hostility to the city and have established a number of residential colleges in monastic rural settings. These try to preserve the flesh from some temptations while exposing the spirit to otherwise forgotten or neglected possibilities.[82] Yet these colleges have never attained the academic reputability of the Jesuits' best institutions, much less of places like Wesleyan or Carleton. And while educated American

[82] St. John's University in Collegeville, Minnesota, is the best known of these institutions, though its principal distinction is its stunning architecture. The nearby Benedictine Abbey has been an innovator in liturgical reform, but the spirit does not seem to have touched many undergraduates. St. John's is unusual, too, in still having a predominantly clerical faculty.

Catholics, both clerical and lay, often distrust the Jesuits, either as too worldly, too organizationally disciplined, or both, they are not interested in a college whose only distinction is spiritual. As a result, the colleges in question attract comparatively few students from urbane college-educated families.

The women's colleges, catering as they do to students who are not especially worried about impressing prospective non-Catholic employers, have had an easier time attracting the children of the Catholic elite. An order such as the Religious of the Sacred Heart is receptive to new intellectual currents and maintains comparatively high academic standards in most of its schools and colleges (which include Manhattanville, Barat, and Newton). At the same time, these sisters have maintained a strict rule and have lived much less in the secular world than the Jesuits. We could not prove it, but they seem to come from more prosperous and cultured families than most Jesuits. They have, moreover, made a conscious effort to attract the Catholic elite to their colleges. This has meant putting money into dormitories rather than expanding to enroll more commuters. Perhaps more important, it has meant dealing with rising applications by restricting enrollment more than the Jesuits have. The Sacred Heart colleges also charge higher tuition than the Jesuit colleges. All this has kept out the less affluent students and has allowed the upper-middle and upper-class Catholic minority to set the tone on some campuses. As a result, a college like Manhattanville is socially more like Wellesley than Notre Dame is like Yale.

It is easier for sisters to cater to upper-strata parental prejudices about feminine higher education than for priests to cater to these same parents' prejudices about masculine higher education. Many fathers who care about the academic and professional standing of their sons' college have no comparable concern about their daughters'. They are interested in a college's capacity to teach poise and gracious living, keep a girl chaste, and prevent her marrying the wrong man, but not in its effect on her intellectual development or career. In the East such a father may acknowledge that Catholic colleges like Manhattanville, New Rochelle, and Trinity are not academically equal to Radcliffe, Bryn Mawr, and Barnard, but may still think this beside the point unless he has an extraordinarily high-powered daughter. Outside the East, even academically oriented parents or students may choose a Catholic college simply because they disapprove of coeducation. If a Midwestern family wants to keep a daughter within a few hundred miles of home and avoid coeducation, a Catholic college like Barat, Rosary, St. Catherine's, or one of their less lively rivals is almost the only option. In California there are a few small non-

Catholic girls' colleges, such as Scripps, Pitzer, and Mills, but they are not patently better than Immaculate Heart in the same state.[83] Nevertheless, many if not most intellectually ambitious Catholic girls seem to feel that no Catholic college quite measures up, just as most comparable Protestant girls feel that no Protestant college does.

Defining a Clientele: Ethnicity

In addition to distinctions of sex and class, the analyst of Catholic higher education must constantly keep an attentive eye on ethnic differences. As already indicated, the Church has historically sought to minimize these differences by encouraging all Catholics from a particular parish to unite around a single church, school, and so forth. Ethnic parishes have mostly been abandoned, and ethnic differences in participation in various Catholic activities have tended to diminish somewhat over time.[84] In higher education, however, ethnicity has sometimes had more opportunity to make its weight felt. Colleges were not organized along strictly geographic lines, but rather by teaching orders free to draw selectively from as large an area as they could. Since many of the teaching orders had historic ties to one or another European country, they were often tempted to aim their American efforts at students who traced their ancestry to the same country and derived at least a few of their attitudes and interests from it. There was nothing in the system, for example, to discourage the Assumptionist Fathers in Worcester, Massachusetts, from setting up overtly French-oriented Assumption College in competition with the Jesuits' traditionally Irish and traditionally middle-class Holy Cross in the same city. Still less was there anything to prevent the Poles in Chicago from making De Paul "their" college while the Irish held to Loyola.

Nonetheless, strictly ethnic colleges have been as exceptional in the Catholic as in the Protestant sector, and for much the same reasons. First, as already indicated, attending a college was a step toward Americanization. Those first- and second-generation immigrants who had reservations about assimilation, who wanted to preserve the old language and the old folkways, were unlikely to send their children to college at all. Catholic colleges tended to avoid any overt activity that might cast doubt on the colleges' complete commitment to the American way. The mere fact of being Catholic seemed to raise

[83] Immaculate Heart is not academically selective, and the majority of its students commute; its quality lies in its faculty, and in terms of "value added."

[84] For trends in the use of parochial as against public schools among various ethnic groups, see Greeley and Rossi, table 2.16.

this doubt among many non-Catholics, including some who made much of America's religious pluralism and tolerance. For a college to fight for ethnic as well as religious separatism would have been to court more trouble than most educators thought necessary, especially when they could preserve the ethnic tradition covertly by identifying it with their particular brand of Catholicism.

A second reason for the relative scarcity of ethnic colleges was economic. Most Catholic colleges had a hard time attracting enough students in their early years, and they simply could not afford to discourage any Catholic applicant, whatever his ethnic background.[85] Even the Irish colleges, which were by far the most common, usually made a point of playing down their ethnic identification.[86] Indeed, even colleges like Assumption, whose initial raison d'être was ethnic, are now seeking a broader Catholic and even non-Catholic clientele. All these colleges now want bright students no matter what their background.

Yet perhaps the foregoing puts matters too cynically. Even where ethnic mixing has had no payoff in terms of institutional growth or academic selectivity, Catholic colleges have often sought it on ideological and moral grounds. There are very few Catholic colleges in the South, for example, but those there are have often led the way in racial integration. There is one Catholic college for Negroes (Xavier in New Orleans) but this is exceptional, if only because there are so few Negro Catholics. As almost always in America, the conflicting claims of religious and ethnic solidarity have eventually been resolved in favor of the former. No American college except perhaps Xavier has been ethnic first and Catholic second. None has tried to unite all Protestant and Catholic Irish-Americans, all Jewish and Catholic Polish-Americans, or all Protestant and Catholic Afro-Americans.

While overtly ethnic colleges have been rare, ethnic images and loyalties have nonetheless exercised a substantial effect on the college choices of many. Ethnic minorities have usually been extremely defensive vis-à-vis established groups. While this defensiveness has focused primarily on the Anglo-American majority, it has at times also included Irish-Americans, who today seem almost as well established and Americanized as the Anglo-Saxons. Many Italian-Americans have

[85] Some early nineteenth-century Catholic colleges were conducted by European priests who knew little or no English. In general, however, these colleges came too early to attract a specialized ethnic constituency, and by the time this came into existence the faculty had learned to work in English (or Irish).

[86] In 1959 when we wrote about Boston College as an "Irish" institution we found this was bitterly resented, presumably because it seemed to perpetuate a narrow identity at a time when BC like almost all Catholic colleges was trying to broaden its appeal. (The essay which evoked this response was later published in slightly revised form in Sanford, ed.)

felt as estranged from the local Irish-Catholic college as from the local Anglo-Protestant one.[87] They have therefore either skipped college entirely or sought out public institutions, especially urban commuter colleges, which were more ethnically anonymous (and also in many cases less expensive).

The influence of ethnic background on Catholics' college choices is illustrated by Table VIII, which gives the ethnic distribution of Catholics graduating from Catholic and non-Catholic colleges both for the over-all period 1927 to 1961, and separately for 1961.

TABLE VIII
ETHNIC BACKGROUND OF CATHOLICS BY TYPE OF COLLEGE

Ethnic Group	All Catholics Born between 1906 and 1940			Catholics Earning B.A.s in June 1961	
	Catholic College	Non-Catholic College	No College	Catholic College	Non-Catholic College
English	5	9	5	10	12
Irish	46	21	14	36	17
German	14	19	16	23	26
Italian	13	17	21	11	17
French	7	5	11	5	4
Polish	6	8	11	6	7
Other East Europe	5	10	10	3	4
Latin American	0	4	8	1	3
Other	5	7	4	5	10
Total	101	100	100	100	100
(N)	(110)	(243)	(1420)	(448)	(395)

SOURCE: Unpublished data from surveys by the National Opinion Research Center. The tabulations were generously made at our request by Father Andrew Greeley of NORC. As indicated in fn. 77, we think the apparent increase in the proportion of Catholics attending Catholic colleges is probably spurious.

The table makes two points clear. First, Catholic colleges have traditionally been overwhelmingly Irish. Whereas less than a quarter of the non-Irish collegians choose Catholic colleges, almost half of the Irish collegians did so. Or to put it another way: whereas the Irish constituted about 16 per cent of the adult Catholic population, they constituted 46 per cent of the Catholic college alumni. The second

---

[87] For a glimpse of Italian self-consciousness at "St. Patrick's College" (presumably Boston College) in the 1930s, see the comments of Chick Morelli in Whyte, p. 55; Morelli campaigned to have a course in Italian taught at what was then an overwhelmingly "Irish" college.

point suggested by the table is that the Irish role in the Catholic colleges has declined somewhat over the years, though it was still very marked in 1961. To what extent the declining proportion of Irish students in Catholic colleges reflects the declining importance of ethnicity, and to what extent it reflects the increased affluence of non-Irish parents who can afford to pay for Catholic as against public colleges, we cannot say. We suspect, however, that the former is as important as the latter.[88]

The Future of the Catholic Colleges

The crucial question confronting America's Catholic colleges today is much like that confronting her Protestant colleges, her Negro colleges, her women's colleges, her community colleges, and all the rest—whether the adjective (in this case "Catholic") has any real meaning in an era when the character of a place calling itself a "college" seems almost wholly prescribed by other established institutions, and especially by the nature of the graduate programs of leading universities.

A century ago there would have been little question that a "Catholic college" was defined in almost every respect primarily by the adjective "Catholic." Indeed, some Catholics and non-Catholics felt the institutions in question could hardly claim to be "colleges" at all, or at least not in the usual Anglo-American sense. Catholic colleges were wholly governed by the religious at a time when Protestant colleges had already begun to yield to lay control. They were staffed entirely by priests (and later nuns) who were trained primarily in theology and philosophy rather than in secular subjects, at a time when non-Catholic colleges were beginning to place growing emphasis on expertise in a particular secular specialty. They offered a program of studies whose form and substance derived from Catholic Europe, at a time when almost all non-Catholic institutions followed a quite different Anglo-American pattern.[89] They recruited Catholic students from the urban lower-middle class, most of whom had second-generation immigrant parents, at a time when most (though certainly not all) other colleges were getting students from more affluent, better-educated, and more fully Americanized families. Their purpose was primarily to strengthen these students' religious faith and commitment and to immunize them against dangerous secular ideas, at a time when

[88] Similar ethnic variations are found in the utilization of parochial schools, where cost is a less important factor. These variations are not eliminated by controlling for number of generations in America. See Greeley and Rossi, table 2.16.

[89] See Gleason; but see also Power, p. 55 and passim.

the leading non-Catholic colleges were beginning to encourage their students to explore secular ideas and trying to help them advance in the secular world.

Today all this has changed. On each of the foregoing counts the Catholic colleges have moved toward the secular norm. They have begun to appoint laymen to their boards of control, and they now seek faculty whose outlook is hard to distinguish from that of faculty at non-Catholic institutions. Even the religious faculty, now only a minority, are often trained in secular graduate schools as well as seminaries. The lay faculty are also more often trained in non-Catholic universities. Clerical and lay faculty alike want to expose their students to "outsiders," both because they want them to know what and how such men think and because they want to impress scholars of all faiths with the fact that Catholic colleges are now dedicated first and foremost to academic excellence—"regardless of race, creed, or color." Not surprisingly, such a faculty offers programs that resemble those of non-Catholic colleges in form and substance.

While most Catholic colleges still have overwhelmingly Catholic student bodies, even this sets them apart from non-Catholic institutions less than it once did. American Catholics are no longer poorer than American Protestants, and national opinion surveys show that Catholics and Protestants have the same range of attitudes on most issues. Leading Catholic universities are beginning to attract Protestants, Jews, and non-believers in much the way that Protestant colleges long ago began to do. These students seldom come to a Catholic college because of emotional or philosophical interest in Catholicism; they come because they cannot find (or get into) a non-Catholic university that offers the right courses at the right time in the right place at a price they can afford. Many nominal Catholics come to Catholic universities for the same reasons, and have only the most marginal interest in the fact that it is Catholic.[90]

Under these circumstances the question is no longer whether the places called "Catholic colleges" will also become "colleges" in the Anglo-American sense; they have almost all done so. The question is now whether the logic of their situation will allow them to remain "Catholic" in any recognizable sense. Will they embrace the academic revolution, warts and all, as many of the nominally Protestant colleges have done? Or will they hold back, continuing to look to the Church as well as to the leading secular universities for ideals and leadership?

Some Catholic educators argue that there is no necessary tension

[90] Some urban Catholic professional schools have been in this situation for a long time. We have the impression that the trend is accelerating, but we know of no national data from earlier times with which to compare recent estimates.

between an institution's becoming academically respectable and its remaining in some way distinctively Catholic. In principle they may be right. Certainly there is no persuasive evidence that at the individual level there is any irreconcilable tension between holding to the Catholic faith and contributing brilliantly to secular scholarship and science. But while a single individual may simultaneously be both a devout Catholic and distinguished scholar, it does not follow that a single institution can long meet both religious and professional payrolls. Many conflicts can be more easily reconciled, and many others more easily ignored, in the privacy of a man's conscience than in the bylaws of an institution.

A college is, among other things, a set of arrangements that enable its faculty and students to live and work together. Its form depends on which habits and values the participants share. Arrangements derived from a common set of religious values differ from arrangements derived from a common set of professional values. Take the single instance of faculty appointments. Academic professionals want their colleagues chosen on the basis of professional accomplishments, and they want them chosen by fellow professionals. An institution that refuses to follow these rules is unlikely to attract appreciable numbers of distinguished scholars over the years, for they will not regard it as a "real university." Yet we find it very hard to see how an institution that accepts these rules can long remain Catholic in any important sense. Surely the idea of a Catholic college or university implies some deviation from this narrowly professional and secular standard for choosing the membership of the community, some commitment to judging the human and more especially the moral qualifications of those who will teach the young. A secular university escapes this challenge by saying that it cannot pass valid judgment on such matters, except perhaps in extreme cases. If a Catholic institution takes the same position, however, what is left of the Church's pastoral commitments?

The leading secular universities are, we would argue, more and more shaped for (though not usually by) their faculties, often at considerable cost to others who have a stake in the institution. Their arrangements are extremely attractive to individuals with academic training and values, regardless of religion. Even devout Catholics who teach at these universities seldom chafe at the occupational culture in which they find themselves; on the contrary, it is the Catholic scholar at a Catholic college or university that deviates from secular academic norms who seems to chafe.[91] Most highly edu-

[91] See Donovan, *The Academic Man*, chap. 8. The stock complaints of Catholic college faculty almost all imply an invidious comparison between Catholic institutions and real or imagined secular alternatives.

cated Americans, Catholic or otherwise, evidently prefer institutions that embody professional aspirations and taboos. They see religion as a largely private affair. This does not necessarily mean they care less about their religion than about their secular work; on the contrary, many would argue in good American style that it was precisely because they cared *more* about their religion that they wanted to build a "wall of separation" protecting it from the claims of their employer.

Be that as it may, any college that insists on making religion a public and institutional matter seems to be fighting against the dominant American ethos—certainly the dominant professional ethos. It may hold out temporarily against secular pressures to "privatize" religion by drawing on nostalgia, institutional loyalty, and other non-professional motives. But while these motives have played an important part in keeping some distinguished institutions at the top of the pile, they are not likely to be very useful to upwardly mobile institutions such as the Catholic colleges and universities.

So while we ourselves are less than enamored of the secular graduate schools as models, we find it hard to see how the Catholic universities will invent acceptable alternatives. Under these circumstances we must return to the question of whether a reputable college or university can really be Catholic in any significant sense. Catholic educators ask themselves this question, and their more critical students ask it of them. We have never heard a really satisfactory answer given to it, and we have none to offer from our own experience. There is a recurrent hope that the richness of Catholic traditions, apart from specific creedal elements, may work against the fragmentation of learning that characterizes the secular university and against the divorce of introverted research from missionary teaching. There is also the hope that the Catholic tradition will help ensure that questions of ultimate concern have priority even if no professionally acceptable methodology has yet been devised for answering them. But the Protestant liberal arts colleges have had somewhat comparable hopes and claims. We can see no persuasive reason to suppose that American Catholicism will ultimately prove any better able than American Protestantism to mute the excesses and channel the energies of the academic profession.

In the short run some Catholic colleges will be able to justify their existence by participating in the renovation of their Church, building morale by attacking the traditionalism that still characterizes so much parish Catholicism (and a good deal of Vatican Catholicism as well). But creative as these colleges' role may be in the Church, and valuable as they may be in mediating between the claims of the Church and of the academic profession on the young, it is not easy to imagine how this will bring them a continuing supply of talented students. To do that they would have somehow to demonstrate that Catholicism helps fertilize the larger society, and especially that it enriches American intellectual life, as well as the other way round. Failing that, perhaps the most that a Catholic college or university can hope to do is to provide a good secular education while also helping its students explore in an informed and disciplined way the question of what it means to be a Catholic. If this is their mission, however, it might be accomplished better through various sorts of "released time" arrangements with secular institutions than through the operation of separate Catholic institutions. It could indeed be argued that this is the current drift of Catholic higher education: handing over most responsibility to laymen and freeing the religious for work on the specifically religious front with those students who are interested.

If we are correct in assuming that most Catholic colleges will embrace the academic disciplines and try to compete with non-Catholic colleges on the latter's terms, the next question is whether they will be able to catch up with what are now the leading secular universities and university colleges. In order to answer this question we must again view the Catholic colleges in two distinct if related ways. First, we must look at them as a species of the larger private genus and ask how they are likely to fare in competition with public institutions. Second, we must look at them as relatively underprivileged private institutions and ask what chance they have of improving their competitive position.

We discussed competition between private and public institutions and the deteriorating position of the former in Chapter VI. Even assuming that the Catholic colleges preserve their present share of the private market, it is unlikely to grow anywhere nearly as fast as the publicly subsidized one. As the private colleges' share of the market declines, Catholic colleges will be forced to define their prospective clientele more and more carefully. To some extent this will be done for them, since like other private colleges they will have to focus primarily on students who are willing to pay steadily rising tuition. Yet if we are right in assuming that Catholic colleges will share the ideals of secular universities, it seems likely that they will also be eager to attract academically promising students regardless of parental income. This will mean raising more money for scholarships, either from the state or from other sources. It will also mean raising academic requirements so as to exclude many students whose families could afford the tuition. The overlap between the well-heeled and the academically promising is, however, great enough so this should not be an insoluble problem.

Will Catholic colleges be able to attract able, sophisticated students? In general the answer is that they will be able to do so only if they significantly improve their present position relative to other private institutions. This raises the question of whether any underprivileged institution, be it Catholic or otherwise, has much chance of upward mobility in the next decade or two. Academic resources, both monetary and intellectual, will clearly be in short supply. Those institutions that have already achieved eminence will find it relatively easy to get more of these resources, while those with an undistinguished record will find this an uphill struggle.

The general rule of the academic world is that the rich grow richer even faster than the poor do. If one looks, for example, at scholarly ratings of universities over the years, one discovers very few new faces.[92] This stability is likely to continue. Quite aside from their Catholicism or lack of it, then, currently second-rank institutions are likely to be second-rank a generation hence. One or two Catholic institutions might break into the charmed circle if the Church were able to come up with a master plan concentrating resources on them, but this is unlikely. The pressure to spread resources is as great in the Church as elsewhere. Tomorrow's Catholic colleges are therefore likely to occupy much the same position in the academic spectrum as today's.

This does not mean that Catholic education cannot be improved. On the contrary, it will have to be improved simply to maintain its present competitive position. By objective indices such as student ability and motivation, faculty erudition and output, or library and laboratory facilities, academic institutions are better today than they were a generation ago, and are likely to be better a generation hence than they are today. Thus Fordham tomorrow may be better than NYU today, just as NYU today is in many ways better than Columbia a generation ago.[93] But Catholics are as competitive as non-Catholics, and sons want not only to do better than their fathers but better than their cousins. To satisfy this ambition Fordham must not only exceed its present level but narrow the gap between itself and the leaders. America seems to have reached the point where it will not allow a university like Columbia to go downhill even if its leadership is bankrupt, its location dysfunctional, and its faculty deteriorating. Faced with such a possibility the Ford Foundation or (in a more discreet way) the federal government will intervene to save the day— or at least try. Like any public utility, Columbia must be kept alive

---

[92] See Cartter, *An Assessment.*

[93] These comparisons are meant to be illustrative, not descriptive. There are plenty of students for whom Fordham is *today* better than NYU, and likewise there are fields in which NYU is now more innovative than Columbia.

and flourishing, rewarded for its blunders as well as its triumphs. The same is true of the other top secular universities with which Catholic institutions must now compete. So while a few elite institutions may slip from the top rung, this is certainly not likely to be common.[94]

The only development we can imagine upsetting this general prognosis would be a radical reorganization of Catholic higher education in America. Today this seems unlikely, but it is certainly not inconceivable. There is enormous ferment within the Church today, and higher education is not only one of the prime instigators but one of the main objects of discussion. More and more Catholics have begun to doubt that their Church has the financial or human resources to compete with public education on all fronts. Some have urged that the Church get out of the education business entirely, on the grounds that the money and personnel now tied up in this effort could be better deployed elsewhere (e.g. in missionary work overseas or in helping the dispossessed at home). Others have urged that the Church concentrate its efforts on higher education, while abandoning elementary education entirely. While no such radical departures seem likely, these and similar proposals may at least encourage the American hierarchy to consider some kind of Master Plan for Catholic education that would set priorities between different levels and within them. In higher education this would almost certainly mean a moratorium on new Catholic colleges. (In the last academic year for which we have data, 1964–65, the number of Catholic colleges listed by the U. S. Office of Education grew from 366 to 381. Some observers think the pace has since slowed, and they may be right.) It would also mean encouraging the consolidation of small struggling colleges in the same diocese. Such colleges could be encouraged to move to adjacent campuses, to share expensive facilities like libraries and laboratories, and to share courses and faculty members in some areas. (At present there is little cooperation even between men's and women's colleges on contiguous campuses, both because historic inter-order rivalries are too fierce and because one institution almost always feels itself superior to its neighbor in some respect.) Church politics would probably not allow a bishop to force such mergers on the unwilling, but he could at least refrain from helping poor colleges escape the logic of their positions. The "natural" rate of mortality among Catholic colleges remains high, and it would be still higher if the

[94] It should be noted that while Catholic universities are well located on the whole, they are almost all in the shadow of an even more favored non-Catholic institution, which makes them acutely aware of the distance they still have to travel. Many could become the second or third university of their city; only Notre Dame and Georgetown or Catholic seem to have a chance to become the first.

hierarchy encouraged lay philanthropists to support only the stronger colleges or groups of colleges.[95]

Sweeping reforms that concentrated religious energy and lay philanthropy on a relatively small number of institutions might well enable leading Catholic colleges and universities to improve their competitive position vis-à-vis non-Catholic institutions. But such reforms are hardly likely. The important question, however, is not whether a few Catholic universities prove capable of competing with Harvard and Berkeley on the latter's terms, but whether Catholicism can provide an ideology or personnel for developing alternatives to the Harvard-Berkeley model of excellence. Our guess is that the ablest Catholic educators will feel obliged to put most of their energies into proving that Catholics can beat non-Catholics at the latter's game. But having proved this, a few may be able to do something more. There is as yet no American Catholic university that manages to fuse academic professionalism with concern for questions of ultimate social and moral importance, but there are Catholic colleges like Immaculate Heart that suggest the possibilities. If Catholicism is to make a distinctive contribution to the over-all academic system, it will have to achieve such a synthesis at the graduate level. It was there that the Protestant colleges failed, and it was that failure that made the Protestant counterparts of Immaculate Heart useful but largely irrelevant to the over-all system. Unless a few Catholic universities can do better, they too will be engulfed by academic professionalism.

[95] Donovan, *The Academic Man*, p. 20, shows that of 268 coeducational and all-male Catholic colleges founded prior to 1957, two-thirds had closed their doors by that date The rate of mortality among Catholic colleges seems to have been somewhat lower than among Protestant ones during the nineteenth century, perhaps because a single Protestant clergyman could found a college during that era whereas it usually took several Catholic priests, working under the authority of an order, to found a Catholic one. In the twentieth century, however, the non-Catholics evidently lost their faith that God would provide and began to found fewer marginal colleges. Catholics, on the other hand, continued to set up new institutions with no money and little prospect of a paying clientele. While the mortality rate among twentieth-century Catholic colleges is marginally lower than among those founded in the nineteenth century, this probably reflects nothing more than the fact that some of the twentieth-century colleges were founded just before 1957 and had not had a chance to prove their lack of seaworthiness when Donovan's tabulations were made. It should be added that these figures do not include Catholic women's colleges, which have been opened even more frequently and heedlessly than coeducational and men's colleges.

X. Negroes and Their Colleges

Negroes in America

Until quite recently almost all Americans, both black and white, have assumed that Negro Americans' problems were unique. Their ancestors were carried to America as slaves, subjected to a centuries-long process of "thought reform" which makes some more recent totalitarian efforts seem both humane and ineffective,[1] liberated from slavery only to be held in a state of near peonage on Southern plantations, and persistently segregated and isolated by laws and customs without parallel in American life. The net result was a state of mind and a way of life almost incomprehensible to most whites. This was officially recognized by classifying Negroes as a separate "race" rather than merely as a distinct "ethnic group" like Jews or Anglo-Saxons.[2] Sociologists also recognized the special position of Negroes by describing them as a "caste" rather than a "class." Nonetheless, the fact of having African ancestors and a black skin does not make *all* a man's hopes and fears unique. *Some* aspects of Negro life are akin to that of whites, and this is perhaps especially true to Negro college life. There is a good deal of bitter controversy, however, about the validity of particular analogies between blacks and whites. A discussion of Negro colleges must therefore begin by outlining the authors' general assumptions about the Negroes' position in America, both yesterday and today.

Southern Negroes never had a revolutionary tradition. There were occasional revolts, and a good deal of muted criticism was expressed through music and religion, but very few Negroes dreamt of a new social order radically different from the existing one, much less elaborating a plan for achieving that order, either by violence or any other way. Marcus Garvey's movement was briefly popular, but only a few Negroes were ready to repudiate their bitter American experience and return to Africa. Nor did their numbers or history

[1] Cf. the discussion in Elkins, chap. 3.

[2] Negroes are not, of course, America's only non-white minority. Indians in the West are often more numerous and more oppressed than Negroes, and for a time Pacific Coast Orientals suffered similarly. But it still seems fair to say that the Negroes' situation has been essentially unique.

lend much credence to the idea that they were oppressed "natives" who might reclaim "their" country from the white colonialists. Like other oppressed American minorities, Southern Negroes evidently accepted the basic legitimacy of the social system under which they lived, and looked up to the men who stood at the top of this order. They asked only that the system not single them out for special hardships, and that their children have the same chance as others of climbing to the top. Their dream, in short, was integration into white society. In this respect they were no different from the Irish, Italian, Jewish, and other minorities who wanted to become "American." There was, of course, plenty of ambivalence about integration, and it was often feared in practice at the same time it was coveted in principle. There were also recurrent religious groups that rejected assimilation into anything as profane as established white institutions. But among Southern Negroes, as among other ethnic minorities, this stance was a deviation from the norm. Whether one looked at hair styles, preferred skin color, the drive to desegregate schools, brand-name choices, or over-all ideology, it seemed clear that for most Negroes "white was right."

The rural South was, however, so ordered that very few Negroes could even hope to join the white social system in their own lifetime. (A few had the right genes and temperament to "pass," but this was hardly an alternative for the majority.) Whatever shady or respectable routes to better status the black metropolis established, the rural South offered at best a few positions within the segregated community. These positions generated the somewhat middle-class outlook described by Franklin Frazier, John Dollard, Allison Davis, Hortense Powdermaker, and others. For a Negro to become a doctor, mortician, or preacher was not, however, a first step toward assimilation into the national upper-middle class as it was for a second- or third-generation Irish-American or Jewish-American. For a Negro, membership in the black bourgeoisie was a dead end. Those who joined this ersatz elite might earn a comfortable living, but they could not hope to rise further, nor even expect their children to do so. Even Negro teachers, who were fiscally and bureaucratically part of the white social system, were never socially or politically part of it. No Negro could pass up through this system into white society, as occasional members of white ethnic minorities did from the very beginning.[3]

Furthermore, unlike other countries with analogous racial situa-

[3] Some exceptions to this rule could perhaps be found in small Northern or Western communities with only a handful of Negroes, such as Great Barrington, Massachusetts, or Seattle before World War I, as pictured in Horace R. Cayton's autobiography, *Long Old Road.*

tions, the rural South did not permit the Negro middle classes to acquire much political power or social status by acting as brokers between the dominant whites and the suppressed Negroes. Southern whites occupied not only the top but most of the intermediate jobs, even when these involved direct contact with poor Negroes. The white sheriff hired white deputies, the white plantation owner usually hired a white supervisor, and the white welfare system usually hired white case workers. The most important exceptions to this pattern were churches, whose Negro ministers sometimes acted as intermediaries between their flocks and local white leaders. In addition, white school boards evolved a system of "indirect rule" through Negro principals which was in some respects analogous to the British colonial system in Africa and Asia.

So long as the overwhelming majority of Negroes remained rural, their plight as an ethnic minority was indeed unique, and it would plainly be misleading to assume that the traditional Southern Negro college was merely a species of the larger ethnic genus. But once Negroes began to move off the farm, and more especially once they began to move out of the predominantly Anglo-Saxon South, the circumstances we have described began to change. Unlike their counterparts in the South, Northern urban leaders were used to playing ethnic politics. They allowed Negroes to vote, and often courted (or bought) those votes. Legal restrictions based on race had never been as widespread or as rigid as in the South, and after the great migration north brought on by the Depression and World War II, they disappeared entirely. The official rhetoric of the white North proclaimed the possibility of creating a "color blind" society, and at times even suggested that this task had already been accomplished. It seemed to follow that blackness might be only one aspect of the Negroes' ethnic heritage, and not necessarily the most important one. More generally, it seemed to follow that Negroes were in fact no different from the other ethnic minorities that had entered the urban melting pot at the bottom, gone through a long, painful, but ultimately effective transformation, and emerged as "red-blooded" Americans. Thus there seemed to be no reason why, with appropriate efforts at self-help and support from sympathetic whites, Negroes could not become fully "assimilated," just as the Irish, Italians, Poles, and Jews were being assimilated.[4]

Having been taught in the South that "white was right," but that nevertheless no Negro should ever *act* as if he were white, the Negro who moved North confronted a new ideology. White was still right,

[4] For an explicit effort to compare the situation of the urban Negro to that of urban white minorities, see Handlin. For a perceptive study of the New York situation, see Glazer and Moynihan. See also Kristol.

but now Negroes were not only permitted but in many respects required to act as if they were white. Just as with other ethnic minorities, assimilation—or integration as it was almost invariably called when Negroes were involved—meant that the minority would adopt most of the customs and concerns of the Anglo-Saxon majority. Having done this, it was presumed Negroes would disperse through the hitherto white occupational structure in an increasingly random pattern, competing on equal terms and presumably achieving equal rewards.

Some prophets of integration also expected that in the long run Negroes would disperse through the hitherto white social system, ultimately intermarrying in substantial numbers and hopefully in this way eliminating skin color as a major issue.[5] This goal had, however, remained elusive even for white ethnic minorities, and most integrationists, especially Negroes, regarded it as much less important than occupational dispersion and economic gains. Most Negroes seem to have limited interest in social integration, since they feel slightly (or at times acutely) uncomfortable or defensive around whites. (The dean of one of the nation's leading Negro colleges underlined this point when he commented that even today his own head often itched when he talked to white men, because as a child he had habitually assumed the "darky" pose of scratching his head and saying "Yassir" to white men.) Since most whites also feel slightly ill at ease with Negroes, off-the-job contact is likely to be limited, just as it is between Jews and Gentiles or between Catholics and non-Catholics. The ambivalence surrounding such contacts will, in turn, continue to be a staple of conversation, fantasy, and action.

The ideology of integration was very much at odds with the reality of the Northern ghetto, but it persisted nonetheless, just as it had among other ethnic minorities. Indeed, it not only persisted but spread. Supported by the mass media and the federal judiciary, it began to have an effect on Southern Negroes, and by the early 1960s it had sparked a mass movement of considerable proportions. For a variety of complex political reasons this movement was able to win at least sporadic support from the federal government and to set in motion changes in the Old South that, while not yet nearly complete, probably spell the end of old-style Southern segregation. The caste system is not dead today, but within a generation the "New South" will probably be dominated by a pattern of racial relationships rather like that now found in the North.

Even if old-style segregation does not die, its importance will fade for purely demographic reasons. Southern agriculture is at long last

[5] See, e.g. Podhoretz.

being mechanized, and Negro hands have little value. Since Negroes have little land and less cash, they are being driven off the farm at a very rapid rate. (In 1950 more than 20 per cent of all Negroes still lived on farms; by 1965 the proportion had fallen to 6 per cent; by 1970 it is likely to be 4 per cent.) This migration has brought a rise in the number of Negroes in Southern hamlets and small towns as well as in large cities. But in the long run the great majority of Negroes will almost certainly find their way to industrial centers, North and South. These will not, of course, all be great cities. There will be plenty of Negroes in places like Savannah as well as places like Atlanta, and in places like Springfield as well as places like Boston. The trend is nonetheless clear.

There was a time—and not so long ago either—when urbanization and the destruction of the legal and quasi-legal pillars of segregation were regarded as sufficient conditions for the eventual assimilation of Negroes into middle-class America. These developments were expected to put Negroes on the same escalator to equality that white ethnic minorities had often ridden. The events of the last few years have, however, made clear that the problem is not so simple. Nearly ten million Negroes have now moved to the urban North and have become fully equal in the eyes of the law if not in the eyes of most law enforcers.[6] Yet in social and economic terms, they are *not* becoming equal. The Northern Negro's position today is clearly better than that of his parents and grandparents or of his Southern cousins, but it is no closer to that of white Northerners than it was a generation ago.

This is not the place to describe in detail the evidence for this assertion, but a few statistics underscore the general point. The simplest quantitative measure is income. Negro family incomes in the rural South still average less than 45 per cent of white family incomes. In the urban South the gap is only slightly smaller, with Negro incomes averaging about half of white incomes. In the urban North, Negro incomes average about 70 per cent of white incomes. There does not appear to have been any significant change in these ratios since the end of World War II. During periods of declining unemployment, such as World War II, Korea, and the 1960s, Negroes tend to catch up slightly. When unemployment rises, they lag behind. When it remains stable, Negroes' position vis-à-vis whites does the same. The fluctuations are, in other words, cyclical; there is no sign of long-term improvement. And while the competitive position of the Negro family as a whole has remained pretty stable, the competitive position of the Negro male has deteriorated.[7] Only the relative im-

---

[6] In 1960 about 40 per cent of all Negroes lived outside the South. The percentage is rising about 1 per cent annually. See 1965 *Statistical Abstract,* table 23.

[7] See Batchelder.

provement in the position of Negro women has kept the total income of Negro families relatively stable compared to whites.[8]

Nor is the physical isolation of the urban Negro diminishing. In almost every big Northern city the proportion of Negroes attending all-Negro schools is rising, despite some ingenious and sincere efforts to arrest the process. In housing, more Negroes are moving to the suburbs, but many of them have moved to what are, or will soon become, all-Negro sections, much like the overwhelmingly Jewish or Italian sections nearby. In both schooling and housing de facto segregation of Negroes has been far more complete than it ever was with other ghettoized ethnic minorities.[9]

Surveying these facts we are forced to conclude that, while what we will call "old-style" Southern segregation is probably dying, "new-style" Northern segregation is enduring. This new-style segregation differs from its ancestor, however, in several important respects. To begin with, it is primarily class segregation rather than race segregation—though the two are obviously related in a society where the urban lower class appears to be increasingly black and most black city dwellers appear to be lower class.[10] New-style segregation allows those Negroes who acquire white middle-class habits and attitudes to move up into the white world; indeed, its vagaries are such that there are some fields and times when it is considerably easier for a Negro with a given level of competence to move ahead than for a

[8] For a comprehensive overview of the gap between Negro and white living standards, see Parsons and Clark, particularly the contributions of Moynihan, Drake, Fein, and Hauser.

[9] On housing, see Hauser, in Parsons and Clark. We know no statistical data comparing school segregation among Negroes to that of white immigrants, so we speak impressionistically. Given the impact of voluntary segregation into parochial schools, we could be wrong.

[10] Statistically, it seems clear that the majority of the urban poor are, and will probably remain, white. In 1964, only 18 per cent of all families in the central cities of Standard Metropolitan Statistical Areas of more than 50,000 were non-white. (It should be borne in mind, that the Census does not use the term "central city" in the vernacular sense, but rather includes all residents of the largest city or cities in a metropolitan area.) Only 34 per cent of the families with less than $3,000 in those cities were non-white. (Bureau of the Census, Current Population Reports (1966), table 1.) The fact remains that in most large cities Negroes now think they constitute the majority of the poor, and middle-class whites generally share this assumption. The reason for this misperception is partly the civil rights movement, which has given poor Negroes a visibility that poor whites only rarely achieve. In addition, racial perceptions inevitably focus on central tendencies, and the typical urban Negro is poor, whereas the typical white is not. In 1964, e.g., the median income of white families in the central cities of SMSAs over 50,000 was $6,034, while the median income of non-white families was $3,656. Then too there is the fact that many of the low-income whites are older people, and many of the others are recent arrivals in the city who expect to do better soon and probably will. For these and other reasons the proportion of low-income whites who "act poor" in a cultural sense is probably smaller than among low-income Negroes. Both white and Negro perceptions of the distribution of poverty are skewed accordingly.

comparable white.[11] But while class segregation allows upward mobility for a minority, it does little to facilitate such mobility for the majority. A Negro who acquires what the white professional and managerial class regards as appropriate skills and virtues may do very well indeed, but very few Negroes can acquire them. Everything about life in the urban Negro ghetto conspires to prevent the young from developing the traits they need for upward mobility. The schools, which are meant to be the first rung on the occupational ladder, almost never afford Negroes an opportunity to meet and mix with children more fortunate than themselves. Their teachers are also likely to be less articulate and worse educated than those whom suburban whites encounter—though occasional exceptions can be found.[12]

[11] Compare e.g. the incomes of Negroes and whites with the same academic skills. Coleman et al., p. 273, shows that the academic value of a year of school for Negroes averages about three-quarters its value for whites, judged by various achievement tests. This same survey suggests (pp. 345 ff.) that a similar pattern probably continues through college, though here the data are less reliable. If one wants to compare the incomes of Negroes and whites with the same academic skills, then one must compare Negroes to whites with three-quarters as much formal education. If this is done, one finds that Negro men earn 10 to 20 per cent less than "comparable" white men, while Negro women earn from 25 to 65 per cent more than "comparable" white women.

Since the above data are likely to be misinterpreted, we must emphasize that when we speak of Negro women having a "competitive advantage" over comparable whites, we do not mean that an employer is likely to favor a Negro over a white when two otherwise identical women apply for a given job. This happens in only a few very special situations, such as color-conscious poverty agencies, which have no significant effect on national income statistics. But many jobs require academic credentials, not academic skills, and Negro women have more of the former than they "deserve" by white standards of academic performance (or, if one prefers, white women have fewer credentials than they "deserve" by Negro standards of performance). On the basis of the data reported by Coleman et al., one would expect e.g. the typical girl graduating from a Southern Negro college to have lower verbal scores than the typical sophomore dropping out of a Southern white college. If both applied for teaching jobs, however, the Negro B.A. would have a better chance of getting a job, even in the South. Nor is this necessarily unreasonable. There is no reason to suppose that tests of academic competence predict on-the-job competence better than the fact of having completed a given number of school or college years. Many employers value diligence, perseverance, willingness to delay gratification, and willingness to do what one is told more than they value verbal or mathematical skills, general information, and the like. It could easily be that these character traits are better correlated with the number of years of school an individual has survived than with his achievement. If so, an employer might be happier with a B.A. who had low achievement scores than with a dropout who had high scores.

It should also be noted that one reason why Negro women make more than white ones with comparable academic skills is that they are more likely to take their careers seriously, staying at a job after childbearing, accumulating seniority, and hence working into higher wage brackets. This is especially important among teachers.

[12] On the importance of various facets of the school in determining student achievement, see Coleman et al., chap. 3. The report suggests that the effects of schools on their students have usually been overestimated, but that insofar as they do have an effect, the class background of an individual pupil's classmates is the most important identifiable variable affecting his performance.

Other public services and private opportunites are for the most part equally deficient, despite exceptions such as the public wards of some teaching hospitals.

Class segregation is not, of course, new to American life. Every urban ethnic minority has suffered from it. The case of the American Negro may, however, be different in several crucial respects. For one thing, each previous ethnic minority escaped its ghettoes at least in part because there was another, more recently urbanized ethnic group to fill the bottom rung of society. The arrival of a new, unskilled minority supported rapid economic growth, creating not only skilled, blue-collar jobs but white-collar and small-business opportunities for better established groups. It also helped redirect the anti-lower-class bias of those who had already made it, or were doing so. The Anglo-Protestant nativists came to accept the Irish more readily once they were exposed to the Italians and Jews, and the Irish in turn lost interest in looking down on the Italians when Negroes arrived in the North in large numbers. Today there is no new minority to take the Negroes' place at the bottom, except perhaps the not very numerous Puerto Ricans and Mexican-Americans.

The fact that Negroes have no successors on the urban escalator should be considered from both an economic and cultural angle. Economically, the harsh fact is that the poorest fifth of the population has gotten between 4 and 5 per cent of the national income for the past forty years. The time has probably passed—if indeed it ever existed—when such an underclass was needed to support the comforts of the middle class. If, for example, the annual increase in output were all channeled to the poorest fifth of society for a mere two years, their incomes could be doubled. But as a practical matter the income distribution seems almost immune to Washington's modest efforts at adjustment, and neither the Negroes nor any of the others who get small shares seem able to alter it. If the income distribution is fixed, somebody must occupy the bottom of the pyramid. The only way for Negroes to move up would be for others to move down. This would be relatively easy to arrange if the "others" could be, say, indigent Latin American immigrants coming from even worse conditions. If they have to be the children of white families who now have higher living standards and more political leverage than Negroes, resistance to upward mobility by Negroes will be greater.

The cultural impact of the Negroes' being the last to join the American industrial club may, however, be even more serious than its economic impact. As Stanley Elkins and others have pointed out, the very fluidity of the class structure in America may have helped direct status anxiety to the one thing that seemed stable: color. Negroes are visible in a way that no other ethnic minority, including Orientals and Indians, has been. They were, moreover, victims of a racial mythology in which they believed almost as strongly as the whites who propagated it. According to this mythology racial categories differ from ethnic ones in that race is unalterably fixed, while ethnicity is a matter of degree. This is taken for granted by almost everyone. The Census, for example, asks respondents whether they or their parents were born in a foreign country, and counts them as part of an ethnic minority if the answer is yes. But the Census Bureau also presumes that there will be too much assimilation and intermarriage after the second generation for such ethnic classifications to remain valid or useful. With "racial" groups, on the other hand, classification is permanent. An American is "white," "Negro," or "Oriental," no matter how many generations removed he may be from Europe, Africa, or Asia, and how much intermarriage or miscegenation has gone on in his family. The Census categories "white" and "non-white" do not even reflect actual skin color; many "non-whites" are as light as many "whites."[13]

This mythology, which tells everyone involved that Negroes are "different," seems to have a self-fulfilling quality. Since whites have generally assumed that Negroes are forever different, most Negroes have come to half believe it. To the extent they believe it, it tends to become so. The existence of differences need not, of course, imply that one group is superior and one inferior. Each can believe itself superior, or better yet, each can accept the other's strengths as complementing his own. Today a vocal Negro minority is beginning to assert that Negroes can, after all, be separate but equal—or even superior. In principle we agree. But we wonder whether such an idea is psychologically viable in an overwhelmingly white society unless it has religious supports. In most instances egalitarian pluralism has been possible in America only *after* a large measure of assimilation. Assimilation, in turn, has usually depended on de-emphasizing or denying basic differences rather than stressing them. But "usually" is not "always." The historical record can be used to show the benefits as well as the dangers of ethnic nationalism. The relevance of these historical parallels to current black nationalist thinking is in any case uncertain.

The analogy between urban Negroes and other ethnic minorities is, then, far from perfect. Nonetheless, important similarities have developed. The old job ceiling for Negroes is, for example, becoming somewhat permeable. There is still plenty of discrimination in hiring and promotion, but there is also beginning to be reverse discrimination

13 While the Census categories reflect racist assumptions, this is *not* an argument for their abandonment. So long as America continues to operate on these assumptions, those who try to understand the consequences must use parallel categories. We cite the Census not to criticize its methods but because its classification scheme reflects the prejudices of society as a whole.

by organizations eager to atone for past injustices or to establish themselves in the vanguard of what is now defined as progress. The search for "qualified Negroes" is particularly conspicuous in the federal government, but can also be seen in many large corporations. While some of these Negroes are hired mainly for public relations purposes, and find that power is in the hands of a white deputy, many are entering middle-level jobs on terms of real equality. Unlike the old Negro middle class, this new class is in continuous contact with whites, usually has to meet white standards of competence, and often competes with white colleagues for advancement. It is thus much more nearly akin to, say, the Irish-Catholic business and professional class than to the old Negro bourgeoisie. The kinship is beginning to extend in another direction as well, for the new Negro middle class is increasingly expected to serve as an intermediary between the white elite and the Negro poor. Negro professionals certainly do not dominate the schools, welfare agencies, police stations, or hospitals that serve Northern ghettoes, but their role is slowly growing. A generation hence it may be comparable to the role they already play in ghetto churches, political machines, and anti-poverty organizations, and thus to the role that upwardly mobile members of other ethnic groups have so frequently played vis-à-vis their less adept fellows.

How different this new Negro middle class will be from the old is difficult to predict. To the extent that it is really part of a national or metropolitan social structure, so that its members mix intellectually and professionally with whites, it will be quite different. But this may not always happen. The development of parallel Catholic institutions enabled many Irish and Italians to move into professional roles without coming into much contact with non-Catholics, and much the same thing may happen among Negroes. We can imagine Harlem Negroes, for example, demanding and getting a school system that would be virtually autonomous within New York City, would hire largely or exclusively Negro principals and teachers, and would probably have minimal contact and little direct competition with white educators elsewhere. While a few of the ablest Negro teachers and administrators would choose to work in such a system out of nationalism and compassion, most would probably take their chances in the larger, more mixed world. Furthermore, with whatever slippage community pressure could create, the virtually separate Negro educational system would nevertheless be obliged to employ people with the same formal credentials as the largely white system. This would generate a continuing demand for teachers who had gone through the motions of getting a higher education, even if they had done so in inferior, perhaps segregated, colleges. Similar developments in health, welfare, religion, politics, and law enforcement could conceivably support the growth of a Negro professional class not very different from its old Southern counterpart. This class would have more power than the old leadership of the separate Negro pyramid, and a standard of living more nearly equal to that of whites, but many of its members would remain relatively isolated and insulated. It would also have to develop a different style of operation from its Southern predecessor, learning to use a violent vocabulary and to participate in the dramatic confrontations which now seem necessary to win the allegiance of the Negro poor and the attention of the mass media. (The old Negro middle-class style was adapted to a white audience, and those who espouse it would have little influence in even partially self-governing ghettoes.)

Comparable developments in profit-making enterprises are harder to imagine. Negro entrepreneurs have not had much luck competing with white-controlled national corporations, and Negroes with a taste for organization life are likely to end up joining white corporations rather than trying to fight them. If the present racial crisis grows worse, however, as it well may, Negro small businessmen may be able to drive most small white businessmen out of Negro ghettoes. To the extent that the Black Muslims and similar organizations can create a patriarchal, prideful, "Protestant," methodical middle class, they may in time assist this development. So far, however, Negro small businessmen have had a hard time winning a clientele in competition with whites. Unlike most immigrant subcultures, the Negro ghetto dweller has not been especially interested in specifically Negro goods on which Negro storekeepers had an inside track. Neither have Negro storekeepers had the advantage of knowing a language their white competitors didn't, in the way that Italian or Puerto Rican storekeepers often did or do. No doubt there are more fundamental cultural factors at work here too, such as the traditional pressure on Negro men to be docile rather than aggressive.

Yet whether or not an individual middle-class Negro chooses to remain largely within a Negro milieu, or to move out into a partially integrated one, the *possibility* of such mobility will almost certainly exercise a profound effect on him. Middle-class Negroes will have contact with one another, and those who remain largely in the ghetto will be influenced by those who move largely outside it. Thus even those middle-class Negroes who are products of new-style segregation will be significantly different from the old Negro middle class. In particular, they will be more likely to have some day-by-day contact with whites, as subordinates, colleagues, and superiors. Their success in their careers will therefore depend in part on white responses to them and judgments about them, in a way that was relatively rare for a Negro doctor with black patients, a Negro teacher in a segregated school, or a Negro clergyman with a black congregation. Not all young

Negroes will find this kind of interdependence with whites appealing. Some, indeed, will undoubtedly go to considerable lengths to minimize their relations with whites once they embark on a career, either by choosing jobs in semi-segregated settings or by helping create such settings as part of a drive for black autonomy. But even these young Negroes, who find the prospect of integration distasteful, will often feel that they should prepare for the worst and learn as much as they can about conning "the man." For such students, just as for students who look forward to integration, a predominantly white college is likely to seem better preparation than a predominantly black one.

The reader of our earlier chapters should not find this judgment surprising. We have, after all, argued that ambitious Catholics usually avoid strictly Catholic colleges, that ambitious women usually avoid egregiously "feminine" colleges, that ambitious small-town boys will usually avoid local colleges, and that talented students from lower-income families mostly bypass cheap public colleges where the tone is set by others from similar families. In each instance a case could be made for delaying integration into the larger world, using a segregated college as a decompression chamber to ease a difficult transition. And in each instance there are some talented youngsters to whom this argument seems decisive. Nonetheless, the general rule is that the longer such transitions are delayed, the less likely they are to take place at all. So too with racial integration. Some students may choose a Negro college as a way of modulating and lubricating their escape from the segregated past to the partially integrated future. Others will choose a Negro college because they expect to move only from the old-style segregation their parents experienced to the new-style segregation that characterizes so many aspects of contemporary Negro life and see no reason to face the intellectual and social strains of an integrated institution. But such choices are likely to become less and less common, especially since Negro colleges are likely to have even greater difficulty assisting such transitions than the other special-interest colleges we have considered. The Negro colleges' special handicaps in this regard derive from the unhappy but seemingly inescapable burden of Southern history which the Negro colleges necessarily carry into the modern world.

The Evolution of the Negro Colleges

The first Negro colleges opened in the North before the Civil War, though none granted a B.A. until after 1865. During Reconstruction, when it became possible for Northern abolitionists and missionaries to operate south of the Mason-Dixon line, the founding of Negro colleges was greatly accelerated. With the help of the Freedman's Bureau and the American Missionary Association, something like two hundred private Negro colleges were established. Like the pre-Civil War clergymen who had fanned out across the South and Midwest to found Protestant colleges, and like the Catholic Fathers and Sisters who were doing the same throughout the nineteenth century, the well-intentioned clerics who founded most of the private Negro colleges usually had more courage and ambition than judgment or resources. Few of their colleges had adequate financial support, and virtually none had a steady supply of qualified applicants. Indeed, only about half the institutions in question were still afloat in 1900, and only half of these had any college-level students.[14] (Which is not to say that they did no useful work with their pre-college students.)

Dozens of these colleges were established to train Negro clergymen —sometimes as missionaries to Africa, sometimes for "home missions." But almost all found it necessary to accept non-clerical students in order to survive. Many became de facto teachers colleges. Yet church subventions remained financially important to many of these colleges long after they had become relatively inconsequential to white sectarian and ethnic institutions. Even today, thirty-seven of the forty-nine surviving private Negro colleges and nineteen of the twenty-one surviving private Negro junior colleges are church-related.[15]

The new Negro colleges differed from white ethnic colleges in several important respects. First, and perhaps most important, Negroes played a much smaller role in founding what were nominally "their" colleges than the Irish, Swedes, or Jews played in founding theirs. The private Negro colleges were for the most part financed by white philanthropists, controlled by white boards of trustees, initially administered by white presidents, and largely staffed by white faculty. In due course the administration and faculty usually became predominantly Negro, but by then a psychological and cultural pattern had been established that was hard to break.[16] Furthermore, even when the staff became predominantly Negro, the board and the donors often remained predominantly white.

It is easy to misunderstand or exaggerate the extent to which white control shaped these private colleges. Some radicals have argued, for

[14] The mortality rate for white colleges founded in the nineteenth century was also well over 50 per cent, and the proportion doing mainly secondary work remained nearly as high until the founding of public high schools became common in the last quarter of the century.

[15] See McGrath, pp. 19–20.

[16] In 1967 there were only two colleges (Xavier in New Orleans and Paine in Augusta) founded for Negroes that had had only white presidents. At least one (Lincoln) had a Negro president some years ago although in 1917 it had a white one. Several others have only recently acquired Negro presidents.

example, that wealthy whites supported Negro colleges in order to head off potentially revolutionary stirrings among the Negro masses. This seems to us almost wholly fanciful. Men like John D. Rockfeller, to take the most famous example, had less reason to feel threatened by impoverished Southern Negroes than by almost any dispossessed group in America—and there were many such groups in the late nineteenth and early twentieth centuries. If wealthy Northerners had been mainly concerned with protecting their class interests— and they certainly *were* concerned with this at times—they would hardly have spent their money in remote places like Tuskegee. The white farmers of the Midwest and the seething urban proletariat threatened established privilege far more than did rural Negro share croppers. Rather than assuming a Machiavellian plot to support "Uncle Toms" like Booker T. Washington against "militants" like W. E. B. DuBois, we would argue that the Northern whites who backed private colleges for Negroes were moved by genuinely philanthropic motives. Unlike Southern segregationists (who feared "uppity" Negroes), the Northern whites saw no necessary conflict between improving the condition of the Southern Negro and preserving their own privileges. Believing in progress on all fronts, they assumed Negroes could be better off without rich whites being worse off.

None of this means that the financial backers, trustees, presidents, or white teachers in the private Negro colleges were uniformly committed to an ideology of racial equality. Many thought there were limits on what Negroes could accomplish, either in school or as adults. Many of the "enlightened" Northerners who took an interest in Negro education differed from their Southern cousins only in being less fearful of the political consequences of educating their presumed inferiors. The missionary spirit of these institutions was sometimes extremely patronizing, and the day-to-day reality was often predicated on the assumption of white supremacy. White faculty, for example, might eat separately from Negro faculty, or send their children to a separate faculty school. On the other hand, other white faculty were thoroughly integrated, sending their children to the Negro colleges where they taught. Their behavior created an interracial model which, while often impressive to the Negroes, also brought reprisals from Southern whites who did not want to see Negroes taught at all, let alone in mixed company.

In any event, we do not believe the basic character of the private Negro colleges was determined primarily by the prejudices or self-interest of their white trustees, any more than the basic character of other colleges has been. Rather, the Negro college was molded by the circumstances in which it found itself locally. That is why the few colleges founded by all-Negro denominations were so similar to those founded by whites—though they were even poorer and less distinguished.[17] The basic fact was that *any* Negro college had to recruit most of its students from the segregated South, and that most of these recruits expected to return to the segregated South. Not only that, but all these colleges depended for survival on the tolerance, or at least the indifference, of local white supremacists. They had few wealthy or loyal alumni to buoy them up or to rally round in times of troubles, and only a few had any endowment on which to rely. Under these circumstances it made relatively little difference whether the white trustees were liberal or conservative—and indeed these colleges' white backers were sometimes more liberal and enlightened than some of the Negroes who came to administer and teach in them. Northern whites could, after all, afford to be liberal; the writ of the Ku Klux Klan never reached into New York City. Even those whites who came South could afford to oppose local mores in ways their Negro colleagues could not. Sometimes they had the advantage of their ignorance of local customs, and violated these without fully appreciating the risks they ran. Sometimes they felt obliged to prove their dedication to colleagues and students, and this occasionally put them on their mettle to be courageous in a way that has happened only very recently and in a few places to Negro faculties under pressure from militant undergraduates. But whatever their motives, the fact remained that if things got too hot there was always the possibility of returning North.

Given most Northern white colleges' reluctance to hire black administrators or faculty, Negroes had no such safety net; if they lost their jobs as professors, the best local alternative might be a poorly paid federal civil service job in the Post Office or elsewhere. So Negroes had to be cautious, for the consequences of a false move looked (and often were) disastrous. Understandably, Negroes living under such pressures were extremely resentful of the relative freedom of their more mobile white colleagues, and were bitter when such men criticized the ways in which Negroes kept the peace with local whites. The whites in turn could often feel that the career sacrifices they were making and the difficulties for their own families were not appreciated or understood by the Negroes, for whom a professorship, even at a Negro college, was one of the best positions a Negro could hope for.[18]

[17] The Negro-initiated-and-financed church colleges are mostly offshoots of the African Methodist Episcopal Church. Of the 6 four-year AME colleges, only Morris Brown in Atlanta and Wilberforce in Ohio are accredited.

[18] On the relative scarcity of other opportunities for educated Negroes and the importance of this in pushing Negroes into college teaching even when this was not an appealing career, see Thompson, "Teachers." See also his summary in "Problems."

The subservience of Negro colleges to local mores was not, however, complete. Some of the better private Negro colleges maintained a tradition of dissent, and some of the most vocal Negro critics of America in general and of segregation in particular were on the faculties of colleges like Fisk, Howard, and the Atlanta group. Even the Negro state colleges sometimes harbored dissenters whose "impolitic" views could be more or less purposely overlooked, under the tacit treaty by which local whites and even state legislators left the Negro state colleges, like the Negro churches, under a quasi-protective screen of silence. (When a Negro college is in the state capital, like Southern University in Baton Rouge, it gets more legislative scrutiny—just as white Louisiana State in the same city does.)

Despite these small apertures, however, dissenters were exceptional. Like other ethnic and sectarian colleges in their early years, most Negro colleges had little use for academic freedom or controversy. They wanted to hire safe, congenial instructors rather than controversial ones. If they made a mistake and got someone who "didn't fit in," or who "didn't understand the local situation," his elimination was as easy as in most white colleges. Nevertheless, the Negro college campus even at its worst provided a freer and more comfortable environment for Negro intellectuals than any other place in the South. Tougaloo College outside Jackson, for example, has been an oasis in a racist desert. A number of other colleges in less beleaguered settings have played a similar if less difficult and dramatic role. Along with the Negro churches, Negro colleges were among the few places where Negroes could meet freely with one another, and often with whites. Integrated professional meetings were possible at Atlanta University when they were still taboo at Georgia Tech or Georgia State in the same city, and the same was true elsewhere. In part this was because the Negro campuses were so completely sealed off from the white world that whites simply did not notice what went on there. But in part it was because the presidents of some of these colleges were willing to protect their faculty and students.

All these possibilities depended very much on the character of the top men—far more so than in a big modern university where the professional guilds and externally financed research barons also play decisive roles. While there were plenty of President Bledsoes in the Negro colleges, there were also courageous and progressive men who did as much as their situations would allow and more. Some of them might appear to the contemporary outsider like Uncle Toms, for more than white college presidents they had to depend on the weapons of the weak: guile, charm, oratory, and seeming compliance. Many of these men had great personal fortitude and dignity. By drawing on their connections with cosmopolitan whites they were able to create some breathing space in the Negro community. Most have unfortunately been left behind by the civil rights movement whose cause they advanced at an earlier point, but without them the years of complete segregation would have been even more stifling than they were.[19]

Thus far we have been talking about private Negro colleges. But every Southern and Border state also had one or more publicly controlled Negro college. Some, such as Alcorn A & M in Mississippi, were set up during Reconstruction, when Negroes and their allies controlled the state legisature. Most, however, came later. Some were established to train Negro teachers for Negro schools. Others were established after 1890 to meet the federal government's new requirement that states either admit Negroes to their land-grant colleges or provide "separate but equal" colleges for them. Every state with a significant Negro population chose the latter alternative, often converting a normal school into an "A and I" or "A and T" college which, while never equal, was at least separate. (A few initially designated a private college such as Hampton Institute to meet the federal requirement.)

None of these land-grant colleges moved very far toward implementing what might loosely be called the "land-grant idea" of public service and practical involvement in the affairs of the surrounding community. They spent less of their tiny budgets on extension and technical services for Negro farmers than white land-grant colleges did for the more prosperous (and therefore more innovative) white farmers. There were few night courses for aspiring lawyers, no refresher courses for middle-aged physicians, no consultants or technical services for Negro businessmen, no extension centers for culture-hungry housewives or job-hungry white-collar workers.[20] In part this absence of services was because the white legislature, not Washington, exercised effective control over these colleges and saw them mainly as institutions for making Negro girls into teachers. But even in the Border states, where Negroes voted and where their enthusiastic support would have helped a public Negro college get more money from the legislature, little was done. The Negro public did not demand such services and Negro educators did not usually try to create such a demand. Everyone talked about Tuskegee, but nobody

[19] One tragic example of this is James Nabrit, who resigned from the presidency of Howard University in the summer of 1967. Long a fierce champion of civil rights, Nabrit had developed a high-handed way of doing business which, while perhaps necessary in a university answerable financially to Southern congressmen, was wholly unacceptable to the new generation of faculty and students.

[20] For evidence of the paucity of extension and adult education programs at Negro colleges see the 1965 *Digest*, table 67. In 1961 the Negro colleges enrolled 2.7 per cent of all students, but only 0.45 per cent of all adult extension students. For evidence that this was not always so true, see Bullock, who also shows that this function was partly performed by Negro high schools.

imitated it. Instead, they accepted W. E. B. DuBois' "radical" thesis that able Negroes were entitled to education as non-utilitarian as that given able whites, and then went him one better by making it pedantic as well. This underlines the fact that the problem was "Southern" as well as "Negro." White land-grant colleges in the South have also had what a Midwesterner or Californian would regard as a comparatively narrow, classical, campus-oriented view of their responsibilities.[21] Nevertheless, the chasm separating Negro educators from their impoverished constituency was probably even wider than that separating Southern white educators from theirs.

The Negro professors' reluctance to mix with less educated people, the white legislatures' reluctance to finance such mixing lest it stir up trouble or enable Negroes to compete with whites, and poor Negroes' assumption that colleges should provide credentials rather than services, all ensured that most Negro land-grant colleges would become (or in some cases simply remain) de facto teachers colleges. A number of states established additional Negro colleges solely to train teachers. By World War I, there were about two dozen public Negro colleges in the Southern and Border states, plus one in Pennsylvania and one in Ohio. In the years between World War I and World War II about half a dozen more private Negro institutions were taken over by Southern states.

Except for Texas Southern, the only additions to the Negro public sector since World War II have been a handful of marginal two-year colleges, mostly in Florida. These have now been merged with Florida's network of white junior colleges. Such colleges have not had the same appeal to Southern Negroes as to whites in comparable economic and intellectual circumstances.[22] Junior college is evidently seen as a gateway to business and commerce, where Negroes have traditionally had little hope of advancement. Four-year colleges, on the other hand, provided entrée into a profession, which could be practiced behind the wall of segregation.[23] For most Negroes, anything less than a B.A. seemed virtually useless.[24] This attitude has

[21] The University of North Carolina at Chapel Hill has had a tradition of interest in state and regional problems, though it is not a land-grant institution.

[22] See Coleman et al., pp. 443–45.

[23] In the Midwest and California, where Negroes have a somewhat better chance of advancing within white-owned enterprises, they enroll at junior colleges in large numbers. A Negro in Watts has to be deaf to all around him not to get the message that Los Angeles City College is available to him if he wants it, virtually as much a part of the local educational culture as the high school.

[24] This attitude seems to have a firm economic foundation only for Negro women, among whom teaching is the principal form of middle-income work. The Negro woman who finishes college typically earns 75 per cent more than the Negro woman who enters but does not finish, whereas a white woman with a B.A. earns only 55 per cent more than a white woman dropout. Among men, on the other hand, the picture is reversed. The Negro man who earns a degree averages only

perhaps been re-enforced by the "shoot for the moon because nothing less is worth the trouble" attitude of many Negro men. Negroes evidently have preferred to enter a four-year college, try for a B.A., and drop out, rather than enter a two-year colleage and settle for an A.A. degree.[25]

Regardless of their clientele or nominal purpose, public Negro colleges have been white-financed and white-controlled. This gave them a certain basic similarity to private Negro colleges and made the relationship of both public and private Negro colleges to their clientele quite different from that of white ethnic colleges to their clientele. The white ethnic colleges had been established at least in part because their founders, trustees, presidents, instructors, and prospective students rejected some aspect of the Anglo-Saxon tradition to which established colleges were committed. In most cases this quarrel was couched in religious terms, but as we tried to show in chapters VIII and IX, it was usually as much a matter of culture as of theology.

The Negro colleges had no such quarrel with Anglo-American culture. Mostly they were founded by whites, financed by whites, and at least in their early years administered and staffed mainly by whites. There were, it is true, a few colleges such as Morris Brown in Atlanta, Wilberforce in Ohio, Shorter in Little Rock, Edward Waters in Jacksonville, Paul Quinn in Texas, Livingstone in North Carolina, and Allen in South Carolina that were controlled by all-Negro denominations. There were some other private Negro colleges that came over a period of years to have predominantly Negro boards of trustees, not to mention Negro presidents and predominantly Negro staffs. Some public Negro colleges were led from the outset by Negro presidents; indeed, some have only recently been allowed by state law or custom to have an integrated faculty.[26] But for reasons already indicated, the "gray" Negroes who played key roles in these colleges were even more deferential to local white expectations and pressures than the white trustees and staffs. So instead of trying to promote a distinctive set of habits and values in their students, the Negro

---

20 per cent more than a Negro dropout, while a white man with a degree averages 28 per cent more than a white dropout. See 1960 *Census*, I, 1, table 223. On this basis one might expect Negro men to be *more* interested in junior colleges than white men, but the differences are probably too small to matter.

[25] Although statistics on attrition are full of pitfalls, Negro men seem to be somewhat more likely to drop out of college than white men, while among women the rates are about the same for Negroes and whites. See 1960 *Census*, I, 1, tables 168 and 173.

[26] East Indians, Chinese, and Cuban refugees have taught at these colleges without white legislators raising questions of "race mixing." These men have, however, been marginal within the Negro college context, never fully accepted as blacks yet never given credit for being altruistic whites who could have done better for themselves.

colleges became purveyors of super-American, ultra-bourgeois prejudices and aspirations. Far from fighting to preserve a separate
subculture, as other ethnic colleges did, the Negro colleges were militantly opposed to almost everything that made Negroes different
from whites, on the grounds that it was "lower class." Other ethnic
colleges confronting this same dilemma chose to attack the lower-
class immigrant subculture in some ways, while legitimizing and
embellishing it in others, usually under a religious umbrella that could
include Europe-oriented theological elements. The Negro colleges,
pious though they were, lacked a religious rationale for their separatism. They were separate only because the white colleges they emulated would not admit their students. Under such circumstances the
Negro colleges could have maintained their self-respect only if they
had viewed themselves as a prerevolutionary holding operation, designed to salvage the victims of injustice. This stance would, however,
have demanded an open and continual attack on segregation and
white supremacy, which the Negro colleges could not afford to make
if they wanted to survive. The price of survival was humility and
humiliation, and those who were willing to pay this price must often
have hated themselves for not fighting back openly, even when they
knew this was hopeless.

The Fruits of Oppression

The cumulative result of all this was that the Negro college of the
1950s was usually an ill-financed, ill-staffed caricature of white higher
education—which was, after all, easy enough to caricature. Or perhaps
it would be more accurate to say that the Negro colleges served as a
living reminder of how bad most white colleges in an earlier era had
been—and a few still are. The authoritarian atmosphere of the typical
Negro college, with its intervening trustees, its domineering but
frightened president, its faculty tyrannized by the president and in turn
tyrannizing the students, and the tendency of the persecuted at all
levels to identify with their persecutors (and in due course to take
their place), all harked back to an earlier period of white academic
history. The emphasis on athletics, fraternities, and sororities at many
of the Negro colleges also classed them with traditional rather than
progressive white institutions.
    Like the bulk of the white population two generations earlier,
American Negroes in the 1950s still lived in a world where most people
were poor and could not change that fact, where success seemed to
depend on winning the favor of some higher power (be it "the man"
or his divine counterpart), and where any form of self-expression,

self-assertion, or self-indulgence threatened to topple one off the straight and narrow path back into hell. Most Negroes, it is true, thought themselves damned no matter what they did, and therefore saw no reason to inhibit their spontaneous impulses. But those who hoped to "better themselves" felt this required even more self-control and discipline than it did for upwardly mobile whites. Sometimes these attitudes were promoted under the auspices of a vengeful religion, sometimes as part of the quest for material comfort, sometimes through a peculiarly noxious combination of mindless materialism and fundamentalist rigidity.

The puritanism of these colleges seems, however, often to have been more external than internal. Students were required to go through the motions of being prim, disciplined models of Victorian virtue, but the self-control that had given New England asceticism its strength was only rarely achieved on these campuses. Like nineteenth-century America at its pious worst, the Negro colleges seemed intent on ignoring the actual qualities of people. The result was a propensity for make-believe. Almost all Negro colleges have been extremely protective of girls, for example, even though it would appear from contemporary studies that most of them, including those from the black bourgeoisie, became sexually knowledgeable quite early.[27] Another form of protectiveness, which is still operative, sprang from the understandable desire of many Negro parents, especially in the middle class, to protect their children not only from disagreeable or traumatic contacts with the white world, but also from inviting and seductive ones. While they wanted their children to have the jobs a white college presumably opened up, they also wanted a safe Negro environment where the young would not be tempted to marry outside the boundaries of race or class, or to land in other sorts of trouble out of idealism or adventurousness. (A similar protectiveness operates in the comparable white worlds, especially for girls.)

Yet to put matters this way judges the Negro colleges in particular and the Negro bourgeoisie in general with what has been called 20-20 hindsight. In the early years after the Civil War and down to very recent times, it could be a prideful accomplishment to show that a Negro was capable of postponing gratification, of scholarly attainment, even of pendantry and intellectual make-work. It is easy to make fun of this "credit to your race" syndrome, with its emphasis on appearances and its indifference to what individual Negroes actually wanted or needed. But appearances *were* important, even if the price paid now seems out of line.

Unfortunately, even appearances were sometimes ignored, and the

[27] See, e.g. Reiss, and Gebhard *et al.*

effort to impose discipline and direction on students was compromised by dishonesty as well as pretense. Dishonesty was not, of course, unique to Negro colleges, but anecdotal evidence suggests that it was more common, especially at the poorer ones. Conversation with both Negroes and whites from these colleges turns up an extraordinary number of cases of petty blackmail and fraud, ranging from such relatively subtle things as college officials' profiteering on textbooks to more egregious incidents like a president's "borrowing" money from a new, untenured faculty member and not repaying it. The grading system was also abused. Professors of all colors use grades to blackmail students into reading books and writing papers. But we have heard frequent reports from Negro colleges of grades being used to blackmail students into mowing lawns, sweeping offices, or even providing sexual favors. This does not mean that sexual relations between faculty and students were or are more common on Negro than on white campuses. We doubt this. What seems to vary, at least according to the second-hand reports we have gotten from both settings, is the basis on which male instructors approach a female student. On a white campus the man is usually at pains to make clear that he is interested in the girl for her own sake and to avoid anything that might give the appearance of blackmail, for he assumes blackmail would both defeat his romantic ambitions and very possibly land him in serious trouble. Negro men who have power seem less concerned about admitting and exploiting it, and girls in turn seem less reluctant to admit that they are using their sexuality for extrinsic purposes.[28]

One reason for the difference between Negro and white colleges in this regard—assuming the difference is more than a by-product of Negro and white imaginations—may be that the men who have become professors at Negro colleges seem to be more interested in personal power than those who have become professors at white colleges. Whites who want power over others have a better chance of getting it in business, public administration, and other fields. Whites who turn to academic life seem to want a high degree of autonomy for themselves, with power over others being of secondary importance. Negroes with a yen for power have had fewer alternatives. Many have turned to education not because of any positive attraction to the inherently rather individualistic and egalitarian pattern of college

28 Women on white campuses are hardly above using their sexuality in the same way. Innumerable girls have found that a pretty face and a tight sweater were an adequate substitute for diligence and cleverness when dealing with a male teacher. Some, having been frustrated in efforts to get by on this basis, have pushed matters further and ended up in bed—though not necessarily with an A. But a white girl concerned with her grade is unlikely to tell her prospective lover this is uppermost in her mind.

life, but because they had nowhere else to go. Perhaps this is one reason why Negro academicians seem more eager to take administrative jobs than their white counterparts. They may also be more interested in "administering" students than the typical white professor.[29]

Yet concern with power and willingness to exploit it are certainly not unknown at white colleges, and invidious comparisons are obviously both risky and inflammatory. This is especially true when no objective indices are available against which to check our impressions. Nonetheless, matters of this kind are crucial to any serious evaluation of colleges and their atmospheres. We are often asked, for example, whether Southern Negro colleges are any more benighted or corrupt than run-of-the-mill Southern white colleges. There are no objective answers to such questions, but we must report our impression that Southern Negro colleges are, with a handful of hopeful exceptions, in something of a class by themselves. We know of no Southern white college, for example, that could match the atmosphere of Ralph Ellison's Negro college in *Invisible Man*. We have known Negro colleges of which this fictional image was a not entirely inaccurate reflection, though it would be hard to find one today where the studen's still accepted the situation in the way Ellison's fictional ones did.

To say this is not to deny the oppressiveness, fakery, and formalism coupled with punitiveness of which some white colleges are capable. Several of these colleges, for example, have turned patriotic anti-communism into a paying proposition. The Negro colleges, conservative though they have been, have never gone into the market in this particular way. Nor are we saying that all Negro colleges are worse than all white colleges. This has never been so. But it *is* true that the great majority of Negro institutions stand near the end of the academic procession in terms of student aptitudes, faculty competence, and intellectual ferment.

This is, of course, a sweeping assertion, and it is not easy to document fully. Certain kinds of data are, however, suggestive. If one looks at students, for example, one finds that the verbal and mathematical aptitude scores at most Negro colleges are lower than at even the worst white colleges in the same states. (There are, of course, plenty of whites with lower scores than the typical Negro college student, but such whites do not usually go to college.) Test scores for Negro and white colleges are not available on a national basis, but the fragmentary data which are available suggest that most Negro college students would probably rank in the bottom quarter

[29] For evidence on the proportion of Negro professors who chose teaching by default, and for comments on the importance of administrative advancement to Negro college faculty, see Thompson, "Problems," pp. 40 and 42.

of their class if they were enrolled in a typical white college.[30] Or to put it another way, a white student with the same aptitude as the typical Negro college entrant has only about one chance in ten of entering college and completing his freshman year in good academic standing.[31]

Yet even these national comparisons seem optimistic when one looks at Scholastic Aptitude Test scores from specific Negro colleges. We know of no Negro college whose mean scores exceed the national mean for those entering college. There are only a handful of Negro colleges where the average freshman scores over 400—approximately the 25th percentile for white freshmen. Most Negro colleges average in the 300s. Some average below 300—approximately the 7th percentile for whites taking the test. There are very few white colleges with mean SAT scores below 400, and we know of none with a mean below 300.

In Georgia, for example, Julian Stanley reports that from 1957 to 1964 freshmen at the four least selective public white colleges (mostly overgrown teachers colleges) had median SAT verbal scores of 400 for men and 419 for women.[32] Freshmen at the four public Negro colleges had median scores of 254 for men and 258 for women. Only 3.2 per cent of the Negro men exceeded the median male score of

[30] Coleman *et al.*, p. 345, gives national estimates of the ability of future teachers from Negro and white colleges. Since large proportions of both college groups plan to teach, and since the future teachers are drawn from the middle ability range in both racial groups, this provides some indication of relative aptitudes at the two sorts of colleges. The Coleman data indicate that the Negroes' average scores put them at about the 10th percentile of the white ability distribution. This estimate is consonant with the estimates (pp. 219 ff.) of the relative standing of Southern Negro high school seniors compared to whites. A somewhat more optimistic picture might be drawn from Jaffe, Adams, and Meyers. These authors collected data in 1965 on academic aptitudes of Southern Negro high school seniors who planned to attend college the following fall. They estimated that a quarter of these Negro students ranked above the national white median for all high school seniors. They would, of course, rank lower in a distribution of college-bound whites—perhaps 15 per cent would exceed the white median. Since many of the abler Southern Negroes were planning to attend integrated colleges, those who enrolled in Negro colleges may well have ranked at around the 10th percentile of the white college student distribution.

[31] Some writers have questioned whether verbal aptitude tests predict academic potential as well for lower-class Negroes as for middle-class whites. Clark and Plotkin reported that Negroes who received scholarships from the National Scholarship Service and Fund for Negro Students to attend integrated colleges were as likely to do well when they had poor verbal scores as when they had good ones. They argued that motivation was the critical variable for these students. On the other hand, Stanley and Porter have summarized a number of studies of this same problem which show that Scholastic Aptitude Test scores predict Negro college grades as accurately as they do white ones. (See also Cleary.) For data on the proportion of white students in various aptitude groups completing high school, entering college, and completing college, see *College Board Score Reports.*

[32] Stanley.

the four worst white colleges, and 1.4 per cent of the Negro women exceeded the median for white women. Nineteen per cent of the Negro freshmen had scores that were below chance. They would, in other words, have done better by closing their eyes and guessing than they did by trying to use the skills they had acquired at home and in Georgia's still-segregated schools. We must therefore assume that at least 38 per cent of these students *did* in effect close their eyes, for if 19 per cent scored below chance, another 19 per cent must have scored above chance only by luck. Reversing the comparison makes the picture even bleaker, for 99 per cent of all freshmen at the four public white colleges outscored the average student at Georgia's public Negro colleges. White-Negro differences on mathematical aptitude tests were comparable. It is true that these comparisons would be less grim if they included the private Negro colleges in the Atlanta complex, such as Spelman and Morehouse, which are more selective than Savannah State, Fort Valley, and the like. But including these colleges would also mean including white institutions such as the University of Georgia, Georgia Tech, and Emory. The results of such a comparison would probably not be very different from the narrower comparisons reported by Dr. Stanley.

Nor, unfortunately, is Georgia atypical. James C. Wallace has presented comparable data for North Carolina public institutions.[33] North Carolina's public Negro colleges averaged around 300 on the verbal test and around 325 on the mathematical test. Only one public white college (Pembroke) averaged below 400, and even it had a higher median than the best public Negro college (North Carolina A and T).

Public colleges in Virginia repeat the same pattern. The two Negro public institutions (Virginia State at Petersburg and at Norfolk) report average verbal scores of about 325 and 300 respectively, while the two least selective coeducational state institutions (Old Dominion and Richmond Professional Institute) report scores of 445 and 435.[34] The typical man entering the most selective public Negro campus in Virginia would have ranked in the 6th percentile if he had instead entered the least selective public white college. The situation would be somewhat more favorable if we compared men entering Hampton Institute to those entering the worst white colleges in Virginia, but relevant data are not available. If we compared Negroes entering Hampton to whites entering the University of Virginia or William and Mary (the state's two elite public institutions), the Negroes' relative position would probably have been about the same as when less academically demanding institutions are compared.

The fact that the Negro colleges get such academically unpromising

33 Wallace.
34 See "Student Admissions 1966."

students should not be surprising. To begin with, their students come from a social milieu and from schools that have done little or nothing to develop intellectual skills. The few who somehow manage to transcend these handicaps and show obvious intellectual ability are now solicited from all sides by white colleges, both Northern and Southern, and many decide to accept the often generous scholarships these institutions can and do offer.[35] Even though we believe that colleges should be judged in terms of what they do with the students they get, the fact that the Negro colleges get unpromising students does pose academic problems. To begin with, as we have suggested over and over, students tend to educate one another. If most of the students entering a college are semiliterate (which is very nearly the case at most Negro colleges, since the typical freshman usually performs at about ninth-grade level) the result will be a semiliterate student culture. It may be possible to develop student subcultures within such colleges that are intellectually stimulating, academically rigorous, or otherwise deviate from the freshman norm. These enclaves may gradually expand over four years to include an appreciable proportion of the student body. But this is clearly an uphill fight, and we do not have the impression that Negro colleges are any more successful at it than are white colleges with inept students. The tendency is for the students to set their sights low, and for the faculty to do likewise. In most cases the result is that students are merely asked to go through the less interesting and less demanding rituals of higher education, in which diligence can often substitute for competence.

Recognizing these handicaps, how well do the Negro colleges perform? If their freshmen do much worse on national tests than most white freshmen, does their relative position change over the next four years? Unfortunately, we know no national data that would answer this question, though it would not be difficult in principle to acquire some. (One could, for example, give Graduate Record aptitude and achievement tests to all seniors at a given Negro college, determine the national percentile rank of the typical B.A., and then go back and look at his national percentile rank on College Board tests when he entered college. If the Negro B.A.'s position relative to white B.A.s had improved, there would be cause for satisfaction. If, on the other hand, it had deteriorated, the worst fears of the Negro colleges' critics would be confirmed.)[36]

Yet even if investigations showed that four years at a Negro college were of less value than four years at a white college, the defenders

[35] On the relative academic aptitudes of Southern Negroes planning to enter Negro and white colleges, see Jaffe, Adams and Meyers.

[36] For some fragmentary and inconclusive evidence that Negroes may be worse off relative to whites after four years at a Negro college, see Coleman *et al.*, p. 345.

of these colleges would have a ready answer. Less money is spent on Negro college students than on white ones, so it would hardly be surprising if the results were less impressive. In 1950 the Negro colleges evidently spent four-fifths as much per student as the national average, which probably put them well above many smaller white institutions. By 1960, however, the Negro colleges' position had evidently deteriorated, and they were spending only two-thirds the national per student average.[37] There are very few altruistic faculty members willing to teach at Negro colleges for appreciably less money than they could earn elsewhere. This means that these colleges must pay relatively competitive wages.[38] In order to make ends meet Negro college administrators resort to various devices. First, they have fewer faculty members per student than the typical white college.[39] Second, they have fewer extensively trained faculty members than the typical white college.[40] Third, among those at any given level of qualification, they tend to hire men who would have the most difficulty landing a job elsewhere, whether because they are refugees with an imperfect command of English, because they have been in personal difficulties elsewhere, or simply because they are black. (This last attribute, which used to be a serious handicap to a Ph.D. looking for a job, has now become an asset, thus further compounding the recruiting problems of the Negro colleges.)

Given the limited academic promise of the students entering Negro colleges, we are by no means sure that the academic qualifications

[37] McGrath, p. 26. Coleman *et al.*, p. 435, present more recent data on expenditures which suggest that there may have been considerable improvement since 1960, more or less restoring the 1950 situation. The data they present on white colleges do not, however, fit with that available from other sources, and in any case it is risky to estimate trends on the basis of point estimates derived from two different sources. We doubt that the relative position of the Negro college is as favorable as Coleman's data suggest.

[38] For evidence that they do so, see Dunham, Wright, and Chandler. Their table 42 shows that the typical Ph.D. at a Negro college makes 85–90 per cent of the national average for Ph.D.s. The gap would be even less if this table were subdivided by both degrees held and the average level of student taught. Men who teach graduate students earn more, and this pulls up the white average. Despite the enormous demand for "qualified" Negroes as consultants and summer school teachers in the early 1960s, the typical Ph.D. at a Negro college came closer to the national average in salary than in outside income. This strongly implies that the demand for his services outside the Negro college was less than within it. It also suggests that the small difference in mean salary for men with comparable qualifications in Negro and white colleges derives from the fact that for one reason or another the men who teach in Negro colleges are less in demand than men who teach in white colleges. If so, they are accepting poor pay out of necessity, not altruism.

[39] The 1965 *Digest,* table 62, shows that the student-faculty ratio at Negro colleges was about 20 per cent higher than at white ones.

[40] Dunham, Wright, and Chandler, table 42, show that 29 per cent of the faculty at Negro colleges held Ph.D.s, compared to 54 per cent at white colleges.

of their faculty are especially relevant. Indeed, we will argue in the
fourth section of this chapter that some Negro colleges would probably
be better off if they stopped trying to compete with top white colleges
and redefined their missions. If they did this, the possession of a
Ph.D. would become even less relevant as a measure of faculty competence than it is today. But that is our judgment, not the Negro
colleges'. They are as concerned with having Ph.D.s as any university
—perhaps more so. Their definition of what they want in a professor
differs from Harvard's or Berkeley's only in that they will tolerate
less personal eccentricity and put more emphasis on not causing
trouble. (Negro college administrators, like all small college spokesmen, also claim that they are more interested in a professor's teaching
ability than Harvard or Berkeley, and less interested in his publications. But we can see little evidence for this. They certainly do not
insist on publication, but demonstrated teaching ability does not seem
to count for any more in the Negro colleges' decisions about whom
to hire or whom to retain than it does at white colleges.) Under these
circumstances we must judge the Negro colleges partly by the same
(often irrelevant) standards of excellence that we and others apply
to their white counterparts. By these standards the Negro colleges do
very poorly indeed.

Nevertheless, as we have already emphasized, Negro colleges are
not all alike. At the head of the Negro academic procession stands a
handful of well-known private institutions, such as Fisk, Morehouse,
Spelman, Hampton, Tuskegee, and Dillard, an even smaller number
of public ones such as Texas Southern and Morgan State, and that
peculiar hybrid, Howard.[41] By most criteria, these institutions would
probably fall near the middle of the national academic procession.
They attract a few brilliant students, employ a few brilliant professors, and run a few very lively programs. On the whole, however,
their faculties are comparable to those of not very distinguished
sectarian colleges or fairly typical state colleges.

In addition to these leaders, there are some 50 relatively large
public colleges and about 60 small private ones. By almost any standard these 110 colleges are academic disaster areas. Badly paid as their
faculty members usually are, many of them could not make as much
elsewhere. Some, indeed, could not get any other academic job. Insecure and marginal, they become insistently pedantic. The better
faculty members are aware that their students cannot master the

[41] Howard is privately controlled but largely federally financed, so that it is
not always put in the private category. Some would argue that Dillard should not
be included above, or that Bennett, Talladega, Knoxville, or Lincoln University
in Pennsylvania ought to be. Fisk, Morehouse, Spelman, and Hampton are sometimes referred to as the Negro Ivy League.

kinds of material they themselves studied during their graduate years at Michigan, Ohio State, Howard, NYU, or Teachers College. But like Nigerians wedded to a University of London syllabus, they cling to a pallid version of the academic tradition, itself in need of renewal. Anxious about their authority, remembering how hard they worked for their degrees, and worried by how much they have forgotten or not kept up with, they require their students to memorize scraps of wisdom in much the same fashion as a bad high school, an old-fashioned Catholic college, or a provincial teachers college does.

Yet these colleges have for several generations been the major agency for selecting and socializing the prospective members of the black bourgeoisie. Their role here may be even more important than the role of white colleges for white society, for upward mobility among Negroes seems to have depended more on professional credentials and less on entrepreneurial or managerial talent than is the case among whites. The fact that these colleges often sift out the rebellious, the creative, and the alienated may therefore have had even more impact on the character of the Negro middle classes than on the white ones. Those who have joined the Negro middle class have been extremely conservative on all issues other than racial equality, and sometimes even on that.

Still, civil rights activism has depended very heavily on Negroes of college age. Like university students elsewhere, these adolescents have not yet been locked into the economy and are relatively free from economic reprisals (though their parents have not been). Correspondingly, they have been less susceptible to temptation and therefore less suspect in Negro communities, which are corrosively skeptical of adult leadership. But the students' activism has seldom been encouraged, even tacitly, by Negro college administrators or faculty, and has often been bitterly opposed. This opposition results partly from knowing that student activism may lead to white retaliation against the college. It also reflects the irritation of the more academically oriented faculty at seeing their best students distracted from schoolwork by what many professors regard as mindless activism, while their worst students often seem to use civil rights as an excuse for goofing off. These faculty members want their students to win Woodrow Wilson Fellowships or get into medical school, not go to jail. Yet even the less academic faculty have often been unsympathetic to civil rights activists. The political gap between white-fearing and God-fearing Negro adults and dissident, rebellious young Negroes has thus been even greater than among whites. This is in some ways surprising, since in strictly cultural terms, such as tastes in music and dancing, there seems to be less of a generation gap among Negroes than among whites. The continued involvement of Negro adults in college-based fraternities and sororities is another sign of this. For this and other reasons, the Negro college student who becomes deeply involved in civil rights work has usually dropped out of college. Very few Student Non-Violent Coordinating Committee activists have B.A.s, though many matriculated at Negro colleges. Nonetheless, the civil rights movement has had an enormous impact on the attitudes of students at Negro colleges during the past few years. There is more open rebelliousness, more racial pride, and more hope than even a few years back. And in 1967 Negro campuses finally became major centers of protest in the South.

One reason for the relative conservatism of the Negro campuses may be the fact that on many of them, women still outnumber men as much as two to one. For Negro colleges as a group, women constitute 54 per cent of enrollment, compared to 38 per cent at white colleges.[42] This imbalance is an endemic problem in all phases of Negro life, and it seems reasonable to assume that the situation at the college level is a cause as well as a consequence of the adult problem. White girls outperform white boys throughout elementary and secondary school. Among whites, however, success begins to be more evenly distributed in college, where the "hard" sciences count for more, where even "soft" subjects can be studied in "hard" ways, and where boys have other ways of asserting themselves than by not learning what they are told to learn. In the Negro colleges these opportunities seem less available, and girls continue to dominate things. This may be one important reason why the matriarchal pattern of lower-class Negro life seems to survive even in the Negro middle class.

The over-all picture at these colleges is, then, grim. Yet when we have visited these institutions we have almost always found pockets of vitality. Almost every college has been touched by the efforts at upgrading of recent years. Almost none is without a small nucleus of faculty, white as well as Negro, who struggle with exemplary passion to overcome the students' previous conditioning, lack of academic motivation, and susceptibility to collegiate distraction. Even the most academically inferior of these colleges has a few students who respond to the zealous efforts of the more imaginative faculty and suggest what might happen if more of their kind could somehow be

[42] 1965 *Digest*, tables 50 and 62. Census data suggest that the ratio of Negro men to women is probably about the same in integrated colleges. Actually, the Census publishes no breakdown of college students by both sex and race, but cautious inferences can be made about Negro sex ratios from those for all non-whites. Allowing for the fact that the Oriental undergraduates are overwhelmingly male, the national male-female ratio for Negroes appears to be about 45:55.

attracted and kept. (Much the same thing is true at the equivalent white institutions.) There seems to be something about a college, as about a nation, that engenders a paradoxical combination of euphoria and paranoia and leads otherwise judicious people to dedicate themselves to its service in spite of somehow knowing better. The spark plug may in one place be the librarian, in another the chaplain, in still another a white academic missionary, and in still others Negro faculty—often women—who might go elsewhere but who stay to suffer and struggle. And as we shall see, outside leverage from leading white universities, from foundations, and from Washington can sometimes buoy these small minorities, giving them the feeling that they are not entirely crazy to stick it out.

The Future of the Negro Colleges: Recruitment

Thus far we have spoken of Negro colleges as by-products of the Southern caste system. This statement is something of an oversimplification, as the existence of two such colleges in Pennsylvania and two in Ohio attests. Nevertheless, few would deny that Negro colleges were in all essential features a response to racism. During the past decade, however, racism in its traditional form has been under mounting attack, both from the Negroes who suffer under it and from much of the white elite, which had hitherto accepted or even actively profited from it. No matter how "backlash" politics develops and no matter what becomes of the Negro poor, the Negro middle classes seem destined to be incorporated into the established institutions that dominate American life, sometimes as brokers dealing with poorer Negroes and sometimes in roles where their color is irrelevant. This development is particularly clear in the urban North, but it is also an emerging pattern in the South. This, as we have already suggested, makes the Negroes' situation more nearly akin to that of other ethnic minorities than was true in the past. It also poses an enormous challenge to the Negro colleges, whose symbiotic relationship with the old Negro middle class has been called into question.

What kinds of students will the Negro colleges get, now that the opportunities and incentives for Negroes to attend predominantly white colleges are expanding? The answer to this question depends in part on established white institutions. To the extent that Negro B.A.s want to move into these institutions, they will have to impress recruiters from major corporations and admissions committees at various kinds of graduate and professional schools. These men will be white in most cases; even when they are black, they will be interested in the usual middle-class virtues, including certain kinds of intellectual skills. There is virtually no chance in the foreseeable future for the development of major national corporations controlled by Negroes, and even if there were it is hard to imagine their having junior management-training programs very different from white corporations. In the professions, too, advancement will usually depend on attending a white professional school. The two Negro medical schools (Meharry and Howard) are said to rank among the worst in the nation, and would probably have been closed long ago had they not been a main source of doctors willing to tend Negro patients.[43] There are five Negro law schools, four of which were founded between 1940 and 1950 by Southern legislatures to meet "separate but equal" requirements and were always one jump ahead of the accrediting agencies. Now that able Negroes in these states have access to white law schools, there is growing pressure to phase the tiny but costly Negro ones out, and this decision has been taken in Florida and, with some reservations, Texas. The fifth school, Howard, is in a different class, and is now recruiting white students. Virtually none of the graduate programs in arts and sciences at Negro colleges is adequate by white academic standards. While the graduate programs in education that most public Negro colleges offer are probably not very different from those in the majority of white colleges, we know of none that can claim distinction. The historical reasons for all this are clear, but that does not make the current situation easier to remedy. Indeed, it seems unlikely that any all-Negro school will ever have a first-rate graduate professional program—though some currently all-Negro schools may establish such programs at the same time they become integrated. If this is so, the Negro B.A. who hopes not just to enter a profession but to advance within it will usually want both the credentials and the training of a predominantly white national university.

[43] When this statement appeared in the earlier version of this chapter published in the *Harvard Educational Review*, it aroused more fury than almost any other. Like much else in this chapter, the statement was based on the judgment of men who had worked closely with these institutions. It can, however, be obliquely confirmed from published data. Reitzes gives aptitude scores for students entering medical school in the 1950s. The Negro schools were evidently admitting students with lower scores than any but a handful of white schools. We are told this has not changed. The Council on Medical Education of the American Medical Association also reports the percentage of students from each medical school failing state medical board exams each year. In 1965 the only schools with higher failure rates than Meharry and Howard were the Chicago Medical School (not to be confused with the University of Chicago School of Medicine) and the Stritch School of Medicine (part of Loyola University in Chicago). The significance of the failure rates for Chicago and Stritch is questionable, since the Illinois boards are among the toughest in the country and the numbers involved are small. The failure rates for Howard and Meharry, on the other hand, almost certainly reflect the limited ability of many of the students admitted.

The question, then, is whether white graduate schools and white corporations will be eager to accept the graduates of Negro colleges. At the moment, both corporations and graduate schools are making special efforts to provide compensatory training for Negroes who have had inadequate undergraduate (not to mention elementary and secondary) education. Recruiters have swarmed onto Negro campuses in recent years, searching for what the skeptics call the "instant Negro." Lincoln University in Pennsylvania reported, for example, that it had more visits from company recruiters in 1966 than it had B.A.s. Some major universities have also established special summer programs to identify and prepare Negro college students for graduate work. A number of universities have even "adopted" one or more Negro colleges, establishing formal links that sometimes make it easier for the graduates of the Negro colleges to get into the "parent" university's graduate schools.

Universities' and corporations' willingness to extend compensatory opportunity to Negroes over the long term will almost certainly depend on whether these programs "work," in the sense that the Negroes in question prove able to compete with whites on relatively equal terms. There will obviously be some white academicians and corporate managers with a personal commitment to extending opportunities for Negroes, and these men will not succumb to a change in fashion or to disappointment when the first recruits are neither Ralph Bunche nor George Washington Carver, John Hope Franklin nor Robert Weaver. But many white professors have been overoptimistic about Negro graduate students, and corporate recruiters have also sometimes made excessive allowance for Negroes' earlier handicaps. When it turns out that poorly prepared Negroes frequently cannot seize the "second chance" they have been given, a reaction is likely to set in and the opportunities are likely to be withdrawn. Such a reaction is particularly likely in the graduate schools which have traditionally been almost unrelievedly meritocratic and have shown almost no concern with inventing new ways to help students learn, whether by reorganizing the disciplines or by instituting the kind of curriculum revision now under way in the elementary and secondary schools. In most cases, then, Negroes will have to respond fairly quickly to compensatory programs and will have to keep fairly close to the pace set by their white classmates. In business, where token Negroes may be hired for more cynical reasons, a double standard may prove more durable and opportunities may not depend so much on performance, which is in any case harder to judge.

Unrealistic white expectations will probably be a problem for most Negro B.A.s who enter white corporations or graduate or professional

schools, regardless of where they attended college. But the problem
may be more acute for those who have been to all-Negro colleges than
for those who have been to predominantly white ones. The latter will
already have shown they can compete with whites academically and
that they can make out in a predominantly white milieu. From the
viewpoint of a company recruiter or a law school dean, a Negro from
San Francisco State, Temple, or Roosevelt will almost certainly seem
less of a risk than a Negro from Alcorn A & M or even Fisk.

When the current wave of interest in "qualified" Negroes began,
people naturally turned to the Negro colleges because these were the
most obvious and most concentrated source of Negro B.A.s. A company that wanted a Negro for its front office, for example, could send
a recruiter to Fisk and be sure that he would come back with a Negro,
even if he was not always the perfect candidate. If they sent a recruiter to, say, Wayne State in Detroit, it was awkward (as well as
illegal) to ask to see only Negroes. Yet it was time-consuming to in-
terview a hundred whites in order to locate the few Negroes the
company wanted, especially since Negroes often assumed that recruiters would be interested only in whites, and therefore did not
sign up to be interviewed. At Fisk, every student knew at least that
if a recruiter came to the campus he was interested in Negro applicants. Nonetheless, more Negro men earn B.A.s from Wayne every
year than from Fisk. Not only that—most Wayne Negroes are probably
readier to enter white professional schools or office jobs. This situation
is not, of course, primarily caused by anything Wayne does or Fisk
fails to do. While there are some Northern Negroes from metropolitan
school systems at Fisk, as at other Negro colleges, the majority of
Wayne Negroes has been better schooled before coming to college,
more carefully screened by the Wayne admissions system, and made
more familiar with a white milieu. Wayne Negroes have been less
visible than their Fisk counterparts, because they are immersed in a
sea of white faces—though there are no doubt tables in the student
union where they congregate. Nevertheless, if they work out better
than Fisk graduates in law schools, graduate chemistry departments,
executive training programs, and other enterprises with national recruiting nets, these organizations will make the efforts needed to
find and favor them.

The Wayne-Fisk comparison is a hypothetical one, since we have
no actual comparative data on the Negro alumni of the two schools.
But it is not an isolated case. A myth has developed to the effect that
virtually all Negro undergraduates are in Negro colleges—a myth
whose corollary is that the growth of an educated Negro middle
class depends on white financial support for Negro colleges. The fact
is, however, that almost half of all Negro undergraduates are already

in predominantly white colleges.[44] If white employers and graduate and professional schools favor Negroes with "white" B.A.s, this proportion will grow. If the financial, academic, and especially the social

[44] Estimates of the total number of Negroes attending college vary widely. Four have come to our attention.

1) *The U. S. Office of Education.* USOE did not collect statistics on Negro enrollment in predominantly white colleges prior to 1965. In that year USOE asked registrars to give their "best estimate" of the number of Negroes in their colleges. About 90 per cent did so. These estimates suggested that 4.6 per cent of all college students were Negroes. It must be emphasized, however, that these were *guesses,* not an enumeration. Since most college officials are eager to prove their institution's commitment to civil rights, and since the Office of Education was thought to favor racial integration, some college registrars probably overestimated the proportion of Negroes at their institutions. We are reluctant to rely on the USOE figure. (For an analysis of the USOE data, see Coleman *et al.,* pp. 368 ff.)

2) *The Census.* Most Census reports classify respondents as "white" or "nonwhite." The latter classification includes not only Negroes but Orientals, American Indians, and other non-Caucasians. Since 92 per cent of all American nonwhites are Negroes, Census data on non-whites are normally presumed to describe Negroes fairly accurately. In the case of college students, however, this assumption turns out to be hazardous. The *School Enrollment* supplement to the 1960 *Census* (Final Report PC(2)-5A, table 1) provides a detailed racial breakdown and shows that only 77 per cent of all "non-white" college students are Negroes. The bulk of the remainder are Orientals, whose college enrollment rate exceeds that of whites. The *School Enrollment* supplement is the only Census report which enumerates Negro students separately from other non-whites. It shows that in the spring of 1960 Negroes constituted 5.2 per cent of all undergraduates and 3.0 per cent of all graduate students—4.9 per cent of total enrollment. "Other non-whites" constituted 1.5 per cent of total enrollment.

3) *The National Opinion Research Center survey.* (James Davis, *Great Aspirations,* pp. 101 ff.) NORC found that 3.0 per cent of the June 1961 B.A.s reported their race as Negro and 2.5 per cent reported their race as Oriental or other non-white. The discrepancy between these figures and those reported to the Census and to USOE might be partly explained by higher undergraduate attrition among Negroes than whites, but neither Census nor USOE data show attrition differentials of this magnitude. Differences in sampling procedures and definitions probably account for part of the variation. It may also be that a disproportionately large number of Negroes refused to answer the racial question or answered "other."

4) *The McGrath mail survey.* (McGrath, p. 21.) McGrath does not describe exactly whom he counted as a college student and whom he did not, but judging by his statistical calculations he seems to have included all regular, degree-credit students, full time and part time, graduate and undergraduate, while excluding extension students. In that case his figures indicate that Negroes constituted 4.1 per cent of college enrollment in 1964. This figure can perhaps be reconciled with NORC's finding that 3.0 per cent of all 1961 *graduates* were Negroes, but not with the 1960 Census finding that 4.9 per cent of all *students* were Negroes, nor with the USOE figure of 4.6 per cent.

Given this contradictory evidence, we can make only approximate guesses about Negro educational patterns. We know that in 1966 about 11 per cent of all eighteen- to twenty-one-year-olds were Negroes; between 4 and 5 per cent of all undergraduates were Negroes; about 2.5 per cent of all undergraduates were enrolled in Negro colleges (projected from McGrath, p. 21, and 1965 *Digest,* table 62). This means that between 50 and 60 per cent of all Negro students were probably in Negro colleges. This percentage is probably falling, but we do not know how fast.

obstacles to Negroes' attending integrated colleges were then eliminated, the Negro colleges would almost certainly lose a large proportion of their applicants.

Yet while white employers and graduate schools may somewhat prefer Negroes who have proven they can make it at a white college, and while Negro high school students may in some cases realize this, such matters are seldom clear-cut. There will, moreover, continue to be some employers and callings (e.g. teaching in predominantly Negro schools) in which it makes relatively little difference where a man or woman went to college, so long as he has the right paper credentials for professional certification. In addition, there are many cases where the contacts made at a Negro college will be much more valuable than the contacts with a smaller number of Negroes and a potentially larger number of whites at an integrated college. This would be true not only of occupations usually practiced within the Negro community, such as the ministry, law, or undertaking, but also of some work for white employers such as insurance companies, which seek Negro employees because they have social connections with other Negroes. Furthermore, even if the advantages of attending an integrated college become greater and every Negro high school student is made aware of them, the obstacles to actually enrolling in such a college will remain formidable for many Negroes for a long time to come.

The legal difficulties confronting a Negro who wants to attend a non-Negro college have never been overwhelming so long as no other problems existed. There have been Northern white colleges open to Negroes since well before the Civil War—*if* the applicant had the proper preparation, enough money to pay tuition and subsistence, and a thick enough skin to endure social isolation and occasional slights. Today almost all white institutions, even in the South, will accept a Negro applicant, and most have done so. Those that have not are mostly small and academically undistinguished sectarian colleges to which relatively few Negroes would want to go even if they expected to be welcome.

The economic obstacles to attending a predominantly white college are also diminishing. It is almost invariably cheaper for a Negro living north of the Mason-Dixon line to attend a public institution in his own state than to go South to a Negro one—and the proportion of Negroes in the North is growing. The cost differential will grow even wider in the next decade, for public universities will by then be available in almost every major Northern city, and public junior colleges with only nominal admission requirements will be within commuting distance of Negroes in most Northern cities of even moderate size.

In the South, public commuter colleges of any sort may be slower coming. Atlanta, Savannah, New Orleans, Houston, and Memphis have such colleges, and Memphis State has already attracted a substantial Negro enrollment. But there are still many sizable Southern cities without a public college, perhaps partly because politicians have anticipated that new institutions of this sort would mix Negroes with whites. In addition, there are still substantial numbers of Negroes in the small towns of the South, and many of these will not have even a junior college in the foreseeable future.

Under these circumstances the economic calculus that determines where it is cheapest for a Southern Negro to go will be more complex than in the North. Today the Southern urban Negro often finds that his cheapest alternative is a private Negro college in his home city. Almost all these colleges now charge substantially less tuition than white colleges in the same area. Since, however, tuition is every-where rising faster than room-and-board charges, it will eventually be cheaper for a student to go away to a public college in most states than to commute to even the cheapest private ones. Since public residential colleges for whites and Negroes almost always have vir-tually the same charges in any given state, economic considerations are likely to have relatively little effect on students' decisions whether or not to integrate, once the private commuter college is priced out of the low-cost field. This day will be hastened by the establishment of public commuter colleges in more and more Southern cities.

The question remains, what should be regarded as a "large" and therefore potentially decisive difference in cost, and what can be dis-counted as a "small" and therefore inconsequential one. Table IX estimates the parental incomes of students at Negro colleges and of all Negro parents with college-age children.

According to the College Scholarship Service's formulae, most of these Negro families were in no position to make any contribution whatever to their children's college expenses.[45] Most nevertheless *did* contribute, often substantially. A price difference of a few hundred dollars could easily have led such families to prefer a Negro college to a white one. This will probably remain true for the foreseeable future.

The Negro who really wants to attend an integrated college, how-ever, whether in the North or the South, need not rely entirely on family support. He can also get a job, borrow, or, if he is lucky, get a scholarship. In the past, Negroes have found it somewhat more difficult than whites to find jobs while attending college, partly be-cause they were Negroes and partly because they often attended

[45] College Scholarship Service, *Manual.*

TABLE IX

1962 INCOMES OF FAMILIES WITH CHILDREN IN NEGRO COLLEGES AND NEGRO FAMILIES WITH HEADS 45 TO 64

Family Income	Negro College Parents	All Negro Parents
Below $4,000	42	51
$4,000 to $5,999	26	22
$6,000 to $9,999	23	19
Above $10,000	10	8
Total	101	100

SOURCES: Negro college students' parental incomes were estimated by the students. See McGrath, p. 39. The students probably underestimated their parents' incomes quite substantially. The data for all Negro families are estimated from the 1960 *Census*, I, 1, table 224, adjusted for income changes between 1959 and 1962. The Census estimates include only families with children under eighteen in their home. They are for the nation as a whole and are not precisely comparable to the predominantly-Southern pool from which Negro college students are drawn.

college in isolated rural areas where jobs were scarce.[46] This handicap should, however, be increasingly offset by the federal government's work-study program, which provides both Negro and white colleges with subsidies to create jobs for undergraduates.

The federal government is also now committed to making almost unlimited loan funds available to undergraduates. Many Negroes have, however, been reluctant to take advantage of these. For one thing, they realized that even if they completed college they would not necessarily be able to earn enough to repay a loan easily—though the partial forgiveness of loans made to future teachers made matters easier for some, especially girls. In addition, many Negro undergraduates had good reason to fear that they would never graduate, and this made the prospect of being saddled with a federal debt doubly alarming. Finally, many Negroes had to borrow up to the statutory limit merely to attend a local Negro college, so that federal loans gave them no additional leeway to attend more expensive integrated institutions. As borrowing becomes a more common way of financing higher education for whites, however, Negro resistance may also diminish.

Finally, there are scholarships. Most applicants to Negro colleges

[46] The 1960 *Census* (*School Enrollment* supplement, Final Report PC(2)-5A, table 8) showed that 39 per cent of all Negro undergraduates were in the labor force, compared to 46 per cent of white undergraduates. Given the differences in family income, one might expect as many as 75 per cent of the Negro undergraduates to work if jobs were available. The percentage of Negroes working to meet expenses has almost certainly increased since 1960 as a result of federal work-study programs and will probably continue to increase if job opportunities for Negro undergraduates do so.

have not had the academic qualifications to apply for scholarships
at Northern institutions, nor even to apply for admission to the
highly competitive private colleges that offer most of the full scholarships. Special programs designed to recruit, tutor, and graduate more
Negro students at these colleges have succeeded in turning up a
number of youngsters who could make it, but the number who plainly
cannot remains much larger. The efforts of the National Merit Scholarship Corporation and the National Scholarship Service and Fund
for Negro Students have been similarly limited in their numerical
effect. This does not mean that such programs are politically or
culturally irrelevant. Increasing the number of "Ivy League Negroes"
could have an enormously positive effect on the national scene a
generation hence. It could also have a conspicuous negative effect
on Negro colleges in the more immediate future. If the various
scholarship programs enable even ten thousand of the most talented
Southern Negroes to attend white institutions, the Negro institutions
will become markedly more depressing than they have been, and
will lose much of their remaining appeal to able faculty.

Another potential threat to the Negro colleges' hold on Negro students is the federal government's small program of "educational opportunity grants" (i.e. scholarships). These are awarded entirely on
the basis of need rather than academic promise, and go to Negroes
in appreciable numbers. They should help those who want to attend
unselective white colleges, North or South, to do so. Finally, the "Cold
War GI Bill," while paying rather modest benefits, should enable a
number of Negro men to attend integrated colleges if they also work
and take advantage of federal loans.

Taking all these factors into account, we conclude that poverty
alone is unlikely to keep a significant number of Negroes in the Negro
colleges in the years ahead. Many Negro students may, of course,
think they cannot afford to attend a white college, and many may not
know about the various programs that would help them pay their
way. Any lower-class culture is characterized by such ignorance of
opportunities that are in principle available. Correspondingly, it is the
poorer Negro colleges that lack the knowledge, resources, ingenuity,
and energy to go after federal or other outside grants.

If we turn from economic to academic obstacles, the path to white
colleges looks considerably rougher. We have already cited test scores
which suggest that the majority of the students now enrolled in
Negro colleges would have great difficulty either getting in or staying
in a typical white college. This is true not only of Southern Negroes
from segregated schools but of some Northern Negroes who now
go south to Negro colleges, sometimes after attending an integrated
high school. The only kind of integrated college these Negroes could

enter would be a junior college that took any high school graduate, or a state college that took students entirely on the basis of their high school grades or rank. Many Negroes now in Negro colleges would have difficulty surviving in any white college without special help—and special help is something that the unselective public commuter college has in the past seldom supplied. Still, if universal higher education becomes a nationally accepted goal—and we think it will—cities and states will be under enormous political pressure (from Negroes, among others) to provide not only colleges that will admit anyone, but also colleges that will graduate anyone who perseveres. In this as in so many other respects, the colleges seem merely to be two generations behind the secondary schools. Looking ahead, it seems likely that unselective junior colleges will be available to the majority of Negroes, North and South, within a generation. It also seems likely that in the more progressive states public four-year colleges will be available in most sizable cities.

The most important obstacle to Negroes' moving into integrated colleges may not, however, be either economic or academic but more broadly social. Most Negroes live in a relatively closed subculture, within which the distinction of "their" colleges is almost inevitably overestimated. There are many reasons for this overestimation. Almost every Negro over forty-five who went to college did so at an all-Negro institution. This means that virtually all the successful Negroes of whom a high school senior might have heard are Negro college alumni.[47] At least in the South, moreover, the Negro high school student is likely to have teachers and guidance counselors all of whom have been to Negro colleges. The counselor, too overworked to keep up with new trends in admissions offices at white colleges, may fear rebuff if he sends a Negro to a white college—even though today the rejection is more likely to be on academic than racial grounds. Then, too, Negro counselors are as prone as white ones to feel that what was good enough for them ought to be good enough for the young. Some have a "Who the hell do you think you are?" attitude toward students who want to go to a white college, even though others take great pride in placing their students in these same colleges. In addition, some Negro college applicants have a parent, and many have a relative or parental friend, who attended a Negro college. These Negro alumni are often fiercely loyal to their alma mater, partly because they so often feel that college made

[47] One suggestive partial exception (and not yet forty-five) was Martin Luther King, Jr. King was an undergraduate at Morehouse, but the fact that both he and a number of other Negro Methodist clergymen also studied at Boston University has added to that institution's considerable appeal to younger Negroes. BU's reputation in African studies has also helped.

everything else (i.e. the escape from lower-class life) possible for them, partly because they often still participate in Negro fraternity or sorority affairs to which their college gave them entrée, and partly because at college they made social contacts of value in their careers.

Taken together, all these adult influences have a conservative effect on the college choices of the young, pushing them toward the institutions of their forefathers. The reader who recalls what we said earlier about most Negroes' belief in white cultural supremacy may find this a bit surprising, and might expect Negro parents, teachers, and other adults to seek vicarious "whiteness" by pushing the young into integrated institutions. Sometimes such pushing does occur, but it is not simple or uniform. Negro feelings about white institutions are even more dramatically ambivalent than the feelings of other ethnic minorities about Anglo-Saxon attitudes and mores, and all these conflicting emotions are brought to bear on college choices. The Negro who accepts the standards of academic competence established at the national universities may nonetheless claim—and in some respects really believe—that Howard is as academically distinguished as Yale, or that a boy can learn as much at Tuskegee as at MIT. This attitude has been in some ways legitimized and re-enforced by the civil rights movement, which has given many Negroes a tentative new pride in their race, and has made them feel that white may not be entirely right after all. The hostility to whites that is much more openly expressed today than it was even a few years back may even make attending a white college look like a sellout. On the other hand, Alexander J. Morin has pointed out to us the paradoxical possibility that some young Negro militants will find the private Negro colleges so offensively "middle class" and so socially and politically regulated that they may prefer to battle it out either at predominantly white colleges or at the larger, public Negro colleges.

In addition to all these adult influences, young Negroes have an important influence on one another, which is unlikely to lead to integration. If Negroes come up through segregated schools and have exclusively Negro friends, peer group pressures may push them toward a Negro college even more relentlessly than the contradictory hopes and admonitions of their elders. A Negro graduating from a Southern high school will almost always have several acquaintances at the nearest public Negro college in his state; he will be less likely to know anyone at the white colleges he might consider. Nor do white admissions systems work in such a way as to facilitate several Negroes from a single Southern high school going off together to a white school. Yet the prospect of going alone is obviously scary. A few white colleges, such as Roosevelt University in Chicago, are widely known to welcome Negroes, but most are unknown quantities, which inspire understandable and often justifiable distrust. Yet unless they are considering a college near home, Negroes often have a difficult time discovering whether there will be a supportive Negro community at a non-Negro institution. Sometimes there is, but it takes time for the word to spread.[48] Without such a community, individual Negroes are likely to be unhappy, for they are even less comfortable as a minority of one—or even half a dozen—than whites are. (The whites, like Englishmen in the colonies, can more easily protect themselves by cultural arrogance.) Negroes may hope to have a lot of white friends, but this seldom means they want to be without Negro friends. This is especially true of dating. Very few Negroes' interest in assimilation extends to serious romance—though, like whites, some are eager to explore the limits (or lack of them) on interracial sex. Still, Negro girls are at least as interested as white ones in marriage, and Negro boys are equally reluctant to spend a Saturday night alone. Even when sex is not an issue, social life can be a problem for Negroes at white colleges. There are seldom, for example, Negro fraternities or sororities at white colleges, and acceptance into a white fraternity, even if possible, is unlikely to provide quite the same feeling of convivial relaxation.

Under these circumstances it is hardly surprising that many college applicants prefer an evil they know (segregation) to a promise they only half believe (integration). Nor is this preference simply a matter of ignorance or paranoia. Every year an appreciable number of Negroes transfer from integrated to all-Negro colleges, and while some of these students make the move for academic or financial reasons, many also cite loneliness and personal unhappiness as major motives. These students may still recognize the academic advantages of an integrated college, and the occupational boost a B.A. from such a college would almost certainly give them, but they find that the personal price is too high. This price is not, we suspect, primarily the result of racial prejudice but of cultural differences. The Negro who goes to

[48] The myth that virtually all Negro undergraduates are at Negro colleges has as its counterpart the myth that there are no white institutions with more than token integration. Tokenism can, of course, mean many different things, and some might argue that 500 Negroes in a student body of 20,000 was tokenism. Reports to the U. S. Office of Education (Coleman et al., p. 419) indicate that in 1965 there were 148 colleges where more than 5 and less than 50 per cent of the students were Negroes. The weighted average size of these institutions was about 10,000 students, but some were quite small. They were found in every part of the country and were evenly divided between the public and private sectors. A survey by the American Council on Education of freshmen entering colleges in 1966, on the other hand, suggests that the number of colleges with between 5 and 50 per cent Negro enrollment was much smaller than this, and that most were private urban colleges. We would be surprised if there were more than 100 traditionally white colleges with over 5 per cent Negro enrollment. Yet even 100 is nearly as many institutions as there are in the Negro system.

a residential white college discovers that social acceptance and intellectual ease depend on his changing in a host of small ways and some big ones. This discovery is not unique to the upwardly mobile Negro. All first-generation collegians, especially those from predominantly lower-class ethnic minorities, make this discovery. Some, having realized this at a private residential college, may transfer back to a commuter college near home. Others anticipate the problem and become the principal clientele of white ethnic colleges. Such colleges provide the upwardly mobile with credentials, and to some extent with skills, while not asking them to change their ways as much as a predominantly Anglo-Saxon, residential college would. By boosting their alumni into middle-class occupations, these colleges encourage further changes later on, and indirectly make it possible for the sons and daughters of their alumni to feel relatively comfortable in non-ethnic institutions. The Negro college is evidently beginning to play a similar role.[49]

This raises the question whether Negro colleges will be able to hold the children of their own alumni, a challenge white ethnic colleges have also faced. As we have said, the Negro middle-class parent often makes great efforts to protect his children from discrimination, just as his own large car could once have been seen in part as an escape from Jim Crow transportation. The defensively closed character of the black bourgeoisie, plus the tendency already referred to of all alumni to overestimate the merits of their alma mater, will help the Negro colleges attract second-generation young people. On the other hand, the Negro middle class seems to be even more education-conscious than its white counterpart, and this is likely to create interests and pressures that lead children toward integrated colleges. The Census reports that 40 per cent of the seventeen- and eighteen-year-old Negro students with white-collar parents are in private schools, and conscientious white schoolmen are trying to encourage this trend in many places.[50] As a result, the abler children of college-educated Negroes are often well enough schooled, well enough heeled, and widely enough sought after to compete on equal terms with white college applicants. Their choice of colleges is likely to be influenced by the same considerations as the choices of comparable whites, and in most places they will want "the best place I can get into." They will therefore usually choose a nationally known college,

[49] One suggestive piece of evidence for this is that two-thirds of the students in Southern Negro colleges want to work in the North (Jaffe, Adams, and Meyers). If they do move north, this in itself will reduce their children's chances of attending a Negro college.

[50] Coleman *et al.*, p. 36. The estimate strikes us as rather improbable and should be treated with caution.

and it will usually be an integrated one.[51] This choice will be most likely for those who realize, as most such Negroes probably will, that college is for them merely a prelude to graduate or professional school.

It is far from clear, moreover, that even upwardly mobile Negroes who are the first in their families to attend college will want to use Negro colleges as decompression chambers. Like other ethnic minorities, especially urban ones, the majority of Negroes may prefer a big, pluralistic, public commuter college. Such a college does not suffer from the stigma of segregation, yet neither does it make the stringent psychological demands of an integrated residential college. It holds out the promise that a Negro with its B.A. will be able to leave the ghetto and enter the white world if he wants, but it does not demand that he make the break today. A Negro can come to such a college, attend classes, take his exams, collect his grades, credits, and diplomas and go home every night to his family and friends around the corner. A commuter college of this kind may be less demanding socially, despite the fact that it is predominantly white, than a residential Negro college would be. The commuter college does not ask its Negro students to acquire the habits and values of the old Negro middle class, much less of white society.

Public commuter colleges need not, of course, be integrated. But of the forty cities with more than fifty thousand Negroes in 1960, only four had public, multipurpose, four-year colleges especially for Negroes. These were Baltimore, Houston, Jackson, and Nashville. In addition, Washington, D.C., had a public teachers college and a federally financed university. The latter, Howard, describes itself as private but charges less than most private universities, Negro or white. Charlotte had a public junior college for Negroes. In addition, and perhaps as a portent of things to come, three of Chicago's eight junior college campuses are now predominantly Negro. Once a college becomes all-Negro it is likely to develop the familiar pathologies of de facto segregation, with separatism coming to mean inferiority. All-Negro colleges tend to be underfinanced, and they often fail to challenge their ablest students. Chicago's Negro campuses, for example, are reported to use less demanding textbooks than the white campuses, and to set lower standards for academic success. Given the inadequacy of elementary and secondary schooling for Negroes in Chicago, and the likelihood that higher standards would mean many

[51] One piece of evidence that supports this inference is that of 740 Negro National Achievement Scholarship winners in 1965–67, only 87 chose Negro colleges. Harvard was the most popular choice, getting about 6 per cent of the winners. Howard was second with 4 per cent. Yale was third, Chicago fourth, and so on down the list of elite white colleges. Fisk ranked fifteenth, and Morehouse sixteenth. No other Negro college got more than 4 of the 740 winners.

more failures, this may make sense. But it also means an able, ambitious Negro should probably go elsewhere. Nonetheless, de facto segregation at the college level is still a relatively remote danger in most cities. Most public colleges have large enough watersheds to pull in whites as well as Negroes, and high enough admissions requirements so that their current worry is getting more Negroes, not holding onto anxious whites.

When all these considerations are taken into account, what kinds of students can we expect to find remaining within the Negro college system, and what kinds can we expect to see opting out? The answer depends, of course, partly on what becomes of the Negro colleges themselves—a question we will discuss in the next section. At this point, we need make clear only that when we talk about Negro colleges we mean just that—colleges not only founded for Negroes but catering almost exclusively to them. We are not talking about the minority of Negro colleges that will attract white students in large numbers and will thus cease to be Negro colleges in any basic sense.

Who, then, will attend the Negro colleges? First, there will be some students who come from homes so isolated from the main currents of American life that they do not sense the occupational advantages of a degree from an integrated school. Second, there will be some whose aspirations are so limited that these advantages are irrelevant— for example, girls who plan to teach school wherever their husbands work and assume that he will be in a big city or small Southern town where there is a chronic shortage of accredited teachers willing to teach Negro children. Third, there will be a shrinking minority that cannot scrape together enough money to attend any white college. Fourth, there will be a sizable minority whose upbringing and schooling have so unfitted them for academic life that they cannot get into any nearby white college, and a larger minority which, while formally eligible for many "open door" white colleges, cannot survive academically in them. Fifth, there will be a substantial group who cannot find an integrated college nearby with a large enough Negro subculture to make them socially comfortable, and who for any one of a dozen reasons will not go away to such a college. Sixth, for a long time, there will be the residual "social" minority, comparable perhaps to some of the Jewish students at Brandeis, whose parents want them to meet the right people, marry the right spouses, and remain within the protective community. Seventh, there will be a small "nationalist" minority that, while aware of the occupational advantages of a white diploma and the academic limitations of Negro colleges, will still have an ideological preference for fighting the black bourgeoisie rather than the white. Finally, there will be a few whites who prefer to spend at least one and occasionally four years at colleges where almost all the other students are Negroes, sometimes because they are idealistic, sometimes because they are curious, sometimes because they are neurotic, and sometimes because the Negro college is the "best buy" in their neighborhood. (In this last rare case, however, the Negro college is likely to become an integrated one.)

As the foregoing list makes clear, there will be a declining number of Negroes for whom an all-Negro college represents the best available academic or occupational choice. We are not saying, however, that *no* Negro should *ever* attend a Negro college. There will be many times when, despite the academic and occupational disadvantages, this choice makes sense on social or psychological grounds. We certainly do not think that most Negroes will be happy in institutions where they are almost the only Negroes around. The chief benefits of such heroism are usually reaped by the whites involved and by later generations of Negroes. There will also be a substantial number of Negroes who want a B.A., are willing to do what they are told to get one, but simply cannot meet the modest standards of even the least selective white colleges. A Negro college will allow them to get the coveted diploma, even if it does not make them competent to do the kinds of work they hope a B.A. implies.

The Future of the Private Negro Colleges

If our analysis of the potential clientele of the all-Negro college is correct, what is to become of the 123 institutions founded for Negroes that were still extant in 1965?[52] They seem likely to be caught in much the same bind as other ethnic colleges have been, but without the legitimacy that comes from transmuting ethnic into religious separatism, without the financial resources available to most white ethnic and religious groups, and with fewer politically powerful friends. Their traditional, first-generation, lower-income constituency will increasingly turn to unselective publicly subsidized commuter colleges, while their prospective second-generation, middle-income constituency will often see no reason to choose their parents' alma mater over a hospitable integrated institution. Like the Catholic colleges discussed in Chapter IX, private Negro institutions can respond to this challenge in one of two ways. Some will undoubtedly try to forget their past and seek students and faculty of all colors, discriminating only against the academically weak. This solution is, however, difficult. A few may reject integration as impractical or undesirable, at

[52] Enumerating Negro colleges is by no means easy, for many are unaccredited, many are tiny, and some do not answer their mail. We rely here on McGrath (appendix A), whose list appears to be the best available.

least on more than a token basis. Some of these may try to legitimize their separatism through one of the quasi-religious mystiques commonly grouped under the rubric of black nationalism. This solution to the racial dilemma is almost as difficult to achieve as full integration. As a result, most Negro colleges are likely to go on very much as they now are.

When asked about the eventual fate of their colleges, virtually all Negro college presidents answer that in due course they hope their college will become integrated. Any other answer would suggest that there was no genuine prospect of establishing a program capable of attracting white students. In theory, a Negro college president might argue that his college is good enough for whites but that he does not want them. If he took this stance, however, he would probably be called an Uncle Tom, a black nationalist, or both.[53] While some Negro college presidents *are* Uncle Toms and others privately sympathize with the advocates of "black power," almost all go along publicly with the ideal of integration. (The most significant exceptions to this rule are a few presidents of public colleges in the Deep South, who find themselves in the difficult position of simultaneously placating both the white supremacists who appoint them and the increasingly assertive Negro students they educate. Such men usually find it expedient to say as little as possible about the future of their institution.)

The fact that Negro college presidents publicly advocate integration does not, however, mean that it will inevitably come. On the contrary, we expect that only a small handful of the colleges founded for Negroes will attract substantial white enrollments in our time. This is not in itself cause for grief. Like every minority group, Negroes need institutions they can call their own, and in the American context a college is one of the most serviceable institutions a special-interest group can have. It provides symbolic assurance of having arrived, a focus for devotion almost comparable to a church, and a platform from which ethnic leaders can speak with more legitimacy than most. Whether these colleges can actually deliver the services or redeem the promises of uplift that give them special status is perhaps no more important than with a church.

In the pages that follow we will examine both the prospects for integration and the prospects for useful service on a segregated basis in various sorts of Negro colleges. We will discuss various sorts of Negro colleges separately, in order to emphasize that Negro colleges are not all alike and probably will not all go the same way. Their futures are linked to one another only insofar as all are linked to the ups and downs of America's seemingly endless struggle with racism.

[53] On the rhetoric and history involved here, compare Brotz, chaps. 4 and 5.

We have already suggested that there are a few privately controlled Negro colleges that are in almost every sense the elite of the Negro academic world. We include in this category the Atlanta group (Atlanta University, Clark College, Morehouse College, Morris Brown College, and Spelman College), Dillard, Fisk, Hampton, Howard, and Tuskegee. These institutions are relatively affluent. In 1964 their combined endowment had a market value of $100 million. At one time the leading foundations were hesitant to help these colleges, on the understandable ground that their help would mean perpetuating segregation. This purist assumption—if one were fighting the evil of segregation, one did not also have to worry about other evils, such as the inadequacy of the colleges the present generation of Southern Negroes would attend—has now been abandoned. Upon its abandonment, the leading private Negro colleges were among the institutions that benefited most. They are also the institutions with loyal alumni, at least some of whom are relatively well off and able to contribute to fund drives.

With the exception of Tuskegee they are all located in fairly large cities, and with the exceptions of Tuskegee and Hampton these cities are among the South's most cosmopolitan. These colleges generally offer prospective faculty more academic freedom, higher salaries, and better schools for their children than do most of their Negro rivals. They are not, it is true, all intellectually exciting or innovative. The pedagogic leaders in the Negro collegiate world include some of these institutions, though also Lincoln in Pennsylvania, Tougaloo, and perhaps others in the private sector, and Texas Southern and Morgan State in the public sector. (Shaw University in Raleigh is one of a number that have sought to insist that entering students, if not academically qualified to be freshmen, must take noncredit remedial courses. But it is a terrific battle to convince students and their parents that they might have to pay more than four years' tuition for a four-year degree. A college that insists too rigidly on such prerequisites may find others drawing its students away by offering a less demanding B.A.) When able young Negro Ph.D.s from leading universities decide which of many tempting offers to accept, these are the only Negro colleges they are likely to consider seriously on a long-term basis. Similarly, although some idealistic young white faculty members will want to spend a year at impoverished commuter colleges like Miles, or try their wings at Talladega or Virginia Union, more will probably be attracted into the Fisk-Morehouse league, especially if they have school-age children. In many cases, what begins as a temporary interlude becomes permanent—especially if a man goes to a Negro college without his Ph.D., finds the routine too exhausting to acquire one, and therefore has no negotiable assets when he wants to leave. But that is hardly a formula for assembling either a competent or a satisfied faculty.

Whether white faculty will be assets in the years ahead is debatable. Some come to Negro colleges with the romantic illusion that the oppressed are more radical, more idealistic, or more "teachable" than the affluent students they have known in Northern white colleges. When such men discover that Negro students have no higher motives and fewer academic interests and aptitudes than the whites they rejected, they often become painfully disillusioned. When they also realize that the psychological damage done by previous home and school life frequently cannot be undone in four years of college, they may want to leave. And their Negro colleagues and administrative superiors may be happy to see them go, both because they have often been a source of political and pedagogic trouble and because their departure confirms the somehow comforting assumption that whites care about Negroes only for neurotic and missionary rather than "sincere" reasons. (We all find a certain security in paranoias of this kind, for it spares us the uncertainty that goes with ambiguity and the risk involved in making subtle distinctions, which often turn out wrong.)

Despite such problems, it seems likely that the wealthier private colleges will be able to maintain the integrated faculties they now have, and that they will be able to attract some professors, both black and white, with good academic pedigrees. Their problems in this regard are likely to be no different from those of second- and third-rank white liberal arts colleges. Like such colleges, they will be tempted to add graduate programs in order to improve their competitive position in the academic market place. As at the comparable white colleges, this will divert some able faculty from teaching promising undergraduates to teaching captive graduate students who lack the energy or resources to attend a leading university. Yet the opportunity to teach such graduate students will also help attract some faculty who would otherwise be totally inaccessible to the undergraduates.

Although these colleges will probably maintain integrated faculties, they are less likely to obtain integrated student bodies. There will be a few liberal white students from the North who find the idea of attending a predominantly Negro college ideologically and culturally attractive, but these cadres are likely to remain scarce. They are, moreover, likely to come from permissive families and to find the puritanical (if often ineffective) paternalism of these Negro colleges hard to accept. Most will also find the collegiate enthusiasms of their fellow students a disappointment, and few will stay four years in a Negro college. If private Negro colleges are to achieve more than token integration, they will have to attract Southern whites from their own environs. Here they will be in direct and hopefully non-ideological competition with Southern white institutions. The white commuter from Atlanta who considers Morehouse will also be considering Emory, Georgia Tech, and Georgia State. Morehouse's only advantage so far as most whites are concerned is likely to be its lower admissions requirements. Similarly, the white student considering Fisk has the alternatives of Vanderbilt and George Peabody in the same city, and the white student considering Dillard on Xavier can also choose Tulane, Newcomb, Loyola, or the New Orleans branch of Louisiana State. Hampton has less impressive competition, and, relative to its own standing, so does Howard.

The top Negro institutions are not going to have an easy time attracting white students. The task might be somewhat simpler if substantial sums were made available for white scholarships, as happened at Howard Law School. But considering the other urgent needs of these colleges, and the other sources of support available to whites, most Negro college presidents will find it hard to justify deploying their limited resources in this way.[54] We therefore doubt that any of these colleges will become predominantly white in the foreseeable future. Indeed, with the possible exception of Howard, whose professional schools are often the cheapest and sometimes the best in the Washington area, we find it hard to imagine any of the leading private Negro colleges attracting even a large minority of whites in the next decade or so.

One alternative would be for these colleges to try to become the Negro counterparts of Brandeis—nearly separate but truly equal. Today there are several serious obstacles to such a course. Jews come from homes which teach them intellectual skills and are likely to have attended the very best elementary and secondary schools in America, while with a handful of exceptions Negroes come from very different homes and are likely to have attended some of the very worst schools. Thus while Negroes are more numerous than Jews in America, academically gifted Negro undergraduates are far scarcer than gifted Jewish ones. In order to put together a student body intellectually comparable to Brandeis, then, a Negro college would

[54] This point was illustrated by student protests at the Howard Law School in the spring of 1967, which charged that whites received preference in competition for scholarships. The alleged reason for this was the administration's desire to integrate Howard "at any price." Actually, we doubt that any formal discrimination was necessary; if scholarships had been given out strictly on the basis of "color-blind" aptitude test scores, most of the whites would probably have gotten help. But while this may be justified in the eyes of the more universalistic or meritocratic members of a faculty like Howard's, it will not placate black students who see that whatever the rationale the money is going to whites and not to them.

have to make itself the first choice of a very large share of all talented
Negro college applicants. Under current conditions, with white colleges combing the country for such students, this seems almost inconceivable.[55] In part, the problem is that no Negro college's B.A.
carries the same weight as one from Harvard, Oberlin, or Berkeley.
Equally serious, not even the best-endowed Negro colleges can match
the combined resources of Northern white colleges in bidding for
promising Negro students. Furthermore, Brandeis succeeded in part
because, aside from Orthodox Yeshiva, it had no Jewish competition.
Too many Negro colleges are within social and academic hailing
distance of one another for any one of them to corner the market
on Negro talent. The Negro college scene is, in this respect, more
akin to the Catholic than the Jewish one. Boston College, Georgetown,
Fordham, and Notre Dame compete with one another as well as
with non-sectarian colleges for promising Catholic students; Fisk,
Howard, and Morehouse do the same. This analogy is imperfect in
other respects, however. Irish Catholic colleges began to achieve
distinction only after their ethnic ties had been attenuated and they
began drawing from the entire American Catholic population. This
gave them a much larger potential constituency than the Negro
colleges, for Catholics are not only twice as numerous as Negroes
but also twice as likely to send their children to college.

Instead of trying to become Negro Brandeises or Notre Dames, the
leading private Negro colleges might try to play the same role vis-à-
vis nearby Negro ghettoes that the Jesuit colleges once played (and
sometimes still do) vis-à-vis Catholic ghettoes. Just as Boston College
helped Americanize the Boston Irish, while at the same time partially
and temporarily sheltering them from Anglo-Saxon competition and
hostility, so Howard might serve Washington Negroes, Fisk might
serve Nashville Negroes, and so on. The problem here is that, with
the partial exception of Tuskegee, these colleges have already moved
"beyond" serving poor local boys. Boston College, Fordham, and St.
Louis University have only recently begun to go residential and
recruit middle-class Catholics from all over the country. The leading
Negro colleges did this some time ago. Indeed, residential education
has been of the most decisive importance in deprovincializing Negroes from farms, small towns, and urban ghettoes, as well as
sheltering them from the punishments of the housing market and
other forms of local white hostility. The Negro residential colleges

[55] One reason for Brandeis' success is that Jews still find it marginally harder
than other students with comparable credentials to get into selective private
colleges. Discrimination against them is sustained by a variety of rationales such
as the quest for geographic diversity ("we've got too many people from New
York") and the quest for "well-rounded leaders."

have truly to act in loco parentis for Negroes out of small, segregated Southern high schools. Yet the very fact that they did this, providing some amenities and embodying some of the symbolism of white middle-class America, has given many poor local Negroes a sense that the elite Negro colleges are pretentious and snobbish. As a result, the elite private colleges would have a hard time reaching the majority of high school graduates in their cities even if they tried. The top Negro private colleges are wedded to the old Negro middle class by their histories and to the new Negro middle class by their aspirations. They may be able to hold their traditional clientele, which continues to look forward to a professional career in a largely segregated setting, but that clientele will shrink. Those who aspire to the new and partially integrated Negro middle class will probably choose integrated colleges. The primary appeal of the elite private Negro colleges will probably remain social rather than intellectual or vocational, and they will therefore find it very hard to alter their present collegiate character even if they want to.

When we turn from the top dozen private Negro colleges to the sixty-odd obscure ones, the prospects of integration diminish to the vanishing point. These colleges typically have no endowment whatever, no alumni capable of supporting them at more than a token level, little time and imagination to develop programs that would get federal or foundation support, few contacts with the men who distribute such funds, and no obvious appeal to white philanthropy, faculty, or students.[56] They tend to be very small—only one or two enroll more than a thousand students, and most have fewer than five hundred. As a result, many operate with a faculty of twenty or thirty, including badly exploited wives, and a budget of less than half a million dollars. Many of these colleges are run as if they were the personal property of their presidents, and a few are.

Recruiting even minimally competent faculty to such colleges is likely to remain difficult. Almost all these colleges are located in small towns or rural areas where local whites are unlikely to be sympathetic, and local Negroes are unlikely to have finished high school. (There are, however, a few exceptions, notably Miles in Birmingham and LeMoyne in Memphis—private commuter colleges that try to play the same role vis-à-vis their urban constituency that the Jesuit colleges have played for theirs.) Faculty considering a job in one of these colleges usually must accept not only starvation wages and poor schools for their children, but grueling teaching loads and isolation from their former friends and colleagues. With little time

[56] There are, however, a few entrepreneurs in the foundations and in federal agencies who will develop a program for a college, fund it, and then hope the college puts the money to good use.

and no money for travel to professional meetings or to centers of cosmopolitan culture, and with only fifteen or twenty educated families in the town, faculty in such institutions are thrown in upon each other, perhaps even more insistently than in a small white college. Gossip rather than ideas inevitably becomes the staple of sociability. The intense pressures from all levels of white society on the one side and from the Negro poor (and increasingly from Negro and white student allies of the poor) on the other side add to faculty tensions. In addition, there is often covert or overt conflict between Negro and white faculty. It is therefore hardly surprising that the faculties at these colleges are almost uniformly poor, the intellectual atmosphere oppressive, and the level of personal tension often high.

Nor are efforts to upgrade faculty at these colleges likely to have more than marginal effects. Negro faculty have, for example, been recruited for summer institutes at leading Northern and Southern universities. These institutes have sought not only to pass on the newest findings in a discipline, but to lessen pedagogic rigidity and encourage an atmosphere of learning rather than teaching in the home institutions. These summer institutes have occasionally given leverage to enterprising younger faculty members who benefit from awareness that they are not alone in their struggles and that the cause is not hopeless. Yet the problems the institutes have faced are grave indeed, as we have learned both from our own experience and vicariously. The models they set may not only be unrealistically high in conventional academic terms, but they may also suffer from the opposite fault of being too unconventional and innovative in terms of the libraries, the administrations, and the entrenched home guard of the Negro institutions. Furthermore, the conservative students aiming at credentials may resent experimental teaching which makes greater demands on them. Brought one-by-one or two-by-two from their colleges, instructors often return home and find they cannot —or dare not—try to change even a textbook in which someone may have a vested interest. They are frequently under the thumb of an older department chairman to whom the president has had to grant almost seignorial rights because he needs men with Ph.D.s to retain or obtain accreditation. The need for Ph.D.s has also made the impoverished private Negro colleges heavily dependent on refugee and émigré faculty, whose foreign credentials look good on paper even when their English is bad and their pedagogy worse. (There are some famous exceptions—men whose very foreignness enables them to cut through racial barriers that native Americans find impenetrable.)

Those who believe in the primacy of either racial integration or academic values are likely to respond to this bleak picture by sug-

gesting that these fifty or sixty least promising private Negro colleges
be closed down entirely, or perhaps consolidated into a dozen hopefully stronger ones. Taken together, these colleges enroll only between an eighth and a tenth of the Negroes now in college. Their
generally low tuitions may make some of them more accessible to
commuters than distant public colleges where the students would
have to pay for their subsistence and might not so readily find part-
time work. Still, most of the students in the poor private colleges
could probably make their way to public ones with little additional
hardship—remembering the very great sacrifice many Negro college
students and their families already make in the way of earnings foregone and college expenses anxiously assembled. As we shall see, the
public institutions to which these students would turn are not always
better staffed, seldom have more freedom of inquiry or action, and
have no better prospect of integration than the majority of private
Negro colleges. It could perhaps be argued that a student's chances of
intellectual and social growth are somewhat better at a public college,
simply because these colleges are larger and therefore more diverse.
The public colleges' academic advantage may, moreover, increase
in the years ahead if Negro voters make their weight felt in legislative appropriations. Nonetheless, the case for closing the poor private Negro colleges does not seem to us persuasive at present. What
must rather be done is to open up more satisfactory alternatives for
those who now attend them.

Whatever the pros and cons of the matter, very few private Negro
colleges *will* close down, any more than their white counterparts
will. They may be academically inadequate, but neither their trustees
nor the general public see that as a sufficient argument for killing
a live institution. So long as these colleges give an otherwise un-
attainable sense of importance to their trustees, administrators, faculty,
and alumni, most will endure. Anybody who thinks these colleges
will just fade away should attend an alumni reunion at one of them.
Negroes are as addicted as whites to ceremonies where modest
achievements can be translated into mutual admiration societies, and
where even these achievements may be momentarily transcended in
loyalty to an older if not larger vision of the self. Negro colleges like
other colleges have their "trade routes," in which ministers send
along promising students from their Sunday schools, politicians boost
the promising or not-so-promising children of local influentials, and
all the rest of it.

Not even loss of accreditation seems to kill them. Seventeen of
the twenty-one private Negro junior colleges and twelve of the forty-
nine private four-year colleges were without accreditation in 1964,
and the proportions will probably rise if the Southern Association

carries through on its promise to apply the same standards to Negro as to white institutions.[57] Yet students keep trickling in, often helped by federal student assistance programs. (The one thing that might kill these colleges would be a federal decision to restrict the use of student assistance funds to, let us say, accredited colleges. This seems politically unlikely.)

For better or for worse, then, most private Negro colleges seem likely to survive. They will continue to recruit most of their students from all-Negro Southern high schools and to send a substantial proportion of their graduates back to teach in those high schools, unable to break out of the cycle of miseducation and deprivation. Eventually their clientele may shrink, partly as a result of the widening price differential between private and public Negro colleges and partly as a result of increases in the proportion of Negroes in the South attending integrated high schools. The latter development is, however, likely to be slow; indeed, it may not take place at all if Washington is forced to let up its pressure on local school boards. For the foreseeable future there will probably be enough devout small-town and small-city Negroes with steady if modest incomes to support the private colleges, even when they cost more and offer less than their public rivals.

This is not an especially attractive prospect, and diverse efforts are therefore being made to transform the colleges in question. The federal government has financed summer institutes of the type already discussed, fellowships for teachers at them, and grants to upgrade their programs. A number of leading universities have also made modest efforts to help. In strictly economic terms none of these efforts amounts to much. Federal programs for "developing institutions" have been small (grants have typically been in four or five figures), have been spread thin, and have mostly gone to poor white rather than Negro colleges, simply because there are so many more of the former than the latter. (No program aimed *exclusively* at Negro colleges appears to be politically viable.) The value of these programs must thus be judged by whether they induce the colleges in question to do particularly worth-while things they otherwise would not have done. Great emphasis has been placed on interinstitutional cooperation, for example. This can take many forms, including cooperation between two local Negro colleges, cooperation between a local Negro college and a nearby white college, or cooperation between a Negro college and a white university in the North. Like home and motherhood, cooperation is unopposable. Unlike home and motherhood, however, it is also almost impossible to achieve. Local institutions may be able to save money here and there

[57] In noting these figures we do not mean to imply that accreditation necessarily represents a good measure of any individual college's educational virtues.

by offering cross-registration in specialized courses, by sharing library
facilities, and by other similar efforts, but the impact of this on the
basic character of the institution is seldom significant. A major university may also help out by sending an exciting lecturer for a day
or even a term, by encouraging some of its graduate students to
take a temporary teaching job at the relevant Negro college, and by
developing personal contacts with professors at the Negro college so
that when they recommend a good prospective graduate student he
is admitted. Occasionally these catalytic efforts may have a decisive
effect on the balance of forces in a particular college, stirring faculty
or students in a way that cannot later be reversed. In general, however, the tone at a college is set by the faculty who spend a lifetime
there, by the regular students, and to a lesser extent by the families,
friends, and future employers of the students. Even the most inflammatory visiting fireman is unlikely to have much effect, precisely because his commitment is so limited.

For this reason we are not optimistic about the success of the
various programs now afoot to "upgrade" the less distinguished private
Negro colleges. These colleges will undoubtedly get somewhat better
academically over the years, just as most other colleges will. But
their position relative to white colleges is likely to remain at least
as unfavorable as it now is, and may very well grow worse. This being
so, it seems reasonable to ask whether they might not be wise to try
to change the terms of the competition.

Alternatives for the Private Negro Colleges

Given the fact that other institutions are now committed to much
the same goals using most of the same means as the private Negro
colleges, and given the virtual certainty that many of these other
institutions will have more resources to do the job, it might make
sense for some of the private Negro colleges to redefine their role in
less orthodox ways. If they did this perhaps the limitations of their
present personnel and resources might loom less large.

One possible road for some of the private Negro colleges would be
to become authentic "community colleges," servicing not just the
young Negro high school graduate in need of credentials, but local
Negroes of all ages and with all kinds of non-academic needs. This
approach is akin to the "land-grant idea" discussed earlier, and also
to the "Tuskegee idea." The basic premise behind this approach is
that in the foreseeable future Southern Negroes will not get the kinds
of help they need from local institutions directly subservient to local
whites. If this is true, private Negro colleges could play an important

role in channeling outside money and ideas to nearby Negro groups and organizing Negro efforts at self-help. Indeed, a number of private Negro colleges have already served as conduits for federal funds aimed at Negroes, running programs no Southern white-controlled public agency would touch. (The most famous case is Mary Holmes Junior College, which provided cover for the Child Development Group of Mississippi to run a federally financed preschool program of extraordinary distinction.) At least in theory, private Negro colleges could become the administrative and organizational base for service programs ranging from precollege training such as the federally sponsored Upward Bound program to adult job training, prenatal health care, and legal assistance.

Such a role would, however, be economically precarious. Resources that were available from Washington for controversial programs in 1965 began to dry up in 1966 as the national political mood about Negroes changed, and this sort of cycle will doubtless be repeated. Nor would a community college of this kind be very academically respectable. In order to serve a still uneducated and impoverished constituency it would have to eschew the pretense and the hope of working only with academically trained professionals and prepro-fessionals. This requires a degree of self-confidence and self-direction few colleges, Negro or white, have. The same problem arises in even more acute form when one thinks not just of reaching out into the surrounding community but of providing a realistic education for those who come out of that community.

We believe, for example, that it may be a mistake to try to teach unsophisticated students traditional academic subjects by traditional academic methods. Regardless of race, such students are unlikely to respond to high culture of the kind that dominates most liberal arts curricula unless they come to it step by step from the popular culture in which they are immersed when they arrive on campus. We would also argue that many skills and principles can be taught by using materials drawn from this popular culture, assuming the teacher is familiar with it and has some appreciation of it. The sports, the pop music, the comics and pulp fiction, the television shows, and the cars that interest the young can be made subjects of discussion and take-off points for deeper study and understanding. But very few faculty at any sort of college agree with this, and we know of no Negro college which has explored these possibilities systematically.

Similarly, we believe that it is important to try to involve late adolescents in what they regard as "real" activities and to use these activities to arouse their curiosity about the ideas and information which college professors think they should be mastering. Almost no white college really does this. A few, such as Antioch, Bennington, and Northeastern, require students to alternate work and study during the academic year, and most give their students three months to work in the summer. But the student's "real" work is only rarely treated as a point of departure for his academic work back on campus. If an attempt is made to integrate the two, it takes the form of finding the student a quasi-academic job, not devising new patterns of study relevant to non-academic job experience. Elite colleges can afford to do this because many of their students are sufficiently pliable and adroit to master a regular curriculum even if they have no spontaneous interest in it and even if it does not connect with any problem they care deeply about. The Negro colleges are not so fortunate, and the failures which result from letting a Negro college faculty replicate the pattern of instruction it remembers from graduate school are more obvious. The case for reorienting the curriculum by making the students' real but disorganized experience a starting point for formal instruction is therefore especially powerful. Both Tougaloo and Miles made small tentative moves in this direction in the mid-1960s, establishing programs that were meant to allow young Negroes to become (or remain) active in the civil rights movement. The colleges then hoped to equip these activists with the intellectual tools they would need to make sense of both their personal experience and the social problems they confronted. Yet neither of these ventures took root and grew. Even the more experimental Negro colleges are reluctant to deviate very far from the pattern of instruction established at the nation's leading universities.

A happier illustration of the ironies implicit in emulating inappropriate models is the recent effort by students at Tougaloo College to establish a Free University of Mississippi in conjunction with white students at neighboring Millsaps, a small Methodist institution. Like most faculty members we have been depressed by the supposedly free universities established on the periphery of major universities, since these seem for the most part to have encouraged self-indulgence and cultism. The need in the academic metropolises is not for additional courses taught by Marxists and acidheads, but for new ways of learning, which the free universities have not for the most part been interested in devising. But a "free university" in Jackson is a somewhat different matter, even though it has the same name. It could become a creative forum for interracial confrontation, and it might well put Southern students, be they black or white, in touch with a world very different from the one they find on campus. It is therefore heartening that the Free University of Mississippi has received faculty support at both Tougaloo and Millsaps. Whether the innovation will prove durable is, however, uncertain.

Another line of innovation for the Negro colleges would be to begin training both black and white students for careers which would help solve the special problems confronting Negroes in America. America desperately needs social workers, ghetto teachers, poverty program executives, and applied social scientists interested in significant social change and technically competent to help bring it about. As returning Peace Corps Volunteers have found to their sorrow, leading white universities have very little programmatic interest and less technical expertise in turning out either revolutionary or reformist professionals. With the exception of Howard Law School, the Negro colleges have done even less. Howard helped train the generation of civil rights lawyers who led the legal attack on racial segregation, and it is increasingly interested in the more general problem of changing the legal relations between the rich and poor. But legal expertise is only a beginning in such matters, and a relatively easy one at that. Most of the medical, educational, social, and economic problems confronting American Negroes demand even more skill, more faith, and more self-sacrifice than the legal ones. Training for such work would require massive resources. It would require extraordinary leadership to mobilize the necessary men and money at any existing Negro college, but it would not necessarily be impossible.

A related but not identical step would be the development of a distinctively "black" curriculum in the humanities and social sciences, aimed primarily at undergraduates. Many Negro educators reject this idea on the political ground that it would look like capitulation to Stokely Carmichael and other flamboyant advocates of Black Power and separatism. Many also feel that it would provide some students and faculty with an excuse for avoiding competition with whites. Many of the least intellectual, least diligent, and least competent students on Negro college campuses today use anti-white slogans to justify their indolence and foolishness, allowing faculty observers to forget that the most promising students are frequently thinking along the same lines. The most serious obstacle to a black curriculum is, however, the almost universal feeling of both black and white faculty at Negro colleges that it would be academically indefensible in strictly scholarly terms. To talk of "Negro sociology" seems to them as regressive as talking of "Negro chemistry," and while some would admit that there is such a thing as "Negro history" and "Negro literature," they mostly prefer to study it as part of "American history" and "American literature."

In this as in most other things, Negro educators are anything but unique. We have already discussed the decline of "Catholic sociology" and "Catholic literature," and similar deracination is going on at other special-interest colleges as well. The logic behind this process is in most ways irresistible, and we are generally sympathetic to it. Yet the quest for cosmopolitanism need not imply complete denial of one's past, either in the personal or the historical sense. To the degree that there are genuine differences in cultural background and aspirations between blacks and whites in America, these can legitimately be incorporated into a college curriculum. Almost all those who argue against "Negro sociology," for example, accept the existence and legitimacy of something called "American sociology," even though American sociology is in principle part of international sociology, and the teaching of strictly American sociology is in this sense provincial. So too those who argue that Negro literature is part of American literature would, if they pushed their logic to its end, as some scholars did in the nineteenth century, have to argue that American literature is an equally spurious subject and is in fact a mere offshoot of English literature or even world literature. No such principle can be taken very far without becoming unworkable.

The white American upper-middle class is today relatively homogeneous, and it is not only the target but the source of the majority of the undergraduates at leading universities. It is thus natural, if not entirely desirable, for these universities to have very similar curricula. But most American Negroes come from a quite different world. Some integrationists argue that students' backgrounds are irrelevant, since the students come to college precisely because they want to transcend their lower-class past and move into the white upper-middle class. To this end hard-line integrationists want Negro undergraduates exposed to precisely the same ideas, information, and attitudes as white ones. Those Negroes who want this will, however, mostly turn to white colleges. Given the existence of some seventy private Negro colleges, only a handful of which have a chance of becoming integrated in the foreseeable future, and given the simultaneous existence of a substantial number of young Negroes who are extremely ambivalent about joining the white upper-middle class, a case can be made for trying to create at least one college dedicated to graduating technically competent, intellectually versatile Negroes who do *not* share the dominant values of the white upper-middle class.

Yet this is an easier objective to proclaim than to realize. It is not enough simply to offer more courses on Negro history and literature, as a number of the Negro colleges are now doing, nor to give political science and sociology courses on what are euphemistically called "urban problems." Even the rediscovery of Africa, symbolized by courses in Yoruba and Swahili at Howard and by African studies at Atlanta University, while valuable in its own right, is unlikely to produce a new breed of alumni. These subjects are already taught in white institutions. If their substance and pedagogic style when taught on Negro campuses simply mirrors that of the white ones, knowledge will be served but the distinctive habits and values of Negro students will not get any more chance to develop than they now do. So too with Negro faculty research. While limited in both quantity and quality, this has for many years focused almost exclusively on "the problem." Yet so long as the style and method of this research is meant to be identical with what would be done in white institutions on the same subject, isolating the researcher in a Negro college can only be a handicap for him and everyone else. If separation is to be an asset as well as a liability, it must somehow be used to develop a distinctive approach—as was done for many years in Catholic institutions.

The formal subject matter of courses and of research may be considerably less important in this regard than the assumptions and attitudes of the instructors and students. If there is a distinctively "black" way of viewing the world, then one can teach white as well as Negro literature from that viewpoint. Conversely, if there is a "white" viewpoint, then it must probably be said that most Negro college courses on nominally "black" subjects now approach their material from this viewpoint. One way to deal with this problem might be to try to build up the international ties of some of the Negro colleges, making them truly international in recruitment of both students and faculty and thus giving American Negroes an alternative reference point to white America. Lincoln in Pennsylvania has tried to do this by keeping in touch with African nationalism over the years, and Howard attracts a very substantial number of foreign students, though not so many foreign faculty. Given the distrust with which non-whites from overseas now view America and the probable distaste of American philanthropy for what would almost certainly be a center of radicalism and revolution, a truly international "third world" university may be impossible in America. Nonetheless, some contact and solidarity with Africa and perhaps also Asia and Latin America seems to be extremely important in maintaining the morale and self-confidence of American Negroes who face overwhelming problems at home.

Yet it is hardly appropriate for upper-middle class whites to become prophets of negritude, and that is not our intention. Americans are always telling one another what their traditions are, and American ethnic groups have for this reason revived many dormant nationalisms, turning themselves into people of one book or many in the process. It is not self-evident that young Negro Americans will be any more interested in Yoruba than young Italian Americans in Dante, though the experiment is worth trying. In a sense it may not even matter whether the traditions revived in this fashion are really authentic. The Muslims talk of a world that never was, but this has not prevented their making convicts literate. They also talk of a world that never will be, and here the dangers may be greater. But it is difficult to make a priori judgments about these matters, and given the gravity of America's present racial crisis virtually any experiment seems worth an initial try, so that its probable consequences can be judged to some extent from observation instead of ideology.

We stress experimentalism because it would be tragic if America developed in such a fashion that young Negroes were *obliged* to become nationalists. There are many Negroes whose strongest impulse is to forget their blackness and "pass," and they too deserve both sympathy and support. The most popular subject taught in the Mississippi Freedom Schools during the summer of 1964 was Negro history, but French was the second choice, presumably because it was remote, non-American, and yet "white." (It was also unavailable in Mississippi's Negro public schools and thus doubly desirable.) Similarly, there are Negro novelists who have grown weary of writing about "their people" and Negro sociologists who are sick of investigating only racial issues. If America is ever to transcend racism it is important that such Negroes feel free to write about whites, and that they find an audience, just as it is important for whites to go on writing about Negroes despite the resentment this arouses.

At the same time, there are many young Negroes who are violently anti-white, and their number is likely to grow. They view public Negro colleges as both repressive and responsive to white legislators, and today's private Negro colleges as accepting white standards of excellence and concentrating their energy on getting students into white graduate schools or white corporations. Seeing no other academic opportunities, they often reject education entirely, as another white conspiracy (like religion).[58] Most drop out before college, and the rest soon after entering, even though this is pretty clearly self-defeating. (Muslims have long argued that a black man who wants to resist the white society around him has a special need for education, perhaps greater than the black man who wants to assimilate. They are probably right.) The problem is to devise a form of education that helps young Negroes cope with the white adult world without making them either completely alienated from it or completely subservient to it. This is part of a larger problem, namely devising forms of upward mobility that allow able Negroes to maintain creative tension between themselves and the white world instead of being wholly co-opted by it.

[58] Compare the description of the "young Negro hangers-on" in Jacobs and Landau, p. 23.

Most Negro college trustees and administrators want no part of anti-white students, and many reject a "black" curriculum partly because they fear it might attract more such students to the campus. The older generation of Negroes often shares the resentments which animate these young "troublemakers," but it has learned to control them, at whatever personal price, and to deal with the white world in subtler and more complicated fashion. The open aggression of the younger Negroes, including some young faculty, is unsettling not just because it threatens the precarious peace the Negro colleges have made with the larger white community but because it threatens the equally precarious peace Negro educators have made with their own pride and anger.

The dangers are real enough. Boycotts, demonstrations, and riots took place in the spring of 1967 on a number of Negro campuses, including many of the most apparently complacent and bourgeois. The style of these upheavals was in many cases remarkably proletarian and was marked by far more violence than, for example, the relatively pacific Berkeley demonstrations in 1964. One might have predicted such developments at Tennessee A & I but hardly at Fisk, at Texas Southern and Southern (in Baton Rouge) but hardly at South Carolina State or Savannah State, at Howard but not at Allen. Yet the students at Allen, picketing in behalf of a white carpetbagger dean supported by a black president, provoked the trustees to fire the latter. The presidents of both Howard and South Carolina also resigned in the wake of protests. Being a Negro college president has become even more precarious than presiding over Berkeley or a Big Ten university, and it is easy to see why such men look askance at proposals which involve embracing their militant critics. Yet this is a time-honored strategy for dealing with dissent in America, and it seems at least conceivable that trustees in one or two of the seventy-odd private Negro colleges will pick a president interested in developing a nationalist institution. Whether this would succeed in redirecting the young militants' energies away from demonstrations to more formal kinds of learning we are not sure.

If neither community service nor black nationalism appeals to a poor private Negro college, another option for some of these institutions would be to stop competing with better situated colleges, white or Negro, and start competing with the still woefully inadequate secondary schools. Poor schooling probably does more damage to 14–17-year-olds than to 18–21-year-olds. Yet Southern Negroes today have few real alternatives to their mediocre local high school; they have many alternatives to a mediocre private Negro college. In principle, a private college might simply become a residential secondary school. In practice, this would entail an intolerable loss of status, a reversion to the very position many of these colleges escaped only a generation back when they were private schools or at least ran large precollege programs. The same result could, however, be accomplished gradually and covertly by establishing an "early admission" program for ninth, tenth, and eleventh graders, along with cooperative arrangements allowing sophomores, juniors, and seniors to do much of their work at big, integrated universities. The marginal colleges would thus provide an escape for students whose local secondary school was hopelessly inadequate, and a gateway to some comparatively lively cooperating university. In theory, such a scheme could be largely financed by the federal government under its Upward Bound program. Even so, few would-be college presidents or professors are likely to find it attractive, and this means it is not likely to be tried. Pressure for such a program from whites such as ourselves is almost certain to be self-defeating, because it is taken as condescension.

The Future of the Public Negro Colleges

As long as old-style segregation persists in the South and middle-class Negroes cannot exercise an effective voice in the operations of predominantly white colleges, there is a generally persuasive argument for the preservation of Negro-run private institutions responsive to the needs and hopes of Negro parents and children. Because they are private, and often in some small measure shielded by a denominational tie (as in the resourceful instance of the American Missionary Association), the possibility for relatively free-wheeling experimentation is always present. The public Negro colleges are clearly less free, because they are responsive to white legislators, to white trustees or state boards of higher education, and to the journalistic monitoring of other watchful whites. Under these conditions, separatism seldom facilitates experimentalism or innovation.

While integration would probably not help in this regard, it might well reduce provinciality for both Negroes and whites. The prospects for integrating most public Negro colleges are, however, poor. In the fourteen years since the *Brown* decision, three public Negro colleges, all in Border states, have attracted substantial numbers of whites. These are Lincoln University in Jefferson City, Missouri; Bluefield State College in West Virginia; and West Virginia State College. Most of the whites coming to these colleges are commuters who have no convenient or economical alternative. They mostly return home when their classes are over, leaving the student union and even the athletic teams in the hands of the residential Negroes. It is, as Southern liberals often say, easier to achieve "vertical" integration in classrooms than "horizontal" integration in dormitories.

The West Virginia and Missouri experience has several unusual features. First, these traditionally Negro public institutions were fortunately located. There were no white public institutions nearby to which commuters could turn, and there were a lot of relatively poor whites nearby for whom a commuter college was the only plausible route to a B.A. Very few other public Negro colleges meet these conditions. Many are located in sparsely settled rural areas and have relatively few students of any color within commuting distance. Most of those in urban areas have a white competitor within commuting distance.

Even where the public Negro college *does* have a large "natural" white clientele, a state legislature may not be willing to do what is necessary to ensure integration. In Maryland, for example, Morgan State was for many years the only public institution in Baltimore. When whites began to demand a public commuter college in the Baltimore area, however, the Maryland legislature never seriously considered developing Morgan to serve this purpose. Instead, a new University of Maryland campus was begun in the Baltimore suburbs, ensuring a large measure of de facto segregation for the foreseeable future. Similarly, Texas Southern was for some years the only public institution in Houston. But when Houston whites began to demand a publicly subsidized commuter college, the Texas legislature met this demand by negotiating a takeover of the hitherto private and undistinguished University of Houston, not by expanding Texas Southern. While poorer Southern states might be harder pressed to maintain a dual system, most of these states would be under even stronger ideological pressure to do so. Even states like North Carolina and Florida, which are relatively liberal on the race issue by Southern standards and have progressive state systems of higher education, do not seem politically ready to attempt the integration of established four-year Negro institutions, even if this were academically feasible. (In many instances, moreover, Negroes are as hostile as whites to proposals for abolishing or merging Negro institutions.)

This need not mean that the public Negro colleges will be starved for money as they have been in the past. Some Southern white political leaders and educators are now eager to make Negro colleges more attractive, in the hope that this will reduce the number of Negroes interested in applying to white colleges. Others are genuinely eager to see more Negroes getting better college educations and better jobs. Between them these two groups have already done a great deal to upgrade the physical facilities of the public Negro colleges. Any Northern visitor can be taken on a tour to see these handsome new plants, "better than for our own." Library budgets and salary scales also tend to be virtually comparable in four-year white and Negro colleges. The white state universities are ordinarily better off in both annual and capital appropriations than any four-year college in their state, white or Negro, but the expenditure gap between white and Negro four-year colleges is usually rather small. Just as in the white academic world, public institutions backed by state taxing power are likely to have a growing competitive advantage over all but the very top private ones in recruiting faculty. But we should again underline the large differences among the Southern states in the financial support and academic leeway given their Negro and indeed their white institutions.

If Southern Negroes choose to employ their unevenly growing electoral power to make a political issue of higher education, they could bring about a more equitable allocation of funds between white and Negro public institutions than already exists. But such pressures are unlikely to bring much integration. Those Negroes who want integration will be able to send their children to predominantly white public colleges. Integrationists, both black and white, may disapprove of all-Negro institutions on principle, but so long as appreciable numbers of Negroes voluntarily choose to attend segregated colleges, these colleges will probably be able to muster the political support they need to stay open. Substantial numbers of Negroes will, moreover, keep choosing these colleges so long as they are easier to get into and easier to stay in than integrated institutions. Practically speaking, this means that separate Negro institutions will almost certainly survive until there is a network of unselective junior colleges and state colleges within commuting distance of most Negroes in a state. They may well linger even after that.

Residential public Negro colleges will, however, find it increasingly difficult to attract big-city Negroes from either the North or the South, since these students will in most cases have better opportunities available to them at the same cost. Instead, residential public Negro colleges will attract mostly Negroes raised in small and medium-sized towns. Some of these students will plan to join the old Negro middle class in their home towns, usually by becoming school teachers. Others will hope to break out of this mold by going to a large city, North or South, where the walls of segregation are more permeable, economic circumstances less pinched, and the round of daily life more tantalizing. The more ambitious of these city-oriented Negroes will, however, presumably want to escape their rigidly segrated small-town past when they enter college, heading for an integrated institution or at least for an urban Negro college like Morgan, Texas Southern, Tennessee A & I in Nashville, or Alabama State in Montgomery. Only the cautious will delay the transition, going to isolated and (at least to their parents) reassuringly provincial colleges like Fort Valley State in

Georgia or Prairie View A & M in Texas. In some cases, these institutions will raise their students' sights to a more cosmopolitan level, ensuring that they "can't go home again." All too often, however, these institutions confirm students in their self-imposed limitations, ensuring that they *will* go home again, albeit in a white-collar job.

Despite the affluence of the public Negro colleges relative to most private ones, both in terms of salaries and working conditions, these institutions will have an extremely difficult time competing for competent faculty, and an even more difficult time persuading whatever faculty they get to deal with their students in an imaginative way. These colleges have very little to tempt a talented professor, whatever his color. Except for such leaders as Texas Southern, the public Negro colleges are among the least favored institutions in the least favored states in the nation. The public Negro colleges, moreover, suffer in many instances from having been until recently de facto teachers colleges, with all that that implies not only for academic prestige but for the character of the faculty against whom a newcomer has to struggle if he wants to innovate. Then, too, all professors require the support of a few gifted students every so often to reassure them that their difficult mission is not in vain. Yet once there are enough Negroes at white public colleges in a given state to make these colleges seem not only academically attractive but socially manageable, the public Negro colleges are likely to get even fewer gifted Negroes than they do now. Such a trend will almost certainly make faculty recruitment even more difficult than it is now. A few faculty may gain satisfaction from academic or political missionary work, but this is unlikely to be common.

Looking a generation ahead, we suspect that the Southern situation will increasingly resemble that in Ohio and Pennsylvania. These are relatively industrialized states with median incomes comparable to what the South might have in a generation. Negroes in these states have had the vote since they arrived in force. The relatively small number of Negroes in these states limits their political influence, but this will be increasingly true in the South too, where the proportion of Negroes in the over-all population is generally declining. Both Ohio and Pennsylvania have a number of public colleges that have long been open to Negroes. But both states have also had a public Negro college for many years. There has been no significant demand to close these two colleges, yet neither has attracted appreciable white enrollment. Neither college has made any great contribution to the lives of Negroes in its state, beyond certifying them for appropriate middle-class jobs. Nonetheless, 40 to 50 per cent of the Ohio Negroes who go to college choose Central State, and 25 to 30 per cent of the

Pennsylvania Negroes who go to college choose Cheyney State.[59]

Like the poorer private Negro colleges, then, public Negro colleges are for the most part likely to remain fourth-rank institutions at the tail end of the academic procession. Perhaps the most important thing that could be done to improve all such colleges, black or white, would be to ensure that their students knew there was a larger and more cosmopolitan world that they might with effort join. Able young professors who teach in such colleges for a year, or even a summer, open this vista for some students. Sometimes, in fact, they can endanger such students by emancipating them too rapidly—as happens in white colleges also of course—without being able to provide them with an alternative to their traditional and safer destination. The more permanent faculty also often feel threatened or antagonistic to the newcomers and hope to see them go back home again without forcing any real change in the status quo. (Local Negroes have often endured as much change as they think they can stand, just in becoming professors. Negro M.A.s will often struggle for the Ph.D. when most comparable whites have either gained that prize or given up, and the struggle is seldom ennobling.) Yet so long as new "carpetbagger" faculty keep coming, they may be able to support more lively resident faculty and to reach a few restless students each year. This will be possible especially if there continue to be summer programs that bring students from these colleges to major university campuses, help them explore ideas in a new way, develop their confidence that they might survive or even flourish in such an environment, and try to give them a realistic sense of the possibilities open to them at the graduate level.

Helpful as such forays may be, however, they do not touch the basic problem of educating large numbers of academically untrained (and in most cases academically though not occupationally unmotivated) students. These students' intellectual limitations differ only in degree from those of their white counterparts in hundreds of colleges across the land, and in some cases they do not even differ in that regard. The academic problem is not likely to be solved by integrating these whites and Negroes into the same institutions—though some

[59] For estimates of total enrollment among Pennsylvania Negroes, see Gray, Jr. Gray's data must, however, be treated with caution. Many colleges reported Negro enrollment in round numbers, which suggests they were guessing. Others did not report at all. If Gray's data were correct, Pennsylvania Negroes would be only a quarter as likely as Pennsylvania whites to enter college. This would be well below the national ratio, which appears to be about 5:2 rather than 4:1. Jaffe, Adams, and Meyers suggest that the over-all college entrance rate of Negroes in the North approximates that for the nation as a whole, and it is hard to see why Pennsylvania should deviate dramatically from the Northern norm. The estimates in the text could easily be off by 10 per cent either way, and perhaps by more. They should be read as illustrative, not descriptive.

other problems might be solved. The most that a college can probably hope to do for such students, white or black, is to improve their basic skills a little, provide them with a foretaste of white-collar life, and give them the diploma they need to enter the white-collar world. As for the life of the mind, we fear that it will remain very much a minority taste among those who spend their first seventeen years in dull schools, unstimulating homes, and aimless socializing with their peers. Yet this is plainly no argument for doing nothing. If a college can revive 5 instead of 2 per cent of its students, it has more than doubled its output.

The problem here is similar to that posed by young people who have been emotionally thwarted in their early years. Some seem to recover spontaneously without any outside help. Psychoanalytic techniques can be worked out to help others. Leadership is needed from the academically exclusive universities to help invent analogous remedial programs that will improve basic skills among despairing and often antagonistic student bodies. Such leadership is necessary, quite apart from the technical and human problems involved, in order to make working with inept students seem respectable as well as productive. But on a large-scale, long-term basis, such programs are unlikely to be any more feasible than mass psychiatry. The burden of mass higher education is likely to fall on the state colleges and junior colleges, which would require enormous resources to inaugurate the necessary programs. Without a united front of needy Negroes and whites, it is hard to see how the necessary intellectual or financial effort will be made. Yet such a united front seems almost as visionary now as when the Populists first broached it, only to sour on it, in the last century. Yet unless some such political pressure group makes its weight felt, state colleges, like state mental hospitals, are likely to play a primarily custodial role for all but their most enterprising students.[60]

Conclusion and Postscript

We have argued that although there are important ideological and political differences between colleges founded to serve Negroes and those founded to serve other ethnic and religious minorities, Negro colleges today face many of the same dilemmas as these white institutions. To the extent that Negroes seek entry into a racially integrated national labor force, they will usually be interested in integrated colleges that prepare them directly for such a life. Some traditionally Negro colleges will try to provide such preparation by

[60] See Riesman and Horton.

attracting white students and becoming largely indistinguishable from traditionally white colleges. Such integration is highly desirable where-ever it is possible, both because it provides symbolic proof that inte-gration can be a two-way street and because it will give the Negroes a feeling of being at home, which they are less likely to feel at traditionally white colleges. But most Negro colleges will not be able to attract whites in appreciable numbers in the foreseeable future. They will also attract relatively few of the young Negroes who expect to work in integrated settings. As a result, they will be left with the less talented, the less ambitious, the more conventional, and the more collegiate Negroes, many of whom will pursue careers behind the wall of segregation. Nonetheless, most Negro colleges are likely to survive and to educate an appreciable proportion of all Negro undergraduates for many years to come. Whether they should all accept this fate is open to question. In the private sector we would argue for re-examination of traditional objectives. Such alternatives as a community college serving adults as well as adolescents, a na-tionalist college attempting to develop the possibilities of a specifically Negro curriculum and extracurriculum, and early admissions pro-grams aimed at getting students out of their local high schools younger should all be given serious consideration. In the public sector this sort of innovation seems less practical. Since the only way to mobilize adequate public financial support for educating relatively slow or hostile learners is likely to be through a racially united front of well-to-do as well as poor Negroes and whites, we would urge politi-cal attempts to do this. The rallying point for such a front would probably have to be integrated "open-door" commuter colleges. These should therefore gradually supplant public residential Negro colleges as the states' major vehicles for providing Negroes with B.A.s.

This is not, we think, an especially remarkable analysis or program. Yet when this chapter was published as an article early in 1967 it caused an extraordinary stir. It was publicized in *The New York Times* and in *Time* magazine, with the latter journal providing an extremely one-sided summary, which quoted our gloomiest judgments, and declining to publish our letter of protest. Nonetheless, even the *Time* article, while more negative than our article and perhaps more negative than the reality of Negro higher education, said hardly anything that detached observers do not say sadly to one another every day. Nonetheless, most spokesmen for the Negro colleges re-acted with considerable anger. Some felt the situation was not as bad as we said, at least relative to the norms established by white colleges. Others felt that we were relying on racial stereotypes to describe Negroes and their colleges, and that the situation was not only not as bad as we said but was qualitatively different too. Still others, while not contesting specific conclusions, objected to our method of inquiry on the ground that it was not objective and hence not scholarly.

There can be no question that our method was personal rather than impersonal. We visited a number of Negro colleges for relatively short periods, talked to or corresponded with many knowledgeable insiders and outsiders, read the better-known books and articles on the subject as well as some obscure ones, listened to critics who said we were wrong on particular points, and made numerous corrections in response to their objections. Other writers who visited the same colleges, talked to the same informants, and read the same materials might well have come to different conclusions. Yet this does not strike us as a serious objection. Few major educational, social, or political questions can be resolved "scientifically" in the sense that different observers can all gather data in a particular way and then be expected to reach a common conclusion. One can hope to approach this kind of objectivity in answering certain specific questions, such as the proportion of Negroes in Negro colleges or the proportion who would be able to survive academically at a given white college. But there can be no hope of such impersonal objectivity when one asks whether Negro colleges will ever be able to assemble resources comparable to those of white colleges, or whether the next generation of Negro students will mostly prefer integrated or segrated colleges. More quantitative research would certainly be useful in illuminating some of these questions, but it would not answer them. Answers necessarily depend partly on untestable axioms derived from personal experience and viewpoint, and disagreement will therefore continue.

Under these circumstances the reader may be interested in knowing who shared our view of the Negro college scene and who rejected it. In general almost everyone who spoke or wrote to us and had attended a white undergraduate college was sympathetic to our view, though some said we were too kind and some said there was a bit more life than we portrayed. This general support came from both whites and Negroes, men who had taught in Negro colleges and men who had only had periodic dealings with these colleges. Those who had attended Negro colleges as undergraduates, on the other hand, were divided but mostly hostile. The few who had gone on to work in white universities mostly seemed to share our prejudices. Most of those who had merely spent a few years in white graduate schools and then became Negro college teachers or administrators were hostile. Negroes currently enrolled in these colleges were usually very ambivalent: on the one hand they found our criticisms, and especially the quotations in *Time*, a useful club with which to beat their elders on the campus; some also made it an excuse for not doing the work their teachers assigned. On the other hand, they bitterly resented two whites telling them that after all their sacrifices their degree might not entitle them to full parity with white B.A.s. We find it hard to believe that these differences in viewpoint could have been eliminated by additional statistics or historical examples. The popular response to the Moynihan Report has surely demonstrated that the mere presence of charts and tables does very little to develop consensus on sensitive issues dealt with in freehand fashion.[61]

What is an outsider to do under such circumstances? The easy course is to keep quiet and wait for Negro intellectuals to tackle the problem. But that is not our style. Furthermore, it is in some ways much harder for a Negro to say these things than for a white to do so. Whoever says them will, after all, antagonize most of the Negro leadership. Black America is still a sufficiently enclosed subculture so that ambitious Negroes are reluctant to do this. Many admire Franklin Frazier, but few wish to endure the persecution he got after writing *Black Bourgeoisie*. Whites, on the other hand, can afford to make such enemies. This gives whites a special freedom and imposes a special responsibility. We have no illusions about most Negroes' response to white criticism at this moment in history. But neither have we any illusions about Negroes' response to uncritical praise. This is a moment when whites can do no right: the critics are viewed as traitors and the supporters as gullible fools to be used as best one can. Under such circumstances one might as well forget about winning friends and do what one thinks right.

But what is right? Many Negro educators argued that even if all we said were true, its publication was a betrayal of the cause. Our description made it harder to raise money and recruit faculty, and our sorrowful predictions thus became self-fulfilling. It is an insignia of the marginality of these colleges that they should assume one article of this kind, written by men who control no resources and have only the most marginal official influence, could seriously affect their future. But suppose they are right? What is one to make of the argument that bad news should be hushed up lest it make the situation even worse?

One reason for publishing bad news is the hope that it will force men to re-examine the course of action that led up to it. This is not easy, either in Vietnam or in the Negro colleges. We said their institutions were academically undistinguished and would in all probability remain that way. Many people heard this as an assertion that the Negro colleges should be closed. That was not, however, our conclusion. Instead of being third-rate imitations of Harvard and

61 On this subject see Rainwater and Yancey.

Berkeley, or perhaps Amherst and Riverside, we suggested that the Negro colleges should reconsider their role and strike out in new directions. As far as we have been able to discover no Negro college president took these suggestions very seriously. Apparently it is Harvard or bust. (While we find this depressing, it confirms our feeling that these colleges are very much part of the white academic system, committed to its academic curriculum and aims, and necessarily judged successful or unsuccessful at least partly in its terms.)

Another reason for publishing bad news is to help the as-yet-uninjured avoid their predecessor's mistakes. We believe that substantial numbers of Negroes grossly overestimate the academic quality of Negro colleges. We think many Negro undergraduates would be better off in an integrated college—especially one that had enough other Negroes to form a partially self-contained subculture. If our article helped create a climate in which this was more likely, we have no regrets. In part this is a matter of trying to end the conspiracy of silence among Negroes and sympathetic whites about these colleges, so that popular imagery becomes more realistic. In part it is a matter of shifting official thinking about "the Negro problem," putting less emphasis on upgrading today's Negro colleges and more on eliminating the financial, academic, and social obstacles to Negroes' attending white colleges. This would, of course, make the position of the Negro colleges even more difficult than it already is. We regret this, but we do not think that individuals should be sacrificed for institutions, however worthy the latter may be and however honorable their historical role.

There are some Negroes for whom a Negro college represents the most sensible choice, but they should have no illusions about what they will get there, any more than they should have illusions about what they will get at integrated colleges. If illusions were eliminated on all scores, we think fewer Negroes would attend Negro colleges. But so long as some continue to attend, whether for good or bad reasons, their choice should be respected. This means that efforts must continue to improve the intellectual and human conditions under which they spend their undergraduate years. We doubt that this can be accomplished by maintaining the fiction that the typical Negro college is just a white college in blackface.

We are, then, prepared to defend both our method and our conclusions. But these were by no means the primary source of criticism. On the contrary, most of the complaints were directed at our tone rather than the substance of what we said. Many readers, especially those who had devoted their lives to the formidable task of trying to build really first-rate Negro colleges in a society that almost never allows Negroes to have anything first-rate, felt that we were blaming them and their friends for the consequences of white supremacists' crimes. In a sense this complaint was just. Oppression corrupts the oppressors as well as the oppressed. Ultimate responsibility for this corruption rests with those who have power, and in the last analysis this means prominent whites. But today most of the men who exercise day-to-day power in Negro colleges are Negroes. They may not be morally responsible for their failures, but they are often administratively responsible. Theirs is a thankless and perhaps impossible task, deserving more sympathy than it usually gets. While we think the preceding discussion makes this clear, the message did not always get across. For that we must doubtless blame our own abrasive prose.

Perhaps no amount of charity would really have affected Negro educator's reactions to our effort. America's Negro colleges are the products of white supremacy and segregation. The malignant consequences of this vicious tradition are still very much in evidence, and no cure is in sight. Describing this malignancy in a way acceptable to its victims is inevitably difficult and perhaps impossible. The temptation is therefore to fall back on optimistic platitudes, talking about the possibility of "massive federal aid" or of a "continuing commitment of talent by the nation's leading universities." We favor these things. But we do not believe them likely, and even if they prove feasible we are by no means convinced that they would do more than temporarily alleviate the patient's symptoms.

XI. *The Anti-University Colleges*

In previous chapters we have argued that the shape of American higher education is largely a response to the assumptions and demands of the academic professions. We have described a variety of different interest groups that had quite divergent ideas about what an educated man ought to know and how a college ought to teach it to him, and we have tried to show how they ended up pursuing increasingly convergent goals by ever more similar means. The primary reason for this convergence, we argued, was the colleges' universal preference for undergraduate faculty trained in the standard disciplines at the leading national graduate schools.

There has been considerable dissidence, however, and some deviation from this highroad. In this chapter we will look briefly at two of the most visible symptoms of such dissidence: the community college movement and the general education movement. We will then comment briefly on some other nodes of resistance to academic claims. The community college movement has found expression in some six hundred publicly controlled two-year commuter colleges. These recruit many of their faculty from the public schools and many others from former teachers colleges, hire relatively few Ph.D.s from major graduate schools, show comparatively little deference to professional academic opinion about how an institution of higher learning should be run, and consequently teach both subjects and students whom most scholars regard as worthless. The general education movement has found expression both in the undergraduate colleges of certain leading universities and in a handful of independent four-year colleges. It has mainly been the work of men with Ph.D.s in traditional disciplines, but these have been dissidents and heretics rather than the reliable stalwarts of the learned societies. Such men have tried to create a viable alternative to the departmentalized, research-oriented model of higher education they encountered in their doctoral studies, usually stressing interdisciplinary teaching with special emphasis on freshmen and sophomores.

The Community College Movement

The public junior college began as a logical extension of the free public high school. Its aim was to provide high school graduates in a given district with two more years of free education before they either took a job or went away to college. Like the comprehensive high school on which it was modeled, the community college was supposed to serve everyone in its district, regardless of previous academic performance. There were to be college-style academic courses for those who planned eventually to transfer to a four-year college, terminal general education programs for those who only wanted two years beyond high school, and vocational and semiprofessional programs for those who needed a salable skill.

Many of these colleges grew up with little sense of distinctive institutional purpose. They were hodgepodges of courses and curricula, established in response to real or imagined local demands, located in cast-off buildings, serving mostly part-time and evening students. Some called themselves junior colleges, some city colleges, some just plain colleges. Few thought the choice vitally important. As time went on, however, the number of men devoting their lives to these enterprises increased, and their enrollments did likewise. Especially in California, they became sufficiently numerous to hold meetings with one another, lobby for special state legislation to facilitate their work, and begin to look for some distinctive ideology to justify their activities. These activities were already so diverse that no single slogan could subsume more than a fraction of them. Nonetheless, the theoreticians of the movement mostly turned to the phrase "community college" to define their essential identity. A "community college" is not a "state college," and still less is it a "national university." It is local, and it is proud of it. Equally important, a "community college" is inclusive rather than exclusive, seeking unity and solidarity rather than hierarchy and exclusion, serving the whole population, not a select minority. Here again the implied contrast with the university is obvious.

The multiplication of such colleges is by no means as recent as some people assume. A handful were established before World War I, and more than a hundred opened during the 1920s. The Depression, far from slowing their growth, seems to have accelerated it, so that there were more than two hundred in operation at the outbreak of World War II. After World War II they multiplied less rapidly, at least until the late 1950s. Since then, however, the movement has shown new fecundity, and several dozen community colleges are now being founded each year. As previous chapters have indicated, they have capitalized on the local backlash against national institutions and cosmopolitan values; on lower-middle and working-class resentment against professional exclusiveness and social snobbery at the universities; and on adult anxiety about the increasing emancipation of the young from adult supervision on residential campuses. In addition to these cultural and political ingredients, the entrepreneurs of the community college movement have also profited from the widespread (though in some ways erroneous) belief that it costs the taxpayers less to educate a given student in a community college than elsewhere, and from the undoubtedly correct belief that it costs parents less to educate their children at home than away. They have also capitalized on a growing demand for part-time education from young and not-so-young adults.

Given their historical origins and political base, the character of most community colleges is hardly surprising. Their governing boards usually consist not of millionaire industrialists, eminent professional men, or the retiring governor's loyal political retainers, but of locally elected or appointed citizens. These men and women are usually prosperous and fairly well educated, but they are not as likely to be products of four-year residential colleges as their counterparts on state boards or regents. Their vision of education is usually less mystical and more mechanical, their hopes for it less cultural and more utilitarian, their assumptions about its clientele less exclusive and more consumer-oriented. The figurative model of excellence for such trustees is New Trier High School, not the University of Chicago or the University of Illinois.

The community colleges' origins in local school districts have, however, also limited their growth. Dependence on local property taxes made budget increases unusually hard to obtain, and organization under the aegis of local school boards limited them to populous districts, since small districts did not have enough high school graduates to run a college of efficient size. (The minimum feasible size for a community college district depends, of course, not only on the absolute number of high school graduates but on the proportion willing to consider a two-year public college where it is available. In California, where more than half of all high school graduates enter such colleges, districts can be quite small.) In recent years some legislatures have therefore moved away from local initiative and control, dividing their states into larger and more inclusive community college districts, shifting the burden of support largely or entirely onto the state's general fund, and sometimes setting up a single statewide board for all community colleges. This trend, while by no means universal, has two offsetting effects. On the one hand, it partially removes the individual colleges from local supervision and gives them trustees more likely to be sympathetic to the ambitions and ideals of an academic faculty. On the other hand, it ties each college to the rules of a larger system, making gradual redefinition of institutional purpose more difficult and inhibiting ambitious administrators from exploiting local civic pride to make theirs a "real four-year college."[1]

The movement away from direct local control and the comprehensive high school model may eventually change the character of the community colleges, but this has not yet happened to any significant extent. Partly as a result of their earlier ties to the public school system, partly as a result of their poor competitive position in bidding for faculty against four-year colleges, and partly as a result of a principled animus against "Ph.D.s who aren't really interested in teaching" and who are "too snobbish to work with the average student," the community colleges continue to recruit their faculty from a manpower pool only partly fed by university graduate schools. Virtually none of the faculty is interested in research, except when the college happens to be near a university and can attract graduate students as faculty. (The community colleges usually pay non-Ph.D.s more than universities pay them as teaching assistants.) Some other community college faculty are dropouts from university graduate departments, but most are men who never even hoped to become regular college teachers. Many are public school teachers who took enough evening courses to earn an M.A. (or a junior college teaching certificate, which some states now require). In recent years growing numbers have been recruited directly from Master's degree programs at the former teachers colleges and other would-be universities.

These "instructors," as they are still often called, have standards and aspirations rather different from "professors" who have successfully completed a standard doctoral program. They usually feel pleased that they are earning more than they would in public schools and are teaching somewhat less. The fact that they are not at a "real" college is often not especially relevant, for this has never been a possibility they took seriously. (They may, indeed, resist efforts to make theirs a more academically respectable college because they fear they would be expendable or at least uncomfortable at such an institution.) The public school atmosphere, reflected in the hegemony of the "front office," the heavy reliance on prescribed syllabi, the inhibitions against teaching things that would offend community sensibilities, the lack of

[1] For discussion of these and other aspects of community college development, see Medsker. Each year a few two-year colleges make the transition to four-year institutions. This seems, however, to happen today mainly in the private sector, where there is no distinctive ideology to justify remaining a two-year college.

academic ranks for the faculty, and even the occasional requirement that arriving and departing teachers punch time clocks, grates on those who compare their lot to professors in four-year institutions but not on those who compare themselves to high school teachers.[2]

It would be pleasant to report that the community colleges' relative freedom from the Ph.D. fixation had enabled them to bring together men of diverse interests and talents. It would be doubly encouraging if these men had provided their students with a wide variety of relevant adult models, employed a panoply of different styles of teaching and learning, and thereby managed to reach students whom more conventional academicians leave untouched. This is exceptional, however, for a variety of reasons.

First, while the community colleges have not been tied to traditional academic definitions of appropriate qualifications for teaching, neither have they been especially imaginative in utilizing new kinds of instructors. They may not have been obsessed with the Ph. D., but like their public school cousins they have often insisted on just enough academic certification to bar the employment of gifted amateurs from other occupations.

Second, community colleges depend for much of their public support on populist hostility to exclusive universities and snobbish scholars. Populists seldom want to supplant academic elitism with some other variety. They have prevented community colleges from offering salaries, working conditions, or social status sufficient to attract large numbers of unusually talented individuals to their staffs. (It is, of course, questionable whether such individuals would be available under any circumstances.)

Third, whatever faculty the community colleges hired have generally been confronted with a quite rigid pattern of instruction. Just as in the public schools, this system has often precluded the development of new learning styles, has limited the kinds of skills that could be cultivated and rewarded, and has encouraged a quite conventional academic vision of what knowledge is and how it is to be acquired. In this sense, then, the community college turns out to be part of the larger academic system.

Perhaps for this very reason, the community colleges have had no difficulty finding a clientele. The typical community college has grown from five hundred students in 1940 to about twenty-five hundred in 1965. The proportion of high school graduates choosing to enter such colleges has also climbed steadily over the years, and now stands at something like one in five.[3] These students fall into four

---

[2] For a discussion of community college faculty attitudes, see Friedman.

[3] Estimates of community college enrollment are extremely risky, because the categories used by the U. S. Office of Education in collecting statistics from these institutions bear almost no relationship to their actual character. In particular,

principal groups: those who do not want to go away to college; those who cannot afford to do so; those whose high school record bars them from a four-year college, or at least from the public ones in their home state; and those who want less than four years of higher education. The relative size of these groups is a matter of some debate.

Substantial numbers of college applicants cannot or will not go away to a residential college. Many of these are employed full time and think of themselves primarily as workers (or mothers), not students. They typically want only part-time instruction, and if they could not find a college within commuting distance of their job they would not attend at all. Others are married and tied to their husbands' (or occasionally wives') place of work. Still others are living at home, working to help support their parental family, and feel they could not make an adequate financial contribution if they went away. Something like 40 per cent of all junior college students enroll part time, and most of these part-timers presumably fall into one of these categories. So do some of the full-timers. Yet it should also be borne in mind that many of these part-time community college students are from cities that also have a public four-year college. On strictly logistical grounds most could enroll part time in a four-year institution. Our semieducated guess is that only around a third of all community college students are tied to a community with a two-year but not a four-year public college.

A second major group said to attend community colleges comes from families that cannot afford to support a child away from home. This group is not as large as one might imagine. The parents of students who enroll at community colleges are slightly *richer* than the parents of students at four-year institutions. Only 22 per cent of the men who entered public junior colleges full time in the fall of 1966 came from families earning less than $6,000 a year, compared to 27 per cent of the men entering public four-year colleges. The median parental income of the public junior college entrants was about $9,000, compared to about $8,000 in the public four-year college and

USOE collects data only on fall entrants, while a substantial proportion of community college students enter in the spring or even the summer. USOE has not until very recently collected data on students enrolled in courses not creditable toward a B.A., even though such students are an important minority at most community colleges. USOE counts a student as "first time" if his college allowed him no credit for previous academic work. This means many students get counted twice if they enroll in college, drop out before the term ends or flunk out when it ends, and then return. USOE does not collect data on the ages of students, so it is difficult to know the size of the total age grade from which they come. USOE data before World War II are, moreover, quite divergent from Census data for the same period, so it is hard to know how much faith to put in them. Some data are, however, available in the 1965 *Digest*, tables 37 and 59, and in the annual reports of *Opening Fall Enrollment*, esp. that for 1959 which provides time series back to 1939 in many different categories.

$6,900 for all American families.[4] This means that most students at community colleges could in principle have gotten as much financial help from their families as those in four-year colleges did. What seems to have distinguished them was not that their parents *couldn't* contribute very much, but that they *didn't*.[5] Whether this was because the community college students were older and more reluctant to ask, or simply because their parents put less of a premium on college, we do not know.

The community college also caters to students with poor high school records and low-aptitude test scores, some of whom cannot get into four-year colleges. We are not sure how many community college students really couldn't find a place in a four-year college, and how many simply think it too much of an effort to try. While a number of state universities have in recent years become rather academically exclusive, these have usually been in states that were converting their former teachers colleges into state colleges with minimal admissions requirements. There are, however, some states where a substantial fraction of the high school graduating class is not eligible for any four-year public institution. (In California, only a third of all high school graduates are academically eligible for either the university or a state college.)

The community college also serves a fourth group of marginal students: those who want less than four years of higher education. If we judged students' intentions by their actions, we would have to assume that this group was very large—about a quarter of all high school seniors and half of all college freshmen. The difficulty is that very few of these freshmen *know* they belong to this group when they enter college.[6] Only about a fifth of all community college students enroll in terminal vocational or technical curricula. Some others merely take a particular course, like painting or French cook-

---

[4] Astin, Panos, and Creager, "National Norms." The data on student incomes applies only to full-time students. The picture might be slightly different if part-time students were included. The relative affluence of the community college students may derive from the fact that community colleges are located in urban areas where incomes exceed the state average, and mainly in prosperous states (though there are exceptions like Florida and Mississippi). Within California and perhaps within other states as well, the family incomes of two-year college students averages less than those of four-year college students, even though they still exceed the national college average. (See Sanders and Palmer.)

[5] Some 21 per cent of full-time community college freshmen reported term-time employment as their major source of support in 1966, compared to 7 per cent of full-time state college freshmen. Conversely, only 41 per cent of community college freshmen reported parents as a major source of help, compared to 54 per cent of state college freshmen. (See Astin, Panos, and Creager.)

[6] About half of all students entering all sorts of colleges never earn degrees, and perhaps 35 per cent of those entering four-year colleges as full-time students fail to do so. Yet only 10 per cent of all full-time freshmen *say* they plan less than a B.A. when they enter. (See Astin, Panos, and Creager.)

ing, which is not part of any sequential program. The overwhelming majority, however, enter hoping eventually to earn a B.A.[7] While their choice of a two-year rather than a four-year college may in some instances betray underlying uncertainty, ambivalence, or eagerness to be seduced by an alternative like work or marriage, it does not lead many students into programs of study that are explicity less than four years.

What have the community colleges been able to offer this potpourri of students? With more than four hundred colleges and a million students, generalizations are risky. Most observers do, however, agree on certain points.

First, while the community college may in principle exist to serve new sorts of students and offer new sorts of programs, most faculty and administrators are still primarily interested in traditional academic programs and in students who will eventually transfer to a four-year college. The community colleges thus resemble other sorts of colleges in placing primary emphasis on the "college" part of their label, with only secondary emphasis on the "community" part. Some may be little more than upward extensions of the comprehensive high school, but they want to offer "college level" instruction, whatever that may mean. The faculty is generally reluctant to "lower academic standards," no matter what the academic aptitudes of the students. Professors want to believe that they are offering instruction of the same quality as that given freshmen and sophomores at the state university, and they usually take this to mean that the community colleges' standards of success and failure must be those of the state university or at least the state colleges. These standards are re-enforced by the fact that most of the entering students deliberately choose the prestige transfer programs. The community college faculty feel some obligation to make clear to these students what traditional academic work is like and how well or badly they are likely to do at it if they transfer. High formal standards are also encouraged by the four-year colleges' understandable insistence that if they are to honor academic credits from two-year institutions, the latter must use the same grading standards as their senior counterparts. While this is certainly not always done, or even approximated, there is steady pressure in this direction.[8]

The same problem arises in even more egregious form when one looks at the substance of the curriculum. The junior colleges do not

[7] Astin, Panos, and Creager found that 77 per cent of the men and 65 per cent of the women entering public two-year colleges as full-time students in the fall of 1966 planned to earn a B.A. or higher degree. *Opening Fall Enrollment* (1965) shows that 71 per cent of the students enrolled in public two-year colleges in the fall of 1965 were taking courses creditable toward a Bachelor's degree.

[8] For evidence that two-year colleges grade somewhat less rigorously than four-year colleges, see Knoell and Medsker. For a general discussion of these problems, see Burton Clark, *The Open Door College*.

feel they can deviate very far from the norms set by the national disciplines about what should be taught in a course called, let us say, "Introduction to English Literature." There are, of course, exceptions. We know some community college instructors, for instance, who use materials drawn from popular culture rather than academic culture to introduce their students to thinking about literature, or who bring their classes alive in other unconventional ways. But, just as in the high schools, there is only limited freedom to innovate. And even where freedom exists and is used, the disease is not often contagious. Pedagogic innovations have only limited visibility within their own institution, and still less beyond it. Spreading the infection depends on the erratic currents of oral communication and myth-making. When an innovation takes place in a community college, these currents must usually flow through the education departments of state colleges and universities. From there the word may conceivably pass back to other community colleges or high schools, but it is unlikely to get to the regular academic departments of the universities. (Academic prejudice against educationists, being non-ethic, does not seem to cause even twinges of guilt among those who indulge themselves in it. Like most enduring prejudices, it embodies part of the truth, and this is thought to excuse missing part of it.) As a result, most community college instructors continue to teach what they were taught in four-year colleges, immunized from new ideas both by isolation and by the prestige of the models they are emulating.

Like other "colonial" enterprises, the two-year college has only the most limited ability to choose its own path. Students are being prepared to transfer on somebody else's terms, and this means that whatever their missionary impulses, instructors must toe a line drawn by someone else.[9] So they concentrate their attention on students whom these outsiders regard as worth educating, not on those whom their own ideology puts at center stage. Under those circumstances the community colleges' "open door" policy is valuable for the handful of "late bloomers" who do better academic work than their high school record implied they would. It is not very helpful to the majority whose high school records are an all-too-accurate indication of academic incompetence or indifference. For such students, the "open door" usually becomes the "revolving door."

Theoretically, most community colleges provide terminal vocational

---

[9] We have heard complaints from faculty teaching in the state colleges of California that their students are more handicapped than junior college students in transferring to the state university, because the junior colleges have been more unquestioning in their subordination to university standards and present more conventional transcripts. The four-year colleges are said to be somewhat more independent, and not to regard themselves as de facto transfer institutions. This is certainly true of San Francisco State College, for a portrait of which see Jencks and Riesman in Sanford, ed.

programs for such students. But here again there are problems. First, the jobs to which a junior college graduate initially aspires often require specialized skill and intelligence. This means that when a dull student is counseled into a technical training program he often finds this just as difficult as the largely rote academic program from which he came. In addition, everyone believes that vocational training leads to less lucrative or at least less prestigious jobs than the transfer program. The transfer program therefore ranks higher in the eyes of the students than do technical programs. When advised to transfer to the latter, community college students usually conclude (often rightly) that they are really being advised to withdraw, and they often take the advice. So while vocational training programs are frequently heralded as playing a crucial role in economic growth, and certainly play a crucial role in mobilizing business support for two-year colleges, they tend to suffer the same kind of neglect—and for some of the same reasons—that their counterparts suffered in nineteenth-century colleges. Those who come to college at all want "the genuine article," while those who would accept practical training tend to shun any place that looks like a college.

But if the community colleges have only rarely devised new sorts of academic programs for students who could not meet traditional payrolls, and if they have provided only a few students with vocational training, how are we to account for their popularity? This is not an easy question to answer, especially since it is clouded with mythology. A comprehensive network of community colleges, for example, is supposed to increase the proportion of high school graduates who go to college. It does increase the proportion who enter college, but it does not appear to increase the proportion who earn B.A.s.[10] Since employers are mainly interested in increasing the proportion of B.A.s rather than the proportion of dropouts, and parents have the same outlook, it is not obvious why the community colleges should win much support on this account.[11]

Nor do community colleges seem to save the taxpayer money in

[10] This generalization rests mainly on the experience of California, which manages to get the great majority of its high school graduates into some sort of college eventually, but is no more successful in getting them through four years than states like New York and Massachusetts. See Sanders and Palmer, table 1, and our chapter on California in *The Academic Enterprise* (forthcoming).

[11] A skeptic might well argue that if four years of college are valuable, then two years ought to be at least half as valuable. But Census data on incomes show this is not so. A man with 1–3 years of college reaps a much smaller return per year of college than a man with four years. (See 1960 *Census*, I, 1, table 223.) This may simply reflect the fact that dropouts are less ambitious or less talented than B.A.s, or it may reflect the so-called "sheepskin effect," which allows B.A.s to command higher salaries simply because they have B.A.s. Whatever the cause, however, the effect is to make most people assume that entering college without finishing it is a waste of time. This is clearly an exaggeration.

the way many legislators expect. The cost of educating a given freshman at a two-year college does not appear to be significantly less than
the cost of educating him at either a four-year college or a big public
university. Since the two-year colleges enroll many freshmen who
would not otherwise go to college at all, the net result is an increase in
both absolute expenditure and expenditure per college graduate.[12]
The savings, such as they are, go to those students who get to live at
home, rather than to the taxpayers.

While the community colleges provide a cheap and academically
accessible path to a B.A. for some impoverished or late maturing students who would otherwise have nowhere to go, their failure to produce a significant increase in the over-all proportions earning B.A.s
suggests that this must be a small group. They also provide a larger
number of local residents with service courses of various kinds. These
are undoubtedly satisfying and useful to some, but this is clearly not
their major activity. Most of their students enter with the conventional
desire for a union card, flounder for a year or two, and then drop out.
This may not be bad for them as individuals, but it is not the sort of
experience that breeds loyal alumni or makes good copy for the
public relations office.

Yet in an ironic way it may be precisely because they attract
the flounderers that the community colleges have grown in popularity
over the past generation. State universities have been getting more
and more students with high academic aptitudes, impressive diligence,
and an interest in mastering the mysteries their professors now command. Their interest in marginal students of modest ability and uncertain plans, always limited, has now entirely vanished. Not only that,
but university propagandists have been quite successful in selling the
public, or at least its elected representatives, on the idea that universities can and should become selective institutions, catering mainly
to students who have "demonstrated an ability to profit from such
opportunities." Yet this gathering consensus has not been accompanied by any diminution in either the number of marginal students

[12] Over-all cost data for four-year colleges and for universities are very misleading on this point, for the cost for freshmen and sophomores is invariably far
below the institution-wide average. We know no good national data on costs for
students at different levels in different kinds of institutions. Data from the 1950s
in California show quite clearly, however, that it cost the California taxpayer as
much to educate a freshman or sophomore at a two-year community college as at
a four-year state college, and only about 15 per cent less than at Berkeley or
UCLA. Only the small university campuses like Davis and Riverside were
appreciably more expensive than the community colleges. Since the freshmen at
two-year colleges were less likely to take B.A.s than freshmen at state colleges
or university campuses, they presumably represented a worse investment, dollar
for dollar. It is true, however, that since part of this cost was borne by local
property taxes, it might appear a better investment from the narrow viewpoint
of a state legislator. See *A Master Plan*, pp. 156 ff.

who want to attend college or the popular feeling that somehow "everyone ought to have a chance to prove himself." The community colleges provide a way out of this dilemma, allowing the universities to become more exclusive without the over-all system's doing likewise. This, we would argue, is one major reason why they have won the support of both politicians and academicians.

The community colleges' failure to reach most of their students must therefore be seen in the context of a long tradition. A generation ago the students in question were admitted to state universities in large numbers. These universities used their freshman year as a protracted but expensive College Board sequence. Half the entering students were often eliminated in this way. Only after this had been done was a somewhat serious effort made to educate the survivors. Today the community colleges get more and more of the marginal students. They usually handle them in much the same way the university did, with much the same result.[13] To the extent that a college is concerned with this kind of selection rather than with education, the brevity of a marginal student's stay is a measure of its efficiency. Quick departures save the staff's time, the taxpayer's money, and probably the student's psyche. The only constraint is that the student should stay long enough so that he feels he has had a fair shake and blames his failure on himself rather than on the system. (This is considerably more likely if he can be induced to drop out rather than being flunked out.)

The interaction between the increasing availability of community colleges and the increasing exclusiveness of public universities is often quite explicit in state planning.[14] Even when it is not explicit, it may be an implicit political consideration. When Michigan State set up a new campus in Oakland, for example, the faculty hoped to make it as academically rigorous as any public university in the country. The residents of Oakland, on the other hand, hoped that the college would provide their children with an accessible and relatively painless road into the diploma elite. A high rate of academic failure was the last thing they wanted, and the potential for conflict with the college was enormous. The opening of Oakland Community College in the same area, along with better freeways allowing migration elsewhere, was expected to take some of the heat off the university campus and allow it to pursue its original vision without a political explosion.

Despite its origins in the anti-academic backlash, then, the community college turns out to be an essential pillar of the academic

13 One important difference may be that the dropouts from state universities usually seem to have returned to college eventually and earned degrees. See Eckland, "College Dropouts." Community college dropouts are probably less persistent, though we know no good long-term follow-up on them.

14 See, e.g. *A Master Plan.*

revolution. It is not primarily an alternative model for other colleges or an alternative path to the top for individuals, but rather a safety valve releasing pressures that might otherwise disrupt the dominant system. It contains these pressures and allows the universities to go their own way without facing the full consequences of excluding the dull-witted or uninterested majority.

Under these circumstances we doubt that the community college movement will lead to significant innovations in academic theory or practice. For reasons suggested in Chapter II we also doubt that the community colleges will compete successfully with four-year colleges for able students. Major assaults on the status quo will therefore have to come from elsewhere.

The General Education Movement

The pattern of resistance to the academic revolution known as "the community college movement" can be readily defined in institutional terms. The pattern of resistance that we will call "the general education movement" is harder to describe and delimit. It clearly does not include all the four-year colleges that call themselves liberal arts colleges. As previous chapters have emphasized, most liberal arts colleges are today supporters of the academic revolution. They are organized along the same departmental lines as graduate schools, they define knowledge in the same way, and with minor variations they select their students by much the same criteria. They hire only faculty trained in the graduate schools, and they judge their pedagogic success in good part by the number of students who enroll in these schools. If they resist the claims of the university at all, it is only at the margins.

What we term the general education movement is in some ways more a mood than a movement, at least if the term "movement" implies organization, program, or a common sense of identity. While some general educationists have had all these things, others with somewhat similar concerns have lacked them all. Many of the men we are talking about would balk at being described as general educationists, or indeed at any label that seemed to put them outside the professional corral. Some label is necessary, however, and despite its currently low estate, "general education" seems to us the best available.

Whatever the label, the mood itself is not new. It had analogues in those old liberal arts colleges that refused (or failed) to become universities, opposed the new emphasis on research, resisted the impulse to hire only Ph.D.s, dragged their feet in establishing new departments, rejected the elective system of course selection, and generally set their faces against what looked like the wave of the future. Today there are relatively few holdouts on these fronts, and these few are for the most part too poor, too benighted, and too isolated to constitute major foci of resistance to academic professionalism. But this does not mean that resistance is dead. Large numbers of B.A.s still decide to become college teachers in the hope of accomplishing something akin to what these old liberal arts colleges claimed to accomplish. They are interested in teaching rather than publishing, and particularly in teaching young and impressionable non-specialists rather than mature and committed departmental majors or doctoral candidates. Many have little commitment to one discipline as against another, and look forward to careers that will allow them to follow their curiosity wherever it leads.

When these students come face to face with the reality of doctoral study, many simply drop out. Others are co-opted. Still others persevere, however, either because they are lucky enough to find a patron or a whole program sympathetic to some of their penchants, or because they are adept enough to win at any game they have to play. Such men are likely to emerge from graduate school with very mixed feelings about the character of the modern university with its emphasis on departmental specialization and individual productivity. Some also dislike the university's preference for playing to an audience of adults rather than undergraduates.

Such men often indulge in sentimental polemics about the virtues of the old liberal arts college, with its smaller numbers, its less specialized faculty, and its exclusively undergraduate student body. This nostalgia does not, however, usually lead them to take jobs at the small denominational colleges that are the living counterparts to the liberal arts college of yore. Instead they tend to scatter through the universities and university colleges of the country in much the same way as their more professional colleagues. Over the years many have found time, energy, and freedom to try out some of their youthful hopes. An unusual course here or there, a distinctive seminar or tutorial program, even an experimental interdepartmental or non-departmental major have all testified to their enduring dissatisfaction with the standard versions of undergraduate instruction. Many of the most exciting moments in individual students' lives stem from such efforts.

Such men have, however, only rarely come together in sufficient numbers and won sufficient freedom to create a whole institution embodying their ideas about undergraduate education. The banner of general education floated for a time over the undergraduate colleges at Columbia and Chicago, and, to some extent, Harvard. A few independent liberal arts colleges, such as St. John's and Shimer, have also gone this route. A variety of other four-year colleges, such as Sarah Lawrence and Bennington, Bard and Goddard, New College and to some extent Antioch, have developed offbeat programs along related lines, though not all of them answer to the slogan of general education. But taken together, all these colleges have at most educated only 1 or 2 per cent of America's undergraduates over the past generation. Their histories are important mainly for what they tell about the problems and prospects of educational reform.

Like most academic innovations of the past century, the general education movement found its first characteristically modern expression at a university: Columbia after World War I. In many respects it was a reaction against the emphasis on graduate professional training and the spread of the elective system at the undergraduate level that had been the major academic achievements of the previous thirty years—especially at universities like Columbia. Even in the 1920s the feeling was abroad that specialization had gotten out of hand, that knowledge was becoming too fragmented, that research was being overemphasized, and that the transcendent truths and eternal verities were being lost in the process. It is probably no accident that the community college movement and the general education movement both became significant at around the same time. Both were reactions, albeit radically different ones, to the rise of academic professionalism in the late nineteenth and early twentieth centuries. Still, few people at Columbia wanted to turn back the clock and re-establish the old sectarian college with all its orthodoxies. Rather, they sought the best of both past and future: a pattern of instruction that would stress unity and community at the undergraduate level, diversity and specialization at the graduate level.[15]

General education at Columbia seems, however, to have had relatively little impact on the larger educational scene. A more historically important development took place at Chicago in the 1930s and 1940s. The arrival of Hutchins in 1929 marked the beginning of an era in which the shapers of the College sought to blend the omnivorous curiosity of avant-garde culture with the technical rigor of the academic disciplines. They also amalgamated the disciplines into somewhat novel shapes and sizes. The Chicago program included sequences in the natural sciences, the humanities, and the social sciences, which were supposed to integrate past and present work within these divisions of knowledge. These sequences were capped by work in philosophy and history. Pedagogically, the emphasis was on small group discussion; lectures were not forbidden but were less highly re-

[15] Daniel Bell's excellent book, *The Reforming of General Education,* gives a good account of these hopes and problems—and of much else.

garded. In order to retain high academic standards and contact with the "frontiers of knowledge," the Chicago pedagogy also stressed reading "original sources" (sometimes though not invariably defined as Great Books). It also employed multiple-choice tests on which purely forensic or rhetorical skills were of limited value. At both Chicago and Columbia an effort was made to offer a permanent career in undergraduate teaching for men who would not train graduate students. These were expected to be men of wide intellectual background and erudition, capable of critical or creative work. But they were not required to do research as that word was defined by the academic disciplines.

There was great internal diversity in the College at Chicago. The physical sciences staff attempted something different from the biological sciences staff, and each of the three year-long sequences in the social sciences was taught by a different staff with different pedagogic aims. These staffs were by no means uniformly hostile to the academic disciplines. Some men (including the second author) held joint appointments, partly in the College and partly in a graduate department. Not all the staffs shared the reverence for the classics. What they did share was a belief that pedagogic issues were of vital importance. They were willing to argue about such issues and to collaborate in a staff-taught course with colleagues of strong views and different persuasions, despite the compromises this necessitated. In addition, the College faculty mostly shared a belief that a man's share in the syllabus of a course (e.g. the widely used *The People Shall Judge,* prepared by the first year social sciences staff for American history) could legitimately be regarded as scholarly output. Some of the true believers even regarded such publications as superior to the allegedly trivial research done by individuals in specialized fields. (If the glory of the College in its balmier days was its unpedantic intellectual tone and its polemical vigor, its more depressing aspect was its air of solemn self-righteousness, characteristic of most academic utopias.)

In addition to these innovations, Hutchins flaunted collegiate tradition by a frontal assault on both college and class spirit. Big-time football was dropped and other sports de-emphasized. Class-wide solidarity was also undermined by placement examinations which enabled a student to take, say, a music course with graduate students, a social science course with second- and third-year undergraduates, and a humanities course with freshmen. As indicated in Chapter II, Hutchins also earned the hostility of many high school principals and counselors by recruiting undergraduates from the tenth and eleventh grades of high school. As if this were not enough, students could earn B.A.s by passing a certain number of comprehensive examinations, irrespective of their formal credit hours. This displeased many graduate schools, including many of the graduate departments of the University of Chicago itself.[16] Finally, Hutchins exploited the University of Chicago as a pulpit for denouncing American education, root and branch, in part for its failure to reform American society, root and branch.

Many of those who participated in or examined the Chicago experiment regarded it as highly successful. Whether one looked at the intense student culture or the records of alumni in graduate and professional schools (where most went), the College made a more impressive showing than almost any other undergraduate institution with similar students. The achievements of the College's alumni were not, however, usually the sort a development office welcomes. Their verbal sharpness, not uncommon bohemianism, and frequent pedagogic and political radicalism all alienated parents, the Chicago business community, Chicago alumni of a more staid era, and many graduate school professors. Even before Hutchins went to the Ford Foundation in 1951, it seemed apparent the College was not attracting sufficient applicants or donors to weather the hostility it was engendering— a hostility sometimes intensified by the doctrinaire reaction of College instructors to criticism. Once Hutchins departed, the College quickly lost its autonomy and was "invaded" by departmental specialists who sought to discipline the "talkie" vagueness and argumentative energy they felt emanated from it. The chemists and physicists, for example, who had criticized the undergraduate natural science courses as being "about science" rather than "science itself" were able to substitute a more conventional science program. Similarly, the historians who had long regarded the undergraduate social science and history courses as pretentious and overgeneral, lacking factuality and rigor, were allowed to edit the program more in their own image. Today, while the College continues and some of the old style remains, its courses tend to be compromises with departmental judgments, taught by faculty members approved by the departments and often members of them.[17]

As is so often the case, however, the innovation crushed at home reappeared in only slightly different form elsewhere. In the late 1950s Wayne State University in Detroit established an experimental undergraduate college called Monteith, which recruited a number of Chicago teachers, adapted the Chicago tradition of staff-taught courses,

[16] Although the majority of the graduate departments and professional schools at the University of Chicago were hostile to the College, sometimes flamboyantly so, there was also support in the Law School, in Sociology, and in such interdisciplinary graduate enterprises as the Committee on Human Development and the Committee on Social Thought, as well as among a few scientists.

[17] This picture may be out of date by the time it reaches our readers. The undergraduate College has now been divided into a set of subcolleges, several of which have attained very considerable freedom for new sorts of experimentation. But when this was written their plans were still on paper.

and retained Chicago's faith—some would say mystique—regarding the virtues of small classes and discussion. The major departure from the Chicago model was that Monteith recruited mainly lower-middle and working-class students instead of getting the precocious children of professionals and intellectually inclined Jews. Yet Monteith, like the College at Chicago, was very much on the defensive vis-à-vis the regular liberal arts faculty at Wayne and owed its existence largely to administrative support and a $700,000 grant from Ford's Fund for the Advancement of Education. After ten years it still has no imitators.

Another version of general education was introduced at Harvard after World War II. The motives behind the Harvard reforms were in many ways similar to those of the Columbia reformers a generation earlier. The faculty was concerned about the fact that high school students came to Harvard innocent of the books and ideas that faculty members had mastered at the same age. Since these students were often inducted into a particular discipline very quickly, they could easily graduate almost as ignorant of "the Western tradition" as when they arrived. But Harvard's attack on this problem was less radical than Columbia's or Chicago's, which may explain why it was so much more widely emulated. No attempt was made to separate the undergraduate College from the Graduate School of Arts and Sciences, nor to pre-empt the bulk of undergraduate time for general education. Instead, a Committee on General Education was established and authorized to give courses, particularly for freshmen and sophomores. The faculty for these courses had to come from the regular departments, but they were free to give courses their departmental colleagues might not have approved. Some of the resulting courses were interdisciplinary, some not. Virtually none was staff-taught in the Chicago sense, though the senior faculty who lectured in these courses were complemented by a staff of graduate assistants who taught small weekly sections.

Whatever its limitations, Harvard's version of general education had the great virtue of providing a rationale for dealing with freshmen and sophomores who had not chosen a departmental major.[18] Since this vacuum exists at virtually every college and since no other ideology or interest group was ready to fill it, the slogan of general education was widely adopted to describe what was done in these years. As at Harvard, the men who actually directed general education courses were almost always drawn from the regular departments. In some cases they were relatively experimental in outlook and had a good deal of freedom to devise their own programs in

[18] There were also general education courses that were mainly for upperclassmen, including one taught by the second author, but these were less central to the over-all program and were not widely emulated elsewhere.

their own way. In other cases they were quite traditional in their view of what freshmen and sophomores should learn and saw general education as little more than a new phrase to describe the old introductory departmental courses. In virtually no instance were these innovators sufficiently powerful to establish an independent center of power within the university, appointing its own faculty in the way that the "real" disciplines did. (Chicago and Columbia were the notable exceptions here.) General education programs existed on the sufferance of the faculty as a whole, which meant the departments, and were continually forced to defend themselves against critics who thought their efforts vague, soft, and dilettantish.

Administrators who hear about successful general education programs at conferences or read about them in the *Journal of General Education* often think they will be easy to establish. They *sound* easy, and sometimes cheap too, since one can presumably use existing talent instead of hiring new specialists in esoteric fields. But on closer inspection the intellectual and managerial problems of general education turn out to be staggering. One of the most serious is the recruitment of faculty sufficiently talented, both intellectually and humanly, to create courses that are genuinely interdisciplinary rather than merely additive. The regular departments are, after all, usually equally interested in men with such gifts, and offer them a chance to teach less strenuous courses at their own pace, without the wear and tear of colleagueship or the endless frustrations of trying to be interdisciplinary.[19] At its worst, an interdisciplinary course is an alibi for lack of intellectual discipline, but at its best it can be an extremely demanding creative feat, requiring a constant effort to see what is common to the disciplines within an area. As with all pedagogic innovation, it takes diplomatic skills of the highest order to secure the agreement and understanding of the relevant faculty committees for such courses. As against this, most research can be carried on pretty much on one's own, or at least with only the approval of an outside funding agency chosen by the researcher, not chosen for him. The results of this research need not be intelligible to faculty members in other fields, much less to freshmen. Yet they bring visibility far beyond what a transitory college course can achieve.

For these and other reasons, which Daniel Bell discusses in *The Reforming of General Education,* the trend seems to be away from interdisciplinary efforts at the undergraduate level and toward renewed acceptance of the value of introductory courses in the academic disciplines. It is mainly in the more backward reaches of higher

---

[19] Cf. Riesman, "Some Problems."

education that general education is being introduced as a new idea. At the leading universities interdisciplinary work goes on mainly in research, and eventuates in an altered curriculum only when a new department like molecular biology is introduced.

Most professional scholars are profoundly offended by the sight of another man they regard as a charlatan talking to impressionable students about their discipline. (Strangely, they feel no such outrage at the idea of a pedantic bore turning hundreds of freshmen entirely against their subject.) They may reluctantly grant presumed charlatans the right to publish, but they are not prepared to grant them free access to students if they can help it. This is true even when they themselves have no particular interest in teaching the students in question. This intolerance provides a rationale for a good deal of departmental imperialism. A department may, for example, have a man it would like to keep on but has no money to pay. The general education program, the experimental college, or whatever it may be, has a budget line but does not want the department's man. It has another candidate of its own whom the department thinks demonstrably weaker, at least on the scholarly side. The department therefore concludes that the general educationists are without judgment and uses the next available opportunity to curtail their power to saddle the university with what seem semicompetent faculty. A cynic might also note that the result of such maneuvers is usually to increase the number of slots the department can fill.

There is a paradox in all this. The College at Chicago demonstrated that its unique combination of administrative and curricular independence was better at recruiting and training candidates for graduate school than were the more orthodox undergraduate programs of other major universities.[20] Yet even Chicago's chemists, historians, *et al.* never accepted this finding, despite the impressive statistical evidence marshaled to support it. Perhaps we should say that *especially* Chicago's graduate faculties did not accept this finding, because they were irritated by the argumentative students and the assertive faculty of the College, in a setting that, by major university standards, was quite small and intimate. Geographically separate institutions producing similar sorts of students, such as New College in Sarasota, may evoke less hostility and defensiveness when students scatter around the graduate school landscape. If faculty see only a few talented students from an experimental college, rather than being physically aware of a whole antagonistic cadre, they may be more open-minded.

[20] Cf. Knapp and Goodrich, and Knapp and Greenbaum. While these studies fail to control for student input, they show that the College of Chicago turned out more future Ph.D.s than most other university colleges with what were presumed to be equally gifted students.

General education has not, of course, been the only attempt to curb the basic professional ethos of the university. We have discussed elsewhere, for example, the relatively small residential colleges for undergraduates at Harvard and Yale. While not overtly opposed to the dominant intellectual style of the graduate schools, these colleges attempted to narrow the gap between the work of professional academicians and the everyday life of the students.[21] Since this meant the faculty had to give time and imagination to items not on the disciplinary agenda, it tended to seem frivolous to the more professionalized scholars and appealing to the more humane. Similar efforts to break up the academic community along non-departmental lines and encourage non-professional relationships among students, among professors, and between students and professors have been made at other large universities, notably the new Santa Cruz campus of the University of California. While these efforts have not always had much in common intellectually with the general education movement, they have sometimes had similar hopes and have almost always run into similar difficulties. In particular, they have had little power over faculty appointments, seeking volunteers only among men already appointed to some department. This has intensified the always difficult problem of finding suitable staff.

Looking at the record of the past half-century, a dispassionate observer would probably have to conclude that major innovations within established universities have depended on strong-minded administrators like Hutchins and Lowell. Once these administrators were gone, the pioneers they brought to clear the departmental jungle were usually driven out too, and the undergraduate landscape reverted to its naturally fragmented and protograduate ecology. Under these circumstances some general educationists have concluded that they cannot lick the academic system and that the only answer is to secede from it. The result has been the establishment of several new, offbeat colleges and the transformation of other existing ones. At the end of World War II, for example, a group of innovators took over sleepy St. John's College in Annapolis and established a Great Books curriculum even more "pure" than the one used at Chicago. In the 1950s a band of Chicago emigrants gained control over Shimer College in Mount Carroll, Illinois, 130 miles west of the University. In the early 1960s St. John's established a second campus in Santa Fe, New Mexico. A number of other new ventures have been founded that in lesser measure reflect the tradition of academic dissent we have been describing.

Most of these colleges are eagerly idiosyncratic, and in many ways

[21] See Jencks and Riesman, "The Harvard House System," and the discussion of Harvard in *The Academic Enterprise* (forthcoming).

as different from one another as from the university colleges against which they define themselves. Virtually all of them, for example, have sought physical isolation and intellectual independence from the academic metropolis. None is located in Cambridge, Morningside Heights, Ann Arbor, Hyde Park, or Berkeley. A few are suburban, like Sarah Lawrence, but the majority are located in small, isolated towns, like Bard in small-town New York State; Bennington, Goddard, and Marlboro in Vermont; Franconia in New Hampshire; Antioch in Ohio; St. John's in both Maryland and New Mexico; New College in Florida; and Shimer in Illinois. (Although most of the above colleges would probably deny the kinship, Parsons College in Iowa also has something in common with them. Its aggressive emphasis on teaching and its attempts to redeem the hitherto apathetic and inept have attracted a handful of faculty who might otherwise have gone to, say, Antioch or Shimer. Its achievements have, however, been overshadowed by the aggressive salesmanship of its president, Millard Roberts, and by the controversies into which he has led the institution.)[22]

While most offbeat colleges are in revolt against the hegemony of the graduate schools and the triumph of the academic revolution, it would be a mistake to assume that they are merely nostalgic throwbacks to an earlier era. One has only to compare them to the small denominational institutions that still dot the American landscape to see that pastoralism, emphasis on community, and de-emphasis of research can mean completely different things in different contexts. A college like St. John's in Annapolis, for example, has some of the same academic conservatism as a denominational college, emphasizing the classics and distrusting new disciplines and new methods. But if St. John's is a community at all, which some doubt, it is certainly a far more competitive one than most denominational colleges. St. John's students enjoy intellectual games and are dialecticians of the most accomplished sort. They reject slovenliness, both mental and physical, in a way that gives them a superficial kinship with the students of a Midwestern Concordia or St. Mary's of the Mountains, but they have none of the sedate piety that also characterizes such students. Culturally, they are closer to Antioch or Chicago than to Middleburg or Prairie Junction.

Unlike other utopian communities, these offbeat colleges have mostly survived and even achieved moderate prosperity. While no experimental college is among the richest or most overapplied in the country, neither are most among the poorest or least sought after.

22 For more detailed treatment of Shimer and New College, see *The Academic Enterprise*, forthcoming. For a discussion of some of the paradoxes of Parsons, see Gusfield and Riesman, "Innovation."

Black Mountain, it is true, went the way of Oneida and New Harmony, but this was atypical. Yet offbeat colleges have had some of the other problems characteristic of utopian communities. Visions and visionaries are always hard to live with, and they tend to produce bitter internal schisms. True believers feel obliged to testify to their faith both in and out of season, and such an atmosphere makes daily life more strenuous than most people can stand for ten or twenty years. This is one reason why almost every experimental college has eventually redefined its goals, or at least the distinctive means by which it initially pursued them, in such a way as to bring it closer to the academic mainstream. In part this has been a matter of consolidating revolutions that have achieved legitimacy in the eyes of outsiders. The permissiveness, the artistic expressiveness, and the curricular freedom of Sarah Lawrence and Bennington, for example, are no longer shocking and novel, and no longer need to be defended as aggressively as they did a generation ago.

But what protagonists describe as consolidating the revolution also means betraying part of it. Every sect tends to become a church once the struggle for mere existence has been won, for the fanaticism that was necessary to sustain morale in the face of overwhelming odds becomes ridiculous when the bankbook balances and the five-year projection shows growth rather than a void. Once it is a going concern, too, an offbeat college begins to attract prospective faculty and students only partially committed to the original revolutionary vision. This in turn helps bring out the underlying ambivalence of some of the founders toward the departmental professionalism in which they were trained before their apostasy. "Sound" faculty are then likely to be hired, on the plausible ground that they will make good teachers. Few questions will be asked about how they view the college's idiosyncrasies, which are taken for granted. But then one fine morning the true believers discover they have become a minority. Despite bitter protests from the old guard, the new majority carries the day and the more traditional norms of the academic profession begin to reassert themselves.

If offbeat colleges were willing and able to devise curricula sufficiently different from those of the leading graduate schools so that they could rely on faculty from completely new sources, this cycle might be broken. As it is, however, they recruit mainly dissident academicians. Some of these men have earned Ph.D.s; others have not. But almost all have tried, at least briefly. Almost all aspiring college teachers rightly feel they must enter a Ph.D. program. Graduate students are less hypnotized by success than many other professional initiates, and often quite alienated from their fields and their faculties, although this varies a good deal. Even so, when they do badly they

are still likely to blame this on themselves more than on their department or the giants who dominate it. More often than not, graduate
students with unusual talent do quite well. This tends to make them
feel that graduate school is a relatively satisfactory model of excellence. Those who reject the graduate school model are apt to be
those who were unable to meet its standards. There are, of course,
plenty of exceptions: incompetents who regard the graduate schools
as the apogee of instructional efficiency, and geniuses who reject the
academic disciplines even though they could rise to the top in them.
But the latter group is small and inchoate. The majority may complain
about small things and feel a generalized sense of dissatisfaction and
resentment, but until the society finds ways of glamorizing the competencies graduate schools now neglect, most talented young men will
have only marginal interest in acquiring them.

It seems to follow that offbeat colleges will never grow in numbers
or influence unless or until they can recruit prospective teachers directly from college, socialize them into a less than completely academic subculture, and then employ them. If, as is generally the case,
the colleges in question believe in general education, they will have
to find ways of training prospective faculty that, while just as rigorous
as existing Ph.D. programs, place more emphasis on the kinds of
erudition needed to connect different kinds of inquiry and different
branches of knowledge and less emphasis on coverage and depth
within a single discipline. The pattern of graduate training must, in
other words, reflect the pattern of undergraduate teaching that will
be expected later on. Not only that, but if able faculty are expected
to get their primary satisfaction from teaching rather than from publication, their graduate training will have to give them clear standards
for judging their pedagogic competence and deciding when the enormous effort required is in fact paying off. This would mean intensive
supervision and discussion of graduate students' day-by-day performance in the classroom; it would mean washing out the poor teachers
in the same way that the authors of poor seminar papers are washed
out; most of all, it would require that those who staffed the program
have the same commitment to classroom competence that the men
in charge of today's graduate schools have to the advancement of
knowledge. Without the development of some such teacher-training
program, competitive with existing ones, offbeat colleges are likely to
remain exciting, useful, but temporary phenomena, touching a few
undergraduates deeply but eventually succumbing to the norms of the
larger academic system rather than helping to transform it.

Or so it will appear. These colleges may, however, have some
subtle impact even when they do not survive in pristine form. The
thoughtful president of a great university commented to us recently

that all the fine venturesome colleges in America—he meant the Reeds, Haverfords, Swarthmores, and Antiochs, but he might also have included the Chicagos, Shimers, and Monteiths—amounted to nothing because they affected such a tiny handful of students. What really mattered, he said, was whether the big universities followed the California model, which ignored the undergraduates, or the Michigan model, which tried in a modest way to do something sensible and sensitive for them. In a sense he was right. But one must ask why Michigan is different from California. The answer, we think, may in part be that there are a number of Michigan faculty members and administrators who have taught in small and unusual colleges, or at least attended them. For them the memory of Chicago, Bennington, Kalamazoo, or some other institution provides a continuing incentive not to abandon the undergraduates to each other. In California, it seems to us, such faculty members are less common. Clark Kerr was a Swarthmore undergraduate, but his efforts to do something about undergraduate education, both at Berkeley and on the new campuses, got little faculty support. (Indeed, his ultimate willingness to accommodate a research-minded faculty earned him a reputation for indifference to undergraduates.) In this sense, then, experiments that seem to fail and models that are never directly emulated may ultimately have some oblique effect.

The disciplines, like other forms of chauvinism, have proved more durable than many reformers anticipated. It does not follow, however, that we should junk general education, any more than we should junk the United Nations. Both have limitations, and both bore many people who support them in principle. But both remain valuable nonetheless. Students and faculty who have taken part in general education at its best have often been indelibly marked by the experience. Most have gone on to work in a particular discipline or gone back to work in one, but they have done so with a noticeably less provincial view of it. It is true that general education has probably done even less than the UN to inspire guilt or doubt among the parishes it tries to unite, and that the departments and the research ethos remain triumphant on every front. But the need remains, and general education still comes closer to meeting it than anything else now on the horizon.

Other Non-Academic Professions and Organizations

If neither the community college movement nor the general education movement threatens the hegemony of the academic profession, what other interest groups might do so? Just as at the elementary and secondary level, some might urge taking undergraduate education away from "subject-matter specialists" and turning it over to men whose special skill and training is in working with late adolescents, i.e. clincial psychologists and psychiatrists. Such men have done a certain amount of research on undergraduate education, have treated some of the students who get into trouble in the existing system, and have made occasional suggestions to the academic profession about how colleges might be better managed. But there are obviously nowhere near enough such men to staff the nation's colleges, and those there are have shown very little interest in running even one such enterprise. They are content to run their professional training programs at the graduate level and leave the work of undergraduate education to others.

Still, there might be some lessons to be learned from these graduate programs. Almost all require the student to apply his skills to a real human problem, to take responsibility for the solution of this problem, and to submit to criticism by his elders for the way in which he carries out his responsibilities. This kind of clinical training has the advantage of engaging all but the most lackadaisical students' interest. It also forces the teacher to recognize—in practice as well as in theory —that education involves more than the transmission of intellectual skills and knowledge. A clinical psychologist or psychiatrist cannot escape responsibility for that elusive entity "the whole student," even if he wishes to do so, for it is "the whole student," or at least a large part of him, whom he is training to work with patients. If undergraduate teachers were equally committed to preparing their students for some sort of responsible work, and if they supervised their students' performance in such work, they might be more sensitive to the fact that the young need non-academic as well as academic help.

Still, it is clear that psychologists and psychiatrists are not going to take responsibility for undergraduate education. What about other professions? Many have played an active role in the past. Not only was there a time when colleges were mostly staffed by clergymen, but there are still many undergraduate professional schools staffed by men trained mainly or exclusively in education, in engineering, in accounting, in optometry, and so forth. Yet none of these non-academic institutions has regularly provided its students with experiences more liberating or more satisfying than those provided by academicians in conventional liberal arts colleges. Nor have such colleges shown the same instinct for survival and growth as colleges staffed by Ph.D.s. As we argued in Chapter V, non-academicians tend to be upwardly mobile, moving out of lower-division and even upper-division undergraduate programs into graduate level instruction. While new sorts of professionals move in and fill the vacuum their more prestigious predecessors have left at the undergraduate level, they too will eventually prefer older students if they can get them.

The withdrawal of the non-academic professions from undergraduate education is in one sense quite beneficial. Most undergraduates are probably better off if they can postpone most of their strictly professional training until graduate school and can use their undergraduate years as a time for exploring who they are and what alternatives are open to them. But for precisely this reason, the *complete* withdrawal of non-academic professionals from undergraduate education is a great loss. A premedical student, for example, can go through his four undergraduate years without ever meeting a doctor, seeing a patient, or even talking to a medical student. If this happens he is not much better able to decide whether he wants to become a doctor after earning his B.A. than he was after finishing high school. This is especially true if, as is usually the case, he has been insulated not only from doctors and medical practice, but from most other non-academic professions to which he might aspire if he was uncertain about medicine.

The only interest groups that have shown a continuing capacity to compete with the academic profession in the training of high school graduates are enormous bureaucratic and corporate enterprises: the Armed Services and the major corporations. These organizations prepare high school graduates and college dropouts for a wide variety of roles, ranging from office management and the pacification of irate customers to aircraft maintenance and counterinsurgency. Perhaps the most important difference between these non-academic programs and their counterparts on college campuses is their brevity. We know of no industrial or military training program (except for the military academies) that requires four years of continuous study. Instead, the typical corporate program alternates much shorter periods of study with longer periods of work. The cumulative result over a career, especially in the military, may well be more than four years of training, coming perhaps at eighteen, twenty-five, thirty-five, and forty-five. Academicians, on the other hand, try to cram everything they can into four years of late adolescence. They do this because unlike GE or the Air Force they cannot bring men back to college at will. Nor can they afford to support older students. (The Department of Defense is said to spend more on education beyond high school than all the state legislatures in the country combined, and General Electric spends more than any but the largest universities.)

Nonetheless, we see little prospect that these in-house training programs will emerge as genuine alternatives to those conducted by academicians. The same organizations that are most committed to expanding their internal education programs are also placing ever-greater emphasis on the B.A. as a prerequisite for both choice training programs and junior management jobs. This is not usually because they think the academicians are doing a better job than the organization's own men could do. It is because they cannot compete with the colleges for able high school graduates. The military academies are the exception that proves the rule. The academies do get very able high school graduates, partly because they look like colleges, and the military prefers their graduates to graduates of conventional academic colleges. Other large organizations (with the partial exception of the Catholic Church) have not been able to compete for able high school graduates, and they have therefore delayed hiring for elite streams until the academicians have finished their turn. Unless large numbers of able students with a bent for organizational life begin to lose interest in academic education, the big organizations are unlikely to make a major effort to create parallel educational programs for them. The post-secondary programs they sponsor will probably continue to have less status, even in their own eyes, than the genuine academic article.

When all is said and done, this is probably just as well. It is true that the academic profession has a quite narrow conception of educational objectives and methods. It is also true that the human products of academic instruction are often a sorry lot. But the alternatives with which we are familiar satisfy us even less. Certainly we feel no yearning for the good old days when colleges were staffed by clergymen interested in moral as well as intellectual rectitude. Nor would we go to the barricades in defense of undergraduate programs run by educationists or engineers. While we know relatively little about the internal programs run by business and the military, our limited experience with them has certainly not convinced us that their alumni are more open-minded, versatile, empathic, self-confident, altruistic, or even competent than the alumni of conventional colleges.[23]

[23] One corporate venture that *did* impress us was the now abandoned Program for the Humanistic Education of Executives, put on for Bell Telephone executives at the University of Pennsylvania. This collected a small number of middle-level executives from all over the country, kept them for an entire academic year, and was free of all directly vocational concerns. Some of its students had not been to college at all and others had attended engineering schools or studied patent law at night. It confronted them with James Joyce and Lewis Mumford, Bela Bartok and Mies Van Der Rohe, Max Weber and Paul Tillich—in person, where possible. Bewildering at first for most, destructive perhaps for a few, it gave many a better education in one year than almost any liberal arts college crams into four. Yet the fact that the program was conducted at the University of Pennsylvania, plus the fact that it has now vanished, suggests that it can hardly be regarded as a prototype for the possibilities of non-academic education. So far as we know, no published work has been done on the careers of the executives who went through it. For a brief description, see Baltzell. For a more extensive discussion, see Peckham.

None of this means that academicians are the only profession that should establish institutions for educating men and women between the ages of eighteen and twenty-one. It means only that the institutions established by other groups, be they corporate administrators, engineers, educationists, or military officers, do not strike us as a conspicuous improvement on the university colleges established by academicians. Quite the contrary.

This being so, it is important to consider more modest reforms which do not depend on the growth of a new non-academic profession to take responsibility for late adolescents. Instead of trying to create institutions run entirely by non-academicians, for example, we might create institutions in which academicians remained the majority shareholders but in which other groups were given a large minority voice. In such an institution the aim would not be to *replace* the academic disciplines but to *supplement* them. The faculty would include substantial numbers to tenured members who were not scholars but doctors, lawyers, administrators, and so forth. The program would include not only regular academic courses in literature, psychology, and chemistry but clinical experience and field work of various kinds. Recognizing that students learn from what they do and whom they meet as well as from what they read, such a college would try to expose them to a wide range of alternatives. Yet perhaps this kind of pluralism is even more visionary than the idea of a college run by non-academicians. It would be workable only if most of the teachers involved respected methods that differed radically from their own and were willing to acknowledge that they had a legitimate place in undergraduate education. Scholars and scientists have not in the past shown such broad-mindedness. Whenever they have had power they have used it to eliminate most non-academicians from undergraduate teaching and to create an undergraduate program of an almost exclusively academic character. In this respect they are even less tolerant than the other professions that conduct undergraduate colleges. Engineers and accountants, for example, while forcing their students to do most of their work in engineering or accounting, usually leave *some* place for academic work in the arts and sciences as well.

The new branch of the State University of New York at Old Westbury on Long Island is hoping to explore these possibilities, but the difficulty of such innovations should not be underestimated. Harris Wofford, the President at Old Westbury, is hoping to involve doctors, lawyers, perhaps theologians, and other professionals in undergraduate education, but neither he nor they have a ready-made curriculum for them to use. The physician or attorney asked to teach at such a college cannot treat undergraduates as he would first-year medical students or law students. He may therefore feel tempted to fall back on anecdotage, meanwhile deriding his presumably more academic colleagues for their lack of experience in the real world and cultivating a similar self-indulgence among his students who have neither academic nor non-academic expertise. Alternatively, he may feel intimidated by the academic tradition he is being asked to enrich and fall into imitative pedantry or deliberately dry abstraction. Any such experiment will inevitably have its share of pretentiousness, sloppiness, and failure. This means it will also have mutual jealousy and recrimination, perhaps especially among men who are uncertain of their own role and therefore intolerant of those who go at it differently. Yet it seems to us that the academic profession is now mature enough and powerful enough to take these risks, and that it no longer needs a protective tariff to maintain its share of the undergraduate market.

XII. *Reforming the Graduate Schools*

The Pitfalls of Nostalgia

If this book has any single message it is that the academic profession increasingly determines the character of undergraduate education in America. Academicians today decide what a student ought to know, how he should be taught it, and who can teach it to him. Not only that—their standards increasingly determine which students attend which colleges, who feels competent once he arrives, and how much time he has for non-academic activities. It is true that the academicians' claims are still resisted with some success by young people who resent adults, by provincials who resent cosmopolitans, by the devout who resent heretics, by the upwardly mobile who resent the arrived, and by the wealthy who resent the application of meritocratic standards to their children. But this resistance is for the most part poorly organized, poorly financed, and poorly thought out. It may help persuade the academicians that they are a beleaguered minority and thus help them rationalize continuing efforts to extend their influence, but it has not provided much basis for creative initiative or reform in undergraduate education.

We see no historical reason to regret the rise of the academicians. Given the character of American society generally, it is hard to identify any other group or groups which would have served undergraduates better. Nor do we see any grounds for nostalgia about the cost of the academic victory. By almost any standard we can think of, the young are better off as a result of it.

If we use a strictly academic yardstick, it seems reasonably clear that today's B.A.s know more in absolute terms than their predecessors in any earlier era. It does not seem to be true, as many observers assume, that the increase in the proportion of young people attending college has brought a decline in average undergraduate IQ. The trend in actual achievement is also up. In good part this reflects changes in the sophistication and competence of college applicants. High schools have generally gotten better, even though some formerly adequate or even distinguished city schools have been swamped with poor students and have seen their abler teachers grow frustrated and depart. In addition, television, paperbacks, LP records, earlier physical maturity, and a host of other influences make today's freshman more precocious than his forerunners. There is a myth that college freshmen used to know three languages, write limpid prose with flawless spelling and punctuation, and had a thorough knowledge of history and literature. But a look at old College Board examinations or freshman courses shows that the general image of decline from an earlier golden era is fantasy. This is particularly clear in science and mathematics, where the competence of today's freshmen can be measured on the same scale as yesterday's. But even in the humanities, where the shift away from the classics toward contemporary problems makes comparisons over time more difficult, it is hard to find much documentary basis for nostalgia. There may have been a decline in some areas of strictly technical competence, such as spelling, which seem less important and more pedantic than they once did, but even this is problematic.

Not only are entering freshmen better prepared, but they appear to learn more during their undergraduate years. For one thing, today's students are more concerned than yesterday's with proving their academic competence. They are more afraid of turning out to be stupid and more inclined to equate academic skills with intelligence. This subjective change is re-enforced by the fact that it is objectively more important to get good grades, for admission to the right graduate or professional school is probably more occupationally significant and certainly more competitive than in the past. In addition, the quality of undergraduate faculty has generally improved. This is partly because today's faculty are products of an improved educational system, partly because the academic profession attracts a larger proportion of America's intellectual talent than it used to (though with considerable variation among fields). The academic profession is also better able to keep its members in contact with the main intellectual currents of their disciplines than it was a generation or two ago. Summer institutes sponsored by the National Science Foundation and other similar efforts encourage college teachers to rethink what they learned years before in poorer places, and perhaps move beyond it. Greater affluence makes travel to more meetings possible, where at least some papers are heard as well as read. There are many more journals, and their general level is much higher.[1]

Not only are the faculty better, but contrary to another legend they are often more interested. Since teachers encounter more students who are well prepared and seem interested in academic work,

[1] Isador Isaac Rabi has commented that when he went to study in Germany in the 1920s, his university there got all the issues of the *Physical Review* once a year to save money. The German physicists felt there was nothing important enough in this leading American journal to be urgent, and probably they were right. This would hardly be the case now.

they are less inclined to see themselves as policemen and less likely to become cynical about the possibility of teaching anyone anything. It is true that the growing emphasis on research has distracted some able senior faculty from undergraduate instruction. But the prestige of teaching remains greater among scholars than among engineers, businessmen, or probably even school administrators. Furthermore, while the teaching assistants who fill in for those senior men who flee the classroom are often deprecated by status-conscious undergraduates, they frequently know more than senior faculty and in the better places may also care more.

Outstanding (as against merely good) teachers have always been scarce, but we know of more today than a generation ago. Indeed, there is more of everything now. There are very few colleges where an enterprising student cannot get an education if he tries, and none we can think of where this is more difficult today than in the past. The undergraduate's problem, especially in the big universities, is to hunt out the good departments and the good teachers (including graduate students) within them. The majority of students have never had the energy or the wit to do this, but have followed conventional tracks through the system. Their creative encounters have depended on luck rather than intelligent search behavior. Advising systems have done little to counter this, for student advising is much less valued than undergraduate instruction. Comity and the fear of seeming malicious have often limited advisors' candor, even when they were genuinely interested, and excessive protectiveness vis-à-vis the students has also been a problem. Student course guides such as the one done by *The Crimson* at Harvard or by SLATE at Berkeley have, however, become more common of late and may have helped freshmen both to save time and do a better job in casing the academic joint.

When we turn from the narrow question of academic competence to the broader question of human growth, the academic revolution again strikes us as a progressive development. Admittedly, progress costs something, and advances in the direction of one value are almost always detrimental to some other values. One cannot, for example, reject gerontocracy and establish equality between age groups without simultaneously making the family less important and the lot of the aged more difficult. Similarly, one cannot free people from the tyranny of their neighbors and encourage them to seek out new worlds where they will be happy without at the same time undermining community solidarity and making the lot of the less competent more difficult. Yet the triumph of academic ideals has helped more undergraduates in what we would regard as the right direction on both these fronts, encouraging the emancipation of the young from adults (at least outside the academic realm) and their exposure to a variety of subversive influences that make them both mentally and physically more mobile. So, too, while we would not everywhere and always insist on integration of ethnic, religious, and sex groups, the academic profession's general distaste for segregation comports with our own.

All in all, then, we see relatively little ground for nostalgia, and considerable reason for satisfaction with the consequences to date of academic power. Changes now taking place in undergraduate education are, moreover, likely to lead to further improvements. Since undergraduates are more competent, sophisticated, and mature than they once were, colleges are treating them more and more as they have traditionally treated graduate students, both socially and intellectually. This is clearest when one looks at the gradual relaxation of social restrictions on most campuses, but it is also true of academic reform. Many reformers now want to induct students into the world of scholarship earlier than was common a generation or two back. This leads to freshman seminars, tutorial programs, honors courses, independent study, comprehensive examinations, senior theses, and the like. (Even the nomenclature is often taken from the graduate schools.) Procedural innovations, such as the abolition of freshman grades and the substitution of long papers for course examinations also turn out on closer scrutiny to be devices for treating undergraduates like more mature graduate students.[2]

Yet these changes, desirable as they are, do not go to the heart of the two central problems of contemporary higher education. The first of these is the academic profession's understandable preference for preaching to the already converted minority instead of doing missionary work among the heathen majority. The second is the inadequacy of the faith most academicians adhere to. The two great challenges are therefore to devise colleges that can touch the lives of those who are now merely going through the motions, and to devise graduate programs—and indeed a style of faculty life—that better develop and exemplify the possibilities of the life of the mind. At the moment very little effort is being made on either front.

Starting at the Top

The American graduate school has become the envy of the world, a mecca for foreign students and a model for foreign institutions. It

---

[2] Since all geological strata coexist, earlier reforms such as General Education are still spreading to the less distinguished undergraduate colleges, even though they have withered in the places of their origin. Syncretism is also common. Thus a typical reform proposal today involves freshmen in seminars like those once reserved for graduate students, but gives these seminars an interdisciplinary approach in the hope of giving freshmen a feeling of relevance and excitement.

has also become one of the central institutions of American culture. Both the best and the worst in undergraduate education emanate from it, and the over-all quality of American intellectual life depends more on it than on any other single institution. The universities have increasingly co-opted all sorts of non-academic intellectuals, beginning with writers and artists in residence but now extending to politicians and bureaucrats (at Harvard's Kennedy Institute for example), journalists, and so on. The university has, indeed, become the new Maecenas, and its decisions to give or withhold patronage shape much of American life. What the graduate schools define as "research" will get done; what they exclude is likely to languish. If scholarly research is too often divorced from the intellectual issues that arise inchoately in men's lives, the graduate school must be named as co-respondent in the case. If professional work is increasingly defined as acting out a role defined by colleagues rather than serving clients and trying to help them understand their needs, the graduate professional schools must bear some share of the blame.

Complaints against the graduate schools are not new, of course. Intellectuals like William James were denouncing what he called "the Ph.D. octopus" before either of the present authors was born, and A. Lawrence Lowell even tried to create an aristocratic alternative to the doctorate by endowing the Society of Fellows at Harvard. On the other side, anti-intellectual newspapermen and legislators still make hay out of apparently (and sometimes actually) ridiculous Ph.D. thesis titles, and any reader of university histories knows that at least until quite recently it has been extremely difficult to raise money for scholarship in fields that lacked an obvious practical application (or, rarely, snob appeal). Caught in this cross-fire between the intellectual elitists and the know-nothings, the graduate schools have inevitably been somewhat defensive, but they have made no concessions. Instead, their faculty mostly concluded that the laity was beyond redemption, that stringent efforts were needed to prevent the subversion of the academy by pragmatism and indolence, and that the primary problem was to raise standards, tighten requirements, and keep the citadel fortified against possible Luddite incursions.

Since World War II the graduate schools have been increasingly successful in winning converts to their point of view. The authors have served on a number of government panels, task forces, private commissions, and committees. These groups have almost all formulated their recommendations on the assumption that the nation's leading graduate schools were in pretty good shape and that America's educational problems were those of quality control further down the academic line. Sometimes this meant that the "underdeveloped" universities needed to be brought up to the level of Berkeley and Harvard. Sometimes it meant that undergraduate colleges had to be upgraded so that their students got a better idea of the kind of scholarship and science being done in the leading graduate schools. Sometimes it meant that the curriculum in the secondary or even the elementary schools had to be revamped to conform to the latest thinking of the top academic professionals. The only failing of the top graduate schools that troubled most of these groups was quantitative: there were not enough Ph.D.s; they were in the wrong fields; they took too long to get through. (A handful of undergraduate colleges have been more critical, on the ground that they were not getting the kinds of teachers they wanted, but this has hardly been typical.) As for the graduate schools themselves, they are astonishingly complacent. A few years ago, for instance, Bernard Berelson published a report on graduate education.[3] He surveyed opinion among graduate deans, faculty, and students on a variety of prickly issues and found general satisfaction with the status quo among all concerned. Despite minor misgivings about details, such as the duration of graduate study, Berelson shared this satisfaction, awarding the graduate schools a certificate of accomplishment and even distinction.

As we have indicated repeatedly throughout this book but especially in our discussion of the academic profession in Chapter V, we number ourselves among the critics rather than among the enthusiasts of graduate education. We are troubled by the rigidity of the departmental and disciplinary categories into which the graduate schools are characteristically organized, and by their emphasis on training men to write papers rather than to communicate with students on a face-to-face basis. More generally, we are troubled by the fact the graduate schools have an essentially imperial relationship with many of the institutions and subcultures on their borders, particularly the undergraduate colleges. Their apparent successes depend in many cases on exploiting these underdeveloped territories. First, the graduate schools import the colleges' most valuable "raw material," i.e. gifted B.A.s. They train these men as scholars. The best of them they keep for themselves; the rest they export to the colleges whence they come, to become teachers. Like all imperial powers, the graduate schools believe they are doing their empire a favor by keeping order and maintaining standards within it. Given their values, this is to some extent true. Nonetheless, their values are not the only imaginable or appealing ones, nor are they necessarily the ones most appropriate to an undergraduate college.

As the foregoing chapters have indicated, we see little prospect that the graduate imperium will yield to outbreaks of unrest among

[3] Berelson.

the natives in the undergraduate colleges. If decolonization comes in our time—and we doubt that it will—it will come as a result of strong initiatives from dissidents within the graduate schools themselves. Such initiatives would succeed only if they had the support of outsiders, but the basic responsibility would almost certainly have to rest on established members of the academic profession. The pages that follow outline some of the possibilities, but they are only a beginning.

"Pure" versus "Applied" Work

We begin with departmentalism and specialization. The basic problem here is how to determine the research agenda of individuals and groups. At present there are two conflicting tendencies. The academic profession is eager to ensure that everyone will draw up his agenda to please his colleagues. This is encouraged by making promotion and tenure dependent on the judgment of departments and by making research funds available partly on the basis of judgments by panels of experts. In this context the test of good research becomes how much influence it has on other scholars. The government and the major foundations, on the other hand, have a different set of priorities. They are primarily interested in non-academic problems, and they finance research in the hope that it will illuminate these problems. Advancing a given discipline is for them a means, not an end. They put more money into "applied" than "pure" research, and in "pure" fields they select subspecialties that seem likely to have some "applied" fallout. Both the government and the foundations tend to support interdisciplinary research, for the problems of the real world often refuse to fit departmental categories.

This divergence about the proper subjects of research does not, however, usually extend to methodology. On the contrary, government agencies and foundations subsidize academic research primarily because they are impressed by the methodological competence of university professors. They may want to redirect this competence into new areas, but they make relatively little effort to influence the technique. That, indeed, is why the marriage between government research agencies and the academic profession has proved fairly satisfactory; many academicians are not particular about the areas in which they work so long as they are free to choose the methods, and the government frequently has no preconceptions about the method so long as it controls the areas. This generalization is admittedly a bit too simple. While most academicians are willing to tailor their research proposals to the concerns of their backers, they often "moonlight" once the grant comes through and work on areas that interest them more. Conversely, some government officials are eager to finance whatever research scholars think important, but cannot get them to stop making proposals aimed at the agency's imagined prejudices.

This pattern of relationships between the pure and the applied is to our mind more satisfactory than that found in most other countries, where universities have resisted outsiders' efforts to dictate even the subjects of inquiry, have gotten relatively little money, and have remained more isolated from the great issues of their times. (This generalization may not hold for the communist countries, of whose institutions we know very little.) Nonetheless, the situation is far from perfect. The means employed in research inevitably shape the ends, often in ways that those who support the research do not fully anticipate or appreciate. More important, the methods employed go a long way toward determining the character of the academician himself, the kind of model he presents to his graduate students, and hence the ideals of those who teach future generations of undergraduates. To the extent that it allows a self-regulating guild to decide how men should answer the great questions that trouble them, society obviously takes a considerable risk.

The genius and the peril of academic research is that it unearths and weighs information in ways very different from those used by laymen. The academic profession places little weight on knowledge derived from individual subjective experience. It insists on knowledge that is objective in the sense that others can be told how it was acquired, can repeat the operation, and can be expected to arrive at the same result. (This book is in this sense largely non-academic, despite its statistical excursions and footnotes.) So long as "hard" data are used to extend the researcher's "soft" experiences and curb his prejudices, the tension between the individual scholar's subjective experience and the profession's emphasis on universalism and replication is likely to remain creative. But "hard" research has a persistent tendency to take on a life of its own, accumulating by an internal logic that takes no account of any one individual's subjective experience. The researcher's work thus ceases to have any effect on the rest of his life, and conversely his life has little effect on his work. This development is, we would argue, one of the crucial ingredients of professionalization. Just as doctors feel they must learn to treat their patients as objects in order to keep their sanity in grisly situations, so too professors struggle to transcend themselves and be dispassionate about subjects they care deeply about. Too often, they succeed in this by ceasing to care. Yet there is also a shrill minority which resolves what should remain a creative tension by emphasizing how much it cares, how little anyone else cares, and how unimportant it therefore is to do competent, accurate, persuasive work.

The result of this quest for impersonality varies from one occupation to another, and within academic life from one field to another. Natural scientists have been able to produce a great deal of valuable work that was completely unrelated to their lives outside their laboratory and that had no immediate or obvious relationship to any practical problem. (This is not to say that *all* natural science falls into this category; only that such work is possible.) It is much harder to think of important social scientists or humanists who did not have a personal or political stake in the substantive outcome of their work. Even among economists, the most "scientific" of the social scientists, the better men have usually been driven by political as well as intellectual commitments. They cared whether the economy worked one way or another, and if they found it worked differently than they had supposed this affected their politics and even at times their way of life. (More often, of course, what they found out about the economy *derived* from their politics and their way of life, so there was no need to reorient the latter. This is not true in any obvious or direct way among natural scientists.)

If this is the case, the critical problem of graduate instruction in the social sciences and the humanities is to narrow the gap between individual students' personal lives and their work. The graduate school must somehow put the student in closer touch with himself, instead of making him believe that the way to get ahead is to repress himself and become a passive instrument "used" by his methods and his disciplinary colleagues. This is no mean task. The difficulty of the job is not, however, an excuse for the present situation, where the student's subjectivity is not even regarded as a problem.

The academy's insistence on objective, verifiable knowledge is unlikely to die easily. It was born in part as a reaction against the excessive moralism of the Protestant ideologues who harassed so many nineteenth-century colleges by insisting that the truth could be neither more complex nor more ambiguous in its social implications than the revelation they thought they had found in the Bible. Unless he teaches in the South or in one of the more cloistered Midwestern church colleges, today's academician no longer confronts many clergymen who take this view, but he does confront young people whose moralism affects him in rather similar ways. These young people may pose even more of a threat to his intellectual integrity than the clergymen of earlier times, for they are figuratively and sometimes literally his own children, sharing many of his political and cultural prejudices. When they tell him that he insists on evidence and refuses to simplify only because he is too cowardly to stick his neck out, they are sometimes close enough to the truth to give him pause. (This does not, of course, mean that cowardice is the only reason for insisting on evidence and rejecting simplifications. Nor does it mean that the world would be a better place if we all had the courage of our prejudices.

Men often act wisely out of cowardice and foolishly because they have more courage than judgment.) Confronted with such threats, the academic majority will probably continue to insist that morality and scholarship do not mix.

Nor is moralism the only threat against which the academy feels obliged to protect itself. Insistence on academic inquiry as an end in itself, with its own criteria of relevance and utility, grew up in response to the mindless expediency of much American life. Many professors had parents who were apt to say about some idea of theirs, "You only read that in a book," as if that were sufficient grounds for dismissing it. There are also plenty of students who feel this way, including many who have had "all the advantages" and therefore feel obliged to elevate their anti-intellectualism into a cult of "experience." Such students will often insist that only a Negro can know what it is like to be black and only a pothead can discuss marijuana. By denying the possibility of vicarious experience such students are, we think, ultimately denying the possibility of human solidarity and morality, which rest on identifying the self with others and with society as a whole. More important for our purposes, however, they are denying the possibility of objectivity, on which the academy has built both its achievements and its pretensions.

Few professors have much sympathy for such narcissism, even though they may humor it in various marginal ways. They seldom see their job as extending the students' experience, either real or vicarious, into new areas. Rather, their hope is to substitute a new mode of learning, which will enable all students to perform the same tasks and use the same skills in the same ways, regardless of where they have come from or what their personal lives may be like. Given the inevitable tendency to group students for instruction on the basis of logistical convenience rather than their having common problems, this approach is hard to alter even where the impulse exists. Relating individual experience to professional knowledge and skills is, after all, extraordinarily difficult on anything other than a one-to-one basis. Yet students could at least be encouraged to link these two modes of knowing in their papers and examinations, and even this is by no means common.

The tension between theorists and practitioners in the humanities often verges on open warfare. Most literary critics, for example, feel quite defensive vis-à-vis writers and poets. They therefore try to establish themselves as a different breed with different standards and objectives. Reading poetry and writing it are said to be totally different activities. In an era where the laity and many students use words like "creative," "human," and "relevant" as weapons to attack those who are in the "Western culture bag," it is understandable that many academicians in the humanities give these same words a derisory connotation. In spite of the temptation, this seems wrong. Reading poetry is not the same thing as writing it, to be sure, and the same men will not reach the top in these two fields. But the two activities are surely related to each other. A graduate training program for literary scholars ought to recognize this, and get the prospective scholar to try his hand at the art he will be criticizing. Many would not perform very well, but that is not the point. We are not suggesting that every Ph.D. in English should have to compose a passable sonnet —though that might be more sensible than requiring him to read Anglo-Saxon. What we are suggesting is that nobody should get a Ph.D. in English who has not *tried* to write a sonnet. More generally, we are arguing that competence as a literary critic and teacher depends on the development of a certain kind of sensibility, and that there are many ways of doing this. Writing papers and examinations about other people's art is one device, but writing about one's own experience and vision is another and not necessarily less effective one.

Both the relation between theory and practice and that between professional objectivity and personal subjectivity are as central in the social sciences as in the humanities. Today a man can become a political scientist without ever having engaged in political activity of any sort. Indeed, some professors would say that such innocence enhanced their academic objectivity. Similarly, a sociologist can earn a Ph.D. without ever talking to anyone from a non-academic group. Some, indeed, do precisely that, for they find it much easier to deal with data collected from an alien subculture than with the subculture itself. A would-be psychologist has a more difficult time avoiding personal involvement with his subject matter, for he must have a non-academic life. But he often finds it not only easy but extremely desirable to separate his life from his work. We know of no psychology department that requires its Ph.D. candidates to undergo any sort of self-analysis, Freudian or otherwise, and many are not even interested in people—no crime were they not so monolithic.

Once again, we are not suggesting that unless a man can "do" he should not be allowed to criticize or teach. Divergent temperaments and limitations of time require that there be a division of labor, and a division that encourages some men to spend most of their time teaching is often a wise one. (On the other hand, we do not think it especially desirable that many people spend *all* their time teaching.) But, just as those who expect to play an active role in society may benefit from theoretical study of the activities they will participate in, so those who expect to theorize or teach may benefit from having participated in a practical way. A man can begin to learn who he is and what life is through a variety of different experiences. A professional training program that concentrates on a single mode of learning and knowing is almost by definition a poor one.

The difficulty in establishing graduate programs with multiple methods and emphases is that students who are, let us say, good at analyzing the interplay of economic interests and political propaganda are not necessarily equally good at lobbying a state legislator or leading a meeting of disgruntled housewives. Since graduate programs exist primarily to certify rather than to teach, this poses a serious problem. If the political science department asks its students to participate in politics as well as studying them, and if it finds that certain students show little skill in participation, what is it to do then? Should it record their failures and penalize them? If it does, some talented individuals with great intellectual gifts will be refused certification. If, on the other hand, the department judges its students only as thinkers and not as doers, the students will quickly figure out that the department is serious only about thinking and not doing and will throw their energies where the main chance lies.

The problem here is obviously akin to the one posed by asking graduate students to teach. Many departments do this, but they make no serious effort to judge the results. Graduate students therefore conclude that the department is not really interested in their teaching but only in their ability to write papers and examinations. Students who draw such conclusions are, moreover, usually right. If adults make no effort to supervise the young in a given area or judge their competence in it, this almost invariably means the adults do not really care about this area—though sometimes they are merely afraid of what they might discover if they looked too closely.

If graduate schools were really committed to broadening their programs, they would not only introduce new ingredients but introduce them on the same basis as the currently favored ones. If, for example, they wanted students to write poetry as well as read it, they would offer writing courses for graduate credit and weigh the results heavily in awarding degrees. Failing this, however, more modest changes would have some value. The present system of teaching assistantships, for example, does not give the student the impression that his elders really care whether he teaches well or badly, but at least it gives him time and a legitimate excuse for attempting to teach if he has an inner impulse to do so. Most other "activist" impulses do not get even this limited re-enforcement. A sociology student cannot get credit for union organizing in the South or for selling textbooks to school systems, even though either of these activities might teach him as much about America as any course. He can, it is true, write a paper about the people he has observed. But he is rewarded only for what he can verbalize, not for what he has become. Similarly, a doc-

toral candidate in English who writes a novel gets no credit for this
effort, nor is any provision made for giving him time or money to try.
At the very least, activities of this sort could be elevated to the same
status as undergraduate teaching, by giving graduate students who
wanted to do such things reduced course loads and financial support.

There is still another way of dealing with non-academic modes of
learning. A graduate program can require students to undertake an
activity and can evaluate their performance, but it can nonetheless
insist that the activity be solely a learning experience. This can be
ensured by refusing to make faculty judgments on student performance
available to outsiders—including other faculty members. An English
department, for example, might require all its doctoral candidates to
take several years of course work in creative writing, but give no
grades in these courses. If the students were sympathetically supervised and criticized, such an experience might be valuable to many.

What we have just said should not be misunderstood. We are not
enthusiastic about simply adding still more requirements to those already established for Ph.D. candidates. Each new requirement seems
to serve as another sieve eliminating a few more promising people
from academic life. This is not because the people in question cannot
meet the requirements but because they will not. Many requirements
seem threatening or irritating to prospective students, and some decide a Ph.D. is just not worth it. There are brilliant students who will
choose one graduate department over another, or even one field of
study over another, because it requires no German. This is not because they have serious language blocs—though a few do. But many
students are skittish about learning anything really new, even at
twenty-two. They have to be led to this with deftness and by in-
direction. If the requirement strikes them as irrelevant and silly their
anxiety can be turned into righteous anger, and their laziness into a
virtue. The same thing can happen with other requirements, such as
field experience of various kinds.

Under these circumstances it is tempting to urge that all requirements be abolished. Yet we fear this would encourage students to
play only from strength, a vice which is already all too common.
What is needed is a system sufficiently structured so that students
will try to learn new things and master new skills, but sufficiently
flexible so that those with real blocks know they can still get through
if they have other valuable skills. A girl who wants to become a
psychologist but thinks she cannot do statistics should, for example,
be encouraged to try, and some effort should be made to explore her
"innumeracy" with her. But if in the end she cannot or will not learn
how to compute Chi-square, this should not be grounds for driving her
out of psychology. There should be a system of weighing assets and

liabilities, so that someone who is really good at, let us say, thera-
peutic work with children can be licensed despite mathematical limitations.

Since most of the more rigid requirements of today's doctoral programs are connected with methodology rather than substance, some
readers may take a call for "flexibility" as an implicit attack on
methodology. Yet we are not against methodologists. Many of the most
important achievements in human understanding have come from
men obsessed with method. Freud's greatest contribution was probably his invention of a tool for getting at the unconscious, namely repeated daily sessions of free association with disturbed individuals.
Newton's development of calculus as a tool for analyzing physical
relationships may likewise have been more important than any of the
substantive uses to which he put it. What we are urging is not de-
emphasis of methodology but recognition that no skill is indispensable for *everyone*. Anthropology can be taught by men with no grasp
of human anatomy, English literature by men who have never read
Chaucer, political science by men innocent of foreign languages, and
so on.

*Disciplines versus Subdisciplines: The Need for More Mobility and
Anarchy*

In addition to encouraging and legitimizing non-academic modes of
learning in the graduate schools, there is also a need for much greater
flexibility in the grouping of strictly academic skills and expertise.
American scholarship has been noteworthy for its ability to cut across
disciplinary boundaries and bring men with different sorts of knowledge together to work on a single problem. This reflects the fact
that research has in recent years been largely supported from outside
the university, so that reverence for traditional disciplinary categories
has been limited. American graduate training has, however, been conspicuously slow to follow this lead and let students look at problems
rather than disciplines. We have experts on Africa, but virtually no
doctoral programs in African studies as distinct from sociology, political science, economics, and so on. We have research centers to
study urbanization, but very few training programs to staff these
centers. We have books about literary movements that cut across
countries and languages, but very few courses of study that do so.

A discipline is at bottom nothing more than an administrative category. The various subdisciplines within biology or history or psychology, for example, have only the most limited intellectual relationship
to one another, and the same is true in every other field. They are

grouped together mainly because the men working in them went through the same sort of graduate program and have some residual feeling of common identity. A good deal of ingenuity has, it is true, been devoted to the rationalization of these traditional ad hoc arrangements. Some of the resulting efforts to show that history, biology, psychology, and so forth are really unified fields built around certain underlying principles are quite brilliant and valuable. But then so are some of the arguments made for regrouping subdisciplines into new patterns. Many research projects regroup subdisciplines in ways that cut across departmental lines, and many individual researchers find they must become expert in subjects nominally outside their discipline. New journals are founded every day to fill the interstices between disciplines and encourage cross-disciplinary contact and fertilization. But the instructional program remains far less flexible. Faculty who want to teach subjects outside their department's traditional boundaries often find this difficult, and graduate students who want to pursue a pattern of studies that does not fall under conventional departmental definitions are likely to run into trouble.

The issue here is not specialization versus generalization. The issue is whether one way of aggregating specialized skills is better than another. In his book *History as Art and as Science*, for example, Stuart Hughes describes some of the things a historian needs to know: anthropology and topography, psychonanalysis and literary criticism, world history and the history of a particular group or time. The agenda is endless, and no man can cover it in a lifetime, much less in a brief doctoral program. Under these circumstances each student might well be told to choose which particular pieces of the picture he will try to sketch and which ones he will paint in detail. Instead, the choice is made for him, willy-nilly, by the administrative organization of the university faculty. First he is assigned to a department. The department is run by its members, and its degree requirements are established on the pork barrel principle. The result is that Ph.D. candidates must know something about the specialty of almost everyone in their department. If the department is history, they must know something about a number of different historical periods and countries. The other items of Hughes's list go by the boards: no anthropology or sociology, no geography or economics, no psychology or literature. If these things happen to be central to the student's interests, they must be postponed until he has met his departmental requirements and gotten his degree. By that time he is likely to have a vested interest in the value and relevance of what he already knows. He is also likely to find that his career depends on making a favorable impression on other men with the same congeries of skills he has just acquired. So he digs deeper into what he already knows and lets the other matters slide indefinitely.

The problem with all this is not really that Ph.D. programs turn out nothing but specialists. The problem is that they turn out generalists who all have the same mix of specialized skills. Every American historian knows a little medieval history and a little German. None is expected to know any sociology or literature or to have any training in analyzing statistics as against documents. Recognizing this, many observers feel that departments should be abolished. But a university faculty cannot govern itself in meetings of the whole. A large academic community needs some sort of formal subgroupings around which individuals can cluster. The departments fill this need; that is the source of their power. If they were abolished, something would have to be put in their place. At any given moment there would be some advantage to regrouping the various subdisciplines into new combinations, simply because the new units would be less hallowed by tradition and more subject to criticism and ad hoc modifications. But over the long haul there is no reason to think new combinations would have any significant advantage over the old ones; all are somewhat arbitrary, and all tend to become houses of worship as well as of work. Abolishing old departments and establishing new ones must, therefore, be a continuing process, like Jefferson's revolution every twenty years.

Like other revolutions, the overthrow of traditional departmental arrangements has drawbacks as well as advantages. Disciplines are, as we have suggested, administrative categories that group particular kinds of specialties together for more or less historical reasons. The fact that a discipline has a history means its practitioners inherit an agenda, but it also means that they inherit knowledge of their predecessors' mistakes and how to avoid repeating them. Those who assemble subdisciplines in some new combination are not so well protected, and they must rediscover some things for themselves instead of relying on their predecessors' experience as a guide. Creating a new field also runs the risk of attracting novices whose primary concern is to avoid the discipline of established departments. But this, we must emphasize, is a problem of selective recruitment rather than an inherent intellectual problem. There is nothing intrinsically unrigorous about new fields of study, which, as we have been using the concept here, are new combinations of subdisciplines from existing fields. Indeed, some of the new combinations (biophysics or bioengineering, for example) are generally thought to be more demanding than traditional natural-history biology. Reassembling the parts of now-divided territories neither adds nor subtracts rigor, though it may alter the ethos or style with which problems are tackled and neophytes socialized. Yet except in the natural sciences, new combinations of subdisciplines have had a hard time winning academic legitimacy or giving recruits a home base and a feeling of control. In part this is because non-scientists feel less certain they can tell fakes from geniuses and are therefore more anxious to keep one another working in traditional fields where the criteria for judgment are clearest.

Nonetheless, a number of new patterns of social science research have proved sufficiently fruitful that doctoral programs are being seriously considered. The objections to such programs are many, but they seem to us misguided. If, to revert to our African example, a doctoral program in African studies were to require its students to master those facets of language, literature, history, economics, political science, anthropology, and geography that are relevant to Africa, it would be more rigorous than any existing doctorate in any of these fields. If it also taught students to manipulate economic and social statistics, to do anthropological field work, and to analyze political and historical documents, it would equip them with a wider variety of tools than almost any conventional Ph.D. program. The difference between a doctorate of this kind and conventional doctorates would not be in the subjects it legitimated or the methods of research it encouraged. The difference would be in the particular combination of these that a student had to master. Combining subjects because they all relate to a particular area is obviously as arbitrary as combining subjects because they all relate to the past or to money. We are not urging the superiority of one combination over another, only the advantages of different combinations. It may well be, for example, that a man is better equipped to teach a course on the economic problems of East Africa if he has studied economics in depth but knows very little about the language, literature, history, social structure, or geography of East Africa. Certainly most economists seem to take this view. Yet we cannot help thinking that this subject might equally profitably be explored with a man who knew East Africa from many angles but had only limited familiarity with mathematical models and econometrics. In any case, whatever the merits of this particular case, the general principle is clear enough, and the merits of the case are so uncertain that experimentation seems in order.

Whatever their character, however, there is a good deal to be said for curtailing the departments' present powers and distributing them to smaller groups. The real unit of intellectual work is the subdiscipline, which usually has only one or two representatives on a small campus and seldom more than half a dozen even on a big one. These subdisciplines are evanescent, arising and disappearing over the lifetime of a single faculty generation. They fertilize one another in unpredictable ways, and the curriculum should be sufficiently flexible to accomodate this tendency. The most obvious way to do this is through ad hoc faculty committees, which set requirements for a particular student's graduate work that are adapted to his special interests.

Harvard, for example, had for some years a doctoral program in social science in which the candidate sought out faculty members who shared his interests, got their approval for a curriculum of his own devising, and was then responsible to them for its completion. This program foundered partly because its graduates had difficulty finding jobs in a departmentalized market place and partly because they had no departmental home in a university where almost everyone else did. A similar approach can, however, be used within a nominally departmental context, as is done in some English universities. Each student in effect writes his own ticket, so long as he can find a few faculty willing to approve his plans. This frees him from the collective demands of the department, which tend to emphasize lowest common denominators like foreign languages, coverage, and great books.

Just as a family can be more oppressive than a college, a relatively small ad hoc doctoral committee can be more oppressive than a larger and more impersonal department. In a department, every faculty member asks for limited fealty; he wants graduate students to take his course and answer his question on the general examinations, but he cannot ask more because other faculty members are around to protect their students from "unreasonable" and "excessive" demands. Only one professor, the candidate's thesis supervisor, is likely to ask for a more basic commitment. A committee system, on the other hand, largely eliminates the protections provided by departmental traditions and formal rules, putting the student entirely at the mercy of his chosen mentors. For this reason we would not urge the complete abolition of departmental programs, but only the creation of alternative routes, worked out on an individual basis between the candidate and a committee of his choice.

In addition, whenever a certain number of faculty members—perhaps five—decide there is a need for a new kind of doctoral program based on a new combination of specialties, they should be free to establish it on their own, setting whatever requirements they think appropriate for the students who enroll. Sociologists interested in professionalization and occupational subcultures might, for instance, join with economists interested in manpower problems and psychologists interested in vocational choice to establish a new program. Or anthropologists, political scientists, and economists concerned with economic development might unite to devise a new set of requirements for those who shared their interests. Such a system would, of course, be anarchic, and subject to some abuse. It would also lead to the proliferation of courses and degrees. But then these same complaints could be made against the present system of research initiatives and support, which seems to be working considerably better than the graduate training system.[4] Without some such assault on the regulatory powers of the collective faculty and of individual departments, the graduate curriculum is almost certain to remain as rigid as any other arrangement that must placate a multitude of competing interest groups.

Thus far we have been talking about simultaneous combinations of subdisciplines in a single doctoral program. It is also important, however, to facilitate sequential combinations, so that students can do their graduate and undergraduate work in different fields. This is far less common than it should be. In part this is because undergraduates choose a field that appeals to them and then want to continue in it because it still interests them. But in part it is because they believe, or actually find, that they cannot get into a graduate department that appeals to them unless they have already done undergraduate work in the same area. Most departments do not want to do the "remedial" work necessary to induct new students into the field, even though this would seldom take more than a year and often only a few months. In addition, most graduate admissions committees seem to assume that a student who has majored in their field as an undergraduate is serious, whereas a student who wants to change fields is likely to be defined as a dilettante. This reflects a characteristic faculty judgment about all interdisciplinary tendencies, which are viewed as "soft" rather than "hard." (Similar prejudices do, however, facilitate downward mobility out of "hard" fields like physics and economics into "soft" fields like sociology and history, so that professors in the latter will usually accept Ph.D. candidates who did their undergraduate work in the former.)

In this context, one of the most useful things universities, foundations, or the federal government could do to enliven graduate training —and also to free undergraduates from the shadow of their professional futures—would be to provide financial support and make academic arrangements for students who wanted an extra transitional year between completing their B.A.s and entering a graduate department. Students who had earned a B.A., felt dissatisfied with the field they were in, and wanted to explore another would be admitted to universities and given fellowships for a year. This idea is akin to the Fulbright and other foreign fellowships that give a student a year or two to retrain himself overseas. Since we think the leading American universities on the whole better than foreign ones, it seems reasonable to make similar opportunities available on the home front,

[4] For a further discussion of this subject, see Jencks, "A New Breed of B.A.s."

and on a larger scale. We believe that a student can prepare himself for first-year graduate work in almost any realm, from medicine to Far Eastern studies, in a single year. At present, however, this year is extremely hard to come by, for it does not fit any established program, and nobody (including parents) is particularly interested in paying for it.

These suggestions are obviously not a blueprint for revolution in the graduate schools. The problems are enormously difficult, the alternatives all filled with obvious and not-so-obvious pitfalls, and the results extremely difficult to measure or even judge impressionistically. We are inclined to believe that innovation must proceed on a case-by-case, place-by-place basis, drawing strength from the particular combination of scholars that happens to have assembled on a particular campus at a particular moment. Yet we also believe that the general direction of change should be toward a more elastic mixture of theory and practice, demanding a wider range of skills from the student and rewarding a wider range of competencies. Graduate schools must allow and even ask their students to take more initiative, exercise more responsibility, and make more moral and political choices, both within academic contexts and, more importantly, outside them. Only if they are asked to do these things, and are judged accordingly, will they come to believe that these activities are part of their professional role. And only if they see themselves and their profession in these terms will they set out to develop such skills among the next generation of undergraduates.

Efforts to go beyond mere professionalism are, of course, filled with evident dangers. To begin with, the academic community is itself divided about moral and political issues, and any effort to develop standards of conduct in these areas will inevitably bring bitter quarrels. That, indeed, is why the university has tended to adopt a civil libertarian position, judging its members almost entirely on the basis of the one set of standards almost all its members accept: professional performance.

The problem is further complicated by the fact that even when the university itself is fairly unified, it may be at odds with part of its outside constituency and may find it more expedient to pretend to neutrality than to defend its convictions. We suspect, for example, that most professors teaching in leading graduate schools feel no alarm at the thought of their students' having premarital sexual affairs. But they prefer to condone these affairs by saying they are not the university's business than by saying they could in principle be the university's business but that in practice the university has no objection to them.

Nonetheless, academic men *are* moral and political men as some of their students have lately been reminding them in far from gentle ways. The doctrine of tolerance is a valuable one, we think, but like all doctrines it has limitations. We believe, for example, that it is better for experts to put their skills to work in the service of the public than for them to put them to work exclusively for their own personal gain, and we believe that this is a legitimate standard for a department to use in evaluating both students and faculty. This is, of course, an easy example, and lengthening the list of generally acceptable standards would be difficult. All we are saying here is that the graduate schools must *try* to lengthen the list, even if this means raising the level of internal conflict and occasionally jeopardizing the harmonious development of technical competence. An institution that trains men to teach can reject traditional religious and business standards of behavior, but it cannot declare *all* such standards irrelevant. If it does, its teachers will come to seem irrelevant to the idealistic young. This has, indeed, already happened in too many cases.

The academic routines of today's graduate schools place a high premium on certain virtues, such as clarity of thought, skepticism, precision, and a capacity to organize one's time and energy. But there are other virtues, which the present system ignores or positively discourages, such as tact, practicality, social inventiveness—and even faith, hope, and charity. There is no new system that will do all those things that are now being left undone. A more open, permissive, flexible system that vested more authority in individual faculty members and less in departments, gave graduate students more freedom to chart their own course, and put them less under the collective thumb of their elders would open up all sorts of possibilities for the best students. But it would also increase the number of abuses and horror stories and usually be less satisfactory for the uncertain or listless student who really wants to be taken charge of. Our own feeling is that different universities should develop different styles in this as in other matters, with some becoming more flexible and others remaining highly structured and disciplined. We are convinced, however, that those departments that put more responsibility on their individual faculty and students will be able to attract many of the ablest students now coming out of college and many of the ablest young faculty. Most of these people now go faute de mieux to the big-name departments, for they cannot see significant differences between one place and another except in terms of the research reputations of their faculties.[5]

[5] Nor, it seems, can faculty see significant differences other than the reputation of faculties. When Allan Cartter surveyed faculty opinion about the relative eminence of departments in various disciplines, he found an almost perfect correlation between rankings of faculty eminence and rankings of teaching effectiveness; see *An Assessment*.

The Art of Teaching

We have already suggested that teaching is not a profession in the way that research is. There is no guild within which successful teaching leads to greater prestige and influence than mediocre teaching, nor any professional training program that develops pedagogic skills in a systematic way. Indeed, there is very little knowledge about which teaching strategies work with which students. Under these circumstances it is hardly surprising that a great deal of teaching at both the graduate and undergraduate level is dull and ineffective. No form of success that depends on luck and individual initiative is ever widespread. No doubt most professors prefer it when their courses are popular, their lectures applauded, and their former students appreciative. But since such successes are of no help in getting a salary increase, moving to a more prestigious campus, or winning their colleagues' admiration, they are unlikely to struggle as hard to create them as to do other things. Indeed, good teaching can be a positive handicap in attempting to meet other payrolls, especially in a place where most teaching is mediocre, for the able teacher finds students beating a path to his door and leaving him little time for anything else. If he is really committed to research he may well find that the only way to make free time is to remain aloof.

Most professors become good teachers only if it comes fairly easily and naturally. Those who do not have much natural flair seldom know how to begin remedying their failings even if they have the impulse. They certainly get little help from their colleagues. The reasons for this are not hard to discover. It seems easier to judge individuals on the basis of papers they turn out than to judge them on the basis of their interaction with other people. A graduate student's performance in comprehensive examinations is said to provide hard evidence of his competence, while visits to his classes provide only soft evidence. A professor's book can be evaluated in "objective" terms, whereas his course syllabi, lectures, and examination questions can be valued only "subjectively." The adjectives re-enforce the prejudices of the profession even though they throw little light on the actual criteria for judgment. These prejudices are not simply a matter of valuing research over teaching. A tenure committee member, for example, who argues for a particular man because of his catalytic qualities in helping his colleagues do better research also finds himself up against an ideology that insists men be judged entirely in terms of their own paper output rather than in terms of their effect on others.

In discussing these matters many critics talk about research versus teaching. We have found no evidence, however, that the two are antagonistic. Teachers cannot remain stimulating unless they also continue to learn, and while this learning may not focus on small, manageable "research problems," it is research by any reasonable definition. When a teacher stops doing it, he begins to repeat himself and eventually loses touch with both the young and the world around him. Research in this general sense does not, of course, necessarily lead to publication, but that is its most common result. Publication is the only way a man can communicate with a significant number of colleagues or other adults. Those who do not publish usually feel they have not learned anything worth communicating to adults. This means they have not learned much worth communicating to the young either. There are, of course, exceptions: men who keep learning but cannot bring themselves to write. Some have unrealistically high standards regarding what deserves publication. Some know no journal which is interested in the kinds of problems that interest them. Some are simply afraid of exposing themselves to their colleagues' criticism, even though their ideas could in fact withstand such scrutiny. Some of these men *are* constantly learning, and some of them are brilliant talkers and teachers. Still, these are the exceptions.

While we do not think there are many brilliant teachers who never publish, we do think many potentially competent teachers do a conspicuously bad job in the classroom because they know that bad teaching is not penalized in any formal way. They have only a limited amount of time and energy, and they know that in terms of professional standing and personal advancement it makes more sense to throw this into research than teaching. Yet even under these circumstances much can be done. Both good and bad teaching have many varieties. Some bad teaching is the result of inadequate preparation, but some is the result of inadequate perception. Most teachers find it hard to realize how they affect students, and critical supervision can be invaluable here. The sarcastic teacher, for example, may be too insecure to let up even when he considers his effect on his students, but that is not always true; at least he should be forced to think about it. The same is true of other pedagogic styles.

Another danger in judging men by their output is that it puts a premium on a particular kind of research for which there is relatively little need. The feverish competition for talent in the contemporary academic market place puts an enormous premium on judging men young and giving them tenure early. This, in turn, creates a climate in which men feel they must produce early, so that their tenure committee will have something to judge and they will not be left behind. The results, at least in the social sciences and humanities, tend to resemble finger exercises for the piano. Such exercises may be useful preparation for something better, and they may even allow a skilled judge to predict whether the man in question will mature into a star performer. The difficulty is that, having gotten tenure on this basis, many never outgrow this stage. Indeed, many do not even see it as a stage, but assume that such work is intrinsically worth while. As a result, a large proportion of the research published in the disciplines we know best exhibits no genuine concern with answering real questions or solving important problems; it is simply a display of professional narcissism. Instead of recording a struggle with methodological and substantive issues that actually matter to either teachers or students, it is simply a roller coaster ride along a well-worn track.

A man who does research of this kind may at times perform a useful service to his colleagues simply because he collects data somebody else can put to use. But such a man is a menace in the classroom, for he re-enforces the anti-academic prejudices of his students. The problem is especially serious among the best students at the best universities. These are not mostly students who demand flashy lectures by professional showmen or easy answers to recalcitrant questions. But they do insist that there be a visible relationship between knowledge and action, between the questions asked in the classroom and the lives they live outside it. Confronted with pedantry and alienated erudition, they are completely turned off. All too often the job of turning them back on goes by default to critics of higher education who encourage the students to believe that all systematic and disciplined intellectual effort is a waste of time and that moral assurance will suffice not only to establish their superiority over their elders but to solve the problems their elders have so obviously botched.

The "research-teaching" dilemma is, then, a false one. The real problem is to marry the two enterprises. But contrary to a good deal that is written by defenders of the status quo this is precisely what the present system fails to do. Teaching is often adjusted to the exigencies of research, but research is almost never shaped by the experience of teaching. We have almost never encountered a professor, for example, who said he was working on a particular research problem because year after year his undergraduate students showed an interest in it. Involved here is not only the understandable fear of one's own showmanship or of sycophancy toward the young, but actual ignorance of what even the most sensitive undergraduates are interested in. Professors do listen to the questions their already socialized graduate students and postdoctoral fellows raise, but most undergraduate courses are so constructed as to provide almost no feedback directly to the professor. Even if they did, it would seldom occur to a professor that the questions raised by bright yet only half-socialized students might be important enough so that, if the answers were not known, an effort should be made to discover them.

The relationship between graduate and undergraduate teaching is equally unsatisfactory. Many undergraduate courses at large universities are taught by one or two senior faculty and a group of graduate assistants. The issues raised in these courses are—or should be—of fundamental importance to graduate students as well as undergraduates. Yet we know no university where the staff of such courses habitually meets together, discusses the intellectual questions being raised, and initiates research in areas where it would be helpful. (Chicago is the closest approximation.) A serious effort along these lines would probably require constituting the staff of big undergraduate courses as a graduate seminar, having the participants meet weekly to discuss the books they were reading with undergraduates, asking them to prepare seminar papers that would also be delivered as course lectures, and discussing individual lectures given in the course in both substantive and pedagogic terms.

This scheme also suggests a possible device for avoiding incompetent amateurism in teaching and developing pedagogic colleagueship. Staff-taught courses that held regular meetings to discuss the intellectual substance of a course could also discuss and evaluate its effect on the students. A staff is by definition a potential colleague group with common problems, common experience, and perhaps even a common objective. If professors are sufficiently secure so that they can elicit and encourage criticism of their performance, and if the graduate students are open enough and interested enough to visit one another's classes, the beginnings of a clinical training program are in hand. These possibilities have been explored on a number of campuses, notably Chicago, and the second author teaches a course at Harvard that tries to achieve this sort of critical perspective on itself. Although there is no quantitative evidence that the staff members of this course are better teachers at the end than the beginning, most of them believe they are.

For one thing, they are encouraged to become more aware of the variety of students they face even in a highly selective college, and this itself is apt to make their teaching more interesting as well as more taxing. Then too, some of the most conscientious come to realize that their tacit hope of reaching every student is an unwarranted demand on both themselves and the students, not all of whom are capable of learning from any particular teacher at a particular moment in their lives. At the same time, staff members seem to become more aware of the often cruel effect they can quite unintentionally have on the more vulnerable students. Since most still think of themselves as inoffensive neophytes, struggling to cope with their own senior professors, the idea that they have power often comes as a shock.

Innovations of this kind are extremely time-consuming and tiring. A course of the sort we have just described, which combined a graduate seminar with an undergraduate course composed partly of lectures and partly of small-group meetings, and in which the staff also made an effort to supervise one another's pedagogic efforts and discuss the effectiveness of books, lectures, and the like, would be virtually a full-time job for all concerned. This does not mean it is impractical: the cost of such a system need be no greater than the present system, and the yield per dollar might be considerably better. But such an effort can be sustained only if the faculty as a whole believes in its importance and has a real conviction that the present less taxing system is failing so badly that it cannot be allowed to continue. Only a minority has had such feelings for the past two generations.

But suppose a cadre of committed faculty and graduate students could be assembled and an effective clinical training program for undergraduate teachers worked out. How should such a program relate to the traditional doctoral program of lectures, seminars, reading courses, comprehensive examinations, and dissertations? Many critics of doctoral programs have argued over the years that, while these programs do an adequate job of research training, a different program is needed to train college teachers, perhaps giving a new degree. Such proposals must grapple with two issues: who would enroll and what would they be taught. On the first score the answer is clear: very few able students would enroll. Only about half of those now taking Ph.D.s take academic jobs. Perhaps half of those who take academic jobs are at universities where research and graduate teaching take as much time as undergraduate work. A program aimed strictly at training undergraduate teachers could thus hope for no more than a quarter of the present doctoral market, plus an indeterminate number of would-be teachers who now drop out of doctoral programs because these do not fit their needs or interests. But even this is optimistic. A teaching doctorate would have less status and attract less talented students than one aimed at training scholars. Its graduates would have difficulty getting good jobs, even in colleges that claim not to be concerned with whether their faculty do research. This would scare away able students interested in teaching, simply because they would not want to settle for a degree that kept many academic doors closed to them. (There is, however, much to be said for awarding a degree to all students who have taken the courses and passed the general examinations for a Ph.D. Such a degree—a Ph.D. without a dissertation—would not be "second-rate," but simply "preliminary."

Anyone who held it would be entitled to submit a thesis and receive a Ph.D. if the thesis was acceptable. Those who did not submit a thesis would have evidence of competence that they could use in seeking teaching jobs in community colleges and perhaps elsewhere.)

Even if prospective college teachers could be siphoned out of traditional doctoral programs into special teacher-training alternatives, this would probably be a mistake on intellectual grounds. As already indicated, we think the divorce of teaching and research is bad for both parties. Teachers need at least as much expertise and technical competence as researchers, and almost anything that has a defensible place in a doctoral program for scholars can also be defended in one for teachers. Everyone, for example, bewails the standard doctoral dissertation, constructed with scissors, paste, five or ten pounds of 3×5 cards, a few hundred obliquely relevant citations, and (in some fields) a few hundred tests of statistical significance. This sort of exercise is usually attacked as irrelevant for future teachers and defended as appropriate for future scholars. In most cases, however, it is irrelevant for anyone, no matter what his plans. In the natural sciences, indeed, where the proportion of future researchers is highest and the proportion of future teachers lowest, book-length dissertations are increasingly rare and have been gradually supplanted by shorter journal articles. The same trend ought to be encouraged in the social sciences and the humanities—not on the ground that dissertations are irrelevant for teachers but that make-work is bad for anyone, be he a future Labor Department economist or a future Antioch professor.

The whole spirit of proposals for a separate teaching degree is, indeed, probably self-defeating. No real progress will ever be made as long as teaching is seen as a soft option for those who cannot make it in research. It is, in truth, a hard option for those who find a research career insufficiently challenging or excessively routinized. A teacher needs to know as much as his research colleagues know, and more. He needs the scholarly competence Ph.D. programs claim to develop, but he also needs expertise in working with late adolescents, both in the classroom and outside it. In this context the present pattern of preparing college teachers, far from looking too extended or too rigorous, looks both too hasty and relatively undemanding.

It is often argued, for example, that since men typically earn their Ph.D.s anywhere from six years (in the natural sciences) to ten years (in the humanities) after their B.A., doctoral programs are too long and should be shortened. The typical Ph.D. does not, however, spend anything like this long actually pursuing his degree. To begin with, only half of all doctoral candidates move directly from undergraduate work to doctoral study. The others take jobs, join the army, or begin graduate work in another field before starting a Ph.D. program.

The elapsed time between actually starting a Ph.D. and finishing it ranges from 4.5 years in the natural sciences to 6 years in the humanities. But even this is misleading, for doctoral candidates seldom work full time at their studies for this long. They take part-time jobs teaching or doing research, drop out for a year or two to work, and so on. This is especially true of those writing dissertations. When this is taken into account it turns out that the typical doctoral candidate spends the equivalent of between three and four full-time years working on his degree. This is true in all fields except education, where the average is less than three.[6] This is a little more than law, a little less than medicine, and hardly seems excessive. To be sure, some doctoral candidates are kept around too long out of compassion or favoritism or indifference to their fate. Other cases of prolongation reflect the decision of individual students, for financial, personal, or intellectual reasons, to mix their doctoral work with other things—though when they delay too long, they often make demands on themselves for a super-dissertation, thus entering a vicious circle.

Under these circumstance it seems to us that the basic problem is not that too much is demanded of Ph.D.s on the scholarly front, but that having met their academic requirements, those who plan to teach get no specific training for this. The need is for an internship and residency program somewhat comparable to those in medicine, which would come *after* the completion of the doctorate. The newly anointed Ph.D. could be inducted into teaching through staff courses and seminars of the kind already described. He would teach undergraduates either at the university where he had just taken his Ph.D. or at another university that offered more attractive conditions. He would be paid a salary comparable to those now offered new Ph.D.s. Such internships would be the pedagogic counterpart of a postdoctoral fellowship for a researcher. If they actually enhanced a man's competence in the classroom, the more student-oriented colleges and universities might eventually begin to make the completion of such an internship a prerequisite to permanent employment as a teacher. The beginnings of such developments can be seen in the Danforth Foundation's Teaching Internships and in the efforts of a few colleges like Monteith to induct novices into interdisciplinary teaching and then send them out as missionaries to other campuses. But here as elsewhere, real progress depends on an institutional commitment from a few leading universities, and this does not seem imminent.

This sort of internship can perhaps best be viewed not as an extension of graduate training but as a modification of the working conditions for assistant professors at leading universities. A number of

6 These calculations are taken from Berelson, pp. 156 ff.

private universities already hire assistant professors for relatively short periods, with the understanding that many will not get tenure. Even those denied tenure, however, get more visibility than they would at a less prominent institution, and usually find attractive jobs at other places. Under the arrangement we are suggesting, the university would merely assume explicit responsibility for putting these novice teachers through a systematic training program, and would certify their competence (or incompetence) to others when this was done. No university we know now does this, for none collects information on either its graduate assistants or its assistant professors that enables it to make intelligent judgments of their classroom strengths and weaknesses. Nor does any university we know make a systematic effort to supervise beginning teachers or give them help in doing a better job.

A program of this kind would have other virtues. For one thing, the staff courses in which young Ph.D.s became involved would in most instances be for freshmen and sophomores, simply because these are the big courses in which a team approach can be justified economically. These are also the courses most likely to deal with issues of interest to laymen, and therefore most likely to provide a useful counterpoint to the emphasis on professional problems characteristic of doctoral training. Involving a new Ph.D. in faculty-level discussion of these issues, forcing him to prepare papers on them and to accept his colleagues' criticisms, and giving him a sense that other men cared enough to listen to him would encourage young scholars to take such matters seriously.

It could be argued that internships of this sort, however valuable, should not be postponed until men have earned their Ph.D., since by then they may have become irreparably committed to a research career. Instead, an attempt might be made to provide more supervision for teaching assistants still working on their doctorate.[7] Yet if the men involved in a staff course all have their Ph.D.s, it may be easier to create an atmosphere of colleagueship and equality than when one man is a tenured professor and the others are "his" graduate students. If interns have completed their Ph.D.s this also gives them added status in the eyes of undergraduates, many of whom refuse to take graduate assistants seriously and therefore cannot learn anything from even the most competent and dedicated. Perhaps most

[7] The most conspicuous efforts to improve doctoral programs in this way have been the Ford Foundation's recent grants to a dozen leading universities for five-year doctoral programs. At least one of these years is to be devoted exclusively to teaching, and the apprentice is supposed to get supervision from senior men. Already established Harvard programs of this sort have, however, done little to develop either faculty or student interest in the technical problems and possibilities of teaching, and have only rarely led to the kind of collaborative teaching we are urging.

important of all, the fact that these men have Ph.D.s would make it impossible to exploit them economically, for they would be in a much stronger bargaining position vis-à-vis the universities than most graduate students now are.[8]

Not only would internships of this kind help focus faculty attention on pedagogic problems, but they might even help redirect research energy in somewhat more fruitful directions. The relatively rigid separation between theoretical inquiry and practical experience as ways of learning is considerably harder to maintain in a setting where students and their problems are taken seriously, for close acquaintance with students makes it perfectly clear that they learn in many ways at once. Conversely, if inability to get through to undergraduates were defined as a serious professional problem, the faculty would almost certainly show more interest in the possible pedagogic value of non-academic experience.

Conclusion

The agenda outlined above is hardly revolutionary. At most, its adoption would marginally reduce the pervasive influence of the academic guilds and enhance the position of men working on applied rather than pure problems. This might give individual students and teachers somewhat more latitude in choosing the audiences to whom they play and make it somewhat easier for them to integrate their academic work with the rest of their lives. But it would not involve any significant redistribution of power between the many interest groups with a stake in the academic system, be these outsiders like state legislators or insiders like students. Yet the relative conservatism of our

[8] Any program which involves a large training component is likely to be underpaid relative to the value of the services being rendered, simply because those who are being trained will accept less than the open market value of their services in order to get the training they want. Internships and residencies in leading hospitals, for example, have traditionally paid less than those in mediocre hospitals because doctors knew interning at, say, Johns Hopkins or the Massachusetts General Hospital would bring them more professional prestige and more income later. Something similar can also happen even when no training is actually offered. Harvard's Faculty of Arts and Sciences offers its young Ph.D.s lower salaries than many less prestigious institutions, but it still gets most of the men it wants. To some extent this reflects the young Ph.D.'s feeling that he will learn more and be happier as an assistant professor at Harvard than at, say, CCNY. But it also reflects the fact that his having been an assistant professor at Harvard will open the door to more lucrative and prestigious jobs later. The man is paying, in other words, for certification more than for training. Nonetheless, there is a limit to the amount of income men will forego for such reasons, as leading teaching hospitals have recently begun to discover. Harvard can pay less, but not *much* less. Since research organizations are also bidding for young Ph.D.s, teaching internships could not offer much less than the market rate for such men's services.

proposals is no reason to take their adoption for granted. Similar proposals have been made many times since the turn of the century, and the academic revolution has gone forward almost unaffected. The graduate departments and the ideology for which they stand have thus far managed to win over or override all the major interest groups which might have forced them to deviate from their chosen path. A realist must therefore ask whether there are now any new forces at work or on the horizon which might upset the existing balance of power.

The most obvious and frequently discussed threat to the academic future is financial. The recent successes of the academic revolution have generated rising expectations all over the country, and there are now perhaps 150 Avis institutions hoping to become Hertz. In practical terms this means that there will be enormous competition for men around whom graduate schools can be built and through whom research grants can be landed. This competition is crucial to the maintenance and growth of academicians' collective power. At least to date, that power has depended on a steady increase in the resources available for higher education. Today higher education consumes nearly 2 per cent of the Gross National Product, and the trend is up. Such a trend obviously cannot continue indefinitely, or the entire country will eventually find itself doing academic work, but it can easily continue for another generation. There is no theoretical reason, for example, why the United States could not devote 3 or 4 per cent of the GNP to higher education in 1985, and this would probably be sufficient to maintain the present momentum and morale of the academic system. The obstacles to such growth are political, not economic. If the federal government continues to give foreign adventures priority over domestic problems, and if state and local tax structures remain as inadequate as they now are, colleges and universities may find they cannot increase their budgets as fast in the next couple of decades as they have in the past one. Yet this is certainly problematic. People have been predicting financial crisis in higher education since the late 1940s, and thus far none has materialized.

Are there any new elements in the political equation which might lead us to expect a reversal of the recent trend toward more generous support of higher education? One possibility is that the racial crisis may divert resources away from the middle classes to institutions which service the Negro poor. If this happens, universities are likely to fare badly, for relatively few Negroes qualify or want to attend them. Indeed, the universities' meritocratic standards could easily become a major target of black criticism, for they symbolize the system of tests and credentials that today legitimizes the privileges of the white-collar and professional classes. Yet for precisely this reason the white majority will probably continue to support "academic standards," even though there may be some modest redirection of resources toward ghetto elementary and secondary schools.

A more likely source of trouble for the academic imperium is generational conflict. The first and less dangerous problem will be direct attacks on universities by their students. As we suggested in Chapter II, many young people raised on television and permissiveness now enter college cynical about the adult world of business, politics, and expertise. Relatively few of them are entirely estranged from adults; the majority are quite eager for guidance in how they might pursue the good life or make sense of the imperfect life they actually live. But few academicians can help the young in this quest, and many do not even try. Those who try often accept the students' professed attitudes at face value. Since the students are usually experimenting with different identities and are ambivalent about them all, they find such uncritical support no more helpful than hostility or indifference. What such angry, rebellious, but idealistic students need is a sense of purpose, direction, discipline, and sympathetic criticism. What they get is a great deal of tolerance, relatively little interest, and a chance to observe the academic profession at work. A few students find this last opportunity catalytic and become converted to academic life. The majority, however, reject the academic world, both as a human environment and as an exemplar of satisfying life and work. In the past few years these disillusioned youngsters have increasingly turned their resentment against the world that has let them down.

Such students' anger is, however, seldom aimed directly at the academic profession. At Berkeley, for example, questionnaires showed students involved in the Free Speech Movement as satisfied with classroom teaching as students who remained aloof, and neither group had many complaints. When Acting Chancellor Martin Meyerson called a meeting to discuss students' ideas about improving the academic program, almost nobody showed up. The students' complaints were directed at the larger society, and at the administration which tried to mediate between them and that society. The faculty was only relevant insofar as it took sides in this struggle. The same has been true on most other campuses.

But while students may not blame their troubles primarily on academicians, the public often does. There is considerable public feeling that college professors are an indolent lot, neglecting their students in order to fly around the country on expense accounts and collect consulting fees. Those who resent academicians also tend to resent youthful protest, whatever its target. Such people often conclude that the answer is to get both students and teachers back in the classroom where they belong, safely out of trouble. If they are legislators they refuse to raise faculty salaries, provide extra teaching assistants who reduce the burden on senior men, or lighten teaching loads. The California legislature reacted this way in the aftermath of the FSM, and other legislatures are likely to do the same. Even private institutions are vulnerable to such reactions. Alumni who believe their gifts will only pay fancy salaries to scholars with no interest in undergraduates tend to give parsimoniously. Parents who think that prestigious universities and university colleges neglect their students and thus foment dissidence and rebellion are likely to look askance at tuition increases, opting for a cheaper and presumptively safer college. The net result of all this could easily be both to curtail over-all financial support for higher education and to redirect some resources away from universities with big, "subversive" graduate schools toward two-year and four-year colleges.

Yet it is far from clear that the academic profession will respond to the threat of what we have called the adult backlash by adopting a reform program of the kind we have been discussing. Again the Berkeley case is revealing. The Free Speech disturbances did lead to some soul-searching, and played a part in the adoption of both the short-lived "Tussman College" and of the "Muscatine Report." The Tussman College was a two-year, interdisciplinary, experimental program for a small group of self-selected students. It died because new faculty could not be found to run it. The Muscatine Report sought to make it easier for experimental faculty members to develop undergraduate courses and programs outside a departmental framework. But three years after the FSM disturbances, the basic pattern of education at Berkely remained unchanged. Indeed, the legislative reprisals provoked by student unrest and the election of Ronald Reagan have in some ways made the situation at Berkeley worse than before the FSM. Budget reductions limited the number of the junior faculty who do most of the teaching, and have made it harder to find money for new non-departmental teaching programs. Senior faculty, chosen for their research competence, have been relatively immune to such pressures. Nor have federal research grants been curtailed as a result of student unrest—though they have been cut back because of Vietnam-related budget problems. The net effect of student unrest, in other words, has evidently been to reduce the proportion of the Berkeley budget spent on instruction and increase its dependency on outside research funds, and thus to strengthen professionalism rather than to redirect it.

More serious than these direct effects, however, may be the indirect consequences of the adult backlash. Academicians are not trained or organized to deal with unruly students, and if they find that teaching makes them responsible for students' behavior they are likely to opt out entirely. The Berkeley faculty, for example, did not feel that it could save its relations with the legislature or Governor Reagan by doing a better collective job with its students; instead, faculty members assumed they would have to save themselves individually if the going got too rough. At this writing very few professors had actually left, but many had given a good deal of thought to the possibility. In practical terms this meant that many professors—especially younger ones—were making sure they had negotiable reputations as scholars, and were devoting their energy to publication rather than "wasting" their time in work with students, which would be of no value in landing another job.

Given the existence of career alternatives in research especially for the abler men outside the humanities, it is hard to imagine any sort of short-term political pressure, whether from students, adults, or other groups, that is likely to improve teaching. Instead, any such pressure seems likely to drive able men into government, industry, or university-based research institutes, where their careers are not dependent on the ups and downs of generational conflict. Over the long haul, however, the prospect is somewhat brighter. The academic world has always had room for an egalitarian, anarchistic, anti-organizational minority. This minority has shared some of the allergies and ideals of dissident students and has helped persuade some of these students that college teaching is the least inhibiting and least compromising way they can earn a living. As a result, the changes in undergraduate character that became visible in the early 1960s are beginning to be reflected in the character of young assistant professors. As these men rise in number and rank they may become a major force in academic politics. It is too soon to be sure what effect they will have. Some seem so anti-organizational in outlook that it is difficult to imagine their having any significant influence on the institutional forms of academic life. Their attitudes could, indeed, alarm their elders and their more moderate age-mates, accentuating adult fears that any change in the established order will mark the beginning of a descent into youthful self-indulgence and chaos. Nonetheless, some of these young men *are* committed to teaching, and some are choosing to work in liberal arts colleges rather than in big universities, since they regard the former as more humane and manageable than the latter. They have rejected conscious careerism, and their lives are therefore less certain to follow the established priorities laid down by the existing academic system.

Aside from nuclear war or a wave of national repression brought on by racial conflict or the defeat of imperial ambitions, generational conflict seems to be the major threat to the stability and growth of the academic system. Whether such conflict will lead to short-run reforms is doubtful. But in the long run the young always displace the old, and they seldom completely resemble them. If they are a different breed, and if they want to build a different world rather than simply destroying the one their elders built, they can do so. Their predecessors, after all, made the academic revolution in colleges that were far less open to reform than today's universities.

References

NOTE: When place of publication is Washington, D.C., publisher is the U. S. Government Printing Office unless otherwise noted.

American Council on Education, *A Fact Book on Higher Education,* Washington, D.C., looseleaf, annual supplements.

C. Arnold Anderson, "Inequalities in Schooling in the South," *American Journal of Sociology,* 60 (May 1955), 547–61.

C. Arnold Anderson, "A Skeptical Note on the Relation of Vertical Mobility to Education," *American Journal of Sociology,* 66 (May 1961), 560–70.

Alexander W. Astin, "Productivity of Undergraduate Institutions," *Science,* 136 (April 13, 1962), 129–35.

Alexander W. Astin, *Who Goes Where to College?* Chicago, Science Research Associates, 1965.

Alexander W. Astin and John L. Holland, "The Distribution of Wealth in Higher Education," *College and University* (Winter 1962), 113–25.

Alexander Astin, Robert Panos, and John Creager. "National Norms for Entering College Freshmen—Fall 1966," *American Council on Education, Research Reports,* Vol. 2, No. 1, Washington, D.C., 1967.

Alexander Astin, Robert Panos, and John Creager, "Supplementary National Norms for Freshmen Entering College in 1966," *American Council on Education Research Reports,* Vol. 2, No. 3, Washington, D.C., 1967.

E. Digby Baltzell, "Bell Telephone's Experiment in Education," *Harper's Magazine* (March 1955), 73–77.

Allen H. Barton, *Studying the Effects of College Education: A Methodological Examination of "Changing Values in College,"* New Haven, Hazen Foundation, 1959.

Alan B. Batchelder, "Decline in the Relative Income of Negro Men," *Quarterly Journal of Economics,* 78 (November 1964), 525–48.

Howard S. Becker, Blanche Geer, Everett C. Hughes, and Anselm Strauss, *Boys in White: Student Culture in Medical School,* University of Chicago Press, 1961.

Daniel Bell, *The Reforming of General Education: The Columbia College Experience in Its National Setting,* Columbia University Press, 1966.

General D. V. Bennett, "The United States Military Academy," *Phi Delta Kappan,* May 1967, pp. 448–49.

Bernard R. Berelson, *Graduate Education in the United States,* New York, McGraw-Hill, 1960.

Jessie S. Bernard, *Academic Women,* Pennsylvania State University Press, 1964.

Biennial Survey of Education: see U. S. Office of Education.

Davis Bitton, "Anti-Intellectualism in Mormon History," *Dialogue: A Journal of Mormon Thought,* 1 (Autumn 1966), 111–34.

Peter M. Blau, "The Flow of Occupational Supply and Recruitment," *American Sociological Review,* 30 (August 1965), 475–90.

Peter M. Blau and Otis Dudley Duncan, *The American Occupational Structure,* New York, Wiley, 1967.

Donald J. Bogue, *The Population of the United States,* Glencoe, The Free Press, 1957.

Daniel J. Boorstin, *The Americans: The National Experience,* New York, Random House, 1965.

Mary Jean Bowman, "The Land-Grant Colleges and Universities in Human Resource Development," *Journal of Economic History,* 22 (1962), 523–46.

Marvin Bressler and Charles F. Westoff, "Catholic Education, Economic Values, and Achievement," *American Journal of Sociology,* 69 (November 1963), 225–33.

Howard Brotz, *The Black Jews of Harlem: Negro Nationalism and the Dilemmas of Negro Leadership,* New York, The Free Press, 1964.

Henry Allen Bullock, *A History of Negro Education in the South from 1619 to the Present,* Harvard University Press, 1967.

John Bushnell, "Student Culture at Vassar," in Nevitt Sanford, ed., *The American College,* New York, Wiley, 1962.

Daniel H. Calhoun, *The American Civil Engineer: Origins and Conflict,* MIT Press, 1960.

Theodore Caplow and Reece J. McGee, *The Academic Marketplace,* New York, Basic Books, 1959; Garden City, N.Y., Anchor Books, 1965.

Jerome H. Carlin, *Lawyers on Their Own: A Study of Individual Practitioners in Chicago,* Rutgers University Press, 1962.

A. M. Carr-Saunders and P. A. Wilson, *The Professions,* Oxford University Press, 1933.

Allan M. Cartter, ed. *American Universities and Colleges,* 9th ed., Washington, D.C., American Council on Education, 1964.

Allan M. Cartter, *An Assessment of Quality in Graduate Education,* Washington, D.C., American Council on Education, 1966.

Allan M. Cartter, "The Supply of and Demand for College Teachers," *Journal of Human Resources,* 1 (Summer 1966), 22–38.

James Cass and Max Birnbaum, *Comparative Guide to American Colleges,* New York, Harper & Row, 1964.

Horace R. Cayton, *Long Old Road,* New York, Trident Press, 1965.

1960 *Census:* see U. S. Bureau of the Census.

John L. Chase and Marguerite G. Wensel, "Doctor's Degrees Awarded in All U. S. Institutions: By State and By Institutions," U. S. Department of Health, Education, and Welfare, n.d. (1964?).

Burton R. Clark, "The 'Cooling Out' Function in Higher Education," *American Journal of Sociology,* 65 (May 1960), 569–76.

Burton R. Clark, *The Open Door College: A Case Study,* New York, McGraw-Hill, 1960.

Harold F. Clark and Harold Sloan, *Classrooms in the Military,* Columbia University, Teachers College, 1964.

Kenneth B. Clark and Lawrence Plotkin, *The Negro Student at Integrated Colleges,* New York, National Scholarship Service and Fund for Negro Students, 1963.

T. Anne Cleary, "Test Bias: Validity of the Scholastic Aptitude Test for Negro and White Students in Integrated Colleges," Princeton, Educational Testing Service, 1966.

Richard J. Clifford, S.J., and William B. Callahan, S.J., "Catholic Higher Education: The Next Twenty Years," *America* (September 19, 1964), 288–91.

James C. Coleman *et al., Equality of Educational Opportunity,* Washington, D.C., U. S. Office of Education, 1966.

College Entrance Examination Board, *College Board Score Reports,* New York, College Entrance Examination Board, 1967.

College Entrance Examination Board, *Manual of Freshman Class Profiles,* New York, College Entrance Examination Board, 1967.

College Scholarship Service, *Manual for Financial Aid Officers,* New York, College Entrance Examination Board, 1965.

James B. Conant, *The Education of American Teachers,* New York, Mc-Graw-Hill, 1963.

Council on Medical Education of the AMA, "Medical Licensure Statistics for 1965," *Journal of the American Medical Association,* June 6, 1966, pp. 882–83.

James D. Cowhig and Charles B. Nam, "Educational Status, College Plans, and Occupational Status of Farm and Non-Farm Youths: October 1959," Series Census-ERS (P-27), No. 30, Washington, D.C., Bureau of the Census, August 1961.

Current Population Reports: see U. S. Bureau of the Census.

André Danière, "Cost-Benefit Analysis of Federal Programs of Financial Aid to College Students," Cambridge, mimeographed, 1967.

André Danière, *Higher Education in the American Economy,* New York, Random House, 1964.

James A. Davis, *Great Aspirations: The Graduate School Plans of America's College Seniors,* Chicago, Aldine, 1964.

James A. Davis, "Higher Education: Selection and Opportunity," *The School Review,* 71 (Autumn 1963), 249–65.

James A. Davis, *Undergraduate Career Decisions: Correlates of Occupational Choice,* Chicago, Aldine, 1965.

Junius Davis, "What College Teachers Value in Students," *College Board Review* (Spring 1965), 15–18.

Edward F. Denison, *The Sources of Economic Growth in the United States and the Alternatives Before Us,* New York, Committee for Economic Development, 1962.

1965 *Digest,* see Kenneth A. Simon and W. Vance Grant.

Gordon J. DiRenzo, "Personality Structures and Orientations Toward Liturgical Change," paper read at the 1966 meeting of the American Catholic Sociological Society.

Humphrey Doermann, "The Market for College Education in the United States," Harvard University, doctoral dissertation, 1967.

Dorothy Dohen, *Nationalism and American Catholicism*, New York, Sheed & Ward, 1967.

John D. Donovan, *The Academic Man in the Catholic College*, New York, Sheed & Ward, 1964.

John D. Donovan, "The American Catholic Hierarchy: a Social Profile," *The American Catholic Sociological Review*, 19 (June 1958), 98–113.

St. Clair Drake, "The Social and Economic Status of the Negro in the United States," in Talcott Parsons and Kenneth B. Clark, eds. *The Negro American*, Boston, Houghton Mifflin, 1966.

Robert Dreeben, *On What Is Learned in School*, Boston, Addison-Wesley, 1968.

Beverly Duncan, "Dropouts and the Unemployed," *Journal of Political Economy*, 73 (April 1956), 121–34.

Otis Dudley Duncan, "The Trend of Occupational Mobility in the United States," *American Sociological Review*, 30 (August 1965), 491–98.

The Duration of Formal Education for High Ability Youth, NSF 61-36, Washington, D.C., National Science Foundation, 1961.

Ralph Dunham, Patricia Wright, and Marjorie Chandler, *Teaching Faculty in Universities and Four-Year Colleges, Spring 1963*, Washington, D.C., Office of Education, 1966.

Bruce K. Eckland, "Academic Ability, Higher Education, and Occupational Mobility," *American Sociological Review*, 30 (October 1965), 735–46.

Bruce K. Eckland, "College Dropouts Who Came Back," *Harvard Educational Review*, 34 (Summer 1964), 402–20.

Bruce K. Eckland, "Genetics and Sociology: A Reconsideration," *American Sociological Review*, 32 (April 1967), 172–93.

Bruce K. Eckland, "Social Class and College Graduation: Some Misconceptions Corrected," *American Journal of Sociology*, 70 (July 1964), 36–50.

The Economic Report of the President, Washington, D.C., 1966.

Education Directory, Part 3, *Higher Education*, Washington, D.C., Office of Education, 1955–56.

Walter Crosby Eells, *Baccalaureate Degrees Conferred by American Colleges in the 17th and 18th Centuries*, Washington, D.C., American Council on Education, 1958.

S. N. Eisenstadt, *From Generation to Generation: Age Grades and the Social Structure*, Glencoe, The Free Press, 1956.

Stanley M. Elkins, *Slavery: A Problem in American Institutional and Intellectual Life*, University of Chicago Press, 1959.

John Tracy Ellis, "American Catholics and the Intellectual Life," *Thought*, Fall 1955.

Robert Ellis and W. Clayton Lane, "Social Mobility and Social Isolation: A Test of Sorokin's Dissociative Hypothesis," *American Sociological Review*, 32 (April 1967), 237–52.

Erik H. Erikson, "Inner and Outer Space: Reflections on Womanhood," in

Robert J. Lifton, ed. *The Woman in America,* Boston, Houghton Mifflin, 1965.

Alvin Eurich, "A Twenty-First Century Look at Higher Education," in *1963 Current Issues in Higher Education,* Proceedings of the 10th Annual National Conference on Higher Education, Washington, D.C., Association for Higher Education (NEA), 1962.

Fact Book: see American Council on Education.

The Federal Government and Education, Washington, D.C., House Committee on Education and Labor, 1963.

Federal Support for Academic Science and Other Educational Activities in Universities and Colleges, Fiscal Year, 1965, Washington, D.C., National Science Foundation, 1965.

Rashi Fein, "An Economic and Social Profile of the Negro American," in Talcott Parsons and Kenneth B. Clark, eds. *The Negro American,* Boston, Houghton Mifflin, 1966.

Joseph Fichter, S.J., *Religion as an Occupation: A Study in the Sociology of Professions,* University of Notre Dame Press, 1961.

Joshua Fishman and A. K. Pasanella, "College Admission-Selection Studies," *Review of Educational Research,* 30 (1960), 298–310.

John C. Flanagan *et al., The American High School Student,* University of Pittsburgh, Project TALENT Office, 1964.

John C. Flanagan *et al., One Year Follow-Up Studies,* University of Pittsburgh, Project TALENT Office, 1966.

Donald H. Fleming, *William H. Welch and the Rise of Modern Medicine,* Boston, Little, Brown, 1954.

John K. Folger, "Explaining Higher Educational Opportunity—Some Problems and Issues," mimeographed paper prepared for Institute for Policy Studies' Congressional Seminar on Education and Public Welfare, Washington, D.C., May 1966.

John K. Folger and Charles B. Nam, *The Education of the American Population,* Washington, D.C., Bureau of the Census, 1967.

John K. Folger and Charles B. Nam, "Trends in Education in Relation to the Occupational Structure," *Sociology of Education,* 38 (Fall 1964), 19–33.

Julian Foster, "Some Effects of Jesuit Education: A Case Study," in Robert Hassenger, ed. *The Shape of Catholic Higher Education,* University of Chicago Press, 1967.

Mervin Freedman, "The Passage Through College," *Journal of Social Issues,* 12 (1956), 13–28.

Norman L. Friedman, "Comprehensiveness and Higher Education: A Sociologist's View of Public Junior College Trends," *American Association of University Presidents Bulletin* (Winter 1966), 417–23.

Erich Fromm, "Sex and Character," in *Man for Himself: An Inquiry into the Psychology of Ethics,* New York, Rinehart, 1947.

Paul H. Gebhard *et al., Pregnancy, Birth, and Abortion,* New York, 1958.

Nathan Glazer and Daniel Patrick Moynihan, *Beyond the Melting Pot: The Negroes, Puerto Ricans, Jews, Italians, and Irish of New York City,* MIT Press, 1963.

Philip Gleason, "American Catholic Higher Education: A Historical Perspective," in Robert Hassenger, ed. *The Shape of Catholic Higher Education*, University of Chicago Press, 1967.

Charles Glock and Rodney Stark, "Is There an American Protestantism?" *Transaction*, 3 (November/December 1965), 8–13.

Erving Goffman, "On Cooling the Mark Out: Some Aspects of Adaptation to Failure," *Psychiatry*, 15 (November 1952), 451–63.

Fred H. Goldner and R. R. Ritti, "Professionalization as Career Immobility," *American Journal of Sociology*, 72 (March 1967), 489–502.

Erich Goode, "Social Class and Church Participation," *American Journal of Sociology*, 72 (July 1966), 100–11.

William H. Gray, Jr., "Pennsylvania College Enrollments," *American Teachers Association Bulletin*, December 1964.

Andrew M. Greeley, "Religion and Academic Career Plans," *American Journal of Sociology*, 72 (May 1967), 668–72.

Andrew M. Greeley, *Religion and Career: A Study of College Graduates*, New York, Sheed & Ward, 1963.

Andrew M. Greeley and Peter Rossi, *The Education of Catholic Americans*, Chicago, Aldine, 1966.

Andrew M. Greeley, William Van Cleve, and Grace Ann Carroll, *The Changing Catholic College*, Chicago, Aldine, 1967.

Ernest Greenwood, "Attributes of a Profession," in Sigmund Nosow and William H. Form, eds. *Man, Work, and Society*, New York, Basic Books, 1962.

Joseph R. Gusfield and David Riesman, "Academic Standards and 'The Two Cultures' in the Context of a New State College," *The School Review*, 74 (Spring 1966), 95–116.

Joseph R. Gusfield and David Riesman, "Innovation in Higher Education: Notes on Students and Faculty Encounters in Three New Colleges," in Howard Becker, Blanche Geer, David Riesman, and Robert S. Weiss, eds. *Institutions and the Person: Essays in Honor of Everett C. Hughes*, Chicago, Aldine, 1968.

A. H. Halsey and Martin Trow, "A Study of the British Teachers," University of California at Berkeley, mimeographed, August 1967.

Oscar Handlin, *Fire-Bell in the Night: The Crisis in Civil Rights*, Boston, Little, Brown, 1964.

Giora Hanoch, "Personal Earnings and Investment in Schooling," University of Chicago, doctoral dissertation, 1965.

Robert Hassenger, ed. *The Shape of Catholic Higher Education*, University of Chicago Press, 1967.

Philip M. Hauser, "Demographic Factors in the Integration of the Negro," in Talcott Parsons and Kenneth B. Clark, eds. *The Negro American*, Boston, Houghton Mifflin, 1966.

Ernest Havemann and Patricia Salter West, *They Went to College: The College Graduate in America Today*, New York, Harcourt Brace, 1952.

Mary Haywood, "Were There but World Enough and Time . . . ," Harvard University, Department of Social Relations Library, undergraduate honors thesis, 1960.

Will Herberg, *Protestant, Catholic, Jew: An Essay in American Religious Sociology*, Garden City, N.Y., Anchor Books, 1960.

Conrad Hilberry and Morris Keeton, eds. *Struggle and Promise: A Future for Private Colleges*, New York, McGraw-Hill, forthcoming.

Historical Statistics: see U. S. Bureau of the Census.

Robert W. Hodge, Paul M. Siegel, and Peter Rossi, "Occupational Prestige in the United States, 1925–63," *American Journal of Sociology*, 70 (November 1964), 289–302.

Richard Hofstadter, *Anti-Intellectualism in American Life*, New York, Knopf, 1963.

Richard Hofstadter and Walter P. Metzger, *The Development of Academic Freedom in the United States*, Columbia University Press, 1955.

Donald P. Hoyt, "The Relationship between College Grades and Adult Achievement," *American College Testing Program, Research Report No. 7*, Iowa City, 1965.

Everett C. Hughes, *Men and Their Work*, Glencoe, The Free Press, 1958.

H. Stuart Hughes, *History as Art and as Science*, New York, Harper & Row, 1964.

Samuel P. Huntington, "Power, Expertise, and the Military Profession," *Daedalus*, Fall 1963.

Samuel P. Huntington, *The Soldier and the State*, Harvard University Press, 1957.

Herbert Hyman, "The Value Systems of Different Classes," in Reinhard Bendix and Seymour Martin Lipset, eds. *Class, Status, and Power: A Reader in Social Stratification*, Glencoe, The Free Press, 1953.

Elton F. Jackson and Harry T. Crockett, Jr., "Occupational Mobility in the United States: A Point Estimate and Trend Comparison," *American Sociological Review*, 29 (February 1964), 5–15.

Philip E. Jacob, *Changing Values in College: An Exploratory Study of the Impact of College Teaching*, New York, Harper, 1957.

Paul Jacobs and Saul Landau, *The New Radicals: A Report with Documents*, New York, Random House, 1966.

Adrian J. Jaffe and Walter Adams, "Trends in College Enrollment," *College Board Review*, Winter 1964–65.

Adrian J. Jaffe, Walter Adams, and Sandra Meyers, "Ethnic Higher Education—Negro Colleges in the 1960's," Columbia University, Bureau of Applied Social Research, mimeographed, 1966.

Morris Janowitz, *The Professional Soldier: A Social and Political Portrait*, Glencoe, The Free Press, 1960.

Christopher Jencks, "A New Breed of B.A.s," *The New Republic*, October 1, 1966.

Christopher Jencks, "Social Stratification and Mass Higher Education," *Harvard Educational Revue*, Spring 1968.

Christopher Jencks and David Riesman, "The Harvard House System," "San Francisco State College," "Boston College," and "The University of Massachusetts," in Nevitt Sanford, ed. *The American College: A Psychological and Social Interpretation of the Higher Learning*, New York, Wiley, 1962.

Joseph Kahl, "Educational and Occupational Aspirations of 'Common Man' Boys," *Harvard Educational Review*, 23 (Summer 1953), 186–203.

Leonard Karel, *Comparisons of Earned Degrees Awarded 1901–1962– with Projections to 2000*, Washington, D.C., National Science Foundation, 1964.

Frederick J. Kelly and Betty A. Patterson, *Residence and Migration of College Students*, Washington, D.C., Office of Education, 1934.

Kenneth Keniston, "The Sources of Student Dissent," *Journal of Social Issues*, forthcoming.

Kenneth Keniston, *The Uncommitted: Alienated Youth in American Society*, New York, Harcourt Brace, 1965.

Clark Kerr, *The Uses of the University*, Harvard University Press, 1963.

Larry King, "The Buckle on the Bible Belt," *Harper's Magazine*, June 1966.

Robert H. Knapp and H. B. Goodrich, *Origins of American Scientists*, University of Chicago Press, 1952.

Robert H. Knapp and J. J. Greenbaum, *The Younger American Scholar: His Collegiate Origins*, University of Chicago Press, 1953.

Dorothy Knoell and Leland Medsker, "Factors Affecting Performance of Transfer Students from Two- to Four-Year Colleges," University of California, Center for the Study of Higher Education, mimeographed, 1964.

James D. Koerner, *The Miseducation of American Teachers*, Boston, Houghton Mifflin, 1963.

Gabriel Kolko, *Wealth and Power in America: An Analysis of Social Class and Income Distribution*, New York, Praeger, 1962.

Mirra Komarovsky, *Women in the Modern World: Their Education and Their Dilemmas*, Boston, Little, Brown, 1954.

Irving Kristol, "The Negro Today Is Like the Immigrant Yesterday," *The New York Times Magazine*, September 11, 1966.

Simon Kuznets, *Shares of Upper Income Groups in Income and Savings*, New York, National Bureau of Economic Research, 1953.

John B. Lansing, Thomas Lorimer, and Chikashi Moriguchi, *How People Pay for College*, Ann Arbor, Survey Research Center, 1960.

Thomas H. A. Le Duc, *Piety and Intellect at Amherst College, 1865–1912*, Columbia University Press, 1946.

Gerhard E. Lenski, *The Religious Factor: A Sociological Study of Religious Impact on Politics, Economics, and Family Life*, New York, Doubleday, 1961.

Gerhard E. Lenski, "Status Crystallization: A Non-Vertical Dimension of Social Status," *American Sociological Review*, 19 (August 1954), 405–13.

Gerhard E. Lenski, "Status Inconsistency and the Vote," *American Sociological Review*, 32 (April 1967), 298–301.

Myron Lieberman, *Education as a Profession*, Englewood Cliffs, N.J., Prentice-Hall, 1956.

Myron Lieberman, *The Future of Public Education*, University of Chicago Press, 1960.

Seymour Martin Lipset and Reinhard Bendix, *Social Mobility in Industrial Society,* University of California Press, 1959.

Michael Maccoby, "The Game Attitude," Harvard University, Department of Social Relations, unpublished doctoral dissertation, 1960.

Manual of Freshman Class Profiles: see College Entrance Examination Board.

David C. McClelland, "Wanted: A New Self-Image for Women," in Robert J. Lifton, ed. *The Woman in America,* Boston, Houghton Mifflin, 1965.

John C. McCullers and Walter T. Plant, "Personality and Social Development: Cultural Influences," *Motivational Research,* 34 (1964), 604–8.

J. Barry McGannon, S.J., Bernard J. Cook, S.J., and George B. Klubertanz, S.J., eds. *Christian Wisdom and Christian Formation: Theology, Philosophy, and the Catholic College Student,* New York, Sheed & Ward, 1964.

Earl J. McGrath, *The Predominantly Negro Colleges and Universities in Transition,* Columbia University, Teachers College, 1965.

Earl J. McGrath and Gerald E. Dupont, S.S.E., "The Future Governance of Catholic Higher Education in America," Columbia University, Institute of Higher Education, Teachers College, mimeographed, 1967.

John W. Masland and Laurence I. Radway, *Scholars and Soldiers: Military Education and National Policy,* Princeton University Press, 1957.

A Master Plan for Higher Education in California, 1960–1975, Sacramento, California State Department of Education, 1960.

David Matza, *Delinquency and Drift,* New York, Wiley, 1963.

Margaret Mead, *Sex and Temperament in Three Primitive Societies,* New York, Morrow, 1935.

Leland L. Medsker, *The Junior College: Progress and Prospects,* New York, McGraw-Hill, 1960.

Robert K. Merton, George Reader, and Patricia Kendall, eds. *The Student Physician: Introductory Studies in the Sociology of Medical Education,* Harvard University Press, 1957.

John A. Michael, "High School Climates and Plans for Entering College," *Public Opinion Quarterly,* 25 (Winter 1961), 585–95.

Herman P. Miller, "Annual and Lifetime Income in Relation to Education." *American Economic Review,* 50 (December 1960), 962–86.

Herman P. Miller, *Income Distribution in the United States,* Washington, D.C., Bureau of the Census, 1966.

C. Wright Mills, *The Power Elite,* Oxford University Press, 1956.

Daniel P. Moynihan, "Employment, Income, and the Ordeal of the Negro Family," in Talcott Parsons and Kenneth B. Clark, eds. *The Negro American,* Boston, Houghton Mifflin, 1966.

Daniel P. Moynihan and James Q. Wilson, "Patronage in New York State," *American Political Science Review,* 58, June 1964.

Paul Mundy, "Some Convergences and the Identity Crisis in the American Catholic Sociological Society," *Sociological Analysis,* 26 (1966), 123–28.

Charles Muscatine *et al., Education at Berkeley,* University of California, Berkeley, Academic Senate, 1966.

Charles B. Nam, "Some Comparisons of Office of Education and Census Bureau Statistics on Education," paper read to the American Statistical Association, September 10, 1962.

Charles B. Nam and James D. Cowhig, "Factors Related to College Attendance of Farm and Non-Farm High School Graduates: 1960," Series Census-ERS (P-27), No. 32, Washington, D.C., Bureau of the Census, June 15, 1962.

George Nash, Patricia Nash, and Martin Goldstein, "Financial Aid Policies and Practices at Accredited Four-Year Universities and Colleges," Columbia University, Bureau of Applied Social Research, 1967.

National Opinion Research Center, "Jobs and Occupations: A Popular Evaluation," in Reinhard Bendix and Seymour Martin Lipset, eds. *Class, Status, and Power*, Glencoe, The Free Press, 1953.

Allan Nevins, *The State Universities and Democracy*, University of Illinois Press, 1962.

Robert C. Nichols, "College Preferences of Eleventh Grade Students," *NMSC Research Reports*, Vol. 2, No. 9, Evanston, National Merit Scholarship Corporation, 1966.

Opening Fall Enrollment: see U. S. Office of Education.

Thomas F. O'Dea, *American Catholic Dilemma: An Inquiry into the Intellectual Life*, New York, Sheed & Ward, 1958.

William Fielding Ogburn, "Technology and the Standard of Living in the United States," *American Journal of Sociology*, 60, January 1955.

Susan Orr and Charles Nam, "Estimates of the 'True' Educational Distribution of the Adult Population of the U.S. from 1910 to 1960," paper prepared for the Population Association of America, mimeographed, April 1967.

Robert Panos and Alexander Astin, "Attrition among College Students," *American Council on Education Research Reports*, Vol. 2, No. 4, Washington, D.C., 1967.

Robert Panos and Alexander Astin, "They Went to College: A Descriptive Summary of the Class of 1965," *American Council on Education Research Reports*, Vol. 2, No. 5, Washington, D.C., 1967.

Talcott Parsons and Kenneth B. Clark, eds. *The Negro American*, Boston, Houghton Mifflin, 1966.

Morse Peckham, *Humanistic Education for Business: An Essay in General Education*, University of Pennsylvania Press, 1960.

Osler Peterson, O. P. Anderson, R. S. Spain, and B. G. Greenberg, "An Analytic Study of North Carolina General Practice," *Journal of Medical Education*, 31, 12, 1956.

Norman Podhoretz, "My Negro Problem—and Ours," *Commentary*, February 1963.

Edward J. Power, *A History of Catholic Higher Education in the United States*, Milwaukee, Bruce, 1958.

Derek J. de Solla Price, *Science Since Babylon*, Yale University Press, 1961.

Lee Rainwater and William Yancey, *The Moynihan Report and the Politics of Controversy*, MIT Press, 1967.

Ira Reiss, "Premarital Sexual Permissiveness Among Negroes and Whites," *American Sociological Review*, 29 (October 1964), 688–98.

Dietrich Reitzes, *Negroes in Medicine*, Harvard University Press, 1958.

Residence and Migration: see U. S. Office of Education and also Frederick J. Kelley and Betty A. Patterson.

O. E. Reynolds, *Social and Economic Status of College Students*, Columbia University, Teachers College Contribution #272, 1927.

David Riesman, "The Academic Procession," in *Constraint and Variety in American Education*, University of Nebraska Press, 1956; Garden City, New York, Anchor Books, 1958.

David Riesman, "Notes on Meritocracy," *Daedalus* (June 1967), 897–908.

David Riesman, "Permissiveness and Sex Roles," *Journal of Marriage and Family Living*, 21 (August 1959), 211–17.

David Riesman, "Review of the Jacob Report," *American Sociological Review*, 23 (December 1958), 732–39.

David Riesman, "Some Continuities and Discontinuities in the Education of Women," in *Abundance for What?*, Garden City, N.Y., Anchor Books, 1964.

David Riesman, "Some Informal Notes on American Churches and Sects," *Confluence*, 4 (July 1955), 151 ff.

David Riesman, "Some Problems of a Course in 'Culture and Personality,'" *Journal of General Education*, 5 (1951), 122–36.

David Riesman, "Two Generations," in Robert J. Lifton, ed. *The Woman in America*, Boston, Houghton Mifflin, 1965.

David Riesman, Reuel Denney, and Nathan Glazer, *The Lonely Crowd: A Study of the Changing American Character*, Yale University Press, 1950.

David Riesman and Donald Horton: "Notes on the Deprived Institution: Illustrations from a State Mental Hospital," *Sociological Quarterly* (Winter 1965), 3–20.

David Riesman, Sr., *Medicine in Modern Society*, Princeton University Press, 1939.

Alice M. Rivlin, *The Role of the Federal Government in Financing Higher Education*, Washington, D.C., The Brookings Institution, 1961.

Natalie Rogoff, "Local Social Structure and Educational Selection," in A. H. Halsey, Jean Floud, and C. Arnold Anderson, eds. *Education, Economy, and Society*, New York, The Free Press, 1961.

Elmo Roper, *Factors Affecting the Admission of High School Seniors to College*, Washington, D.C., American Council on Education, 1949.

Alice S. Rossi, "Equality between the Sexes: An Immodest Proposal," in Robert J. Lifton, ed. *The Woman in America*, Boston, Houghton Mifflin, 1965.

Frederick Rudolph, *The American College and University*, New York, Knopf, 1962.

Edward Sanders and Hans Palmer, "The Financial Barrier to College Attendance in California," Los Angeles, California State Scholarship Commission, mimeographed, 1965.

Nevitt Sanford, ed. *The American College: A Psychological and Social Interpretation of The Higher Learning*, New York, Wiley, 1962.

Mildred A. Schwartz, *The United States College-Educated Population: 1960*, Chicago, National Opinion Research Center, 1965.

John Finley Scott, "The American College Sorority: Its Role in Class and Ethnic Endogamy" *American Sociological Review*, 30 (June 1965), 514–27.

William H. Sewell, "Community of Residence and College Plans," *American Sociological Review*, 26 (February 1964), 24–37.

William H. Sewell and Michael Armer, "Neighborhood Context and College Plans," *American Sociological Review*, 31 (April 1966), 159–68.

Laura Sharpe, "Five Years After the College Degree, Part I, Graduate and Professional Education," Washington, D.C., Bureau of Social Science Research, mimeographed, 1965.

Laura Sharpe, *Two Years After the College Degree*, Washington, D.C., National Science Foundation, 1963.

Kenneth A. Simon and W. Vance Grant, *Digest of Educational Statistics*, Washington, D.C., Office of Education, 1965.

William Spady, "Educational Mobility and Access in the United States: Growth and Paradoxes," *American Journal of Sociology*, forthcoming.

Julian C. Stanley, letter to the *Harvard Educational Review*, 37 (Summer 1967), 275–76.

Julian C. Stanley and Andrew C. Porter, "Predicting College Grades of Negroes versus Whites," University of Wisconsin, mimeographed, 1966.

1965 Statistical Abstract: see U. S. Bureau of the Census.

Richard J. Storr, *The Beginnings of Graduate Education in America*, University of Chicago Press, 1953.

Richard J. Storr, *Harper's University: The Beginnings: A History of the University of Chicago*, University of Chicago Press, 1966.

"Student Admissions/Virginia State-controlled Institutions of Higher Education/Fall 1966," Richmond, State Council of Higher Education for Virginia, 1966.

Summary of Catholic Education, National Catholic Welfare Conference, annual.

John Summerskill, "Dropouts from College," in Nevitt Sanford, ed. *The American College*, New York, Wiley, 1962.

Donald G. Tewksbury, *The Founding of American Colleges and Universities before the Civil War: With Particular Reference to the Religious Influences Bearing upon the College Movement*, Columbia University, Teachers College, 1932.

Stephan A. Thernstrom, *Poverty and Progress: Social Mobility in a 19th Century City*, Harvard University Press, 1964.

Hugh Thomas, ed. *The Establishment: A Symposium*, London, Blond, 1959.

Daniel C. Thompson, "Problems of Faculty Morale," *Journal of Negro Education* (Winter 1960), 37–46.

Daniel C. Thompson, "Teachers in Negro Colleges," Columbia University, unpublished doctoral dissertation, 1955.

James Trent, *Catholics in College: Religious Commitment and the Intellectual Life*, University of Chicago Press, 1967.

Martin Trow, "Notes on Undergraduate Teaching at Large State Universities," Berkeley, mimeographed, 1966.

Martin Trow, "The Second Transformation of American Secondary Education," *International Journal of Comparative Sociology*, 2 (1961), 145–66.

Ralph H. Turner, *The Social Context of Ambition: A Study of High School Seniors in Los Angeles*, San Francisco, Chandler, 1964.

Ralph H. Turner, "Sponsored and Contest Mobility and the School System," *American Sociological Review*, 25 (December 1960), 855–67.

Ralph H. Turner, John A. Michael, William H. Sewell, and Michael Armer, exchange of views in *American Sociological Review*, 31 (October 1966), 698–712.

U. S. Bureau of the Census, *Current Population Reports*, Series P-20, No. 132, "Educational Change in a Generation," Washington, D.C., 1964.

U. S. Bureau of the Census, *Current Population Reports*, Series P-23, No. 24, "Social and Economic Conditions of Negroes in the United States," Washington, D.C., 1967.

U. S. Bureau of the Census, *Current Population Reports*, Series P-60, No. 48, "Income in 1964 of Families and Unrelated Individuals by Metropolitan and Non-Metropolitan Residence," Washington, D.C., 1966.

U. S. Bureau of the Census, *Current Population Reports*, Series P-60, No. 51, "Income in 1965 of Families and Persons in the United States." Washington, D.C., 1967.

U. S. Bureau of the Census, *Historical Statistics of the United States: Colonial Times to 1957.* Washington, D.C., 1960.

U. S. Bureau of the Census, *Statistical Abstract of the United States: 1965,* Washington, D.C., 1965.

U. S. Bureau of the Census, *U. S. Census of Population, 1960, Volume I, Characteristics of the Population, Part 1, U. S. Summary,* Washington, D.C., 1964. (Cited in text as 1960 *Census*, I, 1.)

U. S. Bureau of the Census, *U. S. Census of Population, 1960, Subject Reports: School Enrollment,* Final Report PC(2)-5A, Washington, D.C., 1964.

U. S. Bureau of the Census, *U. S. Census of Population, 1960, Subject Reports: Educational Attainment,* Final Report PC(2)-5B, Washington, D.C., 1963.

U. S. Office of Education, *Biennial Survey of Education,* Washington, D.C., biennial.

U. S. Office of Education, *Opening Fall Enrollment in Higher Education,* Washington, D.C., annual.

U. S. Office of Education, "Residence and Migration of College Students, Fall 1963," Washington, D.C., duplicated.

Laurence R. Veysey, *The Emergence of the American University,* University of Chicago Press, 1965.

Edward Wakin, *The Catholic Campus,* New York, Macmillan, 1963.

James C. Wallace, *Chapel Hill Weekly*, June 19, 1966.

Gustave Weigel, "American Catholic Intellectualism: A Theologian's Reflections," *The Review of Politics*, 19, July 1957.

Patricia Salter West, "Social Mobility Among College Graduates," in Reinhard Bendix and Seymour Martin Lipset, eds. *Class, Status, and Power*, Glencoe, The Free Press, 1953.

William Foote Whyte, *Street Corner Society*, University of Chicago Press, 1943.

Alan Wilson, "Residential Segregation of Social Classes and Aspirations of High School Boys," *American Sociological Review*, 24 (December 1959), 836–45.

Stephen Wright, Benjamin Mays, Hugh Gloster, Albert Dent, "The American Negro College, Four Responses," *Harvard Educational Review*, 37 (Summer 1967), 451–464.

Michael Young, *The Rise of the Meritocracy, 1870–2033*, New York, Random House, 1959.

Index

"Academic Ability" (Eckland), 103n.

Academic administrators, 16–18, 25, 261; training program for, 18n.; and regulation and restriction of today's students, 59; of public institutions, 266–67

Academic credentials, relative importance of different kinds of, 99

Academic distinctiveness: and advantages of private over public institutions, 287–88; and crisis in private higher education today, 289–90

"Academic" distinguished from "intellectual," 242–44

Academic Enterprise, The (Jencks–Riesman), 55n., 183n., 489n., 500n., 501n.

Academic Man, The (Donovan), 349n., 353n., 368n., 373n., 400n., 405n.

"Academic Procession, The" (Riesman), 25n.

Academic professionalism, 160–61, 197, 237, 257, 261, 312, 517, 529; and women, 299; and the anti-university colleges, 480–509

Academic reform, and a more open society, 140–46

Academic research: and rise of university, 13, 92; federal support for, 14, 162, 189, 516; and enhanced status of productive scholars, 14–15; shortage of scholars capable of conducting externally financed projects, 113–14; role of, in shaping technology and social policy, 114; support of foundations for, 162, 516; conducted for the military, 223; "pure" versus "applied," 516–23, 539; professional objectivity in, as against personal subjectivity, 517–20

"Academic Standards" (Gusfield–Riesman), 39n.

Academicians: and academic administrators, 17–18; and definitions of who could or should be educated, 197–98; and teaching of graduate and undergraduate students, 245–46; resistance of, to pedagogic potential of practitioners, 249; and character of undergraduate education of today, 510; *see also* Scholars

Accrediting agencies, and uniformity in distinction between secondary and higher education, 30

Adams, Walter, 429n., 431n., 473n., 448n.

Admission requirements for college: lowering of, 141–42; criteria favoring mobile outsider, 142–43; changes in, to be justified in terms of national needs or general welfare, 143; for out-of-staters, 170; differentials in public and private institutions, 264, 265, 279–86; increased emphasis on selectivity after mid-1950s, 281–82; trend toward making more academically competitive, 282–83; *see also* College admission policy

Adolescence, extension of, for today's students, 42–43, 47, 56

Adult authority, increasing questioning of legitimacy of, 37

Adult backlash from student subcultures, 50–60, 542

Adult colleges, 38

Adult world, and today's students, 43–45, 49, 540–41

Age distribution: of undergraduates, 31–34; of graduate students, 34–35

70; and extracurricular activities, 370–73; conservative campus attitudes of, 371–72; influence of the religious on, 372–75; sex segregation predominant in, 375–79; admission of women to universities graduate programs, 377; class analysis of, 382–95; and percentage of enrollment in private sector, 386; and ethnicity, 395–98 (table); future of, 398–405

Catholic nuns, and women's colleges, 376–79

Catholic parochial schools, 365, 383

Catholic priests, training of, 209n., 211, 357

Catholic University of America, 163, 166, 246, 344, 359, 379n., 380, 388, 392, 404n.

Catholicism in America, 334–43, 370, 380

Cayton, Horace R., 407n.

Certification: as function of college, 61–64; divorcing education from, 62–63; requirements for, 63

Chandler, Marjorie, 432n.

Changing Catholic College, The (Greeley *et al.*), 352n.

Chase, John L., 359n.

Cheyney State College, 473

Chicago, University of, 13, 62, 160, 162, 246, 356, 392, 449n., 482, 534; Hutchins' scheme for lowering age of entrance to College of, 32–33, 34, 495; undergraduate college of, 173; general education movement at, 493, 494–96, 499, 501, 504

Childhood and Society (Erikson), 192n.

Church colleges, 4–6, 51–52, 165–66, 195–96, 269, 328; *see also* Catholic colleges; Protestant colleges

Citadel, The, in South Carolina, 160, 221

Civil War, as catalyst for changes in America's industrial organization, 9–10

Claremont Colleges, of California, 177, 356

Claremont Men's College, 300, 305n.

Clark, Burton, 100n., 487n.

Clark College, Atlanta, 453

Clark, Harold, 221n.

Clark, Kenneth B., 411n., 429n.

Clark University, 13, 160, 163, 246, 260, 344

Clarke College, Dubuque, 367–68

Class differentials: and college enrollment, 95, 96; and college graduation, 95, 96, 97; and college opportunities, 131, 132, 134–35, 146–47; and universal higher education, 153–54

Class segregation at secondary educational level, 135

Classes in America: as socioeconomically based, 64–74; as culturally based, 74–90; and tendency toward congruence between social and cultural, 75, 85–90

Cleary, T. Anne, 124n., 429n.

Clergy, professionalization of, 202, 209

Clifford, Richard J., 348n., 386n.

Coeducation, rise of, 291–302; and feminist movement, 291–92; sexual segregation at coeducational institutions, academically, socially, residentially, 295–96; reaction of male students to, 301–2

Colby College, 171

Coleman, James C., 125n., 132n., 174n., 412n., 423n., 429n., 431n., 432n., 447n., 448n.

College: application of term "college" to an institution, 28; socialization as central purpose of, 28, 35; intergenerational confrontation in, and age of participants, 28–29; twelve years of preparation obligatory for admission to, 30; four-year undergraduate curriculum of, 31; age distribution of undergraduates in, 31–34; delays in entrance and in graduation, 31–32; anxiety of parents about sending "school age" children away to, 33–34; and separation of young from their elders, 37; gradations of college prestige, 41; and giving students larger voice in full range of affairs of, 58

College admission policy: Hutchins' scheme for lowering age of entrance, 32–33, 34, 495; debates over, 122; use of aptitude tests,

Wakin, Edward, 379n.
Wallace, James C., 430
Warner, Lloyd, 74, 341n.
Washington, Booker T., 419
Washington, George, 156
Washington University, 392
Washington, University of, 319
Wayne State University, 53, 439, 496–97
Weber, Max, 333, 365
Webster College, 346
Weigel, Gustave, 390n.
Wellesley College, 302
Wensel, Marguerite G., 359n.
"Were There but World Enough and Time . . . ," (Haywood), 310n.
Wesley Foundations, 328
Wesleyan University, Connecticut, 327
West, Patricia Salter, 110n., 114n., 377n.
West Virginia State College, 469
Western colleges, founding of, and "Western" culture, 4, 159
Westoff, Charles F., 358n.
Wheaton College, Illinois, 144, 332n.
Wheaton College, Massachusetts, 168
White, Andrew, 13, 260
White-collar mentality of most of today's students, 47
White-collar workers, 65
White, Lynn, Jr., 305
White supremacy, college admission requirements as screen for perpetuating, 141
Who Goes Where (Astin), 339n.
Whyte, William Foote, 397n.
Wilberforce University, 420n., 424
William and Mary College, 156, 208, 316, 430
Williams College, 159, 314, 320
Wilson, Alan, 135n.
Wilson, James Q., 317, 318n.
Wilson, P. A., 202n.
Winthrop College, 304
Wisconsin, University of, 160, 178

Wofford, Harris, 508
Women: increase in number entering college after Civil War, 93; college enrollment and graduation, by mid-1960s, 95; and the liberal arts, 200; higher education for, and feminine movement, 291–92, 376; and rise of coeducation, 291–302; discrimination against in college admission, 294–95; career-orientation of, 297
Women's colleges, 5–6, 168, 302–10; "the Seven Sisters," 302, 303, 304, 305, 311; in the South, 303–4; private junior colleges, 304; experimental colleges, 304–5; number of, 305; financial situation of, 305; and graduate schools, 305–6; advantages and disadvantages of separate education for women, 306–7; and extracurricular activities, 307–8; and preparation for roles and problems after graduation, 308–9; as probable anachronism, 310; Catholic, 357, 364, 376–79, 380, 382, 388–89, 394
Woodrow Wilson Fellowships, 367, 434
Working class, 66; college enrollment from, 95; child of, and college entrance, 131
Wright, Patricia, 432n.

Xavier University of Louisiana, 396, 418n., 455

Yale University, 13, 24, 149, 156, 157, 162n., 167, 211, 224, 300, 314, 316, 449n., 500; Yale Law School, 249n.
Yancey, William, 477n.
Yeshiva University, 166, 318, 456
YMCA, adult colleges of, 38
Young, Michael, 12